SIEGFRIED SASSOON

Also by Jean Moorcroft Wilson

SIEGFRIED SASSOON:
The Making of a War Poet

SIEGFRIED SASSOON:
The Journey from the Trenches

ISAAC ROSENBERG:
Poet and Painter

ISAAC ROSENBERG:
The Making of a Great War Poet

I WAS AN ENGLISH POET:
A Critical Biography of Sir William Watson

CHARLES HAMILTON SORLEY:
A Biography

VIRGINIA WOOLF, LIFE AND LONDON:
Bloomsbury & Beyond

ISAAC ROSENBERG:
The Making of a Great War Poet

SIEGFRIED SASSOON

Soldier, Poet, Lover, Friend

Jean Moorcroft Wilson

Duckworth Overlook

First published in the UK and the US in 2013 by
Duckworth Overlook

LONDON
30 Calvin Street, London E1 6NW
T: 020 7490 7300
E: info@duckworth-publishers.co.uk
www.ducknet.co.uk
For bulk and special sales please contact sales@duckworth-publishers.co.uk,
or write to us at the above address.

NEW YORK
141 Wooster Street
New York, NY 10012
www.overlookpress.com
For bulk and special sales please contact sales@overlookny.com,
or write us at the above address.

A catalogue record for this book is available
from the British Library
Cataloging-in-Publication Data is available
from the Library of Congress

ISBNs
UK: 978-0-7156-3389-2
US: 978-1-4683-0852-5

Book design and formatting by Ray Davies
Printed and bound in Great Britain by
Berforts Information Press, Stevenage

Contents

*For my brother, Findlay Wilson
and my husband, Cecil Woolf.*

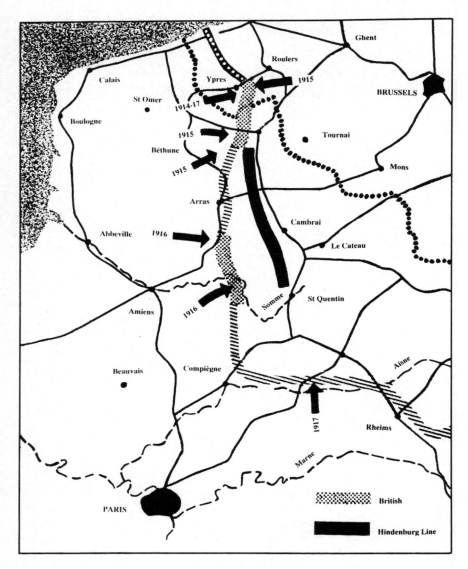

Part of the Western Front in Belgium and France (1915-17).

List of Illustrations

(*between pages 182 and 183*)

Introduction

Few biographers are able to revisit past work and add the new material which often surfaces as a result of the original publication. So I consider myself fortunate in being given the chance to add significant fresh information to this new one-volume account of Siegfried Sassoon's life, including unpublished poems from a 1916 trench journal and shocking evidence of Allied atrocities in the First World War. Sassoon's draft of 'Atrocities', where the narrator congratulates a soldier on 'butcher[ing] some Saxon prisoners' and confesses to 'lov[ing] to hear how Germans die' is horrifying enough in itself, but the letter to C.K. Ogden accompanying it reveals how restrained Sassoon was in his published accounts of the War. 'Only the other day' he tells the editor of the pacifist *Cambridge Magazine* from incarceration in Craiglockhart Hospital on 12 November 1917, 'an officer of a Scotch regiment (one of the many "lead-swinging" cases here)' had 'regaled' him 'with stories of how his chaps put bombs in prisoners' pockets and then shoved them into shell-holes full of water'.[1] I was also able to study a previously buried notebook from the 1920s containing over thirty drafts of hitherto unknown poems.

*

A century has passed since the outbreak of the First World War, but the interest in Sassoon continues to grow. Dame Felicitas Corrigan, who admired him greatly both as a man and writer, summarised the extent of his significance when she wrote to him in 1966, the year before his death: 'To me you are a twentieth century portent: you have summed up in your personal experience the war-tortured, spiritually-bewildered, forsaken and blindly-seeking men of our times.'[2] A similar claim can now be made for Sassoon's status in the twenty-first century. While still symbolizing for many all the heroisms and horrors of the Great War, he has also come to represent the craving for both sexual and spiritual fulfilment which marks our increasingly complex civilization.

More than any other figure from that period, with the possible exception of Rupert Brooke, however, Sassoon has become the prototype of the brave young soldier-poet, a serving officer who entered the war ready to lay down his life for his men and country. His courageous public protest about the handling of the conflict, once he encountered it at first hand, does not quite fit the stereotype, but his qualifications for the role in almost every other respect are impeccable. He came from the right social background: though half-Jewish, his paternal relatives were wealthy merchant princes, who hobnobbed with King Edward

VII, and his maternal ones well-known sculptors, painters and engineers. He had received the 'correct' education at Marlborough and Cambridge, though he did poorly at both. He was an officer adored by his men. Moreover, he was a conspicuously brave officer, awarded an M.C. for bringing in his wounded Corporal under intense fire in May 1916, and involved in several other daring raids. Finally, like Brooke who died before he could qualify fully for the role, Sassoon was extremely handsome, an inestimable advantage for iconhood.

The one condition Sassoon failed to satisfy was that he did not die in the war, though he told Charles Causeley as late as 1952 that 'most people' thought he had.[3] Yet his life after 1918 is as interesting, if not more so, than before it, and not just in personal terms. He produced some of his finest work between 1919 and his death in 1967. This includes his three great war novels, *Memoirs of a Fox-Hunting Man* (1928), *Memoirs of an Infantry Officer* (1930) and *Sherston's Progress* (1936), and also (contrary to the usual perception) some excellent poetry. *The Heart's Journey* (1928), for instance, contains some of the best verse he ever wrote. And as he struggled to find meaning in his life in the late 1940s and 50s, years filled with extreme personal conflict, he produced poetry of an intensity to equal that of his war satires. In fact, he himself believed that the verse written in his later years was far better than his war poems, which he viewed as 'the improvisations of an impulsive, intolerant, immature young creature, under the extreme stress of experience'.[4]

It is as a war poet, however, that Sassoon will be remembered. Yet the importance of his life goes far beyond that, throwing light on a significant segment of the twentieth-century cultural world. Before and during the First World War he was a close friend of well-known patrons of the day, such as Edmund Gosse, Edward Marsh, Ottoline Morrell and Robbie Ross. He also knew a number of the war poets intimately – Robert Graves, Robert Nichols and Wilfred Owen – and exercised a palpable influence on all three. Though Charles Hamilton Sorley died before he had a chance to meet him, Sassoon recognized his fellow-Marlburian's power. Then, after the war, he helped to promote the work of another outstanding but neglected war poet, Isaac Rosenberg. He also became a lifelong friend of Edmund Blunden.

In the years following the war Sassoon got to know many other writers, including Thomas Hardy, H.G. Wells, Arnold Bennett, Walter de la Mare, Max Beerbohm, T.H. White and Edith and Osbert Sitwell. He was a prolific letter-writer – 'many of his missives', as T.H. White points out, being 'small works of art in themselves'[5] – and his correspondence with some of the greatest names of the day adds immeasurably to our knowledge of them. A study of his life is a study of his age.

Sassoon himself wrote three volumes of autobiography, but because of the legislation outlawing homosexuality (in effect) during his lifetime, was never able to write the much franker book he had envisaged in 1921:

It is to be one of the stepping-stones across the raging (or lethargic) river of intolerance which divides creatures of my temperament from a free and unsecretive existence among their fellow men. A mere self-revelation, however spontaneous and clearly-expressed, can never achieve as much as – well, imagine another Madame Bovary dealing with sexual inversion, a book that the world must recognize and learn to understand.[6]

Fortunately, Sassoon did leave his diaries, which give a much clearer picture of him. However, though it is now possible to write relatively freely about his sexuality, it is virtually impossible in our less restrictive age to convey the problems he faced in a society which forbade him full expression of what he called his 'temperament'.

In this and in many other respects, Sassoon is a difficult person to pin down. His was a particularly complex character, more contradictory than most. Perhaps because he came from two very different backgrounds, he seemed to be pulling in opposite directions most of his life. On the one hand there was the hearty extrovert, 'Mad Jack', physically daring, even bloodthirsty at times; on the other a timid, hypersensitive introvert with strong spiritual needs. Known as a great warrior, he nevertheless spent less than a month at the Front. He could write an almost completely autobiographical account of just one side of his personality, *Sherston's Progress*, and fill three books, yet leave his more private, creative side out altogether.

Rather than a 'contradictory' character, however, he preferred to think of himself as a 'multiple personality'.[7] It seemed to him in 1918 that he was a different person with each new poet he met, and in the 1920s he felt positively 'kaleidoscopic'.[8] There is no one label, or set of labels, which will cover Sassoon. Just as he felt himself to be a different person with each poet he met, so each person who met him saw him differently.

The one quality no one questioned was his generosity, which became legendary, especially after he inherited money. His 'spiritual' biographer, Dame Felicitas Corrigan, also claims that no one has ever doubted that he was a gentleman.[9] But there are many who would challenge what that term implies. Sassoon was certainly gentle, kind, honourable and extremely altruistic at times, but there is no doubt that he could also be snobbish, arrogant, even unkind. Ottoline Morrell, who detected a streak of cruelty in him, nevertheless went on to describe him as 'very sympathetic'.[10] Likewise she follows charges of self-centredness and aloofness with praise of his perceptiveness of all things around him. Geoffrey Keynes talked of his 'patent egocentricity' yet thought him a 'wonderful friend'.[11] And Osbert Sitwell found him timid as a writer, but far from timid in other directions. The dichotomy between the contemplative aesthete and man of action, implicit in Sitwell's comment, is perhaps the least controversial description of Sassoon's personality.

Sassoon said that he became a 'ruminant onlooker' after the War was over,[12] but even before it began that side of his personality was well developed. At the same time, when the opportunity arose he stepped into the role of literary lion and successful socialite as though to the manner born. For someone who was almost pathologically shy – so much so that when he gave his first public reading in 1917 he was practically inaudible – it is puzzling to witness the ease with which he took to his meteoric social rise in the 1920s. It is likewise difficult to reconcile his undoubtedly exhibitionist streak with his later craving for anonymity and his hermit-like existence in the country.

He claimed to be non-intellectual, even simple-minded, suggesting that *Sherston's Progress* should really have been called *Simpleton's Progress*, yet he was clearly an astute judge of characters and situations. His deep pessimism was balanced by an unusually optimistic belief in life; no one but Sassoon, for example, would seriously have believed that his public protest against the conduct of the War could have had any real effect on the War Cabinet and High Command.

Though Stephen Tennant, one of his most intimate friends, found him extremely 'moody' at times, Tennant also informed a researcher that 'in a good mood he told funny stories, and then he roared with laughter and charmed every one'.[13]

The contradictions seem endless: the basically conservative countryman contemplating life as a Socialist Member of Parliament in a London constituency, the dandyish youth being mistaken for a tramp at a friend's wedding in later life, the physically adroit sportsman being so clumsy that he dropped his meal from a restaurant balcony on to the diners below, the ultra-conformist who became an arch-rebel, the quintessential Englishman of the middle-class, public school, horsey variety who stemmed from an exotic Middle Eastern background, the practising homosexual who married and had a child, the Jew who became a Roman Catholic.

No biography of such a complex character can be entirely straightforward. Sassoon himself claimed: 'My real biography is my poetry'.[14] Writing his life of George Meredith he added:

> In imagination I am confronted by [Meredith's] protesting presence as he was in his prime. He reminds me that though I have been thinking about him for many months with concentrated industry while exploring a mass of printed material concerning his career, I am still far from justified in generalizing about what he was like. He asks me to consider the impossibility of unshrouding an author who preferred his personality to be private .... What I was in my forties (he concludes) can never be known to you or anyone else. You can see *through* me, but you will never see *into* me. The best of me is in my books .... Make what you can of them, particularly the poems ....[15]

Fortunately, making what *I* can of Sassoon, his life as well as his work, has proved a rewarding challenge, since his development is far from predictable in either case. Few people, reading his juvenile imitations of the Romantics and Pre-Raphaelites, would have guessed at his emergence as one of the finest satirists of the First World War. His is a dramatic journey from his lutes and nightingales to his 'scarlet majors at the base'.

Sassoon's life, too, is full of surprises. Unlike the many writers who lead sedentary lives, he was a man of action caught up in the bloodiest conflict in history. Much has been written about a war in which ten million men were killed, thirty-six million wounded and countless others profoundly affected, but I hope that telling it from Sassoon's singular viewpoint will illuminate new areas. No one who participated in that War wrote about it more frankly than he did. Essentially he was two people. One was an excitable young man caught up in the exhilaration of things such as patrolling at night in No Man's Land. The other was the one who, back at home, had the time to think about the War and never hesitated to say that, in the light of the German peace overtures, what was happening to his friends and to his men was wrong. His conversion from unquestioning support of the Allies to fierce denunciation of their conduct has rightly become a *cause célèbre*.

His life after 1918 is equally interesting, despite the common misconception that it became an arid desert. Over and over again, just as he appears to be settling into a predictable pattern, he changes. This unpredictability, together with the unfamiliarity of many of the details of this period, makes the story of the second half of his life as fascinating as the first. For example, while recognizing that his homosexual affairs were unlikely to lead to lasting happiness, he appeared to see no alternative in the 1920s and early 1930s. So that it comes as a shock to find him marrying suddenly in 1933. Perhaps the most unexpected turn in the life of the man who wrote that deeply sardonic line about the carnage in the trenches – 'And the Bishop said, "The ways of God are strange!"' ('They') – the man who turned against his childhood Anglican faith during the First World War, however, is his entry into the Catholic Church at the age of seventy.

Sassoon's interest transcends both his life and his work. We live in an age of protest and he remains for us what he represented for his contemporaries, one of whom exclaimed at news of his imminent death, 'If Sassoon dies, the Somme is over.'[16]

1

Heredities

> Our heredities are, I think, of all things the most fascinating notion.
>   Letter from Siegfried Sassoon to
>   H.M. Tomlinson, 15 March 1956

A tall, athletic figure in army service dress stood at the mouth of the River Mersey, watching a scrap of purple and white material bobbing lightly on the waves. It was the ribbon of his Military Cross awarded to him for conspicuous courage on the Western Front. Looking back on the scene with the detachment of thirteen years, Siegfried Sassoon was deeply aware of both the irony and futility of his gesture:

> Wandering along the sand dunes I felt outlawed, bitter, and baited. I wanted something to smash and trample on, and in a paroxysm of exasperation I performed the time-honoured gesture of shaking my clenched fists at the sky. Feeling no better for that, I ripped the M.C. ribbon off my tunic and threw it into the mouth of the Mersey. Weighted with significance though this action was, it would have felt more conclusive had the ribbon been heavier. As it was, the poor little thing fell weakly on to the water and floated away as though aware of its own futility. One of my point-to-point cups would have served my purpose more satisfyingly, and they'd meant much the same to me as my Military Cross.
>
> Watching a big boat which was steaming along the horizon, I realized that protesting against the prolongation of the War was about as much use as shouting at the people on board that ship.[1]

In many ways Sassoon's was a highly individual response to a deeply emotional conflict. But it was also one which was determined by multiple influences, not least those resulting from his family background.

*

Siegfried Sassoon was the product of two very different cultures. His father's family, the Sassoons, often referred to as the Rothschilds of the East, were almost completely Oriental in outlook, manners and dress until the arrival of Siegfried's grandfather in England in 1858.[2] This made their rapid acclimatization to Europe within one generation all the more remarkable. They claimed to trace their ancestry back to King David himself, but it is not until the birth of Sason ben Saleh in 1750 that any reliable documentary evidence exists. By this time the family had settled in Baghdad, Mesopotamia (modern day Iraq), among the first Jews to do so.

Sason ben Saleh was the last in a line to serve as 'Nasi' (prince of the captivity) to the Caliph's court in Baghdad. As the city decayed under the Ottoman Empire and governors came and went at an alarming speed, Sheik Sason's own position grew increasingly precarious. By the time he retired from public life in 1817, it was clear that his eldest surviving son David, born in 1792, would not be chosen to succeed him at court. Forced to flee Baghdad, by 1830 David had started a small export trade from Basra to India and in 1832 settled in Bombay. Here the trading venture mushroomed, refounding the Sassoon dynasty. To his great-grandson Siegfried Sassoon the story of 'old David' starting the enormous merchant business' from scratch was the main interest of his father's family.[3]

David had continued to expand his business, finally sending his third son, Sassoon David ('S.D.') Sassoon, the first child of his second marriage, to open a small branch in London at the end of 1858. (S.D.'s grandson Siegfried inherited his height and his shyness from S.D. rather than from his father, Alfred Ezra, a small man full of social confidence.) S.D. set out for England in 1858, leaving his young wife Fahra (anglicized to Flora) to follow a few months later with their three-year-old son, Joseph, and baby daughter, Rachel.

S.D.'s next to youngest child, Alfred (Siegfried's father) was the first Sassoon to be born in England, in 1861. Together with the death of David, the family's Oriental founder, and the arrival of two more Sassoon brothers in London, these events, all in just over a decade, mark a turning-point in the Sassoons' history. From the 1860s onwards their fate is increasingly bound up with England. Siegfried's father's generation of the family no longer needed to earn its own living, though many of them continued to work for the family business. When Alfred grew up, he turned to the arts, which his immediate ancestors had had little time for. He became first a gifted violinist, and then a student in sculpture at the Royal Academy, and his sister, Rachel, took up writing professionally if a little erratically.

By strong contrast Siegfried's mother's family, the Thornycrofts, had been dedicated to art, for three generations in some cases, by the time he was born. His mother's maternal grandfather, John Francis (1780-1861) had begun life as a farmer at Thornham on the Norfolk coast but become a sculptor.

A similar spontaneous impulse to sculpt in almost identical circumstances possessed Siegfried's maternal grandfather – and Francis's future son-in-law – Thomas Thornycroft. Intended, like Francis, for farming, Thomas had from his earliest years shown far more interest in drawing and carving. In 1835, supported by an unusually understanding mother, Thomas set out from his home in Cheshire for London to become apprenticed to John Francis at his house at 56 Albany Street near Regent's Park. He almost immediately fell in love with Francis's sculptor daughter, Mary, whom he married in 1840.

It was, however, not only a strong dedication to art which distinguished the Thornycrofts from the Sassoons. In sharp contrast to the Eastern family of merchants who gravitated naturally towards the city to carry on their trading, the thoroughly English Thornycrofts had farmed lands in Cheshire for generations. Their roots were deep in English soil.

Neither as rich as the first and last Sassoons, nor as poor as David in flight from Baghdad, the Thornycrofts were comfortably established. Their farm was said to produce the finest cheese in Cheshire and they survived the various problems which affected farming during their tenancy of it. Theirs was a middle course without the exoticism, drama and glamour of the Sassoons, but with its own strong appeal. They had a deep love of the countryside around them, which Thomas's children came to share when they returned, as they frequently did, to visit their relatives.

Another salient feature distinguishing the Thornycrofts from the Sassoons is the dominance of women in its family history. While the Jewish Sassoons, with their matriarchal bias, produced no significant example of female influence, the Thornycroft family is marked by its strong women, from Siegfried's maternal great-grandmother, Ann Cheetham, who became a successful female farmer, through her daughter-in-law (his grandmother) Mary Thornycroft, a distinguished sculptor of Queen Victoria's children, and Mary's daughter, Helen, who eventually became Vice-President of the Society of Women Artists. Mary's granddaughter (and Siegfried's cousin), Blanche Thornycroft helped her father, John, with many of his famous engineering achievements, and became an engineer in her own right long before it was common for women to be so. Even Siegfried's mother, Theresa, who chose marriage over painting, showed remarkable strength of character when her husband abandoned her and their three young sons. None of these Thornycroft women had set out deliberately to challenge the male-dominated areas in which they found themselves, but by comparison with the Sassoon women and many other women of their time, their achievements are remarkable.

Siegfried Sassoon made similar generalizations about the two families and their probable influence on his own temperament. In early and middle life he felt he was more of a Thornycroft.[4] Growing up in the country like his Thornycroft ancestors, when his life was peopled almost exclusively with Thornycroft relatives, he identified closely with them. His mother, moreover, was antagonistic to the Sassoons who had, with one exception, rejected her, and for many years they hardly entered his consciousness.

Siegfried's first real awareness of his father's side of the family came abruptly when, at the age of eight, he met his Sassoon grandmother at his father's death-bed. Having never seen her before, he was fascinated by her foreignness and aura of wealth. It was on the same occasion that he was first shown the Sassoon family tree, starting with his great-grandfather David. Though very miserable about his father's hopeless condition and particularly unhappy about his mother's exclusion from the scene, he clearly remembered wondering what 'all those other Sassoons' were like.[5]

A few months later, just after his father's death and Siegfried's subsequent illness, he thought again of his Sassoon ancestors, whom he was already beginning to romanticize. He had borrowed a filigreed scent-bottle from his mother which had been given to her by his father and had once contained attar of roses. As he lay recuperating in a little tent on the lawn, the faint smell of the scent, which he imagined to have come from his father's ancestral home of Persia, seemed to him 'a sort of essence of my father's Oriental extraction'.[6]

In his day-dreaming Siegfried always placed his ancestors in Persia, though some of them had lived in India for two generations by the time his father was born. Presumably Persia seemed to him more romantic. It also fitted in neatly with another memento of his father which he treasured, Alfred's copy of Fitzgerald's *Rubaiyat of Omar Khayyam*. For, though he had been constantly reminded of the wealth of his father's family, it was their exoticism and esoteric beliefs which appealed to him as a child. His somewhat clichéd view of the Sassoons at this time is best summed up in an early poem, 'Ancestors', written some time between 1908 and 1915 (one of his few poems on the subject):

Behold these jewelled, merchant Ancestors,
Foregathered in some chancellery of death;
Calm, provident, discreet, they stroke their beards
And move their faces slowly in the gloom,
And barter monstrous wealth with speech subdued,
Lustreless eyes and acquiescent lids ...   (*CP*, pp. 46-7)

Siegfried saw himself as a 'poor relation' of the legendarily rich Sassoons, and relatively speaking he was, but it was never primarily their money which fascinated him. His attitude towards Sassoon money was both disdainful and apologetic. Sending Robert Graves £23 for his twenty-third birthday in 1918, he refers to his 'Semitic sovereigns none of which I have the least right to call my own'.[7] Nonetheless, as he grew older, his attitude towards his father's family mellowed until by his seventies he felt that his eastern ancestry was stronger in him than that of the Thornycrofts.

There is little doubt that Siegfried did inherit something from the Sassoons, if only physically. Like his grandfather and great-grandfather, he was tall, spare and muscular, unlike the Thornycroft men who tended to be short. His friends attributed other characteristics to his Oriental ancestry, not all of them entirely convincing. One warned him that his hands 'were somewhat over-illustrative', for example, and another detected in him 'a very definite Oriental streak' of cruelty.[8] A third suggested that his early 'deals' in books showed his Sassoon blood coming out, and a fourth, more fancifully, that 'in the Hebrew fashion of the Bible, Jew in this as in so much else, Sassoon always wrote with his heart as well as his head, the heart being the seat of understanding'.[9] One of his closest friends felt that Sassoon, 'like *all Oriental men* was *very secretive* – Reticent, and very eccentric'.[10] And in Sassoon's own later choice of pseudonyms there were many oblique but none too subtle references to his Jewishness, as well as some bad puns – 'Elim Urge', 'Solly Sizzum', 'Sigma Sashun'.

Sassoon himself stated that an obviously inherited Sassoon feature was his tendency to adopt a mystic role in his poetry. 'As a poetic spirit', he wrote, 'I have always felt myself – or wanted to be – a kind of minor prophet' and he refers in his autobiography to 'some angry prophet in my remote ancestry'.[11]

It is far easier and more tempting to speculate about the traits Sassoon inherited from the Thornycrofts, partly because he himself was more articulate on this subject. While he entirely omitted his Jewish side from his thinly-veiled autobiographical novel, *Memoirs of a Fox-Hunting Man* in 1928, he made much of his hero's love of the country, something he firmly believed he had inherited from his mother's yeoman stock. In the straight autobiography which followed his fictionalized trilogy in the late 1930s and early 1940s, he states categorically that being a 'poor relation' of the Sassoons was compensated 'by being half a Thornycroft in blood and more than that in hereditary characteristics'.[12] Welcoming Stanley Jackson's plan to write a history of the Sassoons in 1965, Siegfried nevertheless felt that a book about the Thornycrofts would be much more worthwhile. He believed that he had inherited from his mother what he called the 'Thornycroft sanity', which enabled him, introspective as he was, to 'stand aside and look at myself – and laugh'.[13] It was a trait shared by both his mother and father, however. And if he meant that he had a balanced approach to life, it can only possibly be true of his later years.

Less controversial is his claim that his artistic talent derived from the Thornycrofts. Their complete dedication to art from his great-grandfather's generation onwards must have had a profound influence on Siegfried, who not only wrote poetry and prose, but also loved and performed music and drew and painted throughout his life. Though the visual arts were his immediate ancestors' main concern, music was an important feature of their family life. This musical side was undoubtedly reinforced by Sassoon's father, who was musically gifted, but it also owed a great deal to his mother's family.

Siegfried himself made a direct link between the Thornycrofts' tradition in sculpture and his own chosen art form, poetry. Writing to a young friend in 1948 he claimed that he was 'essentially, *sculptural* in my conceptions of verse, (probably because my mother's family were sculptors – she herself was a *designer* rather than a painter) I want verse to be strongly shaped'.[14]

Another trait Siegfried attributed to his mother's family was his frugality: 'Like a true Thornycroft I detest waste and luxury and excess in anything' he wrote to a friend in 1942, rejoicing in the fact that he was saving money through the wartime shortage of servants.[15] Though extravagant as a young man, particularly where horses were concerned, he grew more careful until, by the time he inherited money in1927, he hardly knew what to do with it.

Surprisingly, Sassoon never theorized about qualities he may have inherited from both sides of his family – industriousness, honesty and ingenuity. He did, however, become convinced that it was not so much what he drew separately from each race which formed his character but the particular way in which these combined. 'You have got it *right* about my Jewish blood,' he wrote to a friendly critic in 1965. 'My artistic talent derives from the Thornycroft side. But what made me different from the gracious serenity of Uncle Hamo [Thornycroft]'s work was the mixture of west and east. The daemon in me is Jewish.'[16] More jocularly he referred elsewhere to being a mixture of 'Cheshire Cheese farmers and Oriental aristocrats'.

Sassoon's most direct link with his family's past came through his maternal grandmother, Mary Thornycroft, who died just after his eighth birthday. When she came to live with his family in the spring of 1894, she seemed to him the epitome of angelic old ladyhood 'dignified in the serene consolations of old age'.[17] On one occasion only – a visit from her eldest son – did he glimpse the 'glorious vitality' she must have had in her prime.[18] He had been told of her distinction as a sculptor and her beautiful long hands symbolized for him the Thornycroft tradition in sculpture. He was sad when she died at the age of eighty-five, after a brief illness in the hard winter of 1894 to 1895, but anxious to know when his mother's mourning would decently allow her to take him ice-skating again.

Mary Thornycroft, who was seven years older than her husband, Thomas, and more successful professionally, had nevertheless looked up to him and promoted his career as a sculptor vigorously. When he turned to engineering, she continued to encourage him despite the domestic chaos this caused and despite bearing their seven children in quick succession.

Even before his patron's death Thomas Thornycroft had busied himself with engineering projects when commissions were scarce. First he designed and built a threshing-machine for his farmer brother, Will. One of the first to be worked by steam, it was in use for the following fifty years. Thomas's next project was an iron-foundry at Stanhope Street. This was followed by a steady stream of inventions, from a six-foot telescope and model railway to a series of progressively larger steam-boats.

This fascination with engineering is perhaps not so surprising as it first seems. Sculptors and engineers must both be able to visualize in three dimensions, as well as have a good grasp of the mathematics of weight and balance. Siegfried's mother told him that her brother John had 'the calculating faculty'. Another feature Thomas passed on to both his sons (but not to his grandson Siegfried) was his practical ingenuity. When the little flat he and Mary rented in Rome in 1843 had no stove, he built one himself, as well as delivering his elder son there. When the house he moved to in Wilton Place in 1861 proved unsatisfactory, possibly because the studio became too crowded, he bought a cabbage field opposite Holland Park in the mid-1870s and had his own home built there with *three* studios, calling it Moreton House.

As a husband and father Thomas was very affectionate. He could be explosive, particularly with his son Hamo, but he genuinely cared for his family. Though his wife was more successful, he showed no signs of jealousy and when his younger son, in turn, began to outstrip him, he was similarly generous-minded. It was his willingness to step down from the Royal Academy's list of nominees which enabled Hamo to become an Academician at the unusually early age of twenty-nine. All things considered, Sassoon's grandfather, Thomas Thornycroft, was an endearing as well as a remarkable man.

Both Thomas and Mary epitomize Victorian virtues in their prodigious industriousness, resourcefulness and multiplicity of interests. Many of these virtues they passed on to their children, together with their outstanding abilities. With the exception of Frances, whose energies were concentrated on her large family, each of the Thornycroft children was preoccupied with design. This entered as strongly into John's engineering inventions as it did into Hamo's sculpting or Alyce, Helen and Theresa's painting.

Siegfried's mother Theresa, known as 'Trees' (from the abbreviation 'Threesa') and later, by extension, 'Ash', was the youngest of the family. Born in 1853, she learnt to carve and model as a child, but quickly turned to painting. She attended Queen's College, Harley Street, where her close friends were the future painters Nellie Epps (later Gosse) and Catherine Brown Hueffer, before being admitted to the Royal Academy Schools in 1890. Very close to her brother

Hamo, whom she nicknamed 'Gull', she made several cultural trips abroad with him, including one to the Paris Salon of 1877. She also modelled for him occasionally. By the age of twenty-two she had exhibited the first of seven paintings at the Royal Academy.

Siegfried insisted that she was primarily a designer and it was her composition which attracted attention. Her most successful picture was one which apparently made a sensation at the Academy Exhibition of 1889; called 'The Hours', it had twenty-four figures floating across the sky from darkness to light. Siegfried knew the picture well and, recalling it on his twenty-first birthday, he wondered if he could ever write as good a poem as 'The Hours' was a picture: 'For in that noble design I had always felt something of the poetry which I could never put into words; and in it I could recognize my kinship with the strength and simplicity of my mother's imagination.'[19]

Theresa carried on painting after her marriage, sometimes using Siegfried and his brothers as models in her largely religious pictures, Siegfried posing on one occasion as the infant Jesus for her 'Nativity'. As the boys grew older and more unmanageable, however, Theresa was forced to give up serious painting, although she did carry on drawing. There was always a drawing-board in her sitting-room and as late as 1930 she produced illustrations for a special edition of her son's *Memoirs of a Fox-Hunting Man*, with Siegfried as her model for Sherston.

Theresa, Helen and Alyce all sat at various times to each other and to the sculptors of the family, Thomas, Mary and Hamo. Frances (1846-1929), nicknamed 'Fanny', though not a professional artist, spent many hours in the studio modelling her head or limbs for various works in progress. Her own ambitions were musical and she flourished in the Glee club the Thornycroft children formed, as well as the more predictable sketching club set up by the girls, called 'The Critics'. Together they went to operas and 'Pop' concerts.[20] It was Theresa's passion for Wagner which led her eventually to call her second son Siegfried in honour of the great musician's work.

Another shared enthusiasm in the Thornycroft family, and related to their love of literature as well as painting, was their admiration of the Pre-Raphaelites. In the late 1860s Hamo had met Burne-Jones, who had introduced him to the William Morris style of decoration, and this had made a deep impression on him. Not long afterwards Theresa went as an RA student to another Pre-Raphaelite's studio, that of Ford Madox Brown. A fellow-student there, as at school, was Edmund Gosse's future wife Nellie, who not only became Theresa's best friend but was also the means of introducing her brother Hamo to Gosse. This started a life-long friendship which undoubtedly encouraged the family's literary interests. The Pre-Raphaelite influence may also have had something to do with the daughters' increasingly High Church leanings, though this may also have been due to the advent of a particularly handsome young curate at their local church. Theresa remained a devout Christian all her life and brought Siegfried up accordingly.

The Thornycrofts were not, however, all piety and culture. They were also united by a love of things physical, swimming, rowing and skating whenever possible. Theresa was also an excellent horsewoman, a skill she passed on to Siegfried, though she could never persuade him to share her love of swimming.

*

When Theresa got to know her future husband, Alfred Sassoon, in 1883, she was at the height of her physical and artistic powers. She was also blessed with a very good sense of humour, which he shared. Their relationship developed from a family acquaintance started in the early 1860s, when Theresa's mother sculpted Alfred's parents, and was reinforced by her brother Hamo's commission to make a half-size statue of Alfred's sister, Rachel, in 1882. Theresa, who became friends with Rachel, started visiting the Sassoons' splendid Elizabethan mansion, Ashley Park, near Walton-on-Thames. Despite the fact that she was eight years older than Alfred, they quickly became emotionally involved.

Alfred Sassoon was only six when his father had dropped dead at the Langham Hotel in 1867. His mother, Flora, partly to compensate for this loss, spoilt him and his younger brother Frederick outrageously. Unaware of how much it took to maintain her glorious but crumbling mansion, its large staff and her children's privileged private education, she spent so lavishly that by the 1880s she had already exhausted a great deal of the money.

Whether from temperament or example, Alfred followed in his mother's footsteps. Slim and handsome, with an attractive cleft in his chin, Alfred sported a thick moustache and, even in his thirties when he was dying of tuberculosis, looked worthy of the description given him of 'a ladies' man'. Whether another charge of 'caddish insouciance' was also appropriate is impossible to say. Certainly he had great personal charm, but then so had Theresa. Alfred also much admired her skill as an artist and, presumably as a result of her influence, enrolled himself as a student in sculpture at the Royal Academy in the autumn of 1883.

Apart from their love of art and well-developed sense of humour, Alfred and Theresa shared a physical adroitness which in Alfred's case showed itself in cricket as well as riding and dancing. Siegfried inherited not only Alfred's aptitude at cricket and riding but also his love of music and his distinctive good looks, even down to the cleft in his chin.

It is not difficult to imagine Alfred and Theresa, two rather spoilt children, fun-loving, generous, physically attractive and attracted to the physical, falling deeply in love. Nor is it hard to understand Alfred's mother's horrified reaction when they started to talk of marriage in 1883. Brought up in strict Jewish orthodoxy herself, surrounded by unquestioning orthodoxy within the Sassoon family, excessively proud of its lineage, Flora simply could not understand her son's desire to marry the eminently English and Christian Theresa. She instantly made her objections very clear – and expected to be obeyed. Her quiet, scholarly, undemonstrative husband had offered very little resistance to his elegant young wife and she was not ready to accept any from her second son. Renowned within the Sassoon family for her indomitability, Flora also had an unpredictable temper which most people feared.

Perhaps because she had indulged him so, Alfred ignored her warnings about marrying out of the Jewish faith. When she threatened to stop his liberal allowance, he went straight to Somerset House to consult his father's will.[21] Having established that his income was independent of his mother's approval, he renewed his offer of marriage to Theresa. Theresa was so deeply in love that she had been quite prepared to accept him without his money and in November 1883 they became secretly engaged. Their first intention was to marry the following April, but such was their impatience that by January 1884 Hamo was called in to help them organize a wedding by special licence. The licence may also have been needed because of Alfred's Jewishness, as well as their eagerness to marry. The secrecy is less puzzling; neither Mrs Sassoon nor Theresa's parents were to know, in case they managed to stop the ceremony.

Hamo arranged for the wedding to take place at their local church, St Mary Abbott's, Kensington, Theresa returned to London with a friend, Eliza Perks. She and Alfred were married on 30 January 1884, with Eliza Perks, Hamo and his friend Edmund Gosse as witnesses – an auspicious literary sponsorship for the future poet.

Theresa's parents were then informed and their reaction was positive. It is clear from Hamo's letter to his fiancée[22] – 'Mrs Sassoon has *not yet* been' [my italics] – that everyone expected her finally to capitulate, but they had reckoned without her stubbornness and genuine distress. Much as she doted on Alfred, she could not condone his marriage out of the faith. For one thing, by marrying a Gentile woman, he ensured that any children of the marriage would be Gentile, since Jewishness is deemed to pass through the female line. With her eldest son, Joseph, already appearing to be a confirmed bachelor and Frederick, her youngest, offering little prospect of marriage, Mrs Sassoon must have been bitterly disappointed by Alfred's depriving her of acceptable grandchildren and heirs. In her rage, she rushed straight to the synagogue to curse any children born of what she saw as an unholy union. She also declared her son officially dead, saying funeral prayers and even sitting the ritual period of mourning for him. Until his last illness she would have nothing to do with him and ordered Joseph, Rachel and Frederick to act similarly. Most significantly of all from her grandson Siegfried's point of view, she cut Alfred out of her will. Though she had spent a great deal of her fortune by the time she died in 1919, even a small part of her money would have made some difference to Siegfried's life at that time.

Alfred's brother, Joseph, obeyed his mother's commands and saw virtually nothing of Alfred or his family after his marriage. His sister Rachel, however, was not prepared to give up her friendship with Theresa, let alone her brother. Slight and delicate as she looked, with her pale skin and large, dark eyes, she had her mother's determination. Frustrated herself by the narrow world of Jewish orthodoxy, she may even have applauded Alfred's action. More than that, she genuinely valued Theresa's friendship and continued to visit her even after Alfred was no longer with her. Artistic herself, but thwarted in her ambition to write seriously or to achieve anything she thought worthwhile, she undoubtedly admired Theresa's gifts and dedication. For a time Rachel consoled herself with unpaid hospital nursing, which her mother grudgingly allowed, but eventually she, too, married 'out'. Though her mother raged, her reaction was not nearly so violent, possibly because Rachel married money and, in any case, would as a female carry on the Jewish line. Flora may also have been badly shaken by the loss of one child and unwilling to risk that of a second.

All these repercussions would probably have seemed both extraordinary and irrelevant to Alfred and Theresa as they set out on their honeymoon, destination unknown. 'We had a festive happy letter from the happy pair this morning,' Hamo reported to his fiancée on 1 February 1884. It was a happiness that lasted just long enough to produce Siegfried and his two brothers.

2

Childhood in the Garden

1886-1895

Siegfried Loraine Sassoon was the second of three sons born to Alfred and Theresa in the four years following their marriage. The first, Michael Thornycroft Sassoon, arrived only eight and a half months after the ceremony, on 14 October 1884. The slight prematurity was probably due to his being the only survivor of twins, since it is unlikely that Theresa's strict religious principles would have allowed her to anticipate marriage.

Siegfried Loraine Sassoon was born two years later on 8 September 1886. Theresa chose to call her second son Siegfried not only because of her admiration for Wagner's operas, but also because he was an exceptionally large baby. 'Loraine' was selected as a tribute to the clergyman who had advised Hamo and Theresa when they were organizing her clandestine marriage in January 1884 and, presumably Siegfried's godfather. Like Michael he was christened at St Stephen's, a High Anglican church in Tunbridge Wells.[1]

Hamo Watts was born less than a year after Siegfried on 4 August 1887, named after Theresa's brother, who had been so helpful in arranging their marriage, and the painter G.F. Watts, the illustrious Thornycroft family friend who also agreed to be their third son's godfather. Siegfried grew up admiring the Watts paintings which surrounded him and was envious of his younger brother's sponsor.

No more children followed after 1887 and, though by today's standards this would not be surprising, in the late-Victorian period it was a small family. One explanation may lie in Theresa's age. When her last child was born she was thirty-four, an age at which some women's fertility starts to decline. Another possible reason for the absence of more children is that Alfred and Theresa, both of whom loved freedom and independence, deliberately limited their family by some form of birth control, though Theresa's religious principles make this unlikely. The most probable explanation is that by 1887 to 1888 their passionate relationship, which was to end tragically for all concerned, was already in crisis.

In 1884, however, Alfred and Theresa were still extremely happy. As soon as they returned from their honeymoon, they started looking for a house in the country. Their eventual choice, Weirleigh, was on a hill just outside the village of Matfield, a few miles further from Tonbridge but only a mile and a half from the railway station at Paddock Wood, Kent. Hamo Thornycroft and his wife, Agatha, had walked over to see it from Tonbridge and obviously thought it worth recommending. By the time Michael was born in October 1884 the Sassoons were comfortably established there. It was to remain Theresa's home for the rest of her long life.

Weirleigh was sold as a 'gentleman's residence' and Alfred was determined to appoint it as such. His will refers to 'all my furniture, plate, plated goods, linen, glass, china, books, manuscripts, pictures, portraits, prints, statuary, musical instruments ... Also my wines, liquors and consumable stores and provisions and all my horses, carriages, harness, saddlery and stable furniture and all my plants and garden and farm utensils, tools and implements.' Not content with that, Alfred also decided to have a studio and stable-block added to the property and commissioned the Thornycrofts' friend, John Belcher, to design these. Theresa intended to carry on painting and Alfred clearly wanted to encourage her, as well as continuing to work at sculpting himself.

It is impossible to exaggerate the importance of Weirleigh to Siegfried, both as a child and as a young man. Though critical of its rather eccentric architecture, particularly its tiled central tower which rose sixty feet from the road to which it was too close, and while he agreed with his mother's criticism that it was 'full of waste space and designed without decorum'[2], he loved Weirleigh deeply. His lyrical account of boyhood in *The Old Century* centres firmly around the rambling Victorian house and lovingly describes its many distinctive features.

Built in the 1860s, it had been added to, probably in the 1870s, by its previous owner, Harrison Weir, from whom it also derived its odd name. Weir, a well-known artist in his day, was so proud of his tower that he had a large lamp lit in it every evening so that it could be seen for miles around.[3] Theresa's reaction to the tower was one of dislike, which turned to apprehension once she found herself with three mischievous boys on her hands. She had the entrance to it altered in an unsuccessful attempt to hide it from her sons.

Siegfried's earliest memories centred round the day and night nurseries at the southern end of the first floor, overlooking the front gate and well away from his parents' and visitors' bedrooms. Alfred and Theresa's world revolved around the spacious, low-windowed drawing-room on the ground floor which led straight out into the garden with its dramatic view of the Weald. An equally large dining-room also looked out over the Weald to the north. The solid stone basement was given over to a servants' hall and kitchen, as well as various store-rooms. The attic floor too was taken up mainly by servants' bedrooms. For a town-dweller from the twenty-first century, to whom every inch of living-space is precious, Weirleigh today seems full not so much of Theresa's dismissive 'waste space' but of elbow-room, an ideal home in which to bring up three energetic boys.

When the adult Siegfried, as his mother's executor, arranged in 1947 to sell Weirleigh, he described it to a friend as 'badly designed, short of bedrooms [there were nine!] and on a main road' but added 'the garden is lovely'.[4] However critical he became of the house, he always remembered its gardens with deep affection. It was not so much the 'lawns and shrubberies' of *The Times'* advertisement[5] as its size, diversity and secret corners where he and his brothers could hide and act out exciting fantasies.

The same varieties of flowers would appear year after year, to be gathered in generous armfuls by the impetuous Theresa to give to departing friends. Flowers, and also trees, figure largely in Siegfried's memories of Weirleigh's garden. He could never think of the garden afterwards without a sense of heartache, as if it contained something which he had never quite been able to discover. Its elusive promise continued to haunt his sleep long after he had left it. 'With a sense of abiding strangeness,' he wrote in his first prose recreation of childhood, 'I see myself looking down from an upper window on a confusion of green branches shaken by the summer breeze. In an endless variety of dream-distorted versions the garden persists as the background of my unconscious existence.'[6]

Weirleigh garden was an Aladdin's cave to a small boy, but the view from it was, if possible, even more magical to Siegfried. The horizon seemed always blue to him as a child, with a mystical haze that encouraged his already pronounced day-dreaming. He claimed to fall into that category of children who are genuinely appreciative of their surroundings. He was able to run his eyes along more than twenty miles of a low-hilled horizon never more than twelve miles away.

It was a magnificent view in all weathers which made a deep impression on an acutely sensitive child, leaving Siegfried with a lasting love of nature. This comes through repeatedly in his work, all but his harshest satires. In 'Before Day', which Edmund Blunden praised as a 'beautiful natural song of personality and England's meaning',[7] he implies that he finds a particular kind of freedom and inspiration in the moment before the day begins. The setting is clearly Weirleigh and the view from its garden:

> Come in this hour to set my spirit free
> When earth is no more mine though night goes out,

And stretching forth these arms I cannot be
Lord of winged sunrise and dim Arcady:
When fieldward boys far off with clack and shout
From orchards scare the birds in sudden rout,
Come, ere my heart grows cold and full of doubt,
In the still summer dawns that waken me ...   (*CP*, p. 64)

The quiet mysticism of this sonnet remains a recognizable feature of Sassoon's poetry throughout his career. So too does his love of nature. Another poem, 'Daybreak in the Garden', based on his habit of stealing downstairs at dawn as a child, dwells on the sounds and sights he experienced in the garden, as well as features of the actual garden – its multiple lawns, May trees and Peony Walk:

I heard the farm cocks crowing, loud, and faint, and thin,
When hooded night was going and one clear planet winked:
I heard shrill notes begin down the spired wood distinct,
When cloudy shoals were chinked and gilt with fires of day.
White-misted was the weald; the lawns were silver-grey;
The lark his lonely field for heaven had forsaken;
And the wind upon its way whispered the boughs of may,
And touched the nodding peony-flowers to bid them waken.
                                                   (*CP*, p. 59)

Siegfried's prose reminiscences of Weirleigh's garden include more mundane details, such as the fact that it was tended by a full-time staff of three – a head-gardener, Mr Reeves, and two under-gardeners, Mabb and Ely. The Sassoon boys appreciated Mr Reeves in particular, since they could always guarantee to provoke his uncertain temper. Mr Reeves, who was short, bearded and brown-bowlered, lived with his wife in rooms above the newly-built stable block just down the hill from Weirleigh. Mabb and Ely were local men and came in daily. So was the odd-job man, who also helped in the garden when he was not too busy trimming and filling oil-lamps, carrying wood and coal for the fires, cleaning shoes or doing other work considered unsuitable for the maids.

Like most middle-class Victorian households, the Sassoons had at least three maids, and a cook, Mrs Battersen, reigned 'below stairs' so that life should run smoothly above. Siegfried's recollection of Weirleigh's kitchen in *The Memoirs of a Fox-Hunting Man* is not particularly sympathetic and displays what he admits was 'a well-developed bump of snobbishness as regards flunkeydom and carriage-and-pair ostentation as a whole'.[8] It also reveals an early suspicion of women in general. As the protagonist, George, returns from his first ride alone, humiliated because his pony has cantered home without him, he passes the 'fat, red-faced cook' in the basement and is immediately surrounded by the 'gaping' kitchen-maid and parlour-maid.[9] He feels himself 'inundated by exasperating female curiosity and concern' and resents the 'feminine fussiness'.

The kitchen-maid to whom he refers so dismissively was the lowliest servant in the household. Sometimes known as the scullery-maid, she would have had to do all the menial tasks below stairs. Her namelessness in Siegfried's autobiography is probably an indication of how low she ranked in the hierarchy. The housemaid, on the other hand, *is* named – Lizzie. She was responsible for most of the cleaning above stairs. It would be her job to clean the bedrooms, make the beds, beeswax the broad oak staircase and the parquet floor in the drawing-room and polish the Spanish leather-screen behind the piano, similarly the Sheraton sideboard in the dining-room and the rest of the furniture.

Emily Eyles, the parlourmaid, was ostensibly in charge of lighter duties in the drawing- and dining-rooms. While Theresa herself arranged the bowls of flowers which filled each room, Emily would set out the blue and yellow eggshell china and 'polite little cakes and sandwiches' which Siegfried remembered as part of the ritual welcome for 'dear old ladies' visiting from their summer retreat at Tunbridge Wells. Besides waiting on guests, Emily's duties were, in theory, to serve the family at meals, answer the front door and to do a little light dusting. In reality, as the boys grew more boisterous and Theresa more harassed, Emily devoted most of her time to them. She was much tougher than her innocent blue eyes and fair hair led people to think, possibly because, as Siegfried suggests, she had inherited her blacksmith father's fortitude. She joined in the boys' roughest games and then, when they finally felt like sitting still in the evenings, would read them their favourite books – *Coral Island*, *Tom Sawyer*, *Around the World in Eighty Days*, *Black Beauty*, *Treasure Island* and, rather unexpectedly, *The Diary of a Nobody*. When she married in 1902, Siegfried showed his affection for her in giving her one of his handwritten poetry books as a present.[10]

The boys' official minder was Mrs Mitchell. Just as Mrs Battersen ruled in the kitchen, so Mrs Mitchell conducted her reign of terror in the nursery. Devoted as Michael, Siegfried and Hamo were to their mother, they took far more notice of Mrs Mitchell. She represented the Old Testament for Siegfried, while his more indulgent 'Mamsy', as he called Theresa, represented the New. Mrs Mitchell was what is commonly called a 'tartar', though Siegfried's 'nursery Jehovah' is perhaps more accurate. With her hard gipsy face, her relish for the lugubrious and a mind as dark as the 'glory-hole' where she kept her prized possessions next to the nursery, Mrs Mitchell tried to frighten her charges into submission. Those who disobeyed were locked into the same 'glory-hole' until they repented. Yet for all her harshness, bad temper and old-fashioned ideas, Siegfried seems to have felt some affection for her, even if only that bred of familiarity.

Mrs Mitchell was very conscious of her superiority to the other servants and Siegfried remembered her dominating proceedings at the 'Servants' Hall Party', held annually in Theresa's large studio, just as she held sway in the nursery. Theresa was a devoted mother but she had less influence than Mrs Mitchell, mainly because of the prevailing system of the day. Siegfried has left no personal memories of his first three years, but it is safe to say that they were dominated by Mrs Mitchell and the nursery routine. As each baby arrived it would be fed and cared for by her and, as each grew old enough, he would eat his meals at the nursery table with her, not with 'Mamsy' and 'Pappy' in the large north-facing dining-room. Since Theresa believed in the virtues of fresh air, there would be daily walks with Mrs Mitchell, rides in the dog-cart[11] and plenty of playing in the garden under nanny's stern eye.

Mrs Mitchell's strict discipline was, however, softened for Siegfried by the presence of his two brothers. As small children Michael, Hamo and he were very close indeed, and not only in age. They had their own private mental territory, as most children do, 'and a very independent one it was', according to Siegfried.[12] The fact that there were three of them enabled them to manage very well without other children and their mother's attempts to introduce 'little friends' were all fruitless.

*

This small self-contained world ran smoothly for Siegfried until at least his fourth year when his parents' relationship began to crumble. Before he was five his father had left home, and one of Siegfried's first clear memories of childhood is of his conflict of feelings when Alfred returns on one of his weekly visits to his sons. The visit itself is eagerly awaited and thrilling: Alfred brings original presents, such as guava jelly, pomegranates and funny unbreakable toys, romps with them on the nursery floor and tells them wonderful jokes. In spite of his joy Siegfried is conscious, even at four, of his mother's extreme unhappiness. This is brought home to him sharply when Theresa, contrary to her usual custom of locking herself in the drawing-room, and perhaps with a forlorn hope of reconciliation, bumps into Alfred and the boys in the garden. All the merriment of a noisy wheelbarrow ride evaporates as Alfred remains stubbornly silent and Theresa looks deeply hurt. As a small, helpless child all Siegfried wants is for them to be reunited – 'for I wanted to enjoy my parents simultaneously – not alternately'.[13]

Alfred and Theresa seem to have been happy together at Weirleigh for at least the first four years of their married life and it is sad that Siegfried was too young to remember or appreciate it. Whilst bearing in quick succession three children whom she adored, Theresa launched herself enthusiastically into the role of Victorian country hostess with Alfred at her side. They gave and received lunches, dinners, teas, even weekends with a prodigality that would overwhelm most twenty-first century mortals.

One of the Sassoons' favourite forms of entertainment, which Theresa had enjoyed before marriage and which gave full reign to Alfred's talents, were musical evenings, when Alfred sometimes played wild gipsy music. He had a collection of old musical instruments – a viola da gamba, some 'dim-gilt' lutes and guitars – but his favourite remained the violin, which he played with an almost diabolical abandon and skill.[14] Theresa's piano playing was sedate and amateurish by comparison but she enjoyed music enormously and made sure it was part of her sons' lives even after her husband had left.

Another interest Theresa shared with Alfred, riding, was indulged freely at Weirleigh. One of their first additions to the property had been to have a large stable-block built. Here they kept several thoroughbreds and at least two ponies, one to pull the lawn-mower and one for the dog-cart. The groom, who slept in the tack-room in those early years, would not only look after the horses but also drive Theresa out in the trap when she travelled locally. Though Alfred shared Theresa's love of horses, he disliked what he called 'horsey-society' and almost certainly did not hunt. Theresa, who was a fearless rider, frequently did, as Siegfried remembered; he claimed it had influenced his own love of the sport.

Alfred and Theresa also shared an interest in their newly-built studio where they worked together, at least to begin with. Not surprisingly, and unlike most modern mothers, Theresa found it easier to carry on painting when her children were little. When Siegfried was only three, for example, she exhibited his favourite picture, 'The Hours', at the Royal Academy. Once the boys were capable of sitting still, she used them as models and took Siegfried on at least one of her painting expeditions.[15] There is no mention of Alfred continuing to sculpt, in spite of having enrolled himself as a sculpture student at the Royal Academy and given 'sculptor' as his profession on his marriage certificate in 1884. Siegfried does, however, refer to a large statue of 'The Dying Gladiator' in the studio, and we know that his Aunt Alyce was sculpting there in the mid-1890s.

One activity Theresa could not join in with Alfred but which Siegfried would emulate was cricket, played on the local village-greens at Matfield and Brenchley. It was not only Alfred's skill which made him popular with the villagers on these occasions, but his sharp sense of humour which they remembered nostalgically long after he had left.

As late as March 1888 Alfred and Theresa were holidaying alone together in Venice and appearing to enjoy it, though this holiday may have been an attempt to revive a flagging interest on Alfred's part. For by May 1889 Theresa appears to be on her own at Weirleigh when Hamo visits her there. She also makes frequent trips to London on her own between the end of 1889 and March 1890, when Hamo finally confirms that her marriage is in pieces. Writing to his wife on 11 March 1890 he also reveals a deep-rooted anti-Semitism which may help to explain Alfred's lack of closeness to Theresa's family: 'Theresa were it not for her three bairns would be very lonely at Weirleigh as her husband is behaving like a madman. He is a caution to us Westerns. Don't be tempted to marry where there [is] Eastern blood and a Sematic [*sic*] nostril. Poor Theresa. She is a plucky one indeed, and a treasure of a woman and one of the brightest of companions possible. For justice sake there should have been a purgatory for such as he.'[16]

By 1891 Alfred has left Weirleigh for good, having run away, according to family rumour, with Theresa's best friend. The relationship does not seem to have lasted long. By 1892 Alfred is established to all appearances on his own at 8 Pembroke Studios, Pembroke Gardens, London, describing himself, in *Kelly's Post Office Directory*, as a 'sculptor'. His neighbours are all aspiring artists and he is once more back in the bohemian world from which Weirleigh had temporarily separated him.

Years later, when Siegfried searched for his father's studio, he went mistakenly to Pembroke Square and failed to find it, but the search in itself is significant. He was 'intensely interested' to discover that his friend Sydney Cockerell had met a Sassoon in the early 1890s in the company of an artist named Randall, telling Cockerell:

> This must have been my father, who was then in his early 30s, pale and delicate looking, with a dark moustache. Anything you can recollect of your impression of him would be of the deepest interest to me – favourable or otherwise. My own memory of him is that he was moody, rather quiet, but extremely good company when in good spirits – (very fond of making jokes). He had the artistic temperament, but no talent, except in his violin-playing, which is described by those who heard him, as really remarkable. At that time, however, he was unhappy and declining into consumption, and his married life had ended in failure through incompatibility of temperament.[17]

Siegfried's low opinion of his father's abilities as a sculptor almost certainly derived from his mother, since he never saw anything executed by him in this discipline. It may also have been Theresa who blamed the failure of their marriage on incompatibility of temperament, a theory which Siegfried would no doubt have found comforting.

Added to an undeniable difference of temperament between the religious, hard-working Theresa and her more light-hearted husband were a number of other factors, Alfred's need for a rich social life and the cultural and religious, as well as age gap between them. When Alfred began to tire of Theresa in 1889, he was still only twenty-eight, whereas she, in her late thirties, was happy to settle down in the country with their three children.

Though Theresa was very unhappy after Alfred left, she was resilient and carried on.[18] As Siegfried wrote of his mother in later life: 'Time teaches one to admire such people, who refuse to pull a long face however deeply life may have hurt them, and whose cheerfulness is born of courage as well as being the outcome of their abundant aliveness.'[19]

Alfred himself was not particularly happy in his new situation, but it was their children who suffered the most, Siegfried possibly most of all. Though he thought that his father was such an incalculable character that it was useless trying to imagine what effect he would have had on his upbringing, he nevertheless remembered Alfred's repeated promise that he would take him to see foreign countries. He cherished all the relics left behind by his father – his musical instruments, his amateurish painting and, in particular, the copy of Fitzgerald's *Rubaiyat* – because they brought back sharp memories of a father he had enjoyed, interruptedly, for too short a time. He was to spend most of his childhood and quite a lot of his adulthood setting up substitute father-figures and reacting to the predominantly female world to which his father had abandoned him.

The most immediate effect of Alfred's departure, however, was to make Siegfried emotionally more dependent on his mother, to whom he felt unusually close. When a friend asked in later life about his relations with Theresa, he replied: 'Yes, in a way I suppose I *was* my mother's favourite. She always said I was her "second self".'[20] He also told a relative that he and Theresa were 'like one person'.[21] His mother, who identified with his imaginative nature more closely than with her two other sons' rather practical outlook, decided early on that Siegfried would become a poet, although she wisely never urged him to write poetry. For his third birthday she had inscribed a copy of Coleridge's lectures on Shakespeare to him, as though hoping to influence events.

When Siegfried did finally start writing poetry it was initially for his mother. In the quarrel between his parents, though he continued to love his father, his sympathies inclined more to his mother, whose unhappiness he witnessed at first hand. This close identification with her from an early age made it very difficult for him to separate himself from her when he grew older. However much they disagreed he found it virtually impossible to oppose her in case he increased her sufferings. His awareness of the sacrifices she had made is evident in a poem he wrote 'To My Mother' in 1928, when he was in his early forties and still unmarried:

> I watch you on your constant way,
> In selfless duty long grown grey;
> And to myself I say
> That I have lived my life to learn
> How lives like your unasking earn
> Aureoles that guide, and burn
> In heart's remembrance ...   (*CP*, pp. 268-9)

*

As a small child the closeness of family relations, even without a father, made for a security which Siegfried constantly looked back on with longing. But his view of the past was not quite so 'golden' as Michael Thorpe has suggested in his introduction to *The Old Century*.[22] His first attempt to write about his life, at the age of six or seven, was, on the contrary, entertainingly realistic: 'Once upon a time there was three brothers. The eldest Michael a [*sic*] the second Siegfried a lazy cowardly boy Hamo a savadge [*sic*] but beautiful boy and they sometimes quarreld [*sic*], a quarrelsome family and that's all I know about that family.'[23] Siegfried's appreciation of male beauty began at an early age.

In spite of their quarrels, until at least 1895, when Siegfried was nine, Michael eleven and Hamo eight, the brothers were united in their tastes and treated in a very similar manner. Theresa kept their hair long and dressed them in smocks for longer than usual. When they were finally promoted to 'boys" clothes, they all wore identical brown jerseys and corduroy shorts.

Their mother's deep suspicion of boarding-schools, particularly the catering arrangements, also led her to keep them at home until long past the usual age for boys of their class. She firmly believed that all her sons were delicate and that it would be a mistake for their 'brains to be overtaxed by a conventional education'.[24] In the context of Alfred's worsening tuberculosis in the early 1890s, her fears are understandable and, in Siegfried's case at least, justified.

As a result of Theresa's distrust of schools Siegfried's education up to the age of eight and a half was, in his own words, 'elementary and irregular'.[25] It was left entirely to his nanny, Mrs Mitchell, and his mother to teach him to read and write. Judging from the first example we have of his work – an exercise book entitled *Celebrated Storeys*, begun in 1893 and inscribed to his mother sometime in 1894 or 1895 – they were neither of them outstanding teachers and he was not a natural scholar. The hand is slightly immature for a child of eight or nine and the spelling, punctuation and grammar are erratic. The coloured illustrations to the book and its lovingly illustrated borders, however, indicate someone of lively imagination. This is confirmed by the numerous stories, which range from those based on giants, kings, princesses, lucky rings and golden apples to more realistic ones, such as the 'Story About Weirleigh' already quoted.

In *Celebrated Storeys* the picture of the three Sassoon boys is particularly interesting: while Siegfried and Michael wear caps, Hamo – 'the savadge but beautiful boy' – has long hair and looks extremely feminine. There are at least five drawings of churches, which played a regular part in the boys' lives, some horses, a number of ships, accurately detailed by the nephew of the naval architect John Thornycroft, and some cartoons, one of Weirleigh's nursery. An illustration of the naval battle between China and Japan suggests that Siegfried was also being taught a little history. His preface – placed with some originality in the middle of the volume – claims not only that 'This book con[t]ains seventeen stories six pictures at the end it is the largest book I have written,' but that he has also produced 'nine small books'. His scholarly 'Index' lists among these 'The Black Fairy Book', 'The Coulerd Fairy Book' and 'Little Storys'. (He freely admitted later that Andrew Lang's *Blue Fairy Book* was his model, for his 'undistracted imagination had been decently nourished' as a child 'on poetry, fairy-tales and fanciful illustrations'.[26])

Theresa believed that the combination of stimulating reading, imaginative writing and copious illustrating were the most important aspects of Siegfried's primary education, and he always retained his early habit of illustrating his work, often very beautifully. His main interest and ability was, however, in words and his mother recognized this. She read aloud to him her favourite poets, primarily the Romantics and the Pre-Raphaelites, his earliest poetic influences.

Another notebook surviving from Siegfried's childhood contains descriptions and illustrations of various butterflies, which suggests that he was also being introduced to some basic natural history in a fairly unsystematic fashion.[27] The only overtly academic subjects Theresa attempted to teach him were arithmetic and, when he was eight, Latin. But since her own knowledge of the language was woefully limited and he had no natural gift in this area, it was not a success and he remained stuck at *mensa*.[28]

Of far greater interest to Siegfried and his brothers was their own world of games and outdoor activities. They had the usual assortment of pets – cats, tortoises, a series of canaries – and, less usually, a grey parrot. One of their favourite games was putting a cat in the dumb-waiter outside the dining-room and sending it down to the kitchen. Mischievous boys, full of physical energy, they preferred sliding down the banisters to walking downstairs, and needed a vent for their high spirits. The garden was much less rule-ridden than the house and in reasonable weather they spent the greater part of the day outdoors. Apart from throwing seed-potatoes at the irascible Mr Reeves, another favourite sport was to crawl in through the vinery window and borrow his 'squirt' which never failed to enrage him.

Siegfried was particularly keen on butterfly-hunting, which they all pursued for a time, but their greatest shared interest was in a ramshackle hut they had made for themselves out of a hundred 'real red bricks' their mother had bought for the purpose.[29] Known as 'The Build', it enabled them to escape from the nursery even in wet weather. Siegfried, fed on Romantic literature, wanted it to have a second storey, which he dreamily imagined as a long loft containing sacks of malt.

It was largely up to the boys to entertain themselves and this they managed to do in a way that would daunt most town children today. In spite of the three years' gap between oldest and youngest, they all behaved as if they were the same age, learning to ride, swim and ice-skate together. Though Siegfried enjoyed these sports, except for swimming, he was extremely timid to begin with. No one watching him on his little black pony would ever have anticipated that he would one day become a hard rider to hounds and winner of several point-to-points.

Theresa did attempt something of a social life for her sons, but her efforts at polite teas and dancing classes in the studio failed dismally. The boys, in their self-contained world, neither needed nor wanted them. More successful were the trips she organized beyond Weirleigh and its immediate surroundings. Because these were rare, they seemed very exciting to Siegfried. By the age of eleven, he claimed, he had been to no more than a dozen public entertainments in his life, and those included the circus, pantomimes, a Paderewski Recital in

Tunbridge Wells and Maskelyne's Mysteries at the Egyptian Hall.[30] He paid a memorable visit to his uncle John Thornycroft's works at Chiswick before he was six. It was not until 1893, his seventh year, that Siegfried started to make a systematic record of events, though the only 'event' as such was the boys' second visit to the Thornycroft works to see the launching of Uncle John's torpedo-gunboat, HMS *Speedy*.

After setting up the Thornycroft ship-building works at Chiswick with the help of his father in 1866, John had made rapid progress, establishing his name with his high-speed launches and his torpedo-boats. By 1885, the year before Siegfried was born, he had built twenty-five torpedo-boats for the Royal Navy, with a guaranteed speed of 19 knots. He also sold torpedo-boats abroad, including the *Ariete* with a speed of 25 knots to the Spanish navy. In 1902 Thornycroft's became a public company and the same year its founder was knighted.

When Siegfried went to see HMS *Speedy* launched in 1893, however, he knew little about his uncle's genius. 'Uncle John invented the tubular boiler' was the rather comic description he had learnt to attach to him as a child.[31] Nor did he have a very intimate knowledge of John's large family. He got to know them much better when he and his brothers were taken by Theresa to spend a month with them at their house on the Isle of Wight two years later. He was never to feel as close to his uncle John as he did to John's younger brother Hamo, but he greatly admired him.

Ten years older than his youngest sister Theresa, John had married fourteen years before her in 1870. His seven children, by Blanche Coules, were, therefore, considerably older than the Sassoon boys. When they went to stay with them on the Isle of Wight in 1895, the eldest son and five daughters were all grown-ups in their eyes. Siegfried was impressed by his highly practical, confident, handsome cousins. While describing the month's holiday as 'glorious', he seems to have been rather overwhelmed by his cousins' physical prowess. The effortless skill with which his cousin Mary set her specimens of butterflies made him feel depressed about his own untidy little collection at home. Even the house, Steyne, which was large and beautiful, overawed him.

In such an uneventful childhood as Siegfried's, it is not surprising that this visit made a deep impression. So regular was the Sassoon boys' existence that, in winter particularly, even softened by hindsight, it seemed monotonous. Sitting day after day on the 'window-shelf' in the nursery passage, watching the rain trickle down the pane, they welcomed diversions; even the robbing of their apple-store provided a thrill.

This monotony was broken in 1894, a year dominated by grandmothers: Grandmama Thornycroft came to live at Weirleigh in the spring and the boys met their Sassoon grandmother for the first time in the autumn. Mary Thornycroft had become increasingly frail since the death of her husband Thomas, who had died at Weirleigh in 1885, the year before Siegfried was born there. By the spring of 1894 Mary, then nearly eighty-five, was installed permanently at Weirleigh, perhaps because her eldest, unmarried daughter, Alyce, lacked her youngest daughter's calm competence as a nurse.

Mary lived peacefully at Weirleigh through the summer and autumn of 1894, her presence probably preventing Theresa from taking the boys away on holiday that year. Siegfried remembered her in a black silk gown with white ruffles, sitting by the drawing room fireside window which had been double-glazed to protect her from draughts. The only sign of agitation he recalled was when she saw her grandsons climbing the Wellingtonia tree in the garden. Whilst Siegfried was aware that his grandmother was someone to be looked up to as well as loved, he did not realize then her true distinction as a sculptress. Her powers of empathy, even with a small child, had shown themselves when she had patched his old toy cow and he was grateful. He was not, however, particularly close to her, and when she died of pneumonia brought on by the severe winter of 1894-5, he could not honestly say that he missed her deeply.

Siegfried recovered rapidly from his grandmother's death. But his father's, less than three months later, left him utterly desolate. By the beginning of 1894 it had become clear that Alfred was seriously ill with what Mrs Mitchell called, with lugubrious relish, 'a galloping consumption'. Giving up all pretences of a carefree bohemian life, he had left his studio in Pembroke Gardens and moved to 50 Grand Parade, Eastbourne, for its sea air, milder climate and proximity to his mother.

Early in 1894 Mrs Mitchell, whom Siegfried suspected of being in collusion with his father against his mother, had taken the boys to stay at Eastbourne for several weeks. Though Alfred talked quite gaily of being well again and taking them abroad, Siegfried found him dreadfully thin and coughing badly. Alfred continued to lose weight and Siegfried began to realize that, however hard he prayed for 'Pappy's' recovery, death was becoming as inevitable as the incoming tide on Eastbourne beach. An awareness of it appears plainly on Alfred's face in the last photograph he arranged to have taken with his sons. As Siegfried points out, the boys look 'much too tidy and smirksome to be real. The only reality was in my father's face.'[32]

After the depressingly wet summer of 1894, it was quite clear to everyone, even the eight-year-old Siegfried, that his father had not much longer to live, however hard he prayed and consulted his toy cow. Alfred made his last will on 14 November and Mrs Mitchell took Siegfried and his brothers to Eastbourne again the same month. It was to say goodbye. This time it was not the shrimp teas Siegfried remembered but his father's relentless cough and his first meeting with his Sassoon grandmother, Flora.

The contrast with Mary Thornycroft, whom he was seeing daily at Weirleigh at this time, was striking. Unlike Mary, Flora was small and, as Siegfried tactfully put it, 'had rather a brown face'. She was very lively and, though equally as kind and delighted to see her grandsons as Mary, was not at all what they expected a grandmother to be. She looked, as indeed she was, much younger than Mary and dressed smartly rather than artistically. She had a disconcerting way of laughing at them when they were not trying to be funny. Though she looked as though she could be dignified, Siegfried found her flaunting of the Sassoon family tree rather vulgar.[33] In contrast Grandmama Thornycroft, sitting in her corner seat at Weirleigh, sipping her port wine and asking magnanimously to be remembered to her erring son-in-law, seemed to him restrained and more truly dignified.

The few days Siegfried spent forlornly in his father's sick-room at Eastbourne, depressed rather than cheered by the profusion of exotic flowers Flora had brought with her from Brighton, were engraved indelibly on his mind:

> From across the years it comes back to me, that picture of the sick-room, with dusk falling and 'Pappy's' face propped up on the pillows, and Grandmama Sassoon bending over us while her other son Joseph stood with his hands in his pockets, staring moodily out at the sunless seaside winter afternoon. And it comes back to me, that sense of being among strangers, with 'Pappy' being killed by that terrible cough, and the queer feeling that although this new grandmama was making such a fuss of us, it would make no difference if we never saw her again .... And I remember my miserable feeling that the only thing which mattered was that my mother ought to be there, and that these people were unfriendly to her who loved my father as they had never done and would have come to him with unquestioning forgiveness.[34]

Alfred lingered on until 18 April 1895. Although Siegfried was told that his death was a 'happy release' his grief was such that he was not allowed to go to the funeral with his brothers. His desolation stemmed from the feeling that 'so much happiness ... could never happen, now that he was dead, for he had made everything seem so promising when we were with him before he was ill'.[35]

Siegfried's grief for his father was complicated by the fact that Alfred, whom he adored, had sent no farewell message to Theresa, whom he also loved deeply. This division of loyalties made him even more unhappy. He could see how brave and unselfish were his mother's attempts to comfort him and his brothers, but he was powerless to help her in return.

Alfred's will, though giving his address as Weirleigh, spelled out his antagonism towards Theresa. Even Mrs Mitchell, whom Siegfried believed had plotted against Theresa, seems to have been treated more kindly, with an annuity of £100. Theresa received a legacy of only £200. It is true that she inherited the personal possessions Alfred had left behind him at Weirleigh, except his Stradivarius. Some of his jewellery was valuable, enabling her to buy the family an occasional luxury, such as a new horse for Siegfried when he outgrew the little black pony. Most of what she was left, however, belonged to Weirleigh, which was held in trust for Alfred's sons.

Another significant aspect of the 1894 will is the change in trustees. In 1885, when Alfred had drawn up a 'post-nuptial' settlement, he had included Theresa's brother, Hamo, and her brother-in-law, John Donaldson, as his trustees. By November 1894 he had dropped Hamo and the third 1885 trustee, Russell Barrington, retaining John Donaldson as trustee and adding the Thornycroft family solicitor, Herbert Lousada. Both Donaldson and Lousada are left as much money as his wife, £200. Alfred's abandonment of Hamo suggests that the latter's strong reaction to his brother-in-law's infidelities had reached his ears. Perhaps Hamo had even tried to talk to him about the situation.

Alfred's will instructs Donaldson and Lousada to invest his money in such stocks as they think fit and to hold it in trust for his children until they reach the age of twenty-one. It is the trustees, rather than Theresa, who are to pay out money for the children's education and make them an allowance if they think it justifiable. Alfred's estate is valued at £5,410 1s. 1d., a great deal of money in 1895 but hardly the kind of sum one would expect from the wealthy Sassoons. (Thomas Thornycroft, for example, when he died ten years earlier had left £11,046 3s. 3d.) By defying his mother, Alfred had cut himself off from her money. He had also increased his expenditure considerably by running two households from about 1890 onwards and he was not in the habit of stinting himself. It is not surprising that Siegfried later saw himself as a 'poor relation' of the almost uniformly rich Sassoons. His own allowance, when he started to receive one, was sufficient for him not to have to work but not enough for him to live as he would have liked.

*

In April 1895, money was far from Siegfried's mind. It had, however, probably caused Mrs Mitchell to leave, an event which was to change his life considerably. Whether it was Alfred's generous annuity or Theresa's deep suspicion of her which prompted the break is not clear, but shortly after the funeral she emptied out her 'glory-hole', packed her bags and left. It was the end of an era. Far from ideal in Siegfried's eyes, Mrs Mitchell nonetheless represented stability and continuity in his already disturbed life. Her departure increased his strong sense of loss and consequent insecurity. On the evening she had gone he remembered how curious it was to be left out in the chilly garden until dusk without anyone coming, as she usually did, to call him in.

The combination of the cold, his own low state and possibly weak lungs (at least so his mother thought) brought on an attack of pneumonia that same evening which took Siegfried into a very different world for the next two months. To begin with, his temperature rose to 105°F and he became delirious. In his own words, he inhabited a strange but fascinating region which was like being outside the world altogether. It seemed to him afterwards that he had had a supernatural revelation: 'Those vague multitudes under enormous flame-lit arches – what could they have been if they were not something to do with death.'[36]

His attempt to follow his father, if that is what it was, failed, mercifully for Theresa. Her feelings as she watched the third person she loved struggling for life that year can only be guessed at. Her joy at his recovery was correspondingly great and her subsequent fussing over him wholly understandable. When her favourite son began to feel better and the May days grew warmer, she had a little tent erected for him on the lawn. Every day he was carried down to spend the day there. Theresa thought him far too weak to walk and Siegfried, who enjoyed being spoilt and still felt fragile, kept up this ritual for as long as he could.

Siegfried dated his first real desire to be a poet from his convalescence in the early summer garden. His senses, already sharpened almost unbearably by the recent experience of his father's death and his own brush with it, responded quiveringly to the beauty of his surroundings and the unaccustomed solitude. He lay there, revelling in the blue visions of the Weald beyond the green treetops, as he listened to the sounds of the garden and the daily household rituals – his brothers playing in the 'Build' or practising their music in the drawing-room, the gruff voices of gardeners, jays squawking, scythes being sharpened in the orchard, or his mother's voice as she set out on her leisurely afternoon ride.

Except for the unavoidable interruptions of the mid-morning egg-nog prescribed by Dr Neild and various meals, he was left almost entirely alone and he loved it: 'I was beginning to discover that solitude could quicken my awareness of aspects within me and around me. My pneumonia had revealed that I had a mind with which I liked to be alone.'[37] It was the beginning of poetic consciousness, if not yet of actual poetry; the poetry was to come only a year later.

3

Lutes and Nightingales
1895-1900

B y 1895 both Siegfried and Michael might reasonably have been expected to be sent away to school, but Theresa Sassoon, now left entirely on her own, could not bring herself to part with them. As Siegfried later realized, she kept her children at home from a growing distrust of the outside world. Having acted recklessly once by rushing into marriage with Alfred, she was not ready to put her faith again in anyone but herself. She did, however, recognize the need for more professional teaching than either she or Mrs Mitchell had been able to provide.

Siegfried's introduction to more formal education was a gentle one. Though Theresa had already planned the change by March 1895, she softened the impact by inviting an old friend of hers, Miss Ellen Batty, to 'do lessons' with her sons in the spring of that year.[1] Siegfried's pneumonia in April left him so weak that he was excused work while recuperating in June. Therefore, instead of introducing him to the harsh world of mathematics, Latin and other traditional school subjects, Miss Batty helped nurse him through his convalescence, becoming his 'devoted slave' in the process.[2] She kept him amused with an endless fund of stories about India, where many of her relatives had gone to rule the Empire. His new teacher's contribution to his education would probably not have resulted in spectacular examination marks, but she clearly stimulated his already active imagination in a way that Mrs Mitchell had failed to do. She also gave Siegfried an entirely different idea of the world from Mrs Mitchell's cramped, suspicious and cynical view of it.

One thing Mrs Mitchell and Miss Batty undeniably had in common, however, was their gender. As women they perpetuated the almost exclusively female world which Siegfried had inhabited since his father's abrupt departure. It was perhaps in an effort to change this that Theresa hired a male tutor for her sons in September 1895, though it is possible that this was her only option. In any case the person who came to take the job was by no means aggressively masculine, a point which the adult Siegfried emphasizes in his autobiography. Conveniently named Mr Moon, he was affectionately dubbed 'Moonie', a name which aptly reflected his gentle character. Describing him as 'one of the mildest of men', Siegfried claimed that 'nobody could have been more like an indulgent tutor and less like a stern taskmaster'.[3] In his fictionalized account of childhood Siegfried, with his love of puns, neatly transforms Mr Moon into Mr Star, but his character remains the same – 'a gentle, semi-clerical old person', who rules with meek authority.[4]

An elementary schoolmaster who had conveniently come to live in the nearby village of Matfield on retirement, Mr Moon was a tall, stooping man with silver hair, dressed always in the same shabby black tail-coat and wide-awake hat. He spoke in measured sentences with a mild, almost apologetic manner. His teaching methods, though not exciting, were moderately successful. He introduced the Sassoon boys to grammar, simple arithmetic, Latin, a little geography, some natural history and the predictable outline of English history. But he also read to them from Lamb's *Tales From Shakespeare* and *Robinson Crusoe*, and started them on some amateur woodwork. Siegfried preferred the reading, his brothers the carpentry. Whatever the response Mr Moon remained patient, methodical and unhurrying. With Siegfried, at least, he had need of all these qualities, particularly when it came to Latin. Looking back, the poet realized that in a curious way his difficulty in learning languages was linked with his intense response to words, already pronounced by the 1890s. He was distracted from the meaning of words not only by their appearance but by their sound. So that when, in the autumn of 1897, Theresa decided that her sons needed a language teacher to supplement Mr Moon's almost exhausted stock of knowledge, Siegfried found himself in trouble.

Fräulein Stoy, unlike Mr Moon, lived in and added yet further to the female presence at Weirleigh. She was, nevertheless, as far away from the feminine fussiness Siegfried dreaded as it is possible to be. Her inevitable nickname, 'Frowsy', seemed to Siegfried, who appreciated her, inappropriate. Small and oldish with shrewd but kind grey eyes and the complexion of a weathered apple, she was 'unchivvying' but determined.[5] She always achieved her end except, ironically, in the vital matter of teaching Siegfried French and German. Putting it as kindly as he could, for he had been fond of her, Siegfried concluded that her teaching, like Mr Moon's, 'lacked illumination'.[6]

Miss Stoy was no more successful at teaching Siegfried music. The explanation seemed to stem from her inability to stimulate his strongest feature, his imagination. Though music later became one of the central interests of his life, with Miss Stoy he showed very little ability. In spite of a genuine desire to play the piano, inspired partly by a growing love of Beethoven's piano sonatas, his progress was so poor that by the end of two years with Miss Stoy they had both lost all confidence in him performing even tolerably well. His brothers fiddled competently through their Corelli and Handel violin sonatas before guests, but Siegfried's painful fumblings at a little Reinecke piece were disastrous. (He was the only one not to have taken up the violin in emulation of their father.)

At the same time as Siegfried's artistic ambitions were suffering setbacks, however, his physical endeavours were unexpectedly flourishing. Though he continued to dislike swimming and was less than enthusiastic about the boxing, fencing and club-swinging that a Sergeant Ryan introduced into the curriculum in 1898, by the summer of that year he suddenly conceived a life-long passion for two activities – riding and cricket. It is unlikely that he would have become addicted to these most English of sports had it not been for the presence of one person, Tom Richardson.

George Thomas Richardson had come to Weirleigh as the Sassoons' coachman in 1890. Then aged about twenty, he had started his working life at fourteen in stables. His career is accurately detailed by Siegfried in *Fox-Hunting Man*, where Tom Dixon is closely modelled on Richardson; a period as 'odd man' to a sporting farmer in the Vale of Aylesbury and a subsequent three years as under-groom to a hard-riding squire who subscribed handsomely to Lord Henry Nevill's Hounds at Eridge Park only twelve miles from Weirleigh. Though Weirleigh was two miles outside Lady Nevill's calling circle, Tom was anxious to maintain contact with Eridge Park and to have a 'young gentleman' who hunted would be one way of satisfying his own passion for the sport. For at least the first eight years of his service with the Sassoons, however, he had to be content with a tamer routine. He ran his stable of three saddle-horses, one carriage-horse and a pony, accompanied Theresa, at a respectful distance, on her afternoon rides and drove her in the trap or carriage whenever necessary. Though Theresa hunted occasionally with the Eridge Hounds it was not an important part of her life nor, consequently, of her groom's.

By the time Siegfried got to know Tom well in 1898, he and his wife were established above the stables and already had two children. On his arrival at Weirleigh in 1890 as a single young man, Tom had been given a tip-up bed in the harness room. Five years later, when he married old Mrs Thornycroft's pretty maid, Emma Wheatley Oakins, who had stayed on at Weirleigh after her employer's death, he was promoted to the two-floor apartment over the coach-house.

Tom was the first of Siegfried's many father-figures, or perhaps more accurately, father-substitutes. There might be more famous ones, but there would never be anyone who inspired quite the same hero-worship. In *Fox-Hunting Man* a thinly-disguised Tom is introduced in the first paragraph and the even more transparently disguised Siegfried, as the protagonist George, tells us on the second page: 'My admiration for him was unqualified.' Tom's son, John Richardson, maintains that Siegfried 'idolized' his father; he certainly *idealized* him in his fiction.

Tom Richardson seemed, even to his son, a rather awesome figure. With his composed features and reserved manner he was 'the embodiment of the efficient groom and the superior private servant'.[7] Tall and handsome, he was always immaculately turned out, either in the Sassoons' livery of blue thigh-length coat with silver buttons, white breeches, high black leg-boots with a tan band round the top, white stock and black top hat or, when following Theresa and later Siegfried to the hunt, in a dark grey suit cut with riding breeches, fawn-coloured gaiters and bowler hat. Siegfried never saw Tom drive even a pony-cart without looking as though it were a carriage and pair.

In spite of a certain aloofness, Tom was persuasive, even artful, in his dealings with Theresa, luring her on to new purchases for the stables in which he took so much pride. Theresa needed little encouragement, and over the years sold many pieces of the jewellery left to her by Alfred to finance the deals.

Together with Tom's persuasiveness went an infinite tact which helps to explain his success in teaching Siegfried not only to ride but to ride extremely well. There was, to use Siegfried's own words, an 'unmanly' element in the nature of this 'dreaming and unpractical' boy, which Tom handled with great delicacy and by 1898 he had gained Siegfried's entire confidence. After a timid and shaky start Siegfried felt sufficiently secure to tackle jumping. Terrified as he was at this new stage, Tom persuaded him to persevere and Siegfried eventually graduated to a full-sized hunter, Sportsman, in 1898.

Sportsman had cost Theresa nothing. A present from someone who wanted him to have a good home, he had done a lot of work and was very much 'over at the knees'. Nevertheless Siegfried adored the handsome chestnut with his three white stockings and Roman nose. Every morning he would run down to the stables to give Sportsman his lump of sugar and discuss his next ride with Tom. Dressed in his brown velveteen riding-suit and matching cap, he would go out for long excursions with Tom, immaculate in his uniform. Their favourite route was through some hilly, remote country which they reached by way of Kipping's Cross on the Tunbridge Wells road. They always stopped on the bridge over the brook by Dundale Farm, because this was the point at which Kent ended and Sussex began. Siegfried could never detect any difference between the two but liked the idea of having a foot in each county. He enjoyed the gentle explorations of the Weald, being 'one of those people on whose minds riding produces a profoundly serenifying effect'. Less gently, Tom would sometimes take him into a neighbouring field for a gallop, in preparation no doubt for the hunting he hoped lay ahead.

When Siegfried eventually tackled his first meet it was with even more trepidation than he had felt at his first jump. However, with an impetuosity and daring which contrasted oddly with his timidity, and which was to characterize him throughout the First World War as 'Mad Jack', he found himself following one of the hardest riders to hounds over a difficult fence. 'Quite a young thruster', the Master of Hounds concluded, but with typical self-effacement Siegfried implies that the truth was very different. The incident shows nevertheless that Tom's training had been a rigorous and successful one.

Before any serious hunting started, however, Tom was also encouraging Siegfried to enjoy cricket. An exceptionally good player himself, he initiated the Sassoon boys into the rudiments of the game on Weirleigh's lower lawn on summer afternoons. He complemented Mr Moon's accurate but gentle lobs with more intimidating overarm bowling and his stylish left-handed batting increased Siegfried's hero-worship, giving him something to emulate. Tom had quickly become captain of the local cricket team, which played its home fixtures a few hundred yards from Weirleigh on Matfield Green.

So great was Siegfried's passion for the game that in 1896 when pains in his hip-joint, diagnosed as 'outgrowing his strength', led to another poetic interlude of lying out on the lawn, he sacrificed it to indulge his 'craving for cricket'.[8] This is one of relatively few references to cricket in his first volume of autobiography, because he had already described it so lovingly and in such detail in *Fox-Hunting Man*. His 'Flower Show Match' chapter in that book has deservedly become a minor classic of cricket literature.

Siegfried's passion for cricket is in an honourable tradition. The only team sport at which he excelled, he appreciated it even more when the time came for him to attend school. It was the only team sport which allowed a self-confessedly dreamy child time to dream at times. Additionally cricket took him into an exclusively male society and offered another opportunity of escape. It would become even more valuable to him as he grew up, a solid bond between him and a number of his closest male friends, Edmund Blunden and Dennis Silk in particular, and a bulwark against chaos. 'In these times,' he was to write in the shadow of War in June 1939, 'one values the humanity of such an occasion [as a cricket match] greatly. It is like the good old England holding its own against the modern pandemonium.'[9]

In the same way he loved horses 'because they were so completely unmodernizable, so independent of fashion' and, like himself, 'refused to move with the times'.[10] He had begun both sports in the beautiful setting of the Weald of Kent and they were linked inextricably for him with a noble tradition he saw endangered by subsequent events. He clung to both not only because he found them physically exhilarating, but because they represented a way of life that was being threatened, particularly with the advent of the First World War.

Whilst fighting in that War he was sustained partly by memories of leisurely cricket matches on village greens and all that they symbolized for him.

What cricket epitomized for him was not entirely solemn, however. His quirky sense of humour and appreciation of eccentricity, well-developed even as a child, led him to create such cricketing characters in *Fox-Hunting Man* as the prosperous saddler, William Dodd, the one-legged umpire Bill Sutler, Crump, Peckham and Parson Yalden, who bring back in all their variety the days before mass communication and media personalities, days for which Siegfried frankly confesses a partiality: 'The players all looked so unlike one another then; and there was an air of alfresco intimacy about their exploits which lent them a fuller flavour than seems perceptible now.'[11]

*

Neither Michael nor Hamo Sassoon appears in Siegfried's two photographs of Matfield Cricket Club, taken in about 1897, which was the beginning of a divergence between himself and his brothers. Clearly both Michael and Hamo took after their grandfather, Thomas Thornycroft, and his eldest son, John. They set up a workshop together on the top floor of the old cottage beyond Theresa's studio and with their lathe and carpenter's bench started to be serious engineers. Siegfried's vague description of their activities comically underlines the difference in temperament between himself and his more scientific brothers: 'They soldered things together, made bits of iron red-hot and then hit them with a hammer ....'[12] (He is unlikely to have been quite as ignorant as this suggests.) Michael and Hamo loved not only making things but finding out how they had been made. Normally Siegfried kept well clear of his brothers' activities and their paths continued to diverge for the rest of their lives, except for a brief truce over cricket. While he devoted himself almost entirely to the arts, both Michael and Hamo became professional engineers.

Michael, who was born two years before Siegfried and died two years after him, devoted his life to engineering. His childhood coincided with the emergence of the motor car and his adolescence with that of the aeroplane, both of which fascinated him. After an undistinguished academic career at Malvern and Cambridge, he came down without a degree, marrying young and serving an engineering apprenticeship with his uncle's firm, Thornycrofts, at Basingstoke. Shortly afterwards he emigrated to Canada, where he started his own car-repair workshop and supervised the mechanical equipment at a nearby salmon fishery-cum-canning factory.

When he returned to England in 1920, shortly after the birth of his third and last child, he helped found a small engineering company, William Godfrey and Partners. His passion for cars led him to collect a number of 'classics', including a steam-driven car, a Riley tri-car, an 8 horsepower de Dion Bouton and a Humberette, which he drove for several years in the London to Brighton Veteran Car run. In the 1930s he also joined the newly opened West Malling Flying Club and in middle age learnt to fly in Amy Johnson's De Havilland

Moth, which he bought. His mother-in-law, Mrs Stroud, aged eighty, and his youngest son, Hamo, aged twelve, learnt with him. Physically daring, like Siegfried, he went in for aerial acrobatics and continued to fly until the end of his long life.[13] His energy and ingenuity also led him in the 1930s to start a loganberry and himalaya-berry (giant blackberry) farm.

Nicknamed 'Billy' in childhood, Michael was quite different from Siegfried. Not so acutely sensitive and far more outgoing, he became known locally as 'Jack-the-lad', a reputation which his middle brother could never have acquired, even though it may have been completely unfounded. Certainly Michael liked women and when his first wife, Violet, died, he quickly remarried.[14] He was, to quote John Richardson, both 'loveable' and 'popular' in Matfield. His violin-playing perhaps best sums up the difference between himself and Siegfried; while he learnt the mechanics of music rapidly, his playing was not sufficiently sensitive to interest Elgar, who had been asked to consider teaching him in 1900. Siegfried, on the other hand, found music-making difficult, as his early fumblings at the piano show, but his response to music itself was both passionate and sensitive. Michael's youngest son, Hamo, did not remember his father sharing Siegfried's interest in family history – 'only in a facetious kind of way'.

The bond between Siegfried and his younger brother Hamo was stronger than with Michael. They were closer in temperament and even closer in age, with less than a year between them. Both seem to have reacted more violently to the loss of their father than Michael. Both were self-confessed homosexuals by the age of twenty-four and Siegfried found comfort in his younger brother's calm acceptance of something which had caused him, in his own words, 'great perplexity and unhappiness'.[15] Hamo's 'intensely humorous way of looking at things', as Siegfried saw it, was another feature they had in common.[16] Hamo is portrayed in his mother's delicate Pre-Raphaelite painting of him as a young man of great sensitivity and is said to have shown promise as a sculptor. Until the brothers' divergence in 1897 Hamo had shared more of Siegfried's interests than Michael.

Though like Siegfried in some ways, Hamo was very different from him in others. In spite of his poetic good looks, he did not share Siegfried's intense response to poetry. When Theresa praised her second son's early poem about a mermaid, Hamo's matter-of-fact mind rebelled. He accused Siegfried of having 'mermaids on the brain'. He remained unmoved by Siegfried's taunt that only people with imagination could understand what mermaids meant. The incident signalled a parting of the ways, all the more painful to Siegfried because he had initially felt closer to Hamo. But Hamo's practical mind seems to have had no time for dreams or nostalgia and, unlike Siegfried's, dwelt little on the past. He loved strenuous occupations, such as chopping or digging and, once the brothers' childhood closeness had passed, planned a grand destruction of the fort which had replaced their 'Build' in the garden.

Though younger than Siegfried, when the two of them finally reached public school, within a term of each other, it became clear that Hamo was the more self-possessed and wise of the two. He was working as an engineer in Argentina when War broke out in 1914 and came home at once to join the army. His early death in the First World War would be partly responsible for the savage turn Siegfried's poetry took in 1916.

*

In *Fox-Hunting Man* not only does the protagonist-narrator lack both father and mother, he also has no siblings, suggesting that Siegfried had a strong sense of isolation in childhood after his brothers' interests began to take them in a different direction from his own. Even before the rift he had felt it necessary to invent an idealized companion in whom he could confide, as though in preparation. This revolved around his toy, Moocow, which became something of a fetish to him and he used to 'converse with' Moocow when he was alone.[17] In the fictional *Fox-Hunting Man*, this 'ideal companion' is masculine – 'that "other boy"' – whereas in his factual accounts of life his 'dream friend' has no sex.

Siegfried had begun to savour solitude in 1895 when convalescing from pneumonia. By 1897 he was able not only to cope with but even to relish it. Apart from riding and sometimes playing cricket without his brothers, he continued his butterfly-collecting without Hamo and took to fishing in the orchard pond or roaming the neighbouring Gedges Wood alone. Looking back on childhood in the poem 'It was the Love of Life', he concluded: 'That loneliness it was which made me wise.'[18] He had already started to write poetry just before the rift came, but its advent speeded up the process. Between 1896 and 1899 he produced at least ten notebooks of poetry, most of them illustrated and with stories included.[19]

Siegfried had started writing poetry in earnest during his second period of lying out alone on the lawn in the spring of 1896. With a few exceptions it was poetry about nature which occupied him throughout these childhood volumes. Larks and swallows were joined by thrushes and nightingales, spring and winter were complemented by summer and autumn, the countryside of Kent supplemented by the seascape of the Isle of Wight, which he visited for a month in August 1896, and that of Norfolk, where Theresa took her sons for two months in the summer of 1897.

Having read the Pre-Raphaelites avidly and devoured Longfellow, Tennyson and Shelley, as well as other Romantics, Siegfried was also anxious to make the connection between autumn and decay, winter and death, the sea and life itself, night and outcast souls. A poem which claims to have been written even earlier than 1896 – 'Autumn 1895' – shows a predilection for melancholy themes, not surprising in view of the deaths of both his father and his grandmother earlier that year.

Siegfried himself claimed that his fascination with death in his earliest poems was a result of reading Shelley, particularly the opening lines of *Queen Mab*:

> How wonderful is Death,
> Death and his brother Sleep!

which had led him to believe that all the best poetry was gloomy, or at any rate solemn. Shelley's poetry made him feel the same way as Tintoretto's *Last Judgement*, a copy of which hung in his mother's studio. Describing his favourite themes at that time as Eternity and the Tomb, he explained his fascination with death as a desire not to disappoint his 'audience', that is his mother, by being 'insipid and unimaginative'.

Apart from fuelling her son's imagination with Romantic poetry, Theresa also fed it with pictures. Not only did she fill the house with the works of her favourite painter, Watts, but she also took Siegfried to see a big Exhibition of his work in London when he was eleven. There he found in Watts's loftiness and grandeur another model for his aims in poetry. When he returned home he tried to put into words the feelings roused in him by one of the painter's most lofty and symbolic works, 'The Court of Death'. This piece duly appeared in *More Poems*, 1897, under the same portentous title.

By the time Siegfried visited the Watts Exhibition in the winter of 1897, he had completed two volumes of poetry, one started in 1896 and the second finished by March 1897 to mark his mother's birthday. He had almost collected a third for her Christmas present. The formula in these second and third volumes is very similar to that of Siegfried's first, but in his fourth volume, dated 1898 and undedicated, some of his own personality begins to emerge in a series of humorous poems which anticipate, very faintly, his satiric war poetry. Portentous poems, on such topics as autumn, winter, twilight and the 'ocean' (rather than the plain old 'sea') are now combined with spirited satires on selected topics. His prose attack on engineers, makes its first appearance in this fourth volume and there is also an equally scornful piece 'To a Motor-Car' (Siegfried shared his mother's extreme distrust of cars and his own experience with them later on suggests that he would have been wise to avoid them):

> If Motor-cars did not stink so
> Perhaps they would not be so bad
> When they go by the folks say, Oh!
> Use their hankerchiefs and look sad.

'To a Pig', 'To a Wasp' and 'The Stork', all humorous, are followed by a ten-stanza poem on 'Natural History', later expanded. Though this attempt at satiric compression fails, it is interesting to see Siegfried experimenting with it so early in his career:

> The Lion is an animal, very unkind
> For he eats Indian babies with toe-nails and rind.[20]

In 1899 Siegfried wrote two new volumes, though again there is a great deal of overlap between them. Indeed some of the poems have already appeared in the 1898 volumes. The most interesting addition to the January 1899 notebook is an ambitious poem on 'The Year', in which he quotes lines from his current favourites, Shakespeare, Shelley and Tennyson, on a left-hand page and gives his own poem on each month on a right-hand page. This tiny, leather-bound, gold-tooled notebook is sparsely illustrated, in contrast to most of the earlier volumes where the pictures sometimes outnumber the poems. Romantic tendencies continue to express themselves in such pieces as 'To a Skylark' and 'To a Nightingale', with their obvious debt to Shelley and Keats. The last production this year – and for some time to come – is 'The Poems by S.L. Sassoon', which largely repeats the contents of the January volume. It is executed in coloured inks, but the illustrations, promised on the title page, are meagre. The childish exuberance of the earlier volumes is giving way to a more self-conscious approach.

There is not a great deal in these juvenile volumes to indicate the poet Siegfried was to become. He himself dismissed them in later life as 'scribblings .... Automatic poetising – not an idea in it – only a delight in the noise of polysyllables.'[21] Some characteristic interests and concerns, however, are already beginning to emerge. He is plainly attempting to emulate one of his models, Tennyson, who made him 'see everything he wrote quite distinctly' and enchanted him 'with his words and cadences'.[22] Siegfried is drunk on words in the 1890s – it comes as no surprise to learn that Swinburne was one of his heroes – and his love of their sound together with their visual impact dominates his poetic technique from the start. The tone is predominantly melancholic:

> Weary and gray, dawn and day
> And the mists of morning rose.
> Damp and dark, and weary lark
> As the shades of evening close.

Here and throughout these volumes Siegfried's attachment to traditional verse forms and his unwillingness to venture far outside them also emerges, his favourite stanza remaining the simple rhymed quatrain. There are moments when a genuine poetic impulse, truly inspired by the natural beauty around him, escapes the heavy weight of nineteenth-century tradition and Siegfried's own voice is heard. An early favourite which reappears in several later volumes, 'To Sylvia, a Horse', describes one of the great loves of his life. Another equally simple poem, 'To the Wild Rose', anticipates the limpidity of much of his later nature poetry:

> In glory grows
> The sweet wild rose.

> In every place
> Of sweet repose
> In kingly grace
> It hangs its petals down
> As though it wore a crown.

Theresa admired this poem so much that she had it set to music and Siegfried had to suffer the excruciating embarrassment of hearing his cousin Mary perform it before guests.

The majority of the poems composed between 1896 and 1899 are, however, largely exercises. The few prose pieces written during the same period tend to be more original and far less romantic. Two stories about cats, 'The Story of Peter' and 'Something About Myself', though somewhat rambling, are full of lively details, much of it drawn from life. At one point Peter, a large tabby of dubious morals, is 'caught on the table with his head in the milkjug', at another he holds a friendly conversation with a rat whom he is 'too fat and too lazey [*sic*]' to chase. 'Something About Myself', which was written nearly a year after 'The Story of Peter', shows more skill in the handling of narrative. The autobiography of a 'common' garden cat, it describes in lurid detail his fight with 'three great vulgar cats' and the subsequent death of his mother: '"That finishes the ole gal" I remarked gaily, for I never did like her piticularly [*sic*]. But here I must end my story, for my uncle is going to give me a snarling lesson. Though, I might tell you, I am a kitchen cat now, and catch lots of mice.'[23]

The liveliness of the narrative, its humour and use of the first-person narrator in 'Something About Myself' anticipate by more than thirty years Siegfried's first novel, *Fox-Hunting Man*. The dramatic monologue was to become his favourite medium of expression in both prose and poetry, his temperament inclining even at an early age to subjective rather than objective expression. He chooses a first-person narrator again for another piece of prose in 1898, 'A Little About Me', the story of a hound called Atalanta. This piece, later jokily renamed 'Atalanta in Kenneldom' with reference to Swinburne's 'Atalanta in Calydon', also allows him to show off his knowledge of hunting terms, learned largely from another favourite writer, the novelist Surtees.

Siegfried's prose and verse at this time have little in common, except for their response to his physical surroundings at Weirleigh. One of his first poems, 'Old Mayfield', for example, is almost certainly a thinly-disguised reference to the local village 'with its houses broad and low'. Based around a large village green and pond, Matfield is still almost as self-contained and picturesque as it was when Siegfried visited its sweet shop a hundred years ago. Because the railway had been expected to go through the village, Matfield had expanded rapidly during the late nineteenth century to overtake its neighbouring 'mother' parish of Brenchley. By Siegfried's day it already boasted, besides three general stores, two bakeries, a butcher's, a Post Office, a cobbler's, a forge, a laundry, a coachbuilding and wheelwright's shop and three public houses, as well as St

Luke's Church (built 1876), Ebenezer Chapel and, by 1890, a Parish Hall. Modern supermarkets and machines have put paid to the forge, the laundry, the wheelwright's and one of the general stores, but the pubs still flourish. Similarly, Squire Marchant's fine Georgian house still dominates the village green, though it is no longer inhabited by Marchants. Its gilded clock no longer strikes in the cobbled courtyard as it did for Siegfried a century ago when he accompanied the Squire's pretty daughters, May and Bessie, home from Weirleigh along his favourite footpath.[24]

Siegfried gives an unashamedly nostalgic vision of his childhood surroundings, which omits the harsh realities he must have glimpsed, or at least guessed at, as a child. *His* Matfield is a 'dawdling homespun' world, full of sunshine and local characters. It is background rather than foreground and he sketches in only a few romantic details – the weatherbeaten village carrier, 'geese going single file across the green', the lame blacksmith and the more colourful members of the cricket-team.

Siegfried's response to Matfield and Brenchley was not just a matter of literary choice; it was also a result of his social position in the district, which separated him from most of its inhabitants. Like George, in *Fox-Hunting Man*, he would not have been allowed to 'associate' with the village boys. Even the sons of neighbouring farmers were considered 'unsuitable'. For his mother, and by extension for himself, the world was divided into people on whom one could, and must, 'call' and those who were 'socially impossible'.[25] It is not surprising, therefore, to find his descriptions of childhood dominated by what he himself dubbed 'the local gentry'.

Theresa's social round of a radius of about ten miles was dictated by the distance she could conveniently travel by carriage or pony-trap. Her friends would, of course, include the vicar, the doctor and any other of the professions, their wives and their children. In reality this translated into a fairly circumscribed world of the vicars of Matfield and Brenchley and their families, the local doctor, Neild, Squires Marchant and Morland and their families, two ex-Army officers, Major Horrocks and Captain Ruxton, and their wives, and several assorted spinsters of genteel background, such as Miss Woodgate and Miss Martin.

Siegfried's favourites, whom he described in both his autobiographical and his fictional accounts of childhood, were Major Edgeworth Horrocks, white-bearded and rubicund, and his ancient, very deaf sister, Clara, Captain Hay Ruxton who farmed at Broad Oak and had been the first Chief Constable of Kent, and Squire Marchant's children, three of whom were either painted or sculpted by his mother.[26] He partially transformed one Marchant son, Richard, into Jack Barchard in *Fox-Hunting Man* and enjoyed trespassing on the land of another brother, Stephen, in nearby Gedges Wood.

Theresa also liked her neighbours, but she found them rather limited. A positive and imaginative person herself, she devised several answers to this problem, some of which livened up Siegfried's childhood considerably. One such attempt was the founding of a Poetry Society in the winter of 1896. Siegfried, who evidently relished the memory, has left us an entertaining account of this society. One incident, when he and his brothers hid in the loft and disrupted a Shelley reading, shows him in an engaging light as a normal, mischievous little boy. Clearly his poetic ambitions did not prevent him enjoying a childish prank which, in the event, ruined the reading of a beautiful poem. There was certainly nothing solemn or priggish about him then and he was never to lose his robust sense of humour. On the contrary, he remained capable of enjoying similar jokes all his life.

In time the Poetry Society was allowed to lapse and Theresa turned her formidable energy to other diversions. The most successful of these, as far as Siegfried was concerned, was a series of *tableaux vivants*, then very much in fashion. Both the designing of the costumes and the painting of the scenery provided an outlet for Theresa's somewhat thwarted artistic impulses. Though the actual sewing of the clothes was left to the long-suffering Emily Eyles, Theresa was kept very busy organizing the cast. Siegfried's own part in proceedings was limited to a scene called 'Queen Margaret and the Robbers', in which he played the young Henry VI, and another from *A Midsummer Night's Dream*, where he was cast as Mustard Seed. Steeped as he was in Romantic literature and art, and acutely sensitive to every type of beauty, he drank it all in.

In the age before cinema or television such simple visual pleasures as *tableaux vivants* created great excitement, particularly in a quiet rural district of Kent, but they could not last, nor be endlessly repeated. Theresa, however, had other distractions which Siegfried registered as welcome diversions in his largely uneventful routine. His mother had a constant stream of visitors to Weirleigh, especially in the summer when the garden was at its loveliest. The ones her son remembered most vividly were her London friends, who came from that mysterious world beyond the Medway.

One of Theresa's oldest London friends was Nellie Gosse, but her visits were not as frequent nor as long as either of them would have liked. Nellie's marriage to the great Edmund Gosse, though it was to prove useful to Siegfried, kept her very busy in London. She had married shortly after her student days at the Royal Academy with Theresa and like Theresa had three children. The eldest, Tessa (named after Theresa), spent the summer of 1897 with the Sassoons in Norfolk and the son, Philip, became friendly with Siegfried later. On the few occasions when their mother managed to visit Weirleigh, far from bringing her London literary world to Kent, she was quite content to sit and gossip with 'Trees', as she affectionately called Theresa, in the garden with an air of 'lulled contentment'.[27]

When Siegfried was only ten he had already reaped the benefit of Nellie's London connections. Theresa had shown Nellie one of his first works, dramatically entitled 'George the Berglerear' ['burglar'?]; Nellie must have realized the strength of his literary ambition, for one of his most treasured birthday presents in 1896 was a copy of Edmund Gosse's *The Naturalist of the Sea Shore*, inscribed with great tact to 'Mr Siegfried Sassoon'.

Much as Siegfried admired Nellie Gosse, there was no doubt in his mind that Helen Wirgman was the most exciting person who came to visit his mother, though she was in her early fifties when he first met her. 'Wirgie', as she was called by adults and children alike, was an old friend of all Theresa's family. She had become acquainted with the Thornycrofts through the relationship of her brother, Theodore Blake Wirgman, with Hamo Thornycroft. Theodore, an artist like Hamo, had painted portraits of Hamo and Hamo's other close friend, Gosse, as well as Gosse's wife Nellie. Wirgie herself had no profession. She lived on a small income and had travelled widely abroad; her French and German were excellent. A highly cultured person, she endured living in London, which she disliked, only for its pictures, music and French and German plays.

Theresa believed that she had had the talent to become a successful actress but Siegfried thought that her real forte was music. Though not of professional standard, she played the piano with such intense imagination, emotional warmth and vitality that she inspired Siegfried to persist in his own woeful fumblings. She was, to use his own words, 'quite the most wonderful musician' he had heard as a child.[28] Wirgie's rendition of the Beethoven piano sonatas seemed to him better even than that of Paderewski, whom he had heard at Tunbridge Wells. Among her favourite composers were Schumann and Beethoven. When she was playing the last movement of the *Moonlight Sonata* or the first page of the *Pathétique*, Siegfried felt 'that she was expressing all the stormy and tremendous things which she couldn't say in any other way' and he longed to be able to emulate her.[29]

Wirgie's was altogether a stormy personality. As Siegfried discovered, she was difficult and easily offended. They had once walked all the way home from Siegfried's favourite 'Watercress Well', at least half an hour from Weirleigh, in complete silence because Wirgie had been so angry with him for prodding a toad rather hard to see how fast it could go. Far from being thrown by Wirgie's bad tempers, Siegfried understood them very well. He himself often suffered similar irrational outbursts and identified closely with her highly emotional response to life. She was unlike any other adult he had met, particularly in her willingness to join in his activities. Whether this meant trampling wildly across the wire-netting Theresa had placed cautiously on the garden pond, in pursuit of butterflies, or acting absurd parts in the miming game of Dumb Crambo with him, she entered into everything with a wholeheartedness and abandonment Siegfried shared.

Unlike most grown-ups too, Wirgie understood nonsense and when Siegfried came out with muddled sentences in his over-excitement, she never said 'Don't be silly', merely that she thought such sentences as 'The studio was playing Ludo with a poodle in a puddle' only occurred in the game of Consequences. Her own sense of humour was highly developed. 'The Honourable Mrs Caboodle' as she sometimes called herself, told Siegfried that she believed laughter was 'almost a greater bond of union than seriousness', though there was undeniably a serious side to their relationship. In some ways Wirgie filled the gap left, not only by his highly emotional and very playful father, but also by his brothers' defection to engineering. She may also have unwittingly encouraged his growing independence from Michael and Hamo.

Wirgie described herself as 'a very old wreck', but she struck Siegfried as 'very distinguished', particularly when she wore her 'old, old mulberry silk garment', as she described her only garden-party dress.[30] (This had been on the occasion of Queen Victoria's Diamond Jubilee, which they had celebrated together in the garden at Weirleigh in 1897.) She spoke slowly and her 'low, mouth-closed laugh' seemed to him to suit her name exactly (was he half-rhyming 'Wirgie' with 'gurgle'?). Her deeply humorous glance remained in his mind, long after he had, to his regret, lost touch with her. Thinking back on his relationship with her sixty-five years after it began, he felt that she had been 'a sort of genius ... imaginative and impulsive', which helped explain her strong appeal for him and other children.[31]

It was no chance, therefore, that Siegfried had dedicated one of his first volumes of poetry to Wirgie. She had very strong views on poetry, as on most subjects, and could be relied on to tell the truth. Her hero was Meredith, whom she had known personally, and she encouraged Siegfried, wisely, to become less vague and more physical in his work, like him. Siegfried thought her a very 'percipient' judge of poetry and continued to seek her advice for more than a decade.

Helen Wirgman fitted completely into the daily routine at Weirleigh, but Aunt Rachel was quite a different matter. After her support of her brother's marriage to Theresa and defiance of her mother's ban on relations with them, she had remained a close friend of Theresa's, even after Alfred's desertion. She visited Weirleigh throughout the 1890s, her visits tending to be both dramatic and brief. If, as often happened, she missed the scheduled train, she would hire a special private one at considerable cost for the journey from Charing Cross to Paddock Wood. However impulsively undertaken, such visits always included lavish boxes of fruit and sweets for the household and parcels of books for the boys.

Rachel's abrupt arrivals and departures and her long conversations with Theresa at Weirleigh were partly caused by her temperament, which was volatile in the extreme. They were also a result of an increasingly desperate personal problem she needed to share with one of her closest friends – a reversal of their roles in 1883 when Theresa had turned to her for support. Her husband, Frederick Beer, the son of a financier from Frankfurt who had made a fortune on the Stock Exchange, was himself a gentle man, too sensitive and unassertive for his father's tastes but well suited to Rachel's artistic temperament. To begin with they were ideally matched. With Frederick's £20,000 a year to add to her own comfortable income, they bought a splendid house at Seven Chesterfield Gardens, Mayfair. Liveried servants, luxurious carriages and priceless works of art completed the scene. Before long, however, it became apparent that Frederick was far from well. Mysterious headaches, bewildering changes of mood and creeping paralysis eventually led doctors to diagnose the tragic cause of his deteriorating health – inherited syphilis. Theresa's evasive explanation to her puzzled sons was that 'poor Mr Beer has a bad heredity'. It was not surprising that Frederick and Rachel had no children, for he in turn had passed the disease on to his wife.

When Siegfried first recalled Aunt Rachel in the 1890s, however, there was little sign of her future fate. She was no vaguer than she had always been and was still capable of becoming animated after a short time with her favourite nephews and sister-in-law. But she was undeniably eccentric. Her vagueness was not an affectation and her lavish spending, which earned her the nickname 'Madame Midas', was carried out in an impulsive and odd manner. Having taken over the *Observer*, which her husband had inherited from his father, she suddenly decided to buy the *Sunday Times* for herself in 1893. (It cost £11,000.) Whilst personally nursing a gravely ill husband through the 1890s, she edited both papers simultaneously and also wrote leaders, book reviews and occasional feature articles. Though both papers declined in circulation during her editorship, neither folded and she did make some impressive decisions. The most memorable of these was her printing of the 'confessions' of Major Esterhazy, the man whose evidence had convicted the Jewish officer, Captain Dreyfus, of treason. Though Esterhazy subsequently retracted the confession and the *Observer* was forced to pay him £500 to settle a libel suit, Rachel had made her mark. Later evidence vindicated her decision, which had been prompted not only by a natural reaction to anti-Semitism but also by a consistent horror of any cruelty or social injustice.

Rachel was still relatively happy when Siegfried became conscious of her presence at Weirleigh in the 1890s. She was his favourite aunt, and not just because she was so generous. Consciously or not, he was deeply attached to the one member of Alfred's family who had stood by his mother, himself and his brothers. This 'queer, brilliant woman', as he called her, also shared many of his father's qualities and, incidentally, his own. All three were witty, charming and volatile. They all loved books and music – Rachel had composed and even published pieces for the piano and other instruments. They were also physically attractive, the same intense expression in their dark eyes compelling attention. Where they differed was in their reaction to town and country. Both Alfred and Rachel flourished in London and seemed out of place in the English countryside. In Siegfried his Thornycroft rural ancestry predominated and ultimately he came to prefer the country.

As a child, of course, his norm *was* the country and London visits to Aunt Rachel were no more than brief interludes in the usual round of events. By the summer of 1899 this routine had changed somewhat with the departure of Michael for prep school and the advent of a new tutor for Siegfried and Hamo, Mr Hamilton. Fresh from Rugby and Cambridge, Clarence Hamilton presented a sharp contrast with Mr Moon in almost every way. Brought in by Theresa in an attempt to drag her younger sons up to standard before they joined Michael at prep school, he was young, sporty and handsome and greatly admired by Siegfried. His clean-shaven good looks, muscular figure and stylish clothes contrasted strikingly with Mr Moon's shabby, stooping appearance. Though planning to become a clergyman after his year with the Sassoons, he had none of Mr Moon's clerical airs. His was, rather, a 'muscular Christianity'.

Unsophisticated as Siegfried was at the age of twelve, he recognized that Mr Hamilton completely eclipsed poor old Mr Moon. Even the determined Fräulein Stoy, who continued to teach him French, German and music, became altogether subsidiary to the new tutor and his fresh approach. 'The Beet', as his two charges nicknamed the ruddy-complexioned graduate, was clearly a welcome masculine presence at Weirleigh. A photograph of Siegfried and Hamo taken by Hamilton in the garden suggests that he was also a very understanding tutor who did not terrorize his pupils. Holding an inside-out umbrella above their heads, though the sun is clearly shining, they are both grinning mischievously at the camera, almost certainly held by Mr Hamilton himself. It is interesting to note too that, in spite of being the elder of the two, Siegfried is half hiding behind Hamo who is the taller and more confident looking. They are in a quasi-uniform of Norfolk jackets with knickerbockers, knee-length woollen socks and stout lace-up shoes. They look very happy.

While Siegfried recognized his tutor's tact, good-nature and modesty and appreciated his more energetic teaching methods, it was Mr Hamilton's sporting abilities he most admired. A member of the Cricket Eleven at Rugby and Captain of his college cricket team at Cambridge, 'the Beet' was an exciting addition to Siegfried's cricketing ambitions in 1899. In his first match at Brenchley, Mr Hamilton lived up to his reputation, knocking up a stylish thirty in an important game. On the highly irregular pitch of Matfield Green, however, he suffered the fate of what locals called 'the toffs' and failed to score at all.

One marked effect of Mr Hamilton's presence on Siegfried was to make him feel that writing poetry was somehow priggish or unmanly. During Mr Hamilton's year with the family he wrote no poetry at all. It was not that Mr Hamilton actively discouraged him, in fact he included poetry in the curriculum. But it was not the kind of poetry to inspire Siegfried to further efforts of his own. Learning by heart such 'public' poems as Tennyson's 'Revenge' and 'Defence of Lucknow' was not calculated to stir the creativity of a boy whose favourite poems included Keats's 'Ode to a Nightingale'.

Siegfried maintained that he was, in any case, beginning to lose his early ecstasies and inspirations, but it may well have been that he could not sustain them in the no-nonsense world of Mr Hamilton, which was not conducive to poetry. His literary tastes, such as they were, ran more to prose and he presented Siegfried with at least one prose work during his stay, Charles Kingsley's *The Heroes, or Greek Fairy Tales for My Children* (1899). He may also have encouraged him to read Scott's stirring adventure stories, which Siegfried was enjoying by the late 1890s. Another possible explanation is that, while desperately trying to catch up on all the conventional schooling that he lacked – he was between four and five years behind boys of his age in the system – Siegfried had no energy left for poetry. These were conflicts he was to experience repeatedly in his career, tensions between the outer and inner worlds, between his sporty, physical side and his introverted, dreamy self. His work is often at its best when he is trying to reconcile the two worlds, as in his war poetry, or *Fox-Hunting Man*.

Whatever Mr Hamilton's negative effects on Siegfried's poetry, Theresa regarded him as her saviour. Her sons began to look as though they would be ready to go to prep school at last and their behaviour also improved under their new tutor's firmer hand. (They had had a reputation for being very naughty in Church, for example.)

Even if Mr Hamilton had not been there, 1899, the last year of the old century, was by its very nature an exciting one. To add to the excitement, the Boer War broke out and everybody began to scan the newspapers anxiously. On a more personal level, their beloved Uncle Don died after a long illness and this time Siegfried attended the funeral. As Siegfried watched his uncle's coffin drawn along by four of his favourite Clydesdales and saw the miserable faces of his ten Donaldson cousins, he felt that his own poems about death had been very shallow indeed. The outside world was beginning to break in on him and for a time poetry seemed both inadequate and inappropriate.

The century ended, however, on a more positive note. Hamo insisted that they celebrate the advent of the new by the destruction of the old. Though Siegfried resisted the idea of burning down their childhood Fort, he was bought off by his more determined brother and felt a certain exhilaration as he watched the past go up in flames. It was the beginning of the end of childhood. In only four more months he would leave Weirleigh for his first sustained visit to the outside world.

4

'Harum-Scarum Schoolboy'

1900-1904

Siegfried's first prolonged sortie to the outside world was to the New Beacon Preparatory School. Situated about a mile and a half from Sevenoaks in the district of Cross Keys, it was only fourteen miles from Weirleigh, a comfort no doubt to his over-protective mother. The New Beacon had been recommended by the boys' governess, Fräulein Stoy, whose previous charge and brightest pupil, Nevill Forbes, had attended it in its former incarnation as The Beacon in Sevenoaks itself.

John Stewart Norman had come to Sevenoaks in 1882 to take over The Beacon, 'a school for the sons of gentlemen preparatory to the great Public Schools of this country'. Founded in 1863 in St John's Road, the school had gradually declined until by 1882 it had no pupils at all. With the help of his dynamic wife, Alice Mary (*née* Square) and two fellow-masters from his previous school, Plymouth Grammar, Norman had set about the revival of The Beacon. Then in his twenty-eighth year, a classical scholar of St Paul's and Corpus Christi, Cambridge, Norman was determined, energetic and imaginative. He was also a perfectionist, who planned his school's curriculum down to the last detail, to include not only all the predictable disciplines of the day – Latin, Greek and Maths – but also less established subjects such as English, French, German, History, Geography, Music and Art. Each of six sets, which were dictated by ability rather than age, had detailed schedules for each subject, carefully defining and limiting the syllabus. His enlightened approach to education also prompted him to broaden extra-curricular activities to include, besides the usual games of cricket, football, hockey and rugger, such things as carpentry, boxing, fencing, swimming, club-swinging and golf.

The Beacon had flourished under Norman's rule and by 1887 had fifty-eight pupils, many from middle-class Sevenoaks families. Before its previous decline it had been well-known for preparing boys mainly for Eton and had had a large clientele among the landed gentry of the county and Southern England. Norman widened its appeal and by the time the first Sassoon arrived at The Beacon in September 1899, the school was also known for its naval, military and Scottish connections, its four chief outlets to public school being Wellington, Charterhouse, Marlborough and the local Tonbridge; it also sent a number of boys to Dartmouth.

The New Beacon was an attractive red-brick building set in spacious grounds, reassuring to a mother like Theresa Sassoon, who worried constantly about her sons; at 600 feet above sea level the New Beacon seemed particularly healthy. The main body of the school, which formed three sides of a square, contained classrooms down the centre and a large dining-room and schoolroom running off at right-angles at either end. Above both wings were two large dormitories called 'Big' and 'Little Big' by the boys, the 'Little' indicating the age of the boys rather than the size of the rooms. When Siegfried and Hamo joined Michael at the New Beacon in its second term on the new premises, Siegfried was in 'Big' and his younger brother in 'Little Big'. Apart from the classrooms, which seem by today's standards rather cramped, all the public rooms were light and airy.

Theresa's main concern, the food, was well looked after, if we are to trust the glowing account of vast roasts and satisfyingly filling puddings given by the founder's son. There was also a matron, Miss Mills, devoted to the boys' welfare even if this meant, as it did in Siegfried's case, finding them shirts that their unworldly mothers had failed to supply. Theresa had dutifully packed knickerbocker suits, Eton collars, 'dickeys' and bowlers for her sons' weekend wear, but had not realized that shirts were necessary. And Siegfried's worst moment as a new boy occurred when a kind master encouraged him to remove his jacket during cricket practice and he was forced to confess to his shirtless state.

When Siegfried and Hamo arrived at the New Beacon in April 1900, Michael was in his third term with Mr Norman. He had started at The Beacon in September 1899, moved to the new premises in January 1900 and was therefore something of an old hand. The impact of leaving home must consequently have been softened somewhat for Siegfried, particularly as he also had his younger brother with him. Nevertheless, he suffered acutely to begin with. It was not only homesickness. The fact that, at nearly fourteen, he was much older and larger than most of the other boys, instead of increasing his confidence, made him feel even more inexperienced and helpless.

One great consolation to Siegfried in his early days was the sympathy of the Chief Assistant Master, Mr Jackson, who on his first day, sensing his misery, encouraged him to go and console himself with a hearty tea. Siegfried found the second-in-command less intimidating than Mr Norman, though he came to like the latter just as much. E.M. Jackson's appeal for a young boy probably lay in his excellence as both a teacher and a sportsman. He not only taught the next to top set in Classics but also coached the first team in one of Siegfried's favourite sports, cricket. (In fact, it was what he was 'keenest on' altogether at the New Beacon.[1]) He also had fond memories of the time Mr Jackson took a group of boys holidaying on the Norfolk Broads.

Most of all, Siegfried was grateful to Mr Jackson for helping him catch up on his education. His backwardness in the most important subject of the time, Classics, had caused him, on entering the school, to be placed in the fourth of six Latin sets and excluded from any of the three Greek sets, even though he was one of the oldest boys at the New Beacon. So determined was he to make up for lost time that by September 1900, his second term, he had moved up in both Latin and Greek to set two. His response to Mr Jackson's skilful teaching there was immediate and after only one term with him Siegfried was again moved up, this time to the top sets in both Latin and Greek.

Here he came into closer contact with the headmaster, whom he found an equally 'magnificent schoolmaster'. Though Siegfried never shone in either subject, Mr Norman enabled him to reach the standard required for public school entrance and he was awarded prizes in both subjects in his final term. Siegfried's admiration for his headmaster was based on more than gratitude. He responded to his headmaster's belief that the three pillars of education were a sense of humour, a sense of proportion and the gift of sympathy. Under Mr Norman's guidance, the New Beacon was disciplined but not repressive; according to Rupert Croft-Cooke, who had been both a boy and a master at the New Beacon: 'The boys were neither coddled nor drilled.'[2] Beaconians were allowed more freedom of activity than was usual for the period.

Mr Norman seems to have been well aware of Siegfried's individuality and to have appealed to one of his stronger traits, his sense of humour. With teasing allusion to his sudden access of dignity in his last few terms at the school, he had christened his pupil 'Dook Sig', or 'Dook' for short. Siegfried in return, and with the usual schoolboy relish for imperfections, referred to his headmaster, who was almost blind in one eye, as 'Cockeye'.

Mr Norman probably also encouraged Siegfried's literary abilities, even though he wrote no actual poetry at the school, since he was to inscribe a copy of one of his earliest printed volumes to his headmaster long after he had left.[3] Mr Norman's own literary enthusiasms revealed themselves in the 'readings' of books like *Moonfleet* he gave to the boys in the big schoolroom at weekends, which the boys found exciting.

Curiously enough, Siegfried had entered the school in the second set at English, though Michael and even Hamo were in the first set. After only one term, however, he was next to top in the first set and stayed there, coming top of the whole school in English in the two terms before he left and winning a prize in the subject. He also won prizes in the two remaining exam subjects, Maths and French, though his progress in both was more erratic and he moved uneasily between the second and first sets during his two years at the New Beacon.

Of all Siegfried's extra-curricular activities, there is no doubt that he enjoyed cricket most. It was one of the few things at which he shone and his arrival at the New Beacon in April 1900 coincided with the completion of a new cricket pitch, which had cost Mr Norman the then large sum of £320 18s. 6d. Siegfried was immediately put into the First Eleven, where he was joined the following year by Hamo. In a 1901 school photograph of the team, taken on the important occasion of their winning the West Kent Preparatory School Cup with the highest score the school was to record until at least the mid-1960s, the two Sassoon brothers tower above their younger fellow cricketers. Cricket and Siegfried's other enthusiasm at the New Beacon, golf, were to form a link which kept him in fairly close touch with the school up to the First World War. He displayed less enthusiasm for the many other physical activities included in the New Beacon timetable.

Returning to school without Michael after the long summer holiday of 1900, Siegfried is elevated from 'Sassoon Minor' to 'Sassoon Major' (one reason perhaps for his increasingly 'Dook'-like behaviour). He discovers the joys of golf while caddying for Mr Jackson and starts to feel more confident about his work. In January 1901, when Queen Victoria dies, it never occurs to him to mark the event in verse as he would once have done. He cannot even remember what 'feeling inspired' is like, though he does occasionally suspect that he has lost something precious. His main response to the momentous death is a fit of giggles when Mr Jackson sits on his bowler hat at the memorial service. Cricket dominates the summer term of 1901, the occasion when Siegfried helps win the West Kent Prep School Cup and gains his 'colours'.

After the memorable holiday with Mr Jackson on the Norfolk Broads in September 1901 he returns for his last term at the New Beacon. In spite of his rather slapdash approach to his entrance exam – Mr Norman makes him do it twice and, with rather dubious morality, destroys his first effort – Siegfried gets his place at Marlborough. When he leaves, at Christmas, he is top of the school in one subject – English.

Siegfried does not appear to have retained any close friends from the New

Beacon, though a number of the pupils were subsequently at Marlborough with him. It may be that the company, first of both his brothers, then of his younger one alone, insulated him a little from the other boys and made him seem more self-sufficient than he felt. Possibly they were put off by his slight 'scattiness' – his nickname at this time, 'Onions', was because he seemed a little 'off his onion', he explained. The fact that he was considerably older than the majority of the boys may also have made close friendships less likely. The most probable explanation is that he was still struggling to survive in the outside world from which his mother had protected him for far longer than normal. That he was happy at the New Beacon is a sign of his resilience and eagerness to catch up.

The one boy with whom Siegfried remained in close touch from the New Beacon, the headmaster's younger son, Cecil Norman, was indirectly the cause of his next choice of school, Marlborough College. In fact, neither Siegfried nor his mother had actually chosen Marlborough, it was the suggestion of Mr Norman, who had already entered Cecil for it. Siegfried was clearly neither academically brilliant nor was he a hopeless case. In addition his family, in spite of its name, was not wealthy. For both reasons Marlborough seemed the right choice. Siegfried later recorded his gratitude that Norman had succeeded in persuading his cautious mother to agree.

Theresa had probably been helped to decide on Marlborough by Fräulein Stoy, whose star pupil, Nevill Forbes, had gone on there from the New Beacon in 1897. She must also have been reassured by what Mr Norman could tell her of the comfortable boarding-house – Cotton – that he had chosen for his own son. At any rate Theresa had put Siegfried's name down for Cotton House and in January 1902 he left home again, this time for a more distant destination.

*

Siegfried was not allowed to travel by himself to Marlborough for his first term, but was accompanied by his anxious mother, still unwilling to let him face the world alone. He was pleased to be going to Marlborough and felt rather important about it, even though he suspected that he could never do outstandingly well at either work or games, the two pillars of public school life at that time. He was determined to do his best but very apprehensive about beginning. To make matters worse, his mother had insisted on arriving early so that she could vet both the Master of the College, the Reverend George Bell, and Siegfried's housemaster, Mr Gould.

Gould was the type of eccentric schoolmaster whom boys love and remember. His habit of riding a lady's bicycle at a snail's pace down the Bath Road from Cotton House into College drew fine taunts from his charges – 'You're scorching, Mr Gould' – which Gould dealt with, genially, in his usual style – 'Shut up, you wretched brute!' It was quite normal for boys to boo him as he entered their classrooms or studies, but the booing was affectionate. He was a deliberate clown who used his buffoonery to win over the boys; they remembered the Greek constructions he taught as well as his jokes. Out of a staff of nearly forty, generations of Marlburians recalled Gould in particular. Charles Hamilton Sorley, for instance, who arrived only six years after Siegfried, thought that his best days at Marlborough were 'the days under Gould'.[4]

Siegfried's later analysis of Herbert Marius Gould was that he was more of a Herbert than a Marius. Though an excellent classicist, as his scholarship to Trinity College, Oxford from Marlborough and First Class degree there showed, and in spite of a taste for good food and wine, his resemblance to Marius the Epicurean was limited. He was perhaps too worldly to resemble his namesake.[5] There was a general feeling at Marlborough that Gould's abilities were wasted as a schoolmaster and that he would have done far better at the Bar or in Parliament. His house, Cotton, was run along very relaxed lines – some said too lax – which helps to explain Siegfried's enjoyment of life there.

In 1902, when Siegfried arrived at Marlborough, Gould was still playing croquet and only halfway through his fifteen years as house-master of Cotton. His pronounced paunch indicated a love of the good things in life, but he was also active in caring for his boys. Siegfried had fond memories of him toddling round the dormitories at night murmuring 'Ho, you big fellow', or 'Hullo, you little fellow'. Gould was attached to them in his own idiosyncratic way and Siegfried's overall response echoed that of many: 'Good old Gould!'

Marlborough had been founded in 1843 by the Reverend Charles Plater, who saw the need for a good public school which the clergy could afford. It opened in what had originally been a country house built by the Seymour family, which then became the famous Castle Inn on the London to Bath road. Shortly afterwards a New House, Junior House and Dining-Hall had been added and many other buildings followed between 1852 and 1902. The College's prospectus for the year of Siegfried's entry, 1902, proudly draws attention to its fine buildings, the most relevant of which to this story is Cotton House, designed by G.E. Street and opened in 1872.

Cotton was one of the first two purpose-built Out-College Houses and living conditions were far more comfortable than In-College, the fees higher. Siegfried, therefore, escaped the austerities and horrors of A-House and Upper School. Louis MacNeice likened A-House, the In-College building for juniors, to a prison and is eloquent on the miseries of Upper School, the communal room for boys on first entering a Senior In-College House. John Betjeman, Sorley, Beverley Nichols and many others have reinforced the grim picture MacNeice paints of physical discomfort and ritual bullying.

As a senior boy entering an Out-House, Sassoon would automatically have escaped these trials. His anxious mother had, nevertheless, taken the precaution of bringing Siegfried his own blankets. Gould, understandably, had been less than enthusiastic about this domestic detail, but the Dame (or Matron), Mrs Bolt, a 'prim but very nice person' according to the embarrassed Siegfried, seemed grateful for the additional bedding.[6] She clearly took Theresa and her son to be 'some of those frightfully rich Sassoons who were always entertaining Royalties'. Not for the first time, Siegfried wished for a more commonplace name, knowing from experience that within a very short time the boys would be calling him 'Stinkweed Bassoon', or something equally awful. (In fact, for some obscure reason, his schoolfellows came up with nothing worse than the nickname 'Gaggers'.)

One of Siegfried's problems in arriving in January, rather than the more usual time of September, was that he found himself the only new boy in Cotton House. The rest of the boys had already paired up. For the first time in his life, therefore, Siegfried was entirely on his own. His memories of this period are of total confusion. The smallest undertaking, such as finding his classroom, or doing up his tie, made him feel panicky. Fortunately Cotton House allowed him a certain amount of privacy. Once Hamo joined Siegfried at the school, they shared a privileged south-facing study on the upper floor. There is no mention of other study-mates or friends.

Another subject Siegfried fails to mention in his description of Marlborough is homosexuality. Yet, like most public schools of the day, the Marlborough authorities clearly feared that the close proximity of teenage boys deprived of female company would result in what they regarded as immoral practices. In an attempt to discourage sexual liaisons and what was known as 'self-abuse' or 'beastliness' (masturbation) there were no doors on the lavatories. Pupils were not allowed to visit dormitories alone in the day and several parts of the school grounds were strictly out of bounds. One housemaster, anxious to stamp out what he called 'impurity', made a close study of the subject and concluded that the most dangerous place was Upper School and that the most tempting times for boys were 'early summer mornings before early school and (most dangerous of all) Sunday mornings when many people are in chapel at early communion'.[7]

Since Siegfried was not In-College, Upper School would not have provided any temptations for him, but he is unlikely to have been entirely free from them. He was to tell a friend sixteen years later that from 'early youth' he had been tortured by the knowledge that women were 'antipathetic' to him and that he could 'only like men'.[8] It is unlikely, however, that his homosexuality found any physical outlet until those same sixteen years had passed. It is probable that his attraction towards his own sex made him both confused and unhappy at Marlborough, all the more so because he was unable to confide in anyone about it.

A more curious omission in Siegfried's account of Marlborough is a description of the countryside. For many Old Marlburians, notably Sorley, the Marlborough Downs were one of the main attractions of the school. Yet Siegfried, who loved his native Kent passionately and wrote endlessly about the countryside in his early verse, makes only passing references to such features of the Marlborough landscape as Savernake Forest and White Horse Hill. Perhaps it was loyalty to Kent that silenced him. It may also have been that his determination to make up as much ground as possible academically left him time for little else.

*

The daily routine at Marlborough was rigorous, starting with a cold wash at 6.30 a.m. in an unheated dormitory and not ending until 6.30 p.m. on Mondays, Wednesdays and Fridays. On Tuesdays, Thursdays and Saturdays afternoons were devoted to mandatory games. Siegfried, who had not played rugger at his prep school, began with hockey. Having had his shin badly bruised in one of his first games, he was rather resentful when Gould swooped down on him one lunchtime and accused him of trying to avoid games by taking organ lessons. Anxious to counteract his housemaster's impression of him as a pampered 'softie', derived no doubt from his affluent surname and his mother's excessive concern for his health, he stood up to Gould who subsequently left him alone. The housemaster's 'choleric performance' towards a new boy, however, had its positive side, since it won him some sympathy and welcome attention from the older boys, who had previously ignored him.

The cause of the row, Siegfried's ambition to play the organ, had led to an embarrassing interview with the school's organist, Mr Bambridge. Convinced that her son was not only an invalid but also a genius, Theresa had written to tell the music master so. It was only as Siegfried prepared nervously to play 'Venetian Gondola' from Mendelssohn's Songs Without Words that he realized what was expected of him. He had, indeed, a real love of music as his mother claimed, but was not yet capable of giving it convincing expression. In fact, in his nervousness he played even less well than usual. Luckily for him Mr Bambridge, whose lean, bearded face gave no sign of it, had a good sense of humour. Stopping Siegfried halfway through the first page, he put down Theresa's letter with a smile and arranged a time for organ lessons.

Siegfried concentrates on such amusing incidents in his autobiography and says little about his education, but it is clear that he carried out his intention of working hard. He still had a great deal of ground to recover in spite of the New Beacon's excellent teaching. Entering the school at fifteen, already two years later than the majority of the new boys, he was placed very near the bottom in the Upper Fourth form of the Lower School. (Scholars, like Sorley and Beverly Nichols, usually entered the school much higher at a much younger age.) He worked so conscientiously in his first term with Mr Meyrick that he came 8th out of 26 in the form lists and even Gould was pleased with him. Promoted to Shell A at the bottom of the Upper School in the summer of 1902, he spent two terms there with Mr O'Regan, coming 19th out of 27 in the summer term but climbing rapidly to 4th out of 26 in the winter of 1902. After a term's absence in the spring of 1903 he found himself promoted again, to Mr Lupton's class, Remove B, where he came a modest 12th out of 28. Winter 1903 brought further promotion, to the Lower Fifth 2B with Mr England, where he remained until he left in the summer of 1904. Perhaps because he knew that, at nearly eighteen, he was not high enough in the school system to be allowed to stay on, his efforts seem to slacken in this class and his initial position of 19th out of 27 is only marginally improved to 15th out of 28 the term he leaves.

Looking back on his education, Siegfried wondered why he found himself so unable to win academic honours. Rather than blaming his teachers, he arrived at the same conclusion as he had over his difficulties in learning languages, that he had a mind which absorbed information slowly and could only learn easily when its visual imagination was stimulated. There were few if any public schools at the beginning of the twentieth century which concerned themselves with the artistic temperament or boys' latent abilities. Siegfried had to confess that he himself had shown little promise of achieving anything out of the ordinary while at Marlborough. Yet, like most imaginative children, he responded, if not to the academic system at least to stimulating teaching. And there was one man at Marlborough who provided that for him. It is no coincidence that, of his four form-masters and numerous teachers between January 1902 and July 1904, and apart from his eccentric housemaster, he describes only one in any detail – John O'Regan.

After referring briefly to the fact that O'Regan had played hockey for England, Siegfried concentrates on his outstanding abilities as a teacher. He found the small, ebullient Irishman so easy to work for that he wanted to stay in his class as long as possible. O'Regan, a First-Class scholar of Balliol who arrived at Marlborough eight years before Siegfried in 1894, wore his learning lightly. Though Senior History Master, he got on extremely well with the younger boys. Very likeable and unaffected, he was according to his biographers, 'a boy among boys'. One of the few teachers who made a direct appeal to their imagination, O'Regan sometimes held tutorials on the roof of an imitation Roman villa he had built for himself in the town. On Sunday evenings he often read to his form after they had written letters home and had had their tea. Siegfried still remembered, thirty-six years later, the 'subdued gusto' with which his form-master read the passage about the young curate and the lady in Kenneth Grahame's *The Golden Age*, a book which gave his pupil 'a pleasant feeling of being away from school and doing things one wasn't allowed to in a shady garden'.[9]

O'Regan made an even stronger appeal to Siegfried's imagination when he read out poetry and then invited the boys to write some themselves, for a prize of half a crown. Siegfried was grateful, not so much for the money, which he nearly always won, but for the encouragement to return to an activity he had begun to look back on with nostalgia. O'Regan had Siegfried's first poem framed and hung on his form-room walls. Though clearly a set-piece, it shows an assurance in the handling of rhythm, form and in particular enjambment that O'Regan must have recognized as unusual in an otherwise backward fifteen-year-old:

> My life at school is fraught with care,
> Replete with many a sorrow.

When evening shadows fall I dare
Not think about tomorrow.
The extra lesson doth correct
My wandering attention;
And other things which I expect
It might give pain to mention.

But extra lessons cannot kill,
And blows don't fall so hard
That they will end the life of this
Ambitious little bard.

The same term that Siegfried produced this poem, and possibly as a result of it, he started to write poetry voluntarily again. This reawakening of the poetic impulse had occurred early in the summer term of 1902 in the library of Cotton House. Alone and at a loose end, he had taken down a volume of *Ward's English Poets* and opened it randomly at Thomas Hood's 'Bridge of Sighs', a poem completely new to him. The effect was immediate and lasting: 'I had always preferred poems which went straight to the point and stayed there, and here was a direct utterance which gave me goose flesh and brought tears to my eyes.'[10] It was not so much the subject of the poem which thrilled the dormant poet in him as Hood's powerful expression and memorable word music. This ability to combine two of his great loves remained one of Siegfried's main aims in poetry throughout his life. He had worshipped it in Swinburne as a child, and it was now revived in him by Hood's strongly rhythmical lines.

Siegfried stresses the apparent randomness of his action in reading Hood, as though he felt himself guided back to his earlier poetic vocation through a higher, unexplained power. He also refers specifically to his childhood belief in himself as 'a prophetic spirit in the making'. There is little doubt that he still believed in the poet as prophet and, therefore, as divinely inspired. Both in his war poetry and in his later work, this prophetic role comes to the fore.

In Cotton House library, with the mundane clatter of the servant laying the long wooden tables in the hall next door for tea, his belief in his calling as a poet was restored. The immediate effect was to liberate him both from his surroundings and from his sense of inadequacy in a world that glorified things at which he could never excel – scholarship and team sports. The 'dreaming boy', his own description of himself as a child, could believe once more in his creative power, unrecognized though this was by the majority of those around him. Emboldened by Hood and other poets – Emily Brontë, Dante Gabriel Rossetti, Byron, Matthew Arnold and Arthur Clough – whose works he copied into his diary, he went on to write poems of his own again.

Siegfried's first serious efforts included a 'dirge-like' piece on the illness of Edward VII, which had delayed the coronation in 1902, and a 'Fragment of Poem Written in Jan. 1903', an allegory which began:

Youth with a joyful heart and mind
Set out his way through life to find,
He thought not of the years before,
But of his childhood left behind.

He went on to write 'Ballad-Land' and an ode on another king, Richard II, an anticipation of a further regal poem on Edward I.[11]

Siegfried may have derived his inspiration for his ode on Richard II from studying Shakespeare's play in his English lessons. He is unlikely to have come across Richard in his History studies, since these were devoted throughout the Classical side of the school to the Roman period. The rest of his educational diet was standard fare: Latin, Maths, Divinity, French and Greek with options in German, Geography, Science and a few other subjects. He must have opted, somewhat surprisingly, for Science since his signed *Inorganic Chemistry* textbook has survived from 1903 with his manuscript notes, scribbles, engravings of Bunsen burners and a pull-out, coloured spectral frontispiece.[12]

Siegfried found it difficult just keeping up with his day-to-day duties, particularly in his first term. These included, apart from lessons and prep, some 'fagging' for senior members of his house. There were strict rules on fagging at Marlborough and his tasks were unlikely to have been onerous. Organ practice was, in theory, another of his duties; in reality it turned out to be a blissful escape from school life. Though his feet refused to operate the pedals in unison with his hands, an example it seemed to him of his 'life-long inability to do two things at once', he enjoyed practising Handel's 'Largo' with the *vox humana* stop pulled out. It was almost the only time his mind could lie fallow, an essential requirement for him in writing poetry.[13]

Though Gould had accused him of using organ-playing to avoid games, this was not possible and Siegfried found himself on the hockey pitch most afternoons. By no means an outstanding player, he probably spent the bulk of his time standing around in the cold, apart from the occasional tackle and inevitable blow to the shin. Weather conditions were particularly severe in early 1902. The year had begun with snow and tobogganing at Weirleigh. The cold had also hastened the death of his Aunt Rachel's husband, which meant an icy journey to the Beer Mausoleum at Highgate Cemetery for the funeral. Once back at school, it had turned so bitter in February that, even in such an intentionally spartan regime, it had been thought necessary to suspend 'early school' (the lesson before breakfast) until conditions improved.

All Siegfried's lessons were abruptly terminated at the end of February by an attack of measles. Though there were strict rules forbidding boys to return to school with an infectious disease, or even if they had been in contact with one, epidemics regularly broke out at Marlborough. If they were particularly serious, the whole school might be sent home. In this case, though the disease was not serious in itself, it had tragic consequences. One of the complications of measles before the advent of antibiotics was secondary bacterial infection brought about by the patient's lowered resistance. The commonest types were ear infections and, as in Siegfried's case, pneumonia. It requires little imagination to envisage his mother's reaction when she was informed by the school that her son, whose life had already been threatened by the disease, now had double pneumonia.

Siegfried himself, after a relatively pleasant week of measles in the sanatorium, was hardly aware of what was happening to him. A sleepless night, in which he had been so thirsty that he had been reduced to drinking from his tepid hot-water bottle, was followed by a blur, punctuated by the dim consciousness of his mother, a large, kind, bearded man and frequent sips of strong beef tea. Theresa, rightly afraid that her son might die, had called for the distinguished physician Sir Thomas Barlow and, presumably on his advice, made Siegfried beef tea with her own hands. The school's medical officer, Dr Edward Penny, may not have liked being overruled in this way, but he must have been grateful that Siegfried did not join the list of those boys who died during the epidemic.

Theresa, whose activities with beefsteaks in the College kitchens had been considered rather *infra dig.* by the authorities, according to her son, was only concerned for his welfare. She had, as Gould generously acknowledged during an early visit to a convalescent Siegfried, probably saved his life. At any rate Siegfried, who had been prayed for in Chapel, felt very important as he lay blissfully recovering. But it was not until the end of March that he was allowed home, looking forward to a game of cribbage with his brothers and the joys of cricket. He may already have started the professional coaching he had decided on after his success in cricket at New Beacon. He had undoubtedly improved by the time he returned to Marlborough for the summer term of 1902, when he was put straight into the House Team. He further distinguished himself by a treble mention in the Lower Games House Matches and was listed among the 'promising' young players who should be 'useful in the future'.

Siegfried's achievements in cricket this term were one sign of his increasing confidence and competence. The advent of his self-assured younger brother, sharing a study with him, his delight in Mr O'Regan's teaching and above all his return to poetry, all helped him to feel less apologetic about himself. He is still inclined to make fun of himself in his memoirs of this period, however, the account of his clumsy performance in the Rifle Volunteer Corps, which he joined in the summer of 1902, being a case in point.[14]

'Siegfried the Maladroit' is clearly one of his favourite themes and personae in his autobiography and not always an entirely convincing one. Nobody who was as uncoordinated as he makes himself seem could have played cricket well enough to get into the House team in his first term. He also played rugby well enough to be awarded his House Colours for it, but represents himself in his autobiography as a 'conscientious but confused ingredient of the "scrum"', who got his colours 'more through discomforts endured than actual merit'.[15] While he can never resist a joke at his own expense, the reader cannot help suspecting that accuracy is sometimes sacrificed to humour.

The truth is that, taking into account his extremely late start in conventional education and his own lack of confidence, Siegfried made good progress at Marlborough to begin with. By the winter of 1902, in his second term with O'Regan, he had climbed from nineteenth to fourth in the form. One result of his efforts, ironically, was that he then missed more school time. For by the middle of November his hard work had led to conjunctivitis and what Matron diagnosed as a 'strained heart' and he was sent home. His mother's ever-present anxieties surfaced and, with Dr Neild's backing, she decided to keep him off school for the Spring term as well. Any hopes he had had of catching up must have begun to seem unrealistic by this time.

*

One positive result of Siegfried's enforced absence from Marlborough, however, was the start of a life-long passion, book-collecting. Bored, no doubt, by his need to continue studying Classics by post with his New Beacon master, Mr Jackson, and prevented from playing golf with him by a spell of bad weather, he conceived the fortuitous idea of making a serious business of books. Until then he had read them enthusiastically but had only collected modern books with coloured illustrations, most of them Christmas presents.

As the sales of his library at Christie's and Sotheby's after his death would show, he succeeded beyond all expectations in building up a superb collection from a modest and haphazard beginning. Grateful for anything which would keep her son occupied, Theresa allowed him to fund his enterprise with the several hundred books left behind by her husband.

Hamo, who had been likewise kept at home for the Spring term of 1903, does not appear to have become involved in Siegfried's book-collecting, but he did help him with cricket practice as the Summer term approached. Both he and Michael had joined Siegfried in setting up their own cricket team in 1902.

Cricket was also the unlikely means of forwarding Siegfried's literary career in April 1903. Despairing of ever getting his poems into the school magazine, *The Marlburian*, which politely ignored his contributions, he had finally sent a piece to *Cricket*, a weekly publication edited by W.A. Bettesworth. To his great surprise, his parody of Charles Kingsley's 'The Sands of Dee', entitled 'The Extra Inch', was accepted, though no payment was made. One can only assume that it was the topicality of Siegfried's subject matter that led to his first appearance in print, since his poem is little more than a humorous exercise, as the opening suggests:[16]

> O batsman, rise and go and stop the rot,
> And go and stop the rot.
> (It was indeed a rot,
> Six down for twenty-three).
> The batsman thought how wretched was his lot,
> And all alone went he.[17]

Siegfried had four more poems accepted by the magazine in the following sixteen months, 'Spring', 'To Wilfred – Bowling', 'Yuletide Thoughts' and 'Dies Irae'.[18]

Siegfried's final year at Marlborough was uneventful. Since by this time it had become clear that he was still too low down the school for his age and would not be able to stay on after summer 1904, he probably felt it was not worth continuing his efforts. After another term's absence in spring 1904, the result of his mother's continuing fear of pneumonia, Siegfried did discover something to interest him at school, calligraphy. Mr England, who tolerated what he describes as his 'semi-idleness', was amused and possibly cheered by his pupil's new-found enthusiasm and allowed him to copy out his weekly Latin prose exercise in pseudo-Gothic characters with ornate initial letters in red, though he drew the line at gilding. Calligraphy, which clearly appealed to Siegfried's highly developed visual sense, continued to delight him throughout his life. He would often copy out his own poems in elaborately beautiful writing as presents. Sometimes, as in the case of a variorum edition of three versions of *The Rubaiyat of Omar Khayyam* in three different coloured inks, he simply created the work for his own pleasure. Like his early childhood notebooks, his handwritten books were at times also illustrated.

There were no prizes for such artistic achievements in Marlborough at the turn of the century, however, and Siegfried left without honours. His failure to succeed at almost everything there seemed to him to explain his recurring dream in later life that he was going back to Marlborough for one more term. In his dream he always relished the idea of being there and 'cutting a fine figure'.[19] In summer 1904, however, Siegfried cut a rather poor one. His final report concluded: 'Lacks power of concentration; shows no particular intelligence or aptitude for any branch of his work; seems unlikely to adopt any special career'.[20] Mr Gould's parting advice to him was 'Try to be more sensible'. He had come to regard Sassoon major, perhaps by comparison with the more diligent and hard-working Hamo, as irresponsible and rather weak. Siegfried's strengths, which were apparent to very few people at that time, could hardly be expected to appeal to an old-fashioned public school master. Their parting was, nevertheless, friendly and Siegfried left regarding his Old Marlburian tie affectionately. More importantly, he also saw it as a sign of his emancipation.

5

The Chancellor's Muddle

1904-1907

Siegfried had entered Marlborough College a child; he left it as a young man, Sassoon. Liberated, as he saw it, from an experience which he had found 'moderately pleasant [but] mentally unprofitable',[1] he could now look forward to a more independent way of life. Though his disappointing performance at Marlborough meant a year's cramming for Cambridge, his middle-class goal, he could at least expect to be treated like a responsible person. So it turned out.

Sassoon's mother, whom he now started to call by her family nickname 'Ash', had had a number of reasons for choosing Henley House; Michael had gone there in 1903 to be coached for Cambridge, as had other members of the Thornycroft family. One advantage was its proximity to Weirleigh. Situated at Frant, less than nine miles away, it was close enough for Siegfried to ride there on the new bicycle he acquired in the summer of 1904 and to return home for visits during the term if he wished. Another advantage, as far as the cyclist was concerned, was that the journey took him through some of his favourite countryside.

Characteristically, Sassoon, in his autobiography, places the advantages of the journey before the more serious reason for choosing Henley House, its excellent academic reputation. He did, however, appreciate its tutoring, which was not quite what might have been expected. For, though Henley House was a full-blown 'crammers', it managed to convey a leisurely, uncompetitive air entirely suited to Sassoon's own dreamy, unworldly temperament. As a result he felt less 'crammed' than he had at school, and worked all the better for it. Whatever its methods, Henley House achieved its ends and succeeded in sending an impressive number of young men to both Oxford and Cambridge, as well as the Armed Forces.

In order to accommodate the twenty or so youths needed to make his establishment a profitable concern the headmaster, Henry Malden, had had to find a sizeable building. Henley House had twenty-two bedrooms and a ground-floor room big enough to be used as a schoolroom. It also had a large drawing-room and all the other accoutrements of a gracious country house. Not the least of its attractions was the house itself and its surroundings. Set in twenty acres of rolling countryside just outside the centre of Frant, it looked down on a lake which could be used as a skating-rink in winter.

There was room not only for two tennis-courts and some cricket nets but also a nine-hole golf course, which Siegfried appreciated greatly. His love of golf was beginning to be something of a passion with him, and Henley House was ideal in this respect. All four members of staff were keen golfers. Henry Malden's cousin, Eustace, was not only a good player but also an expert in laying out golf courses.

Eustace, or 'Uncle' as he was affectionately known to the pupils, was deputy head at Henley House. The establishment had been started by his more enterprizing cousin, Henry, who was also Eustace's brother-in-law, having married Eustace's sister. At the age of twenty-five Henry had opened a small school in Tunbridge Wells, but in 1897 he had decided to move to larger premises at Frant. He was joined there by the newly-married Eustace, who was accommodated in Henley House Lodge. The school continued to flourish and by the time Sassoon arrived in September 1904 he noted that there were over twenty young men studying for either the Oxford or Cambridge entrance exam.

'The Boss', as Henry was called, earned his nickname but it was given with affection. His methods of keeping control over his still schoolboyish pupils were low-keyed. When he found the Old Marlburian actively directing a sousing campaign against an unfortunate youth who had made himself objectionable, instead of ordering him to stop he merely asked Sassoon if he minded using *metal* jugs to pour water over the victim, since the earthenware ones were 'apt to come away from the handles'.

Eustace, on the other hand, seems to have managed to carry out his duties as a teacher and pursue his numerous hobbies at the same time. Besides taking Siegfried through Paley's *Evidences*,[2] and teaching Wellington's campaigns to army candidates, he kept bees and made his own beehives as well as golf-clubs. He was a keen photographer at a time when the art was less commonly practised than today, and took many pictures, on glass, of Henley House. Thanks to him there is a contemporary photograph of Sassoon playing a game of golf near the school lake with two other members of staff. Eustace's own eccentric game sometimes won him the annual Henley House Golf Cup. (Sassoon's even more erratic performance did not, though his golf improved steadily.) Eustace also excelled at another of Siegfried's passions, cricket, and had, to his pupil's great admiration, kept wicket for Kent twelve times between 1892 and 1893. In addition, he was a skilled billiards player.

Sassoon was equally admiring of the two remaining members of staff at Henley House, George Wilson, who taught him classics, and Mr Rawsthorne, who tried to teach him French. George Wilson, was more colourful than Rawsthorne and even more admirable as far as Sassoon was concerned, an excellent all-round athlete who had played rugby for Cambridge, as well as a good teacher. The two were afterwards to become close friends and thus to preserve a link for Sassoon with Henley House until well into the 1920s. For 'George', as he was simply known, was to marry Henry Malden's daughter Jane and to retain close ties with the school even after he had left to start up an establishment of his own in Cambridge. Their friendship started at Henley House and marks the beginning of a period in which Sassoon at last seems ready to make and keep friends. It may be no coincidence that it was also the second time in his life that he had had to face the outside world without the protection of either of his brothers. Michael, who had completed his year at Henley House successfully, was about to go up to Cambridge, and Hamo was still at Marlborough when Siegfried arrived at Henley House; so for one term in the autumn of 1904 he had to fend for himself. During that short period he formed two of his closest early friendships.

The first of these was with a fellow-student, Norman Loder, whom Sassoon used as a model for Denis Milden in *Fox-Hunting Man* to illustrate his theory that for many years he himself was almost a split personality. There was his dreamy, poetical self but also the sporty, physical side. Not only did Loder share his love of sport, hunting and golf in particular, but he also served, in Sassoon's words, as an 'antidote to my poetical-mindedness and indulgence in dreamy sensibility'.[3] Born of an upper-middle-class Sussex family and educated at Eton, where he did little but hunt with the beagles, Loder represented a class and way of life that both attracted and repelled Sassoon.

It took Sassoon many years to overcome the temptation Loder's company afforded to indulge his hearty, extrovert self at the expense of his poetic side. Nor was the choice at all straightforward. The county set, symbolized for Sassoon by Loder, had its virtues. While he felt that it generally lacked subtlety and rarely had either aesthetic or intellectual interests, he could also admire its positive qualities, as epitomized in Loder. He was simple, direct, conscientious and good-natured. Though blunt and matter-of-fact, this only made him seem more solid and reliable, the kind of person often referred to as 'the backbone of England'. He was in addition an outstanding sportsman, something Sassoon could not dismiss. Matching Sassoon's adult height of over six feet, he was the very picture of an English sporting gentleman, as Sassoon implies: 'tall and limber-built, with his neatly-gaitered legs and deliberate way of walking, his brown felt hat tilted over his eyes and a long-stemmed pipe between his teeth'. A mutual friend was to sum up Norman as 'the perfect knight of the saddle, a gallant English gentleman'.[4]

Another friendship strengthened by sport at Henley House was with Henry Thompson. Ill-health had interrupted Thompson's education and he was struggling to get into Oxford. Again it seems to have been largely an attraction of opposites, Thompson complementing him in almost every respect. Unlike Sassoon, 'Tommy' was mature for his age and got on well with his elders. A native of Cumberland, he had a certain north-country shrewdness which contrasted sharply with Sassoon's naïveté. Physically he was much smaller than his friend and his red hair was more striking than Sassoon's, which was nearer to auburn. His slight build and delicate health gave the more robust Sassoon an advantage in golf, since Tommy simply lacked the physique for long, straight drives against a head-wind. Besides a passion for golf, Tommy shared with Sassoon what the latter calls a 'delightfully cronyish quality' and they were to spend many happy days in each other's company. They took a number of long golfing holidays together in their early twenties and paid several visits to each other's houses. Tommy got on particularly well with Theresa, who liked him a great deal better than she was to like most of Sassoon's later male friends.

There was one area of his life that Sassoon did not share with Thompson or Loder, his growing commitment to poetry. Though no poems survive from his time at Henley House, apart from a piece called 'Yuletide' in the *Cricket* magazine, his autobiography suggests that he was planning to write an epic in twelve volumes after he had passed his Cambridge entrance exam. By September 1904 he had apparently written the first two lines, which reflect somewhat portentously his sense of isolation and approaching adulthood after leaving Marlborough: 'Sundered from earth and utterly alone,/ Upon the heights of manhood stood a soul ....'[5] It is also likely that during this year he started to draft some of the poems which appear in *A Pageant of Dreams*, a handwritten volume dedicated to 'Ash' and given to her as a Christmas present in 1905. 'Praise of Spring', for example, could well have been written in the last term of 1905 when, he remembers, 'poetry was awakening [his] senses to ignorant rapture'.[6]

*

Shortly after Sassoon wrote 'Praise of Spring', he was formally admitted to Clare College, Cambridge, though he did not go into residence until the autumn of 1905. On the same day, 29 April 1905, Hamo was also formally admitted to Clare. Their elder brother, Michael, who had been admitted on 13 October 1904 and gone up that term, was still at Clare when Siegfried and Hamo arrived in October 1905.[7]

In choosing Cambridge for her sons rather than Oxford, Theresa was rejecting her husband's family traditions. The wealthier Sassoons generally sent their sons to Eton and Christ Church, Oxford. Whereas, when the Thornycrofts started sending their sons regularly to university in Sassoon's generation, they chose Cambridge. His Donaldson cousin, Malcolm, was the first to go, to Trinity in 1902. Hamo's son, Oliver Thornycroft, followed in 1903 and dictated Theresa's choice for her sons by selecting Clare College, which was smaller than Trinity and approximately the same size as King's. When Michael Sassoon entered Clare in 1904, he set the pattern for his younger brothers.[8]

Sassoon opens his section on Cambridge in *The Old Century* with a description of a family gathering there in June 1906. A dozen of them, all young, all cousins, had met together for the Trinity Boat Club Ball. Apart from the three Sassoon brothers, there were two, possibly three of Hamo Thornycroft's children and the rest were Donaldsons. It is an interesting confirmation of the close family ties maintained by Thomas and Mary Thornycroft's offspring, connexions which Sassoon himself rarely mentions in his autobiography, where he concentrates far more on his moments of isolation, bewilderment and solitary pleasures.

Theresa's decision to follow her brother's choice of college for his son seems entirely understandable. Clare was, and still is, an attractive place. Founded by the Lady Elizabeth, sister and co-heir of Gilbert, Earl of Clare, in 1326, it is the second oldest of all the colleges. With his Pre-Raphaelite love of the medieval, Sassoon could not have helped but enjoy its architecture and cloistered calm. He filled his low-ceilinged third-floor rooms at 4 Market Hill, overlooking the Market Square, with pictures by Burne-Jones and Rossetti and one of his first purchases was a six-volume set of Swinburne's *Poems*, which he had had specially bound in half parchment gilt.[9]

Situated between the River Cam and the Market Square and only a few minutes' walk from the University Library, Clare placed Sassoon at the centre of Cambridge life. And he took advantage of his privileged position in a number of ways. His allowance of £80 per term, while not a fortune, was fairly generous for a young man who as yet neither smoked nor drank. Since his love of book-collecting had continued to grow, some of his money went on buying handsome books in vellum bindings, which he rarely read. Some was spent on entertaining. When his uncle Hamo came to visit, for example, he fêted him with lobster mayonnaise, the best College hock and any other luxury he could find.

Having started to make friends at Henley House, Sassoon appreciated the social life that university offered. Looking back on his time at Clare, he saw himself as a fatuous undergraduate 'sprawl[ing] about in other people's rooms, talking my irrepressible nonsense or listening to someone playing Chopin *scherzos* on the pianola'.[10] Apart from his brothers and cousins, he got to know other students, though none of these friendships was to prove as lasting as those with Loder and Thompson. Cambridge also offered him an opportunity to improve his golf and cricket. Many afternoons when he should have been studying he spent golfing at Mildenhall, Coton or Royston, and he maintained a sufficiently high standard at cricket to feel that it helped conceal his other shortcomings as well as keeping him fit.[11]

Sassoon's greatest inadequacy, he felt, lay in the crucial area of work. Having just scraped into Cambridge with the help of an excellent crammers, he had neither the self-discipline nor the motivation needed to benefit academically there. The problem was not simply one of maturity. As he argued emphatically throughout his memoirs, his academic failure lay deeper than that. It had to do with the poetic temperament, which rejected hard facts in favour of a more imaginative existence. Though this may sound like a cliché, it cannot be dismissed as an explanation. There is no doubt that Sassoon was highly intelligent, hard-working and effectual when his imagination was engaged. When forced, by his conscientious and well-meaning guardians, uncle Hamo and the family solicitor, to study Law, however, motivation failed him completely.

Persuaded initially by the fact that a Law degree required less mathematics than most other degrees, Sassoon quickly found himself bogged down in such dry and bulky works as the *Edicts of Gaius and Justinian*. He felt himself becoming a complete absurdity in the eyes of his quick-witted Law Coach, whose patience finally gave out: 'If I were to go out into the street and interrogate the first errand-boy I met,' he exclaimed, 'he couldn't know less than you do about Maine's *International Law*.'[12]

It was almost certainly this remark which decided Sassoon to give up Law. To his great relief, his senior tutor, W.L. Mollison ('Molly'), who admired his poetry, seemed to understand that Law allowed little scope for the poetic imagination and suggested History as an alternative. His head filled with picturesque scenes from his favourite books, Sassoon gladly embraced the idea. With a burst of characteristically disorganized energy, he started to study the reign of Louis XI, but was soon floundering again. He wanted history to be like Stanley Weyman's novels or Shakespeare's plays and almost entirely lacked a grasp of its constructive elements and political implications. If he could make a poem out of a subject, it interested him; if not, he instantly forgot it. The career of Joan of Arc, for instance, fascinated him and he planned to celebrate it with a long poem in blank verse. The struggle between the Empire and the Papacy, on the other hand, which his History Coach insisted was more important, had no appeal for him at all.

It was the narrative aspect of history, particularly at its dramatic points, which Sassoon absorbed. His choice of Medieval History, not necessarily a wise one, was clearly linked to his continuing interest in the Pre-Raphaelites. When he should have been studying Thatcher and Schwill's *General History of Europe* in the summer term of 1906, he was spending the time reading William Morris's *Earthly Paradise* in a punt, as Oscar Wilde had before him at Oxford. Whether he would have done any better at Cambridge if he had been allowed to study English Literature formally is an interesting but academic question since the English Literature Tripos was not established at Cambridge until 1917, in contrast to Oxford where the English Honours school had been established in 1893.

Sassoon's first year at Cambridge was a time when, to use his own words, he was 'bursting with poetic feeling ... though so immature'. In October 1905 he started to compile an anthology of his favourite poems. Dante Gabriel and Christina Rossetti compete with Swinburne, Browning and Tennyson for top place. A number of minor contemporary poets, such as William Watson, Austin Dobson, Stephen Phillips, John Davidson, Alfred Noyes, Charles Doughty, Robert Louis Stevenson and Ethel Clifford take up most of the rest of the collection. Shakespeare is allowed only one entry, together with Ronsard and Arthur Clough. In keeping with his Romantic tastes at the time, Keats is represented by five sonnets. A less predictable inclusion is Kipling, though his romantic as well as his jingoistic verse is included.

Of his five favourite poets Swinburne was his main influence. Though he still loved Tennyson he was beginning to feel incapable of imitating the older poet's 'distinctness'. Dante Gabriel Rossetti and Browning were now more influential, the latter's *Saul* being his 'prime favourite'.[13] And it was his admiration for Browning's dramatic monologues, as well as a growing interest in blank verse, which led him to attempt his most ambitious poem of this year, 'St Joan'. Written in a state of what he called 'rapt afflatus',[14] it was part of a poetic outpouring that might have resulted from the removal of rigid academic discipline.

The poetic flood had started after he left Henley House in July 1905. By Christmas, apart from this anthology, he had also filled a beautifully bound grey cloth and cream leather notebook tooled in gold with exquisitely handwritten poems of his own for his mother. The bulk of them appear to date from his first three months at Cambridge. The poetry, though still highly derivative, is much more accomplished and assured than that of his childhood notebooks. It is still Romantic in influence, with specifically Pre-Raphaelite emphasis on the medieval in both language and content. At least two of the poems appear to be based on Pre-Raphaelite pictures, one of them, 'Slow Music', describing a warrior being carried to his grave, while: 'Maidens pace slowly by, and knights well mailed,/ Across wet gleaming sand.' 'Love Triumphant' concerns allegorical forms of Love, Mortality and Time, with Joy 'uprising like a prayer' and 'soar[ing] upon the tireless wings of ecstacy [*sic*]'. There are many similar echoes of Keats and other Romantic poets, the main influences, as the numerous epigraphs indicate, being Keats, Tennyson, Rossetti, Swinburne and their ardent disciple Sir William Watson.[15]

Sassoon's subject matter is also predictably late-Romantic – the too-swift passing of time, the arrival of spring, death, creation, the seasons. There is one 'occasional' poem, 'Dies Irae', but for the most part the poems are a vague, generalized examination of the passions. Love is frequently cited, but there is no personal love poetry, a noticeable omission for a young man of nineteen. But if he experienced such impulses, as he almost certainly did, he also felt that he must keep them to himself. He was ashamed of his attraction towards men and was still trying hard to suppress such feelings even from himself. There are hints in some of the poems that he was fighting what he saw as defilement and impurity. The tone in these poems alternates between resolution and despair.

The language of these 1905 poems, like the subject matter, is largely lacking in freshness, being full of archaisms and poeticisms, most of them borrowed from other poets, 'purpureate' being a particularly lurid example. There is clearly a striving for originality, as 'vampired clouds' shows, but, as it also suggests, this can lead to an unfortunate straining after effect. All the 'big' things in life are personified, or at least given capital letters, though even this is not consistent. Life, Love, Joy and Hope fight with Death, Hate, Misery and Despair. Ambition and Lust strive to gain control over Honour and Shame. The imagery itself is likewise largely clichéd: Music strikes her golden lyre, Poetry pours in a flood from the poet's lips, Hope is the dawning of a brighter day, Time's myrmidons 'work their wild way no more'. Sometimes the metaphors are exuberantly mixed. Occasionally, when the description is of something known personally to Sassoon, it is fresh and stimulating: in 'A Vision of Seasons', for example, a tired allegory of the poet dreaming of Spring, Summer and Autumn in an 'enchanted woodland vale', we are reminded of the orchards of Kent in spring:

> For without the song of many birds
> Fell, as scattered blossoms on the air
> Fall when orchards rock in winds of May.

Under the influence of Swinburne and Watson, Sassoon's passion for alliteration is freely indulged, his intoxication with sound extending also to rhythm. He relishes hexameters and experiments freely with odd combinations of metre.

At the end of *A Pageant of Dreams*, written in quite a different hand and clearly added after it had been presented as a Christmas gift to his mother, Sassoon included five poems, three of which indicate a more vigorous poetic impulse. 'Sea-Faring', for example, is much more personal than anything that appears before it. Though couched in fairly stilted language and conventional metaphor, it deals with Sassoon's own struggle to remain 'pure':

> Adrift upon an ocean tempest-toss'd,
> We cast our manhood to the winds, till fain
> To ask a little mercy of the Main
> That hurls us on the rocks, defiled and lost;
> The sullied hours are number'd, and their cost
> Measured by endless misery; – free from stain –
> The shores of godlihead how may we gain –
> Is not this gulf too turbulent to be cross't?

The final poem in the volume, 'A Thought', is another of the few poems based on personal experience and is, correspondingly, less tired and derivative. This gives it a certain amount of vigour, unlike the majority of the pieces in this his first adult volume.

After presenting his mother with *A Pageant of Dreams* at Christmas 1905, Sassoon continued to write feverishly. By June he had had four poems published in the University magazine, *Granta*, and one in the *Cambridge Review*.[16] Though all were parodies, of Stephen Phillips, Robert Browning, Swinburne and the Psalmist, they are exuberant proof of his love of words and sounds.

Sassoon had fed this love of sounds with Swinburne's *Atalanta in Calydon* and other lush verse. The Pre-Raphaelite poems and pictures in which he immersed himself provided an ideal escape into a dream world which seemed both more attractive and, ironically, more real than either Law or History. He filled a blue notebook, originally entitled 'Roman Law II' with 'Rough Drafts' for his poems rather than lecture notes. By September 1906 he had enough poems to contemplate publication. Either he lacked the confidence, or did not wish to approach a commercial publisher. Certainly he was not at all sure of the worth of his poems. A privately printed volume of modest size but attractive appearance seemed the answer. It could also be anonymous and thus avoid the possibility of hostile criticism. (It was a pattern that was to be repeated with variations throughout his life.)

Sassoon finally made his decision on the 8 September 1906, his twentieth birthday, and tentatively approached the publishers of his favourite magazine, the *Athenaeum*. When they readily agreed to print fifty copies of what he titled simply *Poems*, with no price mentioned, he was so grateful that he sent the manuscript off without further enquiry on 20 September. In mid-December he finally received the book, just in time for Christmas.[17] It numbered thirty-six pages and was bound in thick white cartridge paper, with a tastefully contrasting dark blue satin marker band. The title was printed on both the cover and the title-page, with no name. There were two extra copies on hand-made paper. Its production seemed to Sassoon remarkably cheap at £7.

Most of the information about the composition of *Poems* (1906) and Sassoon's reaction to it come from letters written to a friend made at Cambridge, Everard Leaver Guilford. This friendship, which shows that Sassoon had managed to form relationships outside the close, almost claustrophobic family network that operated even at Cambridge, provided him with a confidant and adviser. He seems to have used Guilford rather as a litmus-paper before braving the opinion of the rest of the world with his work.

Guilford's most significant role as far as posterity is concerned, however, was as a sounding-board for Sassoon's ideas on poetry during and just after his Cambridge days. Sassoon clearly trusts Guilford's judgement and sends him a detailed description of his aims in *Poems*, together with an attractive little notebook filled with handwritten copies of his work. When the book itself appears Guilford is the first to receive a copy and, in his enthusiasm, requests a second. Though later Sassoon was to invite another friend to laugh at some of their 'poeticizings, their naive moralizings, verbal imprecision and auto-intoxication with word-sounds', he also pointed out the main significance of *Poems*: that he was 'doing it all on [his] own steam, with no one to tell [him] how to do it professionally'.[18] He told a third friend that '*Poems 1906* is mostly weak imitation of Tennyson, Swinburne and D.G. Rossetti and is full of didactic moralizing and humbug'.[19] But, looking back, he was thankful that he had not been a 'sophisticated youth' but had really experienced all 'those aspirations and vague upliftments'.[20] *Poems* does not differ substantially from the Romantic outpourings of *A Pageant of Dreams*, though there are a few moments in the volume when Sassoon's own observations animate the verse.

The most sustained effort in *Poems* is 'St Joan'. A dramatic monologue, written under the spell of Browning and early history, it manages to steer clear of much of the weariness of language in the less original lyrics. It is no surprise to learn that Sassoon wrote its 220 lines almost at one sitting. It has a directness and thrust lacking in the shorter poems and is far more powerfully conceived. Spoken by Joan on the eve of her execution, it also has pathos while managing to avoid mawkishness.

Sassoon's friends and relatives responded encouragingly to his first printed volume, but it would probably have seemed churlish to react otherwise to a Christmas present. Had he realized what he acknowledged afterwards, that his ideas in *Poems* 'lacked originality' and that his language was 'hopelessly hackneyed', he might well have stopped writing then and there. As it was, he continued with undiminished energy to pour forth poetry.

While *Poems* was at the printers, for example, he was busily preparing an entry for the Chancellor's Medal in poetry. His uncle Hamo, visiting him at Cambridge in the summer of 1906 and hearing of his poetic activity, had diffidently suggested that his nephew try for it and his senior tutor, Mollison, having admired some of his erratic student's work, also urged him to enter. Introduced by His Royal Highness William Frederick, Duke of Gloucester, Chancellor of Cambridge University from 1811 to 1834, the Chancellor's

Medal was the equivalent of the Newdigate Prize at Oxford and had been won by some subsequently well-known poets. One reason Sassoon wanted to try for it was that it seemed to him his only chance of earning academic distinction. He was comforted by the fact that it had been won by Tennyson, who had left Cambridge without taking a degree.

By the time the subject was eventually announced in October 1906, Sassoon's *Poems* were ready for the press and he was, therefore, free to concentrate on the prize. Ironically, the subject turned out to be historical – 'Edward the First'. To begin with, Sassoon felt this to be propitious, since his uncle Hamo had made an equestrian statue of the king. With a photograph of the statue on his desk, he set to work enthusiastically to produce the requisite 200 lines.

Sassoon was hampered by a conviction that the poem would not benefit from his usual Pre-Raphaelite or 1890s treatment, both of which seemed entirely inappropriate to the austere Plantagenet Edward. After rejecting the idea of a soliloquy delivered by the young king on one of his Crusades, he decided on a straightforward retrospect dictated by Edward to an anonymous chronicler towards the end of his reign. Another one hundred flat lines later, however, he realized that he had still not found the correct formula, and put the piece away, consoling himself by seeing his *Poems* through the press.

When Sassoon returned to Edward in December, with most of Tout's indigestible facts about Edward conveniently forgotten and after further encouragement from his tutor, Mollison, inspiration returned. So, too, did the Pre-Raphaelite influence. In what even he recognized as an echo of Tennyson's rendering of King Arthur's end, he gave Edward the 'death-bed' treatment: 'All his inherent nobility of nature was finding solemn expression in blank verse which almost made me feel as if I were bidding farewell to the world myself.'[21] It was an unfortunate choice of treatment, its lack of originality allowing him to indulge in all his favourite clichés. The opening lines, from a handwritten copy sent to Guilford, give the flavour of the whole:

> I have no strength to urge these Scottish wars
> Further, so here at Burgh-on-the-Sands,
> In the last slow surrendering of life
> Will pray that I be brought unto repose,
> And the valley of the shadows, which is Peace.

Even Sassoon recognised that his poem was unlikely to win the Chancellor's Medal. In desperation, weighed down by the heaviness of Stubb's *Constitutional History and Select Charters*, which he was trying unsuccessfully to assimilate during the Christmas vacation, he made the winning of the Medal his condition for returning to Cambridge at the beginning of 1907. Facing certain failure in his second-year exams, it seemed to him the only possible way to maintain credibility. Since the results were not due until March 1907, he stayed on at Weirleigh after Christmas, making a mild attack of flu his excuse for not returning to Cambridge at the beginning of the Lent term.

This was not, however, a simple matter. Sassoon's guardians could not be expected to accept a decision they would certainly consider unwise and irresponsible. The family solicitor, Mr Lousada, caused his charge little concern. Sassoon was used to being reproved by him for his expensive tastes in books and clothes. It was his uncle Hamo, for whom he had great affection and respect, who worried him.

In the absence of Alfred Sassoon, Hamo Thornycroft had become something of a substitute father for Sassoon, the main male influence in his young life. He viewed the small, spare man in many ways as a role model. Hamo and his wife Agatha (on whom, in part, Hardy is reputed to have based Tess in *Tess of the d'Urbervilles*) frequently visited Weirleigh with their children during the troubled years of Alfred's abandonment of his wife and sons. Sassoon showed his affection for his uncle in a number of ways, notably dedicating what he called his *Red Poetry Book* to him in 1898. He admired his uncle not so much for his outstanding achievements in sculpture as for his modesty and self-effacing simplicity, describing him as 'a simple enthusiastic soul'.[22]

When detailing the elaborate lunch he gave Hamo at Cambridge in June 1906, Sassoon reflects: 'If I could have the ordering of that meal again I would give him some good Cheshire cheese, a nice brown loaf, and a tankard of home-brewed ale, and possibly a cold gooseberry tart. Simple country things were what he liked best, and he always had the look of an open-air man, as well he might, since he came of a line of thriving gentleman farmers in Cheshire.'[23] Hamo himself had grown up in the country. His father and mother, short of money and struggling to maintain their large family, had reluctantly agreed to send him at the age of four to live with his uncle, William Thornycroft, on his prosperous cheese farm at Great Tidnock, Cheshire. The plan to pass the childless William's farm on to Hamo failed because of one quality the adults had not taken into account, Hamo's determination. Though he greatly enjoyed his nine years on the farm and retained a love of rural pursuits and the countryside for the rest of his life, he decided quite early on that he wanted to return to London, 'to be something', as he put it.

His father, disillusioned by his own lack of success in sculpture and increasingly drawn towards his eldest son's experiments in engineering, tried hard to deflect Hamo's interests that way. With quiet but iron-willed persistence Hamo went his own way, secretly modelling a figure of a dancing faun which gained him early admission to the Royal Academy School, where he quickly established himself as a sculptor in the classical tradition. Later, under the influence of William Morris, he became something of an innovator, his 'Mower' being the first successful statue of a man in working-clothes. Followed by 'The Sower' and other examples of men and their trades, it portrayed working men with dignity rather than sentimentality, and with an authenticity doubtless gained from his own early experience on a farm.

Edmund Gosse, who became a life-long friend of Hamo's, greatly helped the young sculptor's career by writing extensively about his art and influencing his many friends to commission work. In addition, and throughout his highly successful life, Hamo received many public commissions, notably for the statues of Oliver Cromwell at the House of Commons, Gladstone opposite the Law Courts, Gordon of Khartoum, now in the Embankment Gardens, and King Alfred at Winchester.

On the face of it, there was not much to encourage Siegfried as he contemplated his uncle's character and achievements. He seemed all that his nephew was not: effective where Sassoon failed, determined where he vacillated. In addition his own son Oliver, born a few months after Michael Sassoon, had just successfully completed his own BA at Clare. Sassoon realized how hard it would be for his uncle to understand his own dilemma. How could such a determined, hard-working and successful man possibly understand his position? His only hope lay in his uncle's sympathy and generosity of spirit, which he trusted would eventually win him over.

As it turned out, when Sassoon heard on 11 March 1907 that he had failed to win the Medal, he felt that he had no choice. After a week's delay he wrote with a mixture of defiance and apology to his uncle:

> I must screw myself up to inform you that I intend to give up Cambridge. I see no use in staying there three years and not getting a degree, and am sure I should never pass the exams.
>
> I expect you will be very sick with me about it, but I don't think I should ever do anything there. I admit that it appears rather idiotic, but I have quite made up my mind about it.
>
> Yr. not at all truculent nephew
> S. Sassoon[24]

In desperation, Hamo wrote to Gosse, whose wife was still a close friend of Sassoon's mother, asking him to use all his powers of persuasion on her. (She was in London at the time.) He also wrote to Sassoon with a mixture of exasperation and sorrow familiar to those who try to advise 20-year-olds:

> 20 March '07
> Dear Siegfried,
> I could have wished that you had asked my advice. I should have advised you to stay on until Oct. at any rate, and I certainly think you should do so.
>
> This modern method of 'chucking work' or chucking College as soon as it becomes in any [way] tedious is a poor development.
>
> At the risk of being prosaic I will say that the moral discipline of work we do not quite like is an excellent thing, and as Xtianity gets less and less a guiding influence, will become more and more necessary.

I do not see why your being at Cambridge should not be an advantage to you in every way – even if you do not take your degree.

Yours affectionately,

Hamo Thornycroft.[25]

Sassoon would probably have acceded to Hamo's wishes had he possessed the faintest hope of passing his Tripos exams. He was quite convinced that his uncle was unable to understand his character, which was so very different from his own. It was perhaps a case of his dilettante father's traits confronting solid Thornycroft virtues.

Though deflated when his poem failed to win the prize, Sassoon was more than ever determined to be a poet. He had not wanted to take a degree in the first place and now felt himself freed from any obligation to try for one. (He would later describe his time at Cambridge as 'Four terms of boredom and discomfort'.[26]) His mother, who had believed in his poetic vocation from an early age, supported his decision wholeheartedly. She had, in any case, never forced him to do anything he disliked. In her positive way she tried to make the best of it with a joke about the Chancellor's 'Muddle', then said no more. Sassoon himself settled down with relief to live the life of a country gentleman.

6

Sporting Squire and Gentleman Writer

1907-1914

Seven months after Sassoon's decision to leave Cambridge he celebrated his twenty-first birthday alone with his mother at Weirleigh. Nearly two-thirds of his twenty-one years had been spent at home with her and, in contrast to most of his male contemporaries, only just over a third away at school and university. He was now to pass yet another seven years at home, bringing the time spent there up to three-quarters of his young life. His own diagnosis of this prolonged childhood was that his 'youthful personality ... had no shape or coherence unless [he] was inside the radius of [his] limited experience'.[1] While knowing at some level that he should leave Kent, perhaps even England, he was still not ready to face the outside world on his own.

One of his main problems at this time was how to fill his days. Loving Weirleigh was not quite enough and so gradually he began to adopt the life of a country gentleman, which became almost a full-time occupation. His spring and autumn would be spent golfing, his summer in playing cricket and his winter in renewed pursuit of his early passion, fox-hunting. To these sports he added an even more challenging one, which, like hunting, brought out the daredevil in him so apparently at odds with his timidity – steeplechasing. Another less predictable enthusiasm was dancing.

In direct contrast to these physical activities, and sometimes conflicting with them, were Sassoon's cultural needs. He continued his book-collecting, made a determined effort to improve his musical skills and added to his store of favourite paintings. Occasional days in London were spent mainly at concerts and art-galleries, though they also included visits to his tailors and bootmakers for smart hunting-clothes. Literature, however, remained his chief artistic outlet, and within that broad category, poetry still dominated. Between 1908 and 1913 he produced nine volumes of verse, as though driven by a need he himself did not wholly understand. He became increasingly aware of himself as two separate selves, one physically daring and outgoing, the other tentative and inward-looking. Thinking back on himself in 1914, he remembered the problems he had amalgamating his 'contrasted worlds of literature and sport'. At twenty-eight he would ask himself: 'Why must I always be adapting my manners – and even my style of speaking – to different sets of people? Was it really necessary to exclude one world in order to find diversity in the other? Couldn't one combine them in "one grand sweet song"?'[2]

Sassoon would ultimately find the conflicting roles of sporting squire and gentleman writer impossible to maintain, but he initially set about qualifying for them both in a rather deliberate manner. At the most obvious level, he took to smoking a pipe. (A 'smoking-room' was immediately created for him out of his father's old study.) And in 1908 he got himself elected to a London club. Since he had neither the money nor the reputation for one of the more prestigious establishments, he had to settle for the less well-known Royal Societies Club. Informing his readers that he had once heard it jokingly misnamed 'The United Nonentities" club, Sassoon paints a picture of a sombre, dull but highly respectable place where it took him seven years to become even faintly friendly with one or two elderly members.

*

Before Sassoon returned to the hunting-field in 1907 he spent the spring and summer in the two sporting activities he had been able to pursue consistently throughout university, golf and cricket. From 1906 to 1910 he played golf regularly in the autumn, spring and early summer, his main partner being his friend Henry Thompson from Henley House. He also played with Loder or the staffs of his old preparatory school and crammers. In between he played many matches at a local golf-course run by Squire Morland at Lamberhurst. His description of its neglected and irregular conditions – it was 'much frequented by sheep'[3] – provided him with an amusing digression in *The Weald of Youth*, yet it is clear that he enjoyed his games there as much as, if rather differently from, anywhere else, in particular its idyllic pastoral surroundings. Sassoon's love of golf stemmed partly from the physical exercise it offered. He also enjoyed being out of doors in attractive surroundings. And the company was almost exclusively male. Most importantly of all, golf allowed him to be what he called 'ruminative', there being plenty of time between strokes for daydreams. With a handicap of six, he was sufficiently good to enjoy the game without worrying too much if he sometimes lost.

The same might also be said of Sassoon's love of cricket, though that was to last a lifetime, while his passion for golf faded away in his thirties. Apart from its strong literary appeal, cricket fulfilled other needs in Sassoon. While helping to keep him fit, like golf, it also brought him into close contact with men of widely varying class and age. In his local cricket teams, Brenchley and Matfield, for example, he played with villagers he would not normally have got to know in the fairly rigid class system of the day. Sassoon was respected in the local teams not because he was the 'gentleman' of independent, if limited, means from Weirleigh but because he was a useful bowler, good batsman and great enthusiast, even willing to help with the scoring. He was a valued member of both Brenchley and Matfield teams and some weeks played as many as five matches.

During the Easter 1904 school holidays, Sassoon had attended the Tonbridge Cricket Club nets while being coached by the Kent professional Humphreys. He appeared more frequently, however, for the Blue Mantles, who also played on the Nevill Ground at Tunbridge Wells.[4] By 1904, when Sassoon joined the Blue Mantles, it was playing some very good club sides and had several players with some limited first-class experience. Sassoon almost certainly struggled at this level. With characteristic modesty and probably some truth he suggested that his selection had more than a little to do with his ready availability. The cricket, he felt, was a good deal better than he was. But he was a reliable club cricketer and was not completely ashamed of his averages, considering them 'quite a creditable record for a poet'.[5]

One strong appeal the game had for Sassoon was its beauty. Cricket on a well-tended village green in dazzling whites, with the reassuring sounds of afternoon tea being prepared by non-participating women in the pavilion, was quite a pleasurable experience. He spent a great deal of his life looking back to his youth and became extremely nostalgic about cricket. Even in his twenties he reminisced about the older, more amateurish cricketers and their idiosyncratic ways. A later cricketing friend of Sassoon's remembered his nostalgia for old Kentish cricketers, especially Frank Woolley, who had once repaired a puncture for him in his little shop by the Angel ground at Tonbridge.[6]

While Sassoon undoubtedly appreciated the all-male environment, it was not the real reason for his enjoyment of the game. Its main appeal for him was, and continued to be, its essential Englishness. And as the writer of an article on Sassoon's later cricketing performance argues, 'Cricket was his game because it gave him space and time.'[7] Cricket became the epitome of all that was peaceful in his past. It remained for him not merely a game but a way of life, symbolizing all that he loved most about rural England in summer.

Winter was another matter. As autumn approached Sassoon's thoughts turned to fox-hunting. Largely unhindered by the doubts and conflicts which trouble the sport today, though there were times when he questioned its humaneness, his main problem was finding the money needed to pursue it. When he was a boy his mother had sold her jewellery to buy him horses, but as a young man with an allowance of his own he was expected not only to buy them himself but to pay for their upkeep as well. His allowance of £400 per annum should have been quite sufficient, since his mother continued to pay all household expenses from her far less generous income of £200. It is not surprising that, eighteen months after he returned home, his uncle had to inform him that his mother's income in 1908 had proved insufficient; nor that he felt obliged to tell his self-absorbed young nephew that he thought he and his younger brother should help with household expenses. When Sassoon did finally pronounce himself 'anxious to help in the housekeeping', however, his uncle pointed out that he could not do that *and* 'do the wealthy patronizing gentleman, subscribing to all the golf clubs etc. and keeping a couple of hunters'.[8] If he, Hamo, had spent '£400 a year on self' at the age of 23, he argued, he would have been 'a fool'.

None of this prevented Sassoon from pursuing his chosen lifestyle, however. Since hunting was as much a social as a sporting activity – and Sassoon himself admitted to being something of a snob at this time – he had, in addition to horses, to spend fairly large amounts on riding equipment ordered from the correct tailors and bootmakers. The not inconsiderable hunt subscription had also to be found. The family solicitor, Mr Lousada, the more worldly and stricter of his two guardians, tried hard to dissuade him from such extravagance, but in 1907, shortly after his twenty-first birthday, Sassoon bought himself a hunter and with it a winter's occupation. For the next seven seasons he was to hunt regularly. Even when war intervened and he joined the army, he would go out with the hounds whenever possible, though it was not until the winter of 1920 that he would again have his own horse.

Dame Felicitas Corrigan suggests that the pleasure Sassoon derived from a day with the hounds 'rose out of the aesthetic love for the English countryside of a young poet at the height of his physical vitality'.[9] Sassoon himself maintained:

For me hunting is inevitably associated with the pleasant country house life of the past which the Second World War has apparently eliminated. There was a traditional flavour about hunting which has never been the same since 1914. Admittedly, it was an undemocratic flavour, since it was derived from the 'design for living' of a prosperous and privileged upper class society which could still feel secure against the distant agitations of Socialism ... Those were indeed the days, and delightful they are to remember, though deplorable to the urban-minded politicians of today's Government which aims at reducing us all to equality of income and mediocrity of mind. Nevertheless, I am unable to believe that the material basis of what is called the fabric of existence will alter the mental attitude of people who love horses and hunting. All the essential ingredients will still be there – the behaviour of the animal, the smell of a winter morning, and the sense of personal adventure and physical well-being in the rider.[10]

There was more to it than that, however. Cocooned as he was in his childhood environment, sheltered by an over-protective mother and an independent income from having to face anything uncongenial, he clearly had a need to take risks, to face danger. As an inexperienced child he had followed the Master over the highest jumps and he continued recklessly to do so.

Sassoon derived an equal amount of pleasure from the less dramatic side of hunting, the early start on a crisp winter's morning, with boiled eggs and cocoa for breakfast, the echo of the horse's hoofs on the frosty road, the gradual dawning of day over the misty countryside and then, after the exhilaration of the galloping, jumping and chasing, the slow ride home on his tired horse, with a break for tea at a country inn by a roaring fire. *Fox-Hunting Man* is full of such nostalgic details.

As Sassoon explains in *The Weald of Youth*, published fourteen years after *Fox-Hunting Man*, he deliberately avoided the subject of fox-hunting in his 'real' autobiography because it had 'already been monopolized by a young man named George Sherston' who he admits was 'only me with a lot left out'.[11] He then goes on to give actual names and dates, together with a long description of the peak of his hunting career – a season with Loder at the Atherstone Hunt from September 1913 to March 1914. By that time he had acquired four hunters, Rubicon, Golumpus, Crusader and his favourite, Cockbird. These he transported together with his groom, Richardson, and a stable boy, to Witherley where Norman was living in a cottage while Witherley Lodge was being renovated for him.

Sassoon had stayed with Loder at Ringmer, Lewes, when Loder was Master of the Southdown Hunt. He had also spent less exciting days with the West Kent Hounds. The Atherstone was quite different. In an area approximately twenty-four miles by eighteen, the Atherstone hunted over grassy open pastureland of ridge and furrow relatively free of the huntsman's curse, barbed wire. But it was an expensive undertaking, which Sassoon knew he would be unlikely to afford again. This gave it a unique added piquancy which comes through in both his fictional and autobiographical accounts.

While enjoying almost every minute of his time with the Atherstone, however, Sassoon had learnt by the end of his six-month stay that physical activities alone could not satisfy him. He was extremely fond of Loder and his abrupt, matter-of-fact ways. He also enjoyed the company of Loder's fellow-Etonian friend, Charles Wiggin, and other friends who came to stay. But he could not talk to them of poetry, art or music. Eventually he began to feel that it was possible to have 'too much unadulterated fox-hunting'. It was not Weirleigh he missed; but by devoting himself entirely to the physical he had lost the precarious balance he was gradually establishing between body and mind.

Meantime he finished off his season with Loder in style by competing in what had become another addictive sport, steeplechasing, and winning narrowly from Loder on a horse he had bought in 1910, Cockbird.[12] He describes the thrills and dangers of steeplechasing as vividly as those of the hunt, and it is clear that both appealed to him for similar reasons. It was not so much to do with winning as the excitement of the thing itself. Another advantage point-to-points offered was that they followed the hunting season and prolonged it by several weeks.

Perhaps the greatest benefit Sassoon derived from steeplechasing was that it brought him into contact in 1908 with someone who was to become the best sporting friend he ever had, Gordon Harbord (Stephen Colwood of *Fox-Hunting Man*). Sassoon stayed with Gordon and his family on many occasions at their rectory in East Hoathley, about thirty miles from Weirleigh. All the Harbords, or at least all the males of the household, were keen horsemen.

Gordon himself was nearly four years older than Sassoon, but he became a closer friend than either of his brothers, Geoffrey, a Gunner Major, or Kenneth, almost the same age as Sassoon and a fellow Marlburian. The fact that Gordon, like his eldest brother Henry, went to Winchester rather than Marlborough and won an Exhibition to London University suggests that he was academically able, though it was evidently not a path that he wished to pursue. Like Sassoon he was sensitive and basically non-intellectual in his approach to life.

According to Sassoon, Gordon had a meditative air, softened by a humorous, at time, whimsical expression. This sense of humour, together with his sensitivity and passion for horses, explains his instant rapport with Sassoon and the strength of their friendship. He had various names for Sassoon, all of them jokey – 'Sig', 'old cocky', 'Sarsoon' or 'Sarson'. Referring to Sassoon's own jokey manner he claimed that it would take 'a very experienced Sig-ologist to distinguish matter from mocker, or sense from Surtees'.[13] They were both avid readers of the sporting writer Surtees and shared many private jokes about his characters.[14]

By a fortunate coincidence, not long after Sassoon's encounter with Gordon and the Southdown Hunt, Norman Loder became the Master of it. Gordon learnt to admire Loder's sportsmanship and solid if unimaginative character as much as Sassoon had, and the three became good friends.

*

In the socially rigid and fairly limited society of the district, a handsome, unattached young man of private income, however modest, was inevitably seen as eligible. Sassoon showed no outward signs of his distaste for women in general and none of the clichés attached to homosexuals at the time fitted him. Far from seeming effeminate, he was the very model of masculinity with his lean sportsman's figure and dark good looks. His sensitivity and love of the arts appeared quite natural in the son of a professional painter and talented musician. Not surprisingly, therefore, he found himself invited to numerous dances and balls.

As an extension of what he called his 'life of action', to which he thought himself '(spasmodically) suited by temperament', Sassoon enjoyed dancing.[15] He maintained that the more romantic associations usually attached to dancing escaped him completely, but that is hard to believe. It is more likely that, when his partner suggested that some particularly soulful tune to which they swayed was playing 'specially for us', he was not unaware of its intimate implications, as he claims, but merely untouched by heterosexual interests, perhaps even threatened. He felt more romantic about the Queen Anne country houses where the balls often took place and in which he frequently stayed. He enjoyed their elegance, their discreet luxury, but above all their sense of history. His description of one such house in *The Weald of Youth* was based on Finchcocks at Goudhurst, only seven miles from Weirleigh, and owned by the Stirling family. The daughter of the house, Marjorie, who had known Sassoon from childhood, was one of his few female friends in his twenties.[16] Once the suggestion of romance or sex was removed Sassoon enjoyed talking to women and was later to make confidantes of a number of them. If he suspected them of a sexual interest, however, he began to see them as voracious harpies.

Two other popular sports of the time were croquet and clock-golf, both of which Sassoon probably enjoyed. He seems to have conformed to the pattern of the young country gentleman in all bar one respect: that of shooting; he had never felt able to shoot either animal or bird.

At no other period of his life did Sassoon feel able to compartmentalize his activities so neatly. He was later to argue that too great a concentration on the physical was detrimental to his artistic side: 'How easy it is to be alive when we demand of life only the simple and crude reward of success in a steeplechase. In such a mood art also seems easy, and I feel tempted to lapse into sloppy emotions and luscious derivative cadences – the drawing-room music of poetry, the melody that snares us into easy-flowing sentiment.'[17]

Certainly during this period of intense physical activity his tastes in art continued to be romantic. After a phase of admiring George Meredith for his 'few lyrical masterpieces', he had become intoxicated by Walter Pater, who began to fill his shelves.[18] He was particularly fond of Pater's *Imaginary Portraits,* despite Helen Wirgman's advice that Meredith would have provided a more useful model. It was the romantic and enigmatic in Pater which he craved. Largely ignoring the don's impressive learning, he wallowed in his studies of sensitive temperaments in the picturesque past. Pater's deliberately stylized prose did nothing to improve the aspiring poet's already ornate phrases.

Other books added to Sassoon's new library-study in 1907, however, suggest that he was not completely dominated by Pater's influence. He began to collect A. Wright's 1902 edition of Shakespeare, for example, and bought at least two books of contemporary poetry, Herbert Trench's *New Poems* (1907) and Andrew Lang's *Ballads and Lyrics of Old France* (1907). One aspect of book-collecting which particularly pleased him and revealed another important aspect of his character was that of arranging his treasures on shelves: 'it is an occupation which appeals to my craving for neatness and order', he wrote in his diary in 1922.[19]

These tastes, as well as Sassoon's romantic leanings, were also satisfied by his growing collection of mainly Pre-Raphaelite paintings in his twenties. Even in his thirties he considered his taste in pictures 'a very lop-sided affair, overbalanced by [his] unaesthetic and unintellectual bias towards "literary interest"'.[20] This remark was made on the occasion he bought the photos of the martyrdom of San Lorenzo by Santa Croce, not for aesthetic reasons but for its 'morbidly sexual appeal to my sexually morbid mind':

> I hurry from one San Sebastian to another: from Ganymede to Narcissus and from Narcissus to Apollo. I hunt for beardless Christs and prostrate Abels, and hang about in front of Isaacs quailing at the crises of immolation by Abraham. Abraham, owing to the intervention of the angel, substitutes a ram for his offspring. I wish I could substitute intellect for the lust of the flesh. Also I find myself drugging my visual senses with *colour* instead of cultivating my appreciation of *design*.

His bias towards literary interest may partly account for his love of landscape painters such as John Sell Cotman, James Pyne and George Mason, which endured throughout his life, unlike his interest in the Pre-Raphaelites which gradually declined. But his tastes in painting were to remain fairly conservative and as late as 1952 he could refer to the great French Modernist as 'that awful Matisse'.

Sassoon's taste in music between 1907 and 1914 was slightly more adventurous; he came to it later and without his mother's dominating influence. Though his impulse was still basically romantic, he was much readier to experiment with contemporary or near contemporary music. Helen Wirgman, who had taught him to love music in the first place, was herself open to new experiences and helped him to explore composers who were still regarded as challenging in the early twentieth century, such as Debussy and Grieg. Grieg was still just alive when Sassoon bought himself a grand piano in 1907. Though he had to resort to hire-purchase – a humiliating necessity as he saw it – his need to play the piano was almost as great as his urge to write poetry, two processes he believed to be closely connected: 'Most of my early verse,' he wrote in *The Weald of Youth*, 'was vague poetic feeling set to remembered music. Unintellectual melodiousness was its main characteristic. Rich harmonies and lingering sonorities induced a relaxation of the nerves and acted on me like stimulating oxygen.'[21] Sometimes he would insert bars of music into his poetry notebooks as a guide to metre and a number of his works lent themselves readily to musical settings.[22]

Though Sassoon found Debussy much too difficult for his amateurish technique, he was excited by his 'delicate descriptiveness and his new and sumptuous subtleties of tone'.[23] It was the romantic melodist that attracted him rather than the experimental technician, as his confessed preference for *Clair de Lune* over *Passepied* indicates.

By 1911 he was again expanding his musical horizons, this time through his renewed friendship with Nevill Forbes. Though Sassoon had initially reacted strongly against Fräulein Stoy's praise of her former pupil's musical and linguistic abilities, he had gradually come to share her admiration. Having kept in touch with the Forbes family after he left the New Beacon, he visited Nevill in 1910 at Oxford, where Forbes – who spoke at least fifteen languages – was Professor of Russian. In 1911 Forbes paid a return visit to Weirleigh. Apart from indulging Sassoon in Debussy, he introduced him to other contemporary composers such as Ravel, Reger, Albéniz, Chausson, Scriabin and César Franck, all of whom Sassoon enjoyed despite their modernity.

Sassoon's musical tastes were to be stretched once again in the 1920s, but, as he himself recognized towards the end of his life, they remained essentially conservative and romantic, as in poetry and art. His range was relatively wide, running from Bach, Handel and Gluck to Grieg, Debussy and Franck, but stopping short of highly experimental twentieth century composers such as Bartok. Above all, he looked for what he somewhat apologetically called 'sentimental melodies' in both music and poetry, a characteristic he found lacking in most music after the early twentieth century.

The work published privately between 1907 and 1913, while Sassoon practised to become a professional poet, opens and closes with works related specifically to music. The first of these, *Orpheus in Diloeryum* (1908) may well have been influenced by his childhood memories of a picture by G.F. Watts entitled 'Orpheus and Eurydice' at his aunt Rachel's house, when his mother had told him their story. It was also at Rachel's house he had heard an act of Gluck's 'Orpheus' sung. The work began life in late 1906 or early 1907, shortly after *Poems* (1906) had gone to press, as a detailed examination of Orpheus's role as an inspired musician and the power of his music.[24] After numerous experiments – the notes run to nine pages of 'Rough Drafts' – he arrives at a fairly restrained treatment of the subject, where Orpheus is used to satirize the false and superficial in art, personified in the characters of the musician Discordia, the poet Dorgrelian and others. Through one note on the lyre Orpheus awakens the music of the natural world, which symbolically drowns even his own. By March 1908 fifty ordinary copies were bound up by the Athenaeum Press in stiff wrappers of pale grey cartridge paper and five special copies more elaborately produced in quarter vellum with white cloth sides, gold lettering and marbled end-papers.

Sassoon himself characterized *Orpheus* as a 'typically juvenile performance', only 'a shade more sophisticated' than his previous volume.[25] It contained specific parody of Swinburne, almost certainly in an attempt to free himself from the older poet's influence. In 1908, however, the main effect of his parody was to give *Orpheus in Diloeryum* a certain 'exuberance', as Sassoon put it. Helen Wirgman, to whom he sent a copy, while 'smil[ing] considerably at it', could not 'help wishing there was more of Orpheus' himself in the piece.[26]

Edmund Gosse, who also received a copy at Uncle Hamo's suggestion, had fewer reservations than either its author or Wirgie, describing it as a 'delicate and accomplished little masque' which reminded him of the 'strange entertainments of the early Renaissance and of Italian humanism generally'. 'You own richness of fancy and command of melodious verse,' he told the gratified Sassoon.[27] It was an important contact and one due largely to Hamo Thornycroft, who had also given him sound advice from his own experience in another artistic field: 'Let your thoughts ring true; and always keep your eye on the object while you write.'[28]

While appreciating the wisdom of his uncle's advice, Sassoon was not yet able to follow it, and the next three years were spent working and reworking a group of largely derivative poems. Having temporarily satisfied his satiric urge in *Orpheus*, from 1909 to 1912 he devoted himself mainly to lyric poetry. His favourite form during this period became the sonnet. He was almost certainly more interested in the natural confines of a form which encouraged the shaping of a small but significant observation than in technical virtuosity. Equally attractive, from his bibliophilic viewpoint, was the sonnet's ability to fill a whole page yet leave room for elegant margins. The visual effect of poetry was always important to him.

At the same time, Sassoon continued to experiment with other verse forms, though he was neither radical nor revolutionary in his approach. Of the thirty-five poems in his next but one volume, *Sonnets and Verses* (1909) he thought only 'Villon', on the medieval French poet, worth preserving in his *Collected Poems*:

> They threw me from the gates; my matted hair
> Was dank with dungeon wetness; my spent frame
> O'erlaid with marish agues: everywhere
> Tortured by leaping pangs of frost and flame,
> So hideous was I that even Lazarus there
> In noisome rags arrayed and leprous shame,
> Beside me set had seemed full sweet and fair,
> And looked on me with loathing ... .   (*CP*, pp. 49-50)

It was the publication of this sonnet which led to Sassoon's debut on the London literary scene. While putting the finishing touches to his third volume for private publication, he had also been trying to get some of the sonnets accepted by the better-known literary journals. After a number of curt rejection slips he had tried the *Academy*. Advertised as 'the liveliest of the literary weeklies' and edited by a poet whose sonnets he admired for their polished technical perfection, it was his last resort. When, unexpectedly, the editor wrote to suggest a meeting to discuss publication of some of his sonnets, however, he panicked. T.W.H. Crosland, the editor in question, was known to him only as 'a powerful but repellently pugilistic literary journalist' and he politely declined the invitation, though at the same time indicating his willingness for Crosland to print some of his poems.[29] The result was a characteristically brusque letter from Crosland returning all his work. After a conciliatory telegram from Sassoon, a meeting was arranged and the apprehensive young poet found himself facing the notoriously dour and outspoken Yorkshireman.

Sassoon's later description of Crosland as an 'out and out blackguard' whom he nevertheless 'couldn't dislike'[30] indicates his ambivalence towards him. Polite, restrained and socially inhibited himself, he was both shocked and fascinated by Crosland's deliberate flouting of social conventions. He seemed to him 'a remarkable man ... a human battleground of good and evil'.[31] Accepting Crosland as 'one of the finest journalists of his time', he genuinely admired his literary abilities and was to benefit from his suggestions as an editor who was himself a poet. As the first professional editor to give him meaningful encouragement, Sassoon felt some kind of obligation to him.

When Sassoon accepted Crosland's offer to publish nine of his sonnets in the *Academy* for payment of a guinea each, a fee that was extremely low even for the time and which never materialized, he had only the haziest notion of his background. Later on he was to discover how ferocious and implacable he could be when, with the owner of the *Academy*, Lord Alfred Douglas, he hunted down all those who had come to Oscar Wilde's rescue in his last sad days. In 1909, when Sassoon first met him, he was best known for two biting parodies, *The Egregious English* (1903) and *The Egregious Scot* (1902). Had Crosland known of Sassoon's own attempt at parody in *Orpheus* he would probably have responded even more positively to him.

Crosland's choice of Sassoon's 'Villon' as his first publication in the *Academy* was shrewd. Though still suffering from excessive archaisms and stilted inversions, the choice of subject matter is fresher than in most of Sassoon's early work and the handling of poetic technique more assured. Sassoon was right to feel a cautious confidence at his entry into the London literary world, as he contemplated his first publication in an important literary magazine. Diffidence and a fear of being teased by his sporting friends had led him to initial his sonnet only, but that could easily be rectified if success followed.

In a reversal of their roles the previous year, this time it was Gosse who had doubts and reservations about Sassoon's poetry in 1909. Sassoon had followed up *Orpheus in Diloeryum* by sending his would-be patron copies of poems he planned to include in *Sonnets and Verses*. Replying to Hamo's anxious queries about his nephew's prospects of 'achiev[ing] something in literature' in May 1909, Gosse wrote that he believed that 'to arrange his life from the point of view of his becoming a poet would be very rash'.

Hamo is unlikely to have shown his nephew Gosse's reply. Had he done so it might have saved Sassoon the seven guineas he spent in June 1909 on the private production of *Sonnets and Verses*, which was to have an extremely brief life-span. Sassoon received copies of his new book from the Athenaeum

Press on the day of his fifth appearance in the *Academy* (26 June). He was pleased with the look of the thirty-five ordinary copies, which with his usual eye for detail had been bound in stiff white cartridge paper covers, and the three 'specials' on hand-made paper bound in black buckram. Resolved to do things 'in style' this time, he had instructed the printers to use some red ink on the title-page: 'Sonnets' was in bold scarlet type, and so was 'Verses'. Where his name might have been expected, there was only a quotation from Pliny in the original Latin, to add what he ironically called 'a touch of scholarship'.[32] Another quotation from Meredith on the reverse of the title-page suggests that his mother's favourite poet had had a dominant influence in the composition of the contents. One of the specials was for himself, one for his mother and one was sent to the author he had quoted at the beginning of the 'Verses', Charles Doughty. The first of the ordinary copies was presented to Helen Wirgman, who happened to be staying at Weirleigh.

This was the only copy to survive. Deeply depressed by the discrepancy between the book's elegant appearance and the undoubted failure of some of its lines, and upset by Wirgie's less than enthusiastic response, Sassoon worked himself up into a tantrum and burnt the remaining ordinary copies. Only its tough black buckram binding saved the special copy intended for but never given to his mother. When he confessed to Wirgie what he had done, she gave him one of her searching looks and told him that he sometimes reminded her of his rather unbalanced Aunt Lula. His impetuosity had suffered no real checks from his indulgent mother and there had been no father to discipline him since the age of five. Only Wirgie ever indicated how undesirable such behaviour might be.

On reflection, Sassoon decided that some of *Sonnets and Verses* deserved a better fate than burning and by August 1909 he had reprinted eleven of the 'Sonnets', heavily revised, together with six new ones, as simply *Sonnets*. (Only one, 'Before Day', was to survive in *Collected Poems*.) The fifty copies printed through Messrs Hatchard were even more sumptuously produced than the previous volume. Printed on hand-made paper and bound in grey paper boards with ivory cloth spine, the end-papers were of the same expensive paper as the book. Significantly, Sassoon does not tell us the cost of this elaborate production, nor does he mention Gosse's rather ambivalent response.

Sassoon's own copy of *Sonnets* has survived, heavily revised in red ink and pencil, in preparation for yet another version of basically the same material. This copy is puzzlingly inscribed, two years after publication:

> To the only begetter of Problems
> these ensuing sonnets –
> with ye author's compts.
> Feb. 1911

The echo of Shakespeare is unmistakable and it is tempting to assume that this book is similarly being presented to a young man. The addition of the word 'problems' would reinforce this interpretation, since it could only have been a 'problem' for Sassoon in 1911 if this romantic poetry were inspired by a man. The inscription could also be read as self-directed, with Sassoon himself becoming 'the only begetter of Problems', though this seems uncharacteristic. It is more likely that he first heavily revised his own copy of *Sonnets* in 1909, the year of its publication, and then presented it two years later to a newly-met friend as a highly personal gift.

An equally interesting question is why he chose, for the third time, to repeat large amounts of material already printed. His own explanation is that, in spite of Wirgie's advice that he should write in a more *physical* way, like her hero George Meredith, by 1910 he was aiming at refinement rather than vigour. As he freely admits: 'Poetry was a dream world into which I escaped through an esoteric door in my mind.'[33] This is borne out in his next volume, privately printed in 1911, *Twelve Sonnets*, in which only two of the twelve pieces are new. Of these one survives in *Collected Poems* as 'Goblin Revel'. Far from showing progress towards a more personal voice, it is, as he suggests, laden down with 'pseudo-archaic preciosities', curious outdated words such as 'fleering', 'loutings', 'brisk' (as a verb) and 'dulcimers' dominating the text.

The most plausible explanation for Sassoon's compulsive reworking of material is that living at home in Weirleigh, whilst it was comforting and safe, did not provide him with new subjects. Most of his energies went towards perfecting his technique, a technique that was already being challenged by other young poets as unfitted to the emerging twentieth century. *Poems*, issued this year, is significant mainly for the fact that its author, emerging cautiously from his anonymity, signed the last piece in the book 'Siegfried Sassoon'. He kept to his usual practice, however, in having thirty-five copies privately printed, this time by the Chiswick Press, who were to remain his printers for some years. Gosse was kind as usual, but advised him ominously to 'work more' and 'write, write, write – even if conscience makes you burn and burn'.[34]

Even Sassoon's prose play, *Hyacinth*, an apparently new departure in 1912, incorporated previous work. For *Hyacinth*, an 'Idyll', drew three of its six verse interludes from a small volume of *Melodies* published earlier that same year. The prose subject matter, however, does occupy new territory. In drawing on the Greek myth of the beautiful youth Hyacinth, who is loved by both Apollo and Zephyrus and finally killed by the latter, Sassoon is moving closer to a description of the homosexual love he dared not openly express. His choice of quotation on the title-page from the great exponent of love between men, Plato, reinforces this idea: 'Not all love, nor every mode of love, is beautiful, or worthy of commendation, but that alone which excites us to love worthily.'

Sassoon's choice of a similarly beautiful young Greek, Amyntas, for another prose play written the same year but never printed in book form, *Amyntas, a Mystery*,[35] shows similar interests. His version has Amyntas, the young shepherd-boy of the Greek legend, as someone of higher social standing, perhaps in order to identify with him more closely. For Duke Amyntas, a sensitive music-loving youth, who hates the noise and swagger of court life, is searching restlessly for a cause in life, very much like his idealistic creator. When a mysterious male prophet appears on the scene, he longs to escape with him to 'the green hills'. His musicians play, at his command, a song about a duke 'who loved but the lily and the rose/ He led no lady to his hall'. At he end of a rather inconclusive action, Amyntas shares with his servant a revelation that Sassoon himself may well have just experienced: 'By love my spirit can be healed and saved from darkness. I do not ask a love so vast as can embrace the whole world and guard all mortal men as one. I desire a love less infinite, a pity more human; eyes that may answer mine, arms that shall hold me fast.'

The realization that an ideal love may not be enough sounds a new note in Sassoon's early writing, though it did not satisfy him. After reading a proof copy, produced by the Chiswick Press, he decided that it was not worth printing and two years later was to dismiss it as 'too bloodless! and silly to a degree'.[36] Even the author could see that the long soliloquies in poetical prose were 'rather absurd' for their time.

It was in 1911, the year before both *Hyacinth* and *Amyntas* were written, that Sassoon first openly declared his homosexuality. In June 1910, while staying with Nevill Forbes at Oxford, he had heard from him of his friend, the great sexual pioneer Edward Carpenter. Almost certainly at Forbes's prompting, he subsequently read at least two of Carpenter's ground-breaking works, *The Intermediate Sex* and *Towards Democracy*, a long, Whitmanesque poem of which the fourth section, 'Who Shall Command the Heart?', was published separately.[37] His immediate identification with Carpenter's proposition that there was an 'intermediate' point in sexuality for both men and women between the wholly masculine and the wholly feminine changed his life.

Carpenter had been almost the same age as Sassoon when he arrived at an acceptance of his own homosexuality through a reading of Walt Whitman in 1869. The 'love of comrades' referred to so movingly in Walt Whitman's 'Calamus' poems (a passage of which is underlined in Sassoon's copy of James Thomson's *Walt Whitman, the Man and the Poet*) and the camaraderie of the working-classes were inseparably linked for many middle-class homosexuals at the beginning of the twentieth century. Both the plight of the working man and that of the homosexual were seen as those of a minority group trying to free itself from oppression.

The only other book Sassoon had read on the subject by 1911 apart from Carpenter's, was John Addington Symonds's *A Problem in Greek Ethics*. What distinguished Carpenter was his relative openness and lack of evasiveness, particularly since his books followed closely on the Oscar Wilde trial and the Cleveland affair. He was revolutionary for his time. In addition, as Jeffrey Weeks suggests, Carpenter's works 'had a particular warmth and insight that struck a chord for the young (especially among the middle class) of the period',[38] Sassoon being of their number. Their puritanical emphasis on the 'dignity' and 'comradeship' of male Platonic love tied in neatly with both Christian and public school ethics:

> ... your words have shown me all that I was blind to before, [Sassoon wrote to Carpenter on 27 July 1911] and have opened up the new life for me, after a time of great perplexity and unhappiness. Until I read the 'Inter[mediate] Sex', I knew absolutely nothing of that subject, (and was entirely *unspotted*, as I *am now*), but life was an empty thing, what ideas I had about homosexuality were absolutely prejudiced, and I was in such a groove that I couldn't allow myself to be what I wished to be, and the intense attraction I felt for my own sex was almost a subconscious thing, and my antipathy for women a mystery to me.[39]

Carpenter's sympathetic and open discussion of a problem Sassoon had suppressed, together with his chance discovery that his younger brother Hamo felt exactly as he did, comforted him greatly though it did not entirely solve his problems. As he confided to Carpenter, he still sometimes felt 'bitter agony' at the 'misunderstanding and injustice' suffered by homosexuals. There was also a sense, however, in which he seems to have partially accepted society's prejudices, as his use of the word 'unspotted' (to denote his virginity) indicates. It also suggests suspicion on his part of physical desires, the fulfilment of which might somehow sully the purity of love.

Whatever the implications of the word, it is clear that Sassoon had not yet experienced a physical sexual relationship by 1911, though he goes on to say that, had he read Carpenter earlier, when he was at Cambridge, things might have been different. His views seem to have been entirely consonant with Carpenter's teachings, which argued that homosexual men were less inclined to 'lust' than others, a convenient way of dealing with activities still frowned on by society and, in any case, prohibited by law.

In reading *The Intermediate Sex* Sassoon drew consolation from the numerous passages which emphasize the artistic nature of many homosexuals, and he was eager to share with Carpenter (himself a poet) his love of poetry and music. Enclosed with the *Twelve Sonnets* he sent Carpenter in 1911 is an extra, handwritten sonnet, 'On Music', which suggests at least one way in which he attempted to sublimate his sexual urges:

> Deep voice that through these lands of Life and Time
> Forever sings with passion to control
> The wayward straying of my human soul,
> Leading me up to summits of sublime
> Beauty eternal, flushed with golden fire; ...[40]

In what looks like an attempt to excuse himself from responsibility for inclinations he still could not wholly accept, Sassoon told Carpenter of his belief that his 'intensely musical' father 'had a strong vein of the homosexual nature in him'. (Alfred Sassoon, whose reputation as a 'womanizer' was probably well merited, might have found such an idea surprising.)

Carpenter had also emphasized in *The Intermediate Sex* that, although sexuality should be seen as a continuum, with heterosexuals at either pole and homosexuals somewhere near the middle, this did not mean that homosexual men would necessarily appear effeminate. On the contrary he argued that they were often muscular and well-built. Sassoon again hastens to identify himself with this: 'I live here mostly, in the country with my mother, cricket in summer, and riding and hunting in winter; and I am thankful to say I am as good as those others in their sports, and have some of their strength and courage.'

This first long letter to Carpenter ends with a confession that he is not religious, but that he has to believe 'that our immortality is *to be* (in those immortals whom our better lives may lead to, and whose immortal ways are marred and kept base by the grossness of unworthy souls)'. The high-flown language points to a spiritual need no longer satisfied by his mother's simple Anglicanism, which he had by now rejected. (He would refer later to 'the torment of his mocking youth that denied the God of priests, and triumphed in the God of skies and waters'.[41]) By denying or ignoring what he sees as the grosser physical element of sex, he attempts to promote his homosexuality into a religious cause. Over the years he was to become more sympathetic towards Carpenter's socialist ideals and by 1918 would be eager to join him near Sheffield at a manual job among the working-classes.[42] Though this plan never materialized, it was to pave the way for other socialist activities after the First World War.

There is no doubt that Carpenter's influence changed Sassoon's attitude towards himself and had a palpable effect on his work. The year 1911 is a turning-point in his life. As a direct result of his new self-confidence his writing becomes bolder. Instead of clinging to old material and endlessly recycling it, in 1912 he not only writes *Hyacinth* and *Amyntas* but also experiments with yet another form, the ode. His 'Ode for Music', whilst basically on the same subject as many of his sonnets and lyrics between 1906 and 1911, is far more expansive and confident in tone. The skill with which the difficult but rewarding form is handled shows that Sassoon had benefited, at least technically, from his prolonged years of apprenticeship.

Sassoon admits that his style in 'Ode for Music' had been influenced by Francis Thompson, and Wordsworth too has left his mark, but the theme sprang from his own deepest feelings. His love of music was a genuine and abiding passion and he had written the poem in a state of 'ecstatic afflatus'.[43] He regarded it as his 'liberation from anaemic madrigals about moonlit gardens thrummed by the lutes of ill-starred lovers'.[44] In spite of the inflated rhetoric, an 'Ode for Music' has more life and energy in it than most of his previous works. Whilst Gosse, to whom he sent the first of the fifty copies he had had elegantly printed by the Chiswick Press, failed to register any admiration, Crosland recognized its authenticity.

Crosland had left the *Academy* in 1910 and two of the nine sonnets he had accepted for publication in the magazine had been returned to Sassoon by the next editor. The unstoppable Crosland had, however, then become a publisher under the name of John Richmond Ltd, and the editor of a new monthly magazine, the *Antidote*. Sassoon gratefully accepted his offer to publish his 'Ode for Music' in the *Antidote*, though Crosland had warned him that he could not pay him for it. Sassoon particularly appreciated Crosland's assessment of the poem, which showed an awareness of both its achievements and failing.[45]

The surly Yorkshireman could be relied upon to tell the truth, whatever else his shortcomings, and Sassoon must have felt more confident of his powers by the end of 1912, as he looked around for new subject matter. He was to find it in an unexpected quarter, yet in a sense it was only another swing of the pendulum from the lyric to the satiric in his work. Confined to his study in December 1912 by a particularly bad spell of wet weather which prevented hunting, he searched his bookshelves for something to cheer him up. He found it, by chance, in John Masefield's long narrative poem, *The Everlasting Mercy* (1911). Masefield's revolutionary style, with its emphasis on the colloquial and natural, had attracted both extravagant praise and criticism, and Sassoon's own reaction seems to have been ambivalent. While admiring its vitality, he could not help finding this realistic story of the conversion of the villainous Saul Kain by a Quaker woman amusing in a way Masefield had certainly never intended. It had already proved an easy target for the parodists and he could not resist joining in.

With his natural gift for imitation he had very little difficulty in parodying Masefield's distinctive style. By transposing Masefield's protagonist and setting into something nearer home – a Sussex farmhand waiting to hang for the accidental killing of the 'chucker-out' or 'bouncer' at his village pub – Sassoon unwittingly provided himself with the first real 'subject' of his poetic career. So intense was his response to his material that, after the first fifty lines or so, he dropped all pretence that he was improvising an exuberant skit: 'While continuing to burlesque Masefield for all I was worth, I was really feeling what I wrote – and doing it not only with abundant delight but a sense of descriptive energy quite unlike anything I had experienced before.'[46]

His parody had turned into a pastiche. With his limited experience of working-class life, he could not claim that his Sussex yokel was entirely convincing but he did feel that he had managed to convey something of the rural Sussex he had absorbed through following the Southdown Hunt. Never before had he been able to do what Wirgie had advised, to write physically. His new-found ability to describe the commonplace poetically emerges with particular clarity in the passage he himself chose to quote in his autobiography, the moment when the protagonist thinks back on the man he has unintentionally killed:

I thought how in the summer weather
When Bill and me was boys together

We'd often come this way when trudgin'
Out by the brooks to fish for gudgeon.
I thought, When me and Bill are deaders
There'll still be buttercups in medders,
And boys with penny floats and hooks
Catching fish in Laughton brooks ...[47]

The Daffodil Murderer shows a distinct increase in Sassoon's powers as a writer, a fact Crosland recognized when he sent it to him. But Sassoon was genuinely surprised when Crosland immediately offered to publish it, on condition that the author contributed ten pounds towards expenses. While gladly accepting Crosland's offer, Sassoon rejected his suggested title, '*The Gentle Murderer* by Peter Expletive' and the pseudonymous and adulatory introduction his publisher wanted to write. He did agree, however, to the title '*The Daffodil Murderer* by Saul Kain', a jokey double reference to Masefield's recently published *The Daffodil Fields* and the protagonist of *The Everlasting Mercy*. In an ironic anticipation of Sassoon's own career, the facetious preface, written ostensibly by 'William Butler' (a jibe at Yeats) but really written by himself, describes the author as a soldier who had 'fought for his country on many a bloody field' but who was 'fonder of poetry than pipe-clay'.[48]

A thousand cheerful yellow and brown pamphlets, costing just sixpence each, were ready for the publisher only three weeks after Sassoon had finished polishing it under Crosland's expert guidance. The author's wish to preserve his anonymity, understandable in the circumstances, also served Crosland's ends, since he apparently wanted it to be believed that he had written yet another brilliant satire along the lines of his *Unspeakable Scot*. In the event the book was virtually ignored, its one reviewer (in the *Athenaeum*) dismissing it in a few words: 'This is a pointless and weak-kneed imitation of *The Everlasting Mercy*. The only conclusion we obtain from its perusal is that it is easy to write worse than Mr Masefield.' Sassoon later consoled himself with the theory that, since Crosland was a bitter enemy of the *Athenaeum*, the attack had sprung from the assumption Crosland had deliberately fostered, that he was its author.

Sassoon later argued that the main significance of *The Daffodil Murderer* was 'that it was the first sign of my being capable of writing as I did during the war, and the first time I used real experience. It also revealed my gift for parody, which is considerable.'[49]

Gosse was far more impressed by *The Daffodil Murderer* than Carpenter, to whom he also sent it. Sassoon had expected either the usual bland reply or none at all. Instead Gosse wrote at once to congratulate him. His letter sets the tone for the relationship which was to follow, being cautious as well as encouraging and, above all, honest. Gosse rarely wrote an unconsidered word and, though his carefulness sometimes amused Sassoon, it was a quality he came to value highly. After Gosse's tactful silence over the poetry he could not honestly praise, Sassoon was the readier to believe him when he did write on 13 February 1913:

My dear Siegfried,

The Daffodil Murderer ... is a very clever, brilliant thing, and displays powers which I had not expected from you. But, apart from the 'Preface', which is a very amusing (and well-deserved) bit of satire, what puzzles me about the poem is that it is not really a parody at all. It is a pastiche. It treats a Masefield subject exactly in Masefield's own manner, as if you had actually got into Masefield's own skin, and spoke with his voice. There is nothing comic about it. A tale of rustic tragedy is told with real pathos and power, only – exactly as Masefield would tell it. The end is extremely beautiful ....[50]

Gosse must have found it a great relief to be able, finally, to believe in the young poet. He had been devoted to Sassoon's uncle, Hamo Thornycroft, since 1879. Though they had known each other slightly through Gosse's wife, Nellie's friendship with Hamo's sister, Theresa, it was not until June 1879 that the acquaintance ripened into friendship. Hamo had invited Gosse to join him in a cruise down the Thames on his father's steamer, *The Waterlily*, and Gosse's response to the trip had been ecstatic. Brought up by a loving but stern father, whom he afterwards immortalized in his minor classic, *Father and Son*, he saw in Hamo's carefree but sensitive and passionate response to nature his ideal. As they bathed and sunbathed nude in the lovely backwaters of the Thames, he thought of the Greek sculptures he had secretly worshipped in his Calvinistic childhood. That Hamo himself was a sculptor and an exponent of the New Sculpture, with its emphasis on the beauty of the human body, made it all the more exciting. In August 1879 he asked permission to dedicate his *New Poems* to him. His affection for Hamo became a passion not easily distinguished from the sexual. Though happily married since 1875, when Hamo himself announced his engagement to Agatha Cox in July 1883, Gosse was moved to write: '... at this crisis of our lives my one great thought is one of gratitude to you for these four wonderful years, the summer of my life, which I have spent in a sort of morning glory walking by your side'.[51] As Gosse's biographer, Ann Thwaite, remarks of a similar letter from Gosse, 'This is lover's talk.' Gosse is not known to have been a practising homosexual, however, and, if his feelings for Hamo were those of a lover, he suppressed any physical manifestations of it. Lytton Strachey may have analyzed the situation correctly when he was asked if he thought Gosse homosexual: 'No,' he replied, 'but he's Hamo-sexual.' Sassoon himself confirmed this view.[52]

Though only a year older than Hamo (he had been born in 1849, Hamo in 1850), Gosse was far more established in his chosen field when they met, though never to achieve the fame he longed for as a poet. Despite the fact that in 1879 his knowledge of art was as limited as Hamo's was of literature, he dedicated himself to furthering his friend's career, an end he undoubtedly achieved. He did not hesitate to use his influence wherever possible. The fortunate chance of being the brother-in-law of the fashionable Victorian painter, Alma Tadema, for example, enabled him to get Hamo elected to the Royal Academy at an unusually early age.

By the time Gosse wrote his cautious letter of praise to Sassoon in 1913, however, Hamo's career was no longer in need of his promotion. It seemed the most natural thing in the world for Gosse to transfer his efforts to Hamo's nephew, especially since his wife continued to be close friends with Sassoon's mother. By 1913 he had even more to offer in the way of patronage and influence than his friendships with Swinburne, Browning and Dante Gabriel Rossetti. Not only had he held the prestigious Clark Lectureship at Trinity College, Cambridge, from 1884 to 1890, but he had also been honoured in 1904 with the position of Librarian to the House of Lords. In addition he had extended his friendships with famous writers to include Robert Louis Stevenson, Henry James and Thomas Hardy, among others. Apart from *Father and Son* (1907) and his innovative work on Ibsen, Gosse was known for his eminently readable critical books, *Seventeenth Century Studies* (1883), *Gossip in a Library* (1891), *Critical Kit-Kats* (1896), *French Profiles* (1905) and *Portraits and Sketches* (1912). H.G. Wells had dubbed him, rather mischievously, 'the official British man of letters'.

In the short time it took Gosse to respond to Sassoon's gift of *The Daffodil Murderer* in February 1913, he had already taken the first practical steps in helping Hamo's nephew, by making sure that the 'choragus' of the new poets, as he somewhat pedantically described Edward Marsh, also had a copy of the bright yellow pamphlet. As he explained to Sassoon, Marsh was the editor of *Georgian Poetry*, an anthology of contemporary verse which had recently made its successful appearance on the literary scene. Since Marsh had expressed a polite interest in Gosse's protégé (it would have been difficult for him to have done otherwise), Gosse advised Sassoon to send him his other booklets: 'It would be useful to you, I think, as you lead so isolated a life, to get into relations with these people, who are of all schools, but represent what is most vivid in the latest poetical writing. It is time, I think, for you to begin to tilt up the bushel under which your light has been burning.' Rarely have the workings of the literary bandwagon been so clearly exposed.

Gosse's momentous letter was followed by an equally exciting invitation to visit him a few weeks later at the House of Lords. It was to be Sassoon's first private talk with a man for whom he had already formed a profound respect. He had been thrilled to be invited to an afternoon party at the Gosses' in 1909 and again in 1911,[53] and had continued to correspond with Gosse since then, but it was not until the publication of *The Daffodil Murderer* in 1913 that he was invited to meet him again alone and in private.

In the event Sassoon's first intimate talk with Gosse turned out to be an uncomfortable affair, quite different from the many delightful chats which were to follow. Still socially unsure of himself, as well as constitutionally shy, Sassoon felt that he had made a poor impression. Though small and unprepossessing in appearance Gosse had a fierce manner at times and could be a formidable enemy. (Aldous Huxley called him 'the bloodiest little old man'.)[54] Usually an urbane host, he failed to put his young guest at his ease on this occasion. Overawed by Gosse and his august surroundings in the House of Lords' library, Sassoon was able to say very little, particularly when his host asked him about Crosland, of whom he clearly disapproved.

Sassoon managed to redeem himself a little by remarking innocently, when given a glimpse of the assembled Lords: 'Anyone would almost think they were all half-asleep!' It gave Gosse a chance to deliver one of his artful, if ponderous, periphrases: 'Some of them, I doubt not, are indulging in a decorous doze. The speaker is one of the most profusely unenlightening of our hereditary legislators!'[55] This humorous note, common to both, helped consolidate their relationship and an invitation to a party on 5 June 1913 followed.

7

'Big London where Poets Live'

May-July 1914

Sassoon's friendship with Gosse was a crucial step in his literary career. Whether it was a positive one in the long run is open to debate. 'No one has done me greater service,' Sassoon was to write to Gosse in 1927. But by identifying with Gosse and his friends in 1913, when a major shift in poetic consciousness was already under way, Sassoon was aligning himself with the old guard in literature. If Crosland's poetic development had stopped short at W.E. Henley in the 1890s, Gosse's had not gone much further. And, though he claimed in his letter to Sassoon of February 1913 that his friend Edward Marsh fostered all that was 'most vivid in the latest poetical writing', Marsh too was suspicious of radical experiment. At the start his *Georgian Poetry* anthology represented innovation but it came increasingly to seem highly conservative and by 1922, when the last volume appeared, even Gosse was moved to remind Marsh that 'poetry should not always be "breathing through silver"'.[1]

Sassoon's diffidence and lack of confidence in 1913 made him particularly vulnerable to any type of influence. Whether his later rejection of modernism was a result of Gosse and his friends is impossible to say. What might have happened had his personal introduction to the literary world come through, say, the Imagists, or the Bloomsbury Group, both flourishing in the contemporary London scene? The Imagist movement, influenced by T.E. Hulme's insistence on hard, clear, precise images and encouraged by Ezra Pound during his stay in London just before the First World War, fought against the two things of which Sassoon was most guilty at this time, romantic fuzziness and facile emotionalism.[2] Though the Bloomsbury Group, which was well established by 1913, did not include any major poets at its centre, its aims in both literature and art were ultimately modernist. By choosing Gosse as his mentor, Sassoon chose Gosse's friends, the most influential of whom in terms of poetry was undoubtedly Edward Marsh.

One has only to look at Marsh's advice to Sassoon, in response to the slim volume he sent him, to see how conservative that influence was. Gosse had urged the young poet in 1909 to defend the 'purity of the language'. In 1913 Marsh wrote in very similar terms. Though he criticized Sassoon's sonnets and lyrics for containing 'far too much of the worn-out stuff and garb of poetry',[3] his own criticism sprang from an acceptance of traditions which were already being rejected in England by poets like Pound, Richard Aldington and D.H. Lawrence. (T.S. Eliot would follow shortly afterwards and become Sassoon's particular *bête noire*.)

When Sassoon first met Edward Marsh at the National Club in Whitehall in March 1913, Marsh was already highly successful. Born twenty-three years after Gosse, in 1872, he himself owed some of his literary influence to Gosse. Introduced to him in 1894 by a mutual friend, Maurice Baring, he then went on to meet others of Gosse's influential circle. It was Gosse's recommendation which enabled him to penetrate the Reform Club, that bastion of social privilege, in 1898. By the time Sassoon came to know them both, they were equally powerful in their separate but related spheres, and known jointly to at least one of their friends as 'the oracles'.[4] The two 'oracles' were, however, very different and were to serve different purposes in Sassoon's poetic career. While Gosse encouraged him in fairly general terms and introduced him to 'useful' people, Marsh was to give him more specific help with his work. An outstanding classicist in his generation at Westminster and Cambridge in the 1890s, he became for the younger and less scholarly Sassoon an authority on such technical problems as metre and diction.

Marsh shared other interests with Sassoon beside poetry. At Cambridge he had been friends not only with writers like Baring but also with those involved in the art world, such as Walter Sickert's brother Oswald, and Roger Fry. Fry, who was far ahead of his time, introduced Marsh to the latest developments in art and infected him with an enthusiasm which never left him. By the time Sassoon met him, he had already bought his first picture, 'Parrot Tulips' by Duncan Grant in 1912, his taste in art being more modern than his taste in literature. From then on he continued to help struggling young artists by buying their work. Mark Gertler, John Currie, Stanley Spencer and the poet-painter Isaac Rosenberg were all to benefit from his generosity, Marsh becoming known as something of a Maecenas.

Though comfortably placed, with a well-paid job in the Civil Service, Marsh did not have unlimited funds and he supported his young friends in a curious way. His mother's grandfather, Sir Spencer Perceval, had the distinction of being the only English Prime Minister to be murdered while in office and the family was compensated by a Government grant, one sixth of which eventually came to Marsh. It was this 'murder money', as he called it, which financed his young protégés. In addition, when the *Georgian Poetry* anthology became an overnight success in 1912, he scrupulously divided the profits among the contributors. *Georgian Poetry* had arisen partly out of Marsh's close friendship with Rupert Brooke, whom he had met in 1906 on one of his many return visits to Cambridge. When Brooke's first slim volume of poems came out in 1911, Francis Meynell had suggested that Marsh review it for his friend Harold Monro's *Poetry Review*, and the team which was to produce *Georgian Poetry* was born. It needed only a chance remark by Brooke to bring the anthology into being. Monro agreed to be the publisher but it was Marsh who was to find the poets, make and arrange the selection and distribute payment. The first number was an instant success and went into thirteen editions. In all there were to be five volumes of *Georgian Poetry*, keeping Marsh very busy indeed over the next decade. Since he had no wife or children of his own, he treated his contributors as his family and looked after them devotedly. The son of a surgeon and a nurse, he worked among his young friends rather in that manner, as his biographer points out. All this had to be combined with his demanding job at Whitehall. By 1913 he was already six years into his close relationship with Winston Churchill. He would twice be Private Secretary to Churchill, from 1917 to 1922 and 1924 to 1929, and his friendship with Sassoon was eventually to be threatened by that connection.

In March 1913, however, Sassoon was too overwhelmed by Marsh and his world to challenge it. Sitting in the National Club opposite the 'monocled young man of fashion' (Marsh was fourteen years older than the 26-year-old Sassoon but retained a youthful air),[5] he felt that he had truly 'arrived', particularly when they were joined at coffee by Gosse's friend and colleague, Austin Dobson.

At his next meeting with Marsh, however, he began to feel less intimidated and started to confide in him. This was early in 1914, during his week off from his strenuous hunting season with Loder. He had written to Marsh from Witherley Lodge, Atherstone on 23 October 1913 to tell him that he was 'getting terribly fit, but quite unpoetical',[6] and again, on St Valentine's Day 1914, to say that he was hoping to see him again. 'Eddie', as he now became, obligingly invited him for an evening. After dinner at the Moulin d'Or, they retired to his rooms in Raymond Buildings, Gray's Inn. By contrast with Sassoon's fairly primitive surroundings in Loder's huntsman's cottage and his somewhat philistine friends there, both Marsh and his rooms seemed highly civilized.

After nearly five months of an almost entirely physical existence, Sassoon was feeling culturally starved, which further heightened his appreciation of Marsh's attractively furnished rooms full of modern pictures. Eddie in his bachelor stronghold provided him with a model of what he himself might be if he ever dared to leave Weirleigh. No sooner had he expressed his discontent with his aimless life in Kent than, according to him, his host had decided on the answer: 'But why don't you come and live in London?' he asked.[7] Sassoon afterwards wrote that he was too excited and insecure to admit that he could not afford it and that in an alarmingly short time Marsh had decided his future. He would organize the whole matter. He was in his element the next day, rushing Sassoon off, after a quick lunch in Whitehall, to view a vacant set of rooms in the same block as his own, and when they turned out to be 'depressingly dilapidated', offering to arrange for their redecoration.[8]

Sassoon almost certainly exaggerated Marsh's part in his decision to live in London; a letter towards the end of February 1914 suggests that he was actively urging Marsh to help him find rooms, rather than being pushed into it by his friend.[9] This is a rather different version from the one given in Sassoon's autobiography, but in either case it is a measure of his impracticality at this time that he did not seriously work out how, on an income of £400 a year, with the expense of keeping four horses, a groom and a stable boy, he could afford not only to pay an extra £100 a year for rent and rates of a flat, but also have it furnished and redecorated. His own retrospective explanation is that he was 'so desperate to get out of my groove' that he simply ignored the problem. He was probably depending on his mother to bail him out, as usual.

It had been an exciting week in London altogether. Apart from the momentous decision to move there, he also had two other stimulating meetings. The more predictable of these, a dinner on 22 February with Gosse at his house in Hanover Terrace, helped cement their relationship. The other guest was dull but the dinner allowed Sassoon a glimpse of Gosse at his most enthusiastic and appealing. Pulling Max Beerbohm's prose parodies, *A Christmas Garland*, down from the bookshelf, he introduced Sassoon to a writer who was to become not only a great favourite but also a close friend. It was Gosse himself who would introduce him to 'dear delicious Max', as he called him.

Sassoon's less predictable lunch with his first editor, Crosland, was equally interesting in its own way. Shockingly changed, from a formidable but basically genial man with a thick moustache to a physical wreck, whose sunken, clean-shaven face gave both his mouth and eyes a saturnine air, Crosland seemed to Sassoon a pitiable figure. Guiltily aware that he had ignored his request for a 'fiver' a few months previously, he was unable to refuse his invitation to lunch.

Clearly someone else had come up with more than five pounds, for Crosland took him to Paganis, a restaurant Sassoon came to know well in the 1920s, for what the Yorkshireman himself might have called a 'slap-up meal'. Over special coffee and Corona cigars he explained to Sassoon his theory that life ought to be 'a Promethean struggle with adversity and injustice'.[10] Perhaps pointedly, he indicated to the rather spoilt young man in front of him that those who had never suffered deprivation could not claim to have lived at all. Neither he nor his guest could have foreseen that in less than a year Sassoon would begin to realize the truth of this for himself. At the time Sassoon took it to be largely a rationalization of Crosland's own intemperate lifestyle, which involved him in periods of great hardship. A heavy gambler, he was rashly generous when winning and an unashamed 'scrounger' when his money ran out. He was not the kind of man Sassoon could possibly understand, though neither could he completely dismiss him. He had had no hesitation in abandoning him the moment Gosse and his far more respectable world beckoned. Yet it is significant that, between Crosland's publication of *The Daffodil Murderer* in February 1913 and their lunch together a year later, Sassoon had written nothing he considered worth publishing. Perhaps Crosland's abrasiveness had had a more stimulating effect on him than Gosse and Marsh's more urbane style. Moreover, it was not until Sassoon's comfortable world was challenged, as the blunt Northerner had suggested, that he began to write with conviction. When he did so, it would be despite the disturbing effect he knew it would have on Gosse and Marsh's establishment views.

*

For the time being, however, it was Marsh who became the catalyst. His willingness to help Sassoon move to London had a profound effect. After seven years of life spent trying to satisfy both his physical and aesthetic needs, Sassoon determined to devote himself solely to poetry. His five months in Warwickshire with Loder had given him a greater degree of independence. 'I was conscious of having somehow outgrown the whole place during my absence', he recorded.[11] Then Marsh had provided the incentive.

Sassoon's bid for freedom was to last less than three months. He moved into his flat at 1 Raymond Buildings, Gray's Inn, in early May and by the end of July he was back at Weirleigh. The reason he gave in his autobiography was financial, but a closer reading of it suggests that he was still emotionally unable to cope on his own. To begin with there was the supervision of the decorating and furnishing of his rooms. Sassoon's flat, originally a set of barrister's chambers, was at the noisiest end of the building, but to him it seemed a haven of peace. As he surveyed his immaculate white bedroom, brightly renovated bathroom and two living-rooms, painted in French grey and his favourite peacock-blue, he felt sure that he would produce some very good poetry there. His view of the terraced lawns and tall plane trees of Gray's Inn gardens in their late spring greenery was inspiring and there would be no golf or cricket to distract him. His cooking and cleaning were to be dealt with by a friend of Marsh's famously efficient housekeeper, Mrs Elgy – a Mrs Fretter.

It was not only Mrs Fretter's admirable cookery which pleased Sassoon to begin with. For the first month at least he woke up 'with a sense of freedom and exhilaration', the kind of feeling he associated with the start of a holiday.[12] Every morning after a cold bath and leisurely breakfast, he would spend between two and three hours at his poetry.

On both Gosse and Marsh's advice, he was studying verse technique with a view to improving his own haphazard methods. Though he found the results disappointing, he kept at it and, in contrast to what he suggests in *The Weald of Youth*, produced at least one poem for his next volume, 'South Wind'.[13] It may be that Sassoon's struggle to be on his own, though not as 'Promethean' as Crosland would have wished, was bearing fruit. Reading the poem three years later in *The Old Huntsman and Other Poems*, Virginia Woolf was to claim in her *TLS* review of that book: 'Here we have evidence not of accomplishment, indeed, but of a gift much more valuable than that, the gift of being a poet, we must call it ....'[14]

Another poem almost certainly conceived at this time, 'Alone', deals specifically with the problem Sassoon was himself facing, loneliness. The mention of 'Bright roofs and towers of towns' suggests that it was also composed at the window of his room in Gray's Inn. It is possible that Sassoon also composed two other poems for his 1915 volume at Raymond Buildings, 'Tree and Sky', as he looked out over Gray's Inn gardens, and 'Rain in June'.

There was certainly torrential rain in June the day he tried to make contact with someone he felt could help him with his problems, the poet Ralph Hodgson. Still suffering from the split between his sporting self (he had been helping Loder sell horses at Tattersalls shortly after his arrival in London) and his poetic side, Sassoon had gradually come to believe that Hodgson had the answer. He had admired his *Song of Honour* when it appeared in 1913 and was intrigued by Marsh's assurance that the bowler-hatted, pipe-smoking Hodgson did not look in the least like a poet. His career as a judge of bull-terriers at Crufts made Sassoon feel that he would understand his own divided loyalties. Sassoon's attempts to visit him at his lodgings in the King's Road, Chelsea, however, were unsuccessful, and it would be another five years before he could, as he put it, 'gain admittance to his many-sided and imaginative mind' or congratulate him on the 'startling freshness' of his poetic voice.[15]

Sassoon's failure to contact Hodgson marked a turning-point for him in London. By the time of his abortive visit to the sporting poet in early June he was beginning to find his daily routine unsatisfactory, even boring. The effect of studying technique, rather than wandering about the countryside or browsing through his favourite books, was to stifle his poetic urge. Rightly or wrongly, he felt that his best poetry was 'inspired'. He might afterwards work on the resulting poem, but without the initial inspiration he felt lost and very depressed. He had come to London not only to counteract cricket and hunting but to lead the kind of existence he thought would give him 'something real' to write about.[16] Ironically, he had found more subjects for poetry in the country.

Equally ironic was the fact that Sassoon felt lonelier in the busy city than in his big house in the country, now empty of his brothers. In the mornings he could pretend to work and from half past twelve until about half past two he could occupy himself by taking the 19 or 38 bus to Piccadilly and strolling to the club in St James's Street for lunch, but the afternoons and evenings remained a problem. After five weeks he had exhausted his appetite for art galleries, museums and churches and was feeling too poor to distract himself with daily concerts or plays.

His social life was almost non-existent. He did take his great-aunt Mozelle to lunch and a matinée and would no doubt be invited back. He had also met his old friend Helen Wirgman, not once but twice by accident at London Zoo, and had taken her to a concert and tea at his new flat, but this had not been an unqualified success. Marsh was very kind and invited him to the occasional concert, but he was too busy with his work and his other protégés to protect Sassoon from a strong sense of isolation. Several times he had been reduced to the extreme step of taking a bus at random, just to see where it went. (A visit to Hornsey Rise seems to have cured him of this particular habit.) He had even, on one of his aimless walks across Regent's Park, dared to call on the Gosses unannounced, only to find that they were away for a month in Portugal.

Anyone who has lived in London on their own in their twenties will sympathize, but they might also ask why he did not do more to make friends. The Poetry Bookshop, for example, open since January 1912 and already becoming a central meeting-point for young poets, was just around the corner from him at 35 Devonshire (now Boswell) Street; while he was not yet sufficiently well known to be invited to read there, at least he could have dropped in for a browse and a chat. Perhaps he did; if so, he fails to mention it and neither does the owner, Harold Monro. It may be that Sassoon had been put off by Marsh, who was not very close to Monro in spite of their joint publishing venture. It is equally likely that he was too diffident or shy, which may also explain why he did not respond to an invitation from Marsh and Gosse's friend, Robbie Ross, on 13 June to 'look [him] up' any evening at about six o'clock.[17]

According to Sassoon, only two things prevented June and July from complete flatness: the Russian Ballet and a meeting with Marsh's most brilliant and famous protégé, Rupert Brooke. Sassoon was invited to meet Brooke when the poet came to stay with Marsh after an adventurous year abroad. By the time he was formally introduced to him at a small breakfast party, he had already glimpsed the legendary young man walking towards Marsh's flat. Both then and at the breakfast Brooke made Sassoon feel something of a failure. Yet Marsh had presumably brought them together because he felt that they would like each other.

They had a number of things in common. Near contemporaries, both had had a comfortable middle-class upbringing culminating in public school and Cambridge. Sassoon had been starting his second year when Brooke arrived at the university in October 1906, though his premature departure meant that they overlapped by only one term. In fact Sassoon had been impressed then by Brooke, without knowing it, when he had admired the striking Greek herald in *Euripides* that term, the same occasion which had led to Marsh's introduction to Brooke. Most significantly of all, both young men were consciously striving to be poets.

Sassoon, however, was far more aware of their differences. Whereas he was still virtually unknown, Brooke had already achieved fame, or at least notoriety, through his 1911 *Poems*, in particular 'Channel Crossing', and his contributions to the *Georgian Poetry* anthology of 1912. Sassoon admitted in a chapter of his autobiography, which he found difficult to write because of his continuing friendship with Marsh in 1942, that, by the time the two poets met in 1914, Brooke's success had already aroused in him 'an admiring antagonism'.[18]

In June 1914 his attitude was influenced more by Brooke's personal effect on him. Self-contained and carefree, he made Sassoon feel even more gauche and inadequate than usual. Whereas he had clearly resolved the conflict between his sporting prowess and intellectual powers by simply concealing the former at Cambridge, Sassoon was still struggling with this dichotomy. And while Sassoon had left the university early only to return to his mother, Brooke had left his equally adoring mother to travel half-way across the world. As a result, Brooke had found the vivid subjects for poetry that Sassoon had so far failed to discover.

It was not surprising that Sassoon responded to Marsh's favourite poet with a mixture of jealousy and unwilling admiration.[19] His presence quite overshadowed that of another 'Georgian' whom Sassoon would, in other circumstances, have greatly enjoyed meeting, W.H. Davies (the 'super-tramp'). As it was Davies seemed rather naive and long-winded by comparison with the sophisticated and very handsome Cambridge graduate. Whether some of Sassoon's hostility sprang from an involuntary physical attraction towards him is a moot point. He certainly described Brooke's appearance in loving detail, with particular emphasis on his long brown-gold hair, 'living blue' eyes, sunburnt complexion and bare feet.

They were left alone together, after Marsh had departed for Whitehall and Davies for another engagement, but conversation was stilted and Sassoon formed the distinct impression that Brooke was bored with him and merely tolerating his continued presence. Feeling rather like a Lower Fifth form boy talking to the Head of School, he did not dare to discuss the one subject that might have brought them together, poetry. It was both a relief and a disappointment when the meeting came to an end. Thanking Marsh afterwards for the breakfast, Sassoon remembered saying that he hoped to meet Brooke again some day – 'he is absolutely delightful' – but it is hard to believe that he was being entirely sincere.[20] In any case, the outbreak of war only two months later was to make another meeting between them impossible.

If Sassoon's meeting with Brooke was really as unsuccessful as he portrayed it, then Marsh had probably been wise not to invite him to meet another future war poet, Isaac Rosenberg, who had visited him at Raymond Buildings earlier, on 8 May 1914. While Sassoon half-shared Rosenberg's Jewishness and his dual interest in poetry and art, their class difference might have made a meeting between them difficult, since both were very class-conscious.

It is, nevertheless, tempting to speculate why Marsh did not introduce them and what might have resulted if he had. Rosenberg's visit occurred shortly after Sassoon moved into number 1 Raymond Buildings, and Marsh must surely have been aware of how lonely his neighbour was feeling. Perhaps he did not think Rosenberg established or respectable enough for the rather snobbish Sassoon. It may be that he thought Sassoon needed time to settle in. As it was, the two poets would never meet, though they were to admire each other's work. (Rosenberg praised the 'power' of Sassoon's verse in *Georgian Poetry* of 1917 and Sassoon respected Rosenberg's sufficiently to write an introduction to his *Collected Works* in 1949.)

Sassoon's lack of contact with Rosenberg, or any of the other aspiring poets known to Marsh by 1914, was unfortunate but not entirely surprising. He was still caught uneasily between at least three worlds, the sporting, the poetic and the social. After a morning studying poetic technique, he continued to don the socially correct uniform of top hat (bowler if it rained), black jacket, wash-leather gloves and, with a rolled umbrella hooked jauntily over his left arm, make his way to his gentleman's club for lunch. At the same time he was secretly yearning for a good game of cricket, one reason he might finally have decided to return to Weirleigh towards the end of July.

The reason Sassoon gives – that of financial necessity – was something of a rationalization. As the family solicitor pointed out when Sassoon appealed unsuccessfully to him for £100 to pay some of his debts, if he had really wanted to live in London and remain solvent he could have done so. The thought of furnished rooms rather than what Helen Wirgman had called his 'swell establishment', decorated and furnished to his own taste, did not, however, appeal to someone who had already acquired expensive tastes and established for himself a certain position in society. Mr Lousada would not have minded Sassoon living in Gray's Inn at all if he had been studying for the Bar, as the address suggested. Had Sassoon really believed that he could write better poetry in London, he should theoretically have been prepared to sacrifice social standing. For all his avowed intentions, he was not yet totally dedicated to his art.

Sassoon demonstrated his order of priorities clearly this summer when he decided to pay a guinea, a great deal of money by 1914 standards, for a ticket to the Gala Performance of the Russian Ballet at the beginning of July. Not only was this something he could not afford, but it was also a further venture into the social world which he professed to despise though still clearly enjoyed. Marsh, whom Sassoon later came to feel was something of a social butterfly ('dear old Eddie was hollow inside', he agreed with a friend[21]), reflected the almost hysterical response of London 'Society' to the Russian Ballet, when he told his ignorant young friend that it was 'simply the most divine thing in the world!'[22] Tempted by such enthusiasm, and possibly intrigued by Marsh's comparison the year before of his poem 'Goblin Revels' to a piece in their repertoire, *Oiseau de feu*, Sassoon embarked on a three-week orgy of Russian ballet and opera.

Sergei Diaghilev had formed his permanent company, the *Ballets russes*, in Paris in 1909 in an attempt to integrate the ideals of music, painting and drama into those of dance. The expressive, mimetic dancing of Fokine, Pavlova, Karsavina and Nijinsky, the exotic sets of his compatriot, Leon Bakst, and the explosive music of another young Russian, Igor Stravinsky, brilliantly realized his aims and revitalized contemporary ballet. The troupe was an instant success in Paris and, when it travelled to England in 1911, took London by storm. The

Ballets russes was in its fourth London season when Sassoon first saw it in July 1914. (By this time Pavlova had left the company and Massine joined it.) The 1914 season was to symbolize for many, in retrospect, the last period of carefree gaiety before the outbreak of war, the end of an epoch.

Sassoon's response at the time to the lively and innovative Company was immediate; he was overwhelmed by the lavishness of its decor and the beauty of its sights and sounds. Almost entirely ignorant of ballet, he went to the first performance more out of curiosity than in expectation of enjoyment. He was particularly enchanted by Schumann's haunting score for *Papillons*, which sent him home charmed, exhilarated and determined to return. He also resolved to visit Diaghilev's Russian Opera Company where the music would be even more important. Though somewhat antagonized by the largely upper middle class audience, who struck him as forming 'an enormous but exclusive party',[23] he realized that he was witnessing a memorable artistic event and continued to make his way almost nightly to Drury Lane for either ballet or opera.

While London suffered under an oppressive heat-wave, suffragettes got themselves arrested in public places and members of his Club sat reading about the burning 'Ulster Question', he was haunted by and perhaps identified with 'the half-oriental sadness of Russian music' and 'the legendary poetic feeling of all that colour and movement which was nocturnally alluring [him] to Drury Lane'.[24] It was 'a romantic discovery' which appealed to his imagination more than any previous dramatic performance.[25] His only consolation when it ended was to buy the piano scores of both *Boris Godounov* and *Prince Igor*.

It was not only the loss of his nightly 'fix' Sassoon had to face when the Russian season ended in the third week of July; he had also to confront the financial consequences of his indulgence. His compulsive attendance of the ballet and opera had brought his financial difficulties to a head. He owed at least £500 but could see no way of finding such a large sum. Yet he must have known in advance what his extravagances would lead to. Either he was incapable of economizing, or he secretly welcomed an excuse to return home to Weirleigh, where his mother would support him.

Had he been convinced that living in London helped his poetry, he would have found a way of remaining there. But he felt that from September 1913 to July 1914 he had got into a 'blind alley of excessive sport and self-imposed artistic solitude' and that neither extreme had been productive. The one positive result of his stay had been the development of an appreciation of the metropolis. He had grown up regarding London as a place in which the dirt and noise made him grateful to be living in the country, but by the end of his three months there he had grown to love 'its back-street smells and busy disregard of my existence'.[26] He became particularly fond of Holborn and, like his near contemporary Virginia Woolf, began to find a poetry in the dingy city streets which fed his mind and 'created stirrings of expectation'.[27] Unwittingly he was being prepared for another kind of ugliness which likewise had its own poetry, life in the trenches.

8

The Happy Warrior

August 1914-November 1915

Sassoon arrived back at Weirleigh in the third week of July 1914 and the outbreak of the First World War on 4 August came at exactly the right moment for him; he felt almost as if he had been waiting for it to happen. Initially the War fulfilled a number of urgent needs for him. Practically, it resolved the problem of his mounting debts, by forcing him to economize and providing him with a small additional income. Emotionally, it finally freed him from his prolonged dependence on his mother and presented him with the cause for which his idealistic nature craved. Even more importantly, it gave him a genuine subject for poetry.

Sassoon's attitude towards the First World War was to change profoundly during its course and to become increasingly complex, a process reflected faithfully in the development of his poetry at this time. To begin with his views were broadly those shared by the majority of English people, that the War was both necessary and just and that he was bound by honour to serve in it. It was an attitude, as he himself later noted, 'uncomplicated by intellectual scruples'.[1] There was also the added incentive of being given a sense of direction, or rather a feeling that he no longer needed to look for one. It was almost a relief to learn from a visiting family friend, Mab Anley – the mother of two colonels on the Active Service List – that war was unavoidable and that young men were needed to fight in it.

Mab Anley's arrival on 25 July followed the announcement of an ultimatum from Austria-Hungary to Serbia on 24 July. The ultimatum had been provoked by a long-standing tension between the two nations which had culminated in the assassination of the Austrian Archduke Ferdinand by a Serb on 28 June. What began as a localized hostility reached international dimensions when Germany, with its own barely concealed global ambitions, took sides with Austria, and France with Serbia. Obliged by her informal alliance with France and Russia to help protect them, Britain felt more or less forced to join in when on 4 August Germany, having officially declared war on France as well as Russia, invaded Belgium, a country whose neutrality Britain was pledged to preserve.

Sassoon's own realization of the inevitability of Britain's involvement came, like many other people's, when he read *The Times*'s leading article of 31 July. Though he had suspected the truth for at least a week, it was not until he read *The Times*'s grave predictions that he fully accepted the situation and its personal implications. His immediate reaction was to set off on a punishing bicycle ride of sixty miles, to Rye and back, ostensibly to consider his next move. In reality he had already accepted the fact that he would have to enlist: the physical exertion, as so often with him, was merely a form of outward release. Far from feeling heroic, he was rather embarrassed by his decision but also very relieved. As he wrote later, it freed him from 'any sense of personal responsibility'.[2] Given his background and upbringing, his decision comes as no surprise. Even Charles Hamilton Sorley, who experienced serious misgivings about the War from the outset, demonstrates that for a middle-class young man with a public school background there really seemed very little choice.[3]

Sassoon's impetuosity makes him one of the first war poets to have enlisted. By 1 August he had been given his Army Medical and at the official outbreak of war on 4 August he was in ill-fitting khaki. Like the majority of British people, who were almost completely ignorant of the War's complicated origins and the strength of Germany's ambitions, he believed that it would last no more than eighteen months. His main reaction was not fear, though he was apprehensive, but indignation. As he was subsequently to admit, he had lived to the age of almost twenty-eight with unquestioning confidence in the stability of the world and his own place in it. Without the intervention of war, it is very likely that he would have continued in the same calm but unstimulating assumptions until his death. As with so many other young men and women of the period, it was the subsequent turmoil and conflict which drove him in self-defence to attempt to shape his experience into art.

To begin with, however, Sassoon was more concerned with practicalities than with poetry. He had already written to Gordon Harbord, a regular soldier in the Artillery since 1912, asking him how to enlist in the Cavalry should the need arise. His first choice (a hasty one which he later regretted) was the Sussex Yeomanry, an old county regiment. It is clear from his later description of cavalry officers that he did not regard the Yeomanry as a satisfactory substitute for the regular Army equivalent, being all too conscious of the cavalryman's 'superior social connections'.[4] He was also aware, however, of the money usually needed to belong to such an élite group and, even more importantly, the time required to go through various formalities. In his impatience to act, he seemed unable to contemplate the delay involved in such a move.

When Sassoon enlisted in the 1st/1st Sussex Yeomanry – later to become the 16th (Sussex Yeomanry) Battalion of the Royal Sussex Regiment – it was a relatively new body. Raised as a Volunteer Force in the closing months of the Boer War, for the first five or six years of its existence it was not brigaded with any other units. On the formation of a Territorial Force in 1907-8, in a wider effort to improve the army, it was amalgamated with the South-Eastern Mounted Brigade, under Brigadier-General Fowle. Brigadier-General Briggs took over the command in 1911, a year which saw increasingly strenuous training in preparation for a war which the army rightly anticipated.

The 1st/1st Sussex Yeomanry, whose headquarters was in Brighton, mobilized by squadrons at Lewes, Brighton, Chichester and Eastbourne. (Sassoon reported to Lewes and became part of C Squadron.) Mobilization went very much to plan, with the notable exception of the supply of horses which broke down very badly. Sassoon, who brought his precious hunter Cockbird with him, must therefore have been doubly welcome to the Sussex Yeomanry staff who, in their desperation to keep the few horses they had managed to requisition, are reputed to have hidden them in cellars.

One of Sassoon's main motives in joining the cavalry had been to avoid separation from Cockbird, and his choice of the Sussex Yeomanry seems on the surface to have been the right one. However, because he felt unable to face the responsibility of being an officer, he made the mistake of enlisting as a private (known in the cavalry as a 'trooper'), a position which cut him off almost completely from men of his own class and culture. Though initially attracted by the 'jokes and jollity' of the 'good chaps' in the ranks[5] (condescending phrases which belie any truly democratic impulse behind his decision), he quickly began to miss the conversation of his peers. Just as quickly he realized that, in order to save Cockbird from the enormous weight of equipment a trooper's horse was expected to carry, he must accept his squadron officer's request to buy him. Though he subsequently enjoyed seeing his former hunter looking unburdened and professionally groomed, his motivation for joining the yeomanry was irreparably undermined. At about the same time his remaining two hunters, Jim Murphy and Golumpus, were requisitioned from Weirleigh. It was the end of an important era in both Sassoon's and his groom Tom Richardson's existence.

Life in the ranks of C Squadron, 1st/1st Sussex Yeomanry – popularly known as 'the jolly Yeo-boys' – had been fun to begin with, rather like an overgrown scout-camp, or, as Sassoon put it, 'a mounted infantry picnic in perfect weather'.[6] But they trained daily for the feared German invasion of the South Coast and Sassoon, whose incompetence in practical matters contrasted oddly with his skill at sports, had to struggle hard to get through the daunting business of preparing himself and his horse for routine inspection. Accustomed to both leisure and servants, the dawn start with mucking out of stables before breakfast must have come as an unpleasant shock. The training, designed mainly for raw recruits, was tough, including such unwelcome features as 'dawn alarms', when the men were expected to 'saddle-up' and 'stand-to' an hour before sunrise. Sassoon's small, well-thumbed, maroon *Yeomanry and Mounted Rifle Training Manual* shows that it included not only 'Equitation' and 'Mounted Drill' but also 'Drill on Foot', with numerous sub-sections to each discipline.

Sassoon was saved from complete ignominy by his superiority once in the saddle and protected, to some extent, by his acquaintance with a number of the officers, who had hunted alongside him in the Southdown. At the same time, as Tom Richardson had predicted, knowing some of the officers also made his position rather uneasy. His refusal of a commission in the Yeomanry puzzled his superiors, but he himself felt 'safe' where he was.[7] It was not fighting of which he was afraid – he had 'serious aspirations to heroism in the field' and had earned kudos by volunteering immediately for foreign service – but responsibility.[8]

He was still unwilling to assume an adult role and it is no coincidence that he compared his 'safe' life in the ranks of the Yeomanry to life at school. The price, he discovered, was 'terrible bored[om]'.[9]

Sassoon's 'escape' (his word) from increasing tedium came unexpectedly. At the end of September his mount had gone lame and, since he was known to be a good horseman, he had been sent out on the chargers of various men in the Squadron, such as the Quartermaster. One morning early in October the farrier-sergeant asked him to take his horse out and give it a little 'sharpening up'. Sassoon's interpretation of this order was to find as many jumpable fences as possible and pretend that he was out hunting again. Ironically, on this occasion he suffered a far worse fall than any he had experienced on the hunting-field and his brief career in the Sussex Yeomanry ended with a badly broken arm when his horse rolled on top of him.

Sassoon's decision to leave the Sussex Yeomanry was not a sudden one. The three months spent recovering from his fracture, which initially refused to knit and had to be operated on, gave him time to realize his mistake. Gordon Harbord had been telling him for some time that he would be 'an awful mug' if he missed the chance of a commission, though he made it quite clear that he hoped Sassoon would not be sent out to France. The deciding factor for Sassoon was almost certainly his belief that, as a cavalry unit in a predominantly infantry war, the sleepy Sussex Yeomanry would never be sent overseas and, therefore, never see fighting.

Would Sassoon's decision have been different had he been able to look into the near future and seen the Sussex Yeomanry in action at Gallipoli as dismounted cavalry? Probably not, for by October 1914 he had already decided that he wanted a change. Though continuing to enjoy the weekly visits of friends from the 'jolly Yeo-boys', particularly that of a farmer's son with whom he had previously hunted, he was mentally separating himself from the regiment, so much so that he was unwilling even to visit them in their new quarters only a short walk away.

Sassoon's desire to see action was almost certainly increased by news from the Front during his convalescence between October 1914 and January 1915. Writing to Marsh on 10 November, for example, he says that he will be very upset if he misses the Battle of the Meuse. By January 1915 self-respect demanded of most able-bodied young Englishmen that they fight to prevent an increasingly threatening situation. Though English newspapers had boosted public morale with glowing reports of the 'Russian steam-roller' (the Russians had scored notable early successes for the Allies in East Prussia and Galicia), their subsequent reports of enormous losses of British and French troops at the battles of Mons, the Marne and Ypres from late August to late October 1914 had made most people realize that this war was on a wholly different scale from previous ones and was likely to continue far longer than first anticipated. Though Paris had been saved and the Germans forced to fall back at the Battle of the Marne in September, they had quickly returned to the offensive just over a month later, at Ypres. By Christmas the opposing armies had dug themselves in along a line from the Belgian coast to Switzerland, a line that was rarely to move more than ten miles either way during the next four years.

By February 1915, back in Weirleigh for the end of his long convalescence with his arm finally healed, Sassoon reluctantly made up his mind to apply for a commission in an Infantry Regiment. This decision was reinforced by the news that Tom Richardson had lied about his forty-four years and had volunteered for service overseas in the Army Veterinary Corps. Nevertheless, it took him some time to carry out his secret resolution. His mother's understandable wish that he should remain in what she saw as a comparatively safe posting, together with the pleasures of mild spring days at the end of February, were undeniable deterrents, as was an invitation to visit his Thornycroft cousins on the Isle of Wight that spring.

Another factor which helps to explain Sassoon's delay was a resurgence of the poetic impulse. Dampened by his initial period of recruitment and training in harsh physical circumstances, it began to reassert itself during the solitude of his convalescence in Canterbury at the end of 1914. His return to Weirleigh, which had been one of his favourite subjects for poetry since childhood, the lovely spring weather and a strong sense of uncertainty about the future provided the final stimulus. By 27 February he was sending Eddie Marsh two poems written some time between October 1914 and February 1915 – 'Storm and Rhapsody' and 'Wisdom'. Marsh admired both pieces, which seems to have given Sassoon the confidence he needed to bring out another private collection of poems.

Discoveries, as Sassoon named his slim volume in green paper wrappers, was printed, like his four previous private productions, by the Chiswick Press in a limited edition. Each of the thirteen poems, however brief, appears on a separate page, giving the book an air of luxury and elegance. By contrast with most of his earlier productions, only one poem in the book had appeared before.[10] An even stronger contrast is the fact that Sassoon thought all but two of the thirteen pieces worthy of inclusion in his *Collected Poems*.

On reading *Discoveries* it is immediately clear why so many of its poems were preserved. It is the first work of Sassoon's maturity. No longer heavily Ninetyish – though still basically romantic in theme and treatment – it reflects both Gosse and Marsh's advice to Sassoon. By persuading him to think more carefully about both subject matter and technique, they appear to have stemmed his earlier gush of undigested emotions.

With Marsh's advice in mind it is possible to see Sassoon now writing for the most part either with his eye on an object or with his mind at grips with a more or less definite idea. Many of the poems contain closely observed descriptions of nature, 'Daybreak in a Garden', for example. In addition – and this is where the most noticeable improvement lies – the poems usually have a 'more or less definite idea' at their centre. It may be a simple structural device, as in 'Companions', where the bird 'sings' and the clouds 'tell a story', or a more self-conscious Wordsworthian 'epiphany' (the 'discovery' of Sassoon's title) as in 'Wonderment':

Then a wind blew;
And he who had forgot he moved
Lonely amid the green and silver morning weather,
Suddenly grew
Aware of clouds and trees
Gleaming and white and shafted, shaken together
And blown to music by the ruffling breeze ....   (*CP*, p. 58)

Both here and in the majority of other poems in this volume, Sassoon has moved away from the safe familiarity of the sonnet form he had favoured for so long. He experiments freely with a number of verse forms, ranging from simple couplets and rhymed quatrains to both blank and free verse. His years of apprentice work have given him a noticeable assurance in the handling of these.

Sassoon had continued to write copiously between June 1912, when *Melodies* was produced, and May 1914, when he left Weirleigh for London, as his MS notebook for the years 1911 to 1914 shows. However, the bulk of the poems in *Discoveries* date from a relatively short period between June 1914 and February 1915. The most interesting poem in the volume, partly because it gives Sassoon's early reaction to the War, is 'To-day'.[11] Ostensibly it is a strikingly simple personification of Time and Nature, but it also touches on a theme clearly evoked by the thought of war, the possibility of the poet's own imminent death: 'This is To-day. To-morrow might bring death, –/ And Life, the gleeful madrigal of birds,/ Be drowned in glimmer of sleep ....' As a result, the poet's appreciation of the moment – 'To-day' – is strengthened and the poem ends with the pantheistic plea:

... Oh take me to yourselves,
Earth, sky, and spirit! Let me stand within
The circle of your transience that my voice
May thrill the lonely silences with song.   (*CP*, p. 58)

Sassoon's thoughts on war may as yet be generalized, but he has already started to see it as a fit subject for poetry.

The language of 'To-day' and the majority of the poems in *Discoveries* is, in keeping with their more sharply focused observation, less archaic and derivative. Though the tone is still frequently elevated, it is an elevation more akin to the heartfelt simplicities of Wordsworth than the deliberate artificialities of Swinburne, as if the poet is more genuinely absorbed in his message. Under Marsh's tuition he is already sounding more like a Georgian.

The suspicion that Sassoon had been reading Wordsworth is reinforced by the title of the longest poem composed in spring 1915, for 'The Old Huntsman', as he called it, is the sub-title of Wordsworth's early ballad, 'Simon Lee'. Though almost certainly the best poem of this period, it is not difficult to see why Sassoon did not include it in *Discoveries*. Quite apart from its length, 'The

Old Huntsman', a colloquial narrative poem of nearly 200 lines of blank verse in which the narrator remembers better days, has more in common with *The Daffodil Murderer* of 1913 than the romantic 'discoveries' of the young nature-worshipper of 1915. Though not without its lyric passages, these are much tougher and written in very different language from the shorter pieces, perhaps a self-conscious attempt by Sassoon to emulate Wordsworth's 'language really used by men'. Ironically, by avoiding *The Daffodil Murderer's* excessive 'realism', Sassoon has made his narrator more realistic. In one sense the poem can be seen as Sassoon's farewell to his privileged pre-war days in the hunting-field; in another as an indirect tribute to his long-standing friend, Norman Loder, to whom the poem is dedicated; and in yet another as a further manifestation of a satiric impulse which contrasted oddly with his lyric vein but which was to feature significantly in his war poetry. It is no coincidence that 'The Old Huntsman' would head his first book of war poems, to which it would also give the title.

Another characteristic which has no chance to express itself in Sassoon's lyrics but will reappear in his fiercest war poems is his grim humour, nicely illustrated by the agnostic old huntsman's concept of hell in terms of a bad day's sport: 'Hell was the coldest scenting land I've known,/And both my whips were always lost, and hounds/Would never get their heads down' (*CP*, p. 6). As the reviewer from the *Cambridge Magazine* argued when 'The Old Huntsman' finally appeared in print in 1917, it sums up in many ways Sassoon's main characteristics, his 'broad humanity and sympathy, his keen sense of the poetry of country life, and a touch of that grotesque cynicism which comes out so strongly in his shorter war poems'.[12]

*

By the time *Discoveries* arrived from the printers in April 1915, Sassoon was about to leave for his new regiment. He had finally taken action at the end of February, after sending his poems to the printers. There is something of a puzzle surrounding the incident. He himself suggests in his closely autobiographical *Memoirs of a Fox-Hunting Man* that his first step was to consult an old family friend in the neighbourhood, Captain Ruxton, yet other facts make this seem unlikely.[13] Nevertheless, it makes a good story and is probably true to the extent that one of his family friends used his influence to smooth the young man's path. Like Captain Ruxton it would probably have been someone who had known him since birth and regarded him as an unofficial godson, someone also who lived near Weirleigh. It could even have been Ruxton himself with the details of his army career slightly altered.

As a result of their talk, Captain Ruxton, or whoever it was, wrote recommending Sassoon for a commission in the Royal Welch Fusiliers. Though he had retired from the army many years before, the Adjutant there happened to be the nephew of a former brother officer of Sassoon's sponsor and the old-boy network ensured Sassoon an instant and positive response.

Within a week he was instructed to make a formal application for a Special Reserve commission. The Special Reserve was a new name for the old Militia and a temporary commission in the New Army would have come to much the same thing. Sassoon's sponsor was, however, an old-fashioned snob, of the rather harmless variety in Sassoon's eyes, and could not help looking down on Kitchener's New Army.

Sassoon, while poking gentle fun at his old friend afterwards, nevertheless went along with his suggestion at the time and a number of his subsequent actions and comments suggest that he himself was not immune from a similar snobbishness. His first act on receiving confirmation of his commission, for example, was to go straight to the best military tailors available to order a very different uniform from his former ill-fitting tunic and breeches, an exercise which reminded him strongly of his previous acquisition of hunting clothes. Both the army and the Hunt, he seems to be reminding his reader, were equally class-ridden worlds. And his account of his first visit to the army tailor, while humorously deflating his own snobbishness – 'I became as wax in his hands' – tacitly acknowledges his complicity in the class system.[14]

Sassoon's choice of regiment the second time around also illustrates his anxiety to do the 'correct' thing, at least as far as his limited means would allow. The Royal Welch Fusiliers had a long and honourable history. From their first engagement at the Battle of the Boyne in 1690, when their commander, Major Toby Purcell, distinguished himself, the Royal Welch Fusiliers were at every one of the numerous wars Britain fought over the succeeding two centuries. Their battle honours read like a crash course in British military history, including such famous names as Namur, Blenheim, Ramillies, Corunna, Salamanca, the Peninsula, Waterloo, Inkerman, Sebastopol, Lucknow and the Relief of Ladysmith.

Like all venerable institutions, the Royal Welch had its own insignia and rituals, the most distinctive of these being the wearing of a 'Flash' consisting of five black ribbons attached to the collar of all ranks. Another ritual, shared with several Welsh regiments, was the custom of being led on parade, and even into battle, by a white goat with gilded and ornamented horns. St David's day, as might be expected, was particularly rich in special rites, which one hopes for Sassoon's sake were suspended during the First World War. (It is difficult to imagine him enjoying eating a raw leek.) The contrast between this ancient regiment with its elaborate rituals and the recently formed company of mainly part-time amateurs which made up the Sussex Yeomanry when Sassoon had joined it in August 1914 could hardly have been greater, and his immediate pride in the Royal Welch Fusiliers is understandable.

When war broke out in 1914 the Royal Welch Fusiliers consisted of two Regular battalions – the 1st and 2nd; one Special Reserve battalion – the 3rd; and four Territorial Units – the 4th, 5th, 6th and 7th. The 2nd Battalion left immediately for France in August, and the 3rd left barracks at Pembroke on 9 August and returned to Headquarters at Wrexham, while the 4th, 5th, 6th and 7th were put on war footing. The 1st Battalion went straight out to Flanders in October 1914. Within one year the original seven battalions had swelled to twenty-one, so enthusiastic had been the initial response to Kitchener's call to arms. After conscription was introduced in 1916 the Regiment again expanded and the final tally of battalions reached was forty-two, eighteen of which saw active service.

By the time Sassoon joined the Regiment in May 1915 the 1st and 2nd Battalion between them had fought bravely in all the major battles in France and Belgium – Mons, Le Cateau, the Marne, the Aisne, Ypres, Neuve Chapelle and Aubers. After Turkey's entry into the War on Germany's side in late October 1914, the 5th, 6th, 7th Battalions and, in June 1915, the 8th were sent out to Gallipoli, where the Allies were planning their ill-fated attempt to gain control of the Dardanelles, Turkey's lifeline to Europe.

Sassoon's own inexperience in matters of war was uppermost in his mind when he reported to the 3rd Battalion at its Wartime Training Depot near Liverpool. Though now technically of the officer class – he had been gazetted Second Lieutenant on 28 May 1915 – he felt something of a fraud. Nothing in his brief period of training as a trooper with a non-combatant cavalry unit seemed to have fitted him for a position of command, however lowly, in a fighting infantry regiment. He felt decidedly apprehensive as he made the tedious journey by train from Paddock Wood to Charing Cross, Euston to Liverpool and Liverpool to the dingy suburb of Litherland. Once in the taxi, which took him through a rash of recent housing developments near Seaforth and Litherland station, over the Leeds and Liverpool canal to the wilderness of an industrial estate, he was probably longing to return to the genteel comforts of Weirleigh and the beauty of the undulating Kent countryside. The tin huts of Litherland Camp, situated between the 'hell-workshop' of Brotherton's Ammunition Factory and a large Roman Catholic cemetery, with the smoking chimneys of Bryant and May's match factory half a mile away, could not have been a cheering sight.[15]

During this journey through the dreary industrial suburbs Sassoon found some consolation in the company of another newcomer, Norman Stansfield, an overweight, middle-aged Canadian who, in rather ripe language, grumbled amusingly about the £800 a year job he had just given up. Nevertheless Sassoon felt completely lost on arrival at the camp. His months with the Sussex Yeomanry at Canterbury, conveniently close to his home, and even his brief bid for independence in London had not prepared him for such feelings of complete isolation. His only comfort, he tells his reader, was Palgrave's *Golden Treasury*.

The majority of Sassoon's fellow-officers were probably experiencing similar reactions. With an average age of twenty-one, many of them had come straight from public school and were younger than the men they were being trained to command. But the atmosphere at Litherland Camp was aggressively cheerful, perhaps to compensate for the rising number of men being killed in action. Some of the new officers, like Stansfield, had come from well-paid jobs in civilian life and were part of what were called Special Battalion Commissions.

With his socially superior Special Reserve Commission and his socially correct uniform ('You can't have [your shirts] too dark' his tailor had warned Sassoon, a remark he had remembered when he first saw the unfortunate Stansfield's straw-coloured ones), Sassoon was part of the Establishment, with reservations. Like Robert Graves, also a Special Reserve officer, Sassoon was almost certainly reminded on arrival of his great good fortune in being granted the privilege of fighting with one or other of the regular battalions, if the War lasted.

Nevertheless Sassoon's Special Reserve Commission would have ensured him a privileged position. And, together with his youthful air, would probably have placed him, in others' eyes, among the public schoolboys and ex-Sandhurst cadets. Though his twenty-eight years theoretically separated him from these younger men, his lack of worldly experience and his public-school background enabled him to identify with them quite easily. Within a few days he began to feel one of this outwardly light-hearted group, whose only purpose, he tells us, was to 'get sent out' as soon as possible.[16]

Sassoon's first overt war poem, written between April and September 1915, just before and just after joining the Royal Welch Fusiliers, shows quite clearly that he shared the group's attitude to begin with. For his initial response to the War was one of unquestioning idealism not easily distinguishable from that of his contemporary, Rupert Brooke:

> *Absolution*
> The anguish of the earth absolves our eyes
> Till beauty shines in all that we can see.
> War is our scourge; yet war has made us wise,
> And, fighting for our freedom, we are free.
>
> Horror of wounds and anger at the foe,
> And loss of things desired; all these must pass.
> We are the happy legion, for we know
> Time's but a golden wind that shakes the grass.
>
> There was an hour when we were loth to part
> From life we longed to share no less than others.
> Now, having claimed this heritage of heart,
> What need we more, my comrades and my brothers?   (*CP*, p. 11)

The lack of originality, together with the inflated and clichéd language of these, to use Sassoon's own words, 'too nobly worded lines', suggests that his response in mid-1915 was still largely unconsidered and untested, the conventional response of a member of the ruling classes.[17] He himself later saw them as typical of 'the self-glorifying feelings of a young man about to go to the Front for the first time'.

Adrian Caesar argues that 'Absolution' reveals both sadism and masochism in

Sassoon's attitude to war, an attitude based largely on earlier war poetry, where sacrifice and the brotherhood of man is glorified.[18] It is true that Sassoon knew poems like Tennyson's 'Revenge' and 'The Defence of Lucknow' by heart, but the imagery of the title, 'Absolution', together with such words as 'anguish', 'scourge' and 'wounds' and the notions of purification through suffering and laying down one's life for others are essentially Christian and come as no surprise in the work of someone who has only just begun to question his Christian faith. Even after he abandoned Christianity Sassoon continued, like so many other First World War poets, to use its imagery.

A note Sassoon later added to 'Absolution' states that 'People used to feel like this when they "joined up" in 1914 and 1915,' and that was no doubt true of the majority of recruits who unthinkingly accepted that 'honour' demanded 'sacrifice'. Yet Sorley, whose approach was far more objective, had questioned this attitude from the outset and it was he who wrote of Rupert Brooke, when he died on 23 April 1915 (perhaps the very day Sassoon started to write his poem): 'He is far too obsessed with his own sacrifice, regarding the going to war of himself (and others) as a highly intense, remarkable and sacrificial exploit, whereas it is merely the conduct demanded of him (and others) by the turn of circumstances, where the non-compliance with this demand would have made life intolerable .... He has clothed his attitude in fine words: but he has taken the sentimental attitude.'[19] These are words which could equally well be applied to Sassoon's first war poem.

It is clear that in his first days at Litherland Sassoon was an unquestioning part of the 'happy legion' (an echo perhaps of Wordsworth's 'happy warrior'), eager to leave for the Front. However, he was already beginning to register the complacency and unawareness of those who were in no danger of being sent out, in particular the staff at the camp.

The younger men could only try not to think about the grim casualty lists from abroad. Meanwhile they naturally distracted themselves as much as they could with all available diversions. Apart from dinners at the Adelphi in Liverpool with fellow officers, Sassoon particularly enjoyed battalion cricket. At weekends and sometimes even on weekdays he indulged in another favourite sport, golf, by courtesy of the Formby Golf Club, which had made all officers of the Royal Welch Fusiliers honorary members for the duration of the War. He also hoped in the autumn to get in some days hunting across the Mersey in Cheshire. He was to discover throughout his army career that to be known as a hunting man to regular officers was as decided an advantage as wearing the right coloured shirts.

In the meantime he often simply took a walk down to Seaforth Sands, where the sight of the sea and the flocks of seagulls helped offset the drabness of the Litherland depot. He hired himself a Bechstein piano – which rapidly went out of tune – and spent an occasional hour playing the music he had loved so much the previous summer, Borodin's *Prince Igor*. In addition he attended every concert he could.

Side by side with these leisure activities, rigorous daily training went on. Young officers arriving in camp were instructed by efficient NCOs, who would teach them, among other things, how to form fours, slope arms and so on, until they could drill a company of recruits with rigid assurance, a state Sassoon felt himself unlikely ever to reach. While senior officers busied themselves with company accounts, kit inspections and other routines, raw recruits like Sassoon would have to learn the rudiments of musketry and field training, the use of Lewis guns, rifles, hand-grenades and mortars. Most of these skills had their own manual and Sassoon spent many hours trying to master such mysteries as the mechanism of the rifle, or the precise order of Company drill. He noted down on several occasions an alliterative mnemonic on what qualities were needed in a Company Commander, a typically literary response to the situation.[20] Headed 'C's and their Consequences', it lists 'care (of Men)' as its top priority, a concern he was to demonstrate throughout his three years with the Royal Welch Fusiliers.

Gradually, in spite of his natural resistance to dry knowledge, Sassoon mastered the contents of his Infantry Training Manual. Learning to be a Second Lieutenant, however tedious, was in some ways a relief. Ironically, it kept his mind off the War and made it seem further away. Only when news came from the 1st and 2nd Battalions in France was he unable to forget his own approaching fate. In April, when the Germans used poison gas for the first time, the 1st Battalion of the Royal Welch Fusiliers lost large numbers of officers and men at Festubert. Meanwhile, another three of their battalions were still in Gallipoli. The first phase of the fighting there had ended in early May with heavy Allied casualties, but the campaign was to be renewed. The continuing threat of Turkey in the Middle East, Bulgaria's alliance with the Central Powers and trouble in Africa from Germany's colonies in 1915 made huge demands on the Allies, who had to withdraw large numbers of troops from the Western Front as a result. By the autumn they were in urgent need of reinforcements there.

*

The threat of departure had overshadowed Sassoon's summer, but it had nevertheless been one of the happiest of his life. With the departure of his first, rather taciturn room-mate had come the arrival of someone who was to mean a great deal to him and who was, indirectly, to change his attitude towards war profoundly – David Cuthbert Thomas. It is clear from the language Sassoon uses in his diary and in his thinly-disguised account of Thomas as 'Dick Tiltwood' in *Fox-Hunting Man* that he fell deeply in love with the young Sandhurst subaltern, whom he nicknamed 'Tommy'.[21]

Ten years Sassoon's junior, Tommy seemed to the older man the embodiment of youth and beauty. The emphasis on his 'slender' figure, 'yellow' hair, 'kind grey' eyes, 'young ... warm' hands and 'brilliant' smile makes the reader aware of Sassoon's physical attraction towards Thomas. Yet one is also aware of his need to idealize the love object, as though to purify the attraction of any grosser elements. He emphasized how old Thomas made him feel, but was clearly attracted to him partly because of his youth and innocence. Though there is no suggestion of a physical relationship in this particular case, Thomas is the first in a long line of younger men with whom Sassoon became infatuated. All his subsequent sexual relationships were with people at least ten years younger than himself, often more.

At a rational level there were obvious explanations for Sassoon's attraction towards Thomas. Thomas, like Gordon Harbord, was the son of a well-to-do clergyman and came, therefore, from a similar middle-class background to Sassoon's own He was also a good sportsman and joined Sassoon at the nets of the neighbouring cricket ground on long summer evenings. Though Thomas had hunted very little, he thought it 'immensely important' and listened to Sassoon's hunting stories eagerly. Since Gordon Harbord's letters to Sassoon, written from France, were full of nostalgic hunting references, he would often read them aloud to Thomas, thus linking indirectly his two greatest friends at that time. Perhaps most importantly of all for Sassoon, Thomas took a keen interest in his poetry, finding 'the poems rightly named "Discoveries"', for instance, 'lovely'.[22]

In more practical terms, Thomas, with his Sandhurst training, proved extremely helpful to Sassoon and patiently guided him through the numerous training manuals. Above all, his cheerful and unquestioning acceptance of his patriotic duty which Sassoon shared at this time, gave the older man a sense of security in a manifestly insecure world.

August brought the two men a month in 'Paradise', as Sassoon saw it. In his description of their four-week training course at Pembroke College, Cambridge, he tells his readers that the room he and Thomas shared had the name of its previous occupant – 'Paradise' – still on the door.[23] Whether this was literally true or not, Sassoon's symbolic intentions are clear: to him it *was* paradise. Though barred from attempting a physical relationship with Thomas by his own moral code, he nevertheless enjoyed every moment of his company, an enjoyment sharpened by his sense that it might be their last time together. Though Thomas did not share Sassoon's sexual leanings, he clearly enjoyed his company. After the day's training was over, they spent long evenings together at the Red Lion pub, enjoying their relative freedom.

It is impossible to recapture Sassoon's precise feelings on returning to Cambridge ten years after his first stay there. However, since Thomas was approximately the same age as he had been then, it is reasonable to suppose that his presence made Sassoon very conscious of his younger self and all that it had taken for granted. The town would have been at its most attractive in the fine summer weather of 1915, though strangely denuded of students under wartime conditions. While he never publicly stated regret for his previous abrupt departure, in later life he was to attempt to make Cambridge his centre again, an indication of his affection for it.

One of the main reasons Sassoon appreciated Cambridge the second time round was that he was introduced to a number of interesting people there, marking the start of several important relationships and putting his Officer's Training programme firmly into the background. The most enduring and richest of these was with Sydney Carlyle Cockerell.

Born in 1867, Cockerell had had an extraordinary career. His close friendship with John Ruskin and William Morris in his youth had led to him becoming secretary to Morris and, eventually, to the Kelmscott Press. After Morris's death in 1896, he had become secretary and factotum to the poet Wilfred Scawen Blunt. A period in process-engraving with Sir Emery Walker in the early 1900s was followed by the position which made his name, Director of the Fitzwilliam Museum in Cambridge. Bringing his enormous energy and business acumen to bear on a traditionally sleepy and conservative occupation, Cockerell transformed a dreary and ill-hung provincial gallery into a fine display of treasures. (Fund-raising was one of his many talents.)

Sassoon had been introduced to the well-known connoisseur by a letter from Edmund Gosse and was invited to dine with him on 1 August 1915 at Jesus College, of which Cockerell was an honorary fellow. Just under a week later, he was again invited to dine with Cockerell, this time at his house, Wayside Cottage in Cavendish Avenue on the outskirts of town. There, in Cockerell's candle-lit study, he was allowed to look at some of the collector's many treasures. Though Cockerell's speciality was medieval illuminated missals and psalters, he chose initially to appeal to Sassoon's more contemporary taste for the Pre-Raphaelites, a taste which he had indulged to the detriment of his studies during his original stay in Cambridge. After an evening handling original manuscripts by such adolescent heroes as William Morris, Francis Thompson and Dante Gabriel Rossetti, Sassoon returned to his camp-bed in Pembroke College in a 'trance of stimulation'.[24] So successful had the visit been that it was repeated the next day and the remaining two Sundays of Sassoon's stay in Cambridge. There were also several visits to the Fitzwilliam to look at beautifully illustrated books by Cockerell's wife, a tactful move on the younger man's part.

Sassoon initially perceived Cockerell as an almost supernatural being – 'a bearded and spectacled magician'[25] – and he was subsequently surprised by his kindly interest in a far from expert enthusiast twenty years his junior. For his part Cockerell found Sassoon entertaining company and admired his poetry greatly. They were to remain friends for the next forty-seven years.

One way in which Cockerell tried to help the virtually unknown Sassoon in 1915 was to introduce him to people he might find either interesting or useful. The most important of these, from several points of view, was Edward Dent. Sassoon may already have heard of him from Marsh, whose protégé Rupert Brooke had known him as a Fellow of King's in the early 1900s; Marsh himself knew Dent well.[26] Nine years Cockerell's junior and only ten years older than Sassoon, Dent was already established as a respected musicologist when he and Sassoon met. He had already written books on Scarlatti and Mozart by 1915 and was to become Professor of Music at Cambridge University in 1926. When he met Sassoon at Cockerell's on 15 August, his immediate response was to invite the younger man to dinner.

In replying to the invitation on the 18th Sassoon made it clear that he saw music as an important aspect of their friendship.[27] He felt particularly deprived of music in the army. In England he was still able to get to occasional concerts, but once in France he was to feel 'starved' of anything worth listening to and it was Dent, his 'dear old music-man' to whom he would turn. Despite Dent's wide knowledge and talent (he had himself composed a number of pieces), he was the opposite of self-important and he and Sassoon quickly became firm friends. While Sassoon's close relationship with Cockerell remained fairly formal for some time, he became intimate with Dent almost immediately. When on leave in February 1916 it was Dent, not Cockerell, he hoped to meet 'to do something together, lunch off macaroni, and look at some pictures and talk, talk'.

One explanation for this intimacy emerges in Sassoon's numerous letters to Dent following their initial meeting – their very similar sense of humour. Alluding to Dent's fondness for Italian food, Sassoon addresses him as 'Dear Bolognese', and sending Dent a copy of an ancient Egyptian glass-cup on 15 October 1915 he cannot resist punning 'My cup is thy cup'.

An even more fundamental bond between Dent and Sassoon was their homosexuality. While Sassoon was only just beginning to come to terms with his, Dent was part of a circle of intellectuals at Cambridge who accepted their sexuality with far more confidence and were able to discuss it frankly among themselves. It was probably Dent who introduced Sassoon to members of this circle, including E.M. Forster, Goldsworthy Lowes Dickinson and A.T. Bartholomew. Certainly Dent made the ideal confidant and his must have been one of the few relationships at the time which did not involve Sassoon in concealment. For Sassoon's own conflicts and the legal position of the time made it virtually impossible for him to discuss his sexual preferences with many people. He was unable to reply honestly to an army friend, for instance, who asked him why there were 'no women' in his verse.[28] It must, therefore, have come as a great relief to be able to talk freely to Dent, who was entirely frank about his numerous homosexual liaisons and kept a flat in London mainly for that purpose. It was not Dent, however, but one of the least-known and temporary members of his circle, Gabriel Atkin, who was to have the greatest effect on Sassoon's attitude. Posted to Cambridge for Officer Training just before Sassoon in 1915, he had already left by the time the latter arrived and it would be three years before Dent managed to bring them together and transform Sassoon's life.

For the time being Sassoon had to be content with nostalgic memories of Cambridge and falling chastely in love again, this time with a young man he had known slightly before the War, Robert Hanmer. Hanmer arrived at the Litherland depot in September and, as Sassoon told Dent, immediately became his new 'angel'. The need for 'purity' in sexual matters is clearly still paramount. While his love is denied physical expression, he implies, it remains 'pure' and it is significant that he is attracted to young men he knows to be heterosexual. (Tommy, for example, is 'very much intrigued with a young nurse in Liverpool', he tells Dent.) Like David Thomas, Hanmer seems to Sassoon the very model of English youth, cheerful, bright-eyed, fair-haired, shining-faced, healthy, simple and good. The picture, as with Thomas, is too good to be true and Graves's more objective description is a salutary corrective: 'a perfectly charming boy of a rather conventional type but absolutely unlike the usual run of Sandhurst subalterns in his nice manners and simple tastes'.[29]

Deprived of the possibilities of sexual gratification with 'Bobbie the Beautiful', Sassoon feels that his only means of satisfaction would be to save his life – 'a Gorgeous idea!'[30] In the interim, he sublimates his feelings in hero-worship and attempts to get closer to 'Bobbie' by the more conventional means of getting close to his sister, Dorothy. He had met the Hanmers while staying with Norman Loder in the winter of 1913 to 1914. According to Sassoon, Dorothy was one of the Belles of the Atherstone Hunt; but his efforts to fall in love with her, as an extension of Bobbie, and their eventual engagement early in 1916 were, understandably, to be a failure.[31]

It was more than love for Bobbie that prompted Sassoon to propose to Dorothy Hanmer, however. As he told Ottoline Morrell, he had become engaged since 'he felt he ought to be as all his brother officers had a girl', but he soon found it impossible as he really only liked men and 'women were antipathy to him'. He did not enjoy the prospect of living on his own, but could not contemplate defying social and moral conventions at this stage of his life. At twenty-nine he was also beginning to want children, a need which was to become more pronounced once he embarked on his first sexual relationship.

Meanwhile Sassoon attempted to sublimate his feelings in ceaseless physical activity. Life at Litherland Camp, after his return from Cambridge on 22 August, continued as before, except for new recruiting marches through Liverpool. Only two days earlier, word had come of Bulgaria's entry into the War on the side of the Central Powers and with it the need for more Allied troops on the Eastern Front. From Gallipoli, where Sassoon's younger brother, Hamo, was serving with the Royal Engineers, the news was no more cheerful. In August the Allies had landed at Suvla Bay but during the long, hot summer sickness had seriously weakened the troops and the Allies were beginning to consider withdrawal. At the same time there was an urgent need for reinforcements on the Western Front, where the British were beginning to plan an attack on Loos in support of the French at Souchez. (The 1st, 2nd, 4th and new 9th Service Battalions of the Royal Welch Fusiliers were to be involved.) It could only be a matter of weeks before Sassoon himself was sent abroad.

When Sassoon's draft finally came it was not, as he had feared, for the Balkans or the Dardanelles but for France. He was delighted to find himself going out with David Thomas but very sad to be leaving Robert Hanmer behind. One consolation was a week's leave, granted by custom before embarkation and called, rather ominously, 'last leave'. Sassoon's took place in mid-October and he spent part of it in London with Marsh, Dent and Gosse. It was at Gosse's that he met someone who was to become more important to him than either Cockerell or Dent – Robbie Ross.[32]

Sassoon and Ross had both attended a party given by the Gosses in June 1913, but Ross, who was under a cloud at the time, had not felt able, as he rather quaintly put it, to 'offer the hand of friendship' to Sassoon in the circumstances.[33] Though Sassoon had sent him *The Daffodil Murderer* and other works in June 1914 and been invited to visit him then, the outbreak of war had delayed their first real meeting for yet another year. When he eventually met Ross at the Gosses' on 17 October 1915, he would certainly have known of him, and not just from his friendship with Gosse and Marsh. For Ross's involvement with Oscar Wilde still marked him out, particularly among homosexuals. Ross, who had been a friend, some said more than a friend, to Oscar Wilde from the mid-1880s, had, at the cost of his own reputation, stood by him throughout his trials in 1895. His devotion had earned him the undying hatred of Lord Alfred Douglas, anxious to prove his own change of heart, and he had been remorselessly hounded in the press and the courts by Douglas and his ally, Crosland. Through all these troubles Gosse had, in spite of his anxiety to remain respectable, unexpectedly stood by Ross. (To some, his sympathy smacked of fellow-feeling.) By October 1915 it looked as though Douglas's spite had exhausted itself, and Ross felt able to respond to Gosse's renewed offer of an introduction to Sassoon.

Ross and Sassoon immediately liked each other, not surprisingly since they had a number of interests and experiences in common. Like Sassoon, Ross had left Cambridge without a degree. He had then started his career as a literary journalist before turning to another of Sassoon's interests, art. After running the Carfax Gallery with his friend More Adey from 1901 to 1909, he had become first an art critic on the *Morning Post*, then Adviser to the Inland Revenue on picture valuation, an unlikely post for someone who enjoyed shocking the Establishment. He had spent his time since war broke out trying to get official status for War Artists, an initiative which eventually led to the founding of the Imperial War Museum.

Despite being seventeen years older than Sassoon, Ross had an almost schoolboyish sense of humour and seemed to Sassoon like 'a benevolent and impulsive bachelor uncle with whom one could feel on easy terms of equality'.[34] He was delighted on one occasion by Robbie's reply to his wondering what had caused a fire at the house of the Poet Laureate, Robert Bridges: 'Dry rot, I expect.'[35] A dapper little man with his light grey alpaca suit, soft black hat, large scarab ring, ebony cane and jade cigarette-holder, Robbie attracted Sassoon both physically and mentally. He admired especially his loyalty to his friends.

Everything Sassoon wrote about Ross emphasizes the same point; he gained his greatest pleasures in life, it seemed, in helping his friends, from

Wilde onwards. In Sassoon's case there was much he could do. Unlike Marsh and Gosse, he was not anxious for the approval of the Establishment, in fact he enjoyed opposing it, and he encouraged Sassoon from the start to express his views honestly and directly, especially in his poetry. With his strong anti-war feelings, it was Ross, more than any other single person, who was to help bring about the distinctive change in Sassoon's war poetry during 1916. Arnold Bennett's remark to Sassoon, that Ross was 'the most indirectly creative person [he had] known',[36] is very similar to what Sassoon said of Sydney Cockerell. Both men delighted in helping younger, more creative men.

Though Sassoon was afterwards to claim that he had never talked to Ross about Oscar Wilde, it is clear from contemporary letters and later remarks to friends that this was an evasion of the truth. He and Ross certainly discussed homosexuality, both their own and others'. Ross, like Dent, allowed Sassoon to articulate feelings he had had to suppress for many years. In practical terms Ross was part of a group of influential men who could exert influence in the literary world for Sassoon when the need arose. At least part of Sassoon's success as a war poet would be due to the efforts of this band of admirers and supporters. Sassoon himself was to acknowledge Ross's prime role in the process by dedicating his second volume of war poetry 'To Robbie Ross'.

*

In October 1915, however, Ross's influence lay in the future and Sassoon continued to write poetry in the same martial vein with which he had begun a few months earlier. The most extraordinary example of this occurs after the death of his brother Hamo at the beginning of November. Hamo, the only one of the Sassoon brothers to get a degree, had worked for several years in the family engineering firm, Thornycrofts, before going out to Argentine in 1913 as a structural engineer in the River Plate area. He had been there just over a year when war was declared, and returned to England to enlist in May 1915. Sassoon, waiting to join the Royal Welch Fusiliers, had overlapped with him at Weirleigh for three days, his first sight of his brother for two years.

Hamo was then gazetted Second Lieutenant with the Royal Engineers and sent out to Gallipoli in August without being able to say goodbye to Siegfried, who was in Cambridge. The situation in the Dardanelles was critical by the time he arrived and by the end of October it seemed hopeless. After eight months of fighting 25,000 Allied troops had died, another 12,000 were reported missing, and 75,000 were wounded. The final figures were to be even more devastating. Hamo himself was among those evacuated in late October, but died of wounds on board a hospital ship on 1 November 1915. It seemed appropriate to Sassoon that his brother, who had always ridiculed the pomposity of funerals and undertakers, should be buried at sea: 'I know he would have liked the idea of his body being given to the sea,' he was to write to Hamo's old form master at Marlborough, John Bain. 'He was a strong, slow patient swimmer.'[37]

It was Hamo's humour and self-possession, which Sassoon noted even as a child, together with his passion for climbing, that Bain brought out in his poem 'In Memory of Lieut. H.W. Sassoon, R.E.',[38] a poem which depends for its effect on an acceptance of the public-school athletic-military code of honour. Sassoon's own tribute to Hamo appeals to the same code. Both are curiously impersonal. Though addressed 'To My Brother', Sassoon's conveys no sense of intimacy, contains no revealing touches. It is, rather, a rallying cry to battle, as 'Absolution' had been:

> Give me your hand, my brother, search my face;
> Look in these eyes lest I should think of shame;
> For we have made an end of all things base.
> We are returning by the road we came.
>
> Your lot is with the ghosts of soldiers dead,
> And I am in the field where men must fight.
> But in the gloom I see your laurell'd head
> And through your victory I shall win the light.   (*CP*, p. 12)

Poeticisms such as 'lest', the padding of 'the field where men must fight', the vagueness of 'we are returning by the road we came', the cliché of 'the laurell'd head' in the 'gloom' and the emulation of Brooke in 'For we have made an end of all things base' make this a tired poem which gives no sense of Sassoon's personal loss. Perhaps he was anxious to emphasize a larger 'brotherhood' than that of blood ties. The notion of comradeship, so vital to both Whitman and Carpenter in elevating homosexuality, was certainly important to Sassoon and it is interesting that he originally entitled this poem 'Brothers', thus allowing it to embrace all comrades in arms. 'Absolution' had ended with an appeal to 'my comrades and my brothers'. It may be that he had to convince himself of the validity of war in order to make Hamo's death meaningful and, therefore, more acceptable.

Another possible explanation for the lack of convincing grief in Sassoon's poem to his brother may lie in an initial failure to grasp the reality of his death. If, as seems likely, the death of 'Stephen Colwood' (based on Gordon Harbord) in *Fox-Hunting Man* is really a description of Hamo's death, then Sassoon was in a state of numb disbelief after he heard the news.[39] Sherston is about to carry out his routine round of inspection as orderly officer when a telegram is handed to him announcing 'Stephen's' (i.e. Hamo's) death: 'It was queer to be doing [my duties], with that dazed feeling and the telegram in my pocket,' he tells the reader.[40]

Writing to Dent shortly after Hamo's death, Sassoon makes it clear that he associated his brother primarily with his early childhood, when they were at their closest, 'hunting moths and playing cricket on summer evenings'.[41] In a sense his death, more than anything else, signalled the real end of Sassoon's childhood. He had finally been exiled from the garden, symbolized so perfectly by Weirleigh. 'And I am far from the garden,' he was to write in his diary after a particularly intense memory of childhood and Hamo in their own paradisal garden.[42] His thoughts turn frequently to it, especially after the horrors of wartime France. The day before he actually pens his poem to Hamo on 18 December 1915, and after his first experience of the trenches, he writes:

> Lovely now seem the summer dawns in Weirleigh garden; lovely the slow music of the dusk, and the chords of the piano-music. Loveliest of all, the delight of weaving words into verses; the building of dream on dream; oh the flowers and the songs, now so far away. The certainty of my power to touch the hearts of men with poetry – all faded now like a glorious sky. And then the July days, the afternoons of cricketing, and the silly joy I had when I managed to stay an hour or two at the wicket.[43]

Sassoon's lament for Hamo is inextricably bound up with his sorrow for the loss of childhood and in this wider grief he fails at first to feel the particularity of Hamo's death. It would take another six months for it to become real to him, and when it did it would contribute significantly to his change of attitude towards the War and the consequent shift in his poetic technique.

Hamo's death made him even more conscious of the possibility of his own. He also worried even more about his mother who was entirely alone. (Her eldest son, Michael, had been in Canada since 1910 and showed no signs of returning.) Her response to her youngest son's death had been predictably intense. Since her husband's abandonment of her twenty-five years earlier, she had relied wholly on her sons for emotional fulfilment. Now one of them was dead, one about to leave for the Front and the third 6,000 miles away. Her grief was terrible. Refusing to accept Hamo's death, she preserved his room exactly as he had left it and insisted on showing it to unwary visitors.[44] Her attempts to contact him through Spiritualism were to make Sassoon deeply unhappy and to cause a serious rift with one of his closest friends.

It was, therefore, with a guilty sense of relief that Sassoon finally left Victoria Station on 17 November 1915 after what one can only imagine to have been an almost unbearable leavetaking. Perhaps this is the reason he fails to describe it in his war diary, which begins the same day. However, he does give us some idea of the pain experienced by both mother and son as the train left for Folkestone: his fictionized Aunt Evelyn's 'last, desperately forced smile' as she sees Sherston off for France in *Fox-Hunting Man* is surely Theresa Sassoon putting on a brave face as her favourite son starts for the Front.[45]

9
'Goodbye to Galahad'
November 1915-March 1916

Remarkable though it may seem, Sassoon, who was in the army from the day war broke out to the day it ended and had the reputation of being a fire-eater, spent barely a month out of a possible fifty-one in the Front Line. There were a number of reasons to account for this and chance also played a part. His early riding accident in the Sussex Yeomanry and subsequent change of regiment, for instance, delayed his active service for well over a year. Then, largely because of his late arrival at the Front, he maintained his 'happy warrior' outlook for at least eighteen months after war began.

When Sassoon set out for France on 17 November 1915, it was to some extent a relief. The boredom of life in Litherland Depot, the tension of waiting to be drafted and the guilt and inadequacy he was experiencing over his mother's sufferings were at least brought to an end. Everything negative seemed behind him and only positive action ahead. There was also the excitement of his first arrival on foreign soil. The lunchtime train from Victoria had deposited him on Folkestone pier at 6 p.m. and by 7 p.m. he was on the reassuringly named *Victoria* steaming out to sea. Not until one in the morning did he and Thomas stumble ashore at Calais, having been diverted from their real destination, Boulogne, by the sinking of a hospital ship in mid-Channel. After a night spent on a hotel floor, they eventually left for Boulogne at 11.15 a.m. next day, rather less wide-eyed about France.

In Boulogne there were more aimless hours spent waiting for orders and it was not until 11.30 p.m. that they reached the Base Camp at Etaples only fourteen miles away, described by one veteran as 'a hellish dump without a single redeeming feature'.[1] Sassoon waited there four days for his posting and his laconic diary entries reflect his frustration and boredom.[2] On the fourth day relief appeared, first in the weather, which became milder, then in the news of imminent departure to the Battalion of his choice, the 1st. Best of all was the knowledge that his request not to be separated from Thomas had been heard, or at least fulfilled.

As the oldest battalion in the Royal Welch Fusiliers, the 1st enjoyed the greatest status. When Sassoon joined it near Béthune on 24 November, many of its original members at the outbreak of war were dead or wounded. They had landed at Zeebrugge with the 7th Division in 1914 and marched through Belgium to Ypres where they had scored a decided victory against the Germans. In their subsequent struggle to help keep the enemy from seizing the Channel ports, however, they had been decimated. Restored by more drafts to its proper strength, the 1st had again distinguished itself at the Battle of Neuve

Chapelle in March 1915, but had once again lost the greater part of its men at the Battle of Festubert two months later. In September 1915 it had suffered further casualties in another great massacre, the Battle of Loos. Sassoon and his fellow officers were being sent out to make up for heavy losses in the Givenchy trenches on the La Bassée canal. He was fortunate enough to join the Battalion at Béthune just as it was preparing for a long rest in the back area.

Béthune is less than fifty miles from Etaples, but it took Sassoon, Thomas and Stansfield, also assigned to the 1st, nearly five hours to reach it by a long, roundabout train journey. To Sassoon's weary eyes the French countryside looked lifeless and unattractive, no good for hunting in, even if that had been possible. The area round Béthune was particularly desolate after months of heavy fighting.

Nevertheless, almost anything was better than the wastes of Litherland and Sassoon gradually became stimulated by the change of scene. He also liked his new fellow officers, apart from his Commanding Officer, Colonel Minshull Ford, whom he commemorated not entirely kindly as 'Winchell' in *Fox-Hunting Man*. Though he was to switch battalions twice more before the end of the War, he would remain close friends with a number of survivors from the 1st.

On arrival at Béthune Sassoon had been told to report to 'C' Company, which was particularly short of officers, and was delighted to learn that 'Birdie' Stansfield and Tommy were again to stay with him. Together they marched the final three miles to their billet at Le Hamel on the Béthune-Le Touret road, where they met their Company Commander, E.J. Greaves. Greaves, like the majority of the battalion officers, was not a regular soldier and made a pleasant introduction to the army in France. Sassoon, who portrayed him as 'Barton' in *Fox-Hunting Man*, found him good-natured and easy-going, not at all what he had imagined a Company Commander to be like. His very presence, big, burly and pince-nezed, made the Front Line seem positively cosy. Older than most of the officers, whose average age was twenty-five, and married, which many were not, Greaves became something of a father-figure to the five platoon commanders under him. He was frequently referred to as 'Father' Greaves, his age further accentuated by the fact that he had a younger brother, Ralph, in the same regiment.

Sassoon grew even more attached to the two other officers who were new to him in C Company – Julian Dadd and Edmund Leslie Orme. He particularly admired Dadd and was to praise him in both prose and verse in terms which Dadd's family thought showed great understanding and affection.[3] He celebrated Dadd's unassertive courage and goodness in *Fox-Hunting Man* under the pseudonym 'Durley', a name taken from Dadd's home address in Stamford Hill, London. Dadd's unselfishness and concern for his men were an example Sassoon quite consciously tried to follow in France, though he was less impressed by his jokes, which reminded him of a bus conductor trying to cheer up his passengers on a wet winter's day.

Like Sassoon, Dadd had two brothers, one of whom had been killed at

Gallipoli, though unlike Sassoon his remaining brother, Edmund, was with him in the 1st Battalion (A Company).[4] Their father, Stephen Dadd, was a black and white sporting artist and their great-uncle the painter Richard Dadd. The older members of the family were ashamed of the latter connection because of what Julian called 'the tragic and gruesome termination of his career as a free member of society' when Richard had killed his own father. Julian's younger brother, Gabriel, had shown outstanding artistic talent before his death in Gallipoli, but Julian himself had been a clerk in Somerset House when war broke out. One of Sassoon's few regrets about their relationship was that his friend, though a fine swimmer, had never hunted, almost certainly as a result of his different social background.

The remaining platoon officer in C Company, E.L. Orme, seems to have been equally attractive to Sassoon, though in a quite different way. In *Fox-Hunting Man*, which Dadd himself felt gave a 'true and kindly' picture of the Royal Welch Fusiliers,[5] Sassoon portrays Orme as 'Ormond', a 'sturdy little' youth straight from public school, who made no secret of his wish to avoid a hero's death. 'He wanted life,' Sassoon writes, 'and he appeared capable of making good use of it, if allowed the opportunity.'[6] With his large round eyes under dark eyebrows, 'young Worm', as his friends called him, was a lively presence in C Company, sometimes too lively. His taste for mawkish popular songs, which he played constantly on his portable gramophone, made Sassoon long for Handel's violin sonatas, or even his mother playing 'The Harmonious Blacksmith' not very skilfully on the piano. Nevertheless he was glad when Orme later accompanied him on his transfer to another battalion, the only officer from the 1st to do so. As Sorley remarked, wartime 'friendships of circumstance' were unpredictable and could prove surprisingly strong.[7]

Another even closer friendship formed in November 1915 was with a young officer from A Company of the 1st Battalion, Robert von Ranke Graves. Sassoon's meeting with Graves is one of the best-known literary encounters of the First World War, partly because it has been described in detail by both participants – fictionally by Sassoon in *Memoirs of an Infantry Officer* and autobiographically by Graves in *Goodbye to All That*.[8] It has also been remembered, perhaps because, like Sassoon's other famous encounter with Owen at Craiglockhart several years later, it seemed almost predestined. For, while it was entirely natural that Graves should have enlisted in a Welsh regiment near his parents' holiday home at Harlech, there appeared no compelling reason for Sassoon to choose the same unit.

Graves himself had started his service abroad in the 2nd Battalion and it was again chance, or fate, that led to his transfer to the 1st at approximately the same time as Sassoon. Once there, however, it was entirely natural that they should have come together, even from their different companies. For, as Graves pointed out, it was an unusual experience to encounter, in a group of forty to fifty officers, one seriously literary person, though this was not true of the RWF, which also included Bernard Adams, Frank Richards, David Jones, Llewelyn

Wyn Griffiths, Vivian de Sola Pinto and 'Hedd Wyn'. When Graves discovered a copy of Lionel Johnson's essays among the usual clutter of military manuals and 'trashy' novels on a visit to C Company's mess, he naturally sought out the owner. Glancing round for someone who looked both literary and Jewish – he had only Sassoon's signature to go on – he had no difficulty in identifying him. So immediate was their rapport that a short time later they were walking into Béthune together to indulge in cream cakes and talk. Sassoon's diary entry on that occasion suggests that his initial reaction to Graves was both condescending and intrigued: 'An interesting creature, overstrung and self-conscious, a defier of convention' he wrote on 28 November 1915, also noting that Graves was 'very much disliked' in the unit.[9]

Though Sassoon's immediate response implies a sense of superiority and difference, in fact, he and Graves had a number of things in common. Apart from the superficial and unfortunate one of having a German name in the British army, both were from cultured middle-class backgrounds which encouraged interest in the arts. Graves's father was the popular poet and song-writer, Alfred Perceval Graves (whom Sassoon knew but secretly thought very 'bad'). They had both been educated at public school, though Graves's career at Charterhouse had been more regular and academically more successful than Sassoon's, culminating in a (deferred) Exhibition to St John's College, Oxford. Both wanted to be poets and had already written a great deal, though neither was yet established, in spite of the efforts of their mutual friend, Marsh. Another important link was their similar attitude towards the War at that time. Finally, and this too was to change with time, they were both what might be called idealistic homosexuals. Though Sassoon's attitude towards sex had almost certainly been influenced by his correspondence with Carpenter and his meetings with Dent and Ross, it was still basically puritanical, as was Graves's. Graves, who had himself written to Carpenter in 1914, had had a platonic friendship with a boy at Charterhouse, but none of any significance with women by 1915.

Looking back on their relationship in 1930, Graves claimed that Sassoon had been sexually attracted to him, a charge that the latter flatly denied: 'For you I felt affection, but physical attraction never existed.'[10] Yet eight years before this statement, in June 1922, he had written about Graves in his diary 'there was some vague sexual element lurking in the background of our war-harnessed relationship. There was always some restless passionate nerve-wracked quality in my friendship with R.G., although he has been one of my most stimulating companions.'[11] This 'vague sexual element' undoubtedly helped bond their friendship in November 1915.

Temperamentally they were very different. In spite of being nine and a half years younger, Graves seemed to Sassoon far more confident than he, the natural leader of the two and something of an oracle to him when they first met. Deeply introverted himself, Sassoon appears to have been fascinated by Graves's extrovert personality. Where he was diffident about his talents, Graves bragged unashamedly of his modest achievements, probably one reason he was not popular with his fellow-officers. While Sassoon was conventional and conformist in both social and artistic matters, Graves gloried in rebellion. 'He is a strange person, full of ideas and originality,' Sassoon reported to Marsh shortly after their first meeting.[12] He felt that it was Graves's originality, rather than his brashness, which provoked hostility in the 1st Battalion.[13] Unlike Sassoon he made no real effort to conform to army standards in manners or dress and seemed slovenly and careless beside his friend. While Sassoon struggled to become a good officer, Graves appeared to care little for such matters. According to Colonel C.I. Stockwell, who was to take over the 1st Battalion shortly after Graves joined it, he was 'an average officer who did his work neither well nor ill – but he lacked something – He did not instil confidence or moral [*sic*].'[14] By contrast he found Sassoon an excellent officer.

Even Graves's and Sassoon's physical appearances highlighted their pronounced difference. It was almost as though Graves's inner irregularity was symbolically represented by his outward aspect. (Sassoon talked of Graves's 'twisted, grieving face'.) Though both were over six feet tall Sassoon was normally graceful, while Graves was, according to both of them, 'clumsy'. And, though both had prominent noses, Sassoon's lent distinction to his face while Graves's took it away. It was not surprising that Lady Ottoline Morrell, who was to get to know them both, would compare Sassoon romantically to a 'stag or faun' and Graves, less flatteringly, to a prizefighter.

Pronounced as the physical differences were, however, the mental ones were greater. Sassoon's approach to both art and life was, by his own admission, emotional and non-intellectual. Indeed, he was deeply suspicious of the intellectual, a suspicion which Graves would inadvertently strengthen in time. For Graves was assertively intellectual, revelling in the play of ideas, often at the expense of emotions. It was no coincidence that he embraced the difficult, strange and modern in art while Sassoon lingered nostalgically in the past, another distinction which was to cause problems in the future.

For the time being, however, their differences provided welcome stimulation for them both. As they talked avidly, more of literature than of war, Sassoon discovered that Graves despised most of the books he venerated, including, to his disbelief, *Paradise Lost*. Graves's hero at this time was the controversial author of *Erewhon*, Samuel Butler, whose iconoclastic impulses he shared. Though both fusiliers loved music, Graves insisted that Northern folk ballads were superior to Beethoven's Fifth Symphony, a typically provocative claim which Sassoon was too timid to refute. It was only when Graves argued that 'fox-hunting was the sport of snobs and half-wits', doubtless a deliberate bait, that Sassoon grew angry, accusing him of being a 'fad-ridden crank'.[15] One crucial difference between them, which again was to change with time, was their approach to war poetry. While they both basically accepted the necessity of the War, Sassoon wanted war at that time to be 'an impressive experience – terrible, but not horrible enough to interfere with [his] heroic emotions'.[16] Graves, on the other hand, distrusted sublimation and seemed to Sassoon to want the War to be 'even uglier than it really was'.[17]

Such divergent attitudes revealed themselves most clearly in their work at that time. While Sassoon's idealism gave rise to 'Absolution', Graves's realism manifested itself in the poems he had prepared for his first volume, *Over the Brazier* (to be published on 1 May 1916). Some of these pieces initially repelled Sassoon, who characterized them as 'very bad, violent and repulsive',[18] though they almost certainly influenced him. Graves was equally critical of Sassoon's work. 'Siegfried Sassoon is here and sends his affectionate remembrances,' he wrote to Marsh on 10 December 1915, 'a very nice chap, but his verses, except occasionally, don't please me very much.'[19]

Despite these pronounced differences, perhaps partly because of them, the relationship flourished. In conscious emulation of another great literary friendship, that between Coleridge and Wordsworth, they even planned to bring out a modern equivalent of *Lyrical Ballads* together.

Sassoon, who adopted a fatherly attitude towards Graves at times, in recognition of their age difference, often made generous gifts of money to him, such as a witty £23 for his twenty-third birthday in 1918. Graves, who seemed unembarrassed by Sassoon's generosity, occasionally gave him books, but his real contribution to the relationship appears to have been intellectual.

With direct reference to his Jewish blood, of which he was becoming increasingly conscious, Sassoon would quip: 'You have given me so many valuable tips about poetry that I may surely tip you in return with some of my semitic sovereigns none of which I have the least right to call my own.' One such 'tip', which Sassoon was to take up enthusiastically, concerned another war poet whom Graves greatly admired, Sorley. Like Sorley, they planned to travel to exotic places after the War, but together. Taking up the Oriental theme and with deference to Sassoon's love of Fitzgerald, Graves was to write in his verse 'Letter to Sassoon from Mametz Wood':

> In old Baghdad we'll call a halt
> At the Sâshun's ancestral vault;
> We'll catch the Persian rose-flowers scent
> And understand what Omar meant.[20]

A year later Sassoon, not to be outdone, would suggest New Zealand and Polynesia. It was a stimulating and fruitful relationship which began at Le Hamel on 28 November 1915, only four days after Sassoon's arrival in France.

Less exciting but equally important to Sassoon was his relationship with the soldiers under his command. Though he had already been in a similar position at Litherland, he had never felt fully responsible for his men's welfare there, as he came to feel he was in France. His platoon, exhausted and reduced in number by its recent experiences in the Givenchy trenches, accepted him 'apathetically' at first, caring only for thoughts of the forthcoming 'Divisional Rest'.[21] In spite of this, he gradually won them over with his growing concern for them.

Only a day after he took charge he was ordered to lead a working-party up to the trenches at Festubert, where a new defence scheme was under way. As he marched the men through the ruined town, across a marsh and up the muddy communication trench in the rain and darkness, he began to realize how unglamorous the reality of war was, particularly for the ordinary soldier. Two nights later, this time in brilliant moonlight and a frost of ten degrees below zero, he again led a patrol through the treacherous area; as the men staggered and slipped beneath their burdens of hurdles and planks, they seemed to him 'inhuman forms going to and from inhuman tasks'.[22] Two more working-parties followed on the two subsequent nights, one of them bitterly cold, the other very wet and, though Sassoon himself returned home soaked, his concerns were already more for his platoon: 'A shocking night for the men, whose billets are wretched.'[23]

Sassoon's increasing involvement with his men comes through very clearly in a poem written between the second and third of these nightmarish sorties (and revised the following March), 'The Redeemer'. In strong contrast with 'Absolution', this is a work full of concrete details of front-line conditions; it is significant that it was started the very day he met Graves:

> Darkness: the rain sluiced down; the mire was deep;
> It was past twelve on a mid-winter night,
> When peaceful folk in beds lay snug asleep;
> There, with much work to do before the light,
> We lugged our clay-sucked boots as best we might
> Along the trench; sometimes a bullet sang,
> And droning shells burst with a hollow bang;
> We were soaked, chilled and wretched, every one;
> Darkness; the distant wink of a large gun.   (*CP*, pp. 16-17)

Sassoon's realism may be noticeably less shocking than Graves's, but it marks a distinct change of direction for him. The word 'darkness', which opens and closes the first stanza, sets the tone for a poem which no longer deals in abstractions but draws attention to the realities of trench warfare, the 'mire', the 'clay-sucked boots', the 'droning shells', the 'soaked, chilled and wretched' soldiers and even their 'woollen caps' (or Balaclavas). If the comparison in the second stanza between the soldier 'floundering in mirk' with his heavy burden and Christ carrying His cross smacks somewhat of the heroic tradition, this is undercut by the irreverent colloquialism and direct speech of the last two lines, with their snatch of convincing blasphemy from the exasperated soldier – a device Sassoon was to repeat in later poems: 'And someone flung his burden in the muck,/ Mumbling: "O Christ Almighty, now I'm stuck!".' Here at last is war poetry based on actual experience rather than literature. Years of apprentice-work at verse forms has paid off in a simple but effective nine-line stanza of neatly interwoven rhyme scheme, in which the slight and matching variation in rhyme-pattern of the first and last verses helps round off the poem and gives Sassoon the benefit of two concluding couplets with which to drive home his satire.

Language too is varied to good effect between the deliberately elevated ending to verse three where the soldier's Christ-like heroism is being emphasized,[24] to the equally calculated colloquialism of the concluding verse, all the more effective for the contrast. Otherwise, apart from the onomatopoeic invention 'mirk' and the insistent repetition of 'I say that He was Christ', the language is simple and unrhetorical, conveying directly the narrator's emotional involvement with the common soldier, particularly in the first four lines of verse three:

> No thorny crown, only a woollen cap
> He wore – an English soldier, white and strong,
> Who loved his time like any simple chap,
> Good days of work and sport and homely song;

Wilfred Owen told his sister in 1917 that 'The Redeemer' was a poem that he had been wanting to write every week for the past three years.

In *Fox-Hunting Man* Sassoon states that his concern for his men was inspired by Julian Dadd, but there were other factors at work. Apart from his active imagination, which could envisage only too vividly how they suffered in the quagmire trenches and cramped cold billets, he also found himself at last in a position where his preference for men could legitimately express itself without the disapproval of society or the law. While it is true that the majority of officers, whatever their sexual concerns, became emotionally involved with their men and were, in turn, often idolized by them, Sassoon's feelings appear to have gone beyond the paternalistic and platonic. Less than a year after taking over his first platoon in France he would compose the following lines 'To My Soldiers':

> I have pitied you, shattered with wounds, and dying, and killed, –
> Lads that I've loved and will never change eyes with again:
> But Oh my dears, did you know I was proud as a king,
> When I heard you grumble and joke, and chatter and sing?[25]

Even if we reject Paul Fussell's theory that the word 'Lads' is homosexually charged, the vocabulary here betrays an unusual warmth of feeling.[26] It was partly this concern which changed Sassoon's attitude towards the War.

There are, however, among the material deposited in Cambridge University Library after George Sassoon's death, seven unpublished poems in Sassoon's 1916 trench diary which suggests that his development from idealistic fervour to bitter criticism of the War did not run in a straight line. Having drafted

'The Redeemer' in late 1915 with its insistence on unpleasant trench details, for instance, Sassoon could almost immediately write 'Glory: 1916', where war is shown as a glorious, heroic undertaking along the lines of Arthurian legend:

> O happy heart, I watch you ride
> Clothed in your destiny of pride,
> And sworn to the fair knightlihood
> For which the names of legend stood.
>
> All courage worthy to be sung
> Dreams in your face forever young;
> And shining thought that keeps you glad
> Is glory won from Galahad –
> You and the winds ride out together,
> Your company the world's great weather,
> The clouds your plume, the glittering sky
> A list of swords in harmony
> With the whole loveliness of light,
> Flung forth to lead you thro' the fight.   Jan 15th [1916]

In this particular case, Sassoon is likely to be thinking of David Thomas, but he was also deeply concerned for the ordinary soldiers, distant though they are from Galahad. Paradoxically, part of their appeal for him may have lain in their working-class origins. Except for cricket there had been very few occasions in his past life when he had come into contact with this end of the social scale. As Peter Parker points out in his biography of another, less reticent homosexual, Joe Ackerley, 'the trenches were to show these men at their very best'. Paul Fussell has discussed at some length the attraction of many middle-class homosexuals to both the working-classes and men in uniforms, and in First World War France Sassoon found the two combined. He never subsequently, in his active homosexual phase, took a working-class lover, however, and the point must not be exaggerated. What is significant is the way in which he channelled his passions into caring for his men as well as possible. This made him an excellent officer and quickly won the affection of his platoon. One of its members, V. King, was to write to him later: 'I wonder if they will really know what kind of officer you were[,] always thinking about your men[,] our food and feet, and seeing that we got a few cigs.'[27]

Sassoon was particularly kind towards his servant in C Company, R. Molyneux, a former railway signalman. His description of him as 'Flook' in *Fox-Hunting Man* shows that he found Molyneux entertaining as well as endearing, especially his broad Lancashire accent and expressive use of expletives, which are echoed in the war poems.

*

Sassoon had ample opportunity to show his concern for Molyneux and the rest of his men in late 1915. At the beginning of December the gruelling working-parties were succeeded by an almost equally punishing journey behind the lines for the eagerly awaited Divisional Rest. Marching via Gonnehem, Bouecq and Lillers, where they entrained for Sadeux, near Lens, the men of the 1st were exhausted on arrival there, but still had to march all night to reach their final destination in the Picardy uplands, Montagne. It had taken seven hours to march sixteen miles, the last two of which were very steep indeed. A journey of approximately sixty-five miles, which would have been an easy three hour drive for the Divisional General in his staff car, had taken them from 30 November to 6 December, a whole week – a fact which underlines one of the less dramatic but pressing problems of the First World War, the simple logistics of moving large groups of men and equipment even short distances.

Sassoon himself, fit and unencumbered as he was, had found the last stage of the journey exhausting, but in a curious way it revived his flagging war-zeal. It may have been the sight of the men marching hour after hour with their heavy packs and inadequate boots often through torrential rain – 'the men that do the dirty work and keep us safe'[28] – that inspired his 'happy warrior' outburst on the fourth day of the journey:

> My inner life is far more real than the hideous realism of this land of the war-zone. I never thought to find such peace. If it were not for Mother and friends I would pray for a speedy death. I want a genuine taste of the horrors, and then – peace. I don't want to go back to the old inane life which always seemed like a prison. I want freedom, not comfort. I have seen beauty in life, in men and in things; but I can never be a great poet, or a great lover. The last fifteen months have unsealed my eyes. I have lived well and truly since the war began, and have made my sacrifices; now I ask that the price be required of me. I must pay my debt. Hamo went; I must follow him. I will. Bobbie [Hanmer] will come out soon. I will be happy with him for a few months. And in the spring – who knows?[29]

There seems little doubt that Sassoon's willingness to sacrifice himself was closely connected with his homosexuality, either as it related to Bobbie or to his men. In an almost Christ-like gesture he appeared ready to suffer for them, as though suffering might bring the fulfilment he was denied. At the same time he saw the harsh conditions as a welcome punishment for some unspecified sin, perhaps that of homosexuality. For, in spite of Carpenter's reassurances, he was still unable to accept it without guilt.

If Sassoon wanted suffering there would be plenty of opportunity for it in France, though not just yet. For life at Montagne was reasonably comfortable. Compared with Béthune his duties were light and not entirely uncongenial. Since Minshull Ford believed, according to Graves, that the enemy's defences would be quickly penetrated and open warfare would ensue, he insisted on training them like a peacetime army.[30] Battalion drill and musketry training alternated with field-days and, although the whole exercise seemed rather irrelevant to men already experienced in the realities of trench-warfare, it was not unenjoyable, particularly the days spent out in the unspoilt Picardy countryside. Twenty miles behind the Front Line, Sassoon and his men could only faintly hear the sound of guns in the distance.

When Sassoon had to instruct his platoon two or three evenings a week, he tried to keep things as undemanding as possible, often reading out the League Football news after simple questions from the Infantry Training Manual.[31] Another distraction for both men and officers were games of football and rugby, which Graves and Thomas joined in. Though Sassoon enjoyed neither sport, and it was the wrong season for cricket, he did have a chance to enjoy some riding.

Since transport at this stage of the War was largely dependent on animals, the 1st Battalion had a number of horses. One of these, the 'little black mare' of *Fox-Hunting Man*, had been blinded in one eye and become almost unmanageable. With great patience and gentleness, however, Sassoon won her over and, with it, the right to ride her whenever he could, which was normally two or three afternoons a week. She became, as far as any horse could, a replacement for Cockbird in his affections and a welcome distraction. His skill with horses, as well as his reputation as a hard rider to hounds, continued to stand him in good stead in France.

It is little wonder that Sassoon described himself as happy in Montagne. Surrounded by rolling countryside which he could explore on horseback, his imagination began to revive. His diary entries, which had started in November 1915 as terse and mainly factual, gradually expanded and became positively lyrical as he responded to the surrounding scene. It seemed to him as though he were walking through 'a living masterpiece of landscape-painting'.[32]

Despite a determination to avoid 'fine writing', Sassoon could not help comparing Montagne to Arcadia, particularly when he saw the old men and boys at the plough and flail, or watched the windmills spinning, or an old shepherd driving his sheep and goats home, even when a nearby cock woke him up at 6.30 a.m. He was still missing serious music – he could hardly count the 'squeaks and shrillings' of the battalion's fife and drum band as such – but he had his books and was grateful for Nellie Gosse's offer to send him more. There is no record of what Nellie decided to send, but we do know some of the books Sassoon found consolation in that winter, among them Housman's *Shropshire Lad*, Conrad's *Nostromo* and at least one anthology of poetry, which encouraged him to get back to his own versifying.

Another incentive to start writing poetry again at Montagne was the peacefulness of his surroundings. For, while he filled in his war-diary whatever the circumstances, he needed relative calm to compose verse. His first Montagne poem, 'To My Brother', a direct result of his revived 'happy warrior' mood, is disappointing, particularly after the promise of 'The Redeemer'. His second,

'The Prince of Wounds' is little better, though it is interesting to note the questioning of the link between religion and war in its closing lines:

> Have we the strength to strive alone
> Who can no longer worship Christ?
> Is He a God of wood and stone,
> While those who served him writhe and moan,
> On warfare's altar sacrificed?[33]

Also of interest is a small personal detail it contains; by Christmas 1915, when this poem was written, the things Sassoon was missing most were 'Music and colour and delight'. It is a theme he was to take up more successfully in his next two poems.

Meantime Christmas was celebrated with reasonable success. The men, like their officers, were allowed a little 'disciplined insobriety' for the event, and Montagne was full of 'maudlin sergeants' and 'paralysed privates', all trying, no doubt, to forget what was in store for them. A week later New Year's Day was an occasion for both men and officers to take more sober stock of what lay ahead in 1916. Though the fighting had quietened down for the winter, the situation was far from hopeful. Sydney Cockerell, who took a close interest in events, voiced the anxieties of many when he wrote in his diary on 1 January 1916: 'The British losses, though far less than those of the French, have been enormous. Our campaigns in the East have been unsuccessful and very costly. In the West we remain where we were 15 m[on]ths ago. We can only hope for a turn of the tide when the winter is over and a forward move can again be attempted.'[34]

It was, of course, the 'forward move' that the soldiers feared. Already the Germans were planning a massive attack at Verdun, where almost 420,000 French and Germans would die, and beyond that lay the British counter-offensive on the Somme, another massacre in which 623,000 Allied troops would become casualties. Both battles were to drag on to the end of the year, leaving the situation looking no more hopeful than at the start. In view of such uncertainties, it is not surprising that Sassoon held his own personal stocktaking on this New Year's Day, 'A Testament'. Here he tried to come to terms with the strong probability of death in the near future. The setting for this poem appears to be a deserted château he passed regularly on his rides:

> If, as I think, I'm warned to pack and go
> On a longer journey than I've made before,
> I must be taking stock of what I leave,
> And what I stand to lose, of all my store,
>
> Cries for completion. Things, that made me weep
> For joy of loveliness, come shining back
> Dazzling my spirit that prepares for sleep ....[35]

Still in his mood of heroic renunciation, Sassoon fails to provide any central tension to this poem, which is little more than an attempted acceptance of death in vague romantic terms. The true interest of the poem lies in its insistence, as in 'The Prince of Wounds', on the importance of music and visual beauty to the poet, a theme which becomes central in his next poem, 'To Victory'.

Blessed for once on 3 January by a sunny day, which lit up the Somme Valley and the rooftops of Airames on its opposite side, Sassoon felt a return of his joy in nature, all the more precious in the face of possible death. Playing on the treble function of Apollo as the bringer of sunshine, the god of his two favourite arts, music and poetry, and Admetus' shepherd, and reminded of him perhaps by the manly youth and beauty of many who marched beside him, he exclaims: 'The ghost of Apollo is on these cornlands – Apollo in Picardy; it was here that he ground the kern and plied the flail, and lived at the farm.'[36]

However lovely the moment, it was soon gone and the next day Sassoon poured out his longing for the old life of beauty. The image of a garden again symbolizes something sacred and apart, a complete contrast to the ugliness of war. The poem provides yet another insight into his state of mind at the beginning of January 1916, when his greatest fear in war was of being blinded:

> *To Victory*
> Return to greet me, colours that were my joy,
> Not in the woeful crimson of men slain,
> But shining as a garden; come with the streaming
> Banners of dawn and sundown after rain.
>
> I want to fill my gaze with blue and silver,
> Radiance through living roses, spires of green
> Rising in young-limbed copse and lovely wood
> Where the hueless wind passes and cries unseen.
>
> I am not sad; only I long for lustre.
> I am tired of the greys and browns and the leafless ash.
> I would have hours that move like a glitter of dancers
> Far from the angry guns that boom and flash ....   (*CP*, pp. 13-14)

Sassoon himself pointed out that this poem was 'a much more conventional and unrealistic production' than most of his subsequent war poems.[37] It seems, therefore, appropriate that he should have dedicated it to Edmund Gosse, whose views on the War he knew to be conventional. Gosse himself admired it greatly when it was sent to him and managed to get it into *The Times* for 15 January 1916. Sassoon had insisted that only his initials be given, but Lady Ottoline Morrell, a colourful patron of the arts to whom its high-flown sentiments appealed, discovered his identity through Gosse and wrote him a glowing letter. Though the two would not meet for another seven months, it marked the start of an intriguing relationship which ended only with Ottoline's death in 1938. 'To Victory' like 'Glory: 1916', was one of a number of 'happy warrior' poems he wrote in January and early February, as he sheltered safely away from the harsh realities of the Front Line.[38]

Though the 1st Battalion was not due to leave until the end of the month, there were rumours of change of plans, and everyone started preparing themselves mentally for the move. They were also issued with gas-masks, clumsy devices at that stage in the War which emphasized its grotesqueness and seemed to bring the fighting nearer. The Quartermaster, Joe Cottrell, a seasoned campaigner much respected in the Battalion, gloomily forecast that they were bound for the Somme, a prediction which did nothing to raise spirits. In the face of such possibilities, it is understandable that Sassoon took refuge in an almost mystic mood of supreme self-sacrifice. He seems deliberately to have tried to strengthen this state with a visit to Amiens Cathedral towards the end of the month, and a further reading of the mystic poet Henry Vaughan. Quoting lines from Vaughan's 'Song to Amoret', he concludes that he is 'fortunate in having come to the blessed state of mind when earth and light are one; I suppose it is what the mystics call finding Reality. I am part of the earth, which for me is soaked in the glory of sunlight and past seasons.'[39] (His retrospective comment on this state is more down to earth: 'I used to persuade myself that I had "found peace" in this new life.')[40]

At a daily level life was fairly mundane. Training continued even more rigorously, and so did Sassoon's rides. Sometimes, when Thomas accompanied him, he pretended he was out hunting, much to his friend's entertainment, and could forget for a while the realities of his situation. He also rode occasionally with the Battalion's Transport Officer, R. Ormrod, with whom he was billeted, and was sad when Ormrod left for England on 18 January. In his absence Sassoon was the natural choice for Transport Officer, a relatively safe job which, in his elevated mood of self-sacrifice, he did not want. It seemed ironic to him that, while he yearned almost masochistically for danger and hardship, he should have been given such a post.

Sassoon's friends rejoiced for him and, since there was no choice, he made the best of it. It was certainly more fun than being a company officer and brought him into even closer contact with horses. Always an individualist, in spite of his conformist exterior, he enjoyed the freedom and took on the responsibility with a confidence impossible to imagine at the beginning of the War when he had shied away from a commission. In the days before motorized vehicles had become the norm, 'Transport' involved a surprisingly large number of animals and men, for all of whom he was technically responsible (though he suspected that Joe Cottrell and the Transport Sergeant could have managed perfectly well without him). There were drivers, officers' grooms, brakesmen and the men who looked after the nine pack animals. On the next rung up were the transport sergeant, his corporal and a farrier-corporal, as well as a shoeing-smith, saddler, carpenter and cook. The vehicles themselves included a General Service wagon, a mess-wagon for carrying officers' kits, some company cookers, a watercart, a 'Maltese' cart for the Quartermaster's special use and, not least importantly, limbers which carried machine-guns and ammunition. All these had to be mobilized for frequent journeys and were vital to the Battalion's well-being.

Sassoon took his responsibilities very seriously and filled a whole army notebook with details of his job. His 'Army Notebook 152' also contained the draft of a poem which suggests that he had some free time and was still in 'happy warrior' mood:

> The silver moment showed him lashed with rain
> Unhappy in his labour: one whose voice
> Must swell the dying roar of legions slain
> That in the end, bright victory may rejoice.[41]

One of the greatest advantages of Sassoon's new job seemed to him his closer contact with the Battalion Quartermaster. He had met Cottrell shortly after joining C Company at Béthune and looked forward to working with him. He knew he would be sharing quarters with Joe, as everyone called him, once they returned to the Front. Between the small, balding, middle-aged, disillusioned, working-class man from Lancashire and the tall, young, idealistic ex-public schoolboy from the Home Counties there developed an unexpected friendship which was to survive the War. Sassoon himself tried to explain what attracted him to Cottrell in a Kiplingesque poem more interesting for its content than its technique:

> *The Quarter-Master*
> Bad stations and good liquor and long service
> Have aged his looks beyond their forty-five;
> For eight and twenty years he's been a soldier;
> And nineteen months of war have made him thrive.
> He's got a face to match his breast of medals,
> All stained and veined with purple and deep red.
> His heart is somewhat bigger than his body,
> And there's a holy anger in his head ....[42]

Sassoon also wrote about Cottrell (as Dottrill) in *Fox-Hunting Man*. Though he was to be transferred from the 1st Battalion before the end of 1916, he would remain in close touch with Joe, who was to write him long letters detailing the progress of mutual friends, or grimly reporting their deaths. Whenever Sassoon was in England he would send Joe presents of kippers, or cakes, and if he thought there was a danger of being killed or wounded he gave his friends Joe's name to write to for information. Cottrell, who was not easily impressed, came to regard Sassoon as one of the bravest soldiers he had ever known. (Joe himself had a D.S.O., rarely awarded to an officer of his rank.)

Thus it was, on the whole, a pleasure being Joe's right-hand man in Transport. Even when the time came to organize the Battalion's return to the Front, Sassoon managed his part of things without undue panic. An arduous three days' march via Vaux and Pont Noyelles brought the Battalion to Morlancourt, a village approximately fifteen miles northeast of Amiens and five miles south of Albert. Occupying a strip of undulating land between the Somme and Ancre rivers, Morlancourt had not yet suffered shellfire, and would not do so for another two years. Centred on the meeting of five roads round a little farm and pond, with a church at each end, it still retained its rural atmosphere and was to provide a strong contrast to the trenches in the coming months. Sassoon had comfortable canvas billets near the transport lines and enjoyed waking up to the sound of birds every morning. The majority of the men had no time to enjoy the relative calm of Morlancourt, however, for the day after they arrived they had to leave for the Front Line trenches five miles away, near enemy-occupied Fricourt, where they were due to relieve the 12th Middlesex.

Trench systems varied considerably in different parts of the line. At the beginning of the War, troops on the Western Front had simply dug ditches in which to shelter from enemy fire, but by February 1916 trenches were far more sophisticated. Much wider and deeper passageways were constructed, usually in several roughly parallel lines, so that if a section of the Front Line were taken, reinforcements could be moved up from the rear via communication trenches. Each line was zig-zagged irregularly to prevent the enemy from firing along it, as well as to reduce the impact of bombs, and small 'dug-outs' were excavated in the back of the trenches to provide room for shelter, sleep and even cooking. Sandbags added further protection against enemy fire, as well as support for the sides of the trenches.

Since mud was one of the most unpleasant features of the Western Front, good trenches were paved with 'duck-boards' to walk on and avoid slipping. In front of the first line tangled masses of barbed wire were laid to prevent enemy penetration and narrow passages, or 'saps', ran out to observation posts in the neutral area between the two forces. Known as No Man's Land, this was usually pitted with deep craters left by exploding shells from both sides. Since German and Allied trench systems stretched from the Alps at one end to the English Channel at the other, a distance of approximately 475 miles, outflanking was impossible. In an attack, therefore, the 'poor bloody' Infantry had to 'go over the top', in other words climb out of their own trenches – generally at dawn – cross No Man's Land and rush the enemy, officers with revolvers, men with .303 Enfield rifles with bayonets fixed. As they followed so-called 'safe' routes up to the enemy trenches, they would throw hand-grenades into them, another hazard of trench warfare. Their attack was generally preceded by heavy artillery bombardments which would theoretically kill some of the enemy and destroy their barbed wire, but in practice the far from accurate howitzers often missed, leaving enemy and wire intact and destroying both the surprise element and No

Man's Land itself, which was frequently churned up into a sea of mud. As the heavily-laden troops floundered towards the enemy line, they were more often than not mown down by a murderous hail of bullets. Sometimes they were held up by their own gas attack, which drifted back in their faces as the wind changed. Of all these hazards, mud seems to have featured most largely in the soldiers' lives, closely followed by noise and smell.

The trenches occupied by the Royal Welch Fusiliers in the Bois Français sector near Fricourt were particularly bad. As their Commanding Officer observed on his first tour of them, they were situated on a bare rolling down of chalk. About 500 yards of the Front consisted of a continuous row of craters. In places the Germans were less than sixty yards away and had established bombing posts within forty yards of the British Front Line. But at least the chalky soil made for relatively dry and well-drained trenches at a time when the French winter could be calculated to turn most trenches into mud baths. Even so, the mud was 'beyond belief', according to Sassoon,[43] and the sludge was ankle-deep beneath the duck-boards. 'Trench-foot', brought about by continually wet and cold feet, was one of the many undramatic curses of First World War France. Another was lice, a third rats and a fourth, more seriously, pneumonia. Sassoon had a constant sore throat, but tried to impress on his men the importance of looking after their feet.

In contrast to the British trench system, the Germans' was a model of efficiency. Since their High Command tried to keep its units in the same place in the line, there was usually a competitive spirit between companies, battalions and regiments in constructing and improving trenches. Each separate trench system was strongly wired in and contained deep dug-outs at regular intervals. The great strength of their Fricourt sector was the linking up of the first and second line systems by a series of fortified positions: each wood and village had been prepared for defence, every advantageous piece of ground had been entrenched, often provided with dug-outs and wired. It was virtually impregnable, except perhaps against massed artillery, prepared for by lengthy bombardments.

Though Sassoon felt himself to be only an onlooker as Transport Officer, he became very familiar with the trenches at Fricourt. During the Battalion's six-day stint there he would ride up regularly every afternoon with the food and water-wagons. After spending a morning attending to the horses, while the cooks prepared dixies of stew and tea, he would accompany Joe and the rations up to the line. They had to take a more devious route than the soldiers, which increased the five miles to seven. The whole journey took never less than seven hours and was extremely hazardous, but Sassoon cared very little for danger, even seemed to relish it, as he had on the hunting-field. He regularly visited C Company in the Front Line and listened avidly to their reports of trench-mortar attacks and machine-gun fire. Though he was glad to get back to Joe's comfortable billets, which were shared by the French interpreter, Monsieur Perrineau, he longed to be with his Company. Physically fearless and hardened as he was, the trenches held very little terror for him. In his semi-mystical, heroic mood, half-longing for death to resolve his inner conflicts, trench warfare seemed to offer the possibility of both sacrifice and resolution.

Unable to alleviate his men's sufferings in any practical way, apart from bringing food, Sassoon expressed his sympathy in what he called his first 'outspoken' war poem, 'In the Pink'. This was composed on 10 February, during the Battalion's rest from its first tour of the trenches, when his own duties were accordingly lighter. He was almost certainly inspired by the sight of the Machine-Gun Officer shivering in his blankets on the floor from a combination of alcoholic poisoning and cold feet, though he denied this. Nevertheless, he noted the circumstances and conceded that his verses refer to 'some typical Welshman who probably got killed on the Somme in July, after months and months of a dog's life and no leave'.[44] He could not have been surprised when the *Westminster Gazette* refused it for publication on the grounds that it might prejudice recruiting. The poem's harsh criticism of fighting conditions distinguishes it sharply from any of his previous war verses, except 'The Redeemer', and it anticipates in both content and technique the works which were to make him famous:

> *In the Pink*
> So Davies wrote: 'This leaves me in the pink.'
> Then scrawled his name: 'Your loving sweetheart Willie.'
> With crosses for a hug. He'd had a drink
> Of rum and tea; and, though the barn was chilly,
> For once his blood ran warm; he had pay to spend.
> Winter was passing; soon the year would mend.
>
> But he couldn't sleep that night; stiff in the dark
> He groaned and thought of Sundays at the farm,
> And how he'd go as cheerful as a lark
> In his best suit, to wander arm in arm
> With brown-eyed Gwen, and whisper in her ear
> The simple, silly things she liked to hear.
>
> And then he thought: tomorrow night we trudge
> Up to the trenches, and my boots are rotten.
> Five miles of stodgy clay and freezing sludge,
> And everything but wretchedness forgotten.
> Tonight he's in the pink; but soon he'll die.
> And still the war goes on – *he* don't know why.   (*CP*, p. 22)

Here already is the foundation of a formula for Sassoon's bitter war-satires. The verse form is simple, with no pyrotechnics to distract from the content, and the six-line stanza ends with a rhyming couplet to drive home the ironic point. The language is also simple and largely colloquial, partly to help create the soldier's working-class background, but also to express more bluntly the nastiness of war. The phrase 'in the pink', used three times in all, ironically underlines the fact that the soldier is not 'in the pink of health' and, even if he were, it would be short-lived. His boots are frankly 'rotten', rather than politely 'inadequate'. And as the narrator concludes in a phrase which does not quite avoid the charge of sounding condescending, he echoes the uneducated soldier's thoughts, while at the same time emphasizing his bewilderment – '*he* don't know why'. The few rhetorical flourishes are kept deliberately simple: the man imagines himself as nothing more sophisticated than 'cheerful as a lark'.

'In the Pink' shows even more clearly than 'The Redeemer' Sassoon's need to escape the subjective lyric approach, largely inadequate in the face of the horrors of the Western Front, to a more objective, dramatic one. In doing so, he is forced to find a different vocabulary, which gives the poem a freshness lacking in most of his earlier work. As in so many later poems, a little scene is set and a brief character sketch presented by an apparently detached narrator, who nevertheless makes his irony felt by the end. Sassoon described his method as 'composing two or three harsh, peremptory, and colloquial stanzas with a knock-out blow in the last line'.[45]

Sassoon's lyric impulse was never far away, however, as the titles of his next few poems – 'Love', 'The Rainbow' and 'Pastoral' – suggest. A fourth poem, 'The Dragon and the Undying', dated February 1916, may not even have been written in France and the true horror of the trenches, therefore, not as fresh in his mind as when he wrote 'In the Pink'. For he was given ten days' leave unexpectedly on 23 February and spent the end of the month and the beginning of March in England.

*

It took Sassoon twenty-four hours to reach London, where he spent the night with his Uncle Hamo and Aunt Fanny at the family house they shared in Melbury Road. He cannot altogether have relished the idea of seeing his mother, who was still very bitter and unhappy about Hamo's death, but he dutifully spent the next few days at Weirleigh with her. His subsequent stay in London was probably more enjoyable, since he passed it visiting friends and attending at least one concert. He had kept up a regular correspondence with Gosse, Marsh and Dent, all of whom he saw during his leave. Gosse celebrated his return by inviting Max Beerbohm and his wife, as well as Robbie Ross, to meet him at a dinner given in his honour at Hanover Terrace on 2 March.

There seems to have been some competition between Sassoon's four mentors, Gosse, Ross, Marsh and Dent, to entertain him, particularly between the two latter, both clearly anxious to influence his poetic development. The greatest influence on his poetry at this time, however, came from neither, but from the more recently made acquaintance, Ross, with whom he stayed at 40 Half Moon Street, just off Piccadilly.

Sassoon quickly realized that Ross was far more hostile to the war than Gosse or Marsh, who had both shown that they preferred what he called 'idealized soldier-poems'.[46] It was during this stay with Ross that his own views, which had already begun to change, responded to the older man's influence. His own attitude to what Ross called 'screaming scarlet Majors', a phrase Sassoon would make memorable, was to harden. It was Ross, rather than Gosse, Marsh or Dent, whom he entrusted with a manuscript book of his recent poems.[47]

From this time Ross's rooms became Sassoon's centre when he was on leave in London. Not only did they delight his eye with their subdued half-Italian, half-Oriental tones and exquisite pictures and furniture, but they also allowed him access to an aesthetic world to which he too aspired. While partly listening to one of Ross's erudite conversations with his Burlington Fine Arts Club cronies, or his old friend More Adey, he could browse through his eclectic collection of poetry and *belles lettres*, savouring the matured artistic judgement which informed it all.

One of the choicest pieces in Ross's collection, according to many friends, was his housekeeper and she, too, Sassoon learnt to appreciate on this visit. The former lady's maid of Robbie's mother, Nellie Burton had taken to letting rooms to 'single gentlemen' after her employer's death. She had naturally offered her protection to Robbie when he needed it in 1914. Known variously as 'Nellie', 'Dame Nellie' or simply (and 'chicly' according to Anthony Powell)[48] as 'Burton', she was an unforgettable character.

Part of this was Nellie's remarkable appearance. Small and stout, with an alarming number of double chins accentuated by what Sassoon's American playwright friend, Sam Behrman, was to call her 'minaret' hairstyle, she was not afraid to draw attention to herself with innumerable pieces of jewellery in both hair and clothes.[49] Her prominent blue eyes and benevolent smile added charm to the effect. It was an effect which stimulated the imagination of more than just Behrman and gave rise to a number of pungent comparisons. Robbie's close friend, Squire Sprigge, coming upon Nellie in a mauve dressing-gown, cigarette in hand, supervising the gilding of Robbie's rooms (he was her favourite tenant), compared her lovingly to 'a bad character from a Hogarth print'.[50] Though Nellie and her rooms were eminently respectable, her colourful appearance made Anthony Powell feel that there was something 'a shade *louche*' in the background.

Yet Nellie was also a motherly figure to the gentlemen she petted and pampered. Respectful, chatty and infinitely understanding – though she could be outspoken at times – she created a home for a number of lonely men. Sassoon himself would become one of her tenants and a great favourite. So, too, would Osbert Sitwell and the composer Lord Berners; Wilfred Owen, recommended by Sassoon, would stay in her rooms on his last leave in London. Dame Nellie became a legend in her own life-time and when she died the *Manchester Guardian* was to celebrate her vivid personality in an article entitled simply 'Miss Burton of Half Moon Street'.[51]

Sassoon, who described Nellie all-embracingly as 'Shakespearean', quickly fell under her spell.[52] Anything that distracted him from the War was welcome. Similarly, when, contrary to his fears, the snow melted and allowed the possibility of hunting, he seized it. One of the things he had most missed in France, he gladly sacrificed the last few days of his leave to hunt with an old friend who was valiantly keeping the Southdown going.[53] He spent three days at Middleham, Ringmer, near Lewes, and took back with him to France memories of 'woods and fields in Sussex, in clear sunlight of early March, and the scarlet-coated huntsman galloping his jaunty little grey nag, cheering his hounds to a find or casting them across the wet ploughs'.[54]

*

Sassoon was back in France on 6 March. His new Commanding Officer, Colonel Stockwell, had arrived to replace Minshull Ford the day before Sassoon's departure for England, so this was his first real opportunity to assess him. It quickly became apparent that Stockwell was a strict disciplinarian and demanded extremely high standards from his men, earning him the nickname 'Buffalo Bill'.[55] Cottrell, who had known him since he had been a subaltern, more affectionately called him 'Stocky', and Sassoon gave him the pseudonym 'Kinjack' in his fiction, perhaps to suggest keenness and fierceness. Though critical of Stockwell's harshness – he would threaten to shoot any man who did not obey to the letter – Sassoon immediately acknowledged his merits: 'He is aggressive efficiency, very blatant, but knows the job' he wrote in his diary the day Stockwell arrived.[56] Stockwell himself recognized Sassoon's potential, though he was wary of his rashness, and thought him wasted as a Transport Officer. Only two weeks after the latter's return from leave he was to transfer him back to the line.

Meantime Sassoon carried on with his job in Transport. The wintry weather which had greeted him on his return to France gave way within a week to spring. Sitting in the sunshine reading Shelley in small doses from Robert Bridges's anthology, *The Spirit of Man*, he felt hope revive in him. In spite of the ceaseless gunfire and the exhausting daily journey to the trenches he was happy. David Thomas had welcomed him back warmly and he had written a second poem attempting to capture his friend's youthful appeal. The first had opened 'I find a clear blue morning in your looks'.[57] The second paints an equally romantic picture of charming youth:

> *A Subaltern*
> He turned to me with his kind, sleepy gaze
> And fresh face slowly brightening to the grin
> That sets my memory back to summer days,
> With twenty runs to make, and last man in ....[58]

'A Subaltern' was written about 8 March, three days after Sassoon had returned from leave. Ten days later Thomas was dead. Sassoon had unwittingly written his epitaph. In his attempt to explain the circumstances of this painful loss in *Fox-Hunting Man*, Sassoon appears to blame Stockwell to some extent. With his 'new broom' energy and exacting standards, the Colonel had insisted that the Battalion attempt to bring its sector of the English Front Line up to German standards and ordered the whole of their Front Line to be re-wired. This meant extra work for the already exhausted men, who had to go out nightly on wiring-parties in addition to their other duties. On the evening of 18 March Thomas had taken his turn, been wounded in the throat by a stray bullet and died a few hours later. Robert Graves, who was back with 'A' Company after eight weeks at Base Camp, was in the trenches that night, busily sandbagging a section of the Front Line. When news of Thomas's wound first reached him, it was reassuring, since Thomas was reported able to walk to the dressing-station. The Battalion doctor, Kelsey Fry, a throat specialist in civilian life, assured Thomas that he would be all right, as long as he lay still for a while. In defiance of his orders Thomas raised his head to take a letter from his pocket for his girl-friend and died instantly. To Sassoon and Graves, both deeply suspicious of women at the time, this must have seemed the final irony.

It was not the only irony in the case. Sassoon, whose strongest motive for wanting to be in the trenches had been to protect his 'little Tommy',[59] was due to return there only two days after his death. Did he ask himself whether he might not have averted that death if he had been present? The recent advent of spring, with its invigorating promise of renewed life, must also have seemed to him a mockery. And, though 'The Subaltern' had suggested that Thomas needed him more than his girlfriend did, at least in France, in reality it was she who had prevailed. It was his concern for her which, according to Graves, had killed him.

Without exaggeration, Sassoon found the loss almost unbearable. While his brother Hamo had died in a faraway place during Sassoon's mood of greatest heroic idealism, he had seen Thomas only the day before his death. Notebook in hand, he had been reading Sassoon's last poem, presumably the one written about himself. As Sassoon watched the sack containing his friend's body being lowered into the ground, he felt that he 'knew Death' for the first time.[60] His initial reaction was extreme grief, which he vented in a little wood alone. His second was a longing for 'the bodily presence that was so fair'.[61] His third, which was to prove transitory, was acceptance in a mood of exalted self-sacrifice.[62] It was in this mood that he wrote a quatrain to his departed love two days after his death, lines which emphasize how much he missed Thomas's actual physical presence:

> For you were glad, and kind, and brave;
> With hands that clasped me, young and warm;
> But I have seen a soldier's grave,
> And I have seen your shrouded form.[63]

Just over a fortnight later Sassoon was again attempting to express his horror and grief in 'Memory'. Like his first effort, 'Love', this poem was never published. Its last stanza returns obsessively to Thomas's spilled blood, an image suggesting Christlike sacrifice, and gives the first hint that such memories would eventually create in Sassoon a desire for revenge:

> I thought of him, and knew that he was dead;
> I thought of his dark hour, and laughter killed,
> And the shroud hiding his dear, happy head –
> And blood that heedless enemies have spilled –
> *His* blood: I thought of rivers flowing red,
> And crimson hands that laid him in his bed.[64]

With a swing back to a more resigned mood Sassoon then wrote 'The Last Meeting', a semi-mystical poem in which he attempts to accept death as a transformation rather than an end. Based on his efforts to recall Thomas's presence a month after his death, it describes Sassoon's journey to a deserted wood in search of his friend. Failing to find him in an empty, half-built house there, he turns back to Nature, where the spirit of Thomas becomes 'the magic of the world,/ And dawn and sunset flame with [his] spilt blood' (*CP*, p. 38). The poem continues in this mystical vein for another thirty-nine lines, when the narrator, won at last to acceptance of irrevocable loss, concludes:

> And, as it was in life, his name shall be
> Wonder awaking in a summer dawn,
> And youth that, dying, touched my lips to song.   (*CP*, p. 40)

It is interesting to note that, in an earlier, franker version of the poem which was subsequently censored, possibly by the more worldly Ross or Marsh, Sassoon referred to Thomas 'wait[ing] to feel my fingers touch his face' and, even more specifically, finished his poem with a direct reference to their stay together in the same Cambridge room with the name of the previous owner, Paradise, on the door – 'And lips that touched me once in Paradise'. This emphasis on the physical was completely omitted in the final version.[65] Whichever way the last line reads, Thomas had indeed touched Sassoon's lips to song, but neither here nor in the last poem he wrote about him, 'A Letter Home', does that song rise above the tired, inherited language of his Romantic and Nineties models.[66] Fortunately for poetry it was not a mood which would last. The reaction, when it came, was violent and stimulated Sassoon to write some of his best poems of the War.

10

'At the Edge of the World'

March-July 1916

During the four months which followed David Thomas's death in March 1916, Sassoon's mood fluctuated wildly. His initial despair and resignation was followed closely by an anger which increased his recklessness and made many people, himself included, wonder if he was trying to get himself killed.[1] As the reality of his brother Hamo's loss grew on him and first-hand experience of the trenches brought home the random destructiveness of war, his hatred of the Germans was re-directed towards those in authority on his own side, the politicians, army staff and 'yellow-press' journalists he began to hold responsible for the continuation of the war. At the same time, and alternating curiously with such bitterness, he still had moods of almost mystical exaltation in which he longed to sacrifice himself for his country. Paradoxically, but not surprisingly, the more he wanted to die, the sweeter life seemed to him and this produced other, more familiar moods of joy in nature.

The backdrop to the period is the Battle of the Somme, with its long build-up as the Allies prepare to mount their most massive attack so far, and the opening of the battle itself. Always in the picture, though never at the centre as he would have wished, Sassoon witnesses unforgettable scenes of carnage as the 1st Royal Welch joins in the long drawn out battle of Mametz Wood.

In March 1916, however, all that lay in the future and the Allies were still at the preparatory stage. For Sassoon the month was marked not only by the death of David Thomas, but also by his first full experience of the trenches. Officially transferred back from Transport to his platoon on 20 March, it was not until 26 March that he set out on his first tour of them. He spent his first night there engaged in nothing more dramatic than helping pile sandbags on the crumbling parapet, but the place reminded him forcibly of Thomas, fatally wounded in those same trenches only eight nights earlier. By an odd coincidence he was also reminded of Hamo's death on his second day there, when a friend of his brother from Cambridge, a Royal Engineer officer named Sisson, came into his gloomy steel dug-out to talk to him about Hamo. It was as if this vivid reminder of Hamo so soon after the loss of Thomas finally brought home to him the reality of his brother's death and, with it, a belated desire for revenge: 'I used to say I couldn't kill anyone in this war' he wrote in his diary, 'but since they shot Tommy I would gladly stick a bayonet into a German by daylight. Someone told me a year ago that love, sorrow and hate were things I had never known (things which every poet *should* know!). Now I've known love for Bobbie and Tommy, and grief for Hamo and Tommy, and hate has come also, and the lust to kill.'[2] He can hardly wait to get out to the Front Line again. Not content to sit tamely in the trench hoping to avoid death, he prefers the excitement and challenge of night raids in No Man's Land. Stockwell has made it clear that he wants a prisoner, but Sassoon knows very well that this is not the reason he goes looking for Germans, bludgeon in hand:

I want to smash someone's skull; I want to have a scrap and get out of the war for a bit or for ever. Sitting in a trench waiting for a rifle grenade isn't fighting: war is clambering out of the top trench at 3 o'clock in the morning with a lot of rum-drugged soldiers who don't know where they're going – half of them to be blasted with machine-guns at point-blank range – trying to get over the wire which our artillery have failed to destroy. I can't get my own back for Hamo and Tommy that way. While I am really angry with the enemy, as I am lately, I must work it off, as these things don't last long with me as a rule. If I get shot it will be rotten for some people at home, but I am bound to get it in the neck sometime, so why not make a creditable show, and let people see that poets can fight as well as anybody else? And death is the best adventure of all ....[3]

Out of such mixed motives of revenge, boredom, recklessness, pride in his calling and what Virginia Woolf has described as the need for 'the danger emotion',[4] emerged 'Mad Jack', a nickname given him by his companions for his fearlessness in the Front Line. Sassoon confessed to Dent that he 'thoroughly enjoyed' his first tour of the trenches, particularly when he bombed a German working party out of a freshly-made mine crater.[5] His modest claim, that he 'got rather famous for a day or two', probably conceals the origin of the 'Mad Jack' legend. He certainly relished the need to take risks. Since he was quite sure that he would be killed, he made no effort to protect himself and went out on raiding parties whenever possible, a military equivalent of Russian roulette.

Crawling up to the German trenches, revolver in one hand, knob-kerrie in the other and three hand-grenades in each pocket, was an exhilarating experience. It reminded him of the start of a steeplechase and he was just as determined to win as when he raced. Added to that was his fascination with the nightmare landscape of No Man's Land, which he visited nightly with a fellow daredevil, Corporal O'Brien, a man for whom he was later to risk his life.[6] Together they would lie flat as the snipers shot at them, watching the white rocket-lights going up and laughing with sheer delight when the danger was over. Another companion on these raids was Private Morgan.

While Sassoon took his own courage for granted, he admired O'Brien and Morgan for theirs. And they were not alone in this. For one of the many results of this first tour of trenches was the increased admiration it brought for his platoon. In elevated but heartfelt cadences he exclaims: 'Their temper is proven, the fibre of their worth is tested and revealed; these men from Welsh farms and Midland cities, from factory and shop and mine, who can ever give them their meed of praise for the patience and tender jollity which seldom forsake them?'[7]

Under the influence of such extreme feelings, Sassoon's prose takes wing. His descriptions of the trenches at this time, at once concrete and poetic, are among his finest writings. Sights, sounds and emotions are all vividly evoked:

> As I sit in the sun in a nook among the sandbags and chalky debris, with shells flying overhead in the blue air, a lark sings high up, and a little weasel comes and runs past me within a foot of my outstretched feet, looking at me with tiny bright eyes. Bullets sing and whistle and hum; so do bits of shell; rifles crack; some small guns and trench-mortars pop and thud; big shells burst with a massive explosion, and the voluminous echoes roll along the valleys, to fade nobly and without haste or consternation.
>
> Bullets are deft and flick your life out with a quick smack. Shells rend and bury, and vibrate and scatter, hurling fragments and lumps and jagged splinters at you; they lift you off your legs and leave you huddled and bleeding and torn and scorched with a blast straight from the pit. Heaven is furious with the smoke and flare and portent of shells, but bullets are a swarm of whizzing hornets, mad, winged and relentless, undeviating in their malicious onset.
>
> The big guns roar their challenge and defiance; but the machine-guns rattle with intermittent bursts of mirthless laughter.
>
> There are still pools in the craters; they reflect the stars like any lovely water, but nothing grows near them; snags of iron jut from their banks, tin cans and coils of wire, and other trench-refuse. If you search carefully, you may find a skull, eyeless, grotesquely matted with what was once hair; eyes once looked from those detestable holes, they made the fabric of a passionate life, they appealed for justice, they were lit with triumph, and beautiful with pity.[8]

Living as he was at the highest pitch of emotion, Sassoon believed that he was at last learning to observe things with more receptiveness and accuracy than he had in his undisciplined past. His poetry bears this out. With first-hand experience of the Front Line, it gains in immediacy and, more gradually, in technical skill. 'The Redeemer', started four months earlier, is now revised. Writing to Eddie Marsh on 16 March 1916 he encloses the amended version but adds that he wants to change the last two lines to provide a more shocking and less ambiguous conclusion. He also writes three new poems, of which 'Golgotha' is almost certainly the first:

> Through darkness curves a spume of falling flares
> That flood the field with shallow, blanching light.
>   The huddled sentry stares
>   On gloom at war with white,
>   And white receding slow, submerged in gloom.
>   Guns into mimic thunder burst and boom,

And mirthless laughter rakes the whistling night.
The sentry keeps his watch where no one stirs
But the brown rats, the nimble scavengers.   (*CP*, pp. 14-15)

On the surface a straightforward description of one sentry's impression of the trenches, 'Golgotha' manages to convey a sense of menace and nightmare, of 'gloom at war with white' in which the white, symbolic of goodness and hope, though at the same time a literal reference to the bleached sandbags, is 'submerged in gloom'. The very title 'Golgotha', with its reference to the extreme agony of the Crucifixion, means 'skull' in Aramaic, echoing the diary entry for 30 March: 'If you search carefully you may find a skull.'[9] Ending as it does with scavenging rats, there is no reprieve from the relentless horror of the scene. Even the verse form is disturbing, shifting uneasily from a five-beat to a three-beat line and back again, to reflect the instability of the situation. The final feminine ending takes away any sense of certainty or closure and is in direct contrast with the insistent alliteration of 'falling flares/ That flood the field' or the guns that 'burst and boom'. The diction, while simple, is carefully chosen and the personification of the machine guns' 'mirthless laughter', with the added metaphor of raking the night, sinister and highly effective.

Where 'Golgotha' is concentrated, 'A Working Party', also written during Sassoon's first tour of the trenches, is discursive. And 'Golgotha's' tight rhyme-scheme is replaced by less demanding blank verse. A curious piece, which seems to fall naturally into two halves, 'A Working Party' would almost certainly have been improved by such a division. As it is, the last four stanzas, which start with a near repetition of the first line, read almost as a self-contained poem. They continue Sassoon's practice of 'In the Pink' by giving a deft thumbnail sketch of 'a young man with a meagre wife/ And two small children in a Midland town'. While remaining impersonal – no names are given – it creates a poignant picture of all the young men with their undernourished wives and children ('pale' rather than 'small' in the original), who have died and will die senselessly and needlessly in the War, simply doing their duty. The man's thoughts are sketched in by details of trench life made convincing by Sassoon's current experience there:

He thought how slow time went, stamping his feet
And blowing on his fingers, pinched with cold.
He thought of getting home by half-past-twelve,
And tot of rum to send him warm to sleep
In draughty dug-out frowsty[10] with the fumes
Of coke, and full of snoring weary men.   (*CP*, p. 20)

The end, though sudden, is prepared for in the fourth stanza ('Now he will never walk that road again'):

He pushed another bag along the top,
Craning his body outward; then a flare
Gave one white glimpse of No Man's Land and wire;
And as he dropped his head the instant split
His startled life with lead, and all went out.

The transferred epithet 'startled' and the staccato alliteration of 't's mimicking the gun which is responsible are particularly effective in the last two lines of this extract. In fact the moment Sassoon moves from the detailed narrative description of the man stumbling up the trench to the mini-drama of his death, the poem comes to life, though the first three stanzas are nevertheless important as one of the earliest examples of realistic description of trench conditions. The whole piece was rigorously revised in its final version, the most significant change being the omission of a last stanza which in the original version diffused the tension with its prolix and redundant 'message'.[11]

Sassoon wrote 'The Working Party', and probably 'Golgotha' too, without benefit of Graves's advice, since his friend had left for England just before the tour started. Once there Graves stayed on for an operation to reset his broken nose, which made breathing difficult and the wearing of the primitive gas-masks of that era impossible. He was not, therefore, to share Sassoon's next two tours of the trenches which took place in April. 'I am missing Robert very much,' Sassoon wrote to their mutual friend Marsh on 19 April: 'there is no-one else to fill the gap.'[12] (His old friend Gordon Harbord had written to him from a few miles north of the 1st Royal Welch Fusiliers' sector, hoping that they could meet, but this had proved impossible.)[13]

While Graves made full use of his rest, Sassoon continued to go in and out of the Front Line. By 23 April, Easter Sunday, he had done eighteen days' trench duty altogether and was feeling the strain. He became increasingly sure he would be killed, and for once Nature seemed unable to cheer him up. Though the sun shone frequently, since the death of Thomas most days appeared to him dark and unhappy. Even writing poetry became an enormous effort and of the few short pieces he produced only one seemed worthy of publication, 'Stand-To: Good Friday Morning'.[14] Written, in fact, the day after Good Friday, this poem successfully conveys his frustration and depression in a colloquial style which contrasts sharply with his lyrics of the period:

I'd been on duty from two till four.
I went and stood at the dug-out door.
Down in the frowst I heard them snore.
'Stand-to!' Somebody grunted and swore.
Dawn was misty; the skies were still;
Larks were singing, discordant, shrill;
They seemed happy; but *I* felt ill.
Deep in water I splashed my way

Up the trench to our bogged front line.
Rain had fallen the whole damned night.
O Jesus, send me a wound today,
And I'll believe in Your bread and wine,
And get my bloody old sins washed white!   (*CP*, p. 24)

Sassoon uses his own experience directly here: he had indeed been 'on duty from 2 till 4' on Good Friday, 21 April, and had gone to rouse his platoon for 'stand-to', the early morning ritual of standing with weapons in readiness for action. (There was another 'stand-to' at dusk.) Out of this routine event he versified, as he himself noted, 'a jaunty scrap of doggerel' which anticipated his later successes in condensed satire.[15] What surprised him, as much as it shocked many of his readers, was his talent for satirical epigram. Nothing in his previous work had led him to predict such a turn and he could think of no precedents for it, though he was able to trace the influence of Hardy's *Satires of Circumstance* in some of his longer war poems.

The laconic tone of the piece, however, is all Sassoon's own and deliberately introduced in conjunction with the sacredness of the day, Good Friday, and the event it marks, the Crucifixion, in order to shock by its irreverence. It is produced partly through the abrupt, matter of fact statements, contained in all but one case in short, end-stopped lines, and partly through the echoes of soldiers' blasphemous language. In view of the day, the reader is led to reflect on the ironic comparison and contrast between Christ hanging on the cross to save mankind through his literally 'bloody' wounds and the soldier-narrator demanding a wound, or 'Blighty one', before he will believe in Christ and his message. As Michael Thorpe points out, this is 'calculated to affront one of the most dearly cherished convictions at home – that the War was a contest sanctioned by Heaven and that the British were God's favourite team'.[16] The blasphemy is a deliberate attempt to shock the reader into making the connection between the apparently pointless blood and wounds of the Front Line and the claims made for Christ's sufferings. And by extension, the soldier who suffers such wounds is equated with Christ as in 'The Redeemer', though it is an ironic comparison.

In a truncated sonnet which mirrors the abruptness of the language the poet sets the scene, drawing a contrast between the apparently happy larks and the narrator, as well as between the joyful, though to the narrator discordant, birdsong and the snoring, grunts and curses of the exhausted men, then leads the reader in the last six lines to the narrator's defiant and outrageous plea. Part of the poem's effect depends on the deliberate ordinariness of the diction, which avoids 'poetic' or archaic words. When an unusual word is introduced, such as 'frowst' in line 3, it is in order realistically to convey the sordidness of the trenches.

*

The day after 'Stand-to' was written, Sassoon was on a bus speeding away from the war-zone. He had been one of two officers chosen from his battalion to join subalterns from other units for a month's course at the Fourth Army School. 'Lucky Kangaroo – to be hopping away for a holiday!' he reports his company commander as saying.[17] Situated at Flixécourt, halfway between Amiens and Abbeville and thirty miles from the Fricourt trenches, the Fourth Army School was a complete, if temporary, escape from the Front Line:

> Coming away from it all [he wrote in his diary for 23 April 1916] – to find the world outside really acknowledging the arrival of spring – oh it was a blessed thing – the journey on a sunny morning, pleasantly blown by a north-west wind ... the landscape looking its best – all the clean colours of late April – the renewal of green grass and young leaves – and fruit-trees in blossom – and to see a civilian population well away from the danger-zone going to church on Easter morning – soldiers contented and at rest – it was like coming back to life, warm and secure – it was to feel how much there is to regain. Children in the streets of towns and villages – I saw a tiny one fall, to be gathered up and dusted, soothed, comforted – one forgets 'little things' like those up in the places where men are killing one another with the best weapons that skill can handle.[18]

With its jumble of whitewashed houses, glossy chestnut trees and burgeoning apple-blossom, Flixécourt seemed homely and welcoming, as did its inhabitants. Several large châteaux and quaint farms added charm to the picture, which promised at every point rest and renewal. Even his billet, a small clean room with tiled floor and shuttered windows in one of the cottages, appeared part of the conspiracy to help him forget war.

Space to spread out his belongings and a table for his books seemed luxuries after the cramped squalor of the trenches. Sassoon viewed his reading-matter with pleasurable anticipation – Lamb's *Essays*, Surtees's *Mr Sponge's Sporting Tour* and Hardy's *Far From the Madding Crowd* in particular, books that seemed to him quintessentially English. In the unlikely event that books palled, there was the nearby Mess shared by fourteen other officers, all of them pleasant. It reminded Sassoon of starting at Marlborough, only without the new boy's dread of doing the wrong thing and being punished.

There were, of course, duties to be attended to at Flixécourt, but to Sassoon these also seemed agreeable, in spite of their exacting nature. Every day there was practical training in some aspect of warfare, followed at 5.30 by lectures on various subjects. Since the army school instructors were as obsessed with open warfare as Colonel Minshull Ford had been, both the lectures and the practical exercises often appeared irrelevant.

One lecture Sassoon could not dismiss as impracticable affected him deeply. Given by a massive Highland Scot, Major Campbell, who would afterwards be awarded a D.S.O. for his murderous eloquence, it centred simply on a few lines from the *Manual of Bayonet Training*. Impressed by the lively performance of the genial, sandy-haired major and his tall, sinewy assistant, who demonstrated each move of the homicidal drill with machine-like efficiency, Sassoon was nevertheless profoundly disturbed by this public acknowledgement of the soldier's one aim – to kill. Though he had admitted to himself the murderous impulses and intentions induced in him by the deaths of Hamo and Tommy, the major's cold, logical exposition of the killing process seems to have greatly shocked him. The final words of the lecture: 'Kill them! Kill them! There's only one good Boche, and that's a dead one!' rang in his ears as he walked up a nearby hill to a little wood of hazel and beech trees. But the peace of the spring-time scenery failed to eradicate the insistent voice: 'The bayonet and the bullet are brother and sister.' 'If you don't kill him, he'll kill you.' 'Stick him between the eyes, in the throat, in the chest, or round the thighs.' And so on.

In his diary entry written shortly after the event, Sassoon makes it clear that he was repelled by the public gloating in violence he had just witnessed: 'I told the trees what I had been hearing; but they hate steel, because axes and bayonets are the same to them. They are dressed in their fresh green, every branch showing through the mist of leaves, and the straight stems most lovely against the white and orange sky beyond. And a blackbird's song cries aloud that April cannot understand what war means.'[19]

The juxtaposition of nature's beauty and peace with the brutality of the major's message is intentionally significant. A later poem written in January 1919 about his brother's sword, which Theresa had hung on the wall to commemorate her son, suggests that Sassoon shared the same loathing for steel as he attributes to the trees:

> ... The sword is her idea of glory,
> Who, hating cruel things, can feel
> A secret passion for cold steel.
> (Perhaps that's why she voted Tory).
>
> I too am proud of my slain brother.
> But, when I see that murderous blade
> Kept bright for honour, I'm afraid
> That Wilson's Points have failed, – with mother.

To argue, as Robert Graves does, that the poem which emerged from Major Campbell's talk was originally meant to be taken at its face value as a celebration of violence, and only later offered as satire, is to ignore both Sassoon's contemporary and later descriptions of his reaction.[20] The poem is meant to shock the reader into a rejection of the major's murderous message by its apparently enthusiastic embracing of it:

To these I turn, in these I trust –
Brother Lead and Sister Steel.
To his blind power I make appeal,
I guard her beauty clean from rust.

He spins and burns and loves the air,
And splits a skull to win my praise;
But up the nobly marching days
She glitters naked, cold and fair.

Sweet Sister, grant your soldier this:
That in good fury he may feel
The body where he sets his heel
Quail from your downward darting kiss.   (*CP*, pp. 15-16)

Read as satire the poem fits convincingly into Sassoon's development in that genre; taken seriously, as a blood-thirsty celebration of killing, it shows a puzzling inconsistency with both his own reaction and the poems he was writing at the time. As a satire it achieves its aims, but as a straight poem it seems little more than clever doggerel organized around the major's banal 'brother/sister' metaphor. Sassoon himself was quite clear as to his intention in writing the poem and continued to be irritated by its misinterpretation.

Four days after 'The Kiss' was written, 'The Redeemer' was published in its revised form in the *Cambridge Magazine*, with which Dent was closely connected. It was the beginning of an important partnership that would last beyond the end of the War. Supported by a group of Cambridge scholars, most of whom were close friends of Dent, in particular the University Librarian, Theo Bartholomew, and Fellow of King's College, Goldsworthy Lowes Dickinson, this paper was the obvious choice. One of the few anti-war journals of the day, it welcomed poems rejected by its more conservative counterparts, such as the *Westminster Gazette*. Its publication of 'The Redeemer' on 29 April 1916 marked the beginning of Sassoon's public recognition as a poet determined not to glorify war.

By the time 'The Redeemer' appeared, however, Sassoon was no longer in the same mood as the one which had produced it. Once away from the trenches, he found it hard to sustain the feelings of bitterness and anger which came naturally there, perhaps as a defence mechanism. Soothed by the absence of palpable suffering and horror, his impulses turn once more towards lyric poetry, his more habitual means of expression. Something of the early patriotism and heroic idealism creeps back into his poetry in the peaceful, almost idyllic surroundings of Flixécourt. Now it seems to him, in 'France', that:

... they are fortunate, who fight
For gleaming landscapes swept and shafted

And crowned by cloud pavilions white;
Hearing such harmonies as might
Only from Heaven be downward wafted –
Voices of victory and delight.　　(*CP*, pp. 12-13)

While at the Front it had seemed to him irrelevant whether he had his poetry published or not, though he had been enthusiastic when Marsh suggested that Harold Monro should produce a slim volume of thirty-two pages for the Poetry Bookshop. In the midst of such 'distracted times' he had resolved, however, not to have his work produced privately any more. But once settled at Flixécourt with what he calls 'glad things' pouring out of him, he asks Dent to have his poems typed because he plans to produce another of his privately printed books.[21]

Even David Thomas's death can be accepted, almost joyfully, in the little copse 'of hazel twigs/ With misty raiment of awakening green', where Sassoon goes 'to find the face of him that I have lost'.[22] It is a temporary reprieve but one which lasts until the Battle of the Somme, over a month later, brings him sharply back to the reality of war, and to satire. Meantime, he allows himself to dream, knowing it to be a dream, as he admits to Graves, his friend with the 'crooked smile and baffling laughter', in a verse letter written from Flixécourt:

Robert, there's a war in France;
...
Yet, through stunning battle storms,
All the while I watch the spark
Lit to guide me; for I know
Dreams will triumph, though the dark
Scowls above me where I go.
You can hear me; you can mingle
Radiant folly with my jingle.
War's a joke for me and you
While we know such dreams are true!　　(*CP*, pp. 42-3)

Thomas's death, which he knows has affected Graves as deeply as himself, is now referred to in dreamy terms of the fairytales and legends so loved by Graves.

One reason for Sassoon's apparent acceptance of Tommy's death, apart from the soothing influence of springtime Flixécourt, may have been his meeting there with another young officer, Marcus Goodall. Though there is no suggestion that Goodall replaced either Tommy or Bobbie Hanmer in his affections, it is clear that he was attracted to him and made plans to travel with him, as with Graves, after the War. Almost the same age as Graves, Goodall had a stronger initial link with Sassoon: they had both been at Marlborough.[23] He had had a more successful career at the school than Sassoon – becoming a Foundation Scholar, Junior Scholar and Prefect – but had not gone on to

University when he left in July 1913, nine years after Sassoon. He had been
working as a solicitor's pupil when war was declared and, like Sassoon, had
joined up at once. By the time they met he was a Captain in the Yorkshire and
Lancashire Regiment. Sassoon described Goodall both in his diary and, by a
neat pun on his name and nature, as 'Allgood' in *Infantry Officer*. Yet there is
no real indication in either of the depth of his feeling for this quiet, scholarly
youth who loved birds and history. It is only in Sassoon's franker letters to Dent
and in his unpublished poetry that this comes through clearly. Writing to Dent
on 6 May about his 'dear Marlburian', he includes an extract from one of two
sonnets he has already written to his 'Marlborough Marcus':

> ... I looked at you
> And caught your side-long glance, unboding, gay, –
> Your whimsical fleet smile, and queer, pale blue
> Eyes like the blown rifts of a rainy day.

This is undoubtedly a romantic poem and helps to explain Sassoon's extreme
happiness at Flixécourt. It casts a new light on his comment in *Infantry Officer*,
when he describes his memories of Flixécourt as haunting – 'almost as though
I were remembering a time when I'd been in love'.[24] It was almost certainly a
time when he *had* been in love but could not say so, since his love was of the
wrong sex.

As Sassoon prepared to leave Flixécourt on 22 May, he felt that Goodall's was
the only face out of hundreds that he would remember. In spite of the coming
separation, and with no certainty of meeting again in a wartime situation, he
was happy, partly with the happiness new love brings.

*

When Sassoon arrived back at Morlancourt the contrast with Flixécourt could
hardly have been greater. Preparations for the Somme summer offensive were
building up and everywhere there was feverish activity. The Front to be attacked,
from Maricourt to Serre, formed a great salient with Fricourt at the apex, and
preparations in this sector were particularly busy. Between the rivers Somme
and Ancre observation on the enemy Front Line was good, mainly because it
generally lay above the British trenches, but practically nothing could be seen
of its rear systems, the second of which was between 3,000 and 5,000 yards
away on the summit of the high ground in front of the Fourth Army.

Since the coming fight would depend largely on a frontal assault by the
infantry, massed artillery and huge stocks of shells were needed, as well as extra
dugouts for shelter, medical aid and storage. After strengthening their own sector
of the line, as Stockwell had demanded, men of the 1st RWF were involved,
like many others, in the work this entailed. Vast stocks of ammunition and
stores had to be accumulated within a convenient distance of the British Front,
which meant laying many miles of new railway, as well as trench tramways.

All available roads were improved, others created and long causeways built over marshy valleys. Scores of miles of deep communication trenches had to be dug, as well as trenches for telephone wires, assembly and assault trenches and numerous gun emplacements and observation posts. Mining operations were crucial, to ensure that charges were laid at various points beneath the enemy's lines. Even something as apparently simple as water created a huge amount of work, since numerous wells and borings had to be sunk and over a hundred pumping stations installed, in order to supply even the basic needs of the thirteen British and five French Divisions and their horses destined for this area.

In the midst of such frantic preparations, Stockwell had been incensed by a new and absurd demand from Staff Headquarters. Before leaving Morlancourt on 23 April Sassoon heard that Brigade had ordered Stockwell to organize a raid on the enemy Front Line, ostensibly to capture and examine a portion of enemy trench, take prisoners, bomb dugouts and kill some Germans. In reality everyone suspected that it was simply an expensive morale-boosting exercise, inspired by a recent and successful effort by some tough Canadian soldiers. Knowing the dangers and difficulties of the sector and unwilling to risk his men needlessly, Stockwell had not hesitated to give the 'brass-hats' at Brigade Headquarters his candid opinion, but to no avail. When Sassoon arrived back from Flixécourt the raid was imminent.

Once back at the Front, Sassoon had reverted to martial mood and was, therefore, extremely disappointed to hear that Stockwell had appointed Stansfield, not himself, to lead the raid. While he recognized that the burly Canadian had more common sense, he nevertheless rightly believed himself to be the superior man when it came to crawling among shell-holes in No Man's Land. Stansfield frankly admitted that he did not want to risk his life in such a foolhardy enterprise, whereas Sassoon was once more longing for the excitement and risk it would bring, possibly one reason Stockwell had not put him in charge of it.

In addition Sassoon wanted specifically to earn himself an M.C. Just as he had been determined to win steeplechases before the War, he now wanted a medal to prove himself the equal of his contemporaries. He no longer actively wished to die, in fact he seems to have feared death on this occasion; but he was already bored by the monotonous drudgery of most trench activities and longing for adventure.

Still hoping that he might persuade Stockwell to change his mind, Sassoon carried on with his usual duties. On 23 May C Company was sent up to the reserve trench. Hidden by sloping ground behind a steep bank, it seemed to Sassoon rather like a busy suburb, and life there was fairly relaxed in spite of occasional shells. But the road which passed it, once the way to Fricourt, now led only to the British Front Line, a constant reminder of the coming conflict. For three days he waited there, then on the evening of the 25 May prepared to join the raid.

Anticipating disaster, Sassoon writes a farewell letter to his mother, strips off his tunic, dons his leather waistcoat and old raincoat – it is raining hard – and with steel helmet on and nail-studded knob-kerrie in hand goes to find the raiding-party. Twenty-five blackened faces greet him, reminding him grotesquely in their burnt cork make-up of a minstrel band and hiding their nervousness with jokes and a little whiskey. Once at the Colonel's headquarters, 400 yards from the Front Line, Sassoon begs to be allowed to accompany the raiders. Stockwell's emphatic negative brooks no argument, however, and Sassoon finds himself with the less exciting job, or so he thinks, of 'counting the men in' when the raid is over. After being led up the support trench by Stockwell's second-in-command, Major Compton Smith, the four parties of five men and their 'evacuating party' with ladders and flashlamps prepare to cross the sixty yards to the German trench. Pitted with deep mine-craters, this is a precarious undertaking in the dark and Stansfield, helped by Sergeant Lyle and Sassoon's daredevil friend, Corporal O'Brien, has already been out to lay a guiding trail of lime across No Man's Land. Since Sassoon's only means of following events is by sound, he listens anxiously. He knows that the British wire has been cut, but fears that the Germans' has not, in spite of preparatory bombardments. After fifteen minutes he can contain himself no longer and, strictly against orders, goes out with the rearguard to join the evacuating party twenty yards into No Man's Land.

After another tense five minutes he is convinced that the raiders have been held up by the German wire, a suspicion confirmed by one of the bayonet-men, who returns to report this. He says that the raiding-party's only choice is to throw bombs and retire. Minutes later a rifle-shot rings out, followed by the explosion of several bombs. What follows is chaos and complete confusion as the Germans, who have been waiting for the raiders in silence, open fire and send them helter-skelter back across the treacherous ground. Sassoon counts sixteen men in, then goes out once more to investigate. He finds Stansfield, wounded but safe, and other injured men crawling in. Only O'Brien, his 'dear bombing corporal', and another man are absent down one of the deep craters.[25]

In the face of continuing rifle shots and bombs, Sassoon searches the craters. ('The bloody sods are firing down at me at point-blank range,' he thinks incredulously as five or six Germans concentrate their fire.)[26] Expecting every moment to be his last, he works his way slowly and painfully around the bottom of the twenty-five foot crater until he finds O'Brien and his companion. O'Brien is badly wounded and so heavy – Sassoon describes him as 'a huge Irishman' – that Sassoon has to crawl back twice more to the British trench for help, the second time in dangerously light conditions. By the time he has finally got O'Brien in from the crater, he is dead and all Sassoon can do is to write an epitaph for his 'fine lad': 'Corporal Mick O'Brien (who often went patrolling with me) was a very fine man and had been with the Battalion since November 1914. He was at Neuve Chapelle, Festubert and Loos.'[27]

Of the twenty-eight men who went out, eleven were wounded, of whom one died, and one was killed. As Stockwell noted in his diary, the raid had been a failure and it was 'largely owing to Sassoon's bravery' that it had not been a complete disaster.[28] Sassoon's action in bringing O'Brien in, as Julian Dadd later pointed out, was only the 'conclusion of a remarkably well co-ordinated piece of work' on his part.[29] Stockwell had no hesitation in recommending him for an M.C., which Sassoon received a month later, the first Special Reserve Officer in his regiment to do so. The citation read: 'For conspicuous gallantry during a raid on the enemy's trenches. He remained for one and a half hours under rifle and bomb fire, collecting and bringing in our wounded. Owing to his courage and determination all the killed and wounded were brought in.' Sassoon later wrote in an 'Autobiographical Outline',[30] that he 'did not believe in decorations' and was, therefore, never 'decorated with M.C. by king for this reason'. He did, however, proudly wear his white and purple M.C. ribbon which the Battalion doctor took from his own tunic the day confirmation of the honour came through, and sewed to Sassoon's uniform with his own hands.

Sassoon himself admitted that he was lucky that Stockwell had refused to allow him to go out with the raiding party, as he 'meant to get through that wire somehow, and it seems to have been almost impossible'.[31] Had he succeeded, however, he realized that the Germans would have been waiting for him. Not unnaturally, he experienced a severe sense of anti-climax after the failed night raid and tried to keep up the excitement. Ignoring the extreme danger he had already undergone, he was out in No Man's Land the next night collecting equipment abandoned in the confusion.

While Sassoon believed his 'quest for beauty' in poetry now 'doomed', he was determined to find beauty of another kind in France, 'not the sort of beauty I used to look for'.[32] His duties as a Company Officer did not allow him sufficient leisure to write poetry about this curious kind of beauty, but neither were they stimulating enough to provide an alternative source of excitement, consisting as they did mainly of reinforcement work and wiring parties.

He did not, however, welcome a change of job, as might have been expected. When he was made Sniping Observing Officer on 7 June, he worried about his qualifications for the post. Yet it was probably less demanding than being a company officer and may well have been given to him by Stockwell as a reward for his courage. His misgivings about it seem to have been a symptom of a more general angst, apparent in many passages of his diary at that time. Even when leave was granted to him on 9 June, a week earlier than expected, he was not sure whether he really wanted it, as his jaundiced diary-entry suggests.[33]

The reason Sassoon was sent on leave on 9 June, rather than the 15th as previously planned, was almost certainly the imminence of the Battle of the Somme. The authorities were anxious to have all officers back in France well before the offensive was due to open at the end of June. So Sassoon left for England on the evening of the 9th and arrived, exhausted, in Southampton nearly two days later. He had dreamed of a peaceful existence and time to enjoy his books and piano under the influence of Weirleigh's clustering roses, green trees and 'bird-sung' dawns,[34] but the contrast with France was too stark. There was also the continuing unhappiness of his mother to spoil his pleasure. Proud as she was of his M.C., having lost one son she quite understandably worried about the dangers he had risked to win it and much of his time at home was spent reassuring her. It was a relief to leave for London again, where his literary friends were all clamouring to see him.

Sassoon had encouraged Dent to come down from Cambridge for a lunch or concert, and Marsh, too, had his claims. Gosse invited him to dine, with only Ross for company, an occasion almost certainly set up to discuss his poetry. For, with the Allies' 'Big Push' ahead, both Sassoon and his friends were anxious to prepare for the not unlikely eventuality of his death. (The greatest casualties in the First World War were predominantly among junior officers.) Marsh's approach to Monro had come to nothing and by 30 April Sassoon had decided on another private production. By May, however, he was agreeing with Marsh and Ross, who both felt that it was better to wait.

In the event, the matter was decided by Monro, who by 5 June had decided not to publish Sassoon at the Poetry Bookshop at all, a decision he must later have rued. Gosse, who wanted Sassoon to get his juvenilia out of his system, certainly regretted it, and his dinner for Ross and Sassoon on 16 June was almost certainly intended as an occasion to discuss the matter further. Ross, who admired Sassoon's anti-war poems most, was keen for him to write more in the same vein before publishing. Gosse, who was dubious about the satires but admired the lyrics, wanted the latter published. A compromise seems to have been reached: that Sassoon should siphon off his lyrics into another private production (which was to become *Morning-Glory*) and concentrate on writing more of the satires Ross admired, so that the latter could approach a respectable commercial publisher with them. Dent, meanwhile, though not present at this discussion, was also encouraging Sassoon to write more of his satires for the *Cambridge Magazine*. It is interesting to see the influence of Gosse and Marsh, so powerful at the start of Sassoon's entry to the literary world, diminishing under the 'alternative' views of Ross and Dent, who prove to have been the shrewder critics.

One friend Sassoon was not able to see during his brief leave was Graves, who was with the 3rd RWF at Litherland, but he looked forward to seeing him back in France, which Graves now regarded as his true 'home'. It was one of a number of reasons why Sassoon was not sorry when his leave ended. Like Sorley, and no doubt many others, he had found a curious freedom in the apparently constricting conditions of trench-life. After the first strangeness of being transported back so suddenly from his comfortable bed and clean clothes to his 'flea-bag' on a hard floor and muddy army uniform had passed off, he looked forward like most of his companions to some action, however dangerous.

*

The 1st Battalion had been moved, in Sassoon's absence, for a last 'rest' behind the lines at Bussy-le-Daours, a pleasant little village on the marshy banks of the River Hallue, a tributary of the Ancre. C Company was billeted in buildings situated round a friendly farmhouse and everyone seemed relaxed. Sitting by the river, all seemed smooth and peaceful to Sassoon, the long green weeds 'swaying with the current like nosing fishes slowly curving their way upstream'.[35] Further up the river, along the marsh, there were yellow irises among the reeds, thousands of tiny dark-green and golden frogs and waterside birds 'crying and calling and swinging on the bullrushes and tufted spires, by the smooth grey-green pools and creeks'. It was a scene Sassoon captured in 'Before the Battle', which underlines the calming effect of Nature on him, even as he contemplated the possibility of his own death:

> Music of whispering trees
> Hushed by a broad-winged breeze
> Where shaken water gleams;
> And evening radiance falling
> With reedy bird-notes calling.
> *O bear me safe through dark, you low-voiced streams.*   (*CP*, p. 33)

When Sassoon wrote this poem and when, the next day, he marched the eleven miles back to Morlancourt, he was expecting to be in action within forty-eight hours. Morlancourt itself was crowded with troops and a new Main Dressing Station had been erected in his absence. As he lay once more in his old billet, even the garish pictures on the walls, of the Eiffel Tower and 'jocular Jesus',[36] seemed precious details of a life he was about to risk.

Sassoon might have spared himself the emotional strain, since the order was changed and the action delayed by another forty-eight hours. Instead of the excitement of a 'show', there was the familiar trudge up to the trenches on the evening of the 28th to relieve the 7th Borderers on the Battalion Front opposite Fricourt Cemetery and Station in the muddy trenches. The English bombardment, intended to destroy the enemy wire, continued noisily as it had done for the past twelve days, but Sassoon's C Company had a quiet night in '85th Street' trench.

The overall plan had been for General Rawlinson's 4th Army, supported by five divisions of the French on its right and two divisions of the 3rd Army round Gommecourt on its left, to attack on a fourteen-mile front between Maricourt and Serre, with the initial objective of breaking the German Front Line in that sector. It was, however, a badly flawed scheme. The original intention had been for the Allies to attack on a much larger front, with forty French divisions taking the area from Lassigny to the Somme and the British throwing twenty-five rather than eighteen divisions into battle. The Germans' ferocious attack on the French at Verdun in the spring and the consequent drain on French resources had forced the change. It had also marked a turning-point in the War, since from the Somme onwards the British were to take up the main burden of the Western Front Campaign.

Another problem was that, since the Germans had the high ground, the Allies had to attack mainly uphill, both a physical and psychological disadvantage for the troops if not for the artillery. Furthermore, the assault, which was frontal, was spread evenly across the whole line without special regard to the enemy's weak points or, indeed, to the Allies' own resources. For the British, attacking on a front almost twice as long as the French, had only half their heavy guns – one to every fifty-seven yards – and only one gun of any kind in every twenty yards.

Additionally, the Staff placed altogether too much faith in a preliminary bombardment. Intended to wipe out the German defences, it not only failed conspicuously in this aim but also warned the enemy of the coming attack. As a result the Germans had accelerated the strengthening of their defences, which by 1 July were virtually impregnable. Consequently, when the British Infantry, fatally slowed down by equipment weighing more than half their body weight, lumbered across No Man's Land in stiff formations, German soldiers, still in many cases secure in their dug-outs, were ready to mow them down with their machine-guns.

Sassoon's 7th Division, together with the 21st (both part of the XV Corps) were involved in a smaller battle within the grander scheme, the Battle of Albert. Centred on Fricourt, their front was approximately two miles long, of which 800 yards was the responsibility of the 1st RWF and one of their partners in the 22nd Brigade, the 20th Manchesters. By 28 June, Colonel Stockwell already knew that their action was to be 'subsidiary' and that 'Scatter' Minshull Ford's Brigade, the 91st, would bear the brunt. Not only that, but the 1st RWFs would be in support only, so that they were even less at risk.

Sassoon's own Company, C, was to be split up into groups for carrying ammunition and would, therefore, not be called upon to fight at all. It was intensely disappointing to Sassoon. As it was he had to be satisfied with some hazardous wire-cutting and spent most of the night of 29 June occupied in this task. It was difficult work, since the English wire was deliberately thick, and it had to be carried out under constant shelling from both the Germans and the English, whose own shells often fell short. Nevertheless he was out again on the 30th in broad daylight frantically making gaps for the next day's attack. The official confirmation of his M.C. the same day no doubt spurred him on to even more daring efforts than usual.

When the great day dawned, Sassoon found himself left ingloriously in the support trench with his fellow-officer, Garnons-Williams, his company officer, Greaves, and no men. All he could do was to observe the progress of the battle from a safe distance, approximately five hundred yards behind the line. Despite the anti-climax, he had a sense of being 'irrevocably involved in something bigger than had ever happened before'.[37]

After a hasty breakfast at 6 a.m. on a beautiful summer morning Sassoon witnesses the start of the action when 'all hell is let loose' at 6.30 a.m. as the

English bombardment theoretically prepares the way for the troops. Since the slight breeze is in the wrong direction, the smoke-screen has had to be cancelled and he can see clearly all that follows, as far as the lie of the land allows. By 7.45 a.m. the artillery barrage is working to the right of Fricourt and he watches the 21st and 7th Divisions advancing to the left of it, with some Germans apparently surrendering about three-quarters of a mile away.

After a quick shave in the dug-out at 9.30 a.m., Sassoon continues to watch the men going across the open with no sign of casualties, though German trench-mortars are wreaking havoc on the ground where his neighbours in the support trench, the Manchesters, are due to attack. The morning drags on, with surprisingly little drama. Men still file across No Man's Land in twenties and thirties, and – except for an occasional explosion in German-held Fricourt, some English observation balloons and aeroplanes overhead and the confused fluttering and cries of bewildered birds – it is difficult to believe that one of the biggest battles in history is underway. 'I am looking at a sunlit picture of Hell,' Sassoon records. 'And still the breeze shakes the yellow charlock, and the poppies glow below Crawley ridge ....'[38] The weather is cloudless and hot. A lark is singing overhead.

By 1.30 p.m. Sassoon hears that Mametz and Montaubon are taken, a fact he is unable to verify for himself because of the rising ground towards Mametz. At 2.30 p.m. the Manchesters are finally instructed to advance. He can see about 400 of them cross No Man's Land, many walking slowly with sloped arms. In spite of intense firing there are only forty or so casualties on the left and he is proud of the risks he has taken to cut the English wire for them. Simultaneously the Germans start shelling his dug-out, but he bears a charmed life. At 5 p.m. he watches men from A Company of the 1st RWF going across to help the Manchesters, who have been held up in the Bois Français support, their Colonel dead. By 8 p.m., he learns that the 7th Division has finally reached its objectives, except on his own Brigade Front where the 20th Manchesters are still in trouble. Eventually, with the help of the 1st RWF's A and B Companies and parties of bombers, they reach Fricourt which, in defiance of Headquarters, Stockwell orders them to take. By 2.30 p.m. on 2 July it is reported captured. Rumour has it that over 2,000 prisoners have been taken by the 7th Division, 200 of these by the 1st RWF alone, clearly a gross exaggeration since history records that the whole of the XV Corps took only 517 prisoners altogether. Not one officer of the 1st Battalion has been killed.

Other sectors of the line were not so fortunate, however, and Sassoon's experience on the first day of the Somme was by no means typical. Situated as he was at Fricourt, on the right centre, he was at the very turning point of the battle. The French, south of the Somme and north of it as far as Maricourt, had gained all their objectives with slight losses. Between Maricourt and Fricourt the British XIII Corps had reached its objectives, though with heavier losses. On its left the XV Corps, of which Sassoon had formed an infinitesimal and passive part, partially achieved its aim of pinching out the stronghold of

Fricourt village and wood. But this marked the boundary of success. All to the north was failure – La Boiselle, Contalmaison, Thiepval and Beaumont Hamel. The French might justifiably have claimed success, but for the British, whose thirteen divisions had taken a small tract of land and less than 2,000 prisoners against only six German divisions, it was a disastrous failure. Of the quarter of a million men who went into battle, on the first day alone 20,000 were killed, the heaviest British loss of any single day's fighting in the War, and one which gave the lie to Haig's optimistic faith in massed artillery. Still unaware of these terrible facts, though news was slowly coming in, Sassoon's initial reaction was mainly personal: he felt 'a bit of a fraud'.[39]

Early on the morning of 3 July, nearly sixty hours after Sassoon had marched up to the support trench with C Company, he left it to join the battalion at 71.North. Their destination was a grassy hollow south of the Carnoy-Mametz road. Here, together with three other battalions of the 22nd Brigade – 20th Manchesters, 2nd Warwicks and the 2nd Royal Irish – they were to spend the day resting in preparation for an attack on Mametz Wood the following day. As Sassoon lay listening to the contented chatter of officers and men, and contemplating his own good luck in the recent event, he once again found consolation in Nature, despite thoughts of the 'cursed Wood' they must attack the next day (see 'At Carnoy').

Sassoon's forebodings about Mametz Wood turned out to be fully justified. Of tactical importance to the British in their push forward to the German second line, it proved far more of an obstacle than anticipated. A rumour had started, and been accepted by the staff, that the Wood was unoccupied and the 1st Battalion, together with the 2nd Royal Irish, was ordered to 'go and make a position' on its southern edge. Armed with trenching tools, barbed wire and other equipment, the Royal Welch Fusiliers started out after some hours' delay on the evening of 3rd to 4th July, through Mametz village and up a long communication trench to Bottom Wood. Stockwell had refused to move until the bewildered guide had found his bearings and it was nearly 2 a.m. before the exhausted men set off.

For the first time Sassoon found himself among the debris of a fierce attack, rags and shreds of bloody clothing, bullet-riddled boots and abandoned equipment. This both horrified and fascinated him. Passing about thirty of the British dead laid out by the side of the road, 'their fingers mingled in blood-stained bunches', he reflected that these Gordon Highlanders, Devons and South Staffordshires were finally beyond regimental rivalry in the companionship of death.[40] As he reached the old German Front Line in his slow progress towards Mametz, he was conscious of a 'sour pervasive stench' which differed from anything he had previously experienced: it was the smell of corpses nearly three days old. Some of these strewed the communication trench out of Mametz, their badly mangled bodies deeply shocking in their distorted attitudes. Though he had been with the 1st Battalion in France for nearly eight months, these were the first newly dead Germans he had seen.

When the Royal Welch Fusiliers arrived at their destination at 3 a.m., Stockwell was disgusted to find that it was an impossible place to consolidate. When, therefore, a bombing fight broke out at the edge of the supposedly empty wood, he had no hesitation in ordering his men back to camp. Meanwhile, the Royal Irish, who had been sent up ahead of the Royal Welch to consolidate trenches close to the south end of Mametz Wood and to clear its outskirts, ran into enemy machine-guns, bombers and snipers. When they tried to bomb the Germans out of the wood they suffered sixty casualties and were only saved from further losses by the English guns firing heavy shells, which enabled them to retreat. It had been eleven hours of muddle and mismanagement caused largely, Sassoon believed, by bad staffwork at Divisional Headquarters. Yet, elated by the promise of action at last and stimulated, as always, by danger, he could still describe the events of the previous forty-eight hours as 'great fun'.[41]

Revising their plans only slightly, Headquarters sent orders on the morning of 4 July that the line which the two battalions had been instructed to consolidate the previous night should now be attacked. Since it was raining hard, visibility was even worse than usual from the British line at Bottom Wood. So that it was in some ignorance and with pardonable trepidation that the 1st Battalion got into position at 12.30 a.m. on 5 July, with the depleted Royal Irish on their right and the 7th Northumberland Fusiliers on their left. Though the wire in front of Quadrangle Trench was reported 'well gapped', that in front of Wood Trench had only one opening and the heavy rain had made the ground a quagmire. The attack was launched fifteen minutes later.

Once again Sassoon was thwarted of a good fight with C Company, as before, split up into carrying parties. At 2.10 a.m., with the news that A and D Companies were under extreme pressure from the Germans, Stockwell finally ordered the remnants of C Company (only twenty-six men) up to the line and Sassoon's moment seemed to have arrived. Once again he was to be disappointed, however, for with the report a few minutes later that only bombs and bombers were needed, not more men, Stockwell countermanded the order and C Company was recalled. What followed is typical of Sassoon's impetuousness, hunger for excitement, physical courage and highly emotional nature.

Frustrated by the lack of action, Sassoon ignored Stockwell's order, though he sent his men back. As he crossed the 500 yards from the support trench at Bottom Wood to the newly captured Quadrangle Trench, which he started to investigate, dawn was breaking. The trench itself offered little protection, since it was still only half-finished, and the enemy was also firing down Quadrangle Alley, the communication trench from Mametz Wood. The greatest threat, however, came from a German sniper at the end of Wood Trench, which provided an ideal sniping post, and already British soldiers were lying killed and wounded as Sassoon made his way to the trench end. Whether he was enraged by the general carnage and the death of one of his own favourites, Lance-Corporal Gibson, in particular, as he suggests in *Infantry Officer*, or whether he craved some excitement of his own after his frustrating inactivity of the previous five days, or whether he simply gave way to one of his many impulses, he suddenly decided to put an end to the sniper who was wreaking so much havoc.

Rushing across the little valley and light railway line which separated him from the Germans in Wood Trench, he pulled the safety-pins out of two Mills bombs as he went and, mounting the bank on the opposite side, threw them into the hidden trench. His own words to Marsh convey vividly what happened next: 'Eddie, I chased 40 Bosches out of a trench by Mametz Wood all by myself. Wasn't that a joyous moment for me? They ran like hell and I chucked bombs and made hunting noises.'[42] The sheer foolhardiness of his action, together with covering fire from his own side, probably saved him.

The attack itself achieved little. Once occupying the roomy German trench Sassoon had no idea what to do next. Unable to consolidate his position he did not relish the idea of the enemy's return. Graves's story, that Sassoon simply pulled out a book of poetry and settled down to read, however attractive, is almost certainly apocryphal. It is far more probable that he tentatively explored the trench, like George Sherston in *Infantry Officer*, and then 'took a deep breath and ran headlong back'.[43]

Unlike Sherston, however, his action, far from earning him a reprimand from his Commanding Officer, caused him to be recommended for a further decoration, either a bar to his M.C. or a D.S.O. However annoyed Stockwell was by his initial disobedience, he believed that Sassoon, like his friend Julian Dadd and another bomber, Stevens, had done 'splendidly'.[44] The decoration was to be disallowed, on the grounds that the overall attack had been a failure, though the Royal Welch Fusiliers had gained their objectives.

While exploring Quadrangle Trench at dawn, Sassoon had come across the body of a young German, clearly killed whilst digging. His gentle, good-looking face, not disfigured by wounds, and his fresh blond hair seem to have made Sassoon particularly aware of the waste and futility of war. Wiping the mud from the youth's eyes and mouth, he carefully propped him up against the side of the trench. On his return later the same day, however, he found him trodden into the mud by a careless English boot. It is significant that, out of the many incidents of what he calls 'The Night Attack', he chose to describe, not his own courage, but the pathos of the young German soldier. By revealing genuine sympathy for the enemy the poem indicates a further shift in Sassoon's attitude towards war at the very moment when he is most enjoying it. After describing the British soldiers' relief as they lie resting twelve miles behind the lines, Sassoon recalls the young Prussian he had seen 'Dead in a squalid, miserable ditch,/ Heedless of toiling feet that trod him down.'[45] In the twelve lines Sassoon added to his original version of 6 July 1916, his sympathy for the German youth and his growing sense of the futility of war emerge starkly: '... Such is defeat, not beautiful nor kind;/ And this was ugly death, a shameless thing,/ Stripped of the sable hood that cloaks his grin.'[46]

Sassoon's sense of the ugly wastage of war was further strengthened the same evening that this incident occurred, as the 1st Battalion was relieved by the 14th Royal Welch Fusiliers, a unit of inexperienced, half-trained civilians. Watching a little platoon officer trying to settle his nervous men down 'with a valiant show of self-assurance', and suspecting the hell and carnage that awaited them, he realized then 'for the first time, how blindly war destroys its victims'.[47] Two days later the 38th (Welsh) Division, of which the 14th Battalion formed a part, was to be massacred in one of the most fiercely fought engagements of the War.

By that time Sassoon himself was resting gratefully twelve miles away at Heilly-sur-l'Ancre, where the Battalion spent an enjoyable five days. They had suffered only fourteen dead out of 132 casualties in the seven days since the great battle started and considered themselves extremely lucky. Sassoon even managed to get into Amiens on 7 July for a luxurious lunch at Godberts with Greaves, Reeves, Cottrell and Julian Dadd. On the 9th he had another treat, when he made contact with Norman Loder, now Assistant Provost Marshall to the XIII Corps Headquarters. Arriving back at camp he learned that the 7th Division was moving up to the line again the next day. Mametz Wood had still not been taken.

At 4 p.m. on 10 July the 1st Battalion, reinforced by five officers and fifty-seven men from the 20th RWF, started back to their camp at the Citadel just south of Fricourt. Between Méricourt and Treux they were passed by the Commander-in-Chief of the British Armies in France, Sir Douglas Haig, a privilege they are unlikely to have appreciated. And at Morlancourt Sassoon noted a solitary doctor in a white coat standing at the church-door, perhaps because it seemed to him an ominous conjunction. They arrived at the Citadel about 9 p.m. and, after a brief rest, were standing-to at 10.45 p.m. At 11.30 p.m. they set off for Mametz, but were brought back, without explanation, after only a quarter of an hour and spent a peaceful night sleeping under the stars.

The next day Sassoon learnt that once again he was to be left out of the action, placed in reserve with Julian Dadd and five other officers. In his fictionalized account Sassoon has Sherston's Colonel threaten good-humouredly to leave him out of the 'next show' as a punishment for his impulsive and unconsolidated attack on Wood Trench,[48] and perhaps that really was the explanation for Stockwell's decision to leave him out of the action once more. In any event Sassoon was to remain for the next eleven days in a state of limbo, while the rest of the battalion fought the Battle of Bazentin Ridge. Whatever his personal feelings, he seems to have been extremely lucky, since at least two officers of the 1st Battalion were killed and three wounded in the fierce fighting there.

Only later did Sassoon appreciate how fortunate he had been. At the time he suffered from both boredom and suspense: as long as the battle continued he could be called on at any moment. In an effort to deal with the mental stagnation which overcame him in such an 'arid and irksome place',[49] he spent much of his time reading Hardy, whose fatalistic outlook suited his state of mind more than ever. Above all Hardy helped him to avoid what he thought of as the 'unreasoning mechanical outlook' of his companions, who irritated and endeared him by turns.[50] Often, as he watched them huddled up asleep, they reminded him of the corpses he had recently seen, giving him irrational fears that they might be dead: 'For at any hour I may come upon them, and find that long silence descended over them, their faces grey and disfigured, dark stains of blood soaking through their torn garments, all their hope and merriment snuffed out for ever, and their voices fading on the winds of thought, from memory to memory, from hour to hour, until they are no more to be recalled.'[51]

One of the few enjoyments in this period of suspense and boredom was an unexpected meeting with Robert Graves. When Graves had left for England in late March on a leave prolonged by an essential nose operation, both he and Sassoon expected him to return to the 1st Battalion. They had kept in close touch during Graves's absence and continued to fantasize about all the places they would visit and the poetry they would write together after the War. Graves had sent 'Sassons', as he affectionately called him, an advance copy of his first book of poems, *Over the Brazier*, in May, another incentive for Sassoon to think seriously about publication. He had also confided to Sassoon his misery over an enforced separation from his Charterhouse 'friend', Peter. There was, therefore, a great deal to be discussed when, as they hoped, Graves rejoined the 1st RWF. They were, understandably, very disappointed when he was assigned instead to the 2nd Battalion, which he joined at Givenchy on 5 July. Their delight was all the keener, therefore, when the 2nd Battalion was then sent to join the 1st at Mametz Wood.

Sassoon's protective attitude towards Graves in his absence gave way to feelings of great excitement in his presence. As they sat talking in the darkness, surrounded by their sleeping men, he thought wildly of 'travels, and adventures, and poetry; and anything but the old groove of cricket and hunting, and dreaming in Weirleigh garden'.[52] When the War ended he would be 'at the crossroads' and he now knew which path to choose. He must 'go out into the night alone'; there could be 'no fat settling down'.

Graves, whom Sassoon found 'as whimsical and queer and human as ever', made his old life seem conventional silliness. And it is no coincidence that he went on to say in the same diary passage that he could never marry Bobbie Hanmer's sister. Even his new role as a soldier, which had to some extent liberated him, seemed shallow and unreal under the intoxicating influence of Graves's vivid imagination and total commitment to art. The dissatisfaction he expressed forcibly in his diary a few days later was undoubtedly a result of this.[53]

He was also busy copying Graves's latest poems into his notebook and composing one of his own in response to Graves's visit, 'The Crown', which reinforces the view that this visit had had an unsettling effect on him.[54] Graves, who moved up to Mametz Wood with his men the next day (15 July), nevertheless found time for poetry too, a verse letter in reply to Sassoon's May epistle from Flixécourt which suggests that he, as much as Sassoon, envisaged a closely shared future travelling together: '... And doing wild, tremendous things/ In free adventure, quest and fight,/ And God! what poetry we'll write!'[55]

Graves, in the 2nd Battalion, was part of the same attack as the 1st Battalion, and had already been in action with the 7th Division by the time he arrived at Mametz Wood. Rawlinson, commanding the 4th Army, frustrated by the 38th Division's failure to take the Wood, had devised a plan to break through the German defences along a four-mile front between Delville Wood on the right and Bazentin-le-Petit Wood on the left. Since direct attack had proved ineffective, he decided on a surprise night attack. With the 9th and 3rd Divisions of the XXII Corps on the right and the 7th and 21st Divisions of the XV Corps on the left, troops would attempt to break through at dawn on 14 July and take the German second line. In this they succeeded, the 1st Battalion helping the 7th Division clear Bazentin-le-Petit Wood and push up the slopes beyond towards High Wood. Graves, who arrived at the new Front Line the same day, had to sit waiting in shell-holes for the next stage of the battle. On the 17th he moved up to a position just north of Bazentin-le-Petit to relieve some Irish troops, and that night he supervised the digging of several strong-points.

On the evening of the 19th Graves's Battalion, reduced by casualties to 400 men, was pulled out of the Line and told that they would be in reserve for the major assault on High Wood the next day. Ironically, it was while Graves was waiting in reserve in a relatively safe position that he was injured. The Germans had put down a barrage on the ridge where he was sheltering and, as he tried to escape, an eight-inch shell burst just behind him, wounding him badly in the leg and chest. The Battalion M.O., Dr Dunn, having announced that there was 'no chance' of him surviving, he was assumed dead.

A shocked Sassoon was informed of Graves's 'death' the following day. His thoughts turned back to David Thomas and forward to his own, possibly similar, fate:

> So he and Tommy are together, and perhaps I'll join them soon. 'Oh my songs never sung, And my plays to darkness blown!' – [Graves's] own poor words written last summer, and now so cruelly true. And only two days ago I was copying his last poem into my notebook, a poem full of his best qualities of sweetness and sincerity, full of heart-breaking gaiety and hope. ... Robert might have been a great poet; he could never have become a dull one. In him I thought I had found a lifelong friend to work with. So I go my way alone again.[56]

By the time the news of Graves's supposed death reached Sassoon, the 1st Battalion was reunited with its Reserve Officers and Transport on a hill south-west of Dernancourt. Sassoon had helped prepare for the returning men on 21 July and had waited six hours with Cottrell to welcome them back. Though they had suffered relatively few casualties in the general carnage (less than a hundred), they arrived back in an exhausted and subdued state after what Sassoon described as 'eight days in hell'.[57] A day later, following a good sleep and a shave, they were a great deal more cheerful and on their way to La Chaussée, a mile from Picquigny, for a fortnight's well-earned rest. The journey was an easy one of approximately twenty-three miles, most of it by train, and Sassoon should, theoretically, have been able to relax. Instead, by 23 July, he was feeling extremely ill with a temperature of 105°F, and by the next morning was in the New Zealand hospital at Amiens.

The initial diagnosis was dysentery, which Sassoon suspected he had caught from the new billets at La Chaussée, left in a far from sanitary state by their previous inhabitants. It is more likely that dysentery was in fact only one of the symptoms of trench fever, since his temperature was so high. At first he felt too ill to care about anything, simply appreciating the luxury of a clean bed away from the Front. But gradually, as his temperature returned to normal, the full impact of Graves's death hit him. He had been too busy with battalion business at Dernancourt fully to register this loss. Now, with time on his hands and the news of the death of yet another friend, Marcus Goodall, he felt it necessary to express his sorrow, to pin it down. To Dent he wrote, on 29 July: 'There was something of bitter charm in [Graves], a sort of sallow, victimised, faithful Jester in the storm – quite impossible to describe – queer twisted smile – ungainly lankiness – rather goggling eyes – and all that's been dumped into a shell-hole and blathered over by a parson (if he was so "lucky" as to get that last piece of patronising attentive impudence thrown at him) ... His rare gaiety was like a young animal hopping in a daisied field.'[58]

The poem which emerged, 'To His Dead Body', originally dedicated to Graves, was subsequently retitled 'The Traveller', revised and rededicated to Marcus Goodall when it emerged that Graves was alive after all. This suggests that it was not so much a personal tribute to one particular soldier but an elegy for all the promising young men who were dying so pointlessly in the War.[59]

Sassoon's grief at the death of two of his dearest friends within a week of each other was made even worse by haunting memories of the putrefying corpses he had seen at Mametz. His state of mind was not helped by the presence of a young officer in the bed opposite his, whose serious condition was concealed by red screens which glowed with deceptive cheerfulness at night. As the dying soldier grew more delirious, he started to rave about a wood which he cursed for the miseries he had experienced there, including the loss of a close friend. His disjointed phrases contained for Sassoon 'all the horror of the Somme',[60] as well as reminding him of his own nightmare experience in Mametz Wood.

Sassoon's first version of the poem, written the day he woke to find the boy's bed empty, was much longer than the final version. By cutting the first two and the last of the original seven verses and reducing his stanzas from five to four lines, he greatly improved the poem, condensing it to its barest and most telling details. His substitution of the official phrase 'Died of Wounds' for the title, in place of the original 'In Hospital', is also an improvement. His use of fragmented snatches of direct speech is particularly effective:

Died of Wounds

His wet white face and miserable eyes
Brought nurses to him more than groans and sighs:
But hoarse and low and rapid rose and fell
His troubled voice: he did the business well.

The ward grew dark; but he was still complaining
And calling out for 'Dickie'. 'Curse the Wood!
'It's time to go. O Christ, and what's the good?
'We'll never take it, and it's always raining.'

I wondered where he'd been; then heard him shout,
'They snipe like hell! O Dickie, don't go out' ...
I fell asleep ... Next morning he was dead;
And some Slight Wound lay smiling on the bed.   (*CP*, p. 28)

In spite of Sassoon's mental suffering, his physical state slowly improved and he fully expected to be back in his unit by the end of July. 'Not lucky enough to be wounded' as he put it frankly to Dent on 29 July, he nevertheless still felt very weak and it later emerged that he was anaemic. More significantly for his future, he was also thought to have shadows on his lungs, possibly a legacy from his childhood bouts of pneumonia. Sassoon himself thought that his M.C. influenced the doctor's decision, though there is no proof of this. Instead of being sent to join his battalion at La Chaussée, as they prepared for another engagement at Ginchy, he found himself first on a train for Rouen, then, more miraculously, on a hospital ship for Southampton. By an extraordinary coincidence, Graves too had been sent to Rouen when he was found to be alive after twenty-four hours presumed dead, and was still there recovering from his wounds when Sassoon arrived at No. 2 Hospital, Rouen, on 30 July. They also landed in England within a day of each other, Sassoon on 2 August, Graves on 3 August. Yet Sassoon still believed that Graves was dead, having been told this by both his Colonel and his Adjutant.

Nevertheless, Sassoon could not help rejoicing as he lay in the hospital train taking him, he thought, to London. Whilst he felt guilty at forsaking his men and believed that three or four weeks' convalescence in France would have enabled him to rejoin them, he longed for a break from the almost unrelieved horrors he had recently witnessed. His thankfulness shows itself in an uncharacteristically mild description of his arrival in England, so mild in fact that it was accepted for publication by the *Westminster Gazette*.[61]

Virginia Woolf used the last four lines of 'Stretcher Case' to argue that

Sassoon's realism was 'of the right, the poetic kind. The real things are put in not merely because they are real, but because at a certain moment of emotion the poet happened to be struck by them and is not afraid of spoiling his effect by calling them by their right names'.[62] Looking at the lines in question, it is hard not to believe that Woolf wrote more from a desire to please Ottoline Morrell, who had asked her to write the review, than from poetic sensibility:

> There shone the blue serene, the prosperous land,
> Trees, cows and hedges; skipping these, he scanned
> Large, friendly names, that change not with the year,
>   Lung Tonic, Mustard, Liver Pills and Beer.   (*CP*, p. 30)

Even taking Sassoon's own description of the poem as 'mildly satirical' into account, it is still a disappointing performance, though it does underline how far he had come from his Romantic beginnings. Dedicated to Edward Marsh, who had tried hard to alleviate Sassoon's grief over Robert Graves, 'Stretcher Case' was written at Oxford, the new 'paradise' in which Sassoon found himself safely installed on 2 August 1916.

11

'My Killed Friends Are With Me Where I Go'

August 1916-January 1917

When Sassoon arrived back in England at the beginning of August 1916 the battle of the Somme was still raging and would do so until November. In the space of four months the British were to see 400,000 dead and wounded for severely limited gains, causing Sassoon to question the war further. In August 1916, however, he was not yet seriously disaffected; he was simply happy to be back in England, and not even wounded. The so-called 'spots' on his lung, which had helped bring about this miracle, had either quickly disappeared or been misdiagnosed in the first place. His vigour, undermined by trench-fever and a more long-standing anaemia, was gradually returning under strict medical care, in a situation which made none of the demands of trench life. Delivered from his one great fear in battle, that of being blinded, he feasted his eyes on the beauty of his surroundings which contrasted sharply with the ugliness of the war zone.

Life at No. 3 Southern General Hospital in his little cream room on the ground floor of Somerville College, with its view of tranquil lawns and trees, was positively as well as negatively enjoyable. He loved the Oxford bells chiming the hour, the sound of a piano from across the lawn and the tall chestnut trees swaying against the blue sky. Better, even, than the physical advantages were the mental ones. There was now time to read and his choice of Fanny Burney's *Evelina* suggests that he gladly embraced the chance to escape the harshness of trench life. He also felt ready to pour out all the poetry which had been bottled up in him. As he himself observed, it was not easy to be both poet and platoon commander. Relieved of the latter responsibility, he felt overflowing with accumulated impressions and emotional reactions to the extraordinary events he had experienced.

Only one thing seriously marred his happiness, the death, as he believed, of his friend Robert Graves. The relationship had seemed to promise so much in so many ways that, though it was nearly two weeks since Graves's death had been reported to him, he was still unable to come to terms with it. His delight, therefore, when Edward Marsh telegraphed him the news that Graves had actually survived was unbounded.

While Sassoon was writing joyfully to Dent in Cambridge, still believing Graves to be in Rouen, Graves was addressing a letter to Sassoon in France from his hospital bed in Highgate. It was a comedy of errors which was quickly resolved and three days later Graves, now correctly informed of Sassoon's whereabouts, writes to invite Sassoon to go with him to Harlech. If anything, his narrow escape from death has strengthened the affection between him and Sassoon. They continue to plan a joint volume of verse, in the manner of Wordsworth and Coleridge's *Lyrical Ballads*, one reason Graves believes it is vital Sassoon should visit him in Harlech.

Meantime, relieved of his greatest anxiety, Sassoon starts to write his own poetry again. In a letter to Dent he includes an 'absurd' poem which he is sure will 'tickle' Dent's 'cynical old gullet', 'The Father', interesting for what it reveals of Sassoon's attitude as well as his working methods. 'It was only when I was writing verse that I tried to concentrate and express my somewhat loose ideas,' he wrote of this period,[1] and 'The Father' shows that he has lost none of his growing cynicism about the War. It also demonstrates clearly how an apparently trivial episode of everyday life can be turned by him into effective satire. As he lay relaxing in the grounds of Somerville College he had noticed a tall, well-preserved man pushing his rather sallow and sulky son across the lawn in a long, wheeled bed. The son had lost a leg and the father appeared all solicitude, but Sassoon suspected that they had not got on well together before the War. From this fleeting impression he builds up a bitter picture of mutual loathing and distrust:

> ... I wheel him slowly out in his long bed, while nurses
> watch my stooping tenderness;
> then he smiles up at me, shifting his head: and what's
> between us there they never guess.
>
> For when my boy gets well and finds his legs, and the War
> ends with 'no one quite the same',

> We shall renew – as sure as eggs are eggs, – our bitter
> feud: but he'll be walking lame.[2]

'The Father', with its condensed narrative, colloquial language and deliberately simple stanza and rhyme scheme, is as effective in its own way as others Sassoon allowed to be published. The reason it remained unpublished was almost certainly its challenging of one of the most cherished of ideals, particularly in wartime – family loyalty.

By the time Sassoon sent Dent 'The Father', he had already completed the poem he dedicated to Edward Marsh, 'Stretcher Case'. A day later, in full flow, he finished a third poem, 'Christ and the Soldier'. Described by Sassoon himself as an 'ambitious failure',[3] this remained unpublished until Dame Felicitas Corrigan included it in her spiritual biography of Sassoon, together with his retrospective comments.[4] He had intended it to be a commentary on the mental condition of most front-line soldiers, himself included, 'for whom a roadside Calvary was merely a reminder of the inability of religion to co-operate with the carnage and catastrophe they experienced'. As far as he could remember, no one at the Front had ever talked to him about religion. In its last verse a disconsolate soldier finally abandons his attempt to find comfort in the crucified Christ-figure:

> 'Lord Jesus, ain't you got no more to say?'
> Bowed hung that head below the crown of thorns.
> The soldier shifted and picked up his pack,
> And slung his gun, and stumbled on his way.
> 'O God', he groaned, 'why ever was I born?'
> The battle boomed, and no reply came back.

The ironic play between the suffering and wounds of Christ and those of soldiers at the Front, together with blasphemous and irreverent phrases like 'O Christ Almighty, stop this bleeding fight' ensured that, even if Sassoon had decided to allow publication, it would not have been easy.

Two more poems followed in quick succession, 'The One-Legged Man' and 'The Hero'. Both pieces were to become very popular with reviewers, each epitomizing in its own way Sassoon's satiric method at its most effective. In both Sassoon almost gleefully set out to provide 'a thoroughly caddish antidote to the glorification of "the supreme sacrifice" and such like prevalent phrases'.[5] In order to do this he had deliberately chosen two deeply ironic situations. In 'The One-Legged Man' a badly wounded soldier, instead of raging against the loss of a leg, is grateful for the amputation which restores him to safety. In 'The Hero', where even the title is heavily ironic, a 'brother officer giv[es] a white-haired mother [a] fictitious account of her cold-footed son's death at the front'. In both poems the mini-drama is played out rapidly in only three verses, though 'The Hero' has a more discursive six-line stanza, and rhyme forms an important part of the satiric thrust. The one-legged man, having come home to what is recognizably Sassoon's own Kentish Weald, seems delighted with life, rather oddly so in view of his amputation:

> And he'd come home again to find it more
> Desirable than ever it was before.
> How right it seemed that he should reach the span
> Of comfortable years allowed to man!   (*CP*, p. 48)

In the last verse the savage meaning, anticipated in the title, becomes all too clear:

> Splendid to eat and sleep and choose a wife,
> Safe with his wound, a citizen of life.
> He hobbled blithely though the garden gate,
> And thought: 'Thank God they had to amputate!'

The use of direct speech and, in particular, the careful choice of diction also figure prominently in the second of these two pieces, 'The Hero'. The poem opens with the poor old Mother's quavering words, 'Jack fell as he'd have wished ...', 'The Colonel writes so nicely...', 'We mothers are so proud/ Of our dead soldiers'. These phrases are then contrasted in the following two verses with the thoughts of the brother officer as he thankfully escapes, his duty done:

> Quietly the Brother Officer went out.
> He'd told the poor old dear some gallant lies
> That she would nourish all her days, no doubt.
> For while he coughed and mumbled, her weak eyes
> Had shone with gentle triumph, brimmed with joy,
> Because he'd been so brave, her glorious boy.
>
> He thought how 'Jack', cold-footed, useless swine,
> Had panicked down the trench that night the mine
> Went up at Wicked Corner; how he'd tried
> To get sent home, and how, at last, he died,
> Blown to small bits. And no one seemed to care
> Except that lonely woman with white hair.   (*CP*, p. 29)

Sassoon came to feel later that there was something rather dubious about the pleasure he derived from perfecting poems based on other people's suffering. At the time, however, he felt it was his duty to disturb civilian complacency, knowing that the average Englishman would hate this poem precisely because it set out to destroy the myths built up in wartime for the protection of civilians' peace of mind. When 'The Hero' first appeared in the *Cambridge Magazine* on 18 November 1916, he would not therefore have been surprised to find an irate reader by the name of Charles Geake writing in to say that 'at least one Englishman [was] pained not to say disgusted by the poem'.

Both poems seemed to Sassoon to resemble satiric drawings designed to shock with deliberately crude lines. Just as he would later come to find Hardy's *Satires* 'unworthy of his greatness', so he would reach the conclusion that his own two pieces were too purely savage. They seemed to him to lack the graphic sincerity of a poem such as 'Died of Wounds'.[6]

Sassoon denied that 'The Hero' was based on anyone he had known, but both 'The Road' and 'Died of Wounds', probably completed during the same period, were entirely autobiographical. 'The Road' differs markedly from other poems at this time. Its largely descriptive account of the road up to Mametz, while starkly realistic, reveals a more tender, less ironic side to Sassoon, which he would develop later in such poems as 'Break of Day' and 'Prelude: the Troops':

> You in the bomb-scorched kilt, poor sprawling Jock,
> You tottered here and fell, and stumbled on,
> Half-dazed for want of sleep. No dreams would mock
> Your reeling brain with comforts lost and gone
> ...
> Too tired for thoughts of home and love and ease,
> The road would serve you well enough for bed.   (*CP*, p. 32)

It is likely that Sassoon wrote most of these poems during his first week in hospital, when he was confined to the grounds of Somerville College. Once allowed out, he began to explore the city, but quickly began to want company. He was, therefore, delighted when Robbie Ross telegraphed his intention of visiting him. But when he saw the dapper, little man in his light grey suit, jaunty black hat and ebony cane approaching him across the College lawn, he was concerned to note how exhausted he looked. Always somewhat careworn for his age, Ross's face was already reflecting further harassment from the implacable Lord Alfred Douglas, who was mounting yet another campaign against Oscar Wilde's staunchest friend. In spite of this Ross's gaiety appeared undiminished and together they planned the afternoon's outing.

According to *Siegfried's Journey*, when Robbie asked where Sassoon would like to go, he mentioned Lady Ottoline Morrell who lived somewhere near Oxford. 'To Victory', the poem which had first attracted Ottoline's attention to Sassoon when it was published anonymously in *The Times*, had appeared nearly seven months earlier on 15 January. Since then Sassoon had paid a number of visits to the man who had revealed his identity to Ottoline, Edmund Gosse, as well as exchanging several gifts and further letters with the mistress of Garsington. Gosse would have told him of Ottoline's well-known position as half-sister of the Duke of Portland, wife of a Liberal M.P. who had taken an extreme pacifist line and a lavish patroness of writers and painters, even if Sassoon had not already heard of it from other sources. (Both Ross and Marsh knew her well.) It is also unlikely that Ottoline, who was very conscious of her position, would not herself have made Sassoon aware of her credentials. Of course, Sassoon's version, that he still believed her to be 'a romantic-minded young lady living in the depths of the country', makes for a better story, but it does alert the reader to the dangers of accepting all his autobiographical writings literally.

In essence, however, Sassoon was right to cast Ottoline Morrell as a romantic-minded young lady. Even though she was already in her forty-fourth year when they met (and thirteen years older than the poet), her sprawling handwriting, 'an arabesque of dots and flourishes' and, even more, her high-flown idealism expressed in gushing language, seemed more appropriate to a less mature woman. Nevertheless he jumped at Robbie's suggestion of a visit to this exotic being.

Sassoon's first view of Ottoline's country retreat, Garsington Manor, only confirmed his romantic impression of her. From the moment they arrived at the tall wrought-iron gates and stood in the shadow of some lofty elms, he felt that he was in enchanted and enchanting territory. Within the gates was a green forecourt, flanked on either side by high yew hedges, and across it a paved path which led to the mellow Tudor manor house. On this first occasion he was to see only the Monastery studio, where the Hon. Dorothy Brett[7] was painting Ottoline's portrait, and the celebrated Italianate gardens where the unexpected guests were invited to have tea with their hostess and her husband, Philip. Later he would discover the charms of the house itself, which was a testimony to Ottoline's strongest gift, her innate decorative flair and tact.

Ottoline's decorative abilities also revealed themselves dramatically in her dress, as Sassoon's first meeting with her confirmed. Nothing could more solidly have reinforced his initial diagnosis of romanticism than her costume of voluminous pale-pink Turkish trousers, orange tunic and, to top her already striking six-foot figure, purple hat on purple hair. (Sassoon claimed that his first sight of her was of the aforesaid baggy pink trousers coming backwards down the studio loft-ladder.) On this occasion she had the excuse of sitting for her portrait, but she had always a tendency towards theatrical dress, an inclination which was to cause the conventional Sassoon acute embarrassment at times. It may have accounted partly for his shyness at their first meeting.

It was perhaps his endearing diffidence which attracted Ottoline, who was already half-inclined to fall in love with the next handsome young man she met, since her long affair with the philosopher, Bertrand Russell, and shorter one with the painter, Henry Lamb, among others, were more or less over. Her private papers show that she fell deeply in love with Sassoon and there is more than a hint of infatuation in her published account of their first meeting:

While he and Philip and Robbie Ross were talking I watched him. He sat up very erect and turned his head in a peculiar stiff movement to one side. Although he talked a good deal he had a trick of hesitating over his sentences as if he were shy, but still he was full of humour and laughed and was gay, always keeping his head erect and looking down, Perhaps it was his way of turning his head, and the lean face with green hazel eyes, his ears large and rather protruding, and the nose with the wide nostrils, that was not exactly *farouche* but he seemed very shy and reserved, he was more *sauvage*; and, as I looked at his full face I said to myself, 'He could be cruel'.[8]

Ottoline found Sassoon, unlike many of her more intellectual friends, 'sympathetic and wonderfully intimate' to her and was intensely moved at meeting someone whose thoughts seemed so akin to her own, 'simple, yet imaginative'.[9] While Sassoon might have agreed with her diagnosis of him as more imaginative than intellectual, he would certainly have been nervous had he read the frustrated longing which concluded it, that someone would 'enter into that chamber of my being whence springs the fountain of romance, where a strange and magical coloured light played upon the intruder'. It was a situation which was to cause her a great deal of pain, wholly unintentional on Sassoon's part. Though he knew of Ottoline's reputation as a 'man-hunter' (she was nicknamed 'Lady Utterly Immoral' by unkind people), it was some time before he suspected that she had designs on him. Since he had, from the start, made it clear that he was fonder of men than women and had first appeared in the company of a well-known homosexual, Ross, it was not an unreasonable assumption. When he accepted Ottoline's invitation to visit Garsington for a stay in September, therefore, he did so in all innocence. For him their bond was poetry and things spiritual; for Ottoline things spiritual had a way of leading on to things physical.

At their first meeting, however, none of these complications had become apparent and Sassoon thoroughly enjoyed his visit to Garsington. He also enjoyed another outing, this time alone, to meet his Uncle Hamo at Burford on 11 August. Sassoon appreciated seeing his simple, unpretentious uncle as much as, if not more than, the exotic chatelaine of Garsington. Sitting in the dilatory train which took him from Oxford to Shipton and then in the even slower horse-bus which completed the twelve miles to Burford, Sassoon felt such serenity was worth all the sacrifices demanded at the Front. The ripe harvest fields, the little stone bridge over the Windrush, Burford's steep street of grey houses and the quaint old inn where his uncle greeted him seemed like a welcome home, so completely different was it from France.

Under such tranquillizing effects, Sassoon's nagging doubts about the War vanished. He enjoyed Uncle Hamo's quiet pride in his nephew's M.C. and relished the one or two local 'characters' he was taken to meet. However, when he was finally led up the steep little street for tea with a local dignitary, Mr Horniman, his doubts began to return.[10] He could not help remembering the men he had left behind on the Somme. Yet he felt that it would have been quite impossible to convey the reality of that carnage to his uncle and his charming old friend. Exposed to the sufferings not only of himself but more particularly of others on the Somme, Sassoon found himself resenting their patriotic suppression of the unpleasant aspects of war, in a way which was new to him. His friendship with Ross, who was recklessly critical of the handling of the War, had shown Sassoon that there were civilians capable of confronting the unpalatable truths about it. It was mainly due to Ross's encouragement that he had started to write candidly about them. Now, in the gentle environment of the sleepy little Oxfordshire village in the company of his well-meaning uncle and friend, he felt an urge to go even further. It was another step towards his public protest.

The most immediate results of his fresh dissatisfaction were three more poems underlining the distance between civilian perceptions of life at the Front and the reality of it, all of them unpublished in his lifetime. The first two emphasize the fact that his sympathies were no longer confined to his own side. 'For England' contrasts the miserable end of an English soldier – 'something smashed his neck; he choked and swore' – with the interpretation his civilian relations place upon it – 'A glorious end; killed in the big attack./ His relatives who thought him such a bore,/ Grew pale with grief and dressed themselves in black.'[11] 'The Stunt' describes the unfeeling slaughter of some German soldiers by a gung-ho Englishman who receives a medal for his callousness: ' "How splendid. O how splendid!" his relations said,/ But what the weeping Saxons said I do not know.'[12] There is also an ironic dig at the idea that 'God is on our side', for it is 'Gentle Jesus' who keeps the Englishman safe while he slaughters the Germans. In the third piece, 'Via Crucis', Christianity is again invoked to suggest that, whilst Christ's suffering and death had at least a purpose, the soldier's equally agonizing lot has not even that with which to dignify it:

> Mangling crumps and bullets through the brain,
> Jesus never guessed them when He died.
> Jesus had a purpose for His pain,
> Ay, like abject beasts we shed our blood,
> Often asking if we die in vain.
> Gloom conceals us in a soaking sack –
> Mud and rain.[13]

Sassoon himself argued, only half-jokingly, that a great deal of his bile arose literally from leading an unhealthy life. Once away from the temptation to over-indulge in food and drink, and under the strict régime of daily physical exertion imposed on him in France, his doubts generally subsided. 'It is impossible to remain cynical when one's liver insists on being utterly in order,' he wrote to Dent; 'only heavy luncheons in London Clubs can produce the genuine ironic vein of the critical pacifist'.[14] While this is clearly an oversimplification, it is true that he needed strenuous physical activity to keep him cheerful. Since Oxford offered him the possibility of neither horse riding, golf nor cricket and as his health rapidly returned, he took to a new sport, canoeing. It demanded all his formidable energy, for the River Cherwell, where he spent most of his afternoons during his last week of convalescence, had been sadly neglected during the War and was full of weeds. Reaching Water Eaton, only a few miles upriver, seemed to him convincing proof that he was fit enough to be discharged from hospital. While his doctors approached the question in a rather more scientific fashion, they came to the same conclusion and by 18 August he was back home.

One of the first things Sassoon did when he arrived at Weirleigh was to incorporate his idyllic days on the Cherwell into a striking poem, which Wilfred Owen was to call 'a perfect piece of art'. Based also on his memory of hospital at Amiens, 'The Death-Bed' is a new departure for Sassoon. Abandoning heavy satire for a method closer to his more lyrical early war poems, he nevertheless does not revert to his earlier glorification of war. Perhaps he felt, as he had with 'Died of Wounds', that graphic sincerity could sometimes be more effective than dextrous sarcasm.

The subject, the death of an innocent young soldier, is certainly very similar to 'Died of Wounds', though the narrator's pity is far more overt in 'The Death-Bed'. Much of the effect is achieved through shifts in the point of view. The first six stanzas are an imaginative reconstruction of the dying soldier's gradual descent into the waters of oblivion, expressed appropriately through imagery taken from Sassoon's days on the Oxfordshire river:

> ... Someone was holding water to his mouth.
> He swallowed, unresisting, moaned and dropped
> Through crimson gloom to darkness; and forgot
> The opiate throb and ache that was his wound.
> Water – calm, sliding green above the weir.
> Water – a sky-lit alley for his boat,
> Bird-voiced, and bordered with reflected flowers
> And shaken lines of summer; drifting down,
> He dipped contented oars, and sighed, and slept. ...   (*CP*, p. 34)

In the seventh verse the narrator steps forward and openly invites compassion for this young man who symbolizes all the unnecessary loss of life in war, drawing the reader directly into the drama:

> Light many lamps and gather round his bed.
> Lend him your eyes, warm blood and will to live,
> Speak to him; rouse him; you may save him yet.
> He's young; he hated War; how should he die
> When cruel old campaigners win safe through?

In the eighth and final stanza the point of view shifts again:

But death replied: 'I choose him.' So he went,
And there was silence in the summer night;
Silence and safety; and the veils of sleep.
Then far away, the thudding of the guns.

This less savage but still heartfelt condemnation of the War was refused, without comment, by the *Westminster Review*, as 'In the Pink' had been six months earlier.

'The Death-Bed' concluded Sassoon's compulsive need to put his Somme experiences into verse, at least for the time being, and he spent most of his stay at Weirleigh mooning about in the overgrown garden and neglected stables. His mother, still unreconciled to Hamo's death ten months earlier, was indifferent company and he was, therefore, guiltily relieved when Graves's promised invitation to Harlech materialized.

*

Graves travelled up to Harlech on 26 August with his sister and Sassoon followed on 29 August. He and his dog Topper, an affectionate little fox-terrier of whom he was very fond, were met at Harlech station by Robert and his younger brother, Charles. Both Sassoon and his dog made a good impression on the Graves clan, particularly on Robert's father, who described Sassoon in his diary as 'a fine, tall manly modest fellow'.[15] Everyone enjoyed his stories which according to Robert's youngest brother, John, were extremely humorous and related in 'a nervous but entrancing way'.[16] The whole fortnight at Harlech went well. Almost fully recovered physically, Sassoon enjoyed numerous games of golf with Charles Graves and went on several outings into the beautiful surrounding hills with the family. Most of his time, however, was spent with Robert in his little cottage, Gwuthdy Bach. It was here they carried out the main purpose of their visit, to work on their planned joint publication together.

They were as close as Wordsworth and Coleridge in the support and help they gave each other. Both perfectionists in their different ways, they had already started suggesting emendations to each other's work, mainly in letters. One of the guiding principles of this collaboration, Graves claimed, was that they should define war 'by making contrasted definitions of peace'.[17] With Sassoon it was hunting, nature, music and pastoral scenes, with Graves it was children. Having already considered Marsh's copious comments, they aimed to have a manuscript ready for Ross's inspection by the middle of September, with a view to publication later in the year.

Before travelling to London to see Ross, however, they seem to have stopped off in Oxford for a night or two with the Morrells at Garsington, though the date of their stay is uncertain.[18] Whenever the visit occurred it made a deep impression on Sassoon, who devotes five pages of his autobiography to it.[19] Though he had seen Ottoline at least once since his introduction to her by Ross, he had not previously been inside her house. When at last he did so his imagination was stirred by its 'sumptuous homeliness'.[20] It was the combination of its ancient charm and irregularity, moderate proportions and Ottoline's exotic decoration which struck not only him but most of those who saw it. Many have commented on the panelled drawing room painted a rich lacquer red and furnished with fine Italian furniture, and he was no exception. He had a general impression of faded silks and velvets, of dusty browns and purples tinged with glints of tarnished gold from coffers and cabinets.

It was an effect Ottoline had consciously cultivated in her house and herself, as though both had stepped out of the Renaissance. While Sassoon remained nervous about being seen with a walking period piece outside her setting, inside it he fully appreciated the effect. As Ottoline sat embroidering of an evening in a Velasquez-like gown of rich brocade, or as he himself sat reading the *Oxford Book of English Verse*, given him by his hostess, in his mullion-windowed room with its four-poster bed, he felt the instinctive tact and harmony of his surroundings. It was an escape, of a kind he had frequently enjoyed in his pre-war existence, into a peaceful and gracious past.

However much of a refuge Garsington seemed, it did not allow Sassoon to escape thinking about the War as he had hoped. Philip Morrell's pacifist views were shared by his wife and they had filled Garsington and its out-buildings with conscientious objectors. Since farm-work was accepted as a legitimate alternative to fighting, they had been able to offer their house and farm as a haven for a number of friends. Many were writers or artists, the more famous including Bertrand Russell, the critic John Middleton Murry and the painter Mark Gertler. (Not surprisingly the farm was not run very efficiently and many of the intellectuals appeared rather ungrateful for the escape route so generously offered them.)

When the day's work was over and the pacifists came in for an evening by the fire, Sassoon was exposed to an entirely different view of the War from any previously offered him, except by Ross. At the Front he had himself been highly critical of its handling, but he had never before heard the Government criticized so roundly and so articulately. Philip Morrell's parliamentary connection gave him an insider's authority and this lent weight to his claim that the Germans had already made tentative peace overtures through neutral channels, which had been turned down. While it suited Sassoon to believe that the soldiers had real cause for dissatisfaction, it was nevertheless a genuine revelation to him and one which contributed significantly to his eventual public protest. It was one thing to sacrifice men idealistically in a necessary war, but quite another to continue to do so for cynical, self-serving reasons. From being a largely emotional reaction to his own and others' gruelling experiences, his dissatisfaction began to acquire an intellectual basis. Ottoline herself, unlike the majority of his other friends, was to encourage Sassoon's impulse to protest.

Apart from his nervousness about Ottoline's amorous intentions, Sassoon also realized, after long talks with her, that she was altogether too intense and perhaps too humourless for his taste. Reading her lofty aspirations in the privacy

1. Siegfried Sassoon, *c.* 1916. (photo © Getty Images)

2. SS's great-grandfather, David Sassoon, with three of his eight sons (*l.* to *r.*): Elias, Abdullah and SS's grandfather, Sassoon David ('S.D.'), the first member of the family to wear Western dress.

3. SS's maternal grandfather, Thomas Thornycroft.

4. SS's maternal grandmother, Mary Thornycroft, seated in the drawing-room at Weirleigh.

5. The earliest photograph of SS, *c.* 1888.

6. SS's paternal aunt Rachel Beer (*née* Sassoon).

7. SS's great-aunt Mozelle, the youngest child of David Sassoon.

8. SS's uncle, Hamo Thornycroft, and his fiancée, Agatha Cox, taken at John Thornycroft's house at Bembridge, Isle of Wight, *c.* 1884.

9. Theresa Sassoon and (*l.* to *r.*): SS, Hamo, and Michael 'artistically' posed, *c.* 1800.

10. Alfred Sassoon shortly before his death at thirty-four, with (*l.* to *r.*): Michael, SS and Hamo at Eastbourne.

11. Tom Richardson ('Dixon' of *Memoirs of a Fox-Hunting Man*) in front of the stables where he and his family also lived at Weirleigh.

12. (*l.* to *r.*): Hamo and SS up to no good in the garden at Weirleigh, inscribed on verso 'S.S. & Hamo, 1899 (taken by C.H. Hamilton)'.

13. The village carrier, Tom Homewood ('John Homeward' of *Memoirs of a Fox-Hunting Man*).

14. Matfield cricket team: back row (*l.* to *r.*): Alec Read – unknown – Mr Moon – Tom Richardson – Richard Marchant – William Larkin – Sam Butler, front row: 'Scunger' Austin – unknown – Tom Homewood – SS – unknown – Harry Fuller – Ned Farris.

15. Weirleigh, bereft of its 'tower'.

16. SS (*centre, holding cricket ball*) at the New Beacon, *c.* 1901.

17. SS and his prizewinning horse 'Cockbird', April 1911. (Courtesy of the late Mrs Leo Sassoon)

18. SS on 'Rubicon', who came second in the Sussex Heavyweight Point-to-point in 1912.

19. Norman Loder (*centre*), Master of the Atherstone Hunt at Measham, Leicestershire, in March 1914, while SS was staying with him at Witherley.

20. Edmund Gosse, SS's first patron. (Courtesy Miss Jennifer Gosse)

21. Edward Marsh, 1912, another important patron.

22. SS at the Army School, Flixécourt, May 1916.

23. David Cuthbert Thomas ('Dick Tiltwood of *Memoirs of a Fox-Hunting Man*), *c*. July 1915.

24. Robert Ross, 'friend of friends', 1916. (Courtesy Robert Baldwin Robertson)

25. Lady Ottoline Morrell from Robert Gathorne-Hardy's photograph album. (Courtesy Lady Anne Hill)

26. 'Dame' Nellie Burton with 'Siegfried'.

27. Sydney Carlyle Cockerell, SS's 'bearded and spectacled magician'.

28. Officer Cadet Wilfred Owen, 1916.

29. Robert von Ranke Graves, taken near the time he met SS in November 1915. (Courtesy William Reese)

30. Captain W.H.R. Rivers, R.A.M.C.

31. Vivian de Sola Pinto, on sick leave, Hampstead Heath, 1917.

32. John Masefield in a photograph inscribed 'for Siegfried Sassoon from John Masefield. Nov. 9, 1918'.

33. Lennel House, Coldstream, as it was when Sassoon was there. (Courtesy Miss Grizel Kennedy)

34. SS at Garsington in the mid-1920s, photographed by Robert Gathorne-Hardy.

35. Gabriel Atkin suffering from the effects of Armistice celebrations (self-caricature).

36. 'Enrico' Festing-Jones and 'Theo' Bartholomew.

37. Walter de la Mare in the 1920s.

38. Beverley Nichols in his early twenties.

39. Sacheverell (*l*.) and Osbert (*r*.) being rowed by their sister Edith, from SS's series of caricatures of the Sitwells.

40. The 'Thursdayers': standing (*l.* to *r.*): Mark Gertler, Prof. A.S. Fulton, Walter Turner, Herbert Milne; seated: Ralph Hodgson, S.S. Koteliansky, J.W.N. Sullivan.

41. Edmund Blunden at Garsington Manor in 1924.

42. T.E. Lawrence, alias Aircraftsman Shaw, *c.* 1922.

43. Thomas Hardy shortly before his death in 1928.

44. Frank Schuster (*far right*) at the White Cloud with (*l.* to *r.*): Roger Fry, Julian Sampson and Robert Nichols.

45. Leslie George Wylde ('Anzie'), as a Captain in the Canterbury Regiment of the ANZAC forces, *c.* 1915.

46. Sir Edward Elgar in relaxed mood at the Long White Cloud.

47. Wendela Boreel's etching of SS, mid-1920s.

48. Prince Philipp of Hesse in the early 1920s.

49. 'Bob' Gathorne-Hardy in the early 1920s.

50. SS and Glen Byam Shaw at the home of Ellen Terry (seated), c. 1926/7, shortly before her death.

51. The New Menin Gate Memorial, shortly after its opening by Field-Marshal Lord Plumer in June 1927.

of his perfect bedroom, he seems to have found what he calls those 'touchingly amateurish pages' a little comic, in spite of their unquestionable sincerity.[21] He was to become genuinely fond of Ottoline, once she had accepted him as a comrade rather than a potential lover. The more he saw of her the more he came to appreciate her genuine desire to share the imaginative life of her artistic friends and to promote it whenever possible. Unlike D.H. Lawrence, Aldous Huxley, Osbert Sitwell and others, he resisted the temptation to caricature such an easy target in his work. In fact, he was unintentionally to hurt Ottoline by not alluding to her at all in *Infantry Officer*, though he would describe her at length in his official autobiography. Apart from a few mild jokes he limited his criticism to the observation that she was 'in some ways an idealist, essentially generous but deficient in constructive comprehension of the problems which she contemplated with such intensity. At that period her idealism was still in the full flush of its immaturity.'[22]

Sassoon is unlikely to have been quite so restrained when he met Ross in London shortly after his first stay at Garsington. He and Graves had to be there for examinations by their respective chest specialists on 13 September. They had already booked rooms with Nellie Burton at 40 Half Moon Street and during their two days there discussed their *Lyrical Ballads* plan with Ross. So involved had they become in the idea of a collaboration that they were very surprised when Ross rejected it outright. Sassoon, he argued, needed a publication of his own and had enough strong poems to warrant one, while Graves, who had only recently put all his worthwhile poetry into *Over the Brazier*, needed more time to build up another collection. Writing to Ross two days after accepting his advice Graves acknowledged its wisdom, but also registered his regret.

Sassoon's letter, if there was one, has not survived, but he was almost certainly excited by the change of plan. He could not have found it entirely easy to accept that his much younger friend had already had a volume of war poems brought out by the publisher who had eventually turned his own poems down, Harold Monro. Private productions brought some satisfaction, but the time had come for wider recognition. It is a measure of his increased confidence that he was at last ready to face public exposure on his own.

Instead, therefore, of working with Graves and Ross, Sassoon found himself working with Ross alone on an initial selection to show first to Gosse, then to the publisher William Heinemann. Gosse's wish that Sassoon should get his early poems out of his system by publishing them persisted and this almost certainly influenced the selection, which was fairly comprehensive, ranging from his early sonnets of 1909 to his most recent war-satires. It was eventually to include poems not even written at the time of submission to Heinemann in late September and was to become, in effect, an early *Selected Poems*.

Directly the selection had been made and dispatched to a typist and after another month's leave had been granted to Sassoon by his chest specialist, he took Graves down to Weirleigh to return his hospitality. What happened next was the cause of one of the more famous literary disputes. It was not the event itself which caused the trouble, but Graves's description of it over thirteen years later in *Goodbye to All That*. His account there is so inaccurate that it is difficult to unravel what actually occurred, particularly since Sassoon omitted the whole incident from his own autobiography, limiting himself to a manuscript note in *Goodbye to All That* to the effect that Graves's remarks were 'unforgivable' and 'almost entirely apocryphal'.[23] The 'almost entirely' does, however, suggest that there was some truth in Graves's version and it is likely that Sassoon himself was suppressing a great deal of painful knowledge about the affair.

It had all started on the evening of Graves's arrival at what he obliquely (and inaccurately) refers to as the house of 'a recently wounded First Battalion friend'.[24] After describing in some detail the way in which the friend's mother (Theresa Sassoon) tried to keep the memory of her dead son alive by preserving his room exactly as it had been, Graves related how he had been continually woken up the first night by sudden rapping noises, followed by sobs, shrieks and laughter which made sleep impossible. His friend explained that it was his mother, who had been reading the spiritualist Sir Oliver Lodge's *Raymond, or Life After Death*, and was trying to get in touch with her dead son. Sassoon himself was to confirm the truth of at least this part of Graves's account and his own irritation with his mother in his diary only four months later.[25] It was not, therefore, what Graves said which angered Sassoon but his disloyalty in retailing such private confidences to the world at large in his characteristically exaggerated and inaccurate fashion.

There was one part of Graves's account which was entirely untrue, however, the claim that he told Sassoon after the first night, 'I'm leaving this place. It's worse than France.'[26] In reality, not only did he stay for nearly another week but he also described Weirleigh to Ross, two days after his arrival there (that is, *after* his disturbed first night) as having 'a congenial atmosphere'.[27] Having accepted Ross's rejection of the *Lyrical Ballads* project, he was attempting to start a prose work, a novel based on his war experiences, and he found Weirleigh the right place for this, despite Mrs Sassoon's nightly vigils.

Though Graves may not have made the remark about Weirleigh being worse than France, that country was very much on both their minds, particularly the 1st RWF's horrifying experiences near Ginchy. Haig, having failed to carry out the third phase of his original Somme plan – to roll up the German Front northwards – had decided to continue his main pressure with his right flank from Guillemont to Bazentin-le-Petit. On his left General Gough aimed to take the Pozières-Thiepval end of the ridge.

As part of one of the three Corps of the Fourth Army chosen to carry out Haig's scheme, the 1st RWF had been involved in bitter fighting throughout August and had moved forward only a few miles from their original position by the end of the month. Their engagement at Delville Wood near Ginchy at the beginning of September was part of a holding operation to prevent the Germans firing into the backs of troops attacking the main objective, Guillemont, which Division after Division had failed to capture. Though the 1st did all that could be expected of it in what – with good reason – became known as 'Devil's Wood' and Guillemont itself was finally taken, the engagement as a whole had been unsuccessful. The Manchesters had failed to take Ginchy, which it would require another week of hard fighting to capture, and the troops, to quote one commentator, were little better than 'compressed cannon-fodder'.[28]

Sassoon's friend and fellow-officer in C Company, Julian Dadd, had been severely wounded in the throat at Ginchy and his last surviving brother, Edmund, killed. Another casualty of Ginchy was the young dark-haired bombing officer, V.F. Newton, described as 'Fernby' in *Infantry Officer*, who died of wounds shortly afterwards. Only two officers out of the whole Battalion had not been hit. Many others had been killed or wounded, leaving the 1st Battalion once more badly depleted.

It seems ironic that, with the knowledge of such bloodshed to fuel his mounting anger against the handling of the war, Sassoon should this same month have brought out another private booklet with the Chiswick Press of the escapist pre-war variety. Of the eleven poems in *Morning-Glory* (a fourteen-page volume on hand-made paper bound in dark-blue) only four – 'To Victory', 'To His Dead Body', 'Brothers' and 'The Dragon and the Undying' – deal with war, and none criticizes it. If anything, they promote the romantic view he had appeared to reject. The remaining seven poems are even more reminiscent of Sassoon's pre-war poetry, though most show a marked improvement in technique. It comes as no surprise to find that at least two of these – 'Wind in the Beechwood' and 'A Poplar and the Moon' – were written during his peaceful interlude at Flixécourt in May.

One poem stands out rather puzzlingly in this collection, 'Ancestors'. Why, it might be asked, has Sassoon chosen this particular moment to reflect on his exotic Jewish forebears? The answer lies possibly in a story related by a descendent of the Ashley Park branch of the family, Jacques Sassoon.[29] He distinctly remembered being told that, when the news of Siegfried's M.C. came through, the Sassoon family broke its long, self-imposed feud with Alfred's widow and invited her son to visit. 'But it was an invitation to tea, not dinner,' Jacques Sassoon pointed out, indicating how suspicious the Sassoons still were of their half-Gentile relative. Though Sassoon himself made no reference to such a visit, he did state later that his only communication from his father's brother, Joseph, was a poem of an assertively patriotic nature in June 1917, which suggests that his uncle felt it necessary to make a point.[30] So that, when Sassoon came to make his public protest only a month after receiving his uncle's poem, he did so in the full knowledge that it would antagonize the closest of his Sassoon relatives. The Sassoons as a whole were far more likely to approve of another family member, Sir Philip Sassoon, who was on the Army's General Staff and took the Establishment view of the War.

'Ancestors' and the other ten poems of *Morning-Glory* were all to be included in Sassoon's next volume and in his *Collected Poems* over thirty years later, suggesting that he was at least as proud of them as of his more celebrated anti-war poems. Certainly they were to be more typical of his poetic output as a whole and the kind of work for which he would prefer to be remembered.

*

At Weirleigh in September 1916, with one collection of poems safely in print and another being typed for Gosse's comments, Sassoon took a short break from poetry, to spend nine days cub-hunting with his old friend Loder's wife, Phyllis. Loder himself was still in France but his job as joint-Master of the Fitzwilliam was being carried out ably by his wife, herself a skilled horsewoman. The contrast with poetry and other mental activities was one Sassoon continued to need throughout his life. He had barely returned from Peterborough on 28 September when he was off again for a week's hunting with the Southdown at Ringmer, followed by a week's golfing at Rye with another old friend, David Ayton. Then he spent a further week with the Southdown Hunt from 17 to 24 November, as though cramming in as much as possible before his leave expired.

These strenuous physical activities, however, did not prevent Sassoon from writing at least eight more poems during the autumn. Spurred on by Heinemann's offer on 1 October to publish a selection of his poetry, he settled down to work at Weirleigh. Having hit on a fruitful vein of satire, he now set about producing more of the same.

The first of these, 'The Tombstone-Maker', is a savage satire on a stonemason who complains about the effect of the War on his 'trade'. Sassoon's language convincingly, if somewhat condescendingly, echoes his uneducated speech. He implies, as in previous poems, that Christianity is fairly meaningless when he has the callous stonemason lean his head against 'a sorrowing angel's breast' in the first verse, and puts pious words into his mouth to underline his hypocrisy in the last, where the narrator concludes mischievously:

> I told him with a sympathetic grin,
> That Germans boil dead soldiers down for fat;
> And he was horrified. 'What shameful sin!
> O sir, that Christian souls should come to that!'   (*CP*, p. 27)

The second poem, 'Two Hundred Years', also written in October 1916, would be included in *Collected Poems*, but was of a rather different kind. Almost certainly a result of reading back over his War diaries, it deals with a less harsh aspect of the conflict, the possibility of the spirits of the dead men surviving, in spite of his dismissal of his mother's Spiritualism.[31]

Unusually, Sassoon wrote his third poem this month during a golfing trip. Apart from his dog Topper, smuggled illicitly into his lodgings at Dormy House, Rye, he was accompanied by a retired Scottish professional, David Ayton, who reminded him strongly of a music-hall comedian, especially when cleaning the ball with his tongue. It may have been his friend's jokey influence which caused Sassoon to produce a piece of doggerel which falls well below his usual standard.

Called simply 'A Ballad', it adopts a deliberately sing-song metre reminiscent of Kipling's *Barrack-Room Ballads* to tell the story of a captain who shot himself in the foot after only a week at the Front and was invalided home. The irony comes predictably in the last line of the last of the three quatrains:

> Now the Captain's at the Depot, lame, but happy as a lark;
> And in billets out in France, the men who knew him tell the story
> Of 'the bloke that 'ad an accident when walking in the dark' –
> While the Captain teaches raw recruits the way to blood and glory.[32]

Sassoon wisely decided not to attempt publication of 'A Ballad' and waited till he was back in London before writing his fourth and last poem that month. It was to prove one of the most popular satires he ever produced. Composed at Ross's house late one night after a long evening in which Ross had been criticizing the Bishop of London, 'They' seemed to Sassoon to write itself. When he showed it to Eddie Marsh, whose taste was still for the more heroic type of war poetry, Marsh had exclaimed 'It's *too* horrible,' but Ross instantly recognized its power. Consisting simply of two six-line stanzas, in which an initial quatrain is followed by a couplet, the form allows Sassoon to maximize the effect of rhyme and to throw emphasis on the most ironic word, especially in the second stanza. As he noted himself in *Siegfried's Journey*, 'it went its wicked way to the twelfth and last line'.[33] His usual device of putting direct speech into the mouths of his characters makes for further irony as the privileged Bishop, with his platitudinous mouthings, is contrasted sharply with the uneducated private soldiers, who relate in a matter-of-fact way the stark results of the Bishop's support of the War. The inadequacy of Christianity and its representatives to deal with the horrors of war emerges with shock effect:

> The Bishop tells us: 'When the boys come back
> They will not be the same; for they'll have fought
> In a just cause: they lead the last attack
> On Anti-Christ: their comrades' blood has bought
> New right to breed an honourable race,
> They have challenged Death and dared him face to face.'
>
> 'We're none of us the same!' the boys reply.
> 'For George lost both his legs; and Bill's stone blind;
> 'Poor Jim's shot through the lungs and like to die;
> 'And Bert's gone syphilitic; you'll not find
> 'A chap that's served that hasn't found *some* change.'
> And the Bishop said: 'The ways of God are strange!'   (*CP*, pp. 23-4)

Sassoon claimed actually to have met the Bishop of London on his return from showing this poem to Marsh, and that the Bishop 'turned a mild shining gaze on me and my M.C.'[34] It is to be hoped that such a good story is true. Even the *Cambridge Magazine*, which readily published the poem on 20 January 1917, found the word 'syphilitic' too bold for the time and omitted it.

In addition to poetry and sport Sassoon managed to fit in a visit to Cambridge in late October, where besides seeing Dent, he met the father of a poet he had grown greatly to admire, Sorley. For both Sassoon and Graves, who had introduced him to Sorley's poetry shortly after the young poet's death at the Battle of Loos in October 1915, Sorley had become a standard of excellence in how to tell the unsentimental truth about the War. When the Somme was at its worst for Sassoon, he had written in his diary: 'I've still got my terrible way to tread before I'm free to sleep with Rupert Brooke and Sorley and all the nameless poets of the war,'[35] as though identifying himself more closely with his fellow-Marlburian.

The visit to Professor Sorley must have gone well, for when Sassoon left he was presented with a collection of Sorley's *Letters from Germany and the Army*, recently edited and privately printed by the professor. Less than two months later, inspired and cheered by the lucidly intelligent and highly entertaining letters, he was to acquire his own copy of Sorley's *Marlborough and Other Poems*, which had gone into a third edition. What he particularly admired about the young poet was that he was 'so ready for all emergencies, so ready to accept the "damnable circumstance of death" – or life'.[36] In the face of yet another trip to the Front he was to find strength in Sorley's philosophical acceptance of death, expressed most vividly for Sassoon in the opening lines of his last poem:

> When you see millions of the mouthless dead
> Across your dreams in pale battalions go,
> Say not soft things as other men have said,
> That you'll remember. For you need not so.[37]

It was a reaction to Brooke and his heroics which Sassoon himself could second. He had come a long way since writing 'Absolution'.

The most intriguing reference to Sorley occurs in Graves's letter to Sassoon of May 1916, which reveals more about the two living poets than the dead one. When Sassoon met another Marlburian, Marcus Goodall, that month at Flixécourt, Graves asked him what Goodall had said about Sorley: '... and was he "so"?' (that is to say homosexual). As Sorley's poetry contained no conventional love-lyrics by the age of twenty, Graves concluded that he must be. Clearly he wished to include his favourite poet in a category to which both he and Sassoon assigned themselves at that time. In fact, Sorley, in his brief life, had shown convincing proof that he was attracted by women, but it is interesting to see Graves's attempts to cast him otherwise.

Professor Sorley and Dent were not the only people Sassoon visited in his last precious weeks of leave. Knowing that his Medical Board was coming up on the 17 or 18 November and that it would almost certainly find him fit, he squeezed in a visit to his great-aunt Mozelle in Hove, as well as several more stays with Ross at 40 Half Moon Street. His great-aunt was still very sprightly at sixty-one and he enjoyed seeing her sufficiently to want to return fairly often after the War.

Much as Sassoon enjoyed his visit to Aunt Mozelle at the seaside, he undoubtedly preferred staying at 40 Half Moon Street. By 31 October, when he paid the second visit of his leave there, Ross's lodgings had become his London base and Nellie Burton would increasingly be asked to reserve rooms for him there. Since he enjoyed the company of both Ross and Burton, he found it far more congenial to stay with them than at the more impersonal Royal Societies Club on the other side of Piccadilly. He was also getting to know a number of Ross's friends, in particular Roderick Meiklejohn. Not quite a father-figure, Meiklejohn became more like an indulgent uncle to Sassoon. Barely ten years his senior, he was outwardly far more sober than the irrepressible and often deliberately outrageous Ross. (Sassoon confessed to finding Meiklejohn's company 'slightly dreary', like 'talking to the family solicitor'.)[38]

Meiklejohn's career, first at St Paul's School, then Oxford and finally in the Civil Service was, like most things about him, eminently respectable. By the time Sassoon met him in 1916 he had been Private Secretary to such elevated figures as Sir Edward Hamilton, the Duke of Devonshire and Asquith, a sign of his trustworthiness, ability and discretion. Though not a practitioner of the arts, Meiklejohn was a connoisseur and something of a patron to the younger men he adopted and discreetly adored.

At one of his first dinners with Meiklejohn, on 16 November 1916, Sassoon would almost certainly have discussed with him his reluctance to return to France. No friend of Ross's could possibly have been completely in sympathy with the handling of the War. Sassoon was expecting his final Medical Board the following day and already dreading the inevitable result. As he had done with many other unpleasant experiences in wartime, however, he managed to turn the occasion to positive use. For his visit to the Medical Board at Caxton Hall, Westminster, gave him material for both a poem and an entertaining prose passage in *Infantry Officer*.[39] The poem, written soon after the event, makes full use of the macabre humour of a notice in the desolate waiting-room, advising amputees on how to get government replacement limbs free of charge, though the irony is a little laboured. Sassoon nicknames his thinly-disguised self 'Captain Croesus', either because he is rich in the full complement of limbs and health, or with an allusion to the wealth implied in the name Sassoon; the Colonel who sends young officers out to risk their lives or possible amputation is, not very subtly, called 'Sawbones'; and the poem's title, 'Arms and the Man', is almost certainly an ironic reference to the famous opening lines of Virgil's *Aeneid*:

> ... The waiting-room was dark and bare.
> He eyed a neat-framed notice there

Above the fireplace hung to show
Disabled heroes where to go,

For arms and legs; with scale of price,
And words of dignified advice
How officers could get them free ...   (*CP*, pp. 27-8)

Conscious of the need to add to his collection before the final choice was made and also before his leave expired, Sassoon wrote three more poems in November. The first of these, 'Decorated', hinges on the irony of rewarding soldiers for 'murdering' other soldiers, but, as Sassoon told Dent, was '*not* up to the usual form'.[40] The other two are more interesting, since both show a fluctuation in feelings which had become almost a commonplace for Sassoon by this time. After a brief description of the 'fair songs' of his pre-war days, the poet resolves to seek God, whom he believes to be 'in the strife', and in the third and final stanza concludes:

I walk the secret way
With anger in my brain
O music through my clay,
When will you sound again?   (*CP*, p. 15)

One critic has seen the phrase 'The secret way' as a reference to 'the life of Sassoon the homosexual artist'.[41] It is, however, more likely to refer to his sense of being separated from ordinary men by his poetic vocation and his feelings about the War, since a diary entry written two months after the poem reads: 'When I go out again I will be mad as ever. And the others will laugh at my secret frenzy.'[42] His use of the word 'secret' in a rather similar poem less than a month later also suggests that it is not a coded reference to homosexuality. 'Secret Music', as it is called, uses the word 'secret' to refer again to his sense of being different because of his poetic vocation and attitude towards the War:

I keep such music in my brain
No din this side of death can quell;
Glory exulting over pain,
And beauty, garlanded in hell.   (*CP*, p. 32)

Both 'A Mystic as Poet' and 'Secret Music' were composed in sudden surges of renewed idealism which did not last long. In Sassoon's third and last poem, written in November, 'The Poet as Hero', he describes a very different mood. From the ironic use of the word 'hero' in the title onwards, this poem seems genuinely engaged with its subject, that is, the poet's reasons for rejecting his former chivalric values for a harsher, less beautiful truth. It is a process which Yeats had already described in similar terms in 'All Things Can Tempt Me', though it is doubtful that Sassoon knew this when he came to write his own. What adds vigour to Sassoon's treatment is the easy, conversational tone of his reply to an imaginary companion who has questioned his change from 'silly sweetness' to 'an ugly cry'. Using an extended metaphor from Arthurian legend (as he had in 'The Glory' in January 1916) the poet explains in the final sestet of this sonnet:

> But now I've said good-bye to Galahad,
> And am no more the knight of dreams and show:
> For lust and senseless hatred make me glad,
> And my killed friends are with me where I go.
> Wound for red wound I burn to smite their wrongs;
> And there is absolution in my songs.[43]

The 'absolution' of the last line will come not through sacrificing his life for his country, as in the earlier poem of that title, but in telling the grim truth about war in his poetry.

Sassoon was to make another attempt to describe his change of poetic technique in 'Conscripts'. Written at the end of two months spent training raw recruits for France at Litherland Depot in early 1917, it uses the metaphor of army conscripts to show how inadequate his former lush descriptiveness has proved in the face of war's harsh realities. In a striking opening to the poem, the narrator addresses his former poetic attitudes as though he were shouting at a bunch of clumsy conscripts on the barrack square:

> 'Fall in, that awkward squad, and strike no more
> Attractive attitudes! Dress by the right!
> The luminous rich colours that you wore
> Have changed to hueless khaki in the night.
> Magic? What's magic got to do with you?
> There's no such thing! Blood's red, and skies are blue.'
>
> (*CP*, pp. 30-1)

In the fourth of the five stanzas, having drilled and lectured his bored conscripts, the narrator ships them off to France:

> Where most of those I'd loved too well got killed.
> Rapture and pale Enchantment and Romance,
> And many a sickly, slender lord who'd filled
> My soul long since with lutanies of sin,
> Went home, because they couldn't stand the din.   (*CP*, p. 31)

Sassoon was amazed, but also amused, when Gosse, who was Librarian at the House of Lords, took his reference to 'many a sickly lord' literally and reprimanded him.[44] Sassoon thought that he had made his meaning quite clear in the last verse, where he praises the 'kind, common' techniques that he had previously despised, but Gosse failed to grasp his metaphorical intent and had to be placated. The lines, Sassoon explained, were meant 'as a joke at the expense of his own pre-war precocities', otherwise he would never have used such clichés as 'lutanies of sin'.[45]

*

Sassoon's last weeks of freedom were spent hunting at Ringmer from 17 to 24 November, followed by a few more days in London, and he was back at the RWF Litherland depot by 2 December. His return to the bleak camp was made easier by Graves who had been there for nearly a fortnight. It was not just the knowledge of Graves's presence, however, that reconciled Sassoon to Litherland. Graves had offered another incentive – Bobbie Hanmer. He had found the young officer just as enchanting as Sassoon had and not nearly as 'conventional' as he had expected, 'only rather charmingly ignorant on certain subjects'.[46] To tempt Sassoon further he told him that he could share a hut with Bobbie, even if it meant Graves having to give up his own place for him. A further attraction was the presence of several old friends from the 1st Battalion, 'Bill' Adams and C.D. Morgan among them, and 'a jolly nice crowd of other folk including Hubert Jones the bloke who plays piano quite pleasantly'.[47]

Beside being welcomed by old friends at Litherland, Sassoon was given a much more respectful reception by those in charge than on his first arrival. With his prestigious purple and white M.C. ribbon and his reputation for daring, he seemed a very different man from the one who had entered the Camp so diffidently in May 1915. His confidence was increased by the conviction that he had also made progress as a poet and was about to have his first important book published by a well-known house.

None of this helped very much when it came to the boredom of camp life. His duties were light and unexacting, but constant interruptions by well-meaning friends made it almost impossible to use his plentiful free time in the way he wanted, writing poetry. A less frustrating way of passing time till the inevitable call to France came lay in sport. Sassoon's weekends and some of his afternoons were, consequently, spent either at Formby Golf Club, or hunting with the Cheshire Hounds with a local officer, Brocklebank. Though he still enjoyed the physical side of these activities, he was increasingly disgusted by the other participants. Most of them belonged to the class he was beginning to regard as a ripe target for his satire, the wealthy non-combatants who profited by the War. Fat businessmen gorging themselves on unheard-of delicacies at the Golf Club, rich socialites dancing wildly in country houses after a day's hunting in Cheshire, but above all the women who seemed to glory in the sacrifice of human lives, all repelled him.

It was a world which Sassoon found increasingly suspect. After a particularly pleasant day hunting near Tarporley, for example, he stayed the night at Wistaston Hall, dancing at Alvaston, and wrote in his diary the following day:

A few hours in the pre-war surroundings – 'Loderism' and so on. Pleasant enough; but what a decayed society, hanging blindly on to the shreds of its traditions. The wet, watery-green meadows and straggling bare hedges and grey winding lanes; the cry of hounds and thud of hoofs, and people galloping bravely along all around me; and the ride home with the hounds in the chilly dusk – those are *real* things. But comfort and respectable squiredom and the futile chatter of women, and their man-hunting glances, and the pomposity of port-wine-drinking buffers – what's all that but emptiness? ... Debrett['s *Peerage*] is on every table; and heaven a sexless peerage, with a suitable array of dependents and equipages where God is.[48]

A page of the diary is torn out at this point, suggesting that Sassoon's scorn had carried him beyond acceptable limits.

Nevertheless, when it came to occupying his evenings, Sassoon found, like most officers, that the most effective antidote to the spartan camp was a trip into the society he despised. Over an expensive dinner at the Adelphi Hotel, where he was gaining a reputation as a *bon viveur*, he was again confronted with people who looked as though they were either unaffected by the War, or doing well out of it. He was conscious of his own dissipation in all this and longed to be alone, either in the garden at Weirleigh or his little study there:

... I dream of a small firelit room
With yellow candles burning straight,
And glowing pictures in the gloom,
And kindly books that hold me late.
Of things like these I choose to think
When I can never be alone:
Then someone says, 'Another drink?'
And turns my living heart to stone.   (*CP*, p. 14)

Graves left for France on 22 January 1917, with a promise from Sassoon to see his small collection of poems, *Goliath and David*, through the press for him. Sassoon also continued to add to his own collection. Two days after checking Graves's proofs on 21 January, for example, he wrote a poem on hearing Elgar's *Violin Concerto* for the first time. He almost certainly attended the concert alone, since most of the other officers preferred to play the popular songs of the day interminably on their gramophones. Returning to his bleak hut he was still filled with the visions which had come to him during the 'noblest' passages. In spite of himself he kept seeing 'the suffering mortal figure on a cross, but the face is my own'.[49] His startling identification with the Christ figure here suggests that he felt ready to sacrifice his life for his men in France. (He had been reading George Moore's fictional life of Christ, *The Brook Kerith*.) It was not conventional religious practices which inspired in him visions of Christ:

> I have seen Christ, when music wove
> Exulting vision; storms of prayer
> Deep-voiced within me marched and strove.
> The sorrows of the world were there ...[50]

The Brook Kerith, which may have left its mark on 'The Elgar *Violin Concerto*', was one of a number of books Sassoon read at Litherland in an attempt to escape his surroundings. His greatest consolation, however, remained his own poetry, which he continued to write in the face of all difficulties. Including the four poems already mentioned, he produced at least eleven poems during his nine weeks at Litherland Depot. 'Secret Music' probably came first in early December and 'A Whispered Tale' second in the middle of the same month, after Julian Dadd's visit to Liverpool. Dadd's throat wound at Ginchy had left him virtually mute and the death of his last surviving brother, Edmund, in the same battle had driven him to the edge of sanity. As Sassoon listened to the grim details of Dadd's 'Whispered Tale' he could not help contrasting it with the bragging account 'fool-heroes' might have given:

> I'd heard fool-heroes brag of where they'd been,
> With stories of the glories that they'd seen.
> ...
> *You* had no babbling phrases; what you said
> Was like a message from the maimed and dead.
> But memory brought the voice I knew, whose note
> Was muted when they shot you in the throat;
> And still you whisper of the war, and find
> Sour jokes for all those horrors left behind.[51]   (*CP*, p. 21)

The idea of Dadd's distorted speech being 'like a message from the maimed and dead' is simple but vivid. Of the five officers who listened to Dadd's account in December 1916, two would be dead and one wounded by May 1917, and Dadd himself would finally take his own life.

Sassoon dedicated 'A Whispered Tale' to Dadd, whose visit almost certainly sent him back to his diary entries for the time they spent together at Morlancourt early in 1916. The result was 'The Distant Song', an almost entirely descriptive poem in which a contrast is made between the sordidness of trench-life and the miracle of spring. But he had already handled the same material more successfully in 'Stand-To: Good Friday Morning' and the main interest of this December version is that he was to use a phrase or two from it for the end of *Fox-Hunting Man*.

Even on Christmas Day, traditionally one of rest, Sassoon was writing verse. He had spent most of the day at Formby Golf Club and, though he had enjoyed the enormous cold spread of goose and turkey for lunch, the sight of such excess in a time of general deprivation increased his anger at those who were having a 'good war'. Among these he included the Army Staff. Reading back over his trench diary had reminded him of 'old wine-faced Rawlinson' taking the salute of 200 officers and NCOs at Flixécourt the previous May: 'and how many of them are alive and hale on Christmas Day?' he asked himself.[52] The result was, in his own words, 'a grim, jeering, heart-rending' poem, 'The March-Past', which ends:

> 'Eyes right!' We passed him with a jaunty stare.
> 'Eyes front!' He'd watched his trusted legions go.
> I wonder if he guessed how many there
> Would get knocked out of time in next week's show.
> 'Eyes right!' The corpse-commander was a Mute;
> And Death leered round him, taking our salute.[53]

The idea of making his Corps-Commander a 'corpse-commander' (a pun he could not resist) and a mute, almost certainly came to Sassoon from his recent meeting with the virtually voiceless Julian Dadd. Thoughts of his previous Christmas at Montagne had made him extra-conscious of death, for of all the officers there then, seven had been killed and ten wounded, leaving only four of the original contingent with the Battalion.

Revived memories of Montagne and Morlancourt brought back a more specific loss to Sassoon, that of David Thomas and the German deaths he had inflicted in his rage at this death. By 6 January 1917 he had produced the first version of yet another poem about him, 'Enemies':

> He stood alone in some queer sunless place
> Where Armageddon ends. Perhaps he longed
> For days he might have lived; but his young face
> Gazed forth untroubled: and suddenly there thronged
> Round him the hulking Germans that I shot
> When for his death my brooding rage was hot.
>
> He stared at them, half-wondering; and then
> They told him how I'd killed them for his sake –
> Those patient, stupid, sullen ghosts of men;
> And still there seemed no answer he could make.
> At last he turned and smiled. One took his hand
> Because his face could make them understand.   (*CP*, p. 26)

It seems likely that 'Enemies' was at least one source for Owen's 'Strange

Meeting', which was written after it but also centres round soldiers from opposite sides meeting in hell. Similarly, Owen's tunnel setting, which becomes hell, is probably indebted to Sassoon's 'The Rear-Guard'. Owen also appears to have echoed the word 'sullen', used to describe the Germans in 'Enemies', and applied it to the 'sullen hall' of hell in 'Strange Meeting'. Edmund Blunden believed in the connection, adding that both poems had 'the voice of that hour, of the war-spirit we were living with'.[54]

Three more poems followed in January, only one of which, 'When I'm Among a Blaze of Lights', was published in his lifetime. Of the other two, 'England has many Heroes' is another sarcastic jibe at the Army Staff: 'Ten thousand soldiers, tabbed with blue and green,/ Who, if they heard one shell, would crouch and bolt.'[55] The other, more unusually, attempts a description of the surrounding countryside to which he was evidently becoming reconciled. He had already explored the beach, but on 23 January he walked out into the 'starved, colourless fields' which bordered the camp and was made unexpectedly happy by the experience. Unlike the Kentish Weald though it was, the northern farmland nevertheless brought back memories of home and childhood, which in turn reminded him of his dead brother. The result was as unpredictable as his pleasure in the landscape, for it was 'Serenity', not misery he felt.[56]

Two weeks later, and in a very different mood, Sassoon produced his most successful poem of his stay at Litherland, just a few days before taking his final leave. Ostensibly the result of an evening spent at the Liverpool Hippodrome with a fellow-officer, 'Blighters' is also another angry reaction to the thought of his own probable death in the face of civilian complacency and unawareness. Its success lies in his ability deftly to sketch in a situation, to echo the banalities of non-combatants' rationalizations in colloquial speech and, above all, to choose exactly the right words for the horror he sees just below the surface; 'cackle', 'shrill' and 'prancing' make the audience and the chorus seem particularly nasty. The 'riddled corpses' of the last line allows no evasion of the realities of war:

> The House is crammed: tier beyond tier they grin
> And cackle at the show, while prancing ranks
> Of harlots shrill the chorus, drunk with din;
> 'We're sure the Kaiser loves our dear old Tanks!'
>
> I'd like to see a Tank come down the stalls,
> Lurching to rag-time tunes, or 'Home, sweet Home',
> And there'd be no more jokes in Music-halls
> To mock the riddled corpses round Bapaume.   (*CP*, p. 21)

From the indictment of the punning title onwards – those who remain in 'Blighty', or England, are 'Blighters', or rogues – the narrator's venom is unmistakable. His violent wish to see a tank come 'lurching' down the stalls, killing the complacent civilians, shocks the reader and forms a grotesque link between two very different worlds. The description of the chorus girls as 'harlots' is both an accusation and a suggestion of his continuing distaste for women, and his use of popular music is a neat, if snobbish, shorthand which indicates the low-brow character of the audience.

Apart from 'The Choral Union', a jokey piece about a drunk who staggers into a chapel and thinks he has reached Heaven, and an equally facetious piece about a Special Constable, 'Blighters' completes the work included in *The Old Huntsman*. Three days after finishing it Sassoon was back at Weirleigh on leave, his last before returning to France. It was neither possible, nor did he want to put off returning indefinitely. In fact, it was a relief when he was passed fit for General Service on 27 January 1917.

During Sassoon's stay at the Depot his loss of belief in the War had shaped itself from 'a ferment of disturbing and disorderly ideas'[57] into a more coherent form, bringing his public protest that much nearer. His contact with the pacifists of Garsington in September and the continuance of Ross's anti-war views had been followed by disappointment at Romania's defeat by Germany in November. By December he felt completely disillusioned about the 'Great Advance' promised by the Allies. Having expected too much of the Battle of the Somme, he had been keenly affected not only by his own experience in it, but more particularly by the virtual massacre of his old Battalion at Ginchy on 3 September.

Ottoline kept the Garsington influence going with long letters accompanying the exotic gifts she sent to cheer up his drab surroundings, and Sassoon increasingly found himself agreeing with her. She echoed his own feelings precisely when she wrote that the 'spirit and purpose of the war, that kept it fine and clean at first, dwindles and gets fainter, leaving it utterly ghastly'.[58] Like her, he was beginning to believe that it was the 'brutal fury of L[loyd] G[eorge] and politicians like him' which allowed it to continue, though he admitted that his own fate as an individual 'about to be involved once again in the crass chancefulness of battle' made him readier to criticize.[59]

Sassoon's most powerful revelation, however, came from reading *Mr Britling Sees It Through* (1917) by H.G. Wells, which illuminated the whole background of the War for him and confirmed his worst suspicions. Wells's words struck a nightmarish chord:

Everywhere cunning, everywhere small feuds and hatreds, distrusts, dishonesties, timidities, feebleness of purpose, dwarfish imaginations, swarm over the great and simple issues ... It is a war now like any other of the mobbing, many aimed cataclysms that have shattered empires and devastated the world; it is a war without point, a war that has lost its soul, it has become mere incoherent fighting and destruction, a demonstration in vast and tragic forms of the stupidity and ineffectiveness of our species.[60]

Yet, with a characteristic mood-swing, Sassoon's feelings changed rapidly as

France loomed. He felt now 'as if a load had been lifted' from his 'sullen' heart and another chance been given him to die a 'decent' death.[61] While his body cries out against it, something within him 'lifts adoring hands, something is filled with noble passion and desire for that benison of promise and freedom'. (The language sounds suspiciously like Ottoline's.) All the 'greatness' that was his in 1916 would be his again. It is an unnerving shift in mood and one that will be repeated a number of times before the end of the War.

12

The Wounded Hero

February–April 1917

Sassoon left for France on 15 February 1917 after a week's leave divided equally between Weirleigh and Half Moon Street. His frantic socializing in London had exhausted him, but it had helped put off thoughts of his uncertain future. As he boarded his train at Waterloo he began to feel 'nervous and rattled',[1] yet once aboard the *Archangel* at Southampton the worried feeling wore off. He himself noted that people seemed to become happy 'in a bovine way' as soon as they were relieved of all responsibility for their future. The usual self-protective change in attitude took place as the boat left the dock, though he felt rather like a cabbage going to Covent Garden Market and did resent the fact that someone stole his greatcoat en route. Resigned as he was to his fate, he could not prevent thoughts of death impinging.

One source of comfort, as always, were his books. Anticipating nightmarish conditions at the Front he had again chosen to take not just the writers he admired, but those who seemed to him most English, Hardy chief among these. Beside bringing out the landscape for him, he found that Hardy's irony helped him 'to fight against the inevitable homesickness for things which really don't matter, such as comfortable rooms and blameless domesticity'. In a different way Lamb and Chaucer promised an escape from the grim surroundings. For the trenches themselves he was saving Shakespeare's tragedies, the only literary equivalent he could imagine for the horrors to come. He was still trying to finish Conrad's *Nostromo* and *A Set of Six* and, though he could not have regarded these works as either very English or very consoling, the Pole's tragic vision seemed to suit the situation.[2]

The journey to the 5th Infantry Base Depot at Rouen took over a day. In his fictionalized account, his arrival at the bleak depot was made worse by the fact that he learnt immediately of his transfer to the 2nd Battalion of the RWF. Yet his letters to Ross and others show that in reality he was still expecting to be posted to the 1st Battalion for another three weeks, which suggests that he predated it in his fiction to underline his sense of desolation. This was not helped by another event which almost certainly *did* occur on his arrival and which gave rise to one of his bleakest satires.

Stumbling around in the dark looking for the store-room, Sassoon found himself instead in a Guard Room, where a man, naked to the waist, was kneeling in the middle of the floor, clutching at his chest and weeping uncontrollably. A patient but unpitying sergeant explained to Sassoon as he guided him to the blanket-store that the man had been under detention for assaulting the military police 'and now 'e's just 'ad news of his brother being killed. Seems to take it to 'eart more than most would. 'Arf crazy, 'e's been, tearing 'is clothes off and cursing the War and the Fritzes.'[3]

When Sassoon came to deal with the incident in his poetry, instead of using the sergeant's working-class speech, as he had in 'In the Pink', he chose to make a middle-class narrator the vehicle for his satire. The inability of the insensitive and unsympathetic officer-narrator to comprehend the man's suffering achieves even more of the shock effect Sassoon intended:

> *Lamentations*
> I found him in the guard-room at the Base.
> From the blind darkness I had heard his crying
> And blundered in. With puzzled, patient face
> A sergeant watched him; it was no good trying
> To stop it; for he howled and beat his chest.
> And, all because his brother had gone west,
> Raved at the bleeding war; his rampant grief
> Moaned, shouted, sobbed, and choked, while he was kneeling
> Half-naked on the floor. In my belief
> Such men have lost all patriotic feeling.   (*CP*, p. 76)

The last line, as in most of his successful satires, carries the weight of the charge, though it is hinted at earlier in the euphemistic cliché 'And, all because his brother had gone west'.

Sassoon found life at the 5th Infantry Base Depot altogether depressing. It was like being in a Military Sorting Office, where everyone waited with ill-concealed anxiety to discover their final destination. And since it was just possible to hear the distant grumble of the guns, there was no escaping the fact that the rumoured 'Spring Offensive' was already underway.

After a whole day of this Sassoon realized that it was not just the camp that was making him feel low; he also had a fever. And when he reported sick on the morning of Sunday, 18 February, German measles was diagnosed. If anything his billet in the isolation hospital, a barbed wire enclosure about 300 yards from the main camp, was worse than his first bed in a narrow segment of a low canvas shed. There were already six patients in the small hospital tent to which he was assigned and his arrival caused further crowding. He felt unwelcome, bored and disaffected.

Instead of joining in with the eternal games of bridge which occupied at least four of his fellow-inmates, Sassoon simply read and observed. Apart from providing him with future material for fiction, the other patients made little difference to his mood of resigned despair. 'I loathe the sacrificial imbecility of war,' Sassoon wrote to Ross four days after arriving in hospital, 'and the whole scheme of things as one sees it out here. I could never have believed that things could be so meaningless and so contemptible.'[4] But much as he hated the War, he was unable to face the idea of returning to England without being 'scarred and tortured once more'.[5]

In this muddled, hopeless state his main comfort was not literature but nature. The only advantage the squalid, little compound offered him was the huge pine-forest which surrounded it. By 23 February he was writing to tell Dent that the worst of his 'blackest horrors' were over.[6] One result, as he knew from past experience, was that he would soon be feeling 'heroic and optimistic' again. It seemed impossible to remain neutral. 'I came out here longing to scarify war,' his letter to Dent continues, 'but I know I shall be writing rhapsodies long before Easter-Day, and *that* will probably produce "An Ode on the Eucharist in a Shell-Hole", or "The Peace that Passeth Understanding", a Paschal Play for Devout Sergeants, or some drivel like that ....' He longed for the kind of simplicity he saw in Bobbie Hanmer, who could kneel down every night to say his prayers and fall asleep, content to lose an arm or a leg, or even die for England. At home with his pacifist friends, it had seemed easy to criticize the mindless stupidity of war, but once in France he was drawn back irrevocably into the machine. Dull acquiescence, if not willing self-sacrifice, seemed inevitable.

Apart from possibly keeping him out of the trenches for another ten days, Sassoon's German measles made no real difference to his fate. When he returned to the main camp on 27 February he was still destined for the Front and his fellow officers seemed just as boring. There were very few, he told Ross scathingly, whose ideas rose above a five franc prostitute: 'Poor weary old harlots,' he fantasized, 'how tired they must be of the Welsh dialect and the Lloyd George embrace!'[7] Having heard a number of the younger officers describing their experiences in lurid detail, he almost wished he had the courage to visit the local brothel, the orgies there seemed such a good subject for satire. Relying on Ross's unshockability, as well as their mutual distaste for women sexually, he tried him out with an extempore verse, begging him not to show it to the more staid Meiklejohn:

> She met me on the stairs in her chemise;
> I grinned and offered her a five franc note;
> Poor girl, no doubt she did her best to please;
> But I'd have been far happier with a goat.

The suggestion that the Welch Fusiliers would prefer sex with their regimental goat to a woman is a particularly virulent manifestation of Sassoon's distaste for heterosexual activity, as well as a reference to rumours that circulated on such practices in wartime.

Sassoon felt isolated in other ways too. He had no inclination to join in the never-ending card games and he despised the popular songs that were churned out incessantly on the gramophone. While waiting to be posted, which he still thought would mean being sent back to the 1st Battalion, he tried to make the most of his stay. He paid at least one overnight visit to the centre of Rouen, where he enjoyed a hot bath, a gourmet dinner and a comfortable bed for the night, an experience which provided material for at least two satires. The first of these, written on 4 March, was inspired by lunch at the Hôtel de la Poste the same day. In a third person prose description of the event he used many of the phrases which were to make his poem on the subject memorable, a revealing glimpse into his creative processes, in particular his dependence on telling words and phrases. After describing a young subaltern (presumably himself) enjoying a second glass of wine, he continues (the italics have been added):

Grey-haired colonels with fierce eyebrows lingered over a chicken casserole with the tenderness of a lover .... A Brigadier-General came and sat down a few feet away. He had the *appearance* of a man with a liver who spends most of the year sitting in London clubs. He began *guzzling* hors d'oeuvres as though his life depended on the solidity of his meal.

The cynical subaltern who was staring at him from the next table felt an almost irrepressible desire to walk across and pour a plate of soup down his neck. 'O you bloody Brigadier! you bloody Brigadier! you are a professional soldier: I am not. Why can't you go and show the Germans how to fight instead of *guzzling at the Base*. You have never been within thirty miles of a front-line trench, and yet you call yourself a general. And *you* will be alive, over-eating yourself in a military club, when I am dead in a shell-hole up on the Somme. *You* will *guzzle* yourself to the grave and gas about the Great War, long after I am dead with all my promise unfulfilled.

'O damn all these *bald-headed* incompetent belly-fillers!' he thought. And he glanced at a Gunner Colonel with a D.S.O. who was cutting himself a big slice of cheese, hoping that he at least might be a brave man. But all the really brave men were dead, or else maimed or *up the line*.[8]

Sassoon confirmed that the phrase 'scarlet Majors' came from Robbie Ross, but the rest of the poem which resulted from the incident, 'Base Details', can be traced directly to this prose passage and to Sassoon's skill at sketching in a character and giving that character a voice. In this case there are two 'voices', that of the complacent Staff Officer and that of the scathing narrator, which undercuts it:

If I were fierce, and bald, and short of breath,
I'd live with scarlet Majors at the Base
And speed glum heroes up the line to death.
You'd see me with my puffy petulant face,
Guzzling and gulping in the best hotel,
Reading the Roll of Honour. 'Poor young chap,'
I'd say – 'I used to know his father well;
Yes, we've lost heavily in this last scrap.'
And when the war is done and youth stone dead,
I'd toddle safely home and die – in bed.   (*CP*, p. 75)

The opening pun of the title – as well as being, literally, details about the Infantry Base, it is a poem full of 'base details' of war and a comment on the 'base', or lowly, soldiers, or 'details', who are sent to fight – is echoed in the multiple word-play of 'scarlet Majors', which implies not only that they are wearing the red tabs of the General Staff on their lapels with red bands round their caps and that their faces are red from the high blood-pressure induced by over-indulgence in food and drink, but also that they are 'scarlet' with sin (and possibly from 'screaming', as Ross saw it).

Both phrases illustrate Sassoon's remarkable powers of condensation, as do the unexpected conjunctions of '*glum heroes*' and 'up the line *to death*' (my italics). The alliterative addition of 'gulping' to his diary word 'guzzling' matches that of 'puffy petulant face' and lends weight to the phrase. The emphatic 'stone dead' of line 9, though unlikely to have been used by the euphemistic Staff Officer, makes an inescapable point, which is rounded off in the last line by Sassoon's inspired device of the colloquial 'toddle', which makes the 'scarlet Major' seem more than a little childish and faintly ludicrous. His original choice had been 'waddle' which he wisely changed after the poem's publication in the *Cambridge Magazine* on 28 April 1917, since 'toddle' is more the kind of euphemism which the Staff Officer might himself have used for his presumably inebriated state.

The fact that the Scarlet Major plans to die 'in bed', rather than at the Front with the men he has sent there, underlines the discrepancy between his sybaritic lifestyle and their sufferings. Sassoon's choice of just the right euphemisms for his complacent speaker – 'Yes, we've lost heavily in this last scrap' – underlines his growing anger with unaware non-combatants still cosily ensconced in the old boys' network ('I knew his father well'). Though this had already expressed itself powerfully in 'The Tombstone-Maker' and 'Blighters', it seems all the more forceful when applied to people within the army itself. Sassoon was to continue this line of attack in 'The General' less than two months later.

A second poem written the same day as 'Base Details' shows that Rouen inspired very different moods in Sassoon. The beauty of its cathedral and, more especially, the church of St Ouen, made him yearn for the consolations of religion, particularly in view of what lay ahead. His poetry, accordingly, becomes more lyrical and elegiac: '[his] spirit longs for prayer;/ And, lost to God, [he] seek[s] him everywhere.'

*

After waiting aimlessly for nine days at the Base, Sassoon finally received orders to join the 2nd RWF at Chipilly, a rest camp on the Somme. It was a bitter disappointment to him not to be returning to the 1st Battalion as he had hoped. Even his expectation of at least joining Graves in the 2nd Battalion was dashed when the younger man was invalided back to England just before Sassoon's orders came through. So it was with a heavy heart that he set off from Rouen, at 4 p.m. on Sunday, 11 March. The first leg of the journey, an eight-hour train ride to Corbie near Amiens, was tedious and he passed part of it trying to express his mixed feelings on returning to the war-zone. As he approached the area around Amiens, which had held him physically and emotionally since December 1915, he became increasingly conscious of the friends who had died there. While reluctant to return, he nevertheless felt he was back where he belonged, with his men, past and present:

> *Return*
> I have come home unnoticed; they are still;
> No greetings pass between us; but they lie
> Hearing the boom of guns along the hill,
> Watching the flashes lick the glowering sky.[9]

After an uncomfortable night's sleep on the floor at Corbie, minus his kit which had been left on the train, Sassoon walked the final seven miles to Camp 13 at Chipilly, a few miles from his old camp at Morlancourt. Though safely behind the Line and in a spot he had once found attractive, it now seemed to him an abominable place. Established only a few months earlier, Camp 13 was already a sea of mud. The food was disgusting and the one hut, in which all the Company Officers were herded together, full of smoke from the adjoining kitchen. There was never a moment of silence or peace, only the sound of whiskey-loosened tongues gabbling war-shop as the officers played their endless card-games. Under such circumstances he found it difficult to think, much less write. The mental attitude of his companions, he told Ross after more than a fortnight of their company, was 'like a lead coffin for any sparks of the imagination one [could] muster'.[10] To make things worse, the weather had been wet and windy. He could hardly have joined the battalion under less attractive conditions.

It took Sassoon nearly three weeks to resign himself to staying with the 2nd Battalion, who were about to leave for the Front. On 1 April, their last day in Camp 13, he wrote to Ross: '*We* [my italics] are off to some battle very soon.' It is a small sign that he was beginning to identify with his new unit, which his account in the Battalion history confirms.[11] By 7 April, when a formal request from the 1st for his transfer back to them came through, he had already decided to stay with the 'good old 2nd'.[12] Not only had he found friends among the officers there, but he had, more importantly, begun to bond with his men.

When Sassoon joined the 2nd Battalion at Chipilly they had recently returned from two months in the Cléry sector of the Somme front, where they had suffered some of the worst weather of the War and buried 200 of their number. They were a very different unit from the one Robert Graves had encountered nearly two years earlier at Laventie. One of the few regular infantry battalions still more or less intact at that time, the 2nd had seemed to Graves then a hot-bed of snobbishness and élitism and very tough even on Special Reserve officers, let alone New Army ones. When he returned for the third time at the beginning of 1917, however, he found them noticeably changed: 'No riding-school, no battalion mess, no Quetta manners, no regular officers except for a couple of Sandhurst boys.'[13]

Nevertheless they still seemed to Sassoon in March 1917 stiff and unfriendly by comparison with the 1st Battalion. Captain W.W. Kirkby, the Officer in Command of B Company, to which he was assigned, repeatedly referred to him as a 'bloody wart', obviously intending him to overhear. Kirkby, who had been a Special Reserve officer with the Battalion since before the War, represented the Old Guard. He seemed to think it only right that newcomers should be treated like dirt for the first six months, or until they 'proved' themselves, rather like new boys in the public school system to which the Regular Army was closely allied. The recent C.O. of the 2nd Battalion, 'Tibs' Crawshay, had told Cottrell that Kirkby was 'a Capital S—'. Another officer from the 2nd described him as a 'potent deteriorating influence'.[14] Dadd, who feared Sassoon would find his new unit 'a somewhat snooty lot', observed that Kirkby *seemed* 'to have a courtly, genial way with him' which made debate very difficult. He advised Sassoon to regard him simply as 'something to study'. Fortunately Sassoon listened to Dadd's advice and the fruits of his careful study of his Company Officer emerge amusingly as Captain Leake in *Infantry Officer*.

A short, red-faced, extremely heavy man, Kirkby invited a certain amount of ridicule, but he also inspired respect and Sassoon learnt to get on with him, as he almost always did with fellow-officers; there is an entertaining account in both *Infantry Officer* and *The War the Infantry Knew* of 'a convivial evening' drinking bad champagne with Kirkby (among others), which ended with him swearing 'eternal fealty' to Kirkby at the door of his poky little billet.[15] (In the more colourful fictionized version, they shake hands 'sholemnly' and Sassoon swears to 'blurry well do [his] damndest' for him.)[16]

Sassoon also learnt to get on with the other officers in B Company, some more easily than others. As second-in-command he had three subalterns under him, each of them, like himself, commanding a platoon. The most experienced of these came from a well-known establishment family, the Soameses, and seems to have had problems with discipline. Given his family connections, there was probably some not very flattering reason for his chequered career and relatively lowly rank. Though Sassoon refrained from giving it, his omission of Soames from *Infantry Officer* almost certainly reflects the lack of warmth which comes through in his diary account.

Sassoon did include his other two subordinates in B Company, Casson and Evans, however, who seemed to him to provide a 'typical war contrast' of the kind which was becoming more familiar as the fighting claimed increasing numbers of the originally mainly middle-class officers. For while Casson, a refined youth of twenty-three, had been at Winchester and Christ Church, Evans, at about the same age, had not enjoyed similar social advantages. Rather ape-like in appearance, he licked his thumb noisily when dealing cards and invariably answered 'Pardon' to any remark, a habit Sassoon snobbishly found rather trying. 'Shirley' and 'Rees' in *Infantry Officer* are based largely on the two men. Whatever their social differences, Casson and Evans were to die together on 26 September 1917 at Polygon Wood in the Third Battle of Ypres.

Apart from those in his own unit, Sassoon also got to know officers from the three other Companies. He had a particular rapport with the O.C. of A Company, Ralph Greaves. Not only had he known Greaves slightly in Kent before the War, an excuse for many nostalgic reminiscences, but Greaves's older brother, E.J. Greaves (the 'Barton' of *Infantry Officer*) had been his Company Commander in the 1st, forming a comforting link with his old battalion. Ralph, who was only three years younger than Sassoon, also shared his love of music. He had studied under Vaughan Williams at Cambridge and played the piano well, as Sassoon discovered on the same drunken evening which witnessed his sentimental reconciliation with Kirkby. This had undoubtedly been an emotional occasion; Greaves, Sassoon remembered, had 'played as though he were saying good-bye to all music for ever'.[17]

Sassoon had already spent a similarly convivial evening with Greaves at the Godbert Restaurant in Amiens on their last day at Camp 13 and his memories of that occasion were equally alcoholic. In the photograph of Sassoon, Greaves and two friends taken the morning after they look surprisingly perky, perhaps facing the camera with determined gaiety. The two other men in the group photograph, also good friends of Sassoon, were Lieutenant T.R. Conning, a 'happy-go-lucky fellow' of 'natural jollity'[18] who appears as 'Dunning' in *Infantry Officer*, and 'kind-hearted' Captain Coster, of D Company. Conning was to die in the coming Battle of Arras, which would also deprive the passionate pianist Greaves of one of his arms and render the other virtually useless. (Coster would be killed later at the 3rd Battle of Ypres.) It was an irony which Sassoon was to make much of in his portrayal of Greaves (as Wilmot) in *Infantry Officer*, to help underline the random cruelty of the War.

There were many other cases Sassoon might have cited to reinforce his criticism. Captain J.C. Mann, one of whose letters to Sassoon has survived, is a case in point. His initial gaiety, not quite destroyed by the time Sassoon met him during Mann's second year in France, gradually turned to taciturnity under the pressures of continued Front-Line experience. His ability won him rapid promotion to the position of Adjutant, but he never took advantage of this relatively safe job at Headquarters. When the situation was bad, which it frequently was for the Battalion, he often voluntarily risked his life in order to help matters. An added incentive for his recklessness was almost certainly the death of his only brother at about the time Sassoon joined the Battalion. This made him hate all Germans, though he continued to treat their prisoners humanely. Sassoon, who included him briefly in *Infantry Officer*, would have been as sad and angry as Dr Dunn, the compiler of the Battalion memoirs, when Mann died in the slaughter at Polygon Wood on 26 September, the same day as Casson and many others.

Sassoon's closest friend amongst the younger officers, Leslie Orme, would be dead already by the time Polygon Wood claimed its toll. He was to be a victim of an earlier but no less bloody engagement at 'Plum Lane', Arras on 27 May, when Battalion casualties were to number ten officers and 155 men, half of whom died. Sassoon had learnt to admire the sturdy little ex-public schoolboy during his time with him in the 1st Battalion. Since then his youthful good looks and the location of a particular skirmish in which he had fought had earned him the intriguing nickname 'the Angel of Crawley Ridge' to add to his other nickname, 'Young Worm'. The two shared trips into Amiens and almost certainly paid a visit to their old rest camp at Heilly sur l'Ancre together.[19] Though Sassoon would not have described their friendship as profound, Orme's death was to affect him deeply and lead to one of his most moving war poems.

Another link with the 1st Battalion was the Quartermaster, Captain Yates ('Bates' of *Infantry Officer*), an old friend of Joe Cottrell.[20] Sassoon viewed Yates as simply 'a burlier prototype of Joe ... with fewer political prejudices'.[21] Like Cottrell, Yates had been a regular with the Royal Welch Fusiliers for many years, almost forty by the time Sassoon met him. Like Cottrell too, he was completely dedicated to his battalion. The only officer bar one to have been with the 2nd since the outbreak of war, he would do almost anything to ensure its well-being. When stores were low he would, as he euphemistically put it, 'scrounge' new supplies from wherever possible. His ingenuity and resourcefulness stopped at nothing in the service of his battalion. His strongest link with Sassoon was through horses. Early in the War he had acquired from the Cavalry a wounded mare, whom he adored. As 'Girlie' grew stronger he started to race her and, when Sassoon appeared, invited him to ride her in the Corps Sports. Though the Sports were cancelled, the bond had been formed and Yates, like Cottrell, became for Sassoon a sterling type of 'old soldier'.

Another 'old soldier', though of a quite different type, was the Battalion Medical Officer, Captain J.C. Dunn. Sassoon, who gave Dunn the pseudonym 'Munro' in *Infantry Officer* to emphasize his nationality, had already heard of the tough Scot by the time he arrived at Chipilly, probably from Graves, who wrote of him: 'Dunn, a hard-bitten Scot, had served as a trooper in the South African War, and there won the Distinguished Conduct Medal. Now he was far more than a doctor: living at battalion headquarters, he became the right-hand man of three or four colonels in succession. Whoever failed to take his advice usually regretted it afterwards.'[22] Like Sassoon, Dunn was awarded an M.C. for his courage.

Courage was not the only quality that the two men shared, though it was the first thing Dunn commented on in Sassoon. Writing to Graves shortly after his arrival at the 2nd Battalion, Sassoon complained of 'a beast of a stiff arm where old Dunn inoculated me today – sticking his needle in, and saying "the toughest skin of the lot – but you're a tough character, I know." (Not so tough as he thinks!).'[23] On that occasion Dunn had given Sassoon a double dose of anti-typhoid injection, commenting as he did so: 'That'll keep you quiet for forty-eight hours.' The grim humour of this remark was evidently appreciated by Sassoon, who repeated it in *Infantry Officer*.[24] It was one of a number of reasons why Sassoon wanted to know Dunn better.

Another reason was his love of books. Inured though he was to the hardships of war, Dunn's one serious complaint was that enforced periods of inactivity became 'most boring when a very limited kit [left] no room for books'.[25] It is the kind of remark Sassoon might have made. When Dunn conceived the idea of a collection of first-hand accounts of the Battalion's war-service in 1926, he was to write a great deal of it himself. He was also to appeal to Sassoon, who would provide the longest continuous narrative, in fact a whole chapter, for him.

Dunn was a highly intelligent observer of the human scene, as his *War the Infantry Knew* makes clear, a book justly described by one authority as 'arguably the foremost narrative account of the British Infantry experience on the Western Front'. It ranges from detailed first-hand accounts of individual battles to entertaining asides, such as the way different nationalities named their trench systems. (While 'Piccadilly' remained a favourite with British units, there was always a 'Grafton Street' with the Irish, and a 'Cowcaddens' with the Scots.) Dunn could also be witty at times: 'The C-in-C tells me "our backs are to the wall",' he reports; then adds: 'His men are asking, "Where's the —— wall?".'[26]

Like Sassoon, Dunn was critical of the conduct of the War, particularly of the remoteness of the General Staff. Impressed by the visits of both an Australian Brigadier and Australian Chief Medical Officer to the Front, he asks: 'Was one of ours ever within the shelled zone when there was the greatest need for him to know how things were being done, and what might be needed?'[27] It could have been Sassoon speaking.

Sassoon admired Dunn greatly. When the doctor wrote to ask for a contribution to his planned Battalion history in February 1926, the poet replied:

> We'd got a Doctor with a D.S.O.
> And much unmedalled merit. In the Line
> Or out of it, he'd taught the troops to know
> That shells, bombs, bullets, gas, or even a mine

Heaving green earth toward heaven, were things he took
For granted, and dismissed with one shrewd look.
No missile, as it seemed, could cause him harm.
So on he went past endless sick-parades;
Jabbed his inoculation in an arm;
Gave 'medicine and duty' to all shades
Of uninfectious ailment. Thus his name
Acquired a most intense, though local, fame.[28]

Sassoon was to remain friends with Dunn long after the War, until increasing age made Dunn 'grumblesome' and 'cussed'. Even then his comment was affectionate: 'The poor old boy can't bear getting old,' he told John Graves in 1947.

One member of the Battalion who was already rather old and fussy by the time Sassoon joined it was the second-in-command, Major Poore, brother of General R.M. Poore. Described kindly but briefly by Sassoon in *Infantry Officer* as a 'gentle middle-aged country solicitor',[29] Poore consoled himself by reminiscing about cricket and hunting with Sassoon.

The Commanding Officer himself, Lt.-Col. W.B. Garnett, was hardly a popular figure in the Battalion. It was not simply that the 2nd had loved 'Tibs' Crawshay so much that he had seemed irreplaceable, but that Garnett appeared almost too indulgent and conciliatory. According to Sassoon, who had his previous Colonel, Stockwell, in mind, greater aggressiveness would have been preferable. Garnett had got off to an unfortunate start with his new officers by showing off his superior powers of spelling, a 'rare accomplishment' which had merely harassed and embarrassed them according to Sassoon.[30] Sassoon was probably not the only one to enjoy the C.O.'s discomfort when he was ordered to dismount while saluting his Corps Commander.[31] He certainly enjoyed retelling the incident, with Garnett as 'Easby' in *Infantry Officer*, particularly the part where the General bellowed 'Are you stuck to that bloody horse?' Garnett's anxiety to prove that his G.O.C. should 'be able to depend on him at all times' was interpreted by his Battalion as a sign of ambitiousness rather than conscientiousness.[32] Dunn maintained, in his outspoken way, that Garnett, like Kirkby, was 'a potent deteriorating influence'.

Garnett notwithstanding, Sassoon felt sufficiently at home with his companions by 1 April, the 2nd Battalion's last day at Chipilly, to accept his future with them philosophically. It would, he feared, be a 'squalid' one, since 'some battle' was imminent, though details were still unsure. Cheered by the technical arrival of Spring, the creative urge returned to him. Since poetry was difficult to write in the crowded, uncomfortable camp, he concentrated on prose, sending a piece of what he ironically described as 'fine writing' to Ross. Though ostensibly dismissive of the late nineteenth century Royal Academy 'Dream Pictures' he advocates for 'homesick officers in the Field', the nostalgic tone of his piece suggests that he found consolation in such memories himself.

It is an insight into his own conservative tastes in art, as well as the influence of his early Kentish background.[33]

Though Sassoon concludes his description of 'Dream Pictures' with the words 'what tripe', his own longing for the English countryside and the calm life it symbolizes shows through. He was also yearning for news from home and complained to Ross that Graves had not written to him since his arrival in France. He was worried that Graves was 'annoyed' that he had changed some of his poems in *Goliath and David* while seeing it through the press. He had no need to be, for Graves had already written to him on 26 March, thanking him for editing the book so successfully, a letter which had not yet reached him by the time he wrote to Ross on 1 April.

'Fine' prose passages gave way to scribbled diary entries when the Battalion set off on 2 April for Arras and the Front. The year 1916 had ended in a sense of defeat for the Allies: the Somme offensive had failed, Russian morale was at a low ebb, Roumania had been overrun and, at sea, Jutland had been, at best, a negative encounter. Only the capture of Baghdad (Sassoon's 'ancient family residence' as he described it in a letter of 18 March 'celebrating' the event) could really be counted as a victory and that seemed to most people too far away to be of much interest. One result of the growing dissatisfaction was a change of political leadership in England, where Lloyd George's Government replaced that of Asquith on 11 December 1916, and a switch in military leadership in France, where General Nivelle (of Verdun fame) replaced Marshal Joffre as Commander-in-Chief of the French Armies. While Lloyd George and his fellow politicians on the Allied side were rejecting German peace proposals in December as insincere, Joffre had been drawing up plans for one more great battle, in the belief that this would finally defeat the enemy.

Since Allied troops in France numbered about 3,900,000 men (one-third of them British) to the Germans' 2,500,000, Joffre had calculated that a concerted attack on them in spring 1917 should exhaust their reserves and bring the War to an end. When Nivelle took command in early 1917, whilst accepting Joffre's plan of a renewal of the Somme offensive on a widened front, in principle, he made several significant changes. He proposed to attack on both flanks of the Lens-Noyon-Rheims salient, with the French striking the greatest blow in Champagne after Allied attacks north and south of the Somme had claimed the Germans' main attention. His plan to avoid the old Somme battlefields but attack each side of it reduced the frontage of the British, who were ordered instead to take over the French Front south of the Somme as far as Roye, in order to release more French troops for the main attack in Champagne. In spite of Haig's reservations, the battle was fixed for 1 April, an unfortunate date.

It was an ingenious scheme, but even before it got under way (slightly later than planned) on 9 April, the Germans had disrupted it. Ludendorff, anticipating the Allies' move and anxious to avoid the Somme experience, had already ordered a new, massively fortified line of defence to be built across the base of the Lens-Noyon-Rheims arc. This new line, completed early in 1917, was known as the Hindenburg Line to the Allies, but the Siegfried Line to the Germans, an irony on which Sassoon did not comment. As the Germans retired behind it in good order during the second half of March 1917, they systematically devastated the area they were leaving. This simple but effective device disrupted British plans and delayed preparations for the main attack. Only the area round Arras, a German-held bulge of which Gommecourt formed the most westerly point, remained unchanged and was, therefore, chosen as the starting point of the spring offensive. The VI and XVII Corps were on the left and on the right the VII Corps, of which Sassoon's 2nd Royal Welch Fusiliers formed a part.

The reaction of the 2nd Battalion to the Arras plan, if Dr Dunn's comments are representative, was sceptical. 'The Battle of Arras, and its brood,' Dunn wrote, 'was the B[ritish] E[xpeditionary] F[orce] share of the ambitious scheme which British and French Governments had accepted from the new Commander-in-Chief of the French Armies [Nivelle]. Converging Franco-British attacks were to envelop the German centre.'[34] The first stage of the Battalion's involvement was a march of fifty miles to the battle area, via Corbie, Villers-Bocage, Beauval, Lucheux and Saulty, which took seven days, including a day's rest on Easter Friday.

It was only as the journey got underway that Sassoon had become fully aware of his own men. On arrival at Camp 13 in March he had been put in charge of no. 8 Platoon of B Company, when they seemed to him a sorry collection on the whole. Several of them had been part of a recent draft of conscripts and he suspected them to be physically and, in some cases, mentally unfitted for the army. A number of his platoon were barely capable of carrying the weight of their equipment and in one case a new recruit did not even know how to load a rifle. (After teaching him, Sassoon felt 'that the poor devil would have been a less perilous ingredient of his command had he been left in his primordial ignorance'.[35]) The total strength of the platoon, including two sergeants, one corporal and six lance-corporals, was thirty-four, but since eight of these were Lewis gunners, the unit shrank considerably on parade, seldom mustering even twenty men. A further problem for their officer, this being a Welsh unit, was the presence of *eight* Private Joneses. He had tried to interest them all at rest camp with novel platoon exercises suited to their limited abilities, such as hide-and-seek, but remained convinced that the majority of them should not have been in the army at all.

It was on the second day's march towards Arras that Sassoon's doubts were confirmed. Several of the weaker members of his little band with others from B Company were 'beat to the world' by the time they reached Villers-Bocage and he covered the last lap trundling two of them in front of him, while another hung on to his belt behind. The Company Sergeant had to carry their rifles. Not one of the three stood more than five feet high. Even those who had marched under their own steam were suffering badly, as a foot-inspection revealed. It stirred all Sassoon's latent love and compassion for what he later called, in a

Whitmanesque phrase, his 'brave brown companions',[36] to see the patience with which they endured their badly blistered feet, as a poem written the same day makes clear:

Foot Inspection

The twilight barn was chinked with gleams; I saw
Soldiers with naked feet stretched on the straw,
Stiff-limbed from the long muddy march we'd done,
And ruddy-faced with April wind and sun.
With pity and stabbing tenderness I see
Those stupid, trustful eyes stare up at me.
Yet, while I stoop to Morgan's blistered toes
And ask about his boots, he never knows
How glad I'd be to die, if dying could make him free
From battles. Shyly grinning at my joke,
He pulls his grimy socks on; lights a smoke,
And thinks 'Our officer's a decent bloke.'[37]

In spite of Sassoon's Christ-like willingness to sacrifice himself for his men, all he could really do for them was to send a large batch of excruciating boots to the Battalion cobblers, knowing that they would come back roughly botched at best. But the incident added fuel to his growing anger with 'profiteers and "Society people" who guzzled their way through the War'.[38]

Fortunately for Sassoon's platoon, the longest march of the journey was over and the next lap, a straightforward eight miles north along the Amiens-Doullens road to Beauval, brought nothing worse than some unseasonal snow. As they marched, they passed out of one 'Army area' (Rawlinson's Fourth) into another (Allenby's Third), slowly but surely approaching their final destination. At Saulty, only twelve miles from Arras, they began to notice clear signs of the Offensive, from ammunition and food dumps to the tents of the Casualty Clearing Station. There was also a large Y.M.C.A. canteen, which delighted the men and gave Sassoon a chance to stock up for them: 'Twelve dozen packets of Woodbines in a pale green cardboard box,' he reminisced, 'were all I could store up for the future consolation of B Company.'[39] His own consolation was to sit in the peaceful park of a nearby château enjoying the sunshine, a few small deer and the various birds, whose song punctuated the thudding of the guns. He reflected, not for the first time and with no great originality, that the threat of death, though terrifying, also made everything seem vivid and valuable:

I don't suppose anyone would believe me if I said I was absolutely happy and contented. Of course this is written after a good meal of coffee and eggs. But the fact remains that if I had the choice between England tomorrow and the battle, I would choose the battle without hesitation. Why on earth is one such a fool as to be pleased at the prospect? I can't understand it. Last year I thought it was because I had never been through it before. But my feeling of quiet elation and absolute confidence now is something even stronger than last summer's passionate longings for death and glory.[40]

Among the troops too, he had observed a growing, almost eager expectancy. Paradoxically, the nearer they got to battle, the more cheerful they seemed. Were they, he wondered, always at their best when they knew they were 'for it'?[41] Perhaps they really believed that the Battle of Arras would end the War, unlike Ottoline Morrell, who thought the Spring Offensive 'pure devilry' and had told him so in one of her numerous letters.[42]

The Battalion had been informed that it would move into its 'final concentration area' on 8 April, Easter Sunday. This was an irony which did not escape Sassoon as he marched his men the last six miles eastwards to Basseux, only a few miles from Arras itself. Having made a relatively early 9 a.m. start the men were installed in their billets by midday and he had time to inspect the old Front Line, from which the Germans had retreated. He was struck, as most British soldiers were, by the superiority of the German trench system. Basseux itself had not suffered badly from shells and its relative calm was enhanced, for the officers at least, by their lodgings in an old château. Seated in one of the attics, his feet sticking out of the window, Sassoon watched some of his friends playing cricket and felt again how good life seemed under threat: 'Cheery voices; glorious sunshine; pigeons flapping about over red and grey roofs. A small church with pointed tower a little way down the street.'[43]

The Battalion was still at Basseux the next day, 9 April, for the opening of the Battle of Arras. This was, on the surface, a brilliant success. Virtually the whole of the German Front Line was taken within three-quarters of an hour and the second line within two hours. Even part of the third, the massively fortified Hindenburg Line, was penetrated by nightfall. (Part of this dramatic opening victory was due to a new artillery strategy, the 'creeping' barrage, in which the artillery moved its fire steadily forward while the infantry followed closely behind.) A few miles away at Basseux the 2nd Battalion talked very loudly about the reported successes but, as Sassoon noted, with 'forced uneasy gaiety'.[44]

For once the rumoured 5,000 German prisoners was an underestimate, the Allies having taken at least 5,600 on this first day. For Sassoon the excitement was marred by his own physical condition. He had gastritis, a sore throat and several festering scratches on each hand. Fastidious by nature, he minded almost as much that he had no clean handkerchiefs or socks left. Minor discomforts as these all were in the context, they coloured most soldiers' experience of the War, though often omitted by military historians, as Sassoon pointed out. He had to confess that a large opium pill, 'to promote constipation "suitable for open warfare"' was of more consolation than Ottoline's present of Keats's poems, a little india-paper edition bound in green vellum which arrived in the post.[45] Nevertheless, he took the opportunity of a full day's rest at Basseux to write to thank Ottoline for the book and also for the opal she had given him for good luck.

By the time the 2nd RWF was ordered up to the Front in the late afternoon of 11 April, British success was already beginning to seem less certain. The Germans' third line held firm against renewed attacks and British tanks, which were meant to precede the Infantry and break through the wire, were held up by a combination of mechanical faults and mud. As the Germans brought up reinforcements Allenby's Third Army found itself making a direct attack on a rapidly strengthening resistance without the help of its artillery, whose horse-drawn guns were delayed by the difficulties of crossing the German trench-system. Though the Canadians scored a famous victory further north at Vimy Ridge, an achievement consolidated by the capture of Fampoux a little further south, the River Scarpe marked the limit of real Allied successes. To the south of the Scarpe German resistance, first at Railway Triangle and Telegraph Hill, then on the Wancourt-Feuchy line, was so strong that it badly delayed British advances in that part of the Line.

It was to this area, to the right of Héninel, that the 2nd Battalion, having been 'lent' to the 21st Division for the occasion, was ordered. (The 21st was to relieve the 30th Division.) They had been marching only half an hour when snow started to fall, concealing whole villages which had already been reduced to rubble by the fighting. (One such village was Ficheux, which the men christened 'Fish-hooks'.) Sassoon and Casson considered themselves very lucky indeed to be able to huddle round a brazier in a tiny coke-filled dug-out with a trench-mortar Sergeant-Major and four others. The misery of B Company was alleviated by Sassoon's thoughtful emergency ration of cigarettes from Saulty.

Not surprisingly daylight found everyone bleary-eyed and dejected. The snow had melted, turning everything to mud, a scene of desolation which intensified the nearer they drew to the Front, and by the afternoon they were less than two miles from it. For a march of about three miles in the rain had brought the Battalion to St Martin-Cojeul, a ruined village north-west of Croisilles and south-west of Wancourt, where the Germans had just counter-attacked. The 2nd Royal Welch Fusiliers, who were relieving the 17th Manchesters in reserve, occupied an old German reserve trench near the Hindenburg Line.

As second-in-command Sassoon was entitled to a place in 'Company Headquarters', but this grand-sounding accommodation turned out to be the nearest thing to a rabbit-hole he had ever experienced. Kirkby's considerable bulk did not help; it left just enough room in the dug-out for Sassoon and a small stove. Rations were short and Sassoon risked damaging his already painful fingers further by fishing his precious half-slice of bacon from the flame which threatened to claim it. He shared his last orange (one of his favourite foods in the trenches) with Casson. Then, since sleep seemed impossible in the cramped, icy conditions, tried to keep himself warm by enlarging the dug-out to make room for Casson and Evans. Kirkby, perhaps because of his cushioning of flesh, showed his usual infuriating ability to sleep soundly wherever he was.

When day eventually dawned there was nothing to do except sit in the dug-out and wait for orders. Rumours abounded. Héninel was said to have been taken by the 56th Division, though Sassoon doubted that it could be held. He was aware that the 62nd Brigade was attacking Fontaine-les-Croisilles and Fontaine Wood from a hill three-quarters of a mile away and, by the end of the day, an ominous Friday 13th, he knew that the attack had failed through lack of support on the left flank. He also knew, as he surveyed the numerous corpses scattered over the hillside by the late afternoon, that his own Brigade would be attacking the same targets the next day at 5.30 a.m. He was to remain in reserve again.

At 9 p.m. on Saturday, 14 April, an evening which reminded Sassoon irresistibly of spring twilights in England at the cricket nets, the 2nd Battalion, being in support to the 1st Cameronians, set off to relieve the 13th Northumberland Fusiliers in Hindenburg Support. It had been a day of such carnage that, as Martin Gilbert points out, 'three British generals defied Army tradition by protesting directly to Haig at the mounting casualties'.[46] Yet once again Sassoon found himself relegated to a passive role, or so he thought.

Though the distance was less than two miles, the Northumberland Fusiliers guides, who had come to fetch B Company, managed to lose their way. Kirkby decided to sit down and wait for daylight, but Sassoon, with his usual mixture of recklessness and courage, tried to rectify the situation. Stumbling off into the darkness he came across a small party of Sappers in a sunken road, one of whom was able to lead B Company to their Battalion rendezvous. It was 4 a.m. by the time they arrived at the cavernous underground communication trench assigned to them and 5 a.m. by the time Sassoon finally got to bed.

Sassoon had spent the intervening hour arranging for his depleted Company to mount sentries along its 900-yard front and, in the absence of anyone sufficiently experienced, had gone out to patrol No Man's Land himself, in a fit of temper at the unawareness of Battalion Headquarters when they issued such orders. The trench itself, lined with grotesque figures of dead or sleeping men – he could not distinguish which – had seemed to him a nightmarish place worthy of a new infernal vision by Dante, Milton or Blake, but No Man's Land was far worse. Alone and unprotected by wire of any kind, since he was now behind the enemy's third line, he could think of nothing more defiant than to relieve himself in the direction of the Germans, an action he found curiously comforting. He was, however, in more danger from his own nervous sentry, as he carefully measured his paces back to the trench, than the enemy, and he was glad to regain the company's left-hand post unharmed as 'a dull, red, rainy dawn rose'.[47] Descending into the chill of the tunnel beneath the support trench he lay, frozen to the bone on his wire-netting bunk, unable to sleep and already anticipating his own death in those diabolical surroundings. He was to remember the scene vividly nine years later and to describe it in a passage reminiscent of Henri Barbusse, whose *Under Fire* he greatly admired: 'Stage by stage we had marched to this monstrous region of death and disaster. From afar it had threatened us with the blink and din of its bombardments. We groped and stumbled along a deep ditch to the place appointed for us in that zone of human havoc. The World War had got our insignificant little unit in its mouth; we were there to be munched, maimed or liberated.'[48]

After only one day in the Hindenburg Trench Sassoon believed that he had seen the most ghastly sights of his life, ones which would haunt him till he died; dead bodies lying about, both inside the tunnel and just in front of it, gruesome beyond belief after the rain. Everywhere he saw mangled Germans or British soldiers in various states of dismemberment, and smelt their decaying bodies. In one of his many attempts to exorcize such memories he wrote 'To the Warmongers':

> I'm back again from hell
> With loathsome thoughts to sell:
> Secrets of death to tell;
> And horrors from the abyss. ...[49]

It was 'the horrors from the abyss', particularly the suffering and carnage witnessed at Arras, which were finally to provoke Sassoon into making his feelings about the War public: 'You *shall* hear things like this' he threatened those who remained behind, safe and unaware in England. But the experience was evidently too raw for finished verse and he chose not to publish these lines.

After an hour's sleep on the morning of Sunday, 15 April – he had not slept for more than an hour at a time since the previous Tuesday – Sassoon was up again and in charge of a carrying party. In order to encourage the equally exhausted men, he himself lugged loads of heavy trench-mortar bombs between St Martin-Cojeul and Croisilles. It rained all day and the trenches were like glue. To Sassoon, sodden and exhausted, the experience seemed typical of infantry life at the Front. He was among ruins of an intense bombardment of two weeks before, which had left concrete emplacements smashed and tilted sideways, the chalky soil pitted with huge shell-holes and dead bodies everywhere: 'I can remember looking down, as I blundered and gasped my way along [he was to write] and seeing a mask-like face floating on the surface of the flooded trench. This face had detached itself from its skull. I can remember two mud-clotted hands protruding from the wet ashen soil like the roots of a tree turned upside down; one hand seemed to be pointing at the sky with an accusing gesture.'[50]

It was nightmare visions like these which were to haunt him later as he walked along Piccadilly, or followed equally innocuous pursuits. His attempt to describe the carnage in 'The Effect' gives an even more vivid impression than the diary account, despite the fact that it was written a few months later. The poem is shaped by the phrase 'he had never seen so many dead before', which

Sassoon had taken from the report of a War Correspondent, using it as an ironic refrain, and ends:

> 'How many dead? As many as ever you wish.
> Don't count 'em; they're too many.
> Who'll buy my nice fresh corpses, two a penny.'   (*CP*, p. 73)

When William Heinemann was shown this poem, he thought the last line 'quite impossible'.[51]

After six and a half hours in the mud and the rain, Sassoon returned to Company Headquarters, only to be informed by Kirkby, snug and dry himself, that he had been detailed to take command of a hundred bombers; they were to act as a reserve for the 1st Cameronians the next day. Though the full strength of the 2nd Royal Welch Fusiliers was only 270, he was to take twenty-five men from each Company for the assignment. That same day, 15 April, Haig had ordered an end to the opening offensive, but the fighting continued. As part of what became known as the Battle of the Scarpe, the 1st Cameronians (to the right of the 2nd Royal Welch Fusiliers) were to negotiate a barrier which blocked both the deep tunnel under the support trench and the Hindenburg Trench itself. They were then to attack the Germans, who were known to be on the other side of the 'block', as it was called. The objective was to clear the trench and tunnel for 500 yards, while other battalions on their left went over the top to attack Fontaine-les-Croisilles. Sassoon's unenviable task was to tackle the Tunnel if the Cameronians failed. Though the friendly Cameronian officers who explained the plan believed that there was little chance of Sassoon being called on to support 'the Cams', he was decidedly apprehensive. He was even more alarmed by the need to present a coherent battle plan to his Adjutant, since technical details made him feel inadequate in a way that direct action never did. Clutching the few smudgy notes he had made, and longing for Dr Dunn to advise him, he made his way to Battalion Headquarters along the Tunnel.

A few inches higher than a tall man and fitted with bunks and recessed rooms, this was an eerie place, reeking of foul decay. Once, when he tripped and recovered himself by grabbing the wall, his torch revealed someone half-hidden by a blanket. It was only after shaking and even kicking the apparently sleeping body that he discovered the truth; it was a dead German he was trying to rouse, his fingers still clutching a blackened gash on his neck. Sickened and even more unnerved he stumbled on until he reached Mann at Battalion Headquarters. To his great relief he learnt that the underground part of the operation had been cancelled, though the trench attack on the 'block' would still go ahead. On his way back he was fortunate enough to discover Ralph Greaves sitting in A Company headquarters and was soon supplied with the required organization scheme by his imperturbable friend.

The attack on Fontaine-les-Croisilles began at 3 a.m. on Monday, 16 April.

As Sassoon waited nervously at the 1st Cameronians' Headquarters in the Tunnel, ready but not anxious to be summoned, he felt intensely self-conscious. He found it difficult to believe that anyone thought him capable of helping. With his hundred bombers lining the fifty steps which led up to the trench he felt something of a charlatan. Yet when the order finally came at 6 a.m. for him to dispatch twenty-five of his weary, chilled men to help the Cameronians' struggling B Company, he insisted on taking them up to the 'show' himself. Stopping only to put on his steel helmet, he led A Company, which happened to be at the top of the steep stairs, into the sunlit but noisy morning of the support trench.

Headed by Sergeant Baldwin ('Baldock' in *Infantry Officer*), an admirably impassive man who 'never ceased to behave like a well-trained and confidential man-servant',[52] the contingent consisted of fifteen bombers, four rifle grenadiers and five carriers, who also acted as bayonet men. Dodging and stumbling up a narrow communication trench to the wide main trench, at the head of this little group, Sassoon says he had not the slightest idea what he was going to do. Fortunately, he was able to conceal his confusion and managed to convince not only his own men but also the retreating Cameronians that he was in full control of the situation. On learning that the latter, after taking several hundred yards of the trench, had run out of bombs and been driven back, he reassured their young Captain (Wright) and set off recklessly to regain the lost ground. As he freely admitted in his detailed account for Dunn's subsequent history:

> ... I never pretended to be a professionally efficient soldier. My methods were always amateurish and unsystematic. I always failed to take necessary precautions and, on the occasion I am trying to describe, my only effective quality consisted in an unreasoning resolve to rush in where The Cameronians were no longer willing to tread. Anyhow my ignorance simplified the situation, and was for the time being an advantage .... A few of our own shells were dropping short. It was half-past six on a fresh mid-April morning .... I was excited and mettlesome. The Cameronian crowd had been legging it, and I was out to show them how easy it was to deal with the Germans.[53]

The most interesting aspect of Sassoon's part in the Battle of Arras, for a biographer, is his own attitude toward it. Nowhere is his upper-middle-class background more apparent. For he consistently portrays himself, in true English fashion, as an amateur who nevertheless succeeds where the professionals have failed. Sassoon might dismiss his behaviour, including what followed next, as 'foolhardy', but it was also, without doubt, courageous. Accompanied by Sergeant Baldwin he climbed over the Block and advanced a hundred yards up the trench, without meeting anyone. He then sent Baldwin back to arrange for the collection of small heaps of precious Mills bombs which he had noticed at twenty yard intervals, and continued alone. Rounding a corner with some apprehension, he encountered a small man, fortunately from his own side. This turned out to be a Cameronian Corporal, still on guard, a bag of bombs slung over his left shoulder.

In complete silence Sassoon joined him, his own bag of bombs at the ready, and together they advanced round the next bend. What Sassoon saw there helps to explain his subsequent recklessness. Propped against the wall of the trench, in a pool of his own blood, was a fair-haired Cameronian private staring vacantly at the sky. Enraged by the sight of the badly-wounded man, Sassoon slung a couple of bombs in the enemy's direction, receiving in reply an egg-bomb which exploded harmlessly behind him. Now completely mindless of danger, he advanced without caution until he noticed the corporal darting into saps, or side-tunnels, as he threw his bombs. Impressed by his artfulness and efficiency, Sassoon followed suit and between them they drove the Germans back nearly 400 yards, until they reached their objective.

It was only then that the aptly named Corporal Smart spoke to Sassoon, who had forgotten about their 'objectives'. He had caught an occasional glimpse of retreating Germans, but the whole exercise had seemed to him, in his excitement, so absurdly easy that he wanted to push on. Following one of his frequent impulses, he started to explore a narrow sap which ran out from the place where they had stopped. A second impulse, prompted by an apparent lull in the attack going on overhead, nearly cost him his life. Sticking his head out of the sap to look at the surrounding countryside, he received what felt like a tremendous blow on the back, between the shoulders. In reality, a sharp-eyed sniper had shot him through the right shoulder from the front. Sassoon firmly believed throughout the War that his luck never deserted him, and this was a case in point. The bullet had missed both his jugular vein and his spine by a fraction of an inch.

At the time Sassoon was convinced that his end had come and, leaning against the wall of the sap, shut his eyes. When he opened them again, Sergeant Baldwin was beside him, discreet and sympathetic, and he realized to his great surprise that he was still alive. After helping him to the main trench and dressing his wound, which had luckily not bled much, Baldwin went off to fetch more men. By the time he returned with Sassoon's fellow officer, Conning, who had been sent to relieve him, Sassoon had recovered sufficiently to want to carry on fighting and was busy organizing a fresh attack. (He was now, as he observed, not only a hero but a wounded hero.) Only Conning's calm behaviour and written order from the Cameronian Colonel, Chaplin, telling him not to advance further – the attack had failed elsewhere – quelled his offensive spirit.

With a distinct sense of anti-climax Sassoon observed the further order to hand over to Conning and, at 9.45 a.m., only three and three-quarter hours after he first set out, was back at Battalion H.Q. After receiving both the Colonel's and the Adjutant's congratulations on his courageous action, he made his way slowly to the Aid Post. From there he was directed first to the Advanced Dressing Station at nearby Hénin, to be officially labelled 'walking wounded', then to

Boyelles, an exhausting walk of three miles through the mud. Fortunately his batman, Mansfield, a quiet, clumsy, middle-aged man, went with him to carry his kit and it was he who put him on a bus for Warlencourt.

An uncomfortable one and a half hours later, for the roads were very bad, he found himself sitting in the 20th Casualty Station hospital, destined for England. His wound was 'hurting like hell', his anti-tetanus injection was making him feel 'very chilly and queer', he was 'half-dead for lack of sleep' and still in the 'same old clothes' he had worn for a week, but he was safe. 'For I've sped through. O Life! O Sun!' he marvelled, quoting in this moment of extreme emotion the words of his friend Robert Graves.[54]

13

'Love Drove Me to Rebel'

April-July 1917

Sassoon's immediate reaction on being told that he was destined for England in April 1917 was extreme relief. This lasted as long as his rather protracted journey home, via Doullens, Abbeville and Camières, where he waited two days. While his pain and exhaustion continued he still felt like a wounded hero and his attitude remained warlike, but once in England, comfortably installed in the 4th London Hospital at Denmark Hill, his self-absorption gave way to thoughts of those he had left behind. He already knew that, in spite of his own modest success, things were going badly at Arras, and all the subsequent news from the 2nd RWF was to confirm his sense of lives wasted in a pointless exercise.

Only two days after his arrival at the 4th London, he was trying to describe the incident which most forcefully expressed for him the horror of Arras – his experience in the Hindenburg Tunnel. Unusually, the poetic version, 'The Rear-Guard', preceded the prose account, which was to follow in *Infantry Officer* many years later:

> Groping along the tunnel, step by step,
> He winked his prying torch with patching glare
> From side to side, and sniffed the unwholesome air.
> Tins, boxes, bottles, shapes too vague to know;
> A mirror smashed, the mattress from a bed;
> And he, exploring fifty feet below
> The rosy gloom of battle overhead.
>
> Tripping, he grabbed the wall; saw some one lie
> Humped at his feet, half-hidden by a rug,

And stooped to give the sleeper's arm a tug.
'I'm looking for headquarters.' No reply.
'God blast your neck!' (For days he'd had no sleep,)
'Get up and guide me through this stinking place.'
Savage, he kicked a soft, unanswering heap,
And flashed his beam across the livid face
Terribly glaring up, whose eyes yet wore
Agony dying hard ten days before;
And fists of fingers clutched a blackening wound.

Alone he staggered on, until he found
Dawn's ghost that filtered down a shafted stair
To the dazed, muttering creatures underground
Who hear the boom of shells in muffled sound.
At last, with sweat of horror in his hair,
He climbed through darkness to the twilight air,
Unloading hell behind him step by step.   (*CP*, pp. 69-70)

Through one small but unforgettable incident, Sassoon manages to convey the nightmare quality of the Hindenburg Tunnel. The experience itself was a fairly common one (his own C.O. had a similar encounter) and a comparison of this final version with his rough draft written the same day suggests that he worked hard to make his own memorable. Apart from the division of an originally continuous poem into four irregular but carefully rhymed stanzas, the changes are mainly to the language. While keeping phrases he liked, such as 'sweat of horror in his hair' and 'Dawn's ghost that filtered down a shafted stair', he made his second version both more evocative and more specific. Thus 'tiny torch' is personified into 'prying torch' and 'whitening glare' becomes 'patching glare'. The 'rosy dusk of battle', in line seven, is changed to 'rosy gloom of battle', presumably in the interests of accuracy, since battles start at dawn not dusk. Sometimes the changes promote a sense of greater restraint, the 'hateful air' of the tunnel becoming 'the unwholesome air', for example, and the 'foul, hunched mattress' becoming simply 'the mattress', as though the narrator himself is restrained by his fear from more elaborate language.

In only one instance is the narrator's emotion made more overt, when he shouts at the apparently sleeping corpse, 'God blast your neck', rather than as originally, 'Wake up, you sod', the effect being heightened by the fact that the soldier has died from a neck wound. Rather than keeping the gruesome phrase 'Bloody fingers clutched a hideous wound', however, Sassoon alters it to the more restrained but more specific 'And fists of fingers clutched a blackening wound'. The dead man's suffering is emphasized by the simple device of throwing 'Agony that died ten days before' into the present and more immediate tense: 'Agony dying hard ten days before'. In a similar way 'clammy creatures' becomes 'dazed, muttering creatures', where the de-humanizing effect of the tunnel is preserved in the word 'creatures' but more specific detail is introduced in the adjectives. With the addition of the last line to the final version – 'Unloading hell behind him step by step' – Sassoon not only spells out his message but also brings the rhyme scheme neatly back to where it started, so rounding off the poem.

Scott Moncrieff described 'The Rear-Guard' as 'an amazing piece of war photography'[1] and Sassoon himself thought it succeeded. He did not deny that he had been strongly affected by his recent experiences, but he saw his poems as a way of exorcizing them rather than manifestations of severe shock. 'To the Warmongers', written on 23 April, powerfully expresses in grim detail the horrors of Arras and his anger at those who condoned the situation. In 'The General', also written in hospital, this anger is focused on those most directly responsible for the soldier's fate. The germ of that brief but highly effective satire may have come from an incident in Sassoon's journey to Arras, when the 2nd RWF had passed their Corps Commander, Lt.-Gen. Maxse, though the General has also been variously thought, or argued to be Snow, Haig, Pinney, even Allenby. (To date his identity, if indeed the reference is a specific rather than generic one, has not been satisfactorily established.) In Sassoon's poem the unsuspecting soldiers' praise of their General's cheerfulness is contrasted starkly with the results of his incompetence. The use of generic names for the soldiers – 'Harry' and 'Jack' – which both personalizes and depersonalizes them, and the General's breezily repeated greeting, together with Harry's unwittingly ironic comment and the shock ending, convey the situation far more vividly than a more discursive piece:

> 'Good-morning; good-morning!' the General said
> When we met him last week on our way to the line.
> Now the soldiers he smiled at are most of 'em dead,
> And we're cursing his staff for incompetent swine.
> 'He's a cheery old card,' grunted Harry to Jack
> As they slogged up to Arras with rifle and pack.
>
> But he did for them both by his plan of attack.   (*CP*, p. 75)

The colloquial 'did for them both', which follows unexpectedly on what appears to be the concluding rhyming couplet, is all the more shocking in its euphemism. It is certainly more effective than Sassoon's original 'murdered them both', to which several of his mentors had objected.

It seemed essential to tell the truth about Arras while it was still fresh in his mind, but the effort exhausted him. Then there were too many letters to answer, from Heinemann, Graves and Dent among others. ('Poor old Sassons', Graves had opened his letter, which had arrived on 22 April, '"Blessé pour la patrie" and according to Robbie rather too slightly to serve any useful purpose'.) He was also encouraging Dent to come, though already overwhelmed by visitors.

That, of course, was part of his problem – the many visitors, who all wanted to talk to him about the War. 'My brain is screwed up like a tight wire,' Sassoon noted in his diary towards the end of April. On one afternoon alone, the 26th, he was visited by Meiklejohn, Ross *and* Gosse, which may explain why he wrote to Ottoline the same day asking her not to visit. Over-excited and still not fully recovered physically, he was unable to sleep. Instead his nights were filled with visions of the horrors he had so recently left behind:

> ... when the lights are out, and the ward is half shadow and half glowing firelight, and the white beds are quiet with drowsy figures, huddled outstretched, then the horrors come creeping across the floor: the floor is littered with parcels of dead flesh and bones, faces glaring at the ceiling, faces turned to the floor, hands clutching neck or belly; a livid grinning face with bristly moustache peers at me over the edge of my bed, the hands clutching my sheets. ... One boy, an English private in full battle order, crawls to me painfully on hands and knees, and lies gasping at the foot of my bed; he is fumbling in his tunic for a letter; just as he reaches forward to give it me his head lolls sideways and he collapses on the floor; there is a hole in his jaw, and the blood spreads across his white face like ink spilt on blotting-paper. I wish I could sleep.[2]

Experiences like this revived Sassoon's anti-war feelings, which he further inflamed by reading Bertrand Russell's *Justice in War-Time*.[3]

There were, however, opposing pressures at work. By the end of April he had received a letter from his Adjutant, Mann, telling him that he had been recommended for another (unspecified) decoration, the two most likely ones being a Distinguished Service Order or a bar to his Military Cross.[4] Had either materialized, Sassoon believed that it would have 'queered [his] criticisms' of the War.[5] As it was his failure to win another medal, because of the failure of the action as a whole, would free him from any vestiges of loyalty to the army.

With the publication of *The Old Huntsman* imminent, Sassoon hoped to make his criticism of the war unavoidable and he looked forward to it eagerly. Its printing had been delayed by a war-time rationing of paper, but by 23 April he finally held it in his hands. Its sombre grey and black dust-jacket enclosed the seventy-two poems that he had chosen to represent him between 1909 and the beginning of 1917. Heinemann had printed a modest thousand copies, of which 260 were sent in sheets to E.P. Dutton of New York.[6]

To Sassoon, whose only trade publication, *The Daffodil Murderer*, had sunk almost without trace, it was a heady moment. As soon as he was allowed out of hospital on 1 May, he lunched with one of his staunchest admirers, Meiklejohn, at the Reform, then again with Meiklejohn and Ross there on the 2nd. He also enjoyed talking to two already well-established writers, H.G. Wells and Arnold Bennett, as well as the future Foreign Editor of *The Times*, Harold Williams.

At this time, as Leonard Woolf noted, Wells and Bennett, together with

Bernard Shaw, stood 'at the zenith of the literary heavens'.[7] Wells, who was the slightly senior of the two novelists, was twenty years older than Sassoon and was to treat him at times like a son. In spite of their differences in both age and background – Wells, the child of an unsuccessful tradesman, had pulled himself up by his bootstraps and was more interested in the sciences than the arts – they formed an immediate *rapport*. Wells, Sassoon remembered, 'behaved as though my opinions were worth listening to, which seemed remarkable in one whose talk was so stimulating and humorous and full of ideas'.[8] (Sassoon would later describe Wells as the 'embodiment' of 'humour, the love child of literature'.[9]) Wells's response seemed all the more gratifying in one who was already famed for his uncertain temper and whose celebrity allowed him to choose virtually any company he pleased. By 1917 he had written many of his most successful novels, including *The Time Machine* (1895), *The Invisible Man* (1897), *The War of the Worlds* (1898), *Love and Mr Lewisham* (1900), *Kipps* (1905) and *The History of Mr Polly* (1910). His most recent work, *Mr Britling Sees It Through* (1916) was a bitter criticism of a war which he had initially welcomed as 'the war to end war', a revelation to Sassoon, as I have suggested. Wells may have fuelled Sassoon's own mounting anger at this first meeting. They would remain friends until the end of the novelist's long life, despite criticism on both sides.

Sassoon's relationship with Arnold Bennett would be even closer, perhaps because he had more in common with him than Wells. Beside coming from a more middle-class background – his father had been a solicitor – Bennett shared Sassoon's love of music and art, as well as literature. Though he did not pretend to be an expert on poetry, he never dismissed it, as Wells did, and admired almost all of Sassoon's work in that field. He was, if anything, even more impressed when Sassoon trespassed onto his own ground, the novel. Sassoon was not able to return the praise quite so enthusiastically; he found Bennett's novels merely 'quite pleasant stuff'.[10] Nevertheless, Bennett had firmly established his reputation with his 'Potteries' novels, *Anna of the Five Towns* (1902), *The Old Wives' Tale* (1908), *Clayhanger* (1910), *Hilda Lessways* (1911) and *These Twain* (1916) and was also a successful playwright by the time they met. About his plays Sassoon was even less complimentary. Nor could he resist satirizing Bennett's marked mannerisms. For all his portentousness, however, Bennett was charming and Sassoon quickly grew very fond of him. He also appreciated Bennett's sharper side. He enjoyed his studied outspokenness, even when it was critical of Sassoon's own work and ideas, because it was usually so witty.

Apart from Bennett's humour, Sassoon appreciated his genuine concern for his welfare. From the start Bennett promoted his poetry in his influential newspaper articles and introduced him to anyone he thought might help in his career. Strictly heterosexual himself, he was nevertheless to be deeply sympathetic over the problems Sassoon's homosexuality would create for him in the 1920s. Their one great area of disagreement at the start of their friendship lay in their attitudes towards the War. Whereas Wells had become highly critical of its handling by 1917, Bennett, who was head of French Propaganda at the Ministry of Information, still approved. His response to Sassoon's anti-war protest would be very fierce indeed. But their friendship survived the crisis and they were to remain close until Bennett's death at the age of sixty-four in 1931.

One of the first books Sassoon presented to Bennett was a copy of *The Old Huntsman* when it eventually came out, five days late, on 8 May.[11] He had quickly added Bennett's name to the presentation list he had drawn up for Ross. Apart from his original mentors, Gosse and Marsh, he had included his more recent friends, Graves and Ottoline, as well as his mother and great-aunt Mozelle. The most significant name on his list was his current hero, Thomas Hardy. Encouraged by his uncle's connection with Hardy, also by Gosse's assurance that 'True Thomas' would like it, Sassoon had written to ask Hardy if he might dedicate *The Old Huntsman* to him. It was his first direct contact with the writer, whom he was not actually to meet until eighteen months later. (The dedication was very simple: 'To Thomas Hardy, O.M.')

Not only did Hardy give immediate permission but, after reading just half of his presentation copy, wrote via Hamo Thornycroft to praise a number of its poems.[12] In a volume which contained less than a dozen satires in its 109 pages, it was the satires he mainly admired, and not just because of his own influence on them. Writing to Graves a fortnight after publication Sassoon reports jubilantly: 'Hardy of Wessex ... praises "The Hero", "Blighters", "They", "When I'm Among a Blaze of Lights", "The Working Party" and "the Tombstone-Maker", which is satisfactory. I did not expect him to be very excited, but to appreciate the grim humour which he is so capable of judging.'[13] Hardy also admired the 'pathos' and 'reticent poignancy' of some of the anti-war poems.[14]

Indeed, it was the satires which drew the public's attention as a whole to *The Old Huntsman*. Though the reviewers were equally divided between those who dealt with the war poetry and those who concentrated on the lyrics, they were far more inclined to quote the former. To some extent this was inevitable; the epigrammatic nature of the war poems lent itself to quotation and the ordering of the book drew more attention to them. After the title poem (put in, according to Wilfred Owen, 'to catch the hunting-people and make 'em read the rest'[15]), the first thirty-six pieces and the last three in the book were about war, with the lyrics sandwiched uneasily between. The earliest poems of all, dating from 1909, were further buried, in the middle of the lyrics. Sassoon himself would have liked to cut out the early verse to make room for 'stronger stuff' but he recognized that its presence illustrated 'the development accomplished by the War'.[16] In the event his juvenilia were largely ignored, though the later lyrics received warm praise from some critics.

Virginia Woolf, after her praise of Sassoon's 'realism' as being 'of the right, of the poetic kind', in his war poetry, then went on to suggest that his lyrics were 'full of a rarer kind of interest'.[17] Her glowing review was the second to appear in the *Times Literary Supplement* in two weeks, probably because Sassoon had complained about the much briefer first one. It had, he told Ottoline, ignored his war poems in favour of quoting one of his weaker lyrics, 'Morning Glory'. The impression created seemed to him that of an 'amiable amateur' and he could only hope that the *Nation* would quote some of the poems Hardy liked. It did, and the review, written by the editor, H.W. Massingham, for whom Sassoon was to work briefly later, was one of the most perceptive he received. Unlike Woolf, Massingham admired the poetry not for its 'realism', which he considered 'one of the supreme artistic failures' of contemporary writers, but for its 'truth':

It is no reflection upon [Mr Sassoon] to say that these war-verses are not poetry, that they have nothing to do with poetry .... Nor are they (to go to the other extreme) simply a convenient instrument for vehement rhetoric and declamation. In a word, they are epigrams – modern epigrams, thrown deliberately into the harsh, peremptory, colloquial kind of versification which we have so often mistaken for poetry. And, to our mind, Mr Sassoon is quite right to select this method .... For into this epigrammatic content, he is able to discharge the hot fluid of honest rage and scorn, heartfelt bitterness and indignation, which must read so very unconventionally, so very disagreeably to those civilians, who have been comfortably nurtured upon the war-poem of the past ....[18]

Massingham went on to quote, either whole or in part, five of the satires, including the one Sassoon pinpointed as the critics' favourite, probably because it was among the most shocking, 'They'.

Only one critic, Scott Moncrieff, dismissed Sassoon's war poetry as 'regrettable', though had it been published a few years earlier in the hey-day of Rupert Brooke and Julian Grenfell it would certainly have roused almost universal anger. Scott Moncrieff's reason for dismissal was not just that he objected to Sassoon's handling of the war material, but that, like Woolf, he thought his lyrics more truly poetic.[19] Sassoon wrote at once to complain – ironically, for he, too, came to believe that his lyrics were superior to his war poetry – and only five days after the review appeared in the *New Witness* Scott Moncrieff replied: 'I enjoyed your book much more than I have said, but I do confidently think that you are too "good at" poetry to waste your talents on such London Mail storyette effects as you have secured in "The Hero". If I had written it I should talk about myself for years after, on the head of cleverness. But that is another matter.'[20]

It was a climb-down which may well have stemmed from a desire not to lose Ross's friendship. For Ross had made it quite clear that he thought Sassoon's war poetry very good indeed and promoted *The Old Huntsman* as hard as he could, buying multiple copies of the book to give away to friends and acquaintances. Sassoon fully recognized Ross's efforts and planned to dedicate his next book to him.

Though Gosse had, as Sassoon put it, 'been terribly windy' about the outspoken war poetry, he too did his best for the book. In his long article on 'Some English Poets' for the *Edinburgh Review* of October 1917 he managed to remain 'sitting on the hedge', as Ross colourfully described it. In literature, specially poetry, Ross argued, Gosse 'waits for the tide: though in all other things he is a pioneer'.[21] After dealing with the poetry of Rupert Brooke, Julian Grenfell, Wyndham Tennant and other war poets more to his conservative taste, Gosse concluded his review awkwardly with an attempt to be both honest and kind about his embarrassing protégé:

> The bitterness of Lieut. Sassoon is not cynical, it is the rage of disenchantment, the violence of a young man eager to pursue other aims, who, finding the age out of joint, resents being called upon to help mend it. His temper is not altogether to be applauded, for such sentiments must tend to relax the effort of the struggle, yet they can hardly be reproved when conducted with so much honesty and courage. Lieut. Sassoon, who, as we know, has twice been severely wounded and has been in the very furnace of the fighting, has reflected, more perhaps than his fellow-singers, about the causes and conditions of the war. He may not always have thought correctly, nor have recorded his impressions with proper circumspection, but his honesty must be respectfully acknowledged.

Sassoon was delighted by the many reviews which praised his satires and equally pleased by the letters of praise which poured in from friends. Even Robert Bridges, a 'rare and grudging praiser', believed that Sassoon had 'got more of the real stuff' in him than almost any other poet of his generation.[22] Another doubter, Edward Marsh, was 'quite enthusiastic' according to Ross,[23] but he must have been keener than that since he was to write less than two months later inviting Sassoon to contribute an impressive number of poems to his next *Georgian Poetry*.[24] Graves, who had encouraged Sassoon to publish the book despite his own disappointment, had written on 27 April from Oxford to report that he had tried to persuade all the booksellers in the town to buy it and had got his father to review it in the *Observer*. He had also persuaded his uncle Charles (Graves) to review *The Old Huntsman* in *The Spectator* and E. Osborne in the popular *Morning Post*. On 19 May he wrote again to predict that Sassoon would 'out-Rupert Rupert [Brooke]'. The most pleasing letter of all was probably from Hamo Thornycroft, whom Sassoon had feared offending with his criticism. Not only did Uncle Hamo find the little book 'stunning' but, more surprisingly, 'especially' admired the war poems. Though Sassoon had written somewhat cynically to Ross on 18 March, 'I think the Thornycroft-Harold Cox-Sidney Olivier [i.e. Hamo and his brothers-in-law] clique will be useful,' he genuinely cared about his uncle's opinion.

With such influential friends to support it, *The Old Huntsman* could hardly fail to be a success. As Ross wrote to him on 18 May, 'The tide has obviously turned'; after years of struggle, he had become famous overnight. Suddenly everyone in the literary establishment seemed anxious to know him. The poet John Drinkwater, to whom Sassoon had been writing hopefully since 1915, told him that *The Old Huntsman* contained 'the real excitement of poetry' and invited him to stay.[25] And on the day after publication Arnold Bennett asked him to lunch with J.C. Squire, another useful contact in the literary world. John (known as 'Jack') Collings Squire, a friend of both Bennett and Marsh, was only two years older than Sassoon but already well-established. A poet, critic and parodist by 1917, he was best known for his literary editorship of the *New Statesman*, which he had held since 1913. Later he would become even better known as the founder and editor of the *London Mercury*, a monthly magazine of some repute for which he would also write. He was, however, already regarded as part of a conservative clique which included Gosse and Marsh. Virginia Woolf described him as 'the very spit and image of mediocrity' and the Sitwells were to attack him and his magazine as boring, pompous and complacent.

The same evening that Bennett's introduction to Squire took place, Sassoon moved from Denmark Hill Hospital to the Princess of Wales Convalescent Home for Officers, temporarily housed at the Great Central Hotel, Marylebone. Three days after that he was convalescing at Chapelwood Manor in Sussex, shamelessly using a letter from a titled lady recommending him for one of the country houses in her organization. Though a sadistic doctor (so it seemed to him) had blocked his first attempt, his persistence was rewarded and he eventually found himself on a train bound for Sussex, anticipating three weeks in his favourite countryside.

Chapelwood Manor was at Nutley, only sixteen miles as the crow flies from Weirleigh and half that distance from his old crammers, Henley House. Grey-timbered and many-gabled, it seemed to Sassoon the most perfect house he had ever stayed in. As he was ushered up to his fragrantly named 'Clematis Room' by a discreet manservant he could hardly believe his luck. From the beautiful view of formal gardens, meadows and the Sussex Downs beyond and the delicate freshness of his room, to the graciousness of his host and hostess, Lord and Lady Brassey, and their splendid dinner, it seemed, as he told Dent, almost too 'heavenly'.[26] Nothing could be more peaceful and harmonious than his first evening, listening to Gluck and Handel played by one of the gentlemanly fellow-officers also staying there.

Thomas, the first Earl Brassey, was an urbane host. Though over eighty and crippled with rheumatism, he was still a lively conversationalist and had once been Master of the Southdown Hunt. Having served in Government for many years, he spoke with the kind of authority that a young officer would find hard to question and Sassoon listened respectfully, he tells us, while his host held forth on public matters. Yet he also found something pathetic in the sight of a once powerful man reduced by time.[27]

Lady Brassey, born Sybil de Vere and herself the daughter of an Earl, presented no such decline. A second wife, she was considerably younger than her husband and still very alert and good-looking. Gracious, sympathetic and beautifully-mannered, she represented for Sassoon 'the patrician distinctions that he had fought for – the climbing woods and green fields that soldiers learn to love when death is over them'.[28] Impulsively he confided his problems to her. He had been to the Front twice, twice been invalided home and his friends were now trying to persuade him to take a safe job as a Cadet Training Officer at Oxford or Cambridge. Possibly as a result of his serene and safe surroundings, he seems to have been contemplating this seriously for the first time. He told Lady Brassey with complete honesty of 'his longing for life and the task that lay before him, setting against it his mystical joy in the idea of sacrifice and the disregard of death'. But her response – that 'death is nothing' and that those who die are helping to win the War from 'up there' – shocked him. He realized that he had appealed to an alien intelligence, which could not begin to understand the way his mind worked. He was still a Romantic, but of a very different kind from the dreamy, religious boy he had once been.[29] He was even more shocked when Lady Brassey concluded the argument: 'It isn't as if you were an only child with a big place to inherit. No; I can't see any excuse for your keeping out of danger.'

Such assumptions, however much he had sympathized before the War, now antagonized Sassoon and pushed him one step nearer to public protest. The very comfort and harmony of his surroundings, which he had appreciated so much at the start, began to oppress him and make him even more conscious of the contrast with the trenches. There was no one to whom he could speak frankly at Chapelwood, not even his fellow-officers, who were too full of polite acquiescence and gratitude to remind the Brasseys of the reality of the War. Lady Brassey's spiritualism, like his own mother's, protected her against uncomfortable thoughts. Nothing could penetrate such a barrier.

For a time Sassoon distracted himself with the sheer beauty of his surroundings. Though he was still having problems sleeping, it seemed miraculous to hear English birds singing their 'maytime madrigals' at dawn, for the first time since 1915, cocks crowing and an owl hooting away in the woods. Typically his mornings at Chapelwood started with the sound of a gardener whetting his scythe beyond the yew-hedges, something which made him think of Marvell's 'The Mower to the Glow-worms'.[30] After breakfast he would sit out in the garden under the oaks and beeches, browsing through something entirely divorced from the war, such as Morley's life of an 18th century Frenchman.

In the afternoons he became a country wanderer again, climbing gates and staring through tangled hedges at the mossy boughs of apple-trees covered with blossom, or listening to the noise of a tiny brook as it forced its way through its narrow channel. He wanted nothing more than a leisurely chat with an old man mending hedges, or the village parson as he leant over his garden gate. For a time the world became, as it had been in youth, 'a leafy labyrinth with clouds floating above the silence of vivid green woods and clean meadows bright with cowslips and purple orchis'.[31]

His contentment could not last. Front-line experiences had imprinted themselves too deeply on his imagination to allow him more than a brief respite. 'A Quiet Walk', written at this time, describes how, after an idyllic three-mile ramble through lanes lined with flowering hawthorns, 'old ugly horrors' came 'crowding back' as he caught sight of a corpse-like figure:

> A man was humped face downward in the grass,
> With clutching hands, full-skirted grey-green coat,
> And something stiff and wrong about the legs.
> He gripped his loathing quick ... some hideous wound ...
> And then the stench ... A stubby-bearded tramp
> Coughed and rolled over and asked him for the time.[32]

War even invaded the garden with corpses of his friends and marred his pleasure in the daily miracle of the dawn chorus, as another poem, 'Death in the Garden', written on 25 May and almost certainly referring to the young subaltern, Brocklebank, whose death Cottrell had recently reported, records: '... He stood before me, a remembered name,/ A twilight face, poor lonely ghost astray.'

When Hamo died Sassoon had felt banished from the garden they had shared as children. Now, attempting to return to the garden, its innocence has gone. Sitting there in the afternoons nibbling cucumber sandwiches with Lord and Lady Brassey's neighbours, thoughts of war tormented him. While outwardly polite to these undeniably pleasant and well-meaning people, he inwardly raged at what seemed to him their criminal unawareness. Even a war-widow, who might reasonably be expected to share his views, did not escape his scorn. In a poem which anticipated his two blistering attacks on women – 'Glory of Women' and 'Their Frailty' – he wrote:

> 'Life is *so* wonderful, so vast! – and yet
> 'We waste it in this senseless war,' she said,
> Staring at me with goggling eye-balls set
> Like large star-sapphires in her empty head.[33]

The complacency of such people and the smugness of the Conservative press they read daily, goaded him towards action, though of what kind he was not yet certain. His discontent was now 'simmering rebelliously'.[34]

Another incentive came from France itself. During his stay at Chapelwood, Sassoon read a copy of a letter Cottrell had sent to Dadd, describing the heavy losses suffered by the 1st RWF during April and early May, and another letter directly from Cottrell full of harrowing details of the 2nd RWF's bloody engagement at Plum Lane, Arras, on 27 May. Two of Sassoon's favourite young officers, Orme and Conning, had been killed, and with one exception all officers in action had become casualties.[35] Lady Brassey's response when he repeated the grim news to her seemed entirely unacceptable, if predictable:

> I told her our Battalion'd got a knock.
> 'Six officers were killed; a hopeless show!'
> Her tired eyes half-confessed she'd felt the shock
> Of ugly war brought home. And then a slow
> Spiritual brightness stole across her face ...
> 'But *they* are safe and happy now,' she said ....[36]

As he wrote to Graves, 'It makes all the placid loveliness of this country of wood and gardens seem like a bit of music by our old friend Mendelssohn, whose sloppy works I perform on the piano of an evening to the huge delight of aged Earls and Countesses, who have outlived their austere emotions.'[37] The War was destroying his romanticism more effectively than Graves had been able to.

Even writing anti-war poetry began to seem an inadequate way of protesting. Of all the poems he produced at Chapelwood between 25 May and 2 June, he found only two worthy of inclusion in future collections – 'The Hawthorn Tree' and 'In an Underground Dressing-Station'. The second of these, though published later, had been started first in April, when the memory of 'two bad cases – abdomen (hopeless) and ankle' he had seen at Hénin Underground Dressing-Station was still fresh in his mind.[38] He may have abandoned the poem temporarily as being, in his own words, 'too horrible', but taken it up again after hearing about the 1st and 2nd Battalions' losses because, as he also said, 'these healthy shocks do people good'.[39] In relating the incident he combined the 'two bad cases' into one to emphasize the suffering:

> Quietly they set their burden down: he tried
> To grin; moaned; moved his head from side to side.
>
> 'O put my leg down, doctor, do!' (He'd got
> A bullet in his ankle; and he'd been shot
> Horribly through the guts.) The surgeon seemed
> So kind and gentle, saying above that crying,
> 'You *must* keep still, my lad.' But he was dying.[40]

The final impression is of pathos rather than tragedy. Neither the soldier's nor the doctor's words seem as significant as Sassoon's direct speech often is and the irony lacks bite. Yet Sassoon wanted it published in the *Cambridge Magazine* in preference to another poem he had just completed, his satire on the press entitled 'Editorial Impressions'.[41]

'The Hawthorn Tree' on the other hand makes a deep impression through its very restraint and understatement. In it Sassoon allows a soldier's mother to express as far as she can and with moving simplicity, reminiscent of Wordsworth and Hardy, her love for her absent son:

> Not much to me is yonder lane
> Where I go every day;
> But when there's been a shower of rain
> And hedge-birds whistle gay,
> I know my lad that's out in France
> With fearsome things to see
> Would give his eyes for just one glance
> At our white hawthorn tree.
>
> ...
>
> Not much to me is yonder lane
> Where *he* so longs to tread:
> But when there's been a shower of rain
> I think I'll never weep again
> Until I've heard he's dead.   (*CP*, p. 80)

If 'A War Widow' is an anticipation of Sassoon's scornful 'The Glory of Women' and 'Their Frailty', then 'The Hawthorn Tree' is a welcome antidote. The language and form are kept apparently very simple to demonstrate the unsophisticated nature of the rural narrator, allowing the strength of the suppressed emotion to come through all the more powerfully. It is an everyday, natural occurrence, a shower of rain, which sparks off the speaker's ominous announcement in the last two lines.

The contrast between the 'weeping' of Nature and the speaker's inability to weep is made particularly striking in the final lines by a departure from what started out as a near repetition of the first stanza. And, while the form leads the reader to expect the fourteen lines of a sonnet, the cutting off at line 13 makes the ending seem abrupt, as though the speaker is too choked with emotion to continue. The curious mixture of formal with colloquial language is convincingly awkward in someone clearly unused to expressing emotions verbally. The word-play on 'give his eyes' introduces the idea that the son might literally have to give his eyes, or even his life, not for the sight of the hawthorn-tree but for his country and that, if so, he will never see the tree again. It also emphasizes the contrast, present throughout, between the 'fearsome things' he is seeing in France and the hawthorn-tree he longs to see, its innocence symbolized simply through its whiteness. Colour was particularly symbolic for Sassoon, who noted for example that the sunsets at Chapelwood were 'yellow and serene – never dyed with crimson';[42] the hawthorn-tree's whiteness is a undoubtedly meant as an ironic contrast to the evil being committed in France.

By the time Sassoon left Chapelwood Manor on 4 June he had completed eight anti-war poems. He had also more or less decided not to try for a safe job in England, though he had yielded to his friends' pressure to the extent of arranging an interview about a cadet-training post at Cambridge for the second week of June.[43] He believed that there were only two honourable courses of action open to him – either to go back to the Front as soon as possible, or to make a formal protest about the War – and he had three weeks' leave in which to choose. In order to consider the matter objectively he refrained from staying with Ross on his return to London and deliberately avoided his company.

Sassoon engaged in only one other activity during this time, but it was one which, far from interfering with his deliberations, probably helped them. Ross had arranged for him to have his portrait done by a fashionable artist of the time, Glyn Philpot. (Sassoon had sent Philpot a signed copy of *The Old Huntsman* in May in preparation.) The original commission had been for Sassoon to have his head drawn for fifty guineas, all he could afford, but when he presented himself at Philpot's studio flat in The Tower House, 28 Tite Street in early June, he was flattered to find that Philpot thought him such a good subject that he wanted to do a half-length portrait in oils for the same price.

By the time Sassoon met the painter in 1917 Philpot had established his own reputation. His career had been partially disrupted by enlistment in the Fusiliers at the outbreak of war, though his poor health dictated a home-service job in the War Office which allowed him to continue some painting. In fact it was while he was still in the army in 1915 that he was elected an associate of the Royal Academy at the early age of thirty. The same year his commission as 2nd Lieutenant had come through, but by early 1917 it was clear that his poor health made him unsuitable for the army. He had just been invalided out when he met Sassoon in June.

Though Sassoon knew very little about Philpot as a painter, he found him immediately attractive as a man. He was particularly struck by Philpot's dark, heavy-lidded eyes and his description makes him seem exotic, an impression reinforced by his surroundings.[44] The elegance of Philpot's interiors and his passion for beautiful furniture, elaborate Oriental screens and carefully chosen pieces of Greek, Egyptian and Gothic sculptures, is reminiscent of his friend Ross and places him in a line of aesthetes who featured in Sassoon's life from Edward Marsh onwards. He himself was to introduce Philpot to another such connoisseur, Frankie Schuster. It was a side to Sassoon which conflicted very sharply at times with his equally pronounced puritanism.

Sassoon came to feel that Philpot had just missed being 'first-rate',[45] but in June 1917 he was greatly impressed by him. Far more assured in his chosen art than the slightly younger man, Philpot nevertheless shared his enthusiasm and wholeheartedness. Though his schooling had been limited by ill-health, he was well-read and, like Sassoon, loved music. Brought up a strict Baptist, he anticipated Sassoon by many years in entering the Roman Catholic Church at twenty-one. Both were sensitive, romantic and handsome young men, physically attracted to their own sex, when they met at the age of thirty-two and thirty respectively.

It is clear from Sassoon's autobiography that he greatly enjoyed his leisurely afternoons with Philpot. The artist, who was something of a dandy himself, had chosen to paint him in a soft grey silk shirt open at the neck, in three-quarter profile, his eyes gazing soulfully into the distance. When the portrait made its first public appearance, the *Tatler* critic was ecstatic:

Philpot has painted rather beautifully the soldier-poet man Siegfried Sassoon – in a very 'artistic' soft grey silk shirt, open to show a youthful neck à la cinema hero, and with no detail left out of fine and sensitive nostril, curved mouth, delicate features, and wavy brown hair. In the deep eyes and on the mouth of this young poet one may see those marks of war on a fine spirit that have led him to protest in verse almost too awfully true and tragic to be borne.[46]

Sassoon himself was less enthusiastic about his undeniably glamorous portrait, which seemed to him just a little 'popular', more suitable for a posthumous volume (he may have been thinking of Rupert Brooke) than a living poet. When, on its completion, he told Philpot he found it rather 'Byronic', the painter simply replied, 'You *are* rather, aren't you?'[47] Neither Ottoline, who had already compared Sassoon romantically to a stag or a faun, nor Ross, who had translated this into an 'offended deerhound', would have been surprised by Philpot's interpretation. Another poet, to whom Philpot would be introduced by Sassoon and whose portrait he would also paint, Robert Nichols, thought Sassoon looked more like a 'sullen falcon', but the imagery is equally romantic and Philpot clearly captured the dominant impression Sassoon made at that time.

Sassoon thought his portrait 'almost scornfully serene and speculative, giving no indication of the conflict that was being enacted behind that mask of physical prosperity'.[48] The *Tatler* critic, however, claimed to have seen in it 'those marks of war on a fine spirit' which had led Sassoon to criticize it and he was almost certainly planning his protest during the peaceful afternoons he spent in Philpot's flat. Though the painter never mentioned war and Sassoon later wrote that the quiet studio flat was 'a perfect place in which to forget about it',[49] it is unlikely that he did so.

On 7 June, only three days after his return from Chapelwood, he was lunching with H.W. Massingham ('Markington' in *Infantry Officer*), the editor of the liberal weekly the *Nation* since 1907, a pale, earnest man who looked as if he had ceased to find human follies amusing. Sassoon wanted to discuss with him the possibility of publishing 'something outspoken' on the War. Three days after that he was at Garsington consulting the pacifist Morrells. Whilst Ottoline urged him to make a public statement, Philip, a Liberal M.P. with a wider knowledge of the world, advised against it. But Sassoon, who had been appalled by Massingham's claim that England's aims were essentially acquisitive, and that she had refused to state her War Aims to the new Russian Government in April or to publish the secret treaties made between England and Russia early in the War, resisted Philip's advice. He gratefully accepted

Ottoline's offer of a meeting with Bertrand Russell, who would go to prison for his pacifist beliefs in 1918.[50]

Two days later, on 12 June, Sassoon was lunching with them both at the Eiffel Tower in Percy Street, having visited Massingham in between for further discussion. Ottoline had also invited another outspoken pacifist, John Middleton Murry, who offered to help Sassoon draft his protest. Sassoon gratefully accepted and went to Murry's Kensington flat for that purpose, possibly the same evening. (Katherine Mansfield was there but hardly spoke.) By 14 June he had a draft ready for Russell, who had offered to act as his 'impresario'. Russell wrote approvingly the next day, asking whether he had begun to write out the statement and, perhaps as a result, Sassoon completed it the same day. A week later, having seen the final version, the philosopher wrote again to say that he liked it *'very much indeed'* and to promise to help publicize it.[51] One of his ideas was to introduce Sassoon to a pacifist M.P. interested in his case, H.B. Lees-Smith,[52] who would try to bring his case to the attention of the House of Commons. All this was taking place within the same fortnight that Sassoon was sitting to Philpot for his portrait. The completion of his picture coincided with that of his statement.

Sassoon maintained in his fictionalized version of events that it was Massingham's revelations about the political background which had finally provoked him to protest. It is true that his statement lays most of the blame at the feet of the politicians, while letting the military off conspicuously lightly.[53]

I am making this statement as an act of wilful defiance of military authority, because I believe that the War is being deliberately prolonged by those who have the power to end it. I am a soldier, convinced that I am acting on behalf of soldiers. I believe that this War, upon which I entered as a war of defence and liberation, has now become a war of aggression and conquest. I believe that the purposes for which I and my fellow-soldiers entered upon this War should have been so clearly stated as to have made it impossible for them to be changed without our knowledge, and that, had this been done, the objects which actuated us would now have been attainable by negotiation.

I have seen and endured the sufferings of the troops, and I can no longer be a party to prolonging those sufferings for ends which I believe to be evil and unjust.

I am not protesting against the military conduct of the War, but against the political errors and insincerities for which the fighting men are being sacrificed.

On behalf of those who are suffering now, I make this protest against the deception which is being practised on them. Also I believe that it may help to destroy the callous complacence with which the majority of those at home regard the continuance of agonies which they do not share and which they have not sufficient imagination to realise.[54]

There were, however, factors other than the political which led Sassoon so uncharacteristically to this open defiance. The military situation, in spite of a spectacular success at the Battle of Messines on 7 June, was still deteriorating. Prospects on the Russian Front had worsened considerably since the February Revolution and Sassoon was not the only person to fear that the Allies were 'losing the War heavily'. He no longer thought that 1917 would mark the end of the fighting, but that it would continue for at least another two or three years, with all the suffering and loss of life that would involve. He now believed that the politicians actually *intended* the War to continue, since 'to carry out [their] scheme of "crushing Kaiserism and Prussianism" by means of brute force, the War *must* go on two more years'.[55]

Sassoon's own personal experience of the Front, and the recent loss of so many men he knew from both the 1st and 2nd RWF, made it impossible to ignore the consequences of more fighting. When he thought of the 'vast anonymity of courage and cheerfulness' represented by a typical Royal Welch Fusilier at his best, and contrasted it with the gross profiteer whom he had heard boasting that 'If the War continued another eighteen months he'd be able to retire from business,' he felt he had no choice but to protest.[56] He could still remember the exact tone of voice in which his friend Orme spoke, so vividly in fact that he wrote the whole of his tribute to him, 'To Any Dead Officer', in that voice.

This poem, which came to him in a flash and almost wrote itself, was composed the same day as his finished statement and seemed to Sassoon to prove the sincerity of his protest. When he first learnt of Orme's death in the 2nd RWF's 'hopeless dud-attack' at Plum Lane, it must have seemed to him particularly cruel since, by rights, Orme should have been back with the 1st Battalion by the time it took place. A further irony was that Orme, who had been taken ill at the beginning of April and ordered to England, was forced to remain in France because the leave boat was full. He had recovered in time to be sent back to the Line, and be killed at the end of May.

Like the pianist, Ralph Greaves's loss of an arm, the situation crystallized for Sassoon the cruel irony of war. In his poem on the subject Orme himself becomes an archetypal subaltern, cut off in his cheerful prime with all his life before him, his very ordinariness an appeal to our pity. By refusing to sentimentalize the young man, Sassoon makes him all the more convincing. His own strong sense of loss is very evident in the last stanza of 'To Any Dead Officer' which leaves little doubt that Orme's death provided one strong incentive to protest against the War. The narrator has been trying to reach the dead officer by telephone in Heaven, an innovative approach which Graves later thought put some people off:

Good-bye, old lad! Remember me to God,
And tell Him that our Politicians swear
They won't give in till Prussian Rule's been trod
Under the Heel of England ... Are you there? ...

Yes ... and the War won't end for at least two years;
But we've got stacks of men ... I'm blind with tears,
Staring into the dark. Cheero!
I wish they'd killed you in a decent show.   (*CP*, p. 85)

Graves also thought that the poem contained too much slang, but Sassoon defended his choice. He told Ottoline that it was an elegy on a subaltern 'written in the language of subalterns, yet tragic and glorious'.[57] The slang was deliberate. He believed people ought to read it because it was 'so different to the countless elegies that [had] been written'.[58] So strongly did he believe this that he was prepared to pay for its printing as a *Cambridge Magazine* pamphlet.

Another strong incentive for his protest came from certain of his friends and from his reading. By June he had almost certainly begun Henri Barbusse's harrowing account of the suffering of soldiers at the Front, *Le Feu*, which had just been translated into English.[59] Weeklies such as the *Cambridge Magazine* and the *Nation* not only gave him a platform for his own verse, but also kept him informed of current anti-war views. Even the Conservative press, by its very smugness and hypocrisy, added to his discontent. He had been particularly enraged by it during his weeks at Chapelwood, perhaps because Lord and Lady Brassey themselves seemed so infuriatingly complacent. It was almost certainly with Lord Brassey in mind that he wrote in his diary only a fortnight after leaving the house and four days after completing his statement: 'Of the elderly male population I can hardly trust myself to speak. Their frame of mind is, in the majority of cases, intolerable. They glory in senseless invective against the enemy. They glory in the mock-heroism of their young men. They glory in the mechanical phrases of the Northcliffe Press.'[60]

He undoubtedly had women of Lady Brassey's type in mind when he fulminated, in the same diary entry: 'Poor heroes! If only they would speak out; and throw their medals in the faces of their masters; and ask their women why it thrills them to know that they, the dauntless warriors, have shed the blood of Germans. Do not the women gloat secretly over the wounds of their lovers? Is there anything inwardly noble in savage sex instincts?'[61] Apart from revealing Sassoon's extremely low opinion of women, this passage is interesting because it shows him already anticipating, perhaps even mentally rehearsing his own action in throwing his personal medal, if not 'into the faces of his masters', then into the River Mersey.

A vital factor in Sassoon's protest was his temperament. Someone equally critical of the War but less impulsive would have thought longer and harder about the consequences, which included the likelihood of a Court Martial and the possibility of being imprisoned for sedition or shot for cowardice. As Sassoon himself pointed out, his behaviour was 'in accordance with the temperament which had led [him] to perform reckless exploits in the front line'.[62] It was that same recklessness, or courage, which would make it so difficult for the military authorities to know how to deal with him.

Sassoon was well aware that his action would be particularly difficult for his fellow-officers to understand. Whilst accepting that it did not stem from cowardice, some of them would regard it as a disgrace to the Regiment and others would assume he had gone mad. How many of them, he wondered, would give him credit for having done it for the sake of the troops at the Front? For that, ultimately, was his strongest motive: 'It was for the fighting men that my appeal was made,' he emphasised in his autobiography.[63] Forty-eight years after the event, complaining to Dame Felicitas Corrigan about being labelled 'less compassionate' than Wilfred Owen, he protested, 'I was bursting with [compassion], wasn't I, when I made my famous and futile protest which many now consider reasonable?'[64] His contemporary notes for the statement in any case clearly show that it was the suffering of the troops which was foremost in his mind: 'Fighting men are victims of conspiracy among (a) politicians; (b) military caste; (c) people who are making money out of the war.' Although the final version departed considerably from such a simple formula, it kept the emphasis on the exploitation of the ordinary soldier.

Sassoon did not send his statement out as soon as it was finished; perhaps dreading the consequences, he wanted to delay them a little. He was due back at Litherland Depot on 27 June, but had no intention of reporting then, since part of his protest would be to refuse to serve in the army. He would wait until he was summoned, then send his statement to his Commanding Officer. The interval he would spend at Weirleigh, where there was only his mother from whom to hide his intentions, no easy matter as it turned out.[65]

Part of the reason Sassoon was not ready to show his protest to anyone until it had been seen by his military superiors was that he rightly suspected that most of his friends would try to dissuade him from such a rash course of action. They would certainly urge him to take the post of Cadet Training Officer which he had been offered at Cambridge when he went for an interview there on 13 June. (This was the day fourteen German bombers, flying at 12,000 feet, attacked London, dropping more than 100 bombs and killing 162 civilians. Sassoon had been lucky to escape unhurt when the area between his bank and Liverpool Street Station had been targeted.[66])

By the end of June, however, the strain had become so great that Sassoon needed to confide in someone and he chose Graves, who had appeared to share his criticisms of the War less than a year previously. Graves had already responded to an earlier letter on 30 June and posted it, when he received a second letter hinting at Sassoon's intentions. Alarmed, he wrote again immediately, urging Sassoon to visit him at Osborne on the Isle of Wight where he was convalescing: 'Do say you're coming: I want to know what characteristic devilment this is. Are you standing as pacifist M.P.? That's the most characteristic thing I can think of next to your bombing Lloyd George.'[67]

Unable to confide in Graves further for the moment, Sassoon continued to wait. The weather was as oppressive as his thoughts, and he longed for refreshing rain. He could not get the War out of his mind, particularly when the faint thud of guns could be heard across the Channel. Everything reminded him of it:

> Now light the candles; one; two; there's a moth;
> What silly beggars they are to blunder in
> And scorch their wings with glory, liquid flame –
> No, no, not that, – it's bad to think of war,
> When thoughts you've gagged all day come back to scare you;
> And it's been proved that soldiers don't go mad
> Unless they lose control of ugly thoughts
> That drive them out to jabber among the trees.   (*CP*, p. 89)

These lines were the beginning of a poem written in early July, retrospectively titled 'Repression of War Experience', after Dr Rivers's lecture of that name in 1917. Continuing the dialogue with himself, the narrator wishes restlessly for a thunderstorm, then tries to settle down to read, but concludes:

>   ... on the ceiling
> There's one big, dizzy moth that bumps and flutters;
> And in the breathless air outside the house
> The garden waits for something that delays.
> There must be crowds of ghosts among the trees, –
> Not people killed in battle – they're in France –
> But horrible shapes in shrouds – old men who died
> Slow natural deaths – old men with ugly souls,
> Who wore their bodies out with nasty sins.
> ...
> You're quiet and peaceful, summering safe at home;
> You'd never think there was a bloody war on! ...
> O yes you would ... why, you can hear the guns.
> Hark! Thud, thud, thud – quite soft ... they never cease –
> Those whispering guns – O Christ, I want to go out
> And screech at them to stop – I'm going crazy;
> I'm going stark, staring mad because of the guns.

A strong sense of foreboding is created by what is in effect a study in contrasts between the ostensibly 'peaceful' England and war-torn France, where the narrator's thoughts keep straying. (It may be a Freudian slip, created by the line-breakage, when he announces three lines from the end 'I want to go out'.) The strain of trying to 'listen to the silence', the ominous sense of waiting 'for something that delays', the suffocation of 'breathless air', the ugliness of old men who die 'slow natural deaths' rather than fighting in France and the sinister deceptiveness of 'soft ... whispering' guns all help to create a scenario which clearly reflects Sassoon's own experience. His nightmares after Arras had not gone away; on the contrary they had begun to invade his waking hours. If he had been tempted to forego his protest in the tranquil surroundings of Weirleigh, his memories would not let him.

When the expected telegram requesting him to 'Join at Litherland immediately' arrived at last on 4 July, Sassoon still delayed two days before responding with a copy of his statement and an explanatory letter to his Commanding Officer, Colonel Jones Williams. This letter shows how unwillingly Sassoon entered his martyrdom; he had always known that the hardest aspect of it would be risking the misunderstanding of his fellow-officers:

> I am writing you this private letter with the greatest possible regret. I must inform you that it is my intention to refuse to perform any further military duties. I am doing this as a protest against the policy of the Government in prolonging the War by failing to state their conditions of peace.
>
> I have written a statement of my reasons, of which I enclose a copy. This statement is being circulated. I would have spared you this unpleasantness had it been possible.
>
> My only desire is to make things as easy as possible for you in dealing with my case. I will come to Litherland immediately I hear from you, if that is your wish.
>
> I am fully aware of what I am letting myself in for.[68]

While waiting for a response to his letter and statement, Sassoon occupied himself by sending copies to a list of people he had drawn up. Apart from friends like Marsh, Bennett and Wells, the names were mainly of people he hoped would be sympathetic to his cause, such as the editors of the *Cambridge Magazine*, *Nation* and *Westminster Review*, Ogden, Massingham and Spender, and the M.P.s Lees-Smith, J.F. Hope, Lord Henry Bentinck and Harold Cox. Copies also went to Hardy, Lord Brassey and, curiously, the sportman, Horatio Hutchinson. People not on the list received copies, too, their names too obvious to need noting down, Ross, Meiklejohn, Ottoline and Bertrand Russell. In addition he sent his statement to Hamo Thornycroft, though he told Harold Cox that he was afraid his uncle would never forgive him. He almost certainly did not send a copy to Gosse, who nevertheless was to hear of it and involve himself.

To a large extent the reactions were predictable. Bertrand Russell had already approved and Ottoline wrote enthusiastically to congratulate him on 'the value and splendour of such a True Act'.[69] His old friend Edward Carpenter, himself a rebel, replied biblically 'Well done, good and faithful!'[70] and Wells, whose own disillusionment had influenced Sassoon, wrote to agree 'that the War was going on through the sheer stupid inability of the responsible people to crystallize out in a plain statement the peace wishes that were practically the same in the minds of reasonable persons everywhere'.[71]

The disapprovers were equally vociferous. Bobbie Hanmer, primed by Graves, wrote briskly from his hospital bed to ask: 'What is this damned nonsense' and to urge, with not a little emotional blackmail: 'For Heaven's sake man don't be such a fool. Don't disgrace yourself and think of us before you do anything so mad.'[72] Marsh wrote more reasonably, expressing surprise that America's entry into the War had not made Sassoon more hopeful of an early resolution and begging him not to be 'more of a martyr than he could help'.[73] Bennett was characteristically more forthright, saying that he thought Sassoon 'very misguided', in no position to judge the situation and guilty of 'spiritual pride'. He concluded his closely argued letter by predicting: 'the Army will ultimately lay it down that you are "daft".'[74] To Sassoon's disappointment Harold Cox, whom he had hoped to have as an ally, also wrote to disagree, though with regret: 'to cease fighting now,' he argued, '[would mean] a Victory for the German military party.'[75] Lord Brassey's reply, if he made one, is not recorded – it may have been unprintable.

The most interesting responses came from those who shared Sassoon's unhappiness about the conduct of the War, but feared for him personally. Chief among these was Ross, who had already seen the son of his great friend, Sir Squire Sprigge, Court-Martialled for a lesser offence[76] and was frightened at what might happen to Sassoon. He made it quite clear that his reaction stemmed from practical rather than philosophical considerations: 'Dearest Siegfried, I am quite appalled at what you have done. I can only hope that the C.O. at Litherland will absolutely ignore your letter. I am terrified lest you should be put under arrest. Let me know at once if anything happens.'[77] For the next fortnight he was in constant touch with Graves and Gosse as to the possible outcome and was able to report to Gosse, whose disagreement did not prevent him wishing Sassoon well, that he had 'promise of powerful help if necessary at the War Office'.[78]

Ironically, Sassoon seemed more concerned about Ross and other friends than himself in the situation: 'Have you recovered from the shock, dear Robbie?' he wrote on about 9 July while still waiting to hear from his Colonel.[79] Hamo Thornycroft, far from casting his nephew off, as Sassoon had feared, went to see if Ross could advise him how to help. Another person who went to see Ross was Hamo's daughter's husband, Herbert Farjeon, who was himself fighting his case as a conscientious objector. Ross told him that, although 'he agreed with every word of Siegfried's protest', he thought things were 'better left as they are – one man can do so little'.[80] A man with a German name like 'Siegfried', he added, was particularly unlikely to do much with a protest of this kind.

The most surprising response came from Joe Cottrell. Instead of condemning it roundly, like Bennett, Joe trod a more difficult line. Fearing a Court Martial for one of his favourites, he tactfully concluded his reply: 'I'm afraid the time is not yet ripe for this. I showed this to [fellow-officers] Reeves and Brunicardi. They, like me, admire your motives but are not so sure of the opportuneness of your action.'[81] Joe had seen too many young officers die unnecessarily to condemn Sassoon's protest outright, as Graves had predicted he would.

The most practical response came from Graves himself, who wrote to Ross on 9 July from the Isle of Wight: 'as soon as I heard I wrote to the dear old Senior Major at Litherland imploring him not to let the Colonel take S. seriously but to give him a special medical board and more convalescent home till I can get an opportunity for getting hold of him to stop him disgracing himself, his regiment and especially his friends'.[82] As usual Graves's own account in *Goodbye To All That* is rather garbled; he claims not to have heard of the protest until the end of July, when Sassoon sent a copy of it published in the *Bradford Pioneer* of 27 July, yet he was already writing to Ross about it on the 9th. His account of his own feelings about Sassoon's actions in the same book is, however, authentic, since it was a point of view he repeated to Sassoon himself at the time:

> I entirely agreed with Sassoon about the 'political errors and insincerities' and thought his action magnificently courageous. But more things had to be considered than the strength of our case against the politicians. In the first place, he was in no proper physical condition to suffer the penalty which the letter invited: namely, to be court-martialled, cashiered and imprisoned. I found myself bitter with the pacifists who had encouraged him to make this gesture. I felt that, not being soldiers, they could not understand what it cost Siegfried emotionally.[83]

Graves did not hesitate to point out to Sassoon, however, that it was not 'good form', nor was it the act of 'an officer and a gentleman', a piece of emotional blackmail Sassoon managed to resist, though he realized that most of their fellow-officers would endorse it.[84] To their mutual friend, Marsh, Graves wrote on 12 July, 'It's an awful thing – completely mad – that he has done.'[85] He was relieved to learn that Marsh did not regard Sassoon as a criminal, since this made it easier to ask his advice. Like Ross, Marsh regarded the War Office as their best hope, though he was unfortunately no longer working for it. Graves claimed in his autobiography that he immediately wrote to a friend there, the Hon. Evan Morgan, Private Secretary to one of the Coalition Ministers, but in fact the letter was not written until the worst of the crisis was over. What he did do, however, was extremely effective. After receiving a sympathetic reply from the 'dear old Senior Major' at Litherland, Major Macartney-Filgate, assuring him that Sassoon would be ordered a Medical Board rather than a Court Martial, he persuaded his own doctors to pass him fit for home service in spite of the fact that he was not yet fully recovered.

Sassoon meantime had been ordered to rejoin the Regiment at Litherland and did so on 13 July in a state of some trepidation. (His promotion to full Lieutenant on 1 July could not have helped matters.) His kind reception by Major Macartney-Filgate, who was acting C.O. in Colonel Jones Williams's absence, made it all the more difficult for him to refuse to withdraw his ultimatum, as gently requested. He felt he was committing 'a breach not so much of discipline as of decorum'. Hoping at least to be arrested, to draw attention to his cause, he was further disconcerted to be told simply to book himself in at the Exchange Hotel in Liverpool while his superiors decided what to do about him.

For the next three days Sassoon waited for developments, his anxiety preventing him leaving the hotel. He may have managed to complete a poem or two[86] but he was in no fit state to settle down to anything satisfactory. After three days spent mainly memorizing poems in preparation for the imprisonment he felt was certain, he was summoned to a Medical Board at Crewe. After a brief struggle with himself he tore up the railway warrant he had been issued, to remove the strong temptation to give in and attend it. As his perplexed C.O. explained the next day, when he came in person to try to persuade him to change his mind, a Royal Army Medical Corps Colonel had come all the way from London for the Board Sassoon had cut. It was shortly after this visit that Sassoon took the train to Formby and in a fit of frustration and anger threw his M.C. ribbon into the Mersey, the most extreme act of rebellion against the army he could conceive.

Sassoon had been alone just over a week when Graves turned up at the Litherland depot on 18 July. His arrival was crucial. Since Sassoon had already rejected the army's face-saving offer of a Medical Board to pronounce him shell-shocked, the situation had reached crisis point. Graves's method was simple but effective. In order to take away Sassoon's motivation for continued rebellion, he merely lied to him about the consequences, assuring him, on an imaginary Bible, that if he refused to be medically boarded, the military authorities would shut him up in a mental hospital for the rest of the War. There would be no martyrdom. Thoroughly defeated by the prospect of such an anti-climactic end to his dramatic gesture, Sassoon finally gave in and agreed to attend a medical. Ignoble as his capitulation seemed to him, he was nevertheless aware of a huge sense of relief, since he had fully expected to be sent to prison. Even after he learned of Graves's lie much later, he was still able to write appreciatively of his act and to admit: 'No doubt I should have done the same for him had our positions been reversed.'[87]

The Medical Board, which was instantly arranged for the next day, had of course been fixed. Whether, as Graves claimed, he 'rigged' it himself with his tearful evidence,[88] or, as seems more likely, Ross's contact at the War Office had given instructions that Sassoon was to be diagnosed as 'shell-shocked', the Board conveniently found him in need of treatment: 'His mental condition is abnormal. His conversation is disconnected and somewhat irrational, his manner nervous and excitable. In addition to this his family history is neuropathic. He is suffering from a nervous breakdown and we do not consider him responsible for his actions.'[89]

It is hard not to suspect that the decision was based on grounds of expediency rather than health, taken as the best way of avoiding the publicity both the

Government and the army feared. H.G. Wells, who sympathized with Sassoon's stand but had advised him not to 'get locked up' or 'do anything excessive', was greatly relieved: 'Take your discharge for "shock" [he wrote] and then let every action show that it was a mere excuse, that you are a grave and balanced man, set upon the peace of the world. Don't develop into a "case".'[90]

To Wells's and other friends' relief Sassoon allowed himself to be sent to a convalescent home for neurasthenics at Craiglockhart near Edinburgh. Reporting to Ross the same day, 19 July, Graves could not resist emphasizing his own part in the affair, though he was forced to admit that '[Sassoon's] views on the War are of course unchanged'. He would be asked to escort Sassoon to Craiglockhart. Julian Dadd, who had been equally worried about the possible consequences of Sassoon's action, was full of admiration for Graves. Writing to Sassoon about it twelve years later, and in spite of severe reservations about *Goodbye to All That*, he pointed out that Graves 'was the master of the situation, and I thought that, for a man of his age his ability and tact were wonderful'.[91]

Sassoon's friends had saved him from the imprisonment meted out to other objectors, but they could not prevent the publicity which the Government was trying so hard to avoid. Despite Sassoon's referral to Craiglockhart War Hospital, Lees-Smith went ahead with his speech to the House of Commons, in which he read out the whole of Sassoon's statement. J.L. Macpherson, Under-Secretary for War, in his response to the M.P., did what he could to limit the damage, ending his moving account of the brave young officer's supposed shell-shock with the hope 'that Hon. Members would hesitate long before they made use of a document written by a young man in such a state of mind, nor did he think their action would be appreciated by the friends of the officer'.[92]

Macpherson's plea produced cheers in the House, but the Press were clearly unmoved by it, since the statement, or references to it, appeared in at least twelve newspapers.[93] Only two papers came out in open support of Sassoon, the *Labour Leader*, which headed the piece 'Lieutenant Sassoon's Defiance', and the *Herald*, which ended its article on 'An Officer as C.O.' with the subversive suggestion 'but those who know him appear to think he is quite as sane and in good health as ever he was'.

There was a curious sequel to this saga. Six months after Sassoon's Liverpool Medical Board, a typewritten copy of his statement was discovered by a Mr S. Sullivan of Saltley, Birmingham, in the luggage-rack of a Birmingham-Preston train. It differed slightly from the *Hansard* version and the one Sassoon was to include in his *Infantry Officer*. Sullivan sent the statement to Lord Derby, the minister responsible for army recruitment, who in turn handed it over to the War Office Intelligence Service. The protest was annotated 'Lieutenant Sassoon was undoubtedly the author but when it was written he was a lunatic. It seems possible that some pacifists are circulating Sassoon's insane efforts.' Sullivan's discovery seems to have drawn attention to Sassoon's verse, which had hitherto escaped the censor's notice; the deputy director of Military Intelligence, Brigadier General George Cockerill, was so disturbed that he wrote to Massingham at the *Nation*, 'If Lieutenant Sassoon is now writing verse such as appeared on page 394, issue of July 13, 1918 [i.e. 'I Stood with the Dead'], it would appear that his mind is still in chaos and that he is not fit to be trusted with men's lives.' The intelligence service was particularly upset by the contents of 'Counter-Attack', which had not been submitted for the censor's approval. But Massingham was deliberately vague about its date of composition and the case was dropped.

Sassoon never regretted his action, though he did later acknowledge that it was unrealistic. He had made his protest in all seriousness, fully prepared to accept the consequences, however grave. Yet looking back on events from 1945 he found it 'difficult to believe that a Peace negotiated in 1917 would have been permanent ... nothing on earth would have prevented a recurrence of Teutonic aggressiveness'.[94] Nevertheless his willingness to be sacrificed for his ideals, however impractical, remains as impressive today as it was then.

14

Strange Meeting

July-November 1917

By the time Sassoon arrived at Craiglockhart on 23 July 1917, Haig was about to embark on what one historian has called 'the gloomiest drama in British military history',[1] the 3rd Battle of Ypres, known otherwise as 'Passchendaele'. The Allied victory at Messines at the beginning of June had provided a much-needed morale booster and Haig planned to follow it up with a single-handed defeat of the Germans in Flanders. He had already decided in May 1917, as the Battle of Arras drew to its doleful end, to transfer the main weight of his offensive northwards to Flanders, hoping to distract the enemy's attention from both the trouble-ridden French and the crisis caused by the submarine campaign at sea. He also trusted such a move would support the offensive still hoped for from Russia, though by the time his campaign was launched on 31 July such considerations seemed irrelevant. Ignoring both his weather forecasters, who predicted only three weeks of fine weather at most, and his engineers, who warned him that to destroy the drainage system of the low-lying area with an initial bombardment would turn the battlefield into a swamp, he pressed on with an attack for which the Germans had had two months to prepare. Long before his empty victory of 4 November, when the British finally reached their objective, Passchendaele, the battleground had become a sea of mud and blood.

In pressing on to the bitter end, Haig used up valuable reserves which might have saved the Allies from the humiliating reverse at Cambrai that followed. Had Sassoon returned to the 2nd RWF when his leave expired in July, he would have marched with them to the Ypres battlefield in August and fought with them there near Polygon Wood in September, when six of his fellow-officers were killed in one day, together with at least sixty other ranks. Had he rejoined the 1st RWF he would not only have had to face the horrors of Ypres but also the rigours of the Italian Front, where the Allies had lost 600,000 men at Caporetto and were being pushed back relentlessly by the enemy. Russia's withdrawal from the War after a second revolution in November and the failure of American troops to make their presence felt as quickly as had been hoped would also add to the Allies' low morale at the end of 1917. Allenby's entry into Jerusalem on 11 December might set the church bells ringing but there would be no real expectation of peace in Europe as the year drew to its close.

In spite of the hopelessness and dangers of life on the Western Front, however, Sassoon would far rather have been there with his men than facing what he regarded as imprisonment in a mental hospital. He was to pass his time at Craiglockhart with a suppressed awareness that he was 'shortening the War' for himself every week he remained there.[2] His protest had been genuine enough, but unless he could believe it to be effective, he felt he was there under false pretences, 'merely skrimshanking snugly along'.[3] So there he was, arriving at a shell-shock hospital in a state of unmilitant defiance of military authority. It was, as he himself pointed out, 'an experience peculiar enough to stimulate [his] speculations about the immediate future',[4] and he had thought about it continuously during his journey up to Edinburgh from Liverpool on 23 July. He was all the freer to do so since his official escorts, Graves and another RWF officer, S.W. Harper, had missed the train at Lime Street, leaving him to travel by himself.[5] On reaching Princes Street station he decided to carry on alone to Craiglockhart War Hospital for Nervous Diseases, which was situated just over two miles from the centre of Edinburgh at Slateford, a name he was to use to conceal the hospital's true identity in his fiction.[6]

A twenty-minute taxi ride south-west through respectable suburbs took him all too quickly to his final destination. Seeing Craiglockhart for the first time on a fine July afternoon, his reactions were mixed. He found the place itself, a heavy Italianate-baronial building of decayed grandeur, rather depressing, while its views struck him as 'prodigiously' beautiful.[7] Set into the side of Wester Craiglockhart Hill, 400 feet above sea-level, it was a very healthy spot. Built in 1880 as a Hydro for wealthy invalids but converted into a war hospital by the Red Cross in October 1916, the house overlooked both the Forth Valley and the Pentland Hills, renowned for their beauty.

Whilst Sassoon's appreciation of the landscape grew even keener during his four months there, his impression of the institution itself did not improve. Though admitting to Dent that it was not a bad place, he never ceased to find it 'gloomy' and 'cavernous'.[8] The pomp of its yellowish-grey façade and three huge towers was echoed in its black and white tiled entrance hall and marble staircase, but that was as far as it went. Whether as a result of conversion or original planning needs, the patients' rooms on the upper three floors led off windowless corridors, which narrowed down claustrophobically on the top floor to a few feet in width. It did not strike him as a suitable place to house 160 depressed, often traumatized officers. Even less ideal was the need to fit two of them to a room. Many had hideous nightmares and some could not sleep at all for fear of them. Sassoon found it the worst aspect of the place. As he pointed out in his thinly disguised account of Craiglockhart in *Sherston's Progress*, the doctors dealt more or less successfully with Craiglockhart's disadvantages by day:

> But by night they lost control and the hospital became sepulchral and oppressive with saturations of war experience. One lay awake and listened to feet padding along passages which smelt of stale cigarette-smoke; for the nurses couldn't prevent insomnia-ridden officers from smoking half the night in their bedrooms, though the locks had been removed from all doors. One became conscious that the place was full of men whose slumbers were morbid and terrifying – men muttering uneasily or suddenly crying out in their sleep. Around me was that underworld of dreams haunted by submerged memories of warfare and its intolerable shocks and self-lacerating failures to achieve the impossible. ... By night each man was back in his doomed sector of a horror-stricken Front Line, where the panic and stampede of some ghastly experience was re-enacted among the livid faces of the dead. No doctor could save him then, when he became the lonely victim of his dream disasters and delusions.[9]

The last two sentences carry the conviction of one who had himself suffered such nightmares, as indeed Sassoon had. But he was never to be reduced to the state of those he described so bitterly at Craiglockhart as 'Survivors':

> No doubt they'll soon get well; the shock and strain
> Have caused their stammering, disconnected talk.
> Of course they're 'longing to go out again,' –
> These boys with old, scared faces, learning to walk.
> They'll soon forget their haunted nights; their cowed
> Subjection to the ghosts of friends who died, –
> Their dreams that drip with murder; and they'll be proud
> Of glorious war that shatter'd all their pride ...
> Men who went out to battle, grim and glad;
> Children, with eyes that hate you, broken and mad.
>   *Craiglockhart, October 1917* (*CP*, p. 90)

Sharing a room with such sufferers was not easy, but an even greater disadvantage for Sassoon was that it prevented him from writing. He had many ideas for poems, but needed time alone to work them out. The after-dinner hours between eight and eleven were what he jokingly called his 'brainy' time, but it was also the time when his companion, a young Scots Captain in tartan breeches, wanted to retire to their joint room. It is a measure of Sassoon's conviction and determination that he produced as many poems as he did at Craiglockhart under such circumstances. He struggled on with his poetry in the evenings and filled the day, as he liked to do, with mainly physical pursuits.

The staff at Craiglockhart, as part of the therapy, offered a wide choice of activities. Golf, badminton, bowls, croquet, billiards, tennis, swimming and cycling were only some of the options available. Patients could even rear their own poultry, garden or help the local farmers bring in the hay. They could also pass the time making model boats, develop their own photographs, join the Debating Society, take French classes or go botanizing. In addition, there was a hospital magazine, a theatre company and an orchestra, all run by the patients.

It was not unlike boarding-school or university, and Sassoon's choices remained similar to those he had made at Henley House and at Cambridge. After passing the first week in long, solitary walks over the Pentland Hills, he spent a large part of most days playing golf. It seemed a natural choice in a city surrounded by fine golf-courses, particularly in the absence of his usual summer favourite, cricket. It also kept him fit, something he still cared about. Most importantly, as he reported to Graves halfway through his stay at Craiglockhart, it enabled him 'to escape from the truly awful atmosphere of this place of wash-outs and shattered heroes'.[10]

Sassoon's freedom to play golf daily was due largely to the encouragement and co-operation of one man at Craiglockhart, his case doctor, W.H.R. Rivers.[11] 'Doc Willie', as he was popularly known, quickly realized Sassoon's need for strenuous physical activity to balance his active mental life, and one which took him away from the hospital and its disturbed inhabitants seemed ideal. He therefore arranged his thrice weekly meetings with his patient rather unusually for the early evening, leaving Sassoon's day free.

Sassoon had met Rivers within minutes of his arrival, a tall, heavy-jowled, bespectacled man in his early fifties, with a thick moustache and bushy eyebrows but thinning hair. Both were already known to each other by name. 'Rivers will look after you,' the neurological member of the Medical Board at Liverpool had assured him after his destination had been decided,[12] and Sassoon had realized even then that Rivers was an important man. Rivers would certainly have been aware in advance of the identity of a patient who had already proved to be so awkward. Sassoon's own account of their relationship, though narrated largely in *Sherston's Progress*, is more reliable than fiction usually is, since Rivers was dead by the time it came out in 1936. 'If he were alive,' Sassoon wrote, 'I could not be writing so freely about him. I might even be obliged to call him by some made-up name, which would seem absurd.'[13]

Rivers was already an eminent man by the time he started work at Craiglockhart in 1917. A fellow of St John's College, Cambridge, his central interest was the biological reaction of man to his environment, which led him into the fields of anthropology, neurology and psychology in its widest sense. His research had taken him as far as the South Seas and involved him in daring experiments on the human nervous system, but it was not until the war that he found his true vocation, a remarkable aptitude for treating psychoneuroses. He had begun his war work as a temporary Major in the Royal Army Medical Corps at Maghull War Hospital near Liverpool and had been transferred to Craiglockhart not long before Sassoon's arrival there. When they met he was already in charge of a hundred of the hospital's 160 patients, while the other three doctors, Captain Brock, Major Ruggles and Lieutenant MacIntyre, had only sixty patients between them.

Building on his peace-time experience and drawing on Freud's work on dreams, though not entirely agreeing with his conclusions, Rivers had gradually evolved a method for treating shell-shocked soldiers, whose basic problem he saw as a conflict between fear and duty. His pioneering work was crucial in gaining acceptance for a condition which had previously been regarded with deep suspicion by most military authorities as either insanity or a form of malingering. Rivers was to write about his work at Craiglockhart in *Conflict and Dream*, a series of lectures published posthumously in 1923, in which Sassoon features as 'patient B'. In these lectures he isolates the war dream from other types of dream in a way which ties in closely with Sassoon's own account of Craiglockhart by night.[14]

Interestingly, it was not Sassoon's dreams Rivers analyzed when he came to discuss him as 'patient B', but his own dream in relation to his patient. For Rivers, as well as Sassoon, the relationship was to produce, in the words of his own title, dreams as well as conflict. It was also to create guilt on both sides. Rivers's guilt related to his dual role as scientist and army-officer. In his dream he was talking to Sassoon in both capacities. The dream had followed his reading, at Sassoon's suggestion, of Barbusse's *Under Fire* and an anti-war article in the *English Review*, during which he remembered wondering what would happen 'if my task of converting a patient from his "pacifist errors" to the conventional attitude should have as its result my own conversion to his point of view'.[15] This particularly worried him, since self-interest might well encourage him to wish for the end of the War to enable him to return to his academic research. His main concern in analyzing his dream was to establish whether he was in uniform:

> ... So long as I was an officer of the R.A.M.C., and of this my uniform was the obvious symbol, my discussions with B. on his attitude towards the war were prejudiced by my sense that I was not a free agent in discussing the matter, but that there was the danger that my attitude might be influenced by my official position. As a scientific student whose only object should be the attainment of what I supposed to be the truth, it was definitely unpleasant to me to suspect that the opinions which I was uttering might be influenced by the needs of my position, and I was fully aware of an element of constraint in my relations with B. on this account. So long as I was in uniform I was not a free agent.[16]

Rivers's uniform was not the only constraint in the relationship. He was almost certainly homosexual by inclination and it must quickly have become clear to him that Sassoon was too. Yet neither is likely to have referred to it. At the same time, as an experienced psychologist Rivers could reasonably expect Sassoon to experience 'transference' and become extremely fond of him. Paul Fussell suggests in *The Great War and Modern Memory* that Rivers became the embodiment of the male 'dream friend' who had been the companion of Sassoon's boyhood fantasies.[17] Sassoon publicly acknowledged that 'there was never any doubt about my liking [Rivers]. He made me feel safe at once, and seemed to know all about me.'[18] Privately he was rather franker, telling Marsh, whom he knew would understand, that he 'loved [Rivers] at first sight'.[19] He quickly began to regard him as a father-confessor, as well as something of a father-figure. Twenty-two years his senior, Rivers was certainly old enough for the latter role and, since the slight cooling-off in relations between Gosse and himself as a result of his anti-war views, Sassoon was in need of a more tolerant replacement. Who better than the man he was later to call his 'fathering friend'?[20]

One qualification of the ideal father is wisdom and Rivers seemed to Sassoon a 'Very Wise Man', the title of one of the poems he was to write about him.[21] In 'Revisitation', written after Rivers's death, he was also to emphasize Rivers's selflessness and ardour, endowing him with a saintliness the doctor himself would have found highly embarrassing.

Rivers was no plaster saint, however. He had a well-developed sense of humour that saved him from being pompous, as well as endearing him to his new patient. In one of their first 'friendly confabulations', as Sassoon called his sessions with his psychiatrist, he asked Rivers whether he thought he *was* suffering from shell-shock, as the authorities claimed:

> 'Certainly not,' he replied.
> 'What *have* I got, then?'
> 'Well, you appear to be suffering from an anti-war complex.' We both of us laughed at that. Rivers never seemed elderly ...[22]

Rivers's case notes make it clear that he was telling Sassoon the truth. After outlining his military career between August 1914 and July 1917 and giving a concise account of how Sassoon himself viewed his recent actions, his notes continue:

> The patient is a healthy-looking man of good physique. There are no physical signs of any disorder of the Nervous System. He discusses his recent actions and their motives in a perfectly intelligent and rational way, and there is no evidence of any excitement or depression. He recognises that his view of warfare is tinged by his feeling about the death of friends and of the men who were under his command in France. At the present

time he lays special stress on the hopelessness of any decision in the War as it is now being conducted, but he left out any reference to this aspect of his opinions in the statement which he sent to his Commanding Officer and which was read in the House of Commons. His view differs from that of the ordinary pacifist in that he would no longer object to the continuance of the War if he saw any reasonable prospect of a rapid decision.[23]

Was Rivers right to dismiss the notion of shell-shock in Sassoon's case? Both Eileen Showalter and Adrian Caesar argue that Sassoon was indeed shell-shocked.[24] Both refer to the nightmares and hallucinations he had experienced in April, common symptoms of shell-shock. Caesar also reminds his reader of a letter written the same month in which Sassoon had referred to being very near 'the snapping point' and the 'considerable mental anguish' shown in his diary entries for May.[25] By June and July, he argues, some of Sassoon's friends thought him mentally unstable, Graves and Ross among them. A diary entry for 9 May 1918, referring to Rivers as 'the only man who can save me if I break down again' constitutes, Caesar believes, an admission by Sassoon of aberrant behaviour in July 1917. Showalter interprets his letter declaring the war a 'deliberately prolonged ... war of aggression and conquest' as a 'bizarre aberration from one whose daredevil valor in combat had earned him the nickname Mad Jack and won him the Military Cross'.[26]

There are, however, as many if not more signs that Sassoon's behaviour was the result of an almost too rational response to the hysteria of patriotism and war-mongering, not shell-shock. Quite apart from the fact that he had none of the physical symptoms of that condition, we have Rivers's expert opinion to that effect. Sassoon himself pointed to one of his most critical anti-war poems, 'The Rear-Guard', as a sign of his complete sanity in May 1917, and a letter to Ottoline, admitted by Caesar as 'conflicting evidence', has this to say: 'My doctor is a sensible man who doesn't say anything silly .... But his arguments don't make any impression on me. He doesn't *pretend* that my nerves are wrong, but regards my attitude as abnormal. I do not know for how long he will go on trying to persuade me to modify my views.'[27] This, surely, is the letter of a man in a rational state of mind. He was certainly right to anticipate an attempt by Rivers to 'persuade' him to modify his views, an attempt which was to make him very miserable indeed.

For the first few weeks, however, Sassoon seems to have been relatively happy at Craiglockhart, managing for the most part to suppress memories of France and the Front. His thoughts turned to pre-war days, perhaps as a refuge, and in the third week of August he started to write a hunting poem, to his old friend Gordon Harbord, a piece which had been started, without his knowing it, the day after Gordon's death. He had kept in touch with Gordon when he left Sussex in 1912 to become a 2nd Lieutenant in the Royal Field Artillery (RFA) and the letters had become more frequent once Gordon left England for France at the end of 1914.[28] Gordon sometimes copied his replies to Sassoon to his brother Geoffrey ('Geoff'), who was also friendly with Sassoon. The three of them were very different types, but they all shared a passion for hunting. Geoff, like Gordon, was in the RFA and remained quite near him in France until he was sent out to Mesopotamia with the Middle Eastern Force in 1916. He, too, reported to Sassoon in letters which are as 'horsey' and facetious as his brother's, a style Sassoon evidently appreciated and probably reciprocated.

In spite of their jokiness, however, both brothers were very serious when it came to fighting and as fearless in battle as on the hunting-field. By May 1915 Geoff had been wounded twice and by early 1917 Gordon, having gained promotion to Captain, then Adjutant, had won an M.C. Each of them was prouder of the other than of himself. Geoff, for example, expressed his admiration – and fears – for his brother in August 1917, when Gordon was fighting at Ypres. The tone of the letter is perceptibly graver than earlier ones, reflecting his fully justified concern for his favourite brother: 'Just think of those sods throwing shells at old Gordon, the best-natured fellow in the world, who never did anybody any harm. What a truly amazing thing war is. I wish to God it was all over.'[29]

This letter, in which strong affection shows through the clichés, was written only the day before Gordon's death on 14 August. Another month was to elapse before Geoff, who evidently found it difficult to write in anything but a jokey way, managed to express his grief to Sassoon, whose one consolation was that Gordon 'died at once'.[30]

The strongest evidence of how hard Gordon's death hit Sassoon comes from the three poems he wrote on the subject. The one written when he first heard the news, 'The Wooden Cross', opens with angry, self-pitying, self-dramatizing and melodramatic phrases, but the most successful of the six stanzas is the last, based on Sassoon's final view of Gordon and their shared passion for fox-hunting:

> ... Only I hoard the hours we spent together
> Ranging brown Sussex woods in wintry weather,
> Till, blotting out today, I half-believe
> That I shall find you home again on leave,
> As I last saw you, riding down the lane,
> And lost in lowering dusk and drizzling rain,
> Contented with the hunt we'd had, and then
> Sad lest we'd never ride a hunt again.[31]

Sassoon's second attempt to write about Gordon's death, 'The Investiture', reverts to the same shared love of hunting. Though better digested, it is still not entirely successful and was to appear only in the *Cambridge Magazine* of 3 November 1917. The same nostalgia for what they both regarded as the true heaven, also informs the last, and most successful, of the three poems on Gordon, 'Together', which Sassoon did allow into his *Collected Poems*. Its success may partly be explained by the fact that, unlike the first two, it would be written after a fresh experience of hunting, which Sassoon took up again in December 1917, the month he composed the poem. The fact that it was with Gordon's own hunt, the Southdown, helps explain the form the poem took. Stripped of the melodrama and rhetoric of 'A Wooden Cross' and the elaborate conceit of 'The Investiture', it is a simple account of the way hunting brought back the reality of Gordon to Sassoon:

> *Together*
> Splashing along the boggy woods all day,
> And over brambled hedge and holding clay,
> I shall not think of him:
> But when the watery fields grow brown and dim,
> And hounds have lost their fox, and horses tire,
> I know that he'll be with me on my way
> Home through the darkness to the evening fire ...   (*CP*, pp. 95-6)

Gordon's death left an emotional void in Sassoon's life which made him particularly glad to welcome a new friend into it the same month, Wilfred Owen.

*

When Sassoon and Owen first met, on 18 August, however, Sassoon was still unaware of Gordon's death and his reception of Owen, while cordial, was hardly warm. Owen, who had arrived at Craiglockhart nearly a month before him, had waited another three weeks before daring to knock on his door. The reason for his visit, he explained, was the hope that Sassoon would be kind enough to sign copies of *The Old Huntsman* for himself and a few friends. Sassoon, who had been sitting on his bed cleaning his golf clubs, was naturally flattered and chatted with his reticent visitor as he signed, ending with a fairly lengthy explanation of his motives in writing the poems. It was only as he was showing his visitor to the door that Owen confessed, rather diffidently, to being a poet himself. 'It amused me to remember,' Sassoon wrote retrospectively, 'that I wondered whether his poems were any good!'[32]

There are a number of other possible explanations for Sassoon's slight condescension towards Owen at this first meeting. Sassoon was six and a half years Owen's senior, though he looked to Owen the same age as himself, that is just under twenty-five. He was also physically more imposing; over six feet tall, his lean figure literally looked down on Owen's stockier 5 feet 5½ inches. He also impressed Owen as 'stately' and 'noble-looking' with 'a fine, firm chisel'd ... head'.[33] After their second meeting on 21 August, when Owen took some of his poems to show Sassoon at his suggestion, he detected a general expression of boredom on Sassoon's face which added to the sense of haughtiness he conveyed. As their contact rapidly grew to almost nightly meetings the bored expression was to give way to something far more animated as Sassoon became increasingly interested in and admiring of Owen.

At their first meeting, however, Sassoon freely admitted that he had felt somewhat superior to Owen, who had struck him as a 'rather ordinary young man, perceptibly provincial, though unobtrusively ardent in his responses to my lordly dictums about poetry'.[34] His own social standing, though relatively obscure by comparison with his rich and titled Sassoon relatives, had given him the confidence to dismiss Owen as 'provincial'. It was a subject on which Owen felt particularly sensitive. Though his mother's family had had money and a certain position in society, his father, as a poorly-paid railway clerk, was on the lowest rung of the middle-class ladder, and Wilfred's childhood had been passed against a background of struggle to maintain respectability. Without money to pay for a 'good' education, he had had to attend local schools (the Birkenhead Institute, followed by Shrewsbury Technical School) while secretly longing for a public school. He had also dreamed of Oxford, but had failed even to win a scholarship to Reading University. Sassoon, on the other hand, had been to Marlborough and Cambridge and, though not very successful at either, the experience had certainly added to his social confidence.

It was not surprising, then, that at their first meeting Owen's manners should have struck Sassoon as 'modest and ingratiating', 'he stood at my elbow, rather as though conferring with a superior officer'. Since they were both somewhat snobbish, these social differences gave Sassoon an initial advantage, though he vigorously rejected Owen's later suggestion that he was Don Quixote to Owen's Sancho Panza. When Stephen Spender later asked him what Owen was like, Sassoon replied 'He was embarrassing. He had a Grammar School accent.'[35] The remark may have been a reaction to Spender's desire to know about Owen rather than himself, but it is significant that he could make it at all. Psychologically Sassoon also had the advantage of Owen. While the latter still stammered slightly and continued to suffer bad dreams, symptoms diagnosed as shell-shock, Sassoon showed no sign of that condition, as Rivers had noted. More importantly, Owen still felt himself under suspicion of cowardice for his reaction to his traumatic experiences at the Front, whereas Sassoon had already won an M.C. for his courage under fire and was widely known as a fearless 'Mad Jack', a nickname Owen himself was to use of him.

The most important reason for Sassoon's initial condescension, however, must have been his established reputation as a poet and Owen's obscurity at that time. Even before the numerous reviews of *The Old Huntsman* had appeared, Sassoon's contacts in the literary world had enabled him to place most of his work in reputable papers, and his name was already familiar to the reading public. Owen, on the other hand, had had no publications at all and felt understandably humble in the company of a poet whom he admired greatly. While determined to succeed as a poet, he believed that he had written only three lines which 'carr[ied] the stamp of maturity' by the time he met Sassoon in August 1917.[36] His praise of Sassoon's work, particularly in a letter written to his mother on 15 August 1917, three days before their first meeting, shows which aspects of it he admired most:

> I have just been reading Siegfried Sassoon, and am feeling at a very high pitch of emotion. Nothing like his trench life sketches has ever been written or ever will be written. Shakespeare reads vapid after these. Not of course because Sassoon is a greater artist, but because of the subjects, I mean, I think if I had the choice of making friends with Tennyson or with Sassoon, I should go to Sassoon.[37]

It was this aspect of Sassoon's poetry, his choice of subject matter and the adjustment of language required by that choice, which was to influence Owen's own work profoundly.

Owen's reference to Tennyson in relation to Sassoon indicates the kind of poetry he had been writing up to August 1917. Like Sassoon he had grown up on a diet of mainly Romantics and Pre-Raphaelites and his style when he met Sassoon was not unlike Sassoon's Swinburnian cadences before the War. 'We have followed parallel trenches all our lives,' he told his mother, 'and have more friends in common, authors I mean, than most people can boast of in a lifetime.'[38] Only recently Owen had started a pseudo-medieval ballad of which Sassoon would probably have approved before his own dramatic change of technique. But when it was shown to him at their second meeting, with other poems, he preferred Owen's 'Song of Songs', which he admired for its simple lyricism and dexterous play with words and sounds. It was almost certainly this common ground, their shared love of the lyrical, which enabled Owen to take the leap he did under Sassoon's influence.

'The Death-Bed', for example, which Owen thought Sassoon's finest poem, offered him lyricism while also making the kind of statement he too wanted to make about the War. Though Owen was not a pacifist, he was very critical of the conduct of the War and particularly moved, like Sassoon, by the suffering of his men at the Front. Under Sassoon's influence his attitude was to harden noticeably, possibly encouraged by Sassoon's suggestion (as with Rivers) that he read Barbusse's *Under Fire*. 'The Redeemer' with its blend of lyricism and anger and its haunting refrain, 'I say that he was Christ', struck Owen as the poem he had been 'wishing to write every week for the last three years'.[39]

It was, however, Sassoon's starkly realistic trench-life sketches, such as 'The General' and 'They', which Owen tried initially to copy, their second meeting stimulating him to write his own satire, 'The Dead-Beat'. (Was this a typical word play on 'The Death-Bed'?) Sassoon approved of the opening and closing stanzas which, in strong contrast to Owen's previous war poetry, could well have been written by himself:

> He dropped, more sullenly than wearily,
> Became a lump of stench, a clot of meat,

And none of us could kick him to his feet.
He blinked at my revolver, blearily ...

I've sent him down at last, he seemed so bad,
Although a strongish chap and quite unhurt.
Next day I heard the Doc's fat laugh: 'That dirt
You sent me down last night has died. So glad!'[40]

But the highly facetious middle three stanzas seemed to Sassoon 'out of keeping' with the rest.[41] Though Owen worked on the poem, it never really succeeded. Nor did any other of his attempts to copy Sassoon's methods slavishly. It was only when he had fully absorbed Sassoon's subject matter and technique and adapted it to his own genius that the full benefit of his influence would be felt.

The first real sign Sassoon had that his 'little friend was much more than the promising minor poet [he] had initially adjudged him to be'[42] was when, some time towards the end of September, he brought him the sonnet which was to become 'Anthem for Doomed Youth'. Even then Owen felt in need of Sassoon's help in perfecting it, and it must have pleased Sassoon greatly in later life to think that he had been responsible for some of its more exquisite touches. The title itself, for example, is almost solely due to Sassoon. Under his guidance too 'Only the solemn/ Monstrous anger of our guns' became 'Only the monstrous anger of the guns' and the 'tenderness of silent/ Sweet white minds' in Owen's fourth draft became the memorable 'tenderness of patient minds'.[43] Owen was grateful for these and other suggestions and adopted nearly all of them, in contrast to his response to Robert Graves a few weeks later. (Graves was to visit Sassoon at Craiglockhart in mid-October, when he was introduced to Owen and shown his 'Disabled', which he then proceeded to correct with his usual aplomb. Owen was to ignore all his suggestions save one.)

Sassoon later dismissed his contributions to 'Anthem' as 'slight'.[44] Even at the time, in spite of difficulties of judging manuscript poems, he had realized that Owen's verse 'with its sumptuous epithets and large-scale imagery, its noble naturalness and depth of meaning, had impressive affinities with Keats'.[45] He was the first to recognize Owen's true potential and the most important catalyst in helping him to realize it. Between the first poem written under Sassoon's spell and his discharge from Craiglockhart at the end of October 1917, Owen drafted over a dozen poems, at least four of which were among his best work. Sassoon was proud of his influence, particularly since he was inclined to think Owen the superior poet of the two in later years.[46]

In thinking of Sassoon's relationship with Owen it is easy to overlook the fact that the traffic was not all one way. Sassoon, too, benefited from the extraordinary coincidence of their meeting at Craiglockhart, just as he had profited from his chance encounter with Graves in France. While *his* influence on Owen's poetry has been frequently cited, Owen's on his is rarely mentioned. Yet not only did Owen's comments hearten and help him, as Sassoon acknowledged, but his method of approach began gradually to change his own. 'To remind people of [war's] realities was still my main purpose,' he would write of the year after their meeting, 'but I now preferred to depict it impersonally, and to be as much "above the battle" as I could. Unconsciously, I was getting nearer to Wilfred Owen's method of approach.'[47] The beginnings of this change can be seen at Craiglockhart.

There was, of course, common ground between them, which explains Sassoon's praise of Owen's 'Song of Songs'. It also helps to explain why Owen asked if he could publish the first poem Sassoon wrote at Craiglockhart, 'Dreamers', in the hospital magazine he edited, *The Hydra*. Sassoon agreed to this, but insisted that Owen also included his own 'Song of Songs'. The unassuming editor did so, but reluctantly and anonymously, and the two of them appeared in print together on 1 September. Rarely can a hospital magazine have witnessed such an august literary pairing.

Like two of the three other poems Sassoon allowed Owen to publish in *The Hydra*, 'Dreamers' shows affinities with Owen's technique. Reading his 'sumptuous epithets' and 'large-scale songs' had given Sassoon a renewed appreciation of verbal patterning and music. This is particularly noticeable in the opening eight lines of the sonnet:

> Soldiers are citizens of death's grey land,
> Drawing no dividend from time's tomorrows.
> In the great hour of destiny they stand,
> Each with his feuds, and jealousies, and sorrows.
> Soldiers are sworn to action; they must win
> Some flaming, fatal climax with their lives.
> Soldiers are dreamers; when the guns begin
> They think of firelit homes, clean beds and wives.   (*CP*, pp. 71-2)

The final six lines, however, revert to Sassoon's fiercer manner in which the use of the first person narrator, harsh details of trench conditions and mundane details of everyday life prevent the reader from losing sight of the reality of war:

> I see them in foul dug-outs, gnawed by rats,
> And in the ruined trenches, lashed with rain,
> Dreaming of things they did with balls and bats,
> And mocked by hopeless longing to regain
> Bank-holidays, and picture-shows, and spats,
> And going to the office in the train.

'Dreamers' became one of Sassoon's most anthologized poems, and this may have prompted him to concentrate on what he, as well as Owen, believed he could do best, trench-life sketches. For his next twelve poems, with one or two exceptions, are in his most sardonic manner. They range from a description of a wiring party by a callous officer, which ends:

Young Hughes was badly hit; I heard him carried away
Moaning at every lurch; no doubt he'll die today.
But *we* can say the front-line wire's been safely mended.[48]

and an equally unfeeling report on 'How to Die',[49] to what feels like a less successful version of 'Base Details', 'The Fathers'. In this two non-combatants discuss their soldier sons' fates – 'But Arthur's getting all the fun/ At Arras with his nine-inch gun' – and the narrator concludes bitterly:

I watched them toddle through the door –
Those impotent old friends of mine.[50]

The last line, Sassoon admitted, was written in 'sheer temper'[51] and caused consternation when he submitted it to the *Cambridge Magazine*. These attacks on callous officers, self-righteous Christians and complacent non-combatants are all familiar themes. So too is a more successful assault on journalists and M.P.s, which Rivers thought 'very dangerous',[52] 'Fight to a Finish'.[53] An allusion to Lloyd George's famous phrase, this poem epitomizes both the strengths and limitations of Sassoon's satires. Its initial impact is considerable, the scene is deftly portrayed and the language subtly modulated, ranging from simple colloquialism to heavy irony. The weak point of such a poem, however, is its obsessive tone which inevitably becomes less forceful with repetition and the passage of time. Sassoon himself thought it 'fairly effective in its way'.[54]

Nowhere is this obsessiveness more clearly seen than in two other poems written at Craiglockhart, 'The Glory of Women' and 'Their Frailty'. What, if anything, provoked the virulence of the pieces, especially the former, remains uncertain. The fact that the narrator of 'The Glory of Women' feels sympathy for the 'German mother dreaming by the fire', unaware that, while she knits her son socks, his face 'is trodden deeper in the mud', suggests that Sassoon's scorn was not provoked by all women. He seems to have been thinking of women who visited him admiringly in hospital, or remembering the vacuous visitors to Lady Brassey's teas. And his increasing closeness to Owen, who shared his distrust of most women, with the exception of his mother, may have stirred up his own latent hostility.

There are passages in letters to another homosexual friend, Meiklejohn, at this time which suggest other possible reasons for Sassoon's antagonism toward the sex. Besides references to meeting 'soldiers in the gorse with trollopes' and the 'embarrassment of disturbing amorous soldiers and their doxies among the ferns', he also refers pityingly to a 'fond lady', who has written to him on his birthday and wants to see him when she comes to Edinburgh, concluding: 'I wish I could find a charming young fox-hunting squire for her, poor dear.' Whatever the reasons for his hostility, it did not make for satisfactory poetry, mainly because his accusations, based on enormous generalizations, are so blatantly unfair:

You love us when we're heroes, home on leave,
Or wounded in a mentionable place.
You worship decorations; you believe
That chivalry redeems the war's disgrace.
You make us shells. You listen with delight,
By tales of dirt and danger fondly thrilled.
You crown our distant ardours while we fight,
And mourn our laurelled memories when we're killed ...   (*CP*, p. 79)

Women here are portrayed as wide-eyed, coy, sadistic and empty-headed, generalizations which are also found in 'Their Frailty', though the tone is not quite so scornful:

> ... Husbands and sons and lovers; everywhere
> They die; War bleeds us white
> Mothers and wives and sweethearts, – they don't care
> So long as He's all right.   (*CP*, p. 80)

Sassoon thought 'The Glory of Women' a '*very good* sonnet'[55] and if, as he argued, its purpose was to 'give [women] beans' it certainly achieved its aim.

Yet the success of Sassoon's satires usually depends on his ability to avoid generalizations. Instead he sketches in a specific situation or scene, a character or two and some snatches of actual speech. The failure of 'The Glory of Women' and 'Their Frailty' can be partly explained by his failure to follow the usual practice, perhaps because he was unable to distance himself sufficiently from the subject. Whereas the most successful satire in this group, 'Does It Matter?', gives us three clear-cut situations – a soldier who has lost his legs, another his sight and a third his senses – sets each briefly in a vivid scene and throws in a few clichés to highlight the inadequacy of the average person's response to such tragedies. This poem was almost certainly Sassoon's own response to at least two specific events, as well as his own fear of being blinded. The first was Ralph Greaves's loss of an arm, which Sassoon reported to Ross on 25 September 1917 shortly before 'Does It Matter?' was written, an irony he must have had in mind when he portrayed another amputee in the first stanza, a keen huntsman who has lost his legs. The second was the news that Julian Dadd, who had lost both his brothers in the War as well as his voice, had suffered a mental breakdown, as Sassoon reported to Ross, on 17 September 1917. He was probably also thinking of the haunted patients of Craiglockhart when he referred to 'those dreams from the pit' in stanza three:

> Does it matter? – losing your legs? ...
> For people will always be kind,
> And you need not show that you mind

When the others come in after hunting
To gobble their muffins and eggs.

Does it matter? – losing your sight? ...
There's such splendid work for the blind;
And people will always be kind,
As you sit on the terrace remembering
And turning your face to the light.

Do they matter? – those dreams from the pit? ...
You can drink and forget and be glad,
And people won't say that you're mad;
For they'll know you've fought for your country
And no-one will worry a bit.   (*CP*, pp. 76-7)

Each of these three stanzas follows the same pattern, starting with a similar question, followed by an obviously unsatisfactory answer. In each the five inter-rhyming lines are interrupted by a longer, unrhymed line, which, with its less certain, feminine ending, introduces a note of doubt and nostalgia into the poem ('As you sit on the terrace remembering'), undercutting the certainty and insensitivity of the speaker. Such patterning sets up certain expectations and the questions themselves touch on situations so distressing – amputation, blindness, madness – that the speaker is condemned out of his own mouth for even asking if they matter.

The effect is to alienate the reader, who is nevertheless unwillingly drawn into the poem by those same rhetorical questions. The reader's shock at the speaker's callous and inadequate response in the second line of each verse provokes the outraged indignation Sassoon aims to elicit from complacent civilians. A similar effect is achieved by the irony of the final line which, though said ostensibly to reassure the man who has gone mad, underlines a general lack of concern for the victims. It is just possible that another heavily ironic line in the poem – 'They'll know that you've fought for your country' – influenced Owen when he came to write 'Dulce et Decorum Est' a few weeks later, though he brands it more straightforwardly 'the old lie'. During the same period Owen produced another poem which suggests the influence of 'Does It Matter?', at least in subject matter, 'Disabled'. Whilst he explores in depth the suffering of his amputee, however, Sassoon makes his treatment an excuse for another attack on civilian callousness.

Despite their different approaches, perhaps even because of them, Sassoon and Owen were to grow increasingly close during the two and a half months they spent together. Owen dated the start of this, for him, as mid-September: while Sassoon still regarded him as 'a tiresome little knocker on [his] door' at that time, he had begun to regard Sassoon 'as Keats & Christ & Elijah & my Colonel & my father-confessor & Amenophis IV in profile',[56] seeing him not only as a poet, but also 'as a man, as a friend'.[57] That phrase was written on 11 or 12 September and it is likely that the change had occurred a few days earlier on 7 September, when Sassoon had called Owen to his room.

After criticizing some of his poems, amending others and praising a few, Sassoon did him what Owen considered the great honour of reading him his latest works, one of which struck Owen as 'the most exquisitely painful war poem of any language or time'.[58] 'I don't tell him so,' Owen added for his mother's benefit, 'or that I am not worthy to light his pipe ... No wonder I was happy last night.' The evening had ended with Sassoon inviting Owen to lunch at his golf club the next day, followed by tea at the Astronomer Royal's house in the Observatory.

Though Owen waited until after he left Craiglockhart to tell Sassoon how he worshipped him, it is clear that he had done so even before they met. It is also likely that at his first sight of Sassoon, sitting on his bed in a purplish-blue dressing-gown, his hero-worship had tipped over into romantic love. Certainly he was to regard that first meeting as an epoch in his life, and to replay the scene frequently in his head, as lovers do. Writing to Sassoon from Scarborough on 27 November 1917 he tells him: 'We have had some strong sunshine; and when it strikes anything blue I see you sitting by the bedside as on That Morning in September.'[59]

When, towards the end of October, he spent a whole day with Sassoon, sharing breakfast, lunch, tea and dinner with him, he enjoyed himself so much that he failed for once to write to his mother. And when he heard, the morning after, that he was to have a Medical Board the following Tuesday (30 October), he was 'rather upset about it' because he was 'so happy with Sassoon'.[60] In the same letter, whilst reassuring his mother of her power over him, he refers to 'all the charm of Edinburgh, and all the love that it has thrown about me'. Though the 'love' is unlikely to refer only to Sassoon, it undoubtedly included him in a special way. The fact that Sassoon destroyed some of Owen's letters, which he had initially promised to show Harold Owen, suggests that there may have been something compromising in them, something at any rate which Sassoon considered very private.[61]

It is less easy to say exactly how Sassoon felt about Owen, since he was not so effusive about his feelings as the younger man. Writing to his mother in early September, Owen reports that, while his 'friend' is 'intensely sympathetic' with him about 'every vital question on the planet or off it, [he] keeps all effusiveness strictly within his pages. In this he is so eminently *English*.'[62]

It was not just a difference of temperament: by Sassoon's own admission it took him longer to appreciate Owen than vice versa. As the older, more confident, more successful of the two, he only slowly realized that 'he could give me as much as I gave him'.[63] Though his appreciation of Owen's poetry came fairly early, his personal appreciation of the man started a full month after Owen's, half-way through October. And while there are many signs of his appreciation of Owen's qualities – his 'unassumingness', his 'selflessness', his far more 'compact and coherent personality' and particularly of his 'beautifully sympathetic nature' at a time when he badly needed support – there is not the same suggestion of romantic attachment as there is with Owen. His reference to Owen's 'calm velvety voice' in *Siegfried's Journey* sounds a slightly romantic note, but his description of Owen's other physical attributes seems too detached to be that of someone in love:

> He wasn't a fine-drawn type. There was a full-blooded robustness about him which implied reserves of mental energy and solid ability. Under ordinary conditions it wasn't a spiritual face. It was of the mould which either coarsens or refines itself in later life. I cannot say that I ever saw what is called 'a look of genius' in it. His mouth was resolute and humorous, his eyes long and heavy-lidded, quiescent rather than penetrating. They were somewhat sleepy eyes, kind, shrewd, and seldom lit up from within. They seemed, like much else in his personality, to be instinctively guarding the secret sources of his inward power and integrity.[64]

For the most part Sassoon's appreciation reads like that of one fellow-poet for another. Though he missed Owen after his departure, he did not write to him nearly as often as Owen wrote to him. They would both have understood each other's sexual preferences, but in Sassoon's case at least those tastes seem not to have been engaged by his new friend. It may be that after losing first David Thomas, then Gordon Harbord, Sassoon simply could not allow himself to feel deeply about Owen. At the same time it is likely that he found Owen something of an emotional substitute for Gordon. Years later, in 1954, he was to dream that Owen had come back and that he was very 'happy at his return and taking charge of him'.[65] That 'taking charge of him' is significant, for it was as a mentor rather than a lover that he saw himself in relation to Owen.

However he perceived himself, Sassoon was not invariably mentor in their relationship. While pursuing a mainly satiric line during his first few months at Craiglockhart, for example, he experimented with two poems which show the effect Owen was having on his technique. 'Sick Leave' and 'Attack', both written by mid-October, differ significantly from the other poems of this period. Both one line short of the sonnet's fourteen lines, they leave the reader with a sense of something unfinished. 'Sick Leave' deals with a subject Sassoon had already touched on at Craiglockhart, dreams, and heralds his growing unease at his own comfortable, relatively contented existence at Craiglockhart. Reminded of the battlefield by the 'bellow ... drone and rumble' of a midnight storm, the narrator dreams of his men, some of them dead:

> They whisper to my heart; their thoughts are mine.
> 'Why are you here with all your watches ended?
> From Ypres to Frise we sought you in the Line.'   (*CP*, p. 85)

In 'bitter safety', the narrator wakes up, 'unfriended', made conscious by the 'slashing rain', which follows the storm, of 'the Battalion in the mud'. (Both the 1st and 2nd RWF were near Ypres at this time.) The poem ends with the voices of the dead, quite different from the harsh colloquial tones of previous poems:

> 'When are you going out to them again?
> Are they not still your brothers through our blood?'

It is the voice of Sassoon's uneasy conscience which speaks.

Sassoon said that 'Attack', was based on a note made in his diary while observing the Hindenburg Line attack.[66] His painter's eye has already noted the telling details of shape and colour, light and shade. In converting it to poetry he fills in his picture with other details – tanks, shovels, the noise of the barrage – and humanizes the scene by conveying vividly what he so clearly remembered, the fear of going into battle. His usual irony is missing, though the poem does end with one of his typical soldier's curses (Masefield considered it Sassoon's 'best war-poem'):

> At dawn the ridge emerges massed and dun
> In wild purple of the glow'ring sun,
> Smouldering through spouts of drifting smoke that shroud
> The menacing scarred slope; and, one by one,
> Tanks creep and topple forward to the wire.
> The barrage roars and lifts. Then, clumsily bowed
> With bombs and guns and shovels and battle-gear,
> Men jostle and climb to meet the bristling fire.
> Lines of grey, muttering faces, masked with fear,
> They leave their trenches, going over the top,
> While time ticks blank and busy on their wrists,
> And hope, with furtive eyes and grappling fists,
> Flounders in mud. O Jesus, make it stop!   (*CP*, p. 71)

With its abundant imagery, alliterative and assonanced patterning, personification and elaborate rhyme-scheme, 'Attack' is more typical of Owen's than Sassoon's technique at this time. The same is also true of 'Thrushes', which suggests that Sassoon was not entirely preoccupied with the War at Craiglockhart.

Indeed it would have been difficult for Sassoon to remain angry all the time. Unlike regimental life, he was under no one's orders at the hospital. Instead of the hectic duties of a platoon commander, he enjoyed a daily round of leisurely golf. Whatever his initial inclinations had been, by mid-October he had also begun to build up a social life in Edinburgh. Thanks to his friends' efforts he had met Herbert Grierson, Professor of English Literature at Edinburgh University, had had tea with its rector, Sir A. Ewing, and lunch with the Astronomer

Royal of Scotland, R.A. Sampson, at the nearby Observatory.[67] Lady Margaret Sackville,[68] a minor poet in her own right and daughter of the 3rd Earl de la Warr, had also invited him to lunch. Though he suspected her verse was 'fairly rotten', Sassoon was intrigued: 'A rival to Lady Ottoline,' he joked with Ross 'and quite ten years younger!'[69] More to his taste was the occasional dinner out with Wilfred Owen, or a meal at the Scottish Conservative Club, of which Rivers had made him a temporary member. Sassoon, who used its headed writing paper, had altered it to read:

I am *not* SCOTTISH
or CONSERVATIVE [CLUB, crossed out] thank God

He enjoyed its facilities, nevertheless. In addition, he sometimes took day-trips to places like North Berwick or Glasgow.

Sassoon also had visitors, Meiklejohn making the long journey north to see him in mid-September and Graves returning for his second visit in mid-October. (On the latter occasion Owen remembered being sent to meet 'the big, rather plain fellow' at Waverley Station because 'nothing could keep [Sassoon] from his morning's golf'.[70]) Sassoon wrote frequently to both Meiklejohn and Graves before and after their respective visits, as well as to other friends. Apart from Ottoline and Ross he wrote most often to Theo Bartholomew, the Cambridge University librarian who helped him with his contributions to the *Cambridge Magazine*, to which he was still submitting on average one poem a week. He also kept in touch with Dent, now anxious to put him in touch with Gabriel Atkin, still stationed at Margate.

One unexpected source of amusement for Sassoon at Craiglockhart were his fellow-patients. While he avoided making fun of the really severe cases, he derived some entertainment from the more mildly afflicted. His second room-mate, who came to replace the young Scots captain, was particularly good value, if *Sherston's Progress* is to be believed. A tall, handsome man with iron-grey hair and a monocle, the 'Theosophist', as Sassoon dubbed him, was outwardly quite normal. It was only when he opened his mouth that his dottiness became apparent. In a good mood he would address Sassoon in stilted language reminiscent of Shakespeare or Rider Haggard. If Sassoon complained that the rattling bedroom window was enough to keep one awake all night, for example, he might respond: 'True, O King', or 'Thou hast uttered wise words, O great white chief.' When Sassoon grumbled about the War and the general state of society one evening, his companion reassured him that we were 'all only on the great stairway which conducts us to higher planes of existence'.

In spite of such distractions there were still times at Craiglockhart when life at the Front seemed more real to Sassoon than his daily existence. When this happened he turned to poetry to express his frustration and guilt. Having finally achieved his own room had made writing easier and the three poems which followed this luxury are more developed than his earlier satires. Nostalgia is the keynote of 'Break of Day', where the narrator, waking at dawn on a cold autumnal morning in the trenches, retreats into a dream of happier autumn days on the hunting-field.[71] Autumn at Craiglockhart had clearly brought back memories of an activity which was always to epitomize for Sassoon the innocence of youth and the freshness and purity of nature, hunting. By juxtaposing it to the 'hell' of the narrator's 'dark, musty' dug-out and the 'outcast immolation' of the doomed men in trenches waiting for a hopeless attack, he emphasizes the foulness of war. While the narrator experiences the 'clean' thrill of past autumn dawns in his poetic daydream, in the trench the soldiers are 'far from clean things', both activities being drawn together by the sound of the horn or bugle. It is a skilful adaptation of a theme he had always favoured, dawn.

The second of these longer poems, 'Prelude: the Troops', is also nostalgic, but for 'the troops' rather than the hunting-field. Dominic Hibberd believes that Owen was referring to the last stanza of this poem when he described having Sassoon read him 'the most exquisitely painful war poem of any language or time'. The aptness of the description is undeniable, although the dates do not tally exactly. It is certainly the nearest Sassoon ever came to Owen in technique, particularly in the last line, where the phrase 'the unreturning army' brings to mind both Owen's title 'The Unreturning' and his alternative sestet to 'Happiness' which opens: 'But the old Happiness is unreturning'.

Like Sassoon's poem too, 'Happiness' concentrates on the 'boys' who were sent to war. The influence of Walt Whitman, another admirer of 'boys' and 'comrades', is also evident in the exclamatory opening line of Sassoon's last stanza: 'O my brave brown companions'. It is an unashamedly Romantic poem, almost certainly drawing on Keats, not only for its blank verse and verbal music, but also for what Edmund Blunden called its 'Greek drama beginning',[72] which echoes Keats's moving description of the fallen gods at the start of *Hyperion*:

> Dim, gradual thinning of the shapeless gloom
> Shudders to drizzling daybreak that reveals
> Disconsolate men who stamp their sodden boots
> And turn dulled, sunken faces to the sky
> Haggard and hopeless. They, who have beaten down
> The stale despair of night, must now renew
> Their desolation in the truce of dawn,
> Murdering the livid hours that grope for peace.
>
> ...
>
> O my brave brown companions, when your souls
> Flock silently away, and the eyeless dead
> Shame the wild beast of battle on the ridge,
> Death will stand grieving in that field of war
> Since your unvanquished hardihood is spent.
> And through some mooned Valhalla there will pass

Battalions and battalions, scarred from hell;
The unreturning army that was youth;
The legions who have suffered and are dust.   (*CP*, p. 67)

Sassoon also continued his attempt to be realistic about the trenches. There is nothing vaguely Romantic or consolatory in the last of his three longer poems written in Craiglockhart, 'Counter-Attack', as its first stanza indicates:

... The place was rotten with dead; green clumsy legs
High-booted, sprawled and grovelled along the saps
And trunks, face downward, in the sucking mud,
Wallowed like trodden sand-bags loosely filled;
And naked sodden buttocks, mats of hair,
Bulged, clotted heads slept in the plastering slime
And then the rain began, – the jolly old rain!   (*CP*, p. 68)

While such unflinching realism is an important milestone in the development of First World War poetry, there is more than that to admire in 'Counter-Attack'. Sassoon had been working on it since July 1916, when the said 'counter-attack' had occurred,[73] and the effort shows. The narrative opens with a general scene of exhausted soldiers holding a trench they had gained 'hours before'. It appears to be a straightforward description of a counter-attack, but a sense of unease is created by the narrator's ominous 'Things seemed all right at first'. In stanza two the focus narrows down to a 'yawning soldier', who wonders 'when the Allemands would get busy', at which point the narrator interposes ironically 'And then, of course, they started'. The stanza ends with a detailed description of the soldier's reaction, which takes us still further away from the general opening:

He crouched and flinched, dizzy with galloping fear,
Sick for escape, – loathing the strangled horror
And butchered, frantic gestures of the dead.

The reader's attention is next directed to another participant, an officer, whose 'blundering' descent into the trench underlines the mounting tension of the situation. An incisive account of developments follows, its close reference to trench details lending authenticity to the scene. Suddenly the focus shifts back to the soldier who, in the confusion, has forgotten to use his rifle. The closing description of his death, with its simultaneously external and internal view of the event, is one of Sassoon's most vivid pieces of writing, resembling Owen's description of a gassed soldier in 'Dulce et Decorum Est', in particular the imagery of 'smothering', 'choking' and 'drowning'. There is no conclusive evidence to prove that either poet was influenced by the other in this respect, but if they were, it is more likely that Owen influenced Sassoon. His piece was written about mid-October, whereas Sassoon's appears to have been completed later. Wherever it originated, Sassoon's is highly effective:

> ... then a bang
> Crumpled and spun him sideways, knocked him out
> To grunt and wriggle: none heeded him; he choked
> And fought the flapping veils of smothering gloom,
> Lost in a blurred confusion of yells and groans ...
> Down, and down, and down, he sank and drowned,
> Bleeding to death ...

The narrator need only add: '... The counter-attack had failed' and the poem is skilfully rounded off.

Poems like 'Counter-Attack' suggest that, however much he tried to forget, Sassoon dwelt a good deal on his war experiences at Craiglockhart. And this, in turn, increased his guilt at being safely out of the trenches and abandoning his men, as he saw it, a feeling spelt out in 'Sick Leave' and further explored in what appear to be the last three poems written at Craiglockhart. In 'Twelve Months After' the narrator imagines meeting his very Welsh platoon again:

> Young Gibson with his grin; and Morgan, tired and white;
> Jordan, who's out to win a D.C.M. some night;
> And Hughes that's keen on wiring; and Davies ('79)
> Who always must be firing at the Bosche front line.   (*CP*, p. 74)

The sing-song rhythms lead naturally to his memory of the reassuring song they used to sing, 'Old soldiers never die', but the poem refuses its optimism and concludes bleakly: 'That's where they are today, knocked over to a man.' In 'Autumn' the poet is reminded by the fall of the leaves of his men's deaths:

> ... Their lives are like the leaves
> Scattered in flocks of ruin, tossed and blown
> Along the westering furnace flaring red.
> O martyred youth and manhood overthrown,
> The burden of your wrongs is on my head.   (*CP*, p. 88)

With its echoes of Shelley's 'Ode to the West Wind', in particular its metaphor of autumn for dying, this poem is far from original, yet it is unquestionably heartfelt, as the last poem in this group, 'Banishment', shows. It is a crucial work, marking a definitive turning point in Sassoon's attitude. Beginning with his sense of banishment 'from the patient men who fight', as though he, not they, is being deprived of a valuable experience, the sonnet turns in its last six lines to describe the dreams which had started to trouble him again and the decision he has finally reached:

The darkness tells how vainly I have striven
To free them from the pit where they must dwell
In outcast gloom convulsed and jagged and riven
By grappling guns. Love drove me to rebel.
Love drives me back to grope with them through hell;
And in their tortured eyes I stand forgiven.   (*CP*, p. 86)

There, in the final three lines, was his problem in a nutshell. He felt guilty if he was away from his men and he felt guilty if he was with them, since that meant fighting in a war he no longer believed justified. It was a guilt that Dr Rivers consciously or unconsciously exploited, though doing so made him feel guilty too. In a letter written to Ottoline, on 11 October, Sassoon notes that Rivers, who has just returned from a fortnight's much-needed rest, has become very 'warlike', asserting that the Germans 'will admit defeat suddenly in the face of superior American power'.[74] Since Rivers's arguments were usually indirect, it must have shocked Sassoon to hear his doctor arguing that to make peace as Sassoon wanted would constitute a victory for Pan-Germanisation.

Sassoon, feeling guilty anyway, though not for Rivers's reasons, said that he was now prepared to return to the Front. He was afraid, however, that if he agreed to go before a Medical Board for a reappraisal of his mental state, the War Office would merely 'shunt him off' to some home-service job.[75] 'If I can't be passed for G[eneral] S[ervice] I won't be passed for anything at all,' Sherston tells Rivers.[76] Rivers, delighted with the concession, implied that he would 'wangle' things with the War Office. His absence had probably given his patient time to think without the sense of pressure his presence imposed. Sassoon, now guilty in a different direction, hastened to explain his decision to Ottoline. Worried by signs of his resolution crumbling, she had written to remind him that the war situation looked more hopeless than ever and to urge him to do something else 'outrageous' to highlight the situation. A wiser and a sadder man after twelve weeks at Craiglockhart, Sassoon replied:

I am afraid I cannot do anything 'outrageous'. They would only say I had a relapse and put me in a padded room. I am at present faced with the prospect of remaining here for an indefinite period, and you can imagine how that affects me. Apparently nothing that I can do will make them take me seriously (and of course it is the obvious course for them to adopt). I have told Rivers that I will not withdraw anything that I have said or written, and that my views are the same, but that I will go back to France if the War Office will give me a guarantee that they really will send me there. I haven't the least idea what they will do. But I hope you and others will try to understand what I mean by it.

After all I made my protest on behalf of my fellow-fighters, and (if it is a question of being treated as an imbecile for the rest of the war) the fittest thing for me to do is to go back and share their ills. By passing me for General Service (which Rivers says is 'the only thing they can do') they admit that I never had any shell-shock, as it is quite out of the question for a man who has been three months in a nerve-hospital to be sent back at once if he really had anything wrong.[77]

Sassoon had not changed his mind in the least, he assured Ottoline, as his poems still appearing in the *Cambridge Magazine* should show: 'How else could I get my own back on them?' he asked. 'Killed in action in order to confute the Under-Secretary for War, who had officially stated that I wasn't responsible for my actions. What a truly glorious death for a promising young pacifist!'[78]

Life was pleasantly busy at the time Sassoon made his decision to return to France and he did not entirely welcome Rivers's news that he had managed to arrange a Medical Board for him a few days later, on 23 October. It is unlikely, however, that he deliberately missed it because he could not face giving up his social life. More probably he walked out of the waiting room, as he did, in a fit of pique at being made to wait. (He *said* it was because he had an appointment for tea with the Astronomer Royal.) Whatever his motive, he had to face Rivers's rare anger on his return. With his customary tolerance, however, he promised to arrange another Board.

In the month which intervened Sassoon stopped worrying about the future and threw himself into his social activities. Having failed to put off Ottoline's threatened visit on 9 November, he made the most of her stay. Though she felt neglected and complained bitterly of his thoughtlessness in booking her into one of Edinburgh's most expensive hotels, The Caledonian, he had accorded her exactly the same treatment as he had Graves, that is, fitted her round his games of golf. And one of his reasons for trying to put her off was that he had wanted to find her suitably grand accommodation with her friend Lady de la Warr.

Ottoline's real reason for being unhappy during her stay was probably because it became clear during the course of it that Sassoon could never care for her in the way she was still hoping he would. It may have been during the long walk they took together the next day that he told her quite specifically that he could 'only like men, that women were antipathetic to him'.[79] It was certainly during this walk that he said how impossible it was to talk seriously to anyone who was so artificial. Clive Bell, who had witnessed Ottoline's nervous departure from Garsington, also remarked on her conspicuous appearance on this visit. Perhaps, as he suggested, she had put on even more make-up, higher heels and grander clothes than usual in the hope of attracting a younger man whom everyone but herself appears to have known was homosexual. Sassoon's response to her was, nevertheless, a cruel one and shows the measure of his self-absorption at the time.

There is no doubt that Ottoline's departure was a relief, but Sassoon was not at the station to see her off. His farewell to Owen, a week earlier, had been quite different, suggesting where his real interests lay. Their 'luminous ... intimacy', as

Sassoon called it in *Siegfried's Journey*, was never more apparent than on their last evening together at the Scottish Conservative Club on 3 November.

When the time came for Sassoon to return to Craiglockhart that evening, besides presenting Owen with Aylmer Strong's poems, which they both found deliciously absurd, he also gave him an envelope containing ten pounds and a letter of introduction to Robbie Ross. Characteristically he makes no mention of the money in his later account. But generous as it was, it was not as generous nor as useful as the letter of introduction to Ross. Much has been made of Sassoon's poetic influence on Owen, but perhaps the most helpful thing he ever did for him was to introduce him to his friend. For, though Owen had already met Harold Monro at the Poetry Bookshop, he was still more or less unknown on the London literary scene. Ross, with a generosity and enthusiasm that matched Sassoon's, was now to introduce him to some of the most influential members of the literary establishment. Within hours of responding to Ross's immediate invitation, Owen had met both Arnold Bennett and H.G. Wells. Ross was also to introduce him to Scott Moncrieff, Osbert Sitwell and William Heinemann.

Sassoon probably hoped to see Owen again when he paid his own visit to London ten days after their farewell dinner. His ostensible reason for this brief trip in mid-November was to meet one of his pre-war friends, a Conservative M.P. who had promised to use his influence at the War Office to get him posted abroad after his Medical, but there were other incentives. Ross had invited him to dine at the Reform with a poet he had wanted to know for some time, Robert Nichols. Not only was Nichols the most popular soldier-poet of the year, his *Ardours and Endurances* far outselling *The Old Huntsman*,[80] but Graves had been enthusing about him to Sassoon since his own meeting with him in January.

Graves, who admired Nichols's earlier poetry and was probably flattered by his request to dedicate part of *Ardours and Endurances* to him, had visited Nichols in London at a private hospital on 21 January 1917. Though officially invalided out of the Royal Artillery with shell shock after only three weeks in action, Nichols was, in fact, suffering from syphilis and had been deprived of his commission on that account, as he confided to Graves. In spite of Graves's shocked reaction, Nichols was immediately drawn to Graves, a feeling the latter somewhat condescendingly reciprocated: 'I liked him in a way: quite enthusiastic about the right things – very well-read – so I gave him a hell of a lecture on his ways and, finding he took it well, made friends with him – It was the usual story – shell-shock, friends all killed, too much champagne, sex, desperate fornication, syphilis.'[81]

Once Graves had rationalized Nichols's sexual relations with women, still an unattractive thought to him personally, he became Nichols's staunchest supporter and by April 1917 he was writing again to Sassoon, 'Robert's an awfully good chap – you'd like him awfully after you'd read his new stuff.'[82] He was evidently still worried by Nichols's heterosexuality, since he euphemistically continued: 'I admit his temperament is not ours but the circumstances I met him in last January were more the exception than the rule and it seems to have been largely bad luck.' By June Sassoon had succumbed and was himself reading Nichols's verse.

Meantime Nichols had sent his poetry to Edward Marsh, who had been sufficiently impressed with Nichols's *Invocations* (1915) to help him prepare *Ardours and Endurances* for the press in July 1917. Its extraordinary success was due in part to Marsh's involvement. The month *Ardours* was published Graves was further enticing Sassoon by quoting a letter from Nichols in which Nichols himself quotes Marsh quoting Masefield: 'Nichols, Graves and Sassoon are singing together like the morning stars.'[83] It was a triangle Graves would try to develop until his attention and energies were diverted elsewhere: 'There are three inevitables,' he wrote to Sassoon, 'two Roberts and a Siegfried rising side by side on the roll of fame all still young and more or less undamaged ....'[84]

How could Sassoon help being intrigued at the thought of meeting someone so warmly recommended and so manifestly successful? And in spite of his high expectations he was not disappointed by Nichols. He enjoyed his exuberant talk about poetry, particularly when it included praise of his own. Though he had not made up his mind about Nichols's work, he liked the man unequivocally. Born in the same year as Owen, 1893, Nichols could not have been a greater contrast to him. The son of a solidly middle-class family, whose pedigree Sassoon was personally to trace back to the minor man of letters, John Nichols (1745-1826), Robert Malise Bowyer Nichols was a product of Winchester and Oxford. At times over-confident both of his poetic and social powers and exuberant to an alarming degree – Sassoon was to receive at least one letter of forty-five pages from him – he was also very moody and needed constant reassurance from his friends. Sassoon came to regard his role with Nichols as quite different from the equally encouraging one he had adopted with the diffident Owen, however. He quickly began to see himself as Nichols's 'psychological antithesis', his own 'dangers' being 'verbal constipation and imaginative and constructive timidity', in contrast to Nichols's uninhibited outpourings. If with Owen he had found himself the more confident and authoritative of the two, with Nichols he was to envy and admire the younger man's 'heroic ambitions and attempts'. But it was also true that his admiration for Nichols's poetry, which increased on meeting him,[85] was to diminish almost as quickly, whereas his initially slower appreciation of the less confident Owen's work was to grow steadily. What seems curious is that he ever admired Nichols's verse at all, since it was the kind of poetry he himself had rejected, its bombastic and rhetorical tone glorifying the War in a way he could no longer approve:

> ... Heads forget heaviness,
> Hearts forget spleen,
> For by that mighty winnowing
> Being is blown clean.

Light in the eyes again,
Strength in the hand,
A spirit dares, dies, forgives,
And can understand!

And, best! Love comes back again
After grief and shame,
And along the wind of death
Throws a clean flame ...[86]

Sassoon's doubts lay in the future, however. At their first meeting in mid-
November 1917 he was impressed by Nichols. His admiration increased when,
after an alcoholic dinner at the Reform Club, he found himself trapped into
sharing a poetry reading with him at the house of the society hostess, Sybil
Colefax, an event he loathed. He had always been shy and the prospect of
reading his poems to a room full of mainly female socialites lived up to his
worst fears:

> I responded by choosing some of my least ingratiating performances [he
> read 'They' and 'The Rear-Guard', among others], though so nervous and
> self-conscious that my muttered undertones must have been inferred rather
> than audible. I had never read to an audience before, and felt that I was
> merely the unwilling object of intelligent curiosity. Robbie was furthering
> his purpose of getting my poems talked about, but his zealousness had
> outrun discretion. I didn't want to be paraded before these cultivated and
> agreeable strangers, and for once I was quite huffy with Robbie.[87]

Nichols, according to Sassoon, revelled in it on the other hand, 'proceeding to
give an emotional rendering of the war poems which had won him reputation.
Sometimes his voice was bold and resonant; sometimes it sank to a plaintive
pianissimo. He also indulged in gesticulation, and when reading a stanza, the
last line of which was "I look up and smile", he looked up and smiled.'[88] In
spite of Sassoon's friendly interest in him and his writings, all this caused him
'acute discomfort'. The difference between the two men could not have been
more clearly demonstrated. Dissimilar as they were, however, they were united
in their dislike of having Ivor Novello play rag-time, at their hostess's request,
between their readings. And they liked each other sufficiently to arrange another
meeting for Sassoon's next London visit.

Robert Graves, whose confidence equalled Nichols's, was quite convinced
that he had been responsible for introducing Sassoon to Nichols. 'Nice for
me to have introduced two such great men,' he wrote to Marsh in January
1918. 'I'm beginning to understand more clearly what Georgian poetry means
and what it's going to mean by God's Grace.'[89] He was referring to the fact
that Marsh had by this time included all three poets in his latest anthology of

Georgian Poetry (1916-1917), published in December 1917. He had chosen eight poems by Sassoon, eight by Graves and seven longer ones by Nichols, and placed them prominently towards the front of the collection, anxious to draw attention to the newcomers.

This, the third volume of *Georgian Poetry*, edited by one of Sassoon's first two mentors, Marsh, was dedicated to the second, Edmund Gosse. Both of them, having reacted strongly to Sassoon's realistic war poetry, had clearly come to accept it, since Marsh's selection includes two forceful examples, 'They' and 'In the Pink'. But Marsh's choice also suggests that he still hankered after the earlier, more heroic variety and Sassoon's Romantic vein: he included 'To Victory' and 'The Kiss', as well as the poem Owen so much admired, 'The Death-Bed'. He opens his selection tactfully with a neutral poem, Sassoon's charming verse 'Letter Home (to Robert Graves)'. Sassoon's prominent place in the third *Georgian Poetry* anthology would consolidate the success of *The Old Huntsman* earlier in the year and keep him firmly at the centre of the London literary scene. As he had prophesied to Ross in August, 'Georgian Poetry w[ould] keep the pot boiling' the following year.[90]

Life at Craiglockhart on Sassoon's return from London in mid-November must have seemed dull by comparison with his brief but flattering literary whirl, which may have helped him to feel more positive about the second Medical Board arranged for him on 26 November. A further incentive was the fact that, just before his first, abortive Medical Board, most of the staff at Craiglockhart had resigned in support of the head doctor. Major Bryce, who was respected and admired by staff and patients alike, had refused to titivate his hospital for inspection. He felt that the visiting General should, for once, see a war hospital as it really was. The result was the dismissal of the Commandant, Bryce, followed by the resignation of most of his loyal staff. Sassoon learnt of Rivers's resignation only after missing his first Medical, but it made it easier to attend his second. As he had written to Graves three days earlier, he could not see beyond the War and no longer cared whether he was alive or dead – 'except to look after the two Roberts, and they can do quite well without me'.[91] In an intriguing postscript describing Owen's successful visit to Ross, he advises Graves to 'make *him* the third in your triangle [my italics]. I am sure he will be a very good poet some day, and he is a very loveable creature.'

It is an ambiguous statement which could mean either that Sassoon himself wanted to opt out of a three-cornered relationship with Nichols and Graves, or that he was anxious to replace the heterosexual Nichols with the homosexual Owen. Either way, Sassoon's response was probably prompted by Graves's change of sexual direction. For Graves had announced his engagement to Nancy Nicholson, daughter of the painter William Nicholson, in a letter of 20 November and had written to Robert Nichols at about the same time:

It's only fair to tell you that since the cataclysm of my friend Peter, my affections are running in the more normal channels and I correspond regularly and warmly with Nancy Nicholson, who is great fun. I only tell you this so that you should get out of your head any misconceptions about my temperament. I should hate you to think I was a confirmed homosexual even if it were only in my thought and went no further.[92]

This marked a distinct change of attitude from that of his April letter to Sassoon, in which he had noted that Nichols's 'temperament [i.e. sexual orientation] is not ours'. A triangle consisting of two heterosexuals, Graves and Nichols, would leave Sassoon in a minority. Graves's defection to the heterosexual camp might also help explain the extremely depressed tone of Sassoon's letter to Graves of 21 November.

It was in a mood of almost complete despair, then, that Sassoon finally went before a Medical Board on 26 November. Not caring much whether he lived or died, he could hardly wait to be passed fit for General Service as Rivers had promised he would be. He was duly passed for Service Abroad. The inconvenient protester had now been silenced and, as a reward, been restored to his former status as 'an officer and a gentleman', a position he had reluctantly sacrificed in pursuit of his principles. But it is unlikely that this played any part in his recantation. Nor is his jokey explanation to Theo Bartholomew – that it was 'the only thing I could do to maintain my well known dignity and limelight business!!' – completely convincing,[93] though there is probably some truth in it. His main motive throughout seems to have been returning to his men who, according to Graves, had said 'We'd follow him anywhere.'[94]

15

'Love Drives Me Back'

November 1917-May 1918

The main problem Sassoon had to face on his return to Litherland Depot at the end of November 1917 was embarrassment. Though unrepentant about both his protest and his apparent abandonment of it, he realized that most of his brother officers would think that he had made 'a proper fool' of himself.[1] Instead of taking the easy home job of cadet instructor he had made a very public stand which, in their eyes, had threatened the honour of the Regiment. Now he was returning sheepishly after four months of safety at Craiglockhart, while they had continued to risk their lives on active service. He did not anticipate rejection – they were too kind and genuine for that – but he did fear their puzzled misunderstanding of his apparent *volte-face*. How could he possibly explain to those trained largely to repress their emotions that it was love of his men which had driven him back?

In the event there was little explanation needed, since the camp was virtually empty. The RWF Depot had been transferred to Ireland only a few days earlier on account of the troubles there. Though the Easter Rising of 1916 had been long since quelled, the situation in Ireland, particularly in the South, remained volatile and a fresh wave of unrest in autumn 1917 called for more British troops there. Most of Sassoon's friends had, therefore, been posted to Limerick, leaving only the Assistant Adjutant and two other officers, out of approximately thirty, known to him. Together with about twenty 'details' and a few hundred recruits and returned hospital cases, they rattled around in a camp designed for thousands.

During his first three days there, from 26 to 29 November, Sassoon led what seemed to him a 'python life',[2] eating and sleeping on the floor in the neglected huts, waiting only for his next posting. It came as a relief to be given ten days' leave (twelve, unofficially) to take another last farewell of his family and friends. Though still feeling angry and defiant and still wanting to sacrifice himself – 'martyred because he could not save mankind'[3] – he was nevertheless resolved to have as good a time as possible on leave. For the most part, this seems to have meant being as 'brainless' as possible.[4] It also involved spending as little time at home as he decently could, since it was clear to him that his mother would never understand his attitude towards the War.

It may have been in an effort to improve the situation, as well as out of liking for him, that Sassoon invited Bob Nichols to share three of his four days at Weirleigh. To Sassoon's relief Nichols, while just as charming as he had been in London, seemed 'much nicer' in Kent than the rather superficial, over-confident young man he had appeared in more cosmopolitan surroundings.[5] The visit, brief as it was, cemented their friendship, which was to continue for at least another decade.

The statutory stay at home over, Sassoon felt that he had done his duty, except for a lunch with his great-aunt Mozelle, which he arranged for the following Saturday. The rest of his leave was to be pure pleasure, which for the most part meant hunting. For as he noted in his diary on 7 December after hunting with the Southdown for the second time that week: 'I forgot the war today for fifty minutes when the hounds were running and I was taking the fences on a jolly old grey horse.'[6] He spent his last day of leave similarly occupied, hunting with the Atherstone.

To satisfy a very different side to his nature Sassoon stayed two separate nights in London, both of them at Half Moon Street. On 5 December he spent the evening with Ross. Heinemann was also invited, ostensibly to see Barrie's *Dear Brutus* with them, but almost certainly as a pretext to discuss Sassoon's next volume, *Counter-Attack*. He also showed Marsh his poems during his second stay in London on 8 and 9 December. Marsh had invited him to breakfast at Raymond Buildings with Robert Nichols to present his two newest contributors – Graves was in Wales – with a copy of *Georgian Poetry 1916-17*. This had already sold over 2,000 copies in its first fortnight, which went some way towards consoling Sassoon for Heinemann's reluctance to rush out another volume of his poems. At least he could be sure that his work was being seen and reviewed. Indeed many of the reviewers were to select his contributions to *Georgian Poetry* for special praise.[7]

Sassoon's whirlwind fortnight of indulgence left him determined to lead a life of 'light-hearted stupidity' whilst he remained at Litherland.[8] 'At least I will try and be peaceful-minded for a few months – after the strain and unhappiness of the last seven months. It is the only way I can hope to face the horrors of the front without breaking down completely. I must try to think as little as possible.'[9] Instead, he told Bob Nichols, he ate 'jam-roly and roast sirloin by the barrowload, and sle[pt] like a log on the floor of a hut'.[10] His spare time was spent playing golf at Formby or eating expensive dinners at the Adelphi. The C.O. of what remained of the 3rd RWF, Lt.-Col. Jones Williams, had either forgotten or forgiven his past sins and invited him out to meals with his family in Crosby, a few miles from the Camp. And on 23 December Sassoon took a train to Manchester to meet Dent's friend, Lawrence Haward, curator of Manchester Corporation Art Galleries, a visit which illustrates in a number of ways what Fussell has called the 'polarities', or 'dichotomies', in Sassoon's life.[11]

Not only was Sassoon crossing from the unthinking, animal-like existence of camp life and golf to the cultural and intellectual milieu of the Manchester art world, but he was also moving from the stiff, socially correct sphere of the Officers' Mess to an underworld into which most committed homosexuals of the period had been forced. The final contrast, made even stronger by an invitation to tea with a German family the same day, was between the official army attitude to the War and the pacifists' condemnation of it. For Dent, who was staying with Haward, introduced Sassoon during his visit to another pacifist and homosexual, Goldsworthy Lowes Dickinson. A close friend of E.M. Forster's at King's College, Dickinson was a philosophical writer and essayist who also contributed numerous pacifist articles to the *Cambridge Magazine* during the War. Sassoon knew of his connection with the magazine and may even have seen him briefly in Cambridge before the December 1917 meeting. He would probably already have read Dickinson's *A Greek View of Life* (1896), a book which was seen by some as a veiled justification for homosexuality and had become a bible for many homosexuals by the beginning of the twentieth century. Sassoon had certainly read a 'dialogue' by Dickinson along the same lines, since he wrote to tell him of his reaction some time after January 1907: 'Why didn't someone tell me all that when I was eating my heart out at Cambridge in 1906? Also I felt firmly convinced that you have handled the thing with amazing discretion, delicacy and completeness. And there is nothing else to say about it, – except to pray that it may be read by many more who feel as we do.'[12] His meeting with Dickinson would have been exciting under any circumstances, but must have been particularly stimulating in contrast to the conventional existence he was leading. It helped to keep alive his other, secret life.

That other life had received a severe shock only two days earlier, when

Sassoon had been forced finally to come to terms with Graves's defection from the homosexual camp. Having already told Sassoon of his intention to marry Nancy Nicholson, Graves felt it necessary to discuss it with him in person. And when Sassoon arrived at the 3rd Battalion Garrison at Kinmel Camp near Rhyl, Graves could only 'apologise' for his act of desertion. While Graves was extremely happy at the thought of marriage, he understood Sassoon and his position well enough to feel that an apology was necessary. He was also sufficiently fond of him to want to keep his friendship. Sassoon, on the other hand, was already beginning to distance himself emotionally from Graves. He had made curiously little effort to see him while on leave and had subsequently turned down an invitation to participate in a second poetry-reading at the Colefaxes with him on 12 December. On 21 November he had written to Lady Ottoline Morrell that Robert Graves was 'very happy' but that he did not think that he felt as deeply as some people, not even as much as Bob Nichols 'with all his egotism'.[13] It was Graves who was anxious to keep the friendship alive, trying to persuade Sassoon that he would like Nancy, even to the rather comic extent of characterizing her as a 'capable farmer's *boy*' [my italics].[14]

It may have been his sense that he was losing a close friend and ally which made Sassoon feel depressed at the beginning of 1918. On the other hand, Christmas at Litherland had not been a cheerful affair; it left him viewing his fellow creatures as 'guzzling gabbing grotesques'.[15] Christmas was also a time when he habitually remembered absent army friends and each year the death toll was rising. His nightmares were worse and his expectations for the future even lower. This mood of hopelessness and fear is reflected in a poem written at this time, but not included in his *Collected Poems*:

> I awoke; evilly tired, and startled from sleep;
> Came home to seeing and thinking; shuddered; and shook
> An ugly dream from my shoulders: death with a look
> Of malice, retreated and vanished. I cowered, a horrible heap ....[16]

Written at Limerick, the day after his arrival there, 'A Moment of Waking' marks a turning-point in Sassoon's mood. His relief at leaving the desolate depot, his interminable rounds of golf and heavy dinners, is marked by a more positive return to poetry, even though this first piece *is* pessimistic. Crossing from Liverpool to Limerick by the night ferry on Sunday, 6 January 1918, with two other officers, Attwater and the Quartermaster, Hickman, he felt he was making a fresh start.

Though Sassoon had never visited Ireland, his expectations were high; he had already enjoyed Somerville and Ross's descriptions of it in *Some Experiences of an Irish R.M.* He certainly thought the people he met there were exactly like characters from the *R.M.* books. Limerick, situated in the south, close to the west coast, was pleasantly rural after the dinginess of industrialized Litherland and the bells of Limerick Cathedral were certainly more melodious than the sirens of Bryant and May's Liverpool factory. In addition the weather was crisp and seasonal, softening everything under a layer of frost and snow.

Best of all, Sassoon was back with old friends. For of the 120 officers, five of them had been out in France with him in the 1st RWF from 1915 to 1916: Colin Dobell, C.D. Morgan, J.V. Higginson, A.F. Freeman and H.F. Garnons-Williams. 'I share a room with little Billy Morgan – the Albert Medal lad from the 15th Batt[alion]' Sassoon reported to Graves. 'He is very good company.'[17] His admiration for Morgan sprang partly from the fact that he had been wounded four times and helped put him into a more cheerful frame of mind, enabling him to envisage a future where a man might stand 'Saved by unnumbered miracles of chance/ ... with war's unholiness behind' (lines taken from his diary poem, 'Journey's End', a poem dedicated 'To W.M.M.', that is, William ('Billy') M. Morgan). Morgan would be one of a few friends to see him off when he was finally posted abroad.

Sassoon also knew at least two of the men in F Company, to which he had been assigned under Jim Ormrod, a further boost to morale. The 'New Barracks' themselves, though hardly 'new' anymore, were much more cheerful than the huts at Litherland and made him feel less like a temporary soldier. He spent hours on the parade-ground there watching young fusiliers drill, or lectured 'roseate' Lance-Corporals on such subjects as 'patrolling', pleasant duties which made it easier for him to avoid thinking.

Apart from enjoying the sight of so many healthy young men, a vivid contrast to the physical and mental wrecks he had encountered at Craiglockhart, Sassoon felt extraordinarily fit himself. There was seldom time or opportunity for brooding. On 9 January he wrote a cautiously optimistic poem, 'In Barracks', the second in two days, which suggests that, though he had long since stopped romanticizing war, he was still inclined to romanticize the troops; it is no coincidence that its last line echoes Housman:

> ... Sleep well, you lusty Fusiliers;
> Shut your brave eyes on sense and sight,
> And banish from your dreamless ears
> The bugle's dying notes that say,
> 'Another night; another day.'   (*CP*, p. 95)

By 12 January Sassoon could write in his diary: 'Peace of mind; freedom from all care; the jollity of health and good companions. What more can one ask for?'[18] But he knew at bottom that it was 'a drugged peace, that *will* not think, dares not think': the 'ranks of youth' had become 'the company of death'.[19] Knowing that he would shortly be posted abroad and expecting it to be France, where the situation was at its worst, he deliberately distracted himself with escapist activities. Towards the end of the second week, when the frost and snow had turned to more characteristically warm and rainy weather, he began to explore the surrounding countryside. It was on one such exploration that he wrote 'The

Dream', a poem inspired by the similarity he glimpsed between rural Ireland and wartime France. So vivid were the recollections this inspired, that he felt himself once more in a 'disconsolate, straggling village street', watching the exhausted troops stumbling into 'some crazy hovel'. But it was their blistered feet, which he had already written about in 'Foot Inspection', that moved him most in memory:

> I'm looking at their blistered feet; young Jones
> Stares up at me, mud-splashed and white and jaded;
> Out of his eyes the morning light has faded.
> Old soldiers with three winters in their bones
> Puff their damp Woodbines, whistle, stretch their toes:
> *They* can still grin at me, for each of 'em knows
> That I'm as tired as they are ... Can they guess
> The secret burden that is always mine?
> Pride in their courage; pity for their distress;
> And burning bitterness
> That I must take them to the accursèd Line.   (*CP*, p. 94)

Sassoon was still a long way from France, however, and he was determined to make as much of that fact as he could. On Saturday, 19 January, for instance, he walked out to Adare, a small town ten miles south-west of Limerick, and saw the Ireland which he had already imagined before his posting there: 'the wide, shallow, washing, hastening, grey river; the ivy-clad stones of a castle-ruin planted on the banks amid trees. Very romantic scene, on a grey evening.'[20] He could think of no better way to enjoy such country than on horseback. So, while his superiors were talking in apprehensive undertones about the growing 'troubles' in the area and the possibility that mobile columns of soldiers might have to be sent out to suppress them, Sassoon started making enquiries about the Limerick Hunt. He was finally introduced to it by a talkative horsedealer at Croome. Somerville and Ross, or Surtees himself, could hardly have invented a more colourful set of people for his delight and they were to provide him with rich material for *Sherston's Progress*. Apart from Dorothea Conyers, a prolific author as well as expert horsewoman, there was Mike Sheeby ('Mike Shehan' in *Sherston's Progress*), who hired Sassoon horses, and Nigel Baring 'Esq', who looked after him in other ways, sometimes driving him home after a hard day's hunting. There were others, too, but by far the most memorable was an elderly man called Harnett, whom Sassoon describes as 'Blarnett', or more familiarly, 'The Mister' in *Sherston's Progress*. Together with his hospitable landlady, Mrs MacDonnell ('O'Donnell' in *Sherston's Progress*), he provides the most vivid scenes in Sassoon's account of his Irish hunting experiences. A short, stout man with light blue eyes, pink face and small white moustache, he appeared just what he was, 'an extraordinarily kind old chap'.[21] Having made his fortune in America, he had returned home to spend it, and was doing so in style. Always ready to buy rounds of drinks for his numerous friends, he was hardly ever sober but seldom so drunk that he was out of control. Sassoon treasured one of his rare utterances, which revealed his philosophy as well as the proverbial Irish gift with words: 'In politics and religion, be pleasant to both sides. Sure, we'll all be dead drunk on the Day of Judgement.'[22] Once he took Sassoon under his wing life became even more enjoyable. Before going on an Anti-Gas course at Cork on 22 January, Sassoon had been out once with the Limerick Hunt, but after his introduction to 'the Mister' he hunted almost daily.

Thus he passed the last week and a half of his stay in a round of pleasure which seemed to him like 'a slice out of 1913'.[23] Generally the Limerick met a few miles from the city, in the hilly country south and south-west of the town, where the names were as romantic as the soulful Irish landscape – Kilfinny Cross, Fedamore, Ballingrane and Ballingarry were only a few of the places Sassoon noted in his diary. Once they strayed as far as the Mullagharierk Mountains and, though the weather was too wild for hunting, Sassoon enjoyed an early luncheon in a spacious and remote old Irish mansion at Glenwilliam and 'rich-flavoured Irish talk' with its aristocratic owner, Tom Atkinson.[24] On one occasion, hilariously recalled and almost certainly embroidered in *Sherston's Progress*, he took young Colin Dobell, who had been with him at Mametz Wood, out for his first real day's hunting. But usually his companions were members of the Hunt, who had welcomed him like an old friend. Mrs Marshall invited him to tea, Mrs MacDonnell to lunch and 'the Mister' bought him drinks at every possible opportunity.

'Happy days', Sassoon noted in his diary on 4 February 1918, but they were days always under the shadow of imminent departure. For he had learnt on 21 January that he was on a list of officers going to Egypt. The biggest advantage, he felt, was that Egypt was an unknown country to him, where conditions – he rightly anticipated Palestine – would not be so trying as in France and there would be less chance of being killed. But he still yearned to be where the action was, however dangerous: 'I want to go back to one of the regular battalions. The other place is only a side-show, and I'd be with an inferior battalion.' Quite understandably, he also wanted to be in a unit where he knew people and was known. Though he concluded by saying that he could not make up his mind, he immediately started trying to have himself transferred to either the 1st Battalion in Italy or the 2nd near Ypres.

Sassoon wrote at once to Marsh about his posting, asking him if he could do anything about it at the War Office, which Marsh could not. His most impassioned plea, however, appears to have been to Rivers. While pronouncing himself ready to do anything he could, Rivers clearly preferred Sassoon to go to Palestine, where he would be in less danger. He was not alone in this: Graves, who was arranging to take a safe job with the No. 17 Cadet Battalion and settle down with his new wife, thought so too.

Sassoon may have been relieved to be dissuaded from trying for France. At any rate he resigned himself to Palestine and enjoyed his hunting all the more.

On his very last day, with the 4.25 p.m. train to catch to Dublin, he rode out even further than usual to Ballingarry, about eighteen miles from Limerick. Staying with the hounds for longer than was wise he waited till 2.30 p.m. to take the ramshackle local taxi back to the Mister's lodgings, Balinacurra, where Mrs MacDonnell gave him a magnificent, if hasty, lunch of salmon, woodcock and champagne. Arriving at the station with less than a minute to spare, he was seen off to London by three friends, Billy Morgan, Jim Ormrod and Kit Owen – plus, of course, the old 'Mister'.

Sassoon had balanced his need for strenuous physical exertion at Limerick with more intellectual pursuits. In the evenings, and on the rare days when he was not supervising parades or hunting, he read and wrote poetry. After feeling poems 'piling themselves up inside [his] head' at Litherland, he had been able to get a few down on paper there, but the majority of them were written at Limerick. Not surprisingly, none of the verses he produced after Craiglockhart but before returning to France are as fierce as those produced during and just after time spent at the Front, though a number are anti-war. Some of them are positively escapist, emerging with what he whimsically called 'bright faces' rather than 'haggard exasperated eyes'.[25] Having successfully escaped from the reality of the War for a few months, Sassoon was able to imagine a world, admittedly after death, which resembled the innocent and romantic landscapes of his childhood: an 'Invocation', written to his muse, suggests that his aims in poetry had not really changed and that it was still 'Beauty' he pursued.[26]

Appropriately, since 'Invocation' is more like the piece which led to Sassoon's introduction to Ottoline ('To Victory') than most of his intervening verse, he sent this poem to her, either in December 1917 when he wrote it, or in early January 1918. He also sent it to the person who had introduced them to each other, someone who shared Ottoline's romantic tastes, Edmund Gosse. Though Gosse had finally managed to accept Sassoon's violent trench-satires, he was evidently relieved to be back on more familiar and (to him) more attractive ground. Gosse pleased him even more by reporting from Marsh that the new Georgian volume was still selling like hot cakes.

Proud of the continuing success of *Georgian Poetry 1916-17*, Sassoon had already sent a copy to Hardy who, in thanking him on 28 December 1917, said he liked half of Sassoon's eight contributions to it. When Sassoon replied immediately, recommending other poems from the volume, Hardy again thanked him, this time for a photographic portrait he had enclosed; it had been given a place of honour in his writing-room, where it 'calmly overlooked a hopeless chaos of scribbler's litter'.[27] Even more excitingly, from the younger poet's point of view, he ended his letter: 'I shall be so glad to see you walk in some day.'

Meantime, as Sassoon's departure for Egypt approached, he retreated further into golden memories of childhood and the Weald of Kent. Revising his third tribute to Gordon Harbord, 'Together', his mind lingered on their youthful hunting days on the borders of the Weald. And his final poem about Gordon, 'Idyll', creates yet another vision of his childhood garden:

In the grey summer garden I shall find you
With day-break and the morning hills behind you.
There will be rain-wet roses; stir of wings;
And down the wood a thrush that wakes and sings ...[28] (*CP*, p. 113)

On the same day that Sassoon wrote 'Idyll', 1 February, he made yet another attempt to conjure up the happiness of youth in 'Memory': 'Out in the fields, with morning in the may,/ Wind on the grass, wings in the orchard bloom ....' The poem ends, however, with a strong sense of present unhappiness, in which joy and beauty are only memories:

But now my heart is heavy-laden. I sit
Burning my dreams away beside the fire:
For death has made me wise and bitter and strong;
And I am rich in all that I have lost.
O starshine on the fields of long-ago,
Bring me the darkness and the nightingale;
Dim wealds of vanished summer, peace of home,
And silence; and the faces of my friends.[29] (*CP*, p. 105)

Sassoon himself felt that this uneasy mixture of romanticism and realism was not 'characteristic' and was 'by no means the strongest' of the poems he had written since 1917,[30] whereas the unashamedly romantic 'Idyll' continued to be one of his favourites. This may explain his decision not to attempt to mix the two sides of his nature in a poem he wrote three days later, 'Remorse'. Crammed as this is with realistic details of trench-life, however, it fails to achieve the forcefulness of works like 'Base Details', 'The General' or 'They', lacking their swift narrative action and punchy last line.

Closer in feel to his trench-satires is a poem which may also have been written at Limerick, 'Suicide in the Trenches', describing 'a simple soldier boy' who 'put a bullet through his brain'. Its subject matter is similar to Owen's 'S.I.W.' but its ballad-like technique is much closer to that of Housman, whom he was still reading, among a host of other poets. He was already accumulating books for the journey to Palestine.

*

Back in London, which he reached at 7 a.m. on 9 February after a night crossing from Dublin, Sassoon tried to pack as much into his last two days as possible. Scorning sleep, he lunched with Ross and Marsh and in the afternoon attempted to catch up on the classical music he missed so much in the largely Philistine army camps. To sit in the Queen's Hall, listening to Beethoven's *Fifth Symphony*, Lalo's *Concerto*, César Franck's *Symphonic Variations* and a new Schmitt *Tone Poem* would be a pleasure by most standards but to one whose ears had been jarred by the constant rag-time and popular tunes of army huts, it must have been bliss.

Yet the popular music he had disliked so much at the start was beginning to have a certain power over Sassoon by early 1918, and the dichotomy between his old life and his new is nowhere so clearly illustrated as in his attitude towards music, as a poem written at Limerick shows. Echoing the syncopated rhythms of the jazz and rag-time which had so irritated him, and incidentally anticipating the modernist experiments of T.S. Eliot and Edith Sitwell, among others, he explores his ambivalent feelings on the subject. After paying tribute to his early favourites, Beethoven, Bach and Mozart, he continues in 'Dead Musicians':

II

Great names, I cannot find you now
In these loud years of youth that strives
Through doom toward peace; upon my brow
I wear a wreath of banished lives.
You have no part with lads who fought
And laughed and suffered at my side.
Your fugues and symphonies have brought
No memory of my friends who died.

III

For when my brain is on their track,
In slangy speech I call them back.
With fox-trot tunes their ghosts I charm.
'Another little drink won't do us any harm.'
I think of rag-time; a bit of rag-time;
And see their faces crowding round
To the sound of the syncopated beat.
They've got such jolly things to tell,
Home from hell with a Blighty wound so neat ...

And so the song breaks off; and I'm alone.
They're dead ... For God's Sake stop that gramophone.

(*CP*, pp. 92-3)

Music apart, Sassoon's leave was spent mainly catching up on friends.[31] He shared another meal with Ross on the evening of his first day and afterwards met Rivers, who must have been relieved that he was not seeing him off to the Western Front. Sassoon's family, whom he visited the next day at his aunt's house in Melbury Road, certainly were. His mother had come up to meet him there and it was a tense occasion: 'Mother brave as usual,' Sassoon reported in his diary. But it was Ross and Meiklejohn who saw him off at Waterloo the next day, not his mother.

Leaving London at 12 noon on Monday, 12 February, Sassoon was in

Southampton in time to have dinner at the Dolphin Hotel before boarding the *Antrim*. Thinking himself bound for Le Havre, the usual crossing, he found himself in Cherbourg the next day, spending the night in a Rest Camp three miles outside the town. As he wandered idly about the grounds of a nearby château the next morning, he experienced, as on each of his previous trips to France 'that rather pleasant feeling of isolation from all worldly business, which comes when one is "at the war". Nothing much to worry or distract one except the ordinary irritations and boredom of "being messed about" by the Army.'[32]

It was the third time in three years that Sassoon had been in France in February, only this time it was not to be his final destination. Instead he was about to board a train which would take him 1,446 miles to Taranto, where he would then be taken by troopship to Alexandria *en route* for Palestine. His main concern for the next few weeks would be how to deal with the inevitable boredom of army journeys. He had already adopted one of his defence mechanisms by exploring the countryside near the Rest Camp. He had also started to make his diary-entries fuller.

Sassoon's greatest resource in the face of boredom continued to be reading. Wisely he chose not too demanding texts – Trollope's *Barchester Towers*, Hardy's *Woodlanders* and Pater's *Renaissance*.[33] It was a choice which suggests a compromise between nostalgia for the rural England he was leaving and an attempt to understand the Italy he was visiting for the first time, that country where, as Pater points out, 'the interest of the Renaissance mainly lies'. A second aspect of Pater which must have seemed particularly pertinent to Sassoon, as he travelled towards yet another war-zone, was Pater's awareness, expressed in Victor Hugo's words in the 'Conclusion' to the *Renaissance*, that 'we are all *condamnés* ... we are all under sentence of death but with a sort of indefinite reprieve'. And it was this conviction which made Sassoon desperate to do what Pater himself saw as the sole antidote to 'the awful brevity of life'; that is, 'to burn always with this hard, gemlike flame', both phrases Sassoon repeats in his response to his own journey into the unknown.

Under Pater's direct influence the 'truth' Sassoon seeks on this journey is truth to sensation, which calls for the kind of impressionistic criticism Pater pioneered in the *Renaissance*. Sassoon's descriptions of the scenery he passed on his way from Cherbourg, through Bourges, Lyons, Genoa, Novi, Voghera, Parma, Bologna, Faenza, Foggia and Brindisi, to Taranto glow as never before with impressionistic fervour. In lyrical passages, such as a set-piece on 'Grottiglie at Sunset', he was preparing himself, consciously or not, for the prose-writing which would follow his war poetry. More particularly he was providing himself with the raw material for the last work in his fictionalized trilogy, *Sherston's Progress*. Time and again he would turn back to his diaries to remind himself of what his impressionistic jottings vividly brought back, that sense of leaving the known and journeying into the unknown, an experience he found both exciting and disturbing.

However, helpful as they were to be in the future, Sassoon was not satisfied with his exploration of the picturesque, either in prose or poetry. (He wrote and destroyed some 'landscape poems' on the journey.[34]) They seemed to him merely exercises. '*Must* concentrate on the tragic, emotional, human episodes in the drama,' he reminded himself: '... I *must* have the heroic. So goodbye to amiable efforts at nature-poems. If I write I'll write tense and bitter and proud and pitiful.'[35] He was not being entirely fair to himself; though there was nothing 'tragic' or 'heroic' for him to describe on the journey, he had not neglected the 'human' and 'emotional' aspects of it. In fact, one of the first things he noted about it was the human element: 'My companions S.W. Harper, M. Robinson and H.G. Howell-Jones, all decent chaps – Harper of course charming,' he wrote in his diary on the first day of his journey. 'It was he who went to Edinburgh with Robert Graves, as my "supposed" escort, last July.'[36]

There is nothing like a long journey for testing relationships, however, and Harper (the 'Hooper' of *Sherston's Progress*), is described five days later as 'rather hipped and fussy – bad campaigner, I fear'.[37] On the other hand, Howell-Jones ('Howell' in *Sherston's Progress*), introduced without comment in his diary, is later praised as 'sensible and philosophical'.[38] But it was the third member of the group, Robinson, who won his heart 'with his dear impetuous ways, kind and willing and cheery'. It was undoubtedly Robinson to whom Sassoon was referring when he wrote to Dent on 19 February 1918: 'Only four in a compartment so there is a fair amount of room. The other three are quite pleasant – (one of them rather *more* than that.)'[39] Not surprisingly Robinson, as 'Marshall', figures far more prominently than the others in *Sherston's Progress*, where, in the guise of fiction, Sassoon's attraction to him is underlined. More like the untidy Graves than the impeccable David Thomas or Bobbie Hanmer, the 21-year-old Robinson nevertheless shared their youthful enthusiasm, which so appealed to Sassoon. And, if we are to believe *Sherston's Progress*, he much preferred Robinson's 'jolly face and simple jokes' to Harper's 'youthful charm and good looks but absence of guts'.[40] Physical attraction was not, in itself, enough, though it was an important ingredient in his sexual relationships. (The fact that he shared a seat, which at night became a bed, with Robinson seemed to him significant.) There was also an element of protectiveness in this, as in most of his other passions. The young man's 'grown-up babyish face' inspired emotions very similar to those he had felt for Thomas and Hanmer. Robinson, for his part, was probably unaware of Sassoon's sexual attraction to him. A more practical person than Sassoon, his main concern seems to have been to look after him in a down-to-earth way. Where Sassoon thought of what books to bring, Robinson had thought of a Primus stove, for example, and was able to supply the poet with *café au lait*, a taste not catered for by the army.

Sassoon needed all the comforts he could get. Not only was the journey long and tedious but for most of it he felt ill with 'a touch of fever and chill' on his insides. Even the greater comfort of a Rest Camp at Taranto on 22 February could not restore his good-humour. The majority of the officers there seemed to him lacking in sensitivity and intelligence, except for the doctors who struck him as uniformly wise and kind. It was the beginning of a hostility towards most commissioned officers, whom he would increasingly compare unfavourably with the 'other ranks'. However superficial the officers seemed, the men struck Sassoon as 'simple and childlike' in the face of danger.[41] Their instinct on the journey was to draw physically closer together in attitudes which delighted Sassoon, partly because they roused a 'sexual emotion' in him.[42] Instead of discussing world-politics and drinking cocktails, they read popular magazines and drank ginger-beer. With no smart uniforms, expensive hair-oils, secret information or media recognition to bolster their sense of self-importance, they were forced into a directness which Sassoon, under the influence of Barbusse and strong homoerotic feelings, romanticized:

> They are part of the huge dun-coloured mass of victims that passes across the shambles of war into the gloom of death where all ranks revert to private. But in their vast patience, in the simplicity of their anger and their mirth, they are as one soul. They are the traditions of human suffering, stripped of all its foolish decorations and ignoble sufferings for individual success and social advancement.[43]

This exaggerated recognition of their virtues, while perfectly genuine, may have sprung partly from his sense of guilt at having deserted them for a time. Sometimes, watching them at a concert party, for example, he could hardly bear the pathos of their situation: 'These men, sitting – standing – tier beyond tier – row beyond row – excluded from life – the show is what they long for – LIFE with its song and dance – life with its brief gaiety.'[44]

Concert parties were mainly for the men rather than the officers, but Sassoon found himself particularly interested in one of them, or at least the preparations for it. Shortly before boarding the liner *Kashgar* on 25 February he had come across members of a Jewish battalion rehearsing behind the camp's tent-lines. What he took to be two well-known London comedians were being admired by other members of the battalion. He particularly noted the 'curved Hebrew beak' of one comedian and the fact that 'another little Jew' whispered something to him.[45] Setting out as he was on the final stages of a journey which would terminate in the Holy Land, he was becoming more aware of Jewishness and his own Jewish roots. 'Oriental adventures', he wrote in a Kiplingesque poem sent to Dent, would 'renew the past' in him.[46] Allowing for the facetious tone Sassoon generally adopted with Dent, it is clear that his 'Hebrew heart' was finally 'awaking', as he claimed, on this journey to Palestine.

After three days in Rest Camp Sassoon found it a relief to board ship for Alexandria. The *Kashgar*, anchored in the gulf of Taranto in readiness, set sail on 25 February and once adjusted to sea-travel, he began to feel better. The Mediterranean was calm, the night-skies beautiful, and Conrad's *Chance*, his choice for this part of the journey, absorbing. Arriving at Alexandria on 28

February, exactly three days after leaving Taranto, Sassoon is still trying to nail down impressions in Pateresque phrases. But as he approached the war-zone, only Tolstoy's epic vision would seem fitting: 'I read *War and Peace* of an evening, a grand and consoling book – a huge vista of life and suffering humankind which makes the present troubles easier to endure, and the loneliness of death a little thing.'[47]

At the beginning of March, on his arrival in Egypt, Sassoon's 'present troubles' had appeared relatively minor. Though his overnight train journey to No. 1 Base Depot, Kantara, on the first day of the month was uncomfortable, it was not dangerous and gave him pleasant views of the Suez Canal and an unexpectedly fertile garden at Ismailia. Even the depot, situated though it was in 'sandy wastes', had cool ante-rooms and onions, which he liked, for lunch. His eight days' stay there may have been boring, but it was not wholly without incident or enjoyment. But despite his easy circumstances he was unhappier in Egypt than he had been on the far more demanding Western Front. After a brief respite on board ship, he was still feeling ill, with severe headaches and a constant cough. The majority of his fellow-officers continued to irritate him, making the camp seem an 'arid waste of officer mentality'.[48] Kantara Base Depot quickly became for him 'the absolute visible expression of time wasted at the war. The sand and the huts and the tents and the faces, all are meaningless. Just a crowd of people killing time. Time wasted in waste places.'[49] After his decision to abandon his protest and return to the War, it must have been an enormous anti-climax to find himself in such an aimless situation. And he was not alone. 'People go "up the line" almost gladly,' he noted 'for it means there's some purpose in life.'[50]

Those words were written on 4 March, the day Sassoon was posted to his new unit, a further cause for discontent. Instead of returning to either the 1st or 2nd RWF, both highly respected 'line' battalions, he found himself with the 25th RWF, a battalion formed at Helmia in Egypt only a year earlier from dismounted Montgomery and Welsh Horse Yeomanry. It became part of the Egyptian Expeditionary Force set up by the British to deal with an attempted Turkish invasion in early 1915. Their main purpose was to protect the Suez Canal from the Turks, who occupied Palestine, the Canal being the main sea-route to the East.

British attempts to break out of the Allied Line, east of the Sinai Desert, had failed until the arrival of General Sir Edmund Allenby in July 1917. Allenby, who had come straight from the fiasco of Arras, devoted his first three months to intensive preparations for an autumn offensive. He cleverly misled the enemy into believing that he would be attacking Gaza for the third time, when he was in reality preparing to take Beersheba. This was successfully achieved on 31 October 1917, though the 25th RWF alone suffered 250 casualties that day. Gaza followed and the way to the British main objective, Jerusalem, was clear. By 9 December the Holy City had surrendered to Allenby and by 11 December he had entered and occupied it. At the end of the month, having beaten off a counter-attack by the Germans and Turks, he had also strengthened the city's perimeters.

Spasmodic fighting in Palestine followed throughout January and February 1918. By 21 February, Allenby's troops had driven the Turks from Jericho and reached the northern end of the Dead Sea. A further British offensive was already under way by the time Sassoon was transferred to the 25th RWF at the beginning of March. Even as he waited at Kantara Base Depot, the 25th Battalion, attached to the 74th (Yeomanry) Division and part of the 231st Brigade, was seeing active service. On 8 March the 74th Division advanced along the Jerusalem-Nablus road, with the 53rd and 10th Divisions on their right and left respectively. On 9 March the 231st Brigade rushed enemy defences at Selwad and on 10 March they helped storm the precipitous ridge of Burj el Lisaneh and successfully defend it against three counter-attacks. Finally, on 11 March, the 231st Brigade captured Selim. This was to be the 25th Battalion's final operation in Palestine, however, and, by the time Sassoon joined it near Ramalleh on 14 March, it was engaged in nothing more exciting than holding the recently captured line in quiet conditions. Had there been dangerous action awaiting him, or even a reasonable number of familiar faces, he might have become reconciled to his new unit as quickly as he had accepted the 2nd RWF in 1917. As it was, instead of rejoicing at his relatively safe position, he longed for France and his old battalion.

It had taken Sassoon four days to reach his new battalion, which was stationed near the Jerusalem-Nablus road nine miles north of Ramalleh. Starting with an overnight train journey along the Mediterranean coast to Gaza, he continued north to the railhead at Ludd on 11 March, a ride of nineteen hours altogether, in a cattle truck. His night's sleep in a rest camp near Ludd was almost equally uncomfortable. Continuing his journey by lorry with eleven other officers, one of whom was Robinson, he travelled from Ludd to Divisional Headquarters at Ramalleh on the 12th.

Ramalleh itself, eight miles north of Jerusalem and captured by the Allies only two months earlier, impressed Sassoon more than Jerusalem. Situated on a hill-top, with a line of cypresses surrounding Divisional Headquarters, it seemed mysterious and faintly sinister. It was also very wet and he spent the morning of the next day, 13 March, sheltering in a tent. He had already talked to someone he recognized from the Sussex Yeomanry, a Sergeant Stone, and now spent nearly an hour chatting to a private from the Middlesex Regiment, an indication that he was becoming more reconciled to his situation perhaps. Another sign of this was his growing appreciation of the countryside. Helped by a change in the weather at midday, the landscape, which had struck him as cruel, desolate and unhappy on arrival, now seemed to him 'full of a shy and lovely austerity'.[51] For four hours he escaped the War completely as he studied the innumerable wildflowers and strange birds the colour of the rocks. It was a scene which took him back to his childhood favourite, *Arabia Deserta*, and his own semitic origins. In this 'Old Testament environment' he felt like 'a budding prophet'.[52] It was a striking contrast to Ramalleh with its lorries, camel-columns, limbers and lines of donkeys carrying supplies, all signs of modern warfare, which sat so oddly in this ancient civilization: the very old *versus* the very new.

Leaving Ramalleh at 8.30 a.m. with Robinson, Sassoon walked nine miles through wild hills, which had until a few days previously, been in enemy hands. They found the 25th Battalion bivouacked on a hillside, along rocky terraces, resting after their recent engagement. With two officers killed, three wounded and several more on leave, the battalion was urgently in need of replacements and Sassoon found himself for the first time in charge of a Company. He was promoted to acting Captain, but found himself commanding only one other officer, Harrison, and the hundred 'ragged' soldiers who constituted C Company.

Though they struck him as a 'very slack lot',[53] Sassoon inevitably became fond of them. Two in particular attracted him. One of them, Jim Linthwaite, he had known in the 1st Battalion a few years earlier. (Linthwaite appears as 'Stonethwaite' in *Sherston's Progress*.) Young, handsome, muscular and 'the embodiment of youthful enterprise',[54] he exercised a powerful physical attraction for Sassoon, as did the other young private, Roberts, described by his officer as 'a sort of Apollo', as he played football 'with nothing on but a pair of tight shorts'.[55] But it was a forbidden attraction and one he kept well under control, allowing only the most obviously paternal of interests to manifest itself. (His concern for Linthwaite's 'rotten' boots was, he admitted, a pretext for conversation.) When Linthwaite was waiting to be Court-Martialled for drunkenness later on, for example, he could show his involvement only by giving him fatherly advice, rather than comforting him physically. It seemed so tame by comparison with his wild dreams of saving his life. It was Linthwaite who prompted the remark, 'There was a great deal of sex floating about in this particular effort.'[56] He would also inspire Sassoon's first sustained effort at prose-writing in 1921, a 13,500-word story, 'Beloved Republic', which would prove 'too full of the heart's music' for publication.[57]

Sassoon's fondness for his men was matched by his suspicion of the officer class, which had not abated, and he made very few exceptions in the 25th Battalion. He dismissed his C.O., Colonel Lord Kensington, as 'a very bad type of British nobleman',[58] found fault with the second-in-command, Major Rees's 'stereotyped manner'[59] and described the adjutant as 'tactless, stupid and diligent'.[60] He was scarcely less critical of the four other captains, whom he mostly found snobbish, pretentious and lazy. Of the remaining thirty officers, none seemed in any way remarkable to Sassoon, though he tolerated the two from B Company with whom he shared a tent; Barker, a garrulous 35-year-old ex-commercial traveller from Welshpool, and Charlesworth, a gentle, somewhat diffident 24-year-old from Magdalen College, Oxford, who admired Kipling.

Only the Medical Officer, Captain W.K. Bigger, stood out. Like Doctors Dunn and Rivers, he was very well-informed, and cultivated his own interests. While the others sat drinking cocktails or talking war-shop, he was out in the hills, grubbing at roots or watching birds. A product of Emmanuel College, Cambridge, his knowledge of birds was immense. 'Lean, grimy and brown' with eyes 'like brown pools in a Scotch burn', he looked rather like an untidy bird himself.[61] Sassoon seems to have found his very roughness – scrubby moustache, foul pipe, muddy voice – a welcome contrast to the polished artificiality of the majority of the other officers. He also admired Bigger's 'tenderness for dumb and piping creatures' and his unwillingness to kill them, which suggested a sensitive and caring man uncoarsened by war.

Sassoon had already begun to appreciate the beauty of the Palestinian landscape and its wildlife. Under Bigger's influence he started to study it in earnest, particularly its birds of which he made long lists in his diary. In spite of his occasional longing for the English countryside – he was still reading Hardy's *Woodlanders* – he began to find the Judean hills 'much finer really'.[62] He learnt to appreciate them in all weathers and at all times of day, but particularly liked the late afternoon and early evening, when frogs croaked in the wet ground up the wadi and wheatears, pipits and whitethroats flitted and chirped among the small thorn-trees, shrubs and rocks. Under such soothing influences, as well as that of a writer who acknowledged the power of Nature above all else, Wordsworth, his poetic instinct gradually revived. After only a fortnight in his new surroundings, in verse clearly affected by Wordsworth's simplifying impulse and more reminiscent of Sassoon's own early pastoral poems than later satires, he tried to describe his surroundings 'In Palestine':

> On the thyme-scented hills
> In the morning and freshness of day
> I heard the voices of rills
> Quickly going their way.
> Warm from the west was the breeze;
> There were wandering bees in the clover;
> Grey were the olive trees;
> And a flight of finches went over. ...[63]

It was in prose not poetry, however, that Sassoon managed to bring his new surroundings alive. Writing to Edmund Gosse on 25 March, his account gives not only a vivid physical picture of the Palestinian landscape but also hints at other reasons for its special appeal:

> We are on the rugged hills looking towards Samaria. These hill-landscapes are magnificent. Our present camp is pitched among fig-trees. The narrow terraces are natural rock-gardens, rich with all kinds of flowers; the wild iris has appeared in great profusion lately – also scarlet tulips. – The red and purple anemones are disappearing after making a great demonstration among the rocks – Cyclamen is still going strong. Now I've given you all the local colour I can muster for the present.

The villages on hill-tops rise out of the grey and faint green like heaps of stones. One scarcely sees them at first. They are full of growing Arabs and Bedouins – not over friendly. Long trains of camels and pack-mules move deliberately along the glens through which the road winds, led by dark skinned ruffians in faded blue-green robes; carrying tins of water and other necessaries of life for the army.

Guns boom and echo among the hills; but it is a silent haunted, ancient sort of country, – I was on a high hill one evening, where one could see a great deal of Palestine.[64]

It is clear from a later part of this letter that Sassoon's sense of his Semitic origins was reinforced still further by the appeal of this historic landscape: 'Personally I should like to do something in the prophetic line,' he tells Gosse. 'The Lamentations of Sâshun; I wonder if Heinemann would publish.' He felt almost as far from what he regarded as the 'real' war in Palestine as he had in Ireland, and a similar sense of peace. The Judean Hills even reminded him of Ireland at times, especially after rain. By the time Sassoon wrote to Gosse, his battalion had moved three miles down the Jerusalem-Nablus road to continue its main task of road-mending. He quickly established a routine suited to his new surroundings, getting out of bed into a cold bath at 6.15 a.m., he told Graves on 4 April, 'and just as I get out of it – the sun looks over the eastern hill and warms me nicely as he shines into my tent'. He took his men out from nine in the morning to four in the afternoon, civilized hours compared with those of trench-warfare. And, though the work was strenuous, it was relatively safe. Supervision was easy and left him ample time for bird-watching, reading and writing. At 8.30 p.m. he would put away either *War and Peace* or the *Oxford Book of English Verse* and go to sleep.

Though Sassoon was sad to see Robinson leave for another battalion at the end of the month, he began to feel more positive about his situation. His sense of freedom was increased on 4 April when the officer commanding C Company, Capt. Freeman, returned from leave, releasing him from the full responsibility he had shouldered as Company Commander. As second-in-command of A Company, to which he was transferred, his life became even pleasanter. The War now seemed to him 'quite subsidiary to the landscape – not a sprawling monster, as in France'.

The 'sprawling monster' in France was never very far from Sassoon's mind. The bulletins from the Western Front were getting steadily worse, and names which meant little to officers who had served only in the Middle East made him aware that the Germans had recaptured all the ground gained in the Somme battles by the end of March. While most of his colleagues remained unconcerned, he grew increasingly apprehensive. In January he had tried to get himself posted to France; now, ironically, he feared such a move. Quite apart from his unwillingness to leave the Judean Hills, he was worried that he might not be able to stand another 'dose' of it.[65]

Even when the news of the 25th Battalion's imminent departure came through in early April, less than a month after Sassoon had arrived in Palestine, he still hoped that they were not destined for France. On 5 April, in what he saw as a 'raffish effort to turn the thing into a joke; for everyone knows we *are* going to France',[66] the Colonel organized a 'selling sweep' on their destination. Sassoon initially refused to join in this 'puerile and ill-bred' show, but finally, in sheer annoyance at the snobbishness of it all, bid £10 for the 'submarined' ticket, a very real threat which no one else dared to acknowledge. Even he did not realize until later how close he had come to being right.

By this time all local maps had been handed in and hot weather kit cancelled, and by 7 April the 25th RWF, together with their neighbours, the 24th Welsh, were on the move. Not only was it the start of their march down to the railhead at Ludd but also, as Sassoon apprehensively noted, 'the first day of our journey to France'.[67] He had nerved himself to face it so many times before that he now felt emotionally exhausted. Like all previous army moves, this one was painfully slow and, at times, extremely boring. The march from their camp to Ludd, for example, a distance of only forty-five miles, took four days and even then the men suffered. As Sassoon watched his men staggering along under the weight of their full equipment, all his latent pity for them was aroused, as he imagined their sufferings.[68]

Though Sassoon did not undergo the same physical hardships as his men – he would certainly not have been carrying his full kit with him and was probably far fitter and better nourished – he did suffer on this march. For he felt, as he had once before at Montagne in December 1915, that he had been in Arcadia: 'It is positive agony to leave these Palestine hills in all their beauty and glory', he noted at the end of the journey.[69] Perhaps it was too beautiful for words, or, it may have seemed to him inappropriate to write pastoral poetry at such a time. Whatever the explanation, he seems to have written only two poems in Palestine and the second of these, 'Shadows', written on the last day of the march, concentrates more on the soldiers than the landscape.[70]

Two days later Sassoon found inspiration for another poem where he least expected it, Kantara. He had been sent ahead from Ludd with the Advance Party on 11 April and, after an uncomfortable overnight train journey in a cattle-truck, arrived back at No. 1 Base Depot. Not expecting to see the 'beastly place' again so soon after leaving it, he cheered himself up by escaping to a salt-lake about a mile from the camp. Hardly less dreary, the lake at least offered him the chance to bathe and the sight of flamingos:

> ... wheeling by,
> Crowd[ing] the air with white,
> Warm-flushed in rosy light
> That *flowered* across the sky ...[71]

Such an unexpected sight reminded him of what war had already taught, that beauty could be found in the most desolate of places.

While both 'Flamingos' and 'Shadows' are of biographical interest, Sassoon felt that neither showed him at his best and published neither in his lifetime. But there was another poem written at Kantara of which he was justly proud, 'Concert Party'. In order to divert the men, condemned to remain at the Base Depot for over a fortnight with nothing more than light training to occupy them, an entertainment was arranged for 17 April. It was given by Lena Ashwell, an actress-impresario who had been organizing concert-parties for soldiers since 1914.[72] She and her group struck Sassoon as particularly good and he was deeply moved by their effect on the men. Watching them as they drank in every movement and sound made by the five entertainers, he felt as though he really was by nature 'a seer and dreamer of dreams', as he had sometimes claimed:[73]

> Suddenly I recognize that this is indeed the true spectacle of war – that these puppets are the fantastic delight of life played to an audience of ghosts and shadows – crowding in like moths to a lamp – to see and hear what they must lose – have lost. In front there are half-lit ruddy faces and glittering eyes, and behind they grow more dusky and indistinct – ghosts, souls of the dead – the doomed – till on the edge high above the rest one sees silhouetted forms motionless, intent – those who were killed three years ago – and beyond them, across the glimmering levels of sand, legions of others come stealing in – till the crowd is limitless; all the dead have come to hear the concert party in this half-lit oasis of Time.
>
> It is too much; I cannot bear it; I must get up and go away. For I too am a ghost, one of the doomed.[74]

Puppets, shadows, moths and ghosts, all testify to Sassoon's haunted state of mind at this stage in the War. Vivid as these images are, only the shadows and moths remain in the poem which follows. Yet it still manages to convey the shifting, uncertain, even haunted nature of the desert scene, partly by its varied metre, partly by its repetitions, and partly through new metaphors of drifting 'shoals', 'shuffling' sand, a 'wall' of faces and the men's 'hunger' for home:

> *Concert Party (Egyptian Base Camp)*
> They are gathering round ...
> Out of the twilight; over the grey-blue sand,
> Shoals of low-jargoning men drift inward to the sound –
> The jangle and throb of a piano ... tum-ti-tum ...
> Drawn by a lamp, they come
> Out of the glimmering lines of their tents, over the shuffling sand.
>
> O Sing us the Songs, the songs of our own land,
> You warbling ladies in white.

Dimness conceals the hunger in our faces,
This wall of faces risen out of the night,
These eyes that keep their memories of the places
So long beyond their sight.

... Sing slowly ... now the chorus ... one by one
We hear them, drink them; till the concert's done.
Silent, I watch the shadowy mass of soldiers stand.
Silent, they drift away, over the glimmering sand.   (*CP*, p. 100)

Apart from this concert party, there was little else to relieve the monotony of life at Kantara. Company training occupied the morning from 6.30 to 10 a.m. and some of the afternoon, but to Sassoon the days seemed wasted by petty details to be worried through. He ended each of them exasperated, exhausted and unable to think clearly. His main impression of the camp was of too much sand and sunlight and he welcomed the smallest distractions. He welcomed a football match between his old Company, C, and his new one, A, on 19 April, for example, enjoying the excuse to admire the scantily clad players who included his favourites, Linthwaite and Roberts. The one ray of hope for Sassoon in this gloomy situation was the simplicity he continued to find in his men.[75] Unlike the officers, who continued to hide their fears under a sophisticated veneer of boastful talk and too many cocktails, the men seemed genuinely pleased to be going at least in the direction of home. Most had been in the Middle East without leave since 1915 and had very little idea how horrific conditions on the Western Front really were. Though Sassoon admired their serenity, he could not emulate it:

... here I am [he wrote the day before leaving Kantara] after nearly four years of this business, faced with the same old haggard aspect of soldier-life – a very small chance of complete escape unblemished – a big chance of being killed outright – ditto of being intolerably injured – a certainty of mental agony and physical discomfort – prolonged and exasperating – a possibility of going mad or breaking down badly: in fact, the whole landscape of the near future bristling with unimaginable perils and horrors, and overshadowed by the gloom of death.[76]

To Sassoon's strained nerves the fear of breaking down was very real. Even his faith in his men might not be sufficient to prevent that, though if he did he believed that Rivers would help restore his sanity. His other great consolation at this time was Tolstoy, whose battle scenes in *War and Peace* reminded him of his own past experiences. In anticipating the wounds and failure he had momentarily forgotten what Tolstoy made so real – the excitement and reckless enthusiasm he felt before the fight, the need to play the hero and, as he puts it in his diary, the 'angry joy of being "up against it"', which would carry him through.

As Sassoon faced his fears in this way, he mentally prepared himself for France and when the 25th RWF left Kantara on the last lap of their Middle Eastern journey on 28 April, he was more or less ready. He still felt confused, intolerant and superficial in his attitude towards the War, but he now believed that the whole business was a pilgrimage towards his death. In this exalted, slightly unreal state, the nearer he got to the War the more he wanted to share its terrors. He was no longer going there to kill people, as he had once wanted; his main purpose now was to look after his men, an escape from his own concerns which he found 'a blessed state'.

Before entirely committing himself to this saintly frame of mind, however, Sassoon indulged in one last selfish wish, to visit E.M. Forster, as Dent had suggested, in Alexandria. Forster ('Morgan' to his friends) had been there since 1915 as a 'searcher' for the Red Cross, and was delighted by the chance to meet someone with whom he felt he would have a great deal in common. Though they had missed each other on his way down to Palestine, they had agreed to meet on his way back. But no one was allowed ashore at Alexandria from the troopship they had boarded, and Sassoon set off on the S.S. *Malwa* at the end of April without seeing Forster.

The 25th RWF was one of three battalions on the 10,833-ton P&O liner, part of a seven-ship convoy whose voyage across the Mediterranean would be protected by ten destroyers. Though the Divisional General, four Brigadiers and numerous staff officers who accompanied them were almost certainly aware, as the ship's Captain was, of the dangers ahead, Sassoon and his fellow-officers were largely ignorant of them. Yet more than a hundred merchant ships had been sunk by German submarines the previous month. (A transport ship in the convoy behind them was to strike a mine just outside Alexandria.[77]) With provision for only 1,000 men in the lifeboats on a ship carrying 3,300 troops alone, it probably seemed wiser not to inform them of the shoals of U-boats through which they had to pass. Sassoon, whose purchase of the 'submarined' ticket in the sweepstake had been done more from annoyance than informed opinion, reported sympathetically that, such was the Captain's relief after their hazardous six-day voyage, that he burst into tears on the bridge.

Sassoon himself was more aware of a different kind of danger as the ship ploughed through the Mediterranean. Especially at night, when the sleeping bodies of soldiers on deck put him in mind of corpses and the noise of heavy waves recalled the sound of guns, he was reminded of France, that country which he was slowly but inexorably approaching. While continuing with *War and Peace*, he had also been re-reading Conrad's *Lord Jim* in preparation for the sea-journey and had started on Forster's most recent novel, *Howard's End*. All three brought home what the War had taught him, that life was a very serious business indeed. It had been possible for a short time in Palestine to forget the War, but once on board ship for Marseilles he was already mentally back on the Western Front. Yet in spite of his fears and a natural wish to survive, he also felt that it was right to return to the fighting:

We are going home. The troop-ship, in a thrill
Of fiery-chamber'd anguish, throbs and rolls.
We are going home ... victims ... three thousand souls.   (*CP*, p. 101)

These lines conclude 'Night on the Convoy', a poem written almost certainly in Marseilles as Sassoon waited for the next stage in his pilgrimage to begin.

16

The Good Soldier

May-July 1918

Sassoon's own army experience may not have been very eventful in the first half of 1918, but the War itself had entered its most crucial phase by the time he arrived back in France in May. The Brest-Litovsk Peace Treaty between Russia and Germany signed on 3 March, combined with Germany's efficient railway system, had enabled the Central Powers to transfer large numbers of troops and weapons swiftly from the Eastern to the Western Front and by mid-March they were poised for the offensive. Up to this point the main military initiatives had been taken by the Allies and only the Germans' superior fortifications had prevented a decisive breakthrough. It was now Germany's turn to try to penetrate the Allies' defences and to do so before the mass of fresh, unscarred American troops promised for the summer reached the war-zone. General Ludendorff opened his campaign with a surprise attack on a forty-three-mile front, Arras-St Quentin-La Fère, his aim being to drive the British back from the Somme, the French from the Aisne and to threaten Paris once more. He was only partially successful, however; in spite of forcing the Allies back forty miles in some areas south of the Somme, the northern part of the line held firm, particularly round Arras. He then launched a second great offensive on 9 April in Flanders which opened up a gap thirty miles wide in the Allied line and, by the time Sassoon arrived back in France on 7 May, was preparing a third attack on the Marne.

Though Sassoon had reconciled himself to a return to France, it is clear from a letter Graves wrote him at the time that he was still rejoicing at Sassoon's absence from that country even as he was sailing towards Marseilles. Besides giving his friend news of the 1st RWF, still in Italy, Graves introduced another topic in his letter which was to worry them both throughout the summer of 1918, the Pemberton Billing affair. On 26 January 1918, Noel Pemberton Billing, an independent Member of Parliament for mid-Hertfordshire, had published a fierce attack on the Government's handling of the War in his magazine, the *Imperialist*. In it he claimed that the German Secret Service had a *Black Book* which contained the names of 47,000 English citizens who were vulnerable to blackmail because of their homosexuality. In a further article in his magazine (by now aptly renamed *The Vigilante*) Robbie Ross was clearly implicated. There was little doubt that Lord Alfred Douglas, still anxious to get his revenge on Ross for his support of Oscar Wilde, was behind the attack.[1]

Another source of concern to Sassoon was the publication of his second volume of war poems, *Counter-Attack*. Heinemann had stalled for some months, ostensibly to give *The Old Huntsman* a chance to sell more copies but partly because he wanted some 'amiable' poems 'to mitigate the horrors' and thought the book too short. He now finally agreed to go ahead. Wartime problems of paper shortage created further delays, but by 5 May the proofs were ready. Marsh, at Sassoon's request, had already read the collection in manuscript and had used his influence with Heinemann. Despite his 'grave doubts whether it [was] right from the national point of view to publish the book at all', he admired it as poetry and believed that it would sell well.[2]

Sassoon had by this time almost certainly left Marseilles, his three-day stay there having proved a gentle re-introduction to France. Five months had elapsed since his departure from Craiglockhart and at last he was going back into action, as he had then wished. Now, after reading the *Daily Mail*'s description of enemy-occupied Morlancourt, which his own battalion had inhabited two years earlier, he was not so sure that he still wanted to. Using a metaphor taken from his recent visit to a music hall, he wrote on 9 May in an appropriately new diary:

> And all my future is 'tomorrow', or at the most two or three weeks of training for battle. Beyond that the fire-proof curtain comes down .... And it is covered with placards advertising my new volume of remarkable and arresting poems. I cannot believe that the curtain will go up this year and disclose the painted scene of Peace and Plenty. But I am quite prepared to leave my seat in the stalls and go away with Mr Mors [i.e. death], in case he calls for me at the theatre. But all this is silliness – the facts are what we want in our notebooks, and events. So here's to the *next* five months, and the harvest.[3]

Sassoon was wrong on a number of counts. His future readers would not want only 'facts' and 'events' in his diaries, though fortunately that was a rule he rarely managed to keep. And, in spite of his gloomy predictions, 'Peace' was to come not long after the '*next* five months' he had allowed himself. But it was his third false prediction – that only two or three weeks' training separated him from battle – that was of most immediate significance. It would be nearly nine weeks before the 25th RWF, trained for desert warfare, were considered ready for the Western Front, weeks which took Sassoon ever nearer to safety. The truth is that for the first time Sassoon was returning to France without wanting to be a hero. In 'Testament', a poem completed by 9 May, he declares:

For the last time I say – War is not glorious,
Though lads march out superb and fall victorious, –
Scrapping like demons, suffering like slaves,
And crowned by peace, the sunlight on their graves.

You swear we crush The Beast: I say we fight
Because men lost their landmarks in the night,
And met in gloom to grapple, stab, and kill,
Yelling the fetish-names of Good and Ill
That have been shamed in history.
      O my heart,
Be still; you have cried your cry; you have played
    your part.[4]

As the last line of this poem suggests, Sassoon was still troubled about his own responsibilities in the War but felt that he had done all he could to prevent its continuance and must resign himself to the situation. His aim now was to be a good officer and poetry, for the time being, became subservient. But before he took up his full responsibilities as second-in-command of A Company, there was a brief respite while the 25th Battalion travelled to their next destination. Nine hundred miles away, in the Noyelles area of northern France, this involved another long train journey during which his duties would be minimal.

Though he was not able to plan books appropriate to the journey, as he had in February, it was almost certainly the thought of three days on a train which prompted him to ask Ottoline the day he set out for a copy of Georges Duhamel's novel, *Vie des Martyrs*. This moving account of an army doctor's compassion for the wounded soldiers in his care had just been published in England as *The New Book of Martyrs* and tied in with Sassoon's own feelings for his men.

Apart from books, Sassoon's second long train journey in three months differed from the first in other ways. This time he was travelling towards the familiar, not away from it, though with none of the safety that familiarity usually implies, and it was towards known danger, as opposed to relative safety, that he went. The bitterly cold nights of his February journey, which had made him ill, were replaced by idyllic May days and nights in which the nightingales sang from every bush and thicket. He had a particular fondness for May and, as the train rumbled along through the Rhone valley, 'green and lovely with early summer',[5] he had what he suspected was an illusory sense of youth and prosperity, a feeling that happiness lay ahead. When he passed the outskirts of Paris on 11 May and gazed down on the city, glowing mysteriously in the evening light, he even allowed himself to wonder if he would ever visit it as a civilian.

Sassoon was in a romantic mood and it is hard not to suspect that he was falling in love again, a suspicion his diary reinforces as it lingers over details of one of the three officers sharing his compartment, Lieutenant Jowett. The 'Howitt' of *Sherston's Progress*, Sassoon was to dub him 'handsome boy' Jowett and to write a poem about him. His diary references to Jowett's 'smooth, sensual face and large limbs', his 'dark-eyed and lover-like and wistful air' suggest that his admiration was not simply for his qualities as an officer.[6] He could see that Jowett, like their fellow-officer, 'Stiffy' Phillips, was inclined to indolence and that he was also rather uncouth, but he found his shyness and gentleness irresistible and believed correctly that, when it came to the test, Jowett would be both reliable and brave.

Jowett is first mentioned during the journey north, which he helped to make enjoyable in spite of its sinister purpose. The weather, too, co-operated and continued fine as they detrained at Noyelles-sur-Mer, seven miles north of Abbeville, on the morning of 12 May. Sassoon found it a pleasure rather than a penance to march the last eleven miles to their billets at Domvast. The village itself, situated eight miles north-east of Abbeville among the orchards of Picardy and only a mile from the forest of Crécy, reminded him strongly of earlier French billets and he felt 'rather ghostlike' returning to such familiar country; buying eggs and butter from 'Madame' at the farm and hearing army servants in the kitchen stammering 'Blighty French' to the girls gave him a strong sense of *déjà-vu*.

To the troops, most of whom had spent their service in Palestine, it was more novel but no less agreeable. Lying so far behind the Front Line, the village had not been spoilt by continuous billeting and the men were in a comfortable barn, while Sassoon was in an actual house. For the third time in his army career he resorted to images of Arcadia – flowering hawthorns, lush orchards, grazing cattle and the sound of church bells. It was perhaps his ability to appreciate the beauty of his surroundings under almost all circumstances which enabled him to remain positive. On his first morning in Domvast, for example, and in spite of rain, he visited the forest of Crécy, where the great battle had been fought 572 years before, and in the 'endless avenues of branching green' was comforted by 'the wind in the beech-wood', a sound which had inspired him to poetry at Flixécourt in 1916.[7]

It was impossible to escape the war for long, however. The constant booming of the heavy guns at Amiens and Albert was only one reminder of what lay ahead. Two days after his arrival at Domvast Sassoon was again in the forest of Crécy, this time for training. Though the surroundings appeared to even greater advantage in the sunshine and the men felt that it was 'like being at home again, sir',[8] the significance of the gas drill and bayonet exercises he supervised could not be ignored. The gas drill itself was an ominous reminder that conditions in the trenches had grown even worse since he was last there in April 1917 and he had always found bayonet training 'loathsome'.[9]

So that when, the following day, Sassoon heard Colonel Campbell delivering his famous lecture on 'the spirit of the bayonet' for the second time, he was completely disgusted at this expression of what he called 'Militarism incarnate'. It was a situation full of contradictions; soldiers marching home beneath a peaceful, spacious landscape, with columns of infantry in tin hats suddenly appearing on the Abbeville road among the hornbeam bushes and young wheat. Even at night when the sound of nightingales dominated the air, there was a menacing rumbling in the background and the sky winked and glowed with flashes of distant bombardment. On his third day in Domvast he felt so depressed that he wrote his will, leaving a generous legacy to Robert Graves.

Despite Sassoon's increased awareness of death, he carried on as normal, settling in to a routine which continued until 23 May. One of his duties was that of Company catering officer, but his chief responsibility was training his men, a mainly outdoor activity which both he and they enjoyed. He tried to make their lectures pleasurable too, spending most evenings studying manuals in an attempt to present his material in an entertaining form. He was determined to become an efficient company officer. Due to take over command of A Company when Captain Bardwell went on leave on 26 May, he wanted to make a better job of it than his superior, whom he despised.

One of the few changes for the better since Sassoon's last tour of duty had been the issue of a manual for *The Training and Employment of Platoons*, a masterpiece of common sense, clarity and condensation by comparison with the heavily academic *Infantry Training, 1914*, which was in any case based on outdated principles. Sassoon made notes in his personal copy of the new manual, the most substantial being his list of '6 C's for Companies': '(i) Care (of Men); (ii) Concentration (in training begets coolness in action); (iii) Confidence (in weapons and leaders); (iv) Common-sense; (v) Co-operation = constructive; (vi) Consolidation (both in Attack and Defence).' 'The Big C' he could not resist adding, was 'Campbell (and the offensive Spirit)'. Carried away by his alliteration, he went on to invent a mnemonic of which he was particularly proud: 'clear commands create complete control'.

Sassoon filled another exercise book with notes on 'the Assault', 'Trench reliefs', 'Principles of Defence', 'Platoon Organization', 'Gas Lectures' and 'Tactical Scheme for Platoon', carefully cross-referencing it. In his anxiety to get his message across he sometimes sounds a little condescending, especially when reminding himself to 'Avoid ... using words which they don't understand. Use very simple, and, when possible, slang words.'[10] But his intentions were completely genuine. Time had brought him even closer to his originally 'ragged' company, whom he now found 'such a decent well-behaved lot that it is a pleasure to work with them and do what one can for their comfort'.[11] Never before had he worked so hard for his men.

Another of Sassoon's duties, which he found both amusing and painful, was censoring the men's letters. One issue which concerned them was leave, particularly when it failed to materialize: 'Well dear I dont sea any sighn of my leave [one man wrote] but if we dont get it soon it will be a grate disappointment to us all ....'[12] A recurring complaint was about sore feet, though Sassoon had done his best on that score. And in spite of more positive remarks, particularly on the weather and fresh farm eggs, it was the men's sufferings which tended to fill their letters: 'And this is the war [Sassoon concluded]. "Everywhere we go here seems such a long way" ... "hope to get leave soon" ... "our officers are fairly putting us through it" ... "expect we'll be going to the line soon" ....'[13]

Sassoon was grateful to Ottoline, who kept up a constant flow of books, which helped him to escape. But there were discordant notes in the Arcadia he was trying once again to build around himself – a 'noisy and vulgar' fellow-officer, for instance, or the apparent mindlessness and absurdity of Army orders, even worse because it affected his men.

However strong his sense of the absurd, Sassoon's bitterness towards those he believed were prolonging the War was greater, particularly when he thought of his men. Reminded by signs of seasonal change that autumn was inexorably approaching, he could not ignore the fact that it would 'bring many of them to oblivion and decay'.[14] Perhaps it was also the news that the battalion was about to leave for its training area which made him so conscious of death. His reading of Duhamel was a constant reminder of the physical devastations of war.

Yet the French doctor was also a comfort, of sorts, as Sassoon noted: 'It was written that you should suffer without purpose and without hope [Duhamel wrote]. But I will not let all your sufferings be lost in the abyss.' The next sentence, which Sassoon marked in his copy of Duhamel but did not reproduce in his diary, reads: 'And so I record them at length.' It was almost certainly his own reason for recording so much about the War himself. All he could do for his men, apart from small things like buying them fresh vegetables with his own money and looking after them generally, was to document their sufferings.

Sassoon turned to Duhamel again when instructions came to start the journey to the Front. The order had reminded him of the previous year's move towards Arras, where 80 per cent of his fellow-officers and a large proportion of other ranks were killed, and he found expression for his feelings in Duhamel's poignant question: 'What became of you, precious lives, poor wonderful souls, for whom I fought so many obscure great battles, and who went off again in the realm of adventure?'[15]

There are at least seven other passages marked by Sassoon in his copy of Duhamel but not included in his diary, most of them describing the extraordinary courage of the common soldier. In one of these he has underlined for extra emphasis the words which seem to have meant most to him in the whole book: '... life here is reduced entirely to terms of suffering'. It was almost certain suffering to which Sassoon and his men were travelling when they set out from Domvast on 23 May 1918.

Their destination was Habarcq, only seven and a half miles from Arras and even less from Basseux, where Sassoon had stayed for three days in April 1917 on his way to Arras. The first stage of the journey, a sixteen-mile march to Rue, followed by a five-mile march to Magnicourt, was an exhausting business. Sassoon, who was still thinking of his journey the previous year, when he had passed within six miles of Magnicourt, felt extremely pessimistic about his future and spent part of the day composing a note on his servant, John Law ('Bond' in *Sherston's Progress*) in case of his death. His evident appreciation of Law's simple goodness shows how far he had come from the young subaltern whose main concern had been the correct shade of khaki shirt. He now clearly aspires to the almost saintlike unselfishness he found in Law.

The second and final day's journey to the 25th RWF's training area was less demanding, though Sassoon found the ten miles in warm weather 'beastly', partly because of the congestion on the way. It was a sign of how much nearer they were to the Front. Having left Magnicourt at 9 a.m., the Battalion arrived about 2 p.m. at Habarcq, a much larger village than Domvast and already overcrowded with troops. The men's quarters were, therefore, not as good as those at Domvast; one of A Company's platoons, for example, was billeted near a burial-ground, which the men referred to as 'the rest camp'. 'No reveilles and route-marches there!' Sassoon heard one exhausted soldier remark.[16] The officers' accommodation was, as usual, a great deal better than the men's, and Sassoon found himself billeted with Bardwell on the third floor of a château with a view of tree tops and a huge cedar. A large, empty building, which seemed to him even more 'barrack-like' after Bardwell left for England the next day, it was to be Sassoon's home for a month.

Bardwell's departure had a number of important effects on Sassoon. First and foremost, it made him wholly responsible for A Company, the second time in less than three months that he had been put in complete command. He worried about their welfare far more than his own and was to write to Ross on 18 June enclosing a letter for Ottoline's brother, Lord Henry Bentinck, asking if anything could be done about the men's lack of leave. Equally, he regretted the absence of any proper form of entertainment for them in the evenings. This meant that the majority of them went to the local bars and spent most of their money there, half of the battalion going to bed drunk every night. A poem Sassoon wrote nearly a fortnight after Bardwell's departure, expresses his very real love for his men:

> *Reward*
> Months and weeks and days go past,
> And my soldiers fall at last.
> Months and weeks and days
> Their ways must be my ways.
> And evermore
> Love guards the door ....[17]

Another important result of Bardwell's absence was that it left Sassoon with a room of his own, where he could retreat from the pettiness and worry of army life. As at Craiglockhart he tried to keep a few hours after dinner free for reading, writing to friends and keeping his diary up to date, though he was frequently interrupted by people wanting either to air their grievances or simply chat. The earlier part of the day also resolved itself into a fairly regular routine. As a Company Commander he was kept busy from the time he got up at 6.30 a.m., or earlier, until dinner was over at about 8 p.m.

Sassoon's keenness, conscientiousness and determination to succeed distinguish him sharply from the rather naive and diffident platoon officer of 1915, going far beyond what his position demanded. Often, after his duties were over, he watched inter-company football matches with his men, for example. He also tried to keep in touch with the platoon officers, generally over dinner in the Company mess. His interest in Jowett and Phillips had continued and he noted after the first week's training that one result of his 'personal efforts' was that 'P. & J. [were] getting keen: *both all right.*' Sometimes he had to attend Commanding Officers' Conferences and listen to speeches from the Brigadier, or yet more lectures on Trench Warfare. Occasionally his routine was varied with an inspection by the Divisional General (who made 'a very pleasant impression'[18]), a march to the firing-range eight miles away (his private opinion was that he never hit the target at all), or Brigade Field Days, but essentially it remained stable. It was a healthy and, for officers, far from austere existence, including as it did good food and wine for dinner. (To the eggs, butter, milk, potatoes and other vegetables of the first week, he had managed as catering officer to add coffee, lettuce and sardines, and had augmented the wine, champagne and cider with beer.)

For the most part Sassoon entered into this existence willingly and was totally absorbed by it. Receiving a letter from Graves on 29 May which talked of leave, for instance, he declared in his diary: 'Damn leave; I don't want it. And I don't want to be wounded and wangle a job at home. I want the next six weeks, and success; do I want death? I don't know yet; but the war is outside of life; and I'm in it.'[19] On 30 May he was writing to Marsh: 'I am very happy and hard at work training a glorious company.'[20] Yet, as he confessed in the same letter, with direct reference to one of his anti-war poems, 'I try not to think of the result of the training, which will be mostly "poor young chap. I knew his father well".' And a panegyric to Graves about his men had concluded: 'And in six months they'll have ceased to exist.'

Sassoon's moods fluctuated as wildly as they had once before, after Thomas's death. On 26 May he felt tired and exasperated and on 28 May was too tired even to read. Yet on 30 May he could claim: 'I am still happy, and healthy, and proud of my Company.'[21] 'Could I but breathe into [Bob Nichols'] haunted mind something of the golden-skinned serenity of my own St Martin's Summer of happy warrior youth!'[22] he yearned.

Sassoon's 'happy warrior' instincts were to be satisfied sooner than he had expected. By 2 June he knew from the newspapers that, with the Germans on the Marne claiming 4,500 prisoners, the situation was critical for the Allies, but he was totally unprepared to be ordered to an emergency meeting of Company officers on 6 June in the Neuville-Vitasse sector of the Front Line, approximately three and a half miles south-east of Arras. The 74th Division were to take over there from the 2nd Canadian Division and the C.O. wanted to inspect his part of the Line in advance. Sassoon had heard conflicting reports of the sector. On the one hand it was said to be the quietest part of the Front, on the other conditions were rumoured to be atrocious, with heavy casualties, a great deal of gas and poor discipline among the conscripts.

Setting out on the morning of 7 June in fine weather, Sassoon, his Company Commander, Ellis, and their Colonel rode a few miles to Avesnes, where they were given a lift by lorry south to Basseux, the headquarters of the 2nd Canadian Division and Sassoon's final billet with the 2nd RWF the year before. From Basseux they turned north-east to Agny, where they lunched at Brigade headquarters before proceeding another two miles on foot to the headquarters of the 24th Victoria Rifles, the battalion they were due to relieve. As Sassoon was guided the last stage of the journey to B Company in the Front Line, the area – which he identified as the place where his friends Orme and Conning had died and Ormrod been fatally wounded – looked to him as devastated as ever. The grass still waved in the breeze, poppies still flamed and larks still sang, but he could not ignore the fact that, after fourteen months of fighting, the Front Line was further back than when he had last seen it.

As Sassoon made his way to the steel hut which constituted B Company headquarters at 7.30 p.m. on a June evening, along the crumbling, dry communication trenches, he noticed how narrow they were and suspected that they would be very muddy when it rained, as it inevitably would. Sassoon felt confidence, however, in B Company's commander, Capt. Duclos, who seemed to him 'a fine chap'.[23] His description of Duclos's demeanour during a raid on his second evening with him, showing how greatly he admired the Canadian, concludes: 'he leaves a feeling of security in his wake. Men finger their bayonets and pull themselves together. The end of his cigarette glows in the dusk – a little planet of unquenchable devotion.'[24]

It is unquestionably how Sassoon himself wished to be with his men.

Whilst appreciating that his visit to the Front after more than a year's absence was a good test of his nerves, Sassoon felt 'a bit of a fool'[25] being there with no responsibilities. After 'Stand-To' at 2.30 a.m., he would go to sleep and wake up with the usual trench-mouth. Except for the increased danger of gas, it all seemed very familiar and any fears he might have had about his nerves were quickly dispelled.

Expecting to see it again very soon, Sassoon and his brother officers left the Front Line at 3 p.m. on the third day, 9 June. After various delays he was back in his quiet, empty room at Habarcq by 11 p.m. The next morning, reminded by the arrival of the Southdown Hunt annual balance sheet of Gordon Harbord's death, he was not as thrilled as he might have been by the news that he had been gazetted Acting Captain again. In fact, there was no immediate need to worry, since a flu epidemic struck the 231st Brigade, putting almost half its men out of action and effectively preventing it from being sent to the Neuville-Vitasse sector as planned. With his usual luck Sassoon had gained another month's grace. Far from being grateful, however, he grew increasingly frustrated by the waiting. Four days after his return from the Front, inflamed no doubt by his visit there and a glass or two of wine at dinner, he declared 'Damn it, I'm fed up with all this training! I want to go up to the line and *fight*!' Only after his two young protégés, Phillips and Jowett, had fervently agreed with him, did he come to his senses, noting in his diary: 'I shivered, and walked quickly up to the Château – to the quiet room where I spend my evenings with one candle, scribbling notes on the monstrous cruelty of war and the horrors of the front line. "I want to go and fight!" Thus had I boasted in a moment of folly, catching my mood from the lads who look to me as their leader.'[26]

It was not as though Sassoon had been allowed to forget the 'monstrous cruelty' of war. Only two days earlier, on 12 June, he had read with great sadness of the death of a friend, Lt Colin Dobell, 'Little Colin', who had been with him at Mametz Wood and hunted with him in Limerick. Reflecting on his friend's harmless wish for a life of fox-hunting, marriage and peace-time soldiering, he resisted the idealized picture and, instead of writing 'fool-poems' like those he read in *The Spectator* about 'our unforgotten dead', produced a heartfelt protest about the waste of young life, 'Colin'.[27] Only a pale echo of his earlier satire (ending 'And still the war goes on – *he* don't know why'), this poem nevertheless signals a revival in poetic impulse. His love of 'lads' like Colin, which had prevented him from writing for some time, had now led him back to it again.

It was partly because of a letter from one such 'lad', thanking him for his help in Egypt, that Sassoon turned again to an exponent of 'lad's love' for inspiration, Walt Whitman. Reading Whitman's *Sea-Drift* he experienced an emotion he had not felt for many months – 'the *passion* of poetry'. 'Of late I've been moody and nerve-ridden' he told Nichols on 19 June. 'Reading Whitman put me right. He is a glorious old lad.'[28] Whitman's stirring words were made even more resonant for him by the memory of Delius's musical setting of them. Starved as he had been of both poetry and music, the effect was electrical and everything else was forgotten as he tried to express his turbulent emotions in verse. Three days later he had completed another poem about his 'lads' under the almost hypnotic influence of Whitman:

> *I Stood With the Dead*
> I stood with the Dead, so forsaken and still:
> When dawn was grey I stood with the Dead.
> And my slow heart said, 'You must kill, you must kill:
> 'Soldier, soldier, morning is red.'
>
> On the shapes of the slain in their crumpled disgrace
> I stared for a while through the thin cold rain ...
> 'O lad that I loved, there is rain on your face,
> And your eyes are blurred and sick like the plain.'

I stood with the Dead ... They were dead; they were dead;
My heart and my head beat a march of dismay:
And gusts of the wind came dulled by the guns.
'Fall in!' I shouted; 'Fall in for your pay!'   (*CP*, p. 103)

This is an important piece which highlights the new direction Sassoon's war poetry was taking. Compassion rather than anger now dominates. In this respect, as in its semi-colloquial language, lyrical repetitions and freely expressed 'lad's love', it shows clear signs of Whitman's influence, though its resolutely regular stanza form and rhyme-scheme are very different from the American's fluid free-verse. It is also possible that Whitman's *Drum-taps*, a collection centring round the poet's experience as a nurse in the Civil War, inspired Sassoon's striking metaphor of his heart and head 'beat[ing] a march of dismay'. Likewise the words 'They were dead; they were dead' may be a response to another admired poet, Sorley's instructions: 'Say only this: they are dead' in 'When You See Millions'.

It was while Sassoon was completing 'I Stood With the Dead' that he finally realized just how difficult it was to combine the roles of soldier and poet, particularly when the poet was also a pacifist. It was virtually impossible to remember the multitude of small details which filled a company officer's day if your head was full of poetry. After a curt reprimand from the Adjutant for failing to return certain books and pamphlets, he reluctantly abandoned poetry, though not before completing his poem and not for long. Only three days after 'I Stood with the Dead' was finished, he was relieved of many of the petty tasks which filled his day and actively encouraged to return to poetry. For on 21 June a second-in-command for A Company finally materialized who proved to be both efficient and an enthusiastic admirer of his work, Vivian de Sola Pinto.

Pinto, who himself wrote poetry and was familiar with Sassoon's work, thought it an extraordinary stroke of luck when he reported to the 25th RWF at Habarcq to find himself assigned to A Company as Sassoon's second-in-command. The guide detailed to take him to A Company's headquarters in the grounds of the partly ruined château led him down a muddy path to a hut, he remembered:

A tall figure came out of the hut to greet me. Ignoring my smart salute, he shook me by the hand:

'I suppose you're my new second-in-command. I've never had one before.'

'Yes, Sir ... er, are you the poet Siegfried Sassoon?'

As I blurted out these words, I knew what the answer was. That splendid, erect figure with the noble head, mane of dark hair, piercing black eyes and strongly sculptured features could only belong to a poet.[29]

Sassoon's response to Pinto was equally positive. Under the guise of 'Velmore' in

Sherston's Progress, he described a tall, dark, bespectacled young man of scholarly appearance. (Pinto had been at Oxford a year when the War interrupted his studies and was to return there to complete them when it was over.) His previous experience at the Front, Sassoon found, 'gave him a solid basis of usefulness and to this was added a temperament in which kindliness, humour and intelligence divided the honours equally, with gentleness and modesty in readiness to assert themselves by the power of non-assertion'.[30]

While Pinto, like all the men in A Company, was to fall under the spell of Sassoon's 'charismatic personality', which seemed to him to radiate 'heroic energy and generosity',[31] Sassoon more prosaically admired Pinto's ability to deal with the piles of paperwork accumulating daily on his desk. Their real meeting-point, and one which was to prolong their friendship well beyond the end of the War, was their shared passion for poetry, though Sassoon privately thought Pinto's verse 'not original in any way'.[32]

Only four days after Pinto joined A Company the 25th RWF made their final move toward the Front. The Germans, as a result of their fierce Spring offensives, had advanced in two large bulges (towards Amiens and Paris) in the south and a smaller one in the north on the Belgian border. It was to the northern, not the southern area, that the 25th RWF, recovered from its flu epidemic, were now ordered. So that, instead of repeating his short journey to the Neuville-Vitasse sector as expected, Sassoon found himself on a much longer one to the area north of Béthune, near Lillers. (The 74th Division was to replace the 61st in the St Venant-St Floris sector.) On 25 June, therefore, his battalion marched twelve miles for a four-hour ride north by train to St Hilaire, near Norrent-Fontes. After a long and exhausting journey, he was disappointed to find that his new billets were rather cramped and that he was not much nearer to the Front than at Habarcq, that is, approximately nine miles. For he was beginning to feel that it was 'about time to be up and doing'.[33] After weeks of energetic training, he now felt 'dead stale'[34] as he lay on a 'frowsty bed in a dingy, fly-buzzing room with a brick floor' with 'a midden-smelling yard full of whistling soldiers outside the window'.[35]

It was a stark contrast to Sassoon's large room in the Château at Habarcq, but he tried to accept the change cheerfully. At least the wearisome training programme had come to an end as the battalion, together with the rest of the 74th Division, worked on rear defences for the next fortnight. There was also consolation in the fact that his second book of war poems was finally published on 27 June, after endless delays. 'I have received an advance copy of the book today,' he tells Gosse on 29 June, in response to Gosse's praise of the 'power and originality' of the new collection, 'and am gloating over it, as only young authors can do; when I had read it through I just sat and looked at it from a distance.'[36]

The title of Sassoon's new book, *Counter-Attack*, taken from the opening poem, suggests that he was still determined to fight the complacency and self-righteousness of the jingoists. Even the colours of the cover, yellow and 'blood-red' (as he pointed out) convey defiance. And its dedication to Ross, his greatest encouragement to anti-war satire, seems highly appropriate, both in terms of his deep sympathy for all his friend was suffering in the Pemberton Billing trial and also in terms of the book's content. For almost all of its thirty-nine poems were fiercely critical of the War, unlike *The Old Huntsman*. Sassoon had to a large extent resisted Heinemann's desire for 'some amiable stuff to mitigate the horrors', though he had yielded to pressure from friends to omit two of the fiercer poems, 'Atrocities' and 'The Dressing Station'.[37]

Sassoon called it his 'undertaker' book and informed Osbert Sitwell, whom he knew would appreciate the point: 'The word death, die, dead, recurs more than 40 times in the 39 poems – Dark and darkness – 16 – War: 15. Night: 13. Gloom: 9. Doom: 7. Killed: 5. Corpses – only 3, I am afraid.'[38] Written between May 1917 and February 1918, *Counter-Attack* summed up for both Sassoon and the public his most consistent attitude to the War, which was no longer as shocking to them as it once had been. It seemed highly paradoxical to Pinto, who received a signed copy from Sassoon, that the author of poems such as 'Base Details', 'The General', 'Lamentations', 'Does It Matter?' and 'Fight to a Finish' should also be 'a first-rate soldier and most aggressive Company Commander'.[39] But, as Pinto himself admitted, Sassoon's attitude was not really very different from a large part of the British army by 1918: 'He was convinced that modern warfare was an unspeakable horror and he deeply distrusted those for whom it had become a vested interest, but, as he put it once to me, we were ruddy well going to beat the Germans.'[40] Sassoon himself no longer attempted to resolve the contradiction, if there was one, and the reviews, when they came, would confirm that his attitude was no longer considered outrageous. The public had finally caught up with him.

After the excitement of receiving *Counter-Attack* Sassoon had to wait another week before anything of note happened. When it did, he fortunately jotted it down in a separate notebook which was not, like his diary, lost. The fact that he found the Deputy-Chaplain General's sermon to the 74th Division on Sunday, 7 July, worthy of a lengthy note – 'What the Bishop Said' – suggests that he had not abandoned his satiric approach.[41] In a masterly introduction Sassoon compares the Bishop to a 'well-nourished Anglican Gramophone' which plays 'well-worn Records: Patriotism, Insular Imperialism, Hun-Hatred', and in the main body of the piece sums up the argument by which the Establishment hoped to bolster the morale of the troops. He could not resist turning his observations about the Bishop later into a satirical poem, 'Vicarious Christ', interesting mainly because it anticipates one direction his poetry would take in the 1920s.[42]

One of the Bishop's claims was that the Germans were 'getting weaker', but riding towards the Front on a battalion reconnaissance the day after his sermon, Sassoon had strong reason to doubt this. As at Neuville-Vitasse, they had driven the Allies back many miles earlier in the year and were holding the line strongly near Merville. The 25th RWF were to relieve the 1st East

Lancashires the next day in the right sub-sector, covering St Venant. Primed with map-references and urgent instructions from the Orderly Room, Sassoon was going up to obtain all possible information from the retiring battalion.

Though the British had been driven back beyond Merville they were still in the flat plain of the Lys Valley, in what had been a quiet back area where peasants still worked their land. Driving across the plain today it is still possible to see the problems which faced both armies in such low, open country. They had been forced to build breastworks rather than trenches for the greater part of their defences, since it was impracticable to dig trenches in such marshy ground. One of the 25th RWF's first duties on taking over the Line would be to cut the crops and clear two wide swathes on either side of the barbed wire. It seems ironic that, after training so vigorously in trench warfare, it would be their earlier Middle Eastern experience of patrolling in open country that would help them most.

So that when Sassoon was allowed to witness a small raid by the 1st East Lancashires, which enabled him to see what the sector was really like, it was not a reassuring sight. Instead of the solid defences of the Canadian trenches at Neuville-Vitasse, there were merely a series of breast-high sentry-posts stretching about three-quarters of a mile and connected by a shallow ditch. No Man's Land was a cornfield, containing more corn than barbed wire and varying in depth from a hundred to two hundred yards.

After an hour or two at the Front Sassoon set off home in the early morning, hoping that his five pages of hastily scribbled notes would be useful. But, in spite of his anxiety, as he rode past the shuttered houses of a sleeping village he experienced a moment of extraordinary exhilaration which he never forgot, 'a sort of personal manifesto of being intensely alive – a sense of physical adventure and improvident jubilation; and also, as [he] looked at the signs of military occupation around [him], a feeling that [he] was in the middle of some interesting historical tale'.[43] Instead of sympathizing with the fighting men involved in the unsuccessful raid he had just witnessed, he found himself resolving to make a better job of it with his own soldiers. Such were the self-contradictions he experienced daily.

Looking back on his reconnaissance trip to the 1st East Lancashires, Sassoon doubted its usefulness. One valuable purpose was served by it, however: when A Company was ordered to lead the 25th RWF up to the Front later the same day, 9 July, at least he knew the way. The unpleasantness of the journey comes through forcefully in 'Battalion Relief', one of his less well known war poems, in which the irony of the title and the reference to 'Harvest soon,/ Up in the line' also show which way his thoughts were tending (*CP*, p. 102).

By 1 a.m. on 10 July Sassoon was back in the same Company shell-hole he had left the previous morning, the only difference being that he was now in charge. He and Pinto personally settled the four platoons at their rather exposed posts before retreating along a shallow ditch to their shell-hole-cum-Company-Headquarters. It was impossible in such conditions to organize regular watches at night, as in a connected trench-system, but Sassoon, who was longing for action, decided that he and his second-in-command should divide the night into two halves, during which one of them would 'hold the fort' in Company Headquarters while the other patrolled the posts. Determined that A Company should demonstrate its superiority to the Germans as soon as possible, he spent most of his turn on duty crawling through the cornfields in No Man's Land with a knob-kerry and some hand-grenades in his pockets. Pinto remembers him actually reaching a German post and bringing back a stick bomb, though Sassoon places the incident in broad daylight on the following day in *Sherston's Progress*, probably to accentuate both his foolhardiness and courage. For him the first evening's experience was marked by a less dramatic but equally significant event.

Sassoon had been out patrolling with Jowett and a number of N.C.O.s for practice and, after sending the others back, had made a second round of the sentry posts alone. On returning to his shell-hole, where a large shallow dug-out served as both dining- and bed-room, he saw that Jowett 'lay dead beat and asleep in an ungainly attitude, with that queer half-sullen look on his face', a 'visible representation' of all 'the dead and sleeping multitudes of the War'.[44] (Sassoon had noted in his diary two months earlier: 'Handsome Jowett asleep on the floor, with his smooth, sensual face and large limbs (as usual, he looks as if dead).')[45] This simple experience became the basis for one of his most moving war poems, a disturbing mixture of passion and compassion expressed in deceptively artless language:

The Dug-Out
Why do you lie with your legs ungainly huddled,
And one arm bent across your sullen, cold,
Exhausted face? It hurts my heart to watch you,
Deep-shadow'd from the candle's guttering gold;
And you wonder why I shake you by the shoulder;
Drowsy, you mumble and sigh and turn your head ...
You are too young to fall asleep for ever;
And when you sleep you remind me of the dead. (*CP*, p. 102)

Sassoon himself thought these 'eight vigil-haunted lines' 'memorable' and wisely cut four lines which he had added for their first publication.[46] It was to be his last war poem based directly on trench experience.

The narrator's apparent unkindness in shaking his sleeping subaltern awake in 'The Dug-Out' is a particularly effective way of underlining his irrational fear that the young man is dead, since lack of sleep was a serious problem at the Front, particularly for company commanders. It did not, however, prevent Sassoon from energetically pursuing plans for an offensive. After his daring raid on the German line, during which he claims to have encountered four enemy soldiers face to face, he continued to lead patrols into No Man's Land.

A bad strafe on the evening of the second day frightened even him and nearly ended his life, when a 5.9 shell scored a direct hit on his dug-out. But the shell was, miraculously, a dud and his ardour only temporarily dampened. By the next day, 12 July, he was in fighting mood again and what he called his 'rather feckless 1916 self'.[47]

The day had been quiet but the weather stormy and the shelling of the pack animals bringing rations to the Front had left A Company short of food, possibly the last straw for Sassoon. The 25th were to be relieved the following night and he was determined to have one last 'really good patrol'.[48] Pinto, far more cautious, argued that it would serve no purpose but Sassoon insisted that they must maintain their supremacy in No Man's Land. Another excuse was that he needed to locate a machine-gun which seemed to be firing from outside the German lines. His real reason for going out, he later felt, was his need to escape from the worry and responsibility of his position, and annoyance at the thought of being blown to bits while he sat in the dug-out.

Fearing the worst, Pinto instructed their Company Sergeant-Major to send an urgent message to neighbouring B Company not to fire on Sassoon as he returned. Meanwhile, Sassoon set out with a young corporal from the last post on A Company's right flank,[49] his plan being to get as near to the rogue machine-gun as possible, then frighten its crew with their Mills bombs. It was 1 a.m. when they set out and pitch-black. But it took them over two hours to crawl across No Man's Land and by the time they were within striking distance dawn was breaking.

Pinto, supervising 'Stand-To' back in their sector, was becoming increasingly anxious. Sassoon and his companion, having managed to throw their bombs, had rapidly retreated like 'a pair of scared badgers',[50] but were still in No Man's Land. As they rested in a sunken road the corporal's fresh young face, lit by the rising sun, seemed to Sassoon to assert not only their supremacy over No Man's Land, but also the supreme satisfaction of being alive on a perfect summer's morning. Throwing caution to the wind in characteristic fashion, he removed his steel helmet and stood up to survey the German Line.

Though well hidden from the enemy, Sassoon was clearly visible to his own men, one of whom took careful aim. Moments later Sassoon felt a terrific blow to the head and assumed that his last moment had come. Pinto, meantime, had set off in search of him and was just in time to witness the incident. He afterwards maintained that the gun was fired by a zealous sergeant from A Company, who had forgotten to check whether his Company Commander was back and had mistaken him for a German. Sassoon supported this view publicly in *Sherston's Progress*, but Robert Nichols, who talked to him shortly after the incident, offered a far more dramatic explanation, noting on a letter received from Sassoon in hospital: 'He had been grazed by a bullet fired by one of his own sentries coming in. Somebody said the sergeant knocked up the recruit's rifle just as he pulled the trigger. There was not wanting talk to the effect that the High Command had decided he should die. I think it was wild talk. But the fact remains that he was a very inconvenient figure.'[51] It is more plausible that the shot was 'friendly fire' from a raw recruit rather than an experienced sergeant, but Sassoon may have preferred the inherent irony of being shot by one of his keenest men. There is nothing to support the conspiracy rumours that 'the High Command had decided he should die', though Sassoon would probably have enjoyed those as well.

Another friend from 25th RWF, Wintringham Stables, implies that Sassoon was something of a problem to his superiors in his version of events. Sassoon made his nightly forays, he maintained, in order to get an accurate sketch of the German Front Line immediately opposite the battalion, but that when their Brigadier learnt of his activities he was angry. Knowing Sassoon as he did, Stables passed this order on in writing, 'so that there could be no possible reason for misunderstanding'. He interpreted Sassoon's final sortie, therefore, as a deliberate flouting of the rules in order to complete his sketch of the German Front.[52]

Pinto's main concern when he reached Sassoon in No Man's Land was not who had fired the shot, but how much damage it had done. Sassoon's face was covered in blood and he assumed the worst. The corporal, however, had already discovered that it was only a flesh wound, though hardly the 'graze on the temple' with which Sassoon reassured Pinto. Medically it was described as a 'glancing wound over the right parietal of the skull' and was more serious than he suggested; had the sentry aimed an inch or two to the right he would certainly have died. As it was, he staggered back to his Company unaided.

Once Sassoon realized that his wound was not fatal, his thoughts turned to his men. 'I won't say goodbye; I'm coming back,' he told his Sergeant-Major as he set off for Battalion Headquarters to have his wound dressed. But as he blundered into the Aid Post there, he had already travelled a mile and a half from the Front. He was equally insistent as he said long farewells to the C.O., the Adjutant and other H.Q. officers: 'You'll see me back in three weeks,' he shouted. But as various ambulances ferried him still further away to the Casualty Clearing Station, near St Omer, his words began to sound hollow.

By 15 July, Sassoon found himself at No. 8 Red Cross Hospital in Boulogne, being fussed over by sympathetic nurses. Still haunted by the memory of his Company, which had become as precious to him as his family, he tried to appear hearty and well, though he felt neither: 'All that was decent in me disliked leaving them to endure what I was escaping from. And somehow the idea of death had beckoned to me – ghastly though it had been when I believed that I had been killed.'[53] It was time for a long rest, and when a nurse informed him of his imminent departure for England he could no longer resist. His 'proud, angry resolve', his 'tenderness' for his men had faded into what he guiltily construed as 'a selfish longing for safety'.[54] A month earlier he had urged Robert Nichols to pay a visit to Weirleigh mainly out of concern for his mother. Now he longed to be there himself. He could already see in his mind's eye 'the door into the garden at home, and Mother coming in with a basket of roses. And my terrier ... and the piano ....'[55]

17

'A Loathsome Ending'

July-November 1918

When Sassoon left France for England on 18 July 1918 it was for the last time, though he did not know it. Determined not to desert his men, as he saw it, he was already planning to return to them even before he left. It was as if he could only justify his tortured physical attraction towards particular men by showing an altruistic, asexual love for all his men: 'I know that it is the only way I can keep my soul clean,' he had written in his diary on 15 July, as he struggled to resist the lure of home. But the matter was not in his hands. His wound was slow to heal, there was a danger of infection and the doctors at Boulogne decided to send him back to England.

Consigned to the American Red Cross Hospital No. 22 at Lancaster Gate, in London, Sassoon arrived there on 18 July and was put in a large ward which overlooked Hyde Park. Occasional visits by Royalty and more frequent ones by Winston Churchill's American mother, Lady Randolph, soothed his ego as well as his brow. There were also numerous visitors to welcome the wounded hero home. They swarmed in on his very first afternoon – his mother, Marsh, Ross, Meiklejohn, Nichols and Osbert Sitwell – and began to merge in his bewildered brain, he wrote in a poem, as 'MarshMoonStreetMeiklejohnArdoursandendurancSitwellitis'.[1] Addressed to Graves, one of the few friends absent on the occasion, this poem also suggests that he found their 'Jabber – Gesture – Jabber – Gesture' too much for his frayed nerves. Complications set in and he was moved to a smaller room. As he battled against fever and sleepless, guilt-ridden nights there, all visitors were banned. He was still in a disturbed state by 24 July, when he composed his verse letter to the one person he believed might understand his state, Graves. This was written partly in response to Graves's jokey congratulations on getting a bullet through his 'napper' and for writing to him more sanely. Continuing their tradition of verse letters, Graves had also included ten lines of a poem which started: 'Poor Fusilier, vexed with the Fate/ That keeps you there in France so late ....'[2]

It was this poem which prompted Sassoon to reply on 24 July in a verse letter which was to become the cause of much trouble later on.[3] Its jumpy, changing staccato rhythms and jumbled contents are convincing proof of Sassoon's extreme nervous tension at this time, the occasional breakdown of the verse reflecting his own unstable condition:

Dear Roberto,
I'd timed my death in action to the minute –
(The Nation with my deathly verses in it) –

> The day told off – 13 – (the month July) –[4]
> The picture planned – O Threshold of the dark!
> And then, the quivering Songster failed to die
> Because the bloody Bullet missed its mark.
>
> Here I am: They *would* send me back –
> Kind M.O. at Base; Sassoon's morale grown slack;
> Swallowed all his proud high thoughts & acquiesced ...
> O Gate of Lancaster, O Blightyland the Blessed ...

After another erratic twenty-two lines exploring, in ironic fashion, his sense of guilt and humiliation Sassoon then reverts to his pride in his Company, whom his (and Graves's) friend, Captain Stable has written to say are doing 'better and better'. His final outburst, full of defiant references to popular songs, must have made Graves realize how shaken his friend was:

> But I don't care; I made them love me although
> they didn't want to do it, and I've sent them a
> glorious Gramophone and God send you back to me
> Over the green eviscerating sea – And I'm
> ill and afraid to go back to them because those
> five-nines are so damned awful
> When you think of them all bursting and you're
> lying on your bed, with the books you loved and
> Longed for on the table; and your head All
> Crammed with village verses about Daffodils and
> Geese ... O Jesu make it cease ...

'Does this break your heart ... What do I care?' Sassoon concluded, though softening his apparent defiance by signing himself with the name Graves had given him, 'Sassons'. To which Graves responded three days later, with a reference to his own ancestry: 'Why keep a German friend unless you grieve him?'

Graves was convinced that Sassoon had been misled by Ottoline and her Pacifist circle: 'God preserve you from your friends the Rottalines and the Bolshevists and the syphilitic young poets!' He believed that the only person who could help Sassoon in his distracted state was the same one who had persuaded him to return to the fighting, Dr Rivers. Graves had admired Rivers greatly when they met at Craiglockhart and knew that he had already visited his ex-patient at Lancaster Gate from two passages in Sassoon's verse letter. Though jokey and playful, with their extended pun on Rivers's name, these passages suggest that Sassoon himself felt that Rivers was his only hope and that he still believed he ought to go back to the Front.

The doctor, now based in London, had visited Sassoon on 23 July, in spite of the efforts of the stern matron, Mrs Fisher, to prevent him. Judging from the description in *Sherston's Progress*, which is placed significantly at the end as the climax to the protagonist's war-experience, he was already having the effect Graves hoped for. 'My futile demons fled him,' Sassoon's narrator records, '– for his presence was a refutation of wrong-headedness ... I knew that I had a lot to learn, and that he was the only man who could help me.'[5] Rivers, the one character to appear as himself in this version of Sassoon's life, is typically reticent during their meeting but his presence brings the comfort and reassurance a loving parent gives to an unhappy child: 'He did not tell me that I had done my best to justify his belief in me. He merely made me feel that he took all that for granted, and now we must go on to something better still. And this was the beginning of the new life toward which he had shown me the way ....'[6]

Even when Sassoon began to feel better at the beginning of August, he was still seeing very few people. 'It is very upsetting,' he explained to Cockerell in one of his rare letters of the period, '– coming back to life after saying goodbye to it!'[7] As his health gradually improved he started to think about his own writing again and by mid-August was in 'full blast', as he put it to Nichols on the 15th: 'making the most gorgeous poetry. I simply can't stop ... it pops out so quick that I can't believe it's any good. And then I read it again and gurgle with bliss.'[8] If Sassoon was as prolific as he suggests at Lancaster Gate, he must have destroyed a number of poems, since, of the four included in his letter to Nichols, at least two had originated elsewhere,[9] leaving only two or three new poems. The first of these, 'Dedication', may help to explain why so few have survived from this period. Ostensibly a lament for a dead soldier-friend, this reads more as a 'cry of desire' for a 'lover slain in sleep' to quote its own ninth and twelfth lines. The lingering physical detail – 'blithe limbs', 'steadfast-gazing eyes', 'proud hands', 'body's loveliness', 'face' and 'brow' – the tender reference to 'the dreams of a boy' and the narrator's passionate involvement in the young soldier's 'death' (a popular Jacobean metaphor for sexual consummation) probably struck Sassoon as revealing too much of his homoerotic feelings and it was never published. It may also explain why Nichols suggested that it needed rewriting.

Another poem written at this time suffered the same fate as 'Dedication' and probably for the same reason, that it was too explicit an outpouring of his sexual longings. Entitled 'The Vigil', Sassoon describes it in a letter to Marsh as 'forty lines of blank verse written round Whitman's "Vigil of silence, love and death, vigil for you my son and my soldier"'.[10] Wishing to escape from his 'bitter little epigrammatic poems', which threatened to become a habit of mind, he felt drawn towards 'larger canvasses, sort of Whitmanesque effects of masses of soldiers'.[11] The 'big poem' which emerged attempts to express 'the biggest thing I feel', a reference no doubt to his overwhelming love and pity for all the young men he had seen die in the War.

One of the two war poems Sassoon did not attempt to suppress from his Lancaster Gate phase, 'Can I Forget?', expresses a similar sense of loss but in less explicit, at times highly derivative terms. Echoing Kipling's 'Lest We Forget',[12] Binyon's 'We Will Remember Them'[13] and Whitman's 'O Captain! my Captain!', Sassoon's poem is yet another attempt to come to terms with his guilt in the comfort and security of his hospital bed:

> ... I will remember you; and from your wrongs
> Shall rise the power and poignance of my songs:
> And this shall comfort me until the end,
> That I have been your captain and your friend.[14]

Sassoon's other war poem of the period, 'Great Men', was inspired by the visit of the Duke of Connaught to Lancaster Gate, two 'bad-tempered verses' dealing scathingly with the 'monstrous tyranny ... brought to birth' by such 'Great Men':

> ... You Marshals, gilt and red,
> You Ministers and Princes, and Great Men,
> Why can't you keep your mouthings for the dead?
> Go round the simple cemeteries; and then
> Talk of our noble sacrifice and losses
> To the wooden crosses.[15]

Writing about his conflicts in this way seems to have helped Sassoon resolve them, and by mid-August he was able to report to Marsh that 'the furies [had] flapped out of the window'.[16] Whether it was this image which inspired the fourth poem Sassoon sent to Nichols on 15 August, or whether 'Butterflies' is simply an expression of his recovering sense of beauty and significance in life, it shows a distinct change of mood. Like its subject, it is a slight poem which looks both backward to his youthful descriptions of summer dawns and forward to one type of work to come, a short pastoral piece where observation of nature leads to reflection on the significance of the poet's own life. In this particular case the butterflies become emblems of a new start, however shaky:

> ... And they are as my soul that wings its way
> Out of the starlit dimness into morn:
> And they are as my tremulous being – born
> To know but this, the phantom glare of the day   (*CP*, pp. 111-12)

'Butterflies' was one of the few poems to please Sassoon at Lancaster Gate, but at least he had some published poetry he could be proud of. For one of the most consoling aspects of life at Lancaster Gate was the praise that began to pour in for *Counter-Attack*. There had been at least sixteen reviews by 4 August and many more were to come. He could not resist drawing Pinto's attention in a letter of that date to three of the best, J.C. Squire's in the *New Statesman* (3

August), Winifred Blatchford's in the *Clarion* (19 July) and Max Plowman's in the *Labour Leader* (25 July). As with *The Old Huntsman*, he saved all the reviews for his press-cutting book, with the noticeable exception of a hostile one in the *Nation* by John Middleton Murry. He had regarded both the magazine and the reviewer as allies, so was particularly shocked by it.

On the whole, though, the critics were positive and showed far more understanding of Sassoon's viewpoint than they had the previous year in reviewing *The Old Huntsman*. The *TLS*'s anonymous critic, for example, represents a number of reviewers who, while still questioning whether such harshly realistic satires could be called poetry, are nevertheless full of admiration. Even the *Morning Post*, a bastion of the jingoistic, allows that, having 'served gallantly in the war', he has 'a right to enter a minority report' and praises him as a poet of 'power and precision'.[17] A number of the more learned reviewers hail him as the English verse equivalent of the French writer he had chosen to preface *Counter-Attack*, Henri Barbusse.

Predictably, praise came from the pacifists, notably from Max Plowman, who had himself faced Court Martial and imprisonment when, like Sassoon, he refused to go on serving in the army. 'What recognition,' Plowman asked in the *Labour Leader*, 'is the country going to give to Mr Sassoon for writing this book?' By publishing *Counter-Attack*, he argued, Sassoon had 'rendered about the best public service it is at present possible to offer. He has delivered the finest counter-attack in the war by making a breach in the sinister ranks of official reticence and unofficial ignorance and self-complacency. *He has told the truth about the war.*' The *Tribunal* was equally fulsome.

One friend who had admired the poems in *Counter-Attack* from the start was Wilfred Owen. Though he and Sassoon had not met since Craiglockhart, where they had discussed many of the pieces in the book, they had remained in close touch. Thanks to Sassoon's introductory letter to Ross, Owen had also met many of Sassoon's friends by August 1918. It was he, not Sassoon, who had attended Graves's marriage to Nancy Nicholson in January 1918 and, during his friend's absence in Ireland, Palestine and France, had dined with faithful Meiklejohn at the Reform Club. He had also become increasingly intimate with the Sitwells, whom Sassoon too hoped to know better. After leaving Edinburgh Owen had spent some time in the Sitwells' home town, Scarborough, to which he returned at the beginning of June 1918. He had also been asked to contribute to Edith Sitwell's *avant-garde* anthology, *Wheels*.

Meantime, Owen had written faithfully to his 'greatest friend', Sassoon, who replied not quite so faithfully. From the moment he heard that Sassoon was wounded and back in London, he had been determined to see him again, but it was not until the third week of August that he was able to do so. In spite of another new friend, Scott Moncrieff's efforts at the War Office, Owen had failed to get the instructorship which would have kept him safely in England and by 9 August was on a list for France. When, at the last moment, he failed to pass his Medical Board, he was nevertheless still entitled to furlough and left for Shrewsbury and London. He was in London by Wednesday, 14 August and on Thursday 15th was dining with Sassoon and Meiklejohn at the Reform.

It is possible that this Reform Club dinner was Sassoon's first venture out of hospital. Certainly he was well enough by 17 August to spend a long afternoon with Owen at Osbert Sitwell's. This was to be the sole occasion when they were all three together. Owen's failure to pass his Medical had encouraged him to hope that Scott Moncrieff might still succeed in getting him an instructorship in England. So that it was a relatively light-hearted occasion, with none of the elegiac overtones it would afterwards acquire.

Both Sassoon and Owen had met Sitwell separately at Ross's the previous winter and liked him very much, and Sassoon's interest in Osbert, and his brother Sacheverell ('Sachie'), had been kept alive by Dent. On the same day that Sassoon was sending his 'love' to the brothers via Dent (26 June), Osbert was writing to beg him to take care of himself: 'We *cannot* afford to lose a *poet* – and especially you.'[18] It was a flattering start and Sassoon replied at once. Towards the end of his letter he asks: 'Have you met Wilfred Owen, my little friend, whose verses were in the Nation recently? He is so nice, and shy, and fervent about poetry, which he is quite good at, and will do *very well* some day.'[19] Osbert had been one of Sassoon's first visitors at Lancaster Gate. It was, therefore, quite natural that, when Owen finally managed to get to London, they should both wish to see Osbert. His invitation to tea was, accordingly, very welcome.

Sassoon's war years had been marked by chance meetings which would fascinate posterity more, but this one was no less intriguing. On the surface there were a number of things the three men had in common. They were all serving army officers, all artistically inclined, all poets and all acknowledged themselves as homosexuals at that time. There were, however, profound differences between them. Their physical distinctiveness – Sitwell the tallest, Owen the smallest – neatly reflected a very marked difference of social class. Sitwell, the eldest son of a baronet, a product of Eton and the Grenadier Guards, was at the top of the social scale, Sassoon, with Marlborough and Cambridge behind him, in the middle and Owen, whose father still occupied a fairly humble job on the railways and was entirely innocent of either public school or university education, on the lower slopes.

Perhaps even more importantly, they also differed greatly in temperament. As Sassoon was to discover, Sitwell was quick and capricious where he was slow, and stimulating and provocative where he longed for restfulness. Owen, too, whose 'unassumingness', 'selflessness', 'lack of egotism' or self-advancement he had already recognized at Craiglockhart, could not have been more different from the other two. Osbert, on the other hand, seems to have suffered none of Owen's diffidence, in spite of the fact that his only significant publications were in his sister's anthology. One of the few differences that might have worked in Owen's favour was that, despite Moncrieff's efforts, he was still expecting to be sent back to the Front, while Osbert, invalided back to England, tamely did duty in Chelsea Barracks and Sassoon was finally accepting that he would be staying in England for the rest of the War. It was a situation which probably gave Owen a slight moral edge.

The greatest difference between the three poets, however, was in their work, a difference which would emerge more distinctly and matter more to Sassoon later on. Sassoon, while finding Sitwell's satiric verse 'a great joy',[20] quickly recognized that his desire to shock went far deeper than his own wish to disturb civilian complacency. 'The stormy petrels of modern literature' seemed to him an entirely appropriate way of describing Osbert and his siblings. Owen, with his readiness to experiment, was slightly nearer to the highly experimental trio, as they had recognized when they invited him to contribute to their modernist magazine. But he was still a long way from their deliberate outrageousness. And Sassoon had already acknowledged the differences between himself and Owen when they worked together at Craiglockhart, though by the time of this meeting he felt he was moving more in Owen's direction. Altogether, it was a meeting of 'true', but very different minds.

One of Sitwell's greatest assets, however, was his social skill, and he made quite sure that the afternoon went harmoniously. Knowing the passion both his guests felt for music and how deprived of it they were in wartime, he had arranged to start with a harpsichord recital given by his friend, Violet Gordon-Woodhouse. The afternoon was hot and cloudless and, following a sumptuous tea at Sitwell's house in Swan Walk, Chelsea, they crossed the road to the ancient Chelsea Physic Garden. Here they wandered happily about among its herbs and flowering shrubs.

Wartime conditions were never far away, however, and eventually Sassoon had to report back to Lancaster Gate. Owen, who had already been too 'listlessly happy' to catch his intended train back to Scarborough, further delayed his return by accompanying Sassoon to his hospital.[21] It was their one opportunity for private talk that day and they must have spent part of the time discussing the likelihood of Owen returning to the Front. Sassoon has often been cited as encouraging him to do so, but the opposite is true. He had already told Marsh that it was a 'great relief' to him that Owen had been prevented from going to France and it was probably during their talk after leaving Sitwell's that he threatened to 'stab him in the leg' if he tried to return to the Front.[22] When it became a *fait accompli*, however, he would do his best to be hopeful, by telling him that it would be 'good for his poetry'.[23]

Owen was too upset at parting to say a coherent goodbye on the steps of the hospital and was quite resolved not to upset Sassoon when his draft came through by telling him so. It would, therefore, be nearly a fortnight before he was to contact his 'dearest of all friends' again – from France. In a brave attempt to face the future unafraid he would write, with not a little truth: 'Battle is easier here; and therefore you will stay and endure old men and women to the End, and wage the bitterer war and more hopeless.'[24] In just over another two months he would be dead, killed by a cruel stroke of Fate a week before the

Armistice. But it was to be several more months before Sassoon learnt of his death, a loss he would never be able to accept philosophically.

Meantime, in August, while Owen faced the possibility of another spell at the Front, Sassoon suffered the opposite problem: what was he to do now that it looked almost certain that he would remain in England? He had already written to Marsh at the end of July, suggesting that he might use his influence to get him a job 'as a sort of official artist in words', the only 'cushy' job he could contemplate.[25] But when Marsh responded by offering him a 'green-tabs and arm-chair soldiering' post, he turned it down. As he had written to Carpenter two days before his visit with Owen to Sitwell:

... Of course it is unthinkable.
I told them that I want to go as an ordinary worker in some works in a large town. (I have Sheffield in my mind's eye.)
I don't know whether I am strong enough to stand the effort, but it is worth trying, isn't it?
I know nothing about Labour, except that the whole world depends on it. And I'm one of those people who can only learn things by coming in the closest possible contact with them. Books tell me nothing. Voices and faces awake 'the fire, the sweet hell within;/ The unknown want, the destiny of me'. – O that old man, how grand he is.[26]

It is clear from his closing reference to Whitman that Sassoon had been profoundly influenced by that poet's attitudes, as well as his poetic technique. The ground had been prepared by his first meaningful contact with working-class men in the army, a contact which had become ever closer and more admiring as the War passed.

Sassoon's next letter to Carpenter came from Scotland and was in the nature of a holding operation, though he repeated his determination 'not to be bluffed into an arm-chair job'.[27] He had known from early August that he was due for convalescence in Berwickshire, but it was not until 18 August that he set out for Scotland and even then he did not go straight to his convalescent home, Lennel, at Coldstream. Instead he took the opportunity to revisit Craiglockhart, where he spent three nights. So that it was 21 August before he reached his final destination.

Sassoon's first impression of Lennel was that it seemed entirely unlike a convalescent home, but simply a country house run by its owners. It was not unlike Chapelwood Manor on a larger scale, offering recuperation to about a dozen officers. Situated on a hillside in a sheltered, south-facing position, it offered magnificent views of the River Tweed, the rolling Cheviots and the brooding Lammermuir Hills. Flodden Field, site of the famous battle, lay only a few miles away and Berwick-on-Tweed and Edinburgh were relatively near at hand.

The house itself was built on an ancient site forming part of the mediaeval

Earldom of Dunbar, the nineteenth-century building replacing earlier ones dating from the twelfth century onwards. After passing first to the Cistercian Abbey of Coldstream in the fifteenth century, Lennel became the property of the first Earl of Haddington in 1634 and remained in his family until 1903. Robert Burns had visited it in 1787 and Beatrix Potter rented it as her holiday home in 1894. But Sassoon's most exciting discovery was that it had a Surtees connexion: Lord Elcho, to whom *Mr Sponge's Sporting Tour* was dedicated, had used it as his hunting lodge. One of Sassoon's greatest pleasures at the start was an attempt to identify other details of the district described by his favourite pre-war author.

Sassoon spent many hours on a bicycle in this escapist pursuit. Riding through the mysterious countryside, or just sitting in the lovely grounds of Lennel listening to the Tweed murmuring below the garden did more for his gloomy state of mind than all his friends' pep talks and he soon found himself in a 'comparatively cheerful and unspeculative frame of mind'.[28] Cycling many miles during the day and writing a little lyrical poetry in the evenings, he felt he could have been back in Kent in 1913 before his life had so drastically changed. His stay at Lennel was to be a very important stage in the winding-down process ahead of him.

Another unexpectedly enjoyable feature of life at Lennel was the company – unexpected because Sassoon had been largely antagonized by the inmates of his previous convalescent home. He says little of his host, Major Walter Waring, but he is full of praise for his hostess, Lady Clementine Waring, a small, businesslike woman, known as 'Clemmie' to her friends. Conscious that most of her guests had mental as well as physical needs, she not only produced a succession of delicious meals but managed her 'supposedly nerve-disordered guests', Sassoon found, 'with undeviating adroitness and good-humour'.[29] Clemmie also provided for her guests' needs in other ways. Like Ottoline at Garsington, she had created a beautiful Italian garden in the grounds and, together with her husband, built up a fine library. Their taste in pictures, unfortunately, seemed 'too awful' to Sassoon,[30] but he spent many hours in their library on rainy days.

Lady Waring clearly enjoyed having such a literary guest in her house and immediately ordered thirty copies of his latest book. She also gave him Richard Burton's *The Kasidaha of Haji Abdu El Yezdi: A Lay of the Higher Law* (1914), perhaps as a recognition of his eastern ancestry. Her inscription – 'A souvenir of days and talks by the Tweed – S.S. from C.W. 1918' – suggests that they got on well together. She was a broad-minded woman, rumoured to be a collector of Oscar Wilde at a time when that was considered very daring, which made for a fairly relaxed atmosphere at Lennel.

One book Sassoon had failed to finish at Lennel was Winston Churchill's life of his father, Lord Randolph, which he found 'too political'.[31] He had probably been prompted to attempt Churchill's book after receiving a note from the great man himself to the effect that he hoped to find Sassoon a sufficiently 'unsavoury, dangerous and exhausting job'. The note was almost certainly a result of Marsh's efforts and Sassoon's somewhat ungracious response to them.

Ottoline, meantime, did her best to keep Sassoon up to scratch politically. In response to his first letter from Lennel she sent a swift reply, enclosing in it a statement by Bertrand Russell, whose friends were trying to find him a replacement fellowship for the one his pacifist stance had cost him. Russell had been sentenced to six months' imprisonment for his anti-war writings early in 1918 and had only recently been released. Sassoon, grateful for Russell's help in composing his own protest, not only offered to donate money for Russell's support, but also suggested other possible supporters wealthier than himself. He duly sent his own contribution to the Russell fund, but by the time he did so it is clear that he was already far more involved with another of Ottoline's potential lovers. Indeed, it may have been a letter from Sassoon on 4 September that first aroused her interest in the man concerned, Frank Prewett.

Born in Canada in 1893 and known simply by the name of his home-town, 'Toronto', Prewett attracted Sassoon both physically and intellectually. He claimed Iroquois ancestry, which Sassoon believed responsible for his striking high-cheek-boned face and his keen insight into human nature. He found Prewett a remarkable as well as a romantic character, delightful when in a cheerful frame of mind, but liable to fits of moodiness and aloofness, which could have been explained by his two years' service in the Ypres salient and other nightmarish spots. (He had been 'delivered' from the Front, Sassoon noted ironically, by a huge shell bursting near him.) His mood-swings from black depression to animation suggested to Sassoon a streak of genius, and he was particularly excited when he discovered that Prewett was an aspiring poet. The poems themselves seemed to him 'blurred and embryonic', but there was something in them which interested him and raised his expectations.[32]

Sassoon was to be of great help to Prewett in the publication of his book, *The Rural Scene*, in 1924, by which time the younger man would be something of a liability, but at Lennel in 1918 their friendship was mutually beneficial. While Sassoon encouraged and advised him in both his reading and writing, the handsome 'Canadian-French-Red Indian', as Sassoon described him to Marsh, provided pleasant company for his bicycling expeditions. Prewett, the son of a farmer, shared Sassoon's countryman's eye for detail, so richly rewarded in the Border country. Unfortunately he did not have Sassoon's physical stamina and often returned tired and taciturn from their long rides. There was one ride he did enjoy, however, but it was one taken by car. Late in September he and Sassoon drove about twenty miles to Lindisfarne Castle, where Heinemann had been staying with the owner, Edward Hudson, the proprietor of *Country Life* magazine. Heinemann had visited Sassoon at Lennel earlier in the month, but by the time the author had managed to respond to Heinemann and Hudson's invitation to visit Lindisfarne, both had been called back to London on business.

So, after driving across the wet sands to Holy Island at low tide, Sassoon and Prewett spent the afternoon with the sole occupant of the castle, the celebrated cellist, Madame Suggia.[33] Hearing her play a Bach suite in 'the reverberant chamber of a lonely and historic castle – her 'cello's eloquence accompanied only by the beat and wash and murmur of waves breaking against the rocks below the windows' remained one of Sassoon's most precious memories of his convalescence.[34] It was the first time that he had felt completely remote and absolved from the deadly constraints of the War.

There is little doubt that part of Sassoon's sense of freedom and romance at Lindisfarne sprang from Prewett's presence with him, which he celebrated in a lyrical poem prompted by seeing the young Canadian in Indian costume, 'Fancy Dress' (*CP*, p. 110). Though this stops short of a declaration of love, it suggests strong physical and romantic feelings towards its subject. There is something dangerous, predatory and fascinating in the picture. Sassoon would admit four years later that his 'intimacy with Toronto Prewett began with a strong sexual attraction' which 'horrified' Toronto when he became aware of it.[35] The relationship remained outwardly platonic at Lennel, though inwardly it coloured Sassoon's existence there. Life had rarely seemed so good. He was quickly regaining his physical strength, his surroundings were idyllic and he was in love. Furthermore, he was writing poetry with pleasure again and knew himself firmly established in the literary world.

*

Whether Sassoon was encouraged by Gosse's praise before he left London, or simply happier and more relaxed at Lennel, he produced at least ten poems there. Apart from his piece on Prewett, their inspiration came mainly from his surroundings, as the title of one of them, 'Sunset at the Borders', suggests. So that when, for example, he returns to one of his favourite themes, 'Beauty', he explores it in terms of the natural wonder that surrounds him:

> O Never hast thou shone before my gaze
> A pure unswerving statue, cold and bright.
> But as a tree, aspiring toward the light
> And changing with the conflict of my days...

The rest of this unpublished sonnet, sent to Robert Nichols from Lennel in late August, deals predictably with the poet's belief that beauty will 'absolve' and 'free' him, even in the 'pit of Death'. In defining beauty Sassoon was constantly aware of Keats's phrase 'Beauty that must pass' and in 'Vision', also written in late August, he continues to explore 'all things that pass' and 'Beauty, born of lovely things that die!' (*CP*, p. 117).

The War had forced on Sassoon an awareness of life's transience and he was resolved to seize the 'moment's passion'. In 'Falling Asleep', a slightly later, more discursive exploration of beauty, both of Nature and Art, he seems to be coming to terms with separation from his men through the soothing effects of that beauty:

... but now the beauty swings
Across my brain, ghost of remembered chords
Which still can make such radiance in my dream
That I can watch the marching of my soldiers,
And count their faces; faces; sunlit faces.   (*CP*, p. 123)

This calmer note, so different from the tortured, bitter tone of the previous three years, marks Sassoon's final acceptance that, for him at least, the War was coming to an end. When the 'Wraiths' do return to haunt him, in the poem of that name, they do so gently:

... Peering from face to face,
Until some heart shall call
And keep them, for a breath,
Half-mortal ...   (*CP*, p. 112)

When he does write two more war poems, one is based on the ancient battle of Flodden Field, now inhabited by 'simple harvest-folk', the other a generalized account of men's need of 'God in Battle'. Neither seemed to him worthy of publication.

Sassoon was far prouder of another poem written at Lennel, 'Ancient History', which Graves also thought 'wonderful'.[36] This is a poem based on the familiar story of Cain and Abel and, I believe, on Sassoon's trips with Captain Bigger in the Judean hills. By looking at Abel's murder from their father Adam's viewpoint and reversing the usual interpretation, Sassoon achieves a powerful effect. His chosen sonnet form naturally lends itself to a consideration of Cain in the first eight lines:

... '*He was the grandest of them all – was Cain!*
'A lion laired in the hills, that none could tire;
'Swift as a stag; a stallion of the plain,
'Hungry and fierce with deeds of huge desire.'   (*CP*, p. 109)

This is followed by Adam's reflections on Abel, an opportunity to describe another kind of male beauty:

Grimly he thought of Abel, soft and fair –
A lover with disaster in his face,
And scarlet blossom twisted in bright hair.
'Afraid to fight; was murder more disgrace? ...'

'Ancient History' manages to suggest that it is about far more than the individuals concerned. It can be read as an allegory on War *versus* Art, the masculine *versus* the feminine, or even as an insight into Sassoon's own struggle to define his masculinity in the light not only of his homosexuality, but also of the conflicting demands of War and Art. T.E. Lawrence, involved in a similar conflict, admired the poem very much indeed.

Another poem Lawrence admired greatly, 'Limitations', also refers to Adam and was almost certainly written at Lennel. Part of Sassoon's attempt to find 'a more flexible form of expression', it opens with a description of his own creative processes and may refer back to his attempt to write a Whitmanesque poem called 'The Vigil'. The narrator-poet, facing his 'limitations', urges himself to *be* himself, to allow himself the emotional release he has resisted for so long:

> You've got your limitations: let them sing,
> And all your life will waken with a cry:
> Why should you halt when rapture's on the wing
> And you've no limit but the cloud-flocked sky? ...   (*CP*, p. 121)

'And all you need,' he tells himself in conclusion, 'Is just that flash of joy above your dream.' Again the tone is calm, the mood positive, both very different from that of the war poems.

The last but one piece Sassoon wrote at Lennel came about in a rather unexpected way. He knew that Winston Churchill, through Marsh's intervention, wanted to talk to him, and he also felt by the end of September that he needed a change. Occasional trips to Edinburgh were pleasant, though no substitute for London. It had been a relief to leave Lancaster Gate, but after six weeks his appreciation of Lennel was beginning to wane. Already by 20 September he had told Gosse: 'All the fire is dying out of me, here with my porridge and five glasses of milk a day ....'[37] Graves had written to him on 25 September asking him to contribute to a miscellany, *The Owl*, which he and his father-in-law, the artist William Nicholson, planned to launch. And only two days later he had received a letter from the Hampstead Labour Party, inviting him to stand as an M.P. for the constituency. All in all, London seemed a great deal more stimulating than the uneventful life he was leading in the Scottish Border country, however beautiful. So on 30 September he set out for five days in the metropolis, which were to prove as hectic if not more so than any of his frantic wartime socializings.

During his stay at Marsh's flat in Raymond Buildings Sassoon came into contact with almost all the important social and cultural groups of the day, some of which overlapped. There was the Ross set, which met mainly at the Reform and his apartment in Half Moon Street, the Marsh set, which was busy welcoming the Russian Ballet back to London, together with Ottoline Morrell's circle, the Bloomsbury Group and the Sitwells' clique. In addition Marsh organized an interview with Winston Churchill, the ostensible purpose of the visit, and Sassoon himself took the opportunity to see Heinemann about the sales of *Counter-Attack*, which he was delighted to find was in the third impression, completing 3,500 copies.

From 1 October till his exhausted departure on 5 October Sassoon found no respite from the relentless social round. And during the course of it he made a bewildering number of new friends, most importantly Lytton Strachey and Desmond MacCarthy of the Bloomsbury group, Maurice Baring at the Reform and Noel Coward at Half Moon Street. Ross also introduced him to the only member of the Sitwell trio he had not met, Edith, with whom he was to have a long if sometimes difficult relationship. In the midst of this frenzied activity Sassoon also found time to see Rivers and his old army friend, Ralph Greaves.

On the third day the long-awaited interview with Churchill took place at the Hotel Metropole. Winston had told Marsh that he might be able to find his protégé a post in the Ministry of Munitions, a job which Sassoon realized in advance would be ludicrously at odds with his various protests against the War. This had apparently not occurred to Churchill. Sassoon expected very little in the way of a job, therefore, but was looking forward to meeting a man who had already established a great reputation for himself.

Both in his manner, which went far beyond official graciousness, and in the time he was prepared to give, Churchill surprised Sassoon. Having established a common interest in hunting and an admiration for his poems, Churchill proceeded to question him at length on his attitude to the War and, though this quickly turned into a monologue on the virtues of warfare, Sassoon was both flattered and impressed. Even though Sassoon knew that he would never agree with Churchill's views and could not, therefore, accept his offer of a job, he left feeling that Churchill was extremely likeable.

Lunch with Ralph Greaves followed and by the end of it Sassoon had already had enough excitement for one day, but he went on with Greaves to yet another performance by the Russian Ballet, *Carnaval*. After taking Greaves to tea at Ross's and ignoring his mounting exhaustion, Sassoon then dined as Maynard Keynes's guest at the United Universities Club and visited the Russian Ballet yet again, in *Cleopatra*. Keynes was becoming emotionally involved with the Russian ballerina, Lydia Lopokova, whom he would eventually marry, and Sassoon was introduced to her and to her co-star, Leonide Massine, after the performance.

Despite his extreme fatigue Sassoon had been thrilled by Massine's virtuoso dancing, which merged in his mind with his talks to Churchill and Greaves about the War. The result, a poem he was to complete the following month, shows that his thoughts were still with his men, as he contrasts the stage death of Massine with the many real deaths he had witnessed:

> *To Leonide Massine in 'Cleopatra'*
> O beauty doomed and perfect for an hour,
> Leaping along the verge of death and night,
> You show me dauntless Youth that went to fight
> Four long years past, discovering pride and power.

You die but in our dreams, who watch you fall
Knowing that tomorrow you will dance again.
But not to ebbing music were they slain
Who sleep in ruined graves, beyond recall;
Who, following phantom-glory, friend and foe,
Into the darkness that was War must go;
Blind; banished from desire. O mortal heart
Be still; you have drained the cup; you have played your part.

(CP, pp. 104-5)

The last two lines of this piece, an echo of his earlier, unpublished poem 'Testament', suggest that Sassoon's struggle was not yet over. He himself described his state after seeing Massine as 'overwrought'. The sensible thing would have been to go straight back to bed at Raymond Buildings, but he knew that it was his last chance to see Ross before returning to Scotland, since Ross was about to leave England for several months as consultant to the Melbourne Art Gallery. So, despite a severe headache and an overdose of socializing, he set off for Half Moon Street, hoping for a last quiet talk with Ross.

Sassoon found Ross alone, as he had said he would be, but looking worried and exhausted. The strains of the Billing trial, together with the preparations for his Australian trip, had taxed his already poor health. He had also exerted himself more than was wise to make Sassoon's London visit a success. They both needed a restful evening, but were not to get it. Shortly after Sassoon's arrival Scott Moncrieff came in with a young, and to Sassoon unknown, friend, Noel Coward. Both men irritated him and not just because they were depriving him of a quiet farewell talk with Ross. He had not forgotten Scott Moncrieff's hostile review of *The Old Huntsman* and, in spite of his efforts to get with one of Robbie's closest friends, he was antagonized by him personally. There may also have been an element of jealousy over Moncrieff's growing intimacy with Owen. Nor did he respond to Coward, still a very young and unknown 'boy actor', as he rather whimsically announced himself to be. Normally delighted by praise of his work and by requests to sign his books, Sassoon found Coward 'gushing' and suspected that even the tolerant Ross thought him too effusive. After an hour, with his headache worse than ever, Sassoon left abruptly. Ross, fortunately, followed him down the stairs and they were at least able to say goodbye in peace. Though neither knew it, it was to be their last meeting. Sassoon later read into the long look that Ross gave him as he held his hand on the doorstep a 'presentiment of final farewell'.[38]

There was no time to see Ross on Sassoon's last day in London, which was the busiest of all. The morning was spent talking to Heinemann, then Rivers, and lunch, at the Eiffel Tower in Soho, was with Ottoline. Her ostensible reason for arranging the lunch was to introduce Sassoon to Desmond MacCarthy, yet another member of the Bloomsbury Group, but she was also desperate to see him before he returned to Lennel. Though she had been very hurt by another of his tactless remarks – that her artificial manner made it impossible for him to talk to her – and in spite of the fact that he had turned down her generous offer of some farm work and a cottage at Garsington, she was still too fond of him for her own peace of mind. For his part Sassoon was far more interested in Toronto Prewett, who had arrived in London with Lady Waring and who dined with him, Marsh and 'Clemmie' at the Carlton that evening. Appropriately, they went on to see *The Man from Toronto* and their meeting with the actress Iris Hoey afterwards was the last social occasion in another exhausting day. Ironically, it was the only day of Sassoon's visit not to include Ross in it, yet it was to be his last day alive.

By the time Sassoon arrived back at Lennel on the evening of 5 October, Ross was dead. But Sassoon was not to hear of his death for another two days and on 6 October, assuming him to be still alive, he wrote him a letter which ended: 'You are the dearest thing ever invented, Robbie.'[39] It may have been the arrival of this letter at Half Moon Street which prompted the distraught Nellie Burton to telegram Sassoon the sad news. Nellie Burton had discovered him when she went to wake him from an afternoon nap. Ross had suffered from chronic bronchitis and gastritis, as well as severe asthma, and the doctor's diagnosis had been heart failure, a diagnosis Sassoon found ironic: 'This was the only occasion on which his heart failed him,' he was to write, 'either in personal courage or in generosity towards his friends.'[40]

Graves, whose soldier brother-in-law, Tony Nicholson, had died the same day, felt equally shocked and deprived: '... there'll never be another Robbie, cynical, kind-hearted, witty champion of lost causes, feeder of the fatherless and widowed and oppressed – I feel his loss more than people could suppose'.[41] Like most of Ross's friends he had been worried about his precarious health, but his sudden death at forty-nine was a great shock.

Ross's defiant stand for homosexuality had made him many grateful friends, particularly among the young, and it was not only Sassoon and Graves who missed him. Wilfred Owen, for instance, told his mother that he found Ross's death 'more affecting ... almost' than many of the deaths he had witnessed at first hand in France.[42] Yet when Sassoon came to pay public tribute to Ross he felt constrained by the punitive laws governing homosexual practices at that time and was unable to mention what many considered Ross's greatest achievement, his championship of homosexuals, Oscar Wilde in particular. This may explain the curious woodenness of his 'Elegy (to Robbie Ross)', the last poem he wrote at Lennel. Its stilted, rather formal phrases were no doubt literally true of Ross but they fail to convey the spontaneous delight Sassoon had felt in his company:

> Your dextrous wit will haunt us long
> Wounding our grief with yesterday.
> Your laughter is a broken song;
> And death has found you, kind and gay...

But loyal love has deathless wings
That rise and triumph out of night.

So, in the days to come, your name
Shall be as music that ascends
When honour turns a heart from shame ...
O heart of hearts! ... O friend of friends.   (*CP*, p. 107)

Ross's death upset Sassoon greatly and blighted his last ten days at Lennel. His only consolation was Prewett, who helped him through the days following Burton's telegram. He was becoming increasingly fond of the young Canadian and had already arranged to see him at Oxford in November. (Prewett was to start at Christ Church in October.) Apart from Prewett and Lady Waring, however, there was no one he would really miss at Lennel. When a Medical Board at Edinburgh cleared him on 17 October, therefore, he was not sorry to leave. Stopping only to visit a friend at Portobello, on the outskirts of Edinburgh, he travelled directly south to spend his four weeks' leave among family and older friends. In his final letter to Ross he had said that he was accepting Arnold Bennett's 'offer', almost certainly a job at the Ministry of Information, but that he wanted to discuss it with Ross first. In Ross's absence he seems to have determined against the job after all. He also decided against spending a night in London as originally planned, but carried straight on to Weirleigh.

*

One of Sassoon's strongest temptations to give in to a 'Blighty' had been the thought of home, of his mother coming in with roses from the garden, of his dog Topper, his book-lined study and his piano. Once back there he seems to have sunk into a state of recuperative vegetation which lasted two and a half weeks. By mid-October the Peace negotiations were coming to a head, a cause for reflection on his own future as he idled through his time there. He wrote little or no poetry, though 'Memorial Tablet', with its references to 'sermon-time' and 'Squire in his pew' is likely to have been inspired by a visit to the local church with his mother. His mother's militarism, which he compared to that of Churchill, made it very difficult for him to get on with her, he told Marsh, but she was still the most unselfish person he knew and he still needed her. His reference to Ottoline as a 'jolly good sort' in his Dent letter suggests that he needed her too and that he was keeping up with his correspondence, but there is no evidence of any other activity. He was simply recharging his batteries, knowing that his strenuous social life was about to begin again. For Marsh, not content with introducing him to Winston Churchill, was now arranging for him to meet someone who was to become equally famous, T.E. Lawrence.

So, in spite of his statement to Dent on 28 October that he 'could not bear the idea of London', Sassoon was there again a week later for dinner with the distinguished Hejaz campaigner, who had specifically asked to meet him. One of the results of *Counter-Attack*'s success was that Sassoon himself was considered worth knowing. Fortunately, his natural modesty had prevented him from becoming blasé about his fame and he was flattered to be asked to meet Marsh's friend, little suspecting how famous he was soon to become.

For the young Colonel, who had only just arrived back in London from the Middle East, was not yet a legend there, though he had already caused a stir the previous week by refusing to be invested with the C.B. and D.S.O. at Buckingham Palace. Partly for security reasons, the fighting in the Middle East had received far less attention than that in France and it was not until the War was over that Lawrence's exploits there would be publicized and attract massive media attention.

As it was, Sassoon knew very little of Lawrence's extraordinary story, though he was better informed than most about the situation in the Middle East and must have heard something of his daring raids on the Turks. When Marsh introduced them over dinner at the Savoy, his first impression of the 'Hejaz Colonel' was of a reticent, rather scholarly man, quite different from the conventional military type he had expected. Lawrence was also smaller and more youthful than his rank had suggested. Unwilling to be drawn out about his military exploits, he was very ready to discuss Arabia in another context, that of Charles Doughty. Sassoon, whose youthful worship of Doughty had led him to read some of his more obscure work, was impressed by Lawrence's own knowledge of Doughty's epic poems, as well as the fact that Lawrence had not only corresponded with Doughty, like Sassoon, but also knew him personally. From Doughty they proceeded to another elaborate stylist, Henry James, whom Marsh imitated with great success. (It was one of his party tricks.)

Sassoon pleased Lawrence at this first meeting by exclaiming rather naively that he could not understand how Lawrence came to be a Colonel, but it became quite clear from his discussion of the Peace settlement which followed that he was very experienced and able. The impression Lawrence left on Sassoon at this first meeting was of a pleasant, unassuming person. 'Had I been told that I was meeting one of the most extraordinary beings I should ever know and idolize,' he was to write, 'I should have refused to believe it. He was, I briefly informed my diary, "the Hejaz general, a little Oxford archeologist, who admires Doughty and called him 'a Viking'".'[43] Yet only a few months later society would be agog about Lawrence and his romantic military exploits and Sassoon would find himself buttonholed by eager hostesses who hoped he might bring 'his friend, Colonel Lawrence' to lunch with them.

Sassoon and Lawrence had a number of things in common. Apart from a love of Doughty and the Middle East, they shared a deep nostalgia for the past which had led both of them to devote their first year at university mainly to William Morris's medieval romances. Like Morris they both loved fine printing and both collected rare books. In each the aesthete was combined rather unusually with the man of action. Both had entered the War at its outset and had gained a reputation for great physical courage, resulting in an M.C. for Sassoon and a D.S.O. for Lawrence. Sassoon was thirty-two and Lawrence thirty when they met, yet neither was married nor seemed likely to be. Sassoon's admiration for Lawrence's prose when he started to write would be matched by Lawrence's appreciation of his poetry. Unable to write poetry himself, Lawrence had an enormous respect for those who could, which explained his wish to meet Sassoon in the first place.

It is therefore odd, as Sassoon noted in retrospect, that at their initial meeting they did not discuss a poet they both admired, Hardy, especially since Sassoon was about to pay his first visit to the great man. Sassoon's decision to visit Hardy had been one result of his final acceptance that his active part in the War was at an end. Even if fighting continued beyond the expiry of his leave, which seemed unlikely, he was now convinced that he would never be sent back to France. His delay in paying a visit which Hardy himself had suggested, and which his disciple longed for, had stemmed mainly from an uncertainty about his future. The War had made him admire Hardy more than any other living writer and now that it was coming to an end, he longed to worship in person.

Marsh had arranged for Sassoon to pay a second visit to Churchill before catching his train to Dorset. Added to the thrill of meeting Hardy for the first time and Lawrence the previous evening, it was all too much and Sassoon slept badly. His 'queer dream' (no pun intended) with 'a bit of Toronto in it'[44] suggests that he was also disturbed by the thought of seeing Prewett, whom he had arranged to visit after Hardy. He seems to have found Prewett physically more disturbing than previous loves, perhaps because the tight hold he had kept on his sexual urges during his time with attractive young soldiers was beginning to relax as the War at last appeared to be ending.

Churchill was full of 'victory talk' when Sassoon met him for a few minutes on the morning of 6 November. Though still impressed, Sassoon could not help thinking that he sounded slightly 'inhuman ... like a leading article'.[45] He suspected that England intended to increase its power enormously in the coming Peace and was proposing to 'skin Germany alive'.[46] It was, therefore, something of a relief to leave Churchill and make his way to Waterloo for the 12.30 train to Dorchester. He carried with him a message from Marsh, with whom he had stayed the night, – the offer of the next dedication of *Georgian Poetry* and a request for a poem by Hardy in his Little Book.[47]

It was dark when the horse cab lumbered up to the porch of Max Gate, and Sassoon had only a vague impression of a small house set among trees. Thomas and Florence Hardy seemed diminutive and Sassoon felt horribly large and hearty. Naturally shy himself, Sassoon realized that the Hardys were equally so to begin with, making Thomas's voice sound worn and slightly discordant. As he became more confident, so it became firmer and less strained, even vibrant at times. His appearance underwent a similar transformation in Sassoon's eyes, from that of extreme frailty (he was seventy-eight at this time and had never seemed physically robust) to unusual agility for a man of his age. In strong light he looked all of his years, 'a dear and delightful old country gentleman', with his bald head, beaky nose and drooping grey moustache, but in shadow he seemed to Sassoon quite ageless:

> ... the wisdom of the ages in human form. For that time-trenched face ... was genius made visible, superhuman in its mystery and magnificence. This was the face of the life-seer who had transmuted the Wessex country into a cosmogony of his imagination, who had humanized it and revealed its unrecorded meanings and showings with patient power and mastery of half-tones and subdued colours ...[48]

The legend, it seemed, could co-exist with everyday reality, as Sassoon noted:

> *At Max Gate*
> Old Mr Hardy, upright in his chair,
> Courteous to visiting acquaintance chatted
> With unaloof alertness while he patted
> The sheep dog whose society he preferred.
> He wore an air of never having heard
> That there was much that needed putting right.
> Hardy, the Wessex wizard wasn't there.
> Good care was taken to keep him out of sight.
>
> Head propped on hand, he sat with me alone,
> Silent, the log fire flickering on his face.
> Here was the seer whose words the world had known.
> Someone had taken Mr Hardy's place.   (*CP*, p. 263)

After Hardy had realized that Sassoon was not the 'huge swell' his Philpot portrait had suggested, he too began to relax. During Sassoon's stay they talked mainly of poets and poetry, of Shakespeare, Shelley, Keats and Browning, but not in a self-consciously intellectual way. 'What I was offered at Max Gate,' Sassoon wrote, 'was homeliness.'[49]

Sassoon gained Hardy's confidence by not trying to seem clever and by his genuine interest in everyday humanity. And Hardy taught him 'the simplicity of true greatness'.[50] He had no children of his own and found Sassoon 'a wonderful pleasure and delight', telling Masefield that he 'loved [him] like a son'.[51] His signed photograph to the younger man was the first of a number of gifts. They went for walks together during Sassoon's two days, both of which continued bright and frosty. He had been grateful for Hardy's vivid evocation of the English countryside while he was in France and found it an unforgettable experience seeing some of it with him. As he commented afterwards, Hardy was 'the nearest thing to Shakespeare' he would 'ever go for a walk with'.[52] He found Hardy's outlook on that occasion both humorous and charmingly gay, contrary to the pessimism and bitterness of some of his writing.

One of the most pessimistic of Hardy's novels is *Jude the Obscure*, set partly in a thinly-disguised Oxford, and Sassoon may well have had it in mind as he left Dorset on 8 November to visit Prewett there, combining it with a stay at nearby Garsington. His introduction of Prewett to Ottoline may have been an attempt to divert her too-ardent attentions from himself. This visit certainly marked the end of her romantic feelings for Sassoon. As she told Virginia Woolf a week after he left, she had found him 'terribly, terribly *spoilt*. I *never* want to see him again – so coarse, so ordinary, so just like any other conceited young guardsman – I felt he had been seeing *odious* people, who had changed him *completely*.'[53] Even allowing for both Ottoline's and Virginia's tendency to exaggerate, Sassoon must have said or done something to provoke such a bitter response.

Yet Ottoline had put herself out to please Sassoon. She had arranged for him to have lunch with John Masefield, who in turn planned to introduce him to the Poet Laureate, Robert Bridges. So on 9 November he set off on a borrowed bicycle for Masefield's house at Boar's Hill, to the south-west of Oxford. It was a longer journey than he had anticipated from Garsington and, by the time he arrived breathless and apologetic, the Masefields had finished lunch. Masefield handled the potentially embarrassing situation well, personally bringing Sassoon the food which had been kept hot for him and chatting to him while he ate it. His warm welcome, together with his calm and unassuming manner, put his guest quickly at his ease.

It was a relief to find that he showed no resentment at all of Sassoon's parody of him in *The Daffodil Murderer*. Sassoon had always insisted that he genuinely admired Masefield's work in spite of parodying it and he still did so. Masefield's feelings about Sassoon's work were expressed in the presentation inscription he wrote in a book he gave him that day: 'For Siegfried, with deepest admiration from John Masefield. Nov 9 1918.' They got on well and Sassoon was to revisit the 'great, kind and simple' man a number of times. On this occasion they visited the Poet Laureate together in the afternoon.

Sassoon had looked forward to this greatly. Bridges's *Spirit of Man* anthology had been of real comfort to him at the Front and he thought the poet himself an 'exquisite writer of verse', who had never been surpassed 'in perfection of form and language'.[54] Together with Hardy, he believed Bridges to be one of the two great poets alive and was proud to know that Bridges had told Gosse in June 1917 that Sassoon had 'more of the real stuff' in him than almost any other poet of his generation.[55] So when he was introduced to the venerable septuagenarian with his magnificent bard-like head and fine patrician features, he quite understandably assumed that Bridges had agreed to the meeting and would be welcoming, if not warm. It was, therefore, a shock when Bridges, in response to Masefield's introduction, simply glared at him. Only after asking Masefield whether it was true that the German Emperor had resigned did he register Sassoon's existence, with one of the most surprising remarks Sassoon had ever experienced: 'What did you say his name was – Siegfried Digweed?'

Bridges was a staunch Conservative who hated Socialism and his first topic of conversation had been, not literature, but 'those Socialists'. It seemed to Sassoon more than likely that his remarks were aimed at himself as a 'reprehensible supporter of Socialist opinion' and that Bridges had awaited his arrival with the deliberate intention of 'taking me down a few pegs'.[56] Viewed in the light of subsequent, far pleasanter experiences of him, Sassoon could also see that it was entirely characteristic of Bridges to hector him in the way he did. The older poet had admired the technique of his war poetry, but could hardly be expected to approve its content. Proud and self-conscious, he was not known for his tolerance. Sassoon came to understand one friend's description of Bridges as 'gloriously grumpy' and to believe that his 'nobility of mind atoned for his inurbanities of behaviour'.[57] In fact, the 'Digweed' episode was to be the only occasion when he would see Bridges in a bad humour. He later blamed his younger self for not understanding that it came about partly because Bridges had been depressed by the four long years of war and the fact that his lovely house, Chilswell, had recently been burnt down.

It had been an emotionally draining day, but there was more to come. With her insatiable appetite for company Ottoline had invited Francis Meynell, a poet, publisher and book designer, his wife, the pianist Hilda Saxe, and Aldous Huxley, at that time an assistant-master at Eton. Sassoon noted that Francis Meynell, the son of Wilfred and Alice Meynell, talked Labour politics, and his wife played Beethoven, Brahms and Moussorgsky, but says nothing of Huxley's contribution. To someone as insecure as Sassoon, Huxley's famous family connections and his socially impeccable education at Eton and Balliol were probably off-putting and Huxley seems to have been equally unresponsive. They must later have reached some kind of accord, since Sassoon was to ask Huxley to write for him when he became a literary editor in 1919.

For the time being relations between the two were noticeably cool. There was one subject, however, which must have united even Sassoon and Huxley that evening, the abdication of the Kaiser, which Meynell announced. The peace process had been going on in earnest since the end of September, when the German General Ludendorff had urged Field-Marshal Hindenburg on the 28th (the day Passchendaele was recaptured by the British) to seek an immediate armistice, and Bulgaria had been forced to accept defeat by the Allies on the 30th. When Allenby finally took Damascus and the British prepared to break through the Hindenburg Line on 1 October, Ludendorff begged the Kaiser in person to issue a German peace offer immediately. Political unrest in Germany was adding to her problems and by 4 October her Chancellor, Prince Max, finally telegraphed Washington requesting an armistice. He made it clear, however, that this was not a surrender, only an attempt to end the War without pre-conditions, and President Wilson rejected his advance. A first condition of any armistice, he insisted, must be the evacuation of all occupied territories. The start of the second Battle of Cambrai on 8 October and the final breakthrough of the Hindenburg Line on the 9th forced Germany to accept Wilson's terms and on the 11th they began to withdraw from France and Belgium, though the fighting continued.

In England Lloyd George was still afraid that, if the Allies made peace too soon, Germany would have time to recover, and an even more militant faction wanted complete defeat. Nevertheless, another important move towards peace occurred on 19 October when all German U-boats were ordered to return to their bases, bringing a virtual end to submarine warfare. By 22 October, however, the German Chancellor was not yet ready to accept what he called 'a peace of violence', but the following day was ordered to prepare realistic armistice terms by Wilson. And on the 24th Ludendorff and Hindenburg were still unwilling to acquiesce in what was now clearly a *fait accompli*. Their 'fight to the finish' telegram to all Army Group commanders alarmed the German Government, which threatened to resign, and Ludendorff was forced to do so instead. By 25 October the Turks had been routed from their northernmost stronghold, Aleppo, and the following day began their own armistice talks with the Allies.

A day later Germany's last great ally, Austria, resolved to seek a separate peace and German sailors mutinied. It was quite clear that Germany was now on her own. But fighting on the Western Front continued, even after war on the Middle Eastern and Italian Fronts had ceased and even after the Allies had agreed on 3 November to a formal German request for an armistice. Ironically, Wilfred Owen, who believed that the Allies had deliberately 'thwarted' earlier peace efforts,[58] died the day after this formal request was made and many more were to die needlessly in the week of negotiations that followed. For in spite of General Groener's warning to the Kaiser that the Armistice must be signed by 9 November at the latest, delegates did not arrive at the Armistice meeting in the Forest of Compiègne until the 7th. The Kaiser himself was still refusing to abdicate and it was not until the 9th that he finally accepted the inevitable. News of his abdication that evening at Ottoline's would have made it quite clear to Sassoon that the Armistice was imminent. The next day the German Government formally accepted the Allies' stringent terms, though the legal documents were not signed until 5.10 a.m. on the morning of the 11 November. The Armistice itself was set for 11 a.m. that day, the eleventh day of the eleventh month.

Sassoon was in no mood for rejoicing. His close contact with Marsh during October and early November and his two meetings with Churchill had made him aware that this time the peace talks were in earnest and his most likely response would have been that of Owen, resentment that Germany's earlier tentative offers had not been taken seriously at the time. This had been the main reason for his public protest in 1917 and he had not changed his position. Though still ignorant of Owen's death on 4 November, he could not forget how many people, some of them dear friends, had died in the War and was sickened by the thought that it had been carried on a moment longer than seemed to him necessary. Safe himself, he had anxiously followed his surviving friends in the 1st, 2nd and 25th Battalions of the RWF through the last months of the fighting, as they took part in some of the fiercest battles on the Western and Italian Fronts.

So instead of going up to London to join in the euphoric Armistice Day celebrations on 11 November, or even going into Oxford to mark the occasion, Sassoon stayed quietly in the country. When a peal of church bells from Garsington village signalled that the actual moment of peace had arrived, he was walking alone in the water-meadows of the river Thame below Cuddesdon. For him the War had ended not with a bang but a whimper. There had been no easy, jingoistic assurances to keep him going and even now, when he found himself on the winning side, he experienced no sense of patriotic triumph, only a desire for 'Reconciliation':

> When you are standing at your hero's grave,
> Or near some homeless village where he died,
> Remember, through your heart's rekindling pride,
> The German soldiers who were loyal and brave.
>
> Men fought like brutes; and hideous things were done;
> And you have nourished hatred, harsh and blind.
> But in that Golgotha perhaps you'll find
> The mothers of the men who killed your son.   (*CP*, p. 99)

Later in the day, unable to resist the temptation to see exactly how the capital was celebrating, Sassoon caught a train to London. There, in the congested streets and undergrounds, he found masses of people, many of them drunk, waving flags and generally, as he thought, making fools of themselves. A display of mob patriotism which disgusted him far more than the foulest of trenches, it seemed to him 'a loathsome ending to the loathsome tragedy of the last four years'.[59]

18

'Pilgrimages to Poets, Post-Armistice Parties and Other Diversions'

November-December 1918

Siegfried Sassoon lay in the arms of a young soldier in a Margate hotel on 20 November 1918, only nine days after the end of a war which had left him with a deepened consciousness of peacetime values and enjoyments, together with a new determination to 'get the best out of life'.[1] While his years in the army had given a certain legitimacy to his love of men, his responsibilities as an officer had prevented him from expressing this in any but the most altruistic way. Once freed of such restraints, however, he had rushed headlong into a relationship which would have been unthinkable to him before the war. He was now experiencing for the first time a physical and emotional fulfilment beyond any previous imaginings. All his early romantic impulses, which had seemed out of place during the War, came flooding back as the young man left him, in the dark with his thoughts:

> ... I am alone: but in the windless night
> I listen to the gurgling rain that veils
> The gloom with peace: and whispering of your white
> Limbs, and your mouth that stormed my throat with bliss,
> The rain becomes your voice, and tells me tales
> That crowd my heart with memories of your kiss. ...[2]

When 'Lovers' was eventually published in *Collected Poems*, this middle stanza with its explicit physical details was omitted, and to many people, even close friends, this aspect of Sassoon's life was unknown. The more familiar image of him remained that of 'Mad Jack', the daring soldier, or the shy, impetuous poet. Only three days before 'Lovers' was written, for example, he had been sitting modestly at the feet of Walter de la Mare, full of reverence for de la Mare's poetic genius, the 'crowding enchantments of his word magic'.[3]

Sassoon's commitment to poetry had been essentially unchanged by the War, but there was yet another side to him which had been affected by it as strongly as his sexual mores. His contact in the army with working-class men, already encouraged by Carpenter in the years preceding 1914, had made him far more socially and politically aware than in his privileged youth. And his return to post-war London increased this consciousness, making him realize that it was the working classes that were bearing the brunt of the immense cost of the fighting, especially in the labour market. Jobs were scarce and wages low, the purchasing power of money being roughly one-third of what it had been in 1914. Though modest pensions and benefits were paid to war widows and war veterans, there was still a great deal of individual hardship. This was already visible in the capital, where disabled ex-servicemen begged in the streets alongside the triumphant crowds. Sassoon's friendship with the psychiatrist Dr Rivers strengthened his growing political awareness.[4] Though he had turned down the Hampstead Labour Party's invitation to become its parliamentary candidate in September 1918, less than two days after the Armistice he was consulting Rivers about a possible future in politics.

There were, then, at least three very different sides to Sassoon at the end of 1918. And his 'reality' seemed, even to himself, 'a mere transitory and fleeting illusion', taking one form one day and another the next according to the prevailing conditions.[5]

*

Though Ross himself was no longer alive by November 1918, Sassoon's first visit on his return to London was to one of Ross's close friends, Richmond Temple, and his second to Ross's constant companion, Meiklejohn.

Sassoon's choice of Temple for his first London contact was deliberate. Since Temple, like Ross, was an ardent admirer of his anti-war poetry, he could be relied on to share Sassoon's disgust at what he dismissed as 'the orgy of patriotic demonstrations' which met him on his arrival in the capital late on Armistice Day.[6] Temple, who was seven years younger than Sassoon's thirty-two and had served in the Air Force, seemed to the poet an 'odd character'.[7] Though he was to move in very different circles from him after the War, as director first of the Savoy and Berkeley hotels, later the Dorchester, like Ross he was anxious to help, presenting Sassoon with a new car in 1924 to encourage him to get out of London, for instance, or lending him money in emergencies. On this occasion he welcomed Sassoon to his Mayfair flat and insisted on taking him to an Armistice dinner, though of a kind calculated to annoy him with its triumphalism. By the end of an evening which both agreed had been an utter 'wash-out', Sassoon felt more than ever convinced that the War had been a 'loathsome tragedy'.[8] Flag-waving, especially by civilians, seemed to him completely out of place, as 'The Patriot' written the next day shows:

> He waved his flag when War began;
> A staunch and thriving English man.
> And now, when fighting's finished,
> He buys the Union Jack again
> And demonstrates with might and main,
> His ardour undiminished ...[9]

Dr Rivers, with whom Sassoon and Temple dined the next day, struck Sassoon as an 'ideal moderator of victorious agitations'.[10] His studies in anthropology and psychiatry had prepared him for a wide range of human behaviour and he was neither shocked nor surprised by the frenzied celebrations. Nor, unlike Sassoon, was he critical. But he was unable to share the crowd's enthusiasm, having been influenced by Sassoon's own criticisms of the War at the very moment he was persuading him to return to the fighting.

It was not that Sassoon felt less affectionate towards his older friends. The day after his dinner with Rivers, he hurried to Hanover Terrace to renew contact with the earliest of his patrons, Gosse. Though now less in awe of that arbiter of public taste and establishment figure and decidedly critical of Gosse's unquestioning acceptance of the War, he was still very grateful to his Uncle Hamo's old friend. He found Gosse, though over seventy and in bed with bronchitis, as charming and witty as ever and was particularly amused by his suggestion that his young friend should write a long poem about rural life.

(This was shrewder than Sassoon realized at the time and would form the germ of one of his most successful books, *Memoirs of a Fox-Hunting Man*.)

He was beginning to find his other early patron, Marsh, less sympathetic, while continuing to admire Marsh's generous support and encouragement of young painters and writers. But his experiences at the Front had made Marsh's lifestyle seem essentially frivolous.[11] Nevertheless, it was to Marsh's flat at Gray's Inn that he lugged his suitcase next on 12 November. (The lease on his own flat in the same building had lapsed in 1917.) Armistice celebrations raged on and he longed for a quiet evening with Eddy. But Marsh was rarely without company and Sassoon found himself instead listening to an interminable reading by John Drinkwater of his latest poems.[12]

He met a number of other Georgian poets during this stay at Marsh's, being taken to dine on 13 November with W.J. Turner[13] and on the 14th with Wilfrid Gibson.[14] Then on the 23rd, during his pilgrimage to de la Mare, he met Gibson again and was introduced to John Freeman.[15] Both Gibson and Freeman he dismissed as worthy but dull. Turner, who struck him as having real imagination, he wanted to know better. But it was de la Mare who, as he himself might have put it, cast a spell on him: 'De la Mare is the most wonderful and interesting and sympathetic and mystery-haunted manuscript he has ever written. He is a human being to whom I respond with the utmost enthusiasm. I am bubbling over with excitement when I am with him ... His mind is an enchanted landscape lit by unearthly gleams and fiery auguries.'[16]

Sassoon's visits to the homes of celebrated authors in November 1918 included one different in almost every way from his trek to Anerley, and reflected his increased status in post-war England. On 3 November he had received an invitation from a leading novelist of the day, John Galsworthy, then still engaged on his *Forsyte Saga*.[17] If de la Mare epitomized the other-worldly, Galsworthy stood for the worldly, or at least worldly success. When Sassoon did finally dine with Galsworthy and his 'super-excellent' wife Ada on 15 November, it was to affluent Hampstead not the depths of south London he went. The house itself, Grove Lodge, was very beautiful and very old, unlike de la Mare's modest dwelling, and everything about it emanated signs of success, from the dark polished dining table to the vintage '87 port.[18]

Galsworthy had invited Sassoon to dinner primarily to discuss a contribution to his magazine, *Reveille*, and in that respect the evening was a complete success.[19] Sassoon had, in fact, spent the whole day promoting his work, having lunch with his publisher, Heinemann, to discuss his next volume and visiting the editor of the *Nation*, H.W. Massingham, to offer him two poems.[20] He had returned from France in July 1918 determined to pursue his ambitions as a poet. The problem was that, with the passing of the War, he was left without a subject, as he had been before its start. His horror at the carnage had resulted in some highly successful poetry, but with the arrival of peace he could no longer mine that rich vein. It was a dilemma that contributed significantly to his restlessness in the immediate post-war years.

*

Like the majority of those who have left home – and it took him far longer than most to do so – Sassoon felt comfortable neither at home nor away from it at the start. When he finally visited his mother on 18 November, he stayed only two nights. The rambling Victorian house had a neglected and melancholy feel to it. His mother, still mourning Hamo's death, was far from stimulating company.[21] She continued to disagree strongly with her middle son about the War and there were few safe subjects left for them to discuss, apart from gardening, food and the weather. Still technically his 'home', Weirleigh had lost its childhood power to enchant. Though he continued trying to recreate its pre-war charm, returning for six days at the beginning of December, for instance, and spending the whole of Christmas and New Year there, Sassoon was finally separating himself emotionally from his childhood.

He made several attempts, however, to re-establish his pre-war existence, where the outward pattern of his life had been shaped round various seasonal sports, cricket in summer, golf in early autumn, followed by hunting. Another, less strenuous, activity, though like hunting he could not afford it, was the ballet. His intense enjoyment of the Russian Ballet in 1914, interrupted by the outbreak of hostilities, was now renewed fervently, either with Marsh or his more recently acquired friend, Osbert Sitwell.

Sitwell moved in social circles as dazzling, if not more so, than Marsh's and there was some vying between them for Sassoon's attention. But Sitwell had stronger artistic aspirations than Marsh and gradually became of more interest to Sassoon. Their relationship was to be of some significance to Sassoon during the 1920s. So, too, would his friendship with Osbert's poet-sister, Edith Sitwell. Sassoon had met Edith briefly in October 1918 and Osbert now reintroduced him to her at his house in Swan Walk, Chelsea, which he shared with their younger brother 'Sachie'.

The pull of all these different worlds and his frantic rush from one to the other made Sassoon 'positively dizzy' to contemplate in later years.[22] His life became, in his own words, 'a rabble of disordered occurrences'.[23] While this seemed to him acceptable in all the circumstances, what troubled him about the 'kaleidoscopic young man' he looked back on was the 'remembered inconsistency' of his response to different people.[24] When he revisited friends in Cambridge, for example, especially Dent and Bartholomew, he was drawn into an explicitly homosexual circle which would have puzzled and shocked people like his mother or Gosse.

By 16 November 1918, the weekend Sassoon visited Cambridge, it is noticeable that Dent is being replaced by Bartholomew.[25] Slightly built, with delicate features, pale complexion and dark brown eyes and hair, 'Theo' was only four years older than Sassoon and much nearer to him in age than Dent. Strongly drawn to Sassoon, he was to become a close confidant for the next few years and to remain on good terms with him until his premature death in 1933. Beside Dent they had several friends in common, notably Carpenter and Forster. Theo would also introduce Sassoon to a writer whose friendship would mean a great deal to him in the 1920s, Henry ('Enrico') Festing-Jones, the former companion and literary executor of Samuel Butler.

Osbert witheringly dismissed Theo as 'one of the Cambridge kittens' because he 'could not agree with the placid and well-ordered life of that backwater, nor care for his rather prim and orderly rooms in Pythagoras House, where every book and picture was chosen with great thought and deliberation'.[26] But it was precisely this aesthetic approach to life which appealed to Sassoon, particularly Theo's great interest in book design. His experience at Cambridge University Library, where he had risen to the rank of Senior Under-Librarian by 1912, had already been useful to Sassoon in the production of several poetry pamphlets during the War and he would continue to supervise his private productions throughout the 1920s, together with his book-designer friend Bruce Rogers.[27]

An even stronger pull was their homosexuality. Theo, like Sassoon at this period, was deeply suspicious of women and moved in a largely male world. Both were drawn to younger men, with whom Cambridge was conveniently filled, and Theo would be responsible for introducing the poet to several attractive youths, with predictable results. In November 1918 he was about to introduce Sassoon to someone who would change his life irrevocably, making him even more conscious of his divided worlds, the young army officer, Gabriel Atkin.[28]

Sassoon had already heard of Atkin from Dent, who had befriended the nineteen-year-old cadet in March 1917 when he came to Cambridge from the Durham Light Infantry on an army training course. And Dent must have mentioned Sassoon to Atkin, who next wrote to Dent from his camp at Margate to tell him how much he wanted to meet a poet he so admired. But when Dent passed this on to Sassoon in November 1917, he had replied rather off-handedly: 'Gabriel Atkins [sic] sounds all right. I wish Margate were nearer.'[29] Sassoon's posting, first to Ireland, then Palestine in the first half of 1918, had intervened and it was not until October 1918 that the subject was reintroduced. By 30 October Atkin was writing to Dent: 'I am most excited by the possibility of meeting Siegfried Sassoon. I think of him as most attractively Byronic in appearance.'[30] Clearly in awe of Sassoon, he feels it might be 'presumptuous' of him to write or send a photograph as Dent suggests, but does hope for a few lines from the famous poet.[31] So that he is thrilled to receive a 'hectic' postcard from Sassoon on Armistice Day, though 'devastated' that it is to defer their meeting. The matchmaking is then taken up by Theo, who has himself been in and out of bed with Atkin for the past year, and it is during Sassoon's stay with Theo in mid-November that another meeting with Atkin is arranged.[32]

When Sassoon finally met Atkin for the first time at Margate station on 20 November 1918, he knew something of his background. Born in 1897 in the South Shields area, William ('Gabriel') Atkin had grown up there and was completing his education at Durham Art College when army service intervened.[33] There was little mention of a father, but many references to his mother, whom he adored. There were also three sisters, a brother and various aunts, but Gabriel was more conscious of his 'Rector uncles' whose 'domination' he was determined to escape.[34] He was already heavily into drink and drugs by the time he left home for the army. The army did nothing to lessen his drinking and on Armistice Day, while Sassoon had been soberly eyeing the inebriated celebrators, Gabriel himself had been chief among them. Sassoon attributed Gabriel's drinking to bad heredity and would try to help him curb it, but he could do little about his exhibitionist love of extraordinary clothes. This was to cause the ultra-conservative Sassoon problems, especially Gabriel's choice of his great-grandfather's red velvet dinner jacket with light blue facings and gold buttons for a visit to the ballet. 'With such a face you can't afford to dress unconventionally, I assure you,' Sassoon wrote to him on 31 December 1918. 'The most I can allow will be a touch of the sportsman, and *that* is bad enough unless done with tact and sobriety.'

There was another side to Gabriel, however, which helps to explain their friends' anxiety to bring him and Sassoon together. He was not only a promising artist, which in itself would have interested Sassoon, but he was also an accomplished pianist.[35] Like Sassoon, he had yearned for a piano in the army and when he came across one, would play his favourite pieces from Puccini, Verdi and Chopin. Even more importantly Gabriel's interests included literature. (He claimed descent from the writer Leigh Hunt, whose work he presented to Sassoon.) He knew Sassoon's poetry well and the month they met was reading H.G. Wells, whom Sassoon also admired. He would complete a novel of his own, a memoir and at least two plays, though none would be published.

When Dent had first tried to interest Sassoon in 'the child "Gabriel"', he had described him as 'a pleasant and amusing lad, fearfully lonely at Margate', appealing in one stroke both to Sassoon's preference for much younger men and his protective instinct.[36] Theo found him 'very charming'.[37] They might also have added that Gabriel, despite his rackety lifestyle, was fairly thoughtful, sensitive and kind. Like Sassoon himself, his approach to life and art was instinctive rather than intellectual. But Gabriel's most important quality of all in relation to Sassoon was probably the one he identified himself, that he was 'very good at listening'.[38] This was a vital prerequisite for any close friend of Sassoon's, particularly in the immediate post-war years.

It is unlikely that Sassoon was thinking of Gabriel's character, however, as he made the slow journey by train from Paddock Wood to meet him on 20 November 1918. Whether he had already decided to embark on the first physical affair of his life, or was simply intending to befriend the lonely young soldier is impossible to say. Most probably his mind was in turmoil, for he could not have been unaware of Dent's and Theo's intentions when they insisted on him meeting the attractive and promiscuous Gabriel. He had also told Carpenter in August 1918 of his 'craving' for something Carpenter had 'advised' him to do.[39]

In the event Gabriel himself seems to have decided the issue. Nicknamed 'Gabriel' because of his angelic appearance, his golden hair and boyish good looks had an immediate effect on Sassoon – 'You are all red and white roses, you darling' – and his poems to Gabriel leave little doubt as to what followed. He certainly felt, as he wrote to Theo after the first meeting, that Gabriel was one of the 'divinest' things that had ever happened to him.[40] His letters to Gabriel are more explicit and more appreciative.

Even Gabriel, who changed sexual partners frequently, thought it was 'the most wonderful thing' that had ever happened to him. 'Siegfried is the most amazing gorgeous person in the universe,' he told Dent on 24 November.[41] And in case Dent had any doubts as to the precise nature of the relationship, he added in a later letter (using a traditional euphemism for sexual intercourse) that he had been 'in the country ... bound on the N, S, E and W by Siegfried Sassoon' and 'much too busy and breathlessly happy while on leave to write at all'.[42]

Their 'lyric time', as Theo discreetly phrased it, continued the week after their first meeting, when Sassoon returned to Margate on 26 November, ostensibly to attend a concert Gabriel was organizing.[43] Sassoon's first visit had made Gabriel suddenly ashamed of his dissolute lifestyle and he had pledged himself to sobriety, vowed to give up promiscuity and resolved to work seriously at his art. Sassoon, in his first ecstasy, and possibly in an attempt to rationalize his strong sexual arousal, had quoted reams of poetry by Walt Whitman, that great exponent of 'lad's-love'. This had had a powerful effect on the impressionable Gabriel, who reported to Dent: 'Walt Whitman swarms over my horizon and makes me feel a little worm.'[44] It is a proof of the strength of Sassoon's idealism that he could make Gabriel stop, however briefly, to consider Whitman's words.

Like many young people from the provinces, Gabriel 'adore[d] London with a wicked foolish and childish adoration'. He was, therefore, thrilled when Sassoon invited him to spend five days in the capital with him, though his main motive was to introduce Gabriel to his friends rather than to new vices. Anxious to impress his young lover, Sassoon had planned an exhausting schedule. In itself a reminder of how many contacts he had made in London during his wartime visits, it puts all his previous socializing into the shade.

In the five days from 16 to 20 December he lunched, had tea and dined out with Gabriel daily, attended numerous parties and took him to three new plays, several concerts and at least one art gallery. With the notable exceptions of Gosse and Rivers, who he suspected would not approve, Gabriel met all his close friends and many of his acquaintances. The sheer profusion of invitations the two received suggests that they all rejoiced in Sassoon's happiness, as well as being naturally concerned to meet the miracle-worker.

For this initial sortie into London society Sassoon had taken lodgings again with Nellie in Half Moon Street. He had already visited Ross's old room the previous month, when Nellie had shown him 'the last dreadful vile attack' on Ross by Lord Alfred Douglas.[45] And, though he knew it could make no difference now to Ross, it seemed to him 'so hideous and monstrous' that he had wept all the way back to Marsh's flat on the top of a bus. But this was a happier occasion and Nellie welcomed one of her favourite 'boys' back with her usual gusto.

It was becoming clear to him, however, that he would need his own base in the city. The visit to Weirleigh with Gabriel which immediately followed made him more sharply conscious of this. For Gabriel was not a success with Sassoon's mother, Theresa. Though both were artists, they had little in common. Where she was religious and strictly principled, Gabriel was lax; where she, like her son, was moderate, Gabriel was excessive. 'Mother always disliked and distrusted G[abriel],' Sassoon was to write later: 'She still talks about him as "that hopeless creature" ... His half-frivolous and wholly pleasure-loving temperament repelled her.'[46] Another attempt to analyse their differences helps to explain something of Gabriel's fascination for him: 'Gabriel represents green chartreuse and Epstein sculpture. Mother is G.F. Watts and holy communion. They can't be mixed.'[47] Part of Theresa's antagonism, no doubt, sprang from a suspicion that her 32-year-old son was more interested in young men than young women. Her great-niece remembered her dismissing Gabriel bitterly as 'another of Sieg's pretty boys'.[48]

*

While Theresa was trying to come to terms with her son's friend at the end of 1918, Sassoon was writing passionate love poetry to him. If, as he would argue, 'repressed sex' was behind his early romantic verse, sexual fulfilment seems equally to have inspired a burst of creativity.[49] 'I lived my poetry *physically* before I wrote it,' he claimed, 'and it was written when I was feeling physically rich.'[50]

He had composed little of significance since leaving France the previous July and his work as a whole had included almost no love poetry.[51] But now, as a critic in the *Cambridge Magazine*, E.B.C. ('Topsy') Jones, noted, he becomes 'a love-poet among other things'.[52] But as Topsy Jones warned, romantic poems are in more danger of cliché than angry war satires and Sassoon treads warily from the start. 'Parted', written while he waited impatiently for his second meeting with Gabriel, shows him trying to maintain what Jones called 'the extreme directness and first-handedness of his diction'. He has also learnt from his war poetry the value of presenting a 'situation', in this case a lover lying in bed alone, waiting for his 'love's release':

> Sleepless I listen to the surge and drone
> And drifting roar of the town's undertone;
> Till through quiet falling rain I hear the bells
> Tolling and chiming their brief tune that tells
> Day's midnight end. And from the day that's over
> No flashes of delight I can recover;

But only dreary winter streets, and faces
Of people moving in loud clanging places:
And I in my loneliness, longing for you ...   (*CP*, p. 114)[53]

Sassoon was to write a number of other poems about Gabriel as their relationship developed, but none more intriguing than the one which followed closely on 'Slumber-Song' in January 1919, 'To a Childless Woman'. This may have been sparked off by an actual encounter with such a woman, but its main interest is Sassoon's close identification with her plight. It is possible that his first real love affair had brought home to him for the first time the full implications of a homosexual relationship. However successful it turned out to be, it could never satisfy his yearning for children, a need which the birth of Graves's first child that month may have increased. And when, more than a decade later, he decided to marry, it would not be only the strain of concealing his homosexual relationships from a society which had branded them criminal, but also a longing for children which would dictate his extraordinary volte-face.

19

'A Simpleton's Progress'[1]

January-March 1919

Memories of the War would continue to dominate this period of Sassoon's life.[2] And though his passion for Gabriel blotted them out, it was for all too short a time. Only two months after their first meeting, there are signs of trouble in his Eden. 'I never asked you to be perfect – did I?' he writes in 'The Imperfect Lover' on 22 January 1919.[3] Yet the same poem strongly suggests that he misses the 'early-morning freshness' he had first found in Gabriel. He may deny having expected his beloved to be 'unsoiled, angelic and inhuman', but it is in religious terms that he describes their initial bliss:

Oh yes, I know the way to heaven was easy.
We found the little kingdom of our passion
That all can share who walk the road of lovers.
In wild and secret happiness we stumbled;
And gods and demons clamoured in our senses.

The reference to 'gods *and* demons' (my italics) is particularly revealing. 'Neither night nor day may I escape thee oh my heavenly hell', he had written to his 'little angel-devil', Gabriel, in his first ecstasy.[4] Now, having initially idealized their physical union, he rejects it as 'lov[ing] like beasts', their 'heaven' turned to 'hell'.[5] For fundamentally he remained a puritan and would never be comfortable with what he called 'the cursed nuisance of sex'.[6] He was already looking back on his sexual gratification with Gabriel only two months after first experiencing it as 'illusions/ That blossom from desire with desperate beauty'.[7] It was a pattern which would repeat itself many times in the 1920s: once his physical needs had been met, he would begin to analyse his feelings, usually with negative results. 'I've grown thoughtful now,' he warns Gabriel in his January 1919 poem and it is clear from the same work that Gabriel has 'learned to fear/ The gloomy stricken places' in his soul and the 'occasional ghosts' that haunt him. The last two phrases refer directly to Sassoon's experiences in the War and point to another complicating factor in his relationships in the 1920s. Gabriel had helped him to forget the horrors he had witnessed – 'all the old wounds in my heart are healed for ever', Sassoon had assured him on 1 December 1918 – but it would take a stronger personality than Gabriel's and a lot more years for him to emerge from what he called his 'devildoms'.[8] He was not, of course, alone in this. Many of those who fought in the First World War never fully recovered from its effects.

Paradoxically, then, though the War had liberated Sassoon from some of his inhibitions, it also prevented him from enjoying his new-found freedom for long. He had written, with ominous prescience, in January 1918: 'For death has made me wise and bitter and strong;/ *And I am rich in all that I have lost*' (my italics).[9] By January 1919 the living could still not compete with the memory of his dead friends. Dame Felicitas Corrigan, in her 'spiritual' biography of Sassoon,[10] dismisses his behaviour at this period as 'post-war deviations ... unlovely but negligible', a 'backlash' against the war.[11] To me it suggests an attempt, however doomed or misguided, to find meaning in an existence turned upside down by the War.

*

Even before the full extent of Gabriel's dissoluteness became apparent, Sassoon began to suffer doubts about him. He was still close to his mother and her disapproval of Gabriel had not been reassuring. He might think of her as old-fashioned and prejudiced, but he could not deny her essential intuitive wisdom. Rivers, who arrived at Weirleigh a week after Gabriel on 27 December 1918, had confirmed this view.[12] Theresa's reaction to Rivers was positive, making her disapproval of Gabriel all the more evident. She had a weakness for the medical profession and believed that the doctor had cured Siegfried of being 'a militant war-resister'.[13] Rivers, a man of wide knowledge, great perception and serious purpose, was in himself such a contrast to Gabriel that he might well have caused Sassoon to wonder what position his immature young friend could occupy in his life.

Of Rivers's place there was little doubt. Sassoon depended increasingly on the man he described to Gabriel as his 'father confessor'.[14] When, after hearing of his intention to join the Labour Movement, Rivers suggested that he should study political economy at either Oxford or Cambridge, he at once agreed. He was to write a poem about Rivers called 'To a Very Wise Man',[15] but had Rivers been wiser he would have steered his young disciple away from his choice of Oxford. Sassoon would claim in his autobiography that he chose Oxford for its nearness to his colourful friend and patron, Lady Ottoline Morrell. But to Ottoline herself he wrote that he had picked Oxford because two other close friends, Graves and Prewett, would be there. His explanation to Gabriel, who was worried that it might mean them seeing less of each other, was that living in London was 'very bad' for him since it involved 'rushing round seeing Society'.[16] 'And when you want to study anatomy,' he joked coyly with him, 'you can come and stay with me.'[17]

He had already made a modest start on his political career by agreeing to help the Labour Party in the December 1918 'Coupon' Election, so called because of the 'Coupon' (Asquith's contemptuous phrase), or letter of endorsement issued by Lloyd George and Bonar Law to sitting M.P.s who supported their Liberal-Conservative coalition. Max Plowman had asked if Sassoon would be willing to speak for another pacifist, the Labour M.P. for Blackburn, Philip Snowden. Playing on the public's patriotic fervour, Lloyd George's party had chosen what Sassoon succinctly called 'a Naval VC (Unionist)' to oppose Snowden and the Labour Party hoped that Sassoon's well-known war record together with his officer's uniform and M.C. ribbon might counteract this cynical ploy.

It was with some apprehension that Sassoon set out for the industrial north on 10 December.[18] His political views seemed to him a 'muddle' and, as he explained to Snowden in reply to his letter of thanks, he was completely inexperienced as a speaker.[19] A great deal, he felt, depended on whether he liked Snowden. Fortunately he did. The politician, while very serious in his aims, had a down-to-earth Yorkshire humour which would have appealed to Sassoon as much as it did to the large audiences he addressed. Sassoon already admired Snowden's anti-war stance in Parliament and his sustained efforts on behalf of private soldiers and their families; meeting him only confirmed his view that Snowden was a 'good' man.[20] He also liked and admired Snowden's wife and a third speaker, Isabella Blow.[21] A fifth member of the team, who went on to become one of the first women M.P.s when she won her Northampton seat in 1923 and the very first female Cabinet Minister, was Margaret Bondfield. The Snowdens were strong supporters of women's rights, for which Bondfield fought, and the three were close friends. Margaret Bondfield and Mrs Snowden would be responsible for Sassoon's election to the 1917 Club, which had been founded by a group of left-wing politicians in honour of the Russian Revolution. Drinking cocoa with the Blackburn team late at night after the day's exertions, Sassoon felt that they were like 'a happy family'.[22]

Snowden, who would eventually become Chancellor of the Exchequer in 1924 and 1929-31 and the first Socialist viscount, was on the right wing of the Labour Party. Described by one contemporary, Leonard Woolf, as 'very honest, unimaginative, conservative – fundamentally reactionary',[23] he probably appealed to the conservative Sassoon. And his lameness, which gave Woolf the impression that he was 'embittered by pain', certainly made the athletic younger man sympathetic.[24] He also understood Snowden's bitterness at being represented as 'unpatriotic'.[25] In spite of Snowden's twelve-year fight to improve working-class conditions in Blackburn, it came as no surprise to any of them when he failed to be returned on this fourth occasion. Even the politically naïve Sassoon could see that the sitting M.P. had fought a losing battle against 'a frenzied intolerance whose catchwords were "Hang the Kaiser" and "Make the Germans Pay". "Snowden, the Arch-Pacifist" was reviled as though he were a public enemy.'[26]

Yet Sassoon claimed that his own remarks against conscription had gone down well, in spite of the fact that the opposition had described him as 'a stage soldier who'd never been near the war but had been got down by the pacifists'.[27] (Fortunately no action had been taken about him appearing in uniform in such a context. Still technically in the army, he had already overstayed his leave by three weeks and did not want further problems.) Inflamed by his modest success, he saw this visit as 'the beginning of a new phase of my life – . I have made a strong appeal to these Blackburn people, but I must justify my words by deeds. A great vista has opened to me in the last few days, and I have escaped – for ever – those reactionary and self-indulgent influences to which I was bred and educated – I have offered myself to the people and they have accepted me – Will I live to be worthy of their trust? Who knows?'[28]

These brave, somewhat high-flown words were followed almost immediately by the London whirl with Gabriel already described, which would have shown the worthy people of Blackburn a very different side to Sassoon. Even after Gabriel's return to Margate, Sassoon was tempted into further socializing by Glyn Philpot, who insisted on taking him to a fancy-dress ball in the costume of a Tartar prince. The ball was given by a man who could have been specially chosen to represent a set of values and way of life completely at odds with Sassoon's Blackburn vision, Frank ('Frankie') Schuster. When Sassoon first met Schuster at Osbert's in November 1918, he had found him 'very pleasant and congenial', but had no idea that he would become a close friend, or that they would attend innumerable concerts together until Schuster's death in 1927. For Schuster, though no musician himself, was an important figure in the musical world, putting a great deal of his wealth and influence at the disposal of struggling composers and performers. His patronage of Elgar, for instance, had been a significant factor in the musician's success.

Nearly eighty when they first met, Schuster was still enjoying the good things of life with an apparent disregard for his age: a house in Old Queen Street, Westminster, in winter, with a flat in Brighton for weekends, a retreat at Bray-on-Thames for summer, a chauffeur-driven Rolls-Royce, a round of social events, and frequent trips abroad. Though unmarried, he was seldom alone and failed totally to understand Sassoon's or anyone else's need for solitude. With his bald, freckled head, his clumsy, almost malformed hands and feet, his Aberdeen terrier on a silver chain, he might have seemed a figure of fun, had it not been for his passion for music, which redeemed him in Sassoon's eyes.

Nevertheless Sassoon was at times highly critical of the man he once described as 'the Frankfurt Jew'.[29] Though his own father was Jewish, this was not intended as praise, the implication being that Schuster was vulgar. In fact he actually stated that Schuster lacked 'essential good breeding', a remark that underlines one of Sassoon's own gravest faults, his snobbishness.[30] He would also become critical of Schuster's 'carefulness' in money matters, while at the same time happy to accept Schuster's hospitality for weeks on end. Similarly, though accusing Schuster of being 'socially frothy', he was quite ready to join in with his plans if it suited him.[31] At this first party, however, there seemed to him something magical about Schuster's world, in which his host appeared as 'a sort of party-giving Prospero'.[32]

*

When Sassoon told Rivers how he had occupied his time after returning from Blackburn, he laughed heartily: 'You'll have to decide which party you really belong to!' was his dry comment.[33] He sensibly suggested that the less Sassoon was in London the less he would be tempted by its social life, and for at least a fortnight after Rivers's departure from Weirleigh on 29 December Sassoon remained soberly at home.

After that, however, Sassoon was off again, this time to Garsington. His relationship with Ottoline had passed through the awkward stage, when he had had to fend off her advances, and settled down into a solid friendship. He now regarded her as a generous and loyal friend and true patron of the arts. An invitation to visit her at her manor house near Oxford was always tempting, since she gathered round her a wide variety of interesting guests and on this occasion the company was particularly intriguing. Apart from Philip Morrell, there were Bertrand Russell, another philosopher, George Santayana, and Prewett, whom Sassoon himself had introduced to Garsington when Prewett enrolled at Christ Church.

Sassoon had written to Ottoline on 4 January 1919 asking her to find him a 'modest' flat in Oxford, a place where he could meet 'a few youngish people'.[34] His excuse for accepting her invitation to visit on the 15th was to inspect her choice. Though her idea of 'modest' turned out to be a fairly luxurious apartment in Merton Street, consisting of a sitting room and two bedrooms overlooking Christ Church meadows at a rent of almost half his income, he was unable to resist it.

It is a sign of Sassoon's inconsistency at this time that, having accepted an invitation to join an elaborate dinner party at Marsh's and having more or less apologized to him for his Blackburn activities, he immediately felt hostile towards what he scornfully called Eddie's 'titled blokes and blokesses'.[35] The evening papers had announced the murder of the leaders of the German Communist Party, Karl Liebknecht and Rosa Luxembourg, and since Liebknecht, like

Snowden, had been a pacifist member of his government, Sassoon identified with him and Luxembourg against Marsh and his guests. He stayed on to listen to Ivor Novello, who struck him as 'very charming in appearance, but really quite fifth-rate – a common little Jew snob with a pretty face and a facility for improvising taking tunes', unaware how much Novello would later make him suffer.[36] At the same time, however, he was haunted by the thought of Liebknecht and Luxembourg, 'those two anti-militarists riddled with bullets in a Berlin Hotel'.[37]

It would be interesting to know whether Sassoon confessed this particular bit of socializing to Rivers when he arrived to stay with him in Cambridge the next day. Rivers had just accepted a fellowship at his old college, St John's. During Sassoon's two-day stay he claimed to have met more Fellows of the Royal Society than in the whole of his previous existence, including an introduction to another Fellow, the composer Cyril Rootham, who would later set some of his works to music.[38]

Famous in his own right by now, Sassoon was persuaded on his second day at St John's to read some of his poems to a silent but seemingly appreciative circle of undergraduates. It is to be hoped that, as on many later occasions, his audience felt that simply meeting him and watching him read his own work was experience enough, since he was rarely audible.[39]

While Sassoon was at Cambridge he also kept his promise to Theo to 'fix up' his next production.[40] So on Monday, 19 January, after leaving Rivers, he took himself and his manuscript to Cockerell, whose experience he valued greatly.[41]

Back in London on 20 January, Sassoon had a brief meeting with his servant from his last battalion, the 25th Royal Welch Fusiliers. John Law had been a miner in South Wales before the army expanded his horizons. He was having problems settling back into civilian life and Sassoon wanted to help. Always generous with his money, he had sent Law at least one food parcel from Harrods after his return from France in July 1918 and was to come to his rescue financially a number of times in the 1920s.[42] It was men like Law who had first made Sassoon aware of the inequalities of the social system. Perhaps meeting him on this occasion reminded him of his new-year resolution, since, resisting the lures of London, he returned straight to Weirleigh. And, apart from one visit to the ballet on 28 January, he remained there quietly until it was time to leave for Oxford.

*

While writing his own account of his life, Sassoon confessed to frequent doubts as to 'what is significant to the story'.[43] Does it really matter, for instance, that in January 1919, at the height of his resolve to help the Labour Party fight social injustice, he accepted membership of one of the most privileged gentlemen's clubs in London, the Reform?[44] It is certainly another sign of his inconsistency, which he himself attributed to 'chuckle-headed immaturity'.[45] Sassoon had been introduced to the Reform by Ross. With Ross dead he needed membership of his own and was grateful to Arnold Bennett for proposing him. Its Pall Mall premises would serve him as a convenient place for meeting and entertaining for the next ten years or so.

Since his introduction to Bennett at the Reform in May 1917, Sassoon had found the novelist 'always the same and always nice'.[46] Another of his friends at the Reform was H.W. Massingham, whose continued support in the *Nation* he valued. Meeting Massingham in the Club on 1 February, the evening before he planned to leave for Oxford, he was offered another chance to show his political commitment in practical terms. News had just broken of rioting in Glasgow, brought on by the prospect of unemployment following rapid demobilization and the end of war-production. The leaders of the protest, William Gallagher, David Kirkwood and Emmanuel Shinwell, were aiming at a general strike, in order to force in a forty-hour working week which would, theoretically, absorb the extra labour about to arrive on the market.

Impulsive by nature, Sassoon rose to the bait and offered his services, which were quickly accepted. So, after only one day in Oxford, he set out for Glasgow by overnight train on Sunday, 2 February, with two letters of introduction from Massingham in his pocket, hoping rather ignobly that 'things wouldn't have quietened down' by the time he got there.[47] Arriving in Glasgow on a 'dismal' Monday morning, two things immediately became clear to him: that the riots were 'all over' and that he was going to have difficulty finding anything new to report for the *Nation*, especially in his ignorant state.[48] He was rescued by a young man called John Langdon Davies, the nephew of a well-known member of the Independent Labour Party.[49] Like most left-wingers, Davies had admired Sassoon's anti-war protest and offered to share some useful contacts he had in Glasgow. He remembered with some amusement what happened when he took the patently middle-class Sassoon to a meeting of the Socialist Labour Party, a forerunner of the Communist Party in Britain:

> A big man said: 'We shall not see the last fight, the fight for the tools.' A very little woman in glasses with straight black hair and bitter thin lips said she did not see why, and then turned on poor Siegfried and must have surprised him very much by saying, in a Glasgow dialect, which I have no ability to imitate: 'Mr Sassoon, we are glad of your sympathy of course, but you will never understand us, Mr Sassoon. For you, Mr Sassoon, never took in Marx with your mother's milk.' She seemed to grow more bitter with every word, and Siegfried more embarrassed. It was so patently true that he had not taken in Marx with his mother's milk nor probably at any later date.[50]

After three days' 'behind the scenes' activity, including a visit to the police courts, a session of the City Corporation, an engineering works and the worst of the city's slums, Sassoon realized that he was completely unqualified to produce the article Massingham needed and asked Davies to write it for him.

'It probably contained a fair number of suggestions made by me,' he explained defensively, but the cheque, when it arrived, went straight to Davies.[51]

*

By 7 February Sassoon was back at Oxford. He had stopped briefly in London to recover at the 1917 Club, thinking it more suitable in his 'tousled unshaven condition' than the Reform.[52] (Word of his affair with Gabriel may already have spread, since he overheard one member confessing to another that he knew very little about Sassoon except that he was said to spend a hundred pounds a year on scent.) But his main focus was now Oxford. Determined to remedy his political ignorance, so apparent to him in Glasgow, he envisaged an austere but rewarding programme of study and poetry-writing. When he needed a little home comfort combined with high-mindedness, there was Garsington only a few miles away.

Oxford had changed since his austere wartime convalescence at Somerville College, however, and though there were serious, mature students there determined to make up what the War had interrupted, there were also many young men whose main purpose was to have a good time. So that instead of the earnest life he had planned, Sassoon found himself immediately caught up in a social whirl even more frenzied than his London one. His own version implies that he had no control over events, but his letters and diaries of the period make it clear that he was not being entirely honest with himself. A letter to Graves, for instance, who was about to take up his deferred scholarship at St John's College, suggests that Sassoon was planning a busy social life among the dreaming spires; despite a passing reference to the prominent Communists, Trotsky and Liebknecht, there would clearly be little time left over for politics.

'My God, we'll have fun at Oxford, old frump!' Graves responded.[53] He planned to spend all his spare time in Sassoon's Merton Street rooms, but fortunately for Sassoon's good intentions, his arrival was delayed, partly by ill health and partly by the birth of his first child, Jenny. Sassoon, after much persuasion, agreed to be Jenny's godfather.

Even without Graves there were plenty of distractions. Gabriel, for whom the second bedroom had been taken, arrived in Oxford early in the month. Lectured at by Sassoon and still full of pious resolutions to study Art at the Slade, his lifestyle remained frivolous. And his presence alone made it difficult for Sassoon to carry out his own plan of study. There were still others to tempt Sassoon from his chosen path, John Masefield, for example, in his élite artistic community on Boar's Hill.[54] A visit to him in February 1919 posed no real threat to his political studies, but its consequences did. 'We have got to write and act a 25-minute play with 5 or 6 characters ... at Masefield's ball,' Sassoon informed Graves, begging him to 'please write the play.'[55]

Sassoon was particularly impressed by Masefield's simplicity, both of character and work, contrasting it favourably with the deliberate difficulty, obscurity and allusiveness of many Modernist poets. T.S. Eliot, whose *Prufrock and Other Observations* had been published in America by 1919, would remain a *bête noire* all his life, with Yeats and Auden rating little better.

The other poet he admired for his 'simplicity', Prewett, also proved a distraction at Oxford. Judging from Sassoon's letters to Graves, the young Canadian's poor health, lack of money and need of a holiday were of far greater concern to Sassoon than books on political theory, or even his own poetry. And Prewett led on to other diversions. By the time Sassoon arrived in Oxford, Prewett had already made friends at Christ Church and introduced at least one of them to Sassoon, William Walton. Walton and Prewett had met through a shared interest in rowing and music and it was at a concert that Prewett first brought Walton and Sassoon together on 12 February 1919.[56]

Walton, who had been a chorister at Christ Church Cathedral School during the War, had become an undergraduate at the college itself in October 1918 at the age of sixteen. He was determined to succeed as a composer but was still struggling to establish himself on very little money. Pale, thin and delicate-looking, he probably appealed to Sassoon's protective instincts as well as his love of music, since he would become one of his most generous patrons, his reward being the dedication of Walton's orchestral suite, *Portsmouth Point*, to him in 1925. Sassoon's greatest favour to Walton, however, took place shortly after they met. Most lives of Walton rightly emphasize the importance of his friendship with Osbert and Sacheverell Sitwell, but none points out that it was Sassoon who introduced the young composer to them in the first place. As Osbert recalls, Sassoon took Sachie to visit Walton, who then invited both Sitwell brothers, Sassoon and Prewett to tea,[57] thus launching his own career. The Sitwells became Walton's early champions, inviting him to live in their London house with them while he worked on his early compositions. And Walton's first real success arrived with his setting of their sister Edith's poems, *Façade*.

Sassoon had contacted the Sitwell brothers when he arrived in Oxford, knowing that Sachie was studying (briefly) at Balliol, with Osbert in close attendance. Since one of his main motives in moving to the university town had been to avoid dissipating his time and energy on social occasions, it was hardly a sensible contact. But it was a highly entertaining one and the Sitwells were responsible for what Sassoon regarded as his 'oddest' encounter in Oxford.[58] With their taste for the eccentric and bizarre, Osbert and Sachie had contacted one of the most exotic writers of the day, Ronald Firbank. Firbank, who, like them, was wealthy enough to follow his own whims, had become a cult figure with his novel *Vainglory* in 1915. He had followed this up with *Inclinations* (1916) and *Caprice* (1917) and was about to publish *Valmouth* when Sassoon was taken to see him by the Sitwells in February 1919.

If the keynote to Firbank's personality and work is artificiality, then his surroundings reflected him to perfection. His novels had led Sassoon to expect 'a somewhat peculiar person' and he was not surprised by the novelist's distinctly 'orchidaceous' appearance.[59] But he was not prepared for the closely curtained room filled with countless candles and hothouse flowers. Nor did he know how to deal with Firbank's strange behaviour, which made all attempts at ordinary conversation seem farcical. As he politely ate the rich cakes and out-of-season fruits in the overheated, heavily scented room, Sassoon found it hard to believe that this 'strange being' could have any relationship with the outer world. It seemed entirely appropriate that, when he asked Firbank his favourite country, he should reply 'Lotus-land'. Altogether he made Sassoon feel very pedestrian.

Sassoon was clearly fascinated by Firbank, a prefiguring of his later obsession with Stephen Tennant's exotic lifestyle. And though at the time he was dismissive of Firbank's novels, regarding them for all their amusement value as 'the elegant triflings of a talented amateur', he was sufficiently intrigued to return his invitation to tea.[60] He also reported the occasion in his autobiography, while many apparently more significant events of his stay, such as a second visit to the poet laureate, Robert Bridges, went unrecorded.

At least one letter from Firbank to Sassoon survives, thanking him for his poems, which he praises. Looked at in the light of Sassoon's autobiography alone their continuing friendship is puzzling, since it omits one of the main contributory factors, Gabriel. For Gabriel, who could not be mentioned in *Siegfried's Journey*, found Firbank 'Simply too marvellous!' as Sassoon explains in his diary: '[Firbank] belongs to the life into whose fringes I am drawn by my "friendship" with G. He is the type of man that G. would have become if he'd never met me. A talented drunken freak without enough strength of character to steer him through the shoals of intellectual Bohemia.'[61] Like Gabriel, however, for all his preciousness Firbank was fairly shrewd. 'I am Pavlova chasing butterflies,' he told Sassoon on meeting him at the Russian Ballet in 1921. 'You are Tolstoi digging for worms.'[62]

Unlike Gabriel or later Tennant, Firbank, a powdered, ninetyish figure the same age as Sassoon, did not attract him physically. But another friend of the Sitwells almost certainly did. Beverley Nichols, a fellow-student of Sachie at Balliol, was handsome, gifted and, crucially for Sassoon, not yet twenty-one.[63] Christened by Osbert 'the original bright young thing', he was just the kind of youth calculated to seduce Sassoon, and not just away from his work.

Sassoon may have met Nichols briefly in Cambridge in 1915 through Dent or Theo, the way in which Gabriel had got to know 'Nicolette', as his Cambridge friends called him, in 1917. The opportunity for their first tête-à-tête arrived a week after their first Oxford meeting, when Nichols went round to Sassoon's rooms to discuss a magazine he was starting, the *Oxford Outlook*. Sassoon may have shown him the poem he planned to submit to it, 'Lovers', with its explicit detail and erotic overtones.[64] He probably encouraged Nichols to approach Masefield for a contribution, which Nichols successfully did. And five days later both poets were addressing one of Nichols's many societies, Masefield having also been persuaded by Sassoon to do so.

Then, on 9 March, a cryptic sentence in Nichols's diary code indicates the likely outcome of his relationship with Sassoon: 'Siegfried came up after.' For Nichols, who was cheerfully promiscuous throughout his life, the encounter seems to have meant very little: he remained friends with both Sassoon and Gabriel. But for Sassoon it was another significant step in the acceptance of his own sexuality. He had tried to idealize his physical relations with Gabriel, but there could be no denying the carnal nature of a one-night stand with an attractive, fairly casual acquaintance. Though no one would ever call him promiscuous, this liaison marked a further crumbling of his resistance to the physical side of sex, as his numerous relationships with young men in the 1920s would show.

*

By the beginning of March Sassoon was forced to admit that Rivers's plan for his education was failing. Even more worryingly he had written little poetry and was still no clearer as to his future direction in that area. His initial passion and subsequent despair over Gabriel had inspired at least eight poems. But the impetus had not lasted and by the middle of March 1919 he had added only three poems.[65] Two of these, 'The Goldsmith' and 'Devotion to Duty', look to the distant past for their inspiration, but indicate no new direction for the future.

The third poem, 'Aftermath', is more successful, though mainly as an 'effective recitation poem' according to Sassoon.[66] Its series of declamatory questions and statements may strike the modern reader as too rhetorical and much of it is highly emotive – 'Look up, and swear by the green of the spring that you'll never forget' – but it paints a vivid picture of trench warfare and conveys convincing concern for the ordinary soldier:

> ... Do you remember the dark months you held the sector at Mametz
> – The nights you watched and wired and dug and piled sandbags on
>   parapets?
> Do you remember the rats; and the stench
> Of corpses rotting in front of the front-line trench –
> And dawn coming, dirty-white, and chill with a hopeless rain?
> Do you ever stop and ask, 'Is it all going to happen again?'
>
> Do you remember that hour of din before the attack –
> And the anger, the blind compassion that seized and shook you then
> As you peered at the doomed and haggard faces of your men?
> Do you remember the stretcher-cases lurching back
> With dying eyes and lolling heads – those ashen-grey
> Masks of the lads who once were keen and kind and gay? ...
>
>   (*CP*, p. 119)

The main problem with 'Aftermath' for Sassoon was that it looked backwards and led him no nearer to a new path. It was almost certainly written in reaction to his demobilization on 12 March 1919.[67] He had refused to accompany

Graves to Limerick for the event, but had nevertheless been officially retired with the rank of captain. Curiously, for someone who was already becoming irritated by a tendency to brand him solely as a war poet, he decided to keep his military title in civilian life, a social solecism for all but regular soldiers. And he would do so to the end of his life. Wilfred Owen's brother, Harold, suggests that while Sassoon repudiated war, he was snobbishly unable to resist 'empty' titles. Dame Felicitas Corrigan, on the other hand, argues that it was probably Hardy's remark to Graves, after the latter had given up his title, that dictated Sassoon's choice: "'But you have a right to it!" Hardy had said. "I should certainly keep my rank if I had one, and feel very proud to be called Captain Hardy".'[68] If so, it was probably a rationalization of a deeper urge to preserve a last link with his men who had meant so much to him. Perhaps he heard the words of Whitman in their mouths: 'O Captain, my Captain!'

Within days of writing 'Aftermath', Sassoon decided to leave Oxford. To his complete surprise, he had been offered the literary editorship of a new Labour paper, the *Daily Herald*. Though he had failed in his own eyes in his political efforts, he was evidently still regarded as a good socialist by the outside world. It seemed to him a heaven-sent chance to 'put an end to [his] purposeless existence at Oxford' and he accepted the post at once.[69]

It was not his only motive. Apart from his failure to study, he had more practical concerns. The army had continued to pay him a modest amount, but this had come to an end with his official retirement. His private income was scarcely enough to cover his expenses, particularly now that he had started to make Gabriel a generous allowance.[70] And there were other obligations: 'It is a cushy job, at £5 a week and extras,' he wrote to Graves, 'and I can't refuse it, as I've got to find at least £300 a year for my brother, who has two boys to educate as snobs at a first-class prep school ....'[71]

His most compelling reason for accepting the *Daily Herald* job, however, was the hope that it would stop him 'worrying so much about leagues of nations and conscription, etc.', the very issues one might expect to find debated in a Labour paper of the period.[72] By taking it he hoped finally to escape the War and the 'picture-show' of memories which still haunted him.

20

'Rootless Re-Beginnings'[1]

April–December 1919

Everyone suddenly burst out singing;
And I was filled with such delight
As prisoned birds must find in freedom,
Winging wildly across the white
Orchards and dark-green fields; on – on – and out of sight.

Everyone's voice was suddenly lifted;
And beauty came like the setting sun:
My heart was shaken with tears; and horror
Drifted away ... O, but Everyone
Was a bird; and the song was wordless; the singing
will never be done.   ('Everyone Sang', *CP*, p. 124)[2]

Sassoon's acceptance of the *Daily Herald* literary editorship had a number of consequences. One of the most immediate was a sense of liberation from the War, as he had hoped. And this, in turn, inspired his popular anthology poem, 'Everyone Sang'.[3] Written during his first few weeks at the *Herald*, it expresses his powerful feeling of release from years of tension and unhappiness. Like floodwaters bursting their dam, his renewed joy in life sweeps all before it in flowing, irresistible lines.

Since 'Everyone Sang' is usually taken to refer to the Armistice, it is traditionally included with Sassoon's war poems, but he himself called it 'a peace celebration', and was proud of Masefield's recognition of it as such.[4] He was also anxious to explain that his poem was really about the social revolution he believed to be at hand in 1919.[5] And the 'singing', which many readers interpreted as a reference to soldiers on the march, really referred to this hope of social change. In the light of Sassoon's gloss it becomes more understandable why he wrote 'Everyone Sang' shortly after starting work on the *Daily Herald*, Britain's only socialist daily in 1919.[6] The *Herald*'s original founder and editor was George Lansbury, a man whom one unsympathetic contemporary described as 'one of those sentimental, muddle-headed Pecksniffian good men who mean so well in theory and do so much harm in practice'.[7]

Sassoon was almost certainly familiar with Lansbury's name, since he would have known the weekly version of the *Herald* published throughout the War, which largely reflected his own anti-war views. Its success had encouraged Lansbury to relaunch it as a daily in 1919, when he continued to make it the mouthpiece of his left-wing and markedly pro-Russian views.[8] Lansbury would go on to be an M.P. and eventually leader of the Labour Party after Ramsay MacDonald's defeat in 1931. His working-class, trade-unionist background was in strong contrast to his much younger associate editor, Gerald Gould, who represented the intellectual element in the party. Only a year older than Sassoon, Gould was an ex-Fellow of Merton College, Oxford, and much closer to him in background. It was he who had written to ask Sassoon to join the *Daily Herald* and almost certainly he who had suggested him in the first place. A poet himself, he admired not just Sassoon's anti-war protest but also his verse, offering to review it at one point if Sassoon, as literary editor, felt inhibited about asking anyone else to do so.[9]

Though Sassoon felt at home neither with intellectuals nor with the working classes, a fact which contributed to his eventual rejection of socialism, he certainly felt more comfortable with fellow-poets of middle-class background like Gould and another member of the *Herald* staff, Francis Meynell. After their brief meeting at Garsington in November 1918[10] he claimed to be 'very fond of' Meynell,[11] but their mutual interest in poetry and book design would not be enough to keep their friendship alive once Sassoon had abandoned socialism.

There were other significant figures on the *Herald*'s staff; Norman Angell, for example, author of *The Great Illusion*.[12] But none of them interested Sassoon as much as the paper's music critic, W.J. Turner (of 'Chimborazo, Cotopaxi' fame).[13] Born in Australia in the 1880s, Turner had come to London as a young man determined to be a poet. He got to know Marsh, Brooke and other Georgians, with whom his own verse became identified. After serving with the Royal Artillery from 1916 to 1918 he continued with the music criticism for the *New Statesman* he had started during the War, accepted a job with the *Daily Herald* and was to become drama critic of the *London Mercury* when it was launched by his friend J.C. Squire later in 1919.

Sassoon had been reading and admiring Turner's exotic poetry since at least 1917, when he had written to Graves: 'Get *The Hunter and Other Poems* by W.J. Turner ... and tell people to buy it. Some very good things in it.'[14] There seems to have been some possessiveness between them over 'Walter' – or 'Wilks', as Sassoon sometimes called him. Sassoon had first met Turner at a dinner given by Osbert Sitwell in late 1918, when their mutual commitment to poetry and music quickly drew them together, but Graves had become friends with Turner just as rapidly, asking him to be his co-editor on a new publishing venture, *The Owl*, during the same period.

Turner must have had a magnetic personality as well as talent for neither his appearance nor voice were prepossessing. Lytton Strachey described him to Virginia Woolf with his usual cruel wit and social assumptions as 'a very small birdlike man with a desolating accent, good deal to say for himself – but punctuated by strange hesitations – impediments – rather distressing; but really a nice little fellow, when one has got over the way in which he says "count"'.[15]

Later on, after Sassoon had grown disillusioned with Turner, he would criticize his 'general rawness and violence of opinion'[16] and other graver faults, such as his compulsive womanizing and general disloyalty to former friends. But in early 1919 he felt nothing but admiration for the small, tough, self-educated Australian. It was largely the attraction of opposites. Sassoon particularly admired Turner's wide aesthetic taste, which included art and drama, as well as music and poetry. He found him 'if anything, more sensitive' than he was and even more involved in London's intellectual and artistic world.[17] Listening to Turner's 'stimulating and provocative talk' made him wish, uncharacteristically, to 'shake off the past'.[18] He longed to enter into Turner's world, where audacious critical opinions and adventurous ideas were the order of the day. And for a time it looked as though Turner might manage to drag him into the twentieth century.

Above all (and, later, in spite of all), Sassoon admired Turner's independence and seriousness. He was enormously attracted to Turner's 'quality of male independence', though not, he insisted, in a sexual way.[19] In fact, he believed that his satisfactory relationship with Turner was based on 'a complete absence of any sex feeling at all'.[20] One of Sassoon's later lovers would argue that Turner was a clear case of 'repressed "peculiarity"' (i.e. homosexuality) and Sassoon felt that there was 'just enough evidence to make it barely possible ...'.[21] But there is no suggestion of any sexual relationship between the two writers. This may account for an important element in their friendship, Sassoon's ability to confide in Turner completely about his sexual problems.[22] As a colonial and disciple of Shaw and Ibsen, whose advanced ideas caused outrage in early twentieth-century England, Turner's outlook was less conventional and hidebound than that of many of Sassoon's friends. He also had a good sense of humour. All in all he was to become very important to Sassoon for a time.

*

The most important member of the *Herald*'s staff in practical terms, however, was Sassoon's secretary, Miss Irene Clephane, who ran his tiny office at 8 Carmelite Street. Since his literary columns came out initially on Wednesdays and Saturdays, she worked only part-time for him on Tuesdays and Fridays, but her help was invaluable.[23] His account in *Siegfried's Journey* stresses his own ignorance and impetuousness, both of which he exaggerated for comic effect,[24] portraying himself, as he did in the First World War, as a bungling amateur. Miss Clephane probably did contribute useful suggestions about his 'Books of To-day and To-morrow' columns.[25] She almost certainly saved him from blunders in his correspondence with contributors, as he claimed.

Sassoon's own attitude towards the *Daily Herald* was a mixture of resolution, excitement and pride, but he quickly realized that not everyone felt so positive about it. He knew that his mother, for example, privately thought of the *Herald* as 'that rabid and pestilent rag'.[26] He had returned yet again to live at Weirleigh and it was with a sense of relief, as well as excitement, that he rode his bicycle down to Paddock Wood on Tuesdays and Fridays to take the train into London and spend the night there.

Marsh, too, disapproved of the *Daily Herald*, dismissing it as 'a very fishy try-on'.[27] He had also been partly responsible for the disapproval of Graves's parents, who were worried about their son reviewing books for Sassoon in a Labour daily. Far from reassuring them, Marsh had strengthened their fears by claiming that Sassoon had 'bolshevized or tried to bolshevize Robert',[28] a charge which must have made Sassoon doubly conscious of the social ostracism he risked in his new position.

For, as Graves himself put it, the *Daily Herald* was 'not respectable'.[29] Its strong anti-militarism, violent criticism of the Versailles Treaty and the blockade of Russia, but above all its protest against social injustice, made uncomfortable reading for the cosy middle classes. Unlike his parents, however, he and Nancy 'took it to heart' and 'called [themselves] socialists'.[30] It was a great comfort to Sassoon that at least one of those closest to him approved of the paper.[31]

The most significant reaction to the *Daily Herald*, however, came not from friends and family but from publishers, who were mainly to the right of the political spectrum. This affected Sassoon's job in a way he had not anticipated. While getting into his editorial stride, he had given no thought to what he called 'the sordid subject of advertisements'.[32] Once he understood that any paper, especially one on such a tight budget as the *Herald*, needed the money from advertising, he dutifully set out on a round of visits to publishing houses to solicit business. But, while the interviews themselves were quite agreeable, it quickly became apparent that most big publishers disliked his paper for what they considered its disruptive ideas and that smaller firms simply did not have the money to advertise.

Sassoon's own publisher, William Heinemann, considered the *Daily Herald* 'a menace to the fabric of the social system',[33] and this had one immediate and unfortunate consequence. In an effort to ensure that publishers sent in review copies to the 'Paper with its Face Towards the Future', the *Herald* had issued an eight-page pamphlet trumpeting 'A Literary Editor for the New London Daily Newspaper', included four of Sassoon's poems from *Counter-Attack*.[34] Unluckily, one of the first to receive the flyer was Heinemann, the publisher of those four poems. Since these had been printed without his permission he was able to express his strong dislike of the *Herald* by demanding the destruction of all undistributed copies of the pamphlet.

Sassoon tried to win Heinemann back by reviewing several of his publications in the following weeks and months, an attempt which explains several puzzling review choices. Heinemann was almost certainly mollified, since his firm would continue to publish Sassoon until 1928, but the main interest of the incident is that it highlights the power Sassoon's new position gave him. Not only could he choose which books to review and which not; he was also responsible for who reviewed them.

An even greater source of power for Sassoon were the 'Literary Notes' he had agreed to provide. These gave him the chance to promote his own favourites directly, which he did, writing at some length about war books in his first batch, for instance, and mentioning his friend H.G. Wells's latest book in passing.

One real problem inherent in his job was that by agreeing to work for a crusading socialist daily, Sassoon is more or less obliged to review important political works, even though he may not think they have intrinsic literary merit. One such book is Professor Nicolai's *Biology of War*, which Gould makes sure is reviewed at length at the first opportunity by someone who understands its significance, Havelock Ellis. For a related, possibly even greater, problem is that Sassoon himself is not qualified to judge such books in political terms, his commitment to Labour being a largely emotional matter. His answer is to enlist a body of professionals, most of them academics or political figures, such as G.D.H. Cole, H.N. Brailsford, W.N. Ewer, Philip Guedalla and Bertrand Russell. For other specialist subjects, too, he does not hesitate to call in experts in their field, such as the philosopher C.E.M. Joad, or the Shakespearian scholar Ivor Brown.

Another problem, which threatens the space he has been allowed, is the rapid drop in advertising on his page over the first few weeks. After an impressive start it falls to virtually nothing.[35] He eventually receives a 'kindly-worded warning' from the Editorial Board that the literary side of the paper has become too expensive and must be abbreviated until it attracts more advertising, a warning he evidently takes to heart, since the advertising picks up noticeably in the twelfth number.

However unbusinesslike Sassoon affected to be, he was clearly capable of action when his own interests were threatened. Not only did he increase the advertising, but he also persuaded the Editorial Board to allow him to replace his modest twice-weekly section with a larger weekly one, as he had originally wanted.[36] Wednesday was the chosen day, though Sassoon managed to get literary articles published occasionally on Saturdays; there was a full-length column by Henry Nevinson on Walt Whitman, 'The People's Poet', on 31 May 1919, for instance, to mark the centenary of Whitman's birth. Strictly speaking, he now needed to visit London only once a week.

With his responsibilities thus reduced, Sassoon appreciated his position even more. He particularly enjoyed being able to pay decent rates to contributors, especially those who were still struggling to establish themselves as writers. (He managed to raise the paper's suggested rate of pay from two to three guineas per 1000 words.) To the impecunious Graves, for instance, he wrote more than a fortnight before the first issue: 'You will have to do a lot of amusing reviews for the *Herald* ... non-pompous.'[37]

Another young writer Sassoon enjoyed helping was Nichols. Though Nichols's war poetry had been even more successful than Sassoon's, he was still finding it difficult to support himself when he returned from America in mid-1919 and appreciated the offer of review work.[38] Though the Sitwells were slightly less in need of support than Nichols, they were famously anxious to promote themselves and responded eagerly to Sassoon's invitation to contribute to his columns.[39] Osbert, in particular, benefited from Sassoon's generosity, since the four satires he submitted led directly to the publication of his first solo poetry collection, *The Winstonburg Line*.[40]

Sassoon's most interesting choice among younger writers was Alec Waugh, Evelyn's older brother. He not only invited Waugh to review a number of books for the *Herald*, but also asked Graves to write about Waugh's latest novel. Waugh's first work, *The Loom of Youth*, which dealt openly with homosexuality, had been a *succès de scandale* at its publication and Sassoon seems to have been anxious to become better acquainted with its author. He had a 'very jolly' lunch with Waugh and another contributor to the *Herald*, E.M. Forster, during his first month as literary editor.[41] But despite the fact that Waugh admired his war poems greatly, had published a volume of his own and shared his passion for cricket, he failed to find him anything but 'extremely uninteresting'.[42]

With Forster it was quite different. One of Sassoon's greatest achievements on the *Herald* was to persuade Forster to become a regular reviewer. Forster's wit, perception and erudition illuminate even the dullest of books and his reviews stand out in Sassoon's literary columns as small works of art. His treatment of *The Price of Things* by the popular novelist Eleanor Glyn, for example, is highly entertaining, though at her and her publisher's expense.[43] It was also an opportunity to become better acquainted with Forster. Their first actual meeting was in the offices of the *Daily Herald*.

On the whole, however, Sassoon stuck to writers he already knew well for reviews. If they were really established, like Wells, Bennett, Masefield or de la Mare, he might commission a 'special' article from them at £10 a time, or arrange for their latest book to be favourably reviewed.[44] Whenever possible, he promoted his favourites, especially if they were a minority taste, like Charles Doughty, Max Beerbohm, Charlotte Mew or Wilfrid Scawen Blunt.

Though familiar with both poets' work, he had known little of Blunt and even less of Mew until Cockerell, a champion of writers he thought unduly neglected, offered to introduce him to them. By 16 May 1919, less than two months into his new job, Sassoon found himself taking tea with Charlotte Mew at her sister Anne's studio in Charlotte Street.[45] Beside Anne there was also Mew's other great ally, Alida Klementaski, the future wife of Harold Monro and his assistant at the Poetry Bookshop. Alida and Harold had done more than anyone else to promote Charlotte's work, publishing in 1916 *The Farmer's Bride*, the collection which had first brought her to Cockerell's attention in 1918.

It must have been an odd gathering that day at 6 Hogarth Studios, the tiny, mannish figure of Mew, then over fifty and white-haired, contrasting strongly with the delicate, exotic beauty of the Polish Alida, the youthful handsomeness of Sassoon and the portly respectability of Cockerell. Both Mew and Sassoon were shy and both preferred their own sex, but Cockerell appears to have succeeded in making them like each other. Whereas T.E. Lawrence, whom Cockerell also tried to enlist, declared himself 'frigid' towards women and therefore untouched by Mew, Sassoon found her 'vividly gay'.[46] His efforts to help Mew, until her suicide in 1928, would include introductions to influential friends like Ottoline [47] and helping to get a Civil List Pension for her in 1923,[48] but his first act was more direct. Knowing that she and her sister had very little money with which to support themselves and their elderly mother, he offered her paid work with the *Herald*. A review by her appeared a month after their first meeting on 11 June.

The situation was reversed in the case of Blunt. Knowing that Cockerell had managed to secure an invitation for him to stay the weekend with the venerable poet, diplomat and Arabist in June, Sassoon commissioned H.W. Nevinson to write a long review of Blunt's *My Diaries* on 7 May in advance of his visit.

When Sassoon eventually visited Blunt from 14 to 16 June, he was already familiar with what he described as his 'admirable sonnets and protean love-lyrics'.[49] He had also heard many stories of Blunt's colourful life, which included marriage to Byron's granddaughter, an affair in the desert with his cousin's daughter, Mary Wemyss, resulting in a child, and fights for Egyptian, Indian and Irish independence that landed him in prison. All of this, together with Blunt's famous stud of Arab horses, appealed to Sassoon's romantic imagination and he anticipated meeting a 'cultivated, picturesque and contentious character'.[50]

In reality, Blunt, who was almost eighty by the time they met in the bedroom of his fine Jacobean house, Newbuildings, in West Sussex, was more fragile and less formidable than Sassoon had expected, with a surprisingly soft voice. His dark eyes appeared to observe Sassoon 'with the mournful scrutiny of a proud spirit resenting age and infirmity'.[51] But Sassoon was impressed, as he so easily was, by Blunt's aristocratic background: 'He was the most perfect example of a thoroughbred human being I had seen ....'[52] It seems appropriate that Sassoon should have described Blunt in terms of a racehorse, since Blunt himself showed more interest in Sassoon's abilities as a horse-racer than as a poet. When they did eventually discuss poetry, Sassoon became convinced that Blunt's 'strong prejudices' against contemporary verse had stunted his development as a poet. Given Sassoon's own negative attitude towards most of the significant experimental poetry of his time, it is a diverting charge. Sassoon preferred to think of Blunt in the context of his 'noble' Arab stallions, and he ends his account of the weekend with a glowing description of Blunt, 'superb' in his white Bedouin cloak, leading his guests to the paddock in his invalid pony-carriage. The scene closes with Blunt being sung an old folksong by his ebullient neighbour, Hilaire Belloc, whom Sassoon has met the previous day. Blunt's failure to praise Sassoon's poetry during this visit may have contributed to Sassoon's reservations about Blunt's own work. Of all the famous writers he had visited since the end of the War Blunt was not, he felt, 'the most notable in achievement'.[53]

That position Sassoon undoubtedly reserved for Hardy, and he happily exercised his new-found power to promote his hero. Not only did he commission a special article from the poet Lascelles Abercrombie to mark Hardy's seventy-ninth birthday on 2 June, but he also used his increased literary authority to organize a tribute to Hardy from the younger poets. (He realized that the traditional time to pay homage would be on Hardy's eightieth birthday but was too eager to wait.) This took the form of an anthology of poems handwritten by each contributor on special paper and beautifully bound up under Cockerell's expert supervision. With Gosse's approval, Sassoon chose a committee of influential figures, all of them friends of his by now – Gosse, Masefield, de la Mare, Newbolt and Bridges, who wrote a short foreword. Sassoon himself was secretary. In all, forty-three poets contributed to the volume, which Sassoon was deputed to present to Hardy at Max Gate.

The whole project smacks of an ambitious young man's attempt to ingratiate himself, but this was almost certainly not the case. While Sassoon was quite ready to use any connection that might prove useful in the literary world, he genuinely wanted to pay tribute to the object of his worship. When he delivered the 'Poets' Tribute' to Hardy, it seemed to him 'as good a moment as any' he had known.[54] Hardy's evident pleasure at the mark of recognition so animated him that the years dropped away from him. It was, however, the last occasion on which Sassoon could forget how old he was. 'Always, when going there again,' he wrote, 'I was in dread that he would show signs of his increasing age.'[55] When the inevitable changes occurred, gradual though they were, he became increasingly careful not to overtax Hardy. Their long discussions, like their walks in the Dorset countryside, were curtailed. And eventually, in order to avoid tiring Hardy in the evenings, Sassoon would stay, not with the Hardys themselves, but in a hotel. So that his visits became a source of some anxiety to him as well as intense pleasure. His most vivid memory of these later years was of Hardy saying, 'You'd better come again soon, or you may find me over at Stinsford churchyard.' To which Florence Hardy replied: 'Don't be so gruesome, T.H.!'[56]

When Hardy eventually died in 1928, Sassoon would find consolation in his friendship with a fellow-enthusiast, H.M. Tomlinson, a writer who appears regularly in the *Herald*'s literary columns in 1919. Hardy himself had praised Tomlinson's *Old Junk* to Sassoon in 1918, the year it was published, and Sassoon may already have met Tomlinson in the offices of the *Nation*, where he was literary editor under Massingham.[57] He may also have met him at the Reform, of which both were members, but the relationship was consolidated at the *Daily Herald*.

'No man alive,' Sassoon told the poet Charles Causley, had a 'deeper love and veneration for Hardy and his work.'[58] And when Causley persuaded Sassoon and Tomlinson to make a radio programme about Hardy in 1955, Tomlinson delighted Causley by referring to his old friend simply as 'Tom'. (Gosse had christened Hardy 'true Thomas'.) Sassoon in turn called Tomlinson 'Tommy', an affectionate echo, perhaps, of his first great love, the young army officer David Thomas. That was as far as the similarity went, however, for no one could have less resembled the handsome ex-public schoolboy than the rugged Tomlinson. Sassoon referred to his 'queer gargoyle face'[59] and Virginia Woolf saw him in terms of 'the hard knob of a walking stick carved by a boy of eight'.[60] Her husband, Leonard, remembered him more neutrally as 'gentle' and 'deaf'.[61]

Born in the dockland area of East London, Tomlinson had left school early and gone into a shipping office. He remained interested in the sea all his life. Largely self-educated, he never lost his cockney accent, as Sassoon rather snobbishly noted in his diary.[62] Yet in spite of his disadvantages, he became a highly respected journalist and prose writer, producing his first successful book, *The Sea and the Jungle* (1912), at the age of thirty-nine. Sassoon thought him a 'great prose writer'.[63] He is remembered nowadays, if at all, for his novels *Gallions Reach* (1927) and *All Our Yesterdays* (1930), a powerful criticism of the First World War.

Only thirteen years older than Sassoon, Tomlinson seemed to him far more than that in experience and would go some way to replacing Hardy as a father-figure. Though he came from a very different background from Hardy, Sassoon found in him the same 'comforting voice, homeliness and profound human philosophy'.[64] He relied greatly on Tomlinson's 'simple wisdom' and 'genuineness'[65] for guidance and would consult him frequently about both work and more personal matters.

Whether Tomlinson was quite as objective a critic of Sassoon's work as he insisted is doubtful.[66] One of the things which drew them together at the start, even more than a shared love of Hardy, a critical attitude towards the First World War and a good sense of humour, was a profound distrust of Modernism. Tommy was one of the few people on whom Sassoon felt he could lean for 'support in my ignoramus pilgrimage through the mazes of modernity'.[67] It seemed to him that they both suffered a good deal from the impact of Modernist writing and he looked to Tomlinson for reassurance. In doing so, he identified with the rearguard rather than the vanguard of literature, as he had done in 1913 when he chose Gosse and Marsh as his mentors. The book of poems he dedicated to Tomlinson in 1956, *Sequences*, would demonstrate all the strengths and weaknesses of that choice.

Another writer from whom he drew 'spiritual sustenance' in his resistance to Modernism, and who also contributed regularly to his literary columns in 1919, was Frank Swinnerton.[68] Born in 1884, he was much closer in age to Sassoon than Tomlinson, but he too became a support-figure. Sassoon had a 'great respect' for his judgement, he told de la Mare, perhaps because Swinnerton confirmed his own prejudice against Modernist poets like Eliot and Auden. Swinnerton was particularly hostile to the writers of the Bloomsbury Group and Sassoon himself would become increasingly critical of them partly under his influence, though he was loath to include Forster in his strictures.[69] He would also rely on Swinnerton for advice on his prose works later on.

When they first met, Swinnerton was one of the foremost critics of the day. He would remain a literary authority until well into the 1950s, writing regularly for the *Evening News* and the *Observer*, among other papers, and producing over twenty books of criticism, such as his popular *Georgian Literary Scene*. In 1919, however, Swinnerton was even better known as the author of his highly successful seventh novel, *Nocturne* (1917), a work which was to overshadow his many later efforts. Both hard-working – he produced nearly forty novels in addition to his critical books – and optimistic, he was an inspiration to Sassoon, who frequently despaired of writing anything at all. Like Tomlinson, he had overcome early hardship by sheer determination.

With men like Swinnerton and Tomlinson to support him, Sassoon could continue to believe in the traditional path he had chosen. Both relationships would survive a lifetime, while friendships with younger, more experimental writers, such as Graves and Osbert Sitwell, would weaken during the 1920s.[70] There was one younger writer, however, also met through his *Herald* work and also a traditionalist, who would become one of his greatest friends, Edmund Blunden.

*

There is a striking photograph of Edmund Blunden which shows him striding onto a cricket pitch with Rupert Hart-Davis, a friend of Blunden and Sassoon in later life. Blunden appears at least a foot shorter than Hart-Davis and looks like a child who has trespassed into an adult's world, his small, pointed face, eager expression and thin, almost stick-like arms giving him an air of extreme vulnerability. So, indeed, most of his close friends saw him, Sassoon in particular. 'Yes,' he wrote in June 1922, three years after their friendship started, 'it is the frailty of Blunden which makes him unique. Perhaps my vanity is flattered by my protective feeling for him. His spirit burns in his body with the apparent fragility of a flame. I want always to be interposing the bulk of my physical robustness between him and the brutish blustering of the winds of the outer world.'[71]

Sassoon was not alone in finding Blunden's frailty appealing; Blunden would be helped and protected all his life by devoted friends of both sexes. Yet, as Sassoon implies, his 'fragility' was to some extent more apparent than real. Like Keats, to whom he was often compared, he was extremely resilient and determined, and could be ruthlessly single-minded on occasions. A man of fierce, if sometimes unconventional principles, he rarely hesitated to follow them, whatever complications it created. His one burning ambition, like Keats, was to serve literature. And in that service he could also be remarkably unselfish, particularly as a teacher and correspondent, when he inspired in many students and friends a similar ambition. As Sassoon himself observed, Blunden lived 'in an atmosphere of intense devotion to the art of poetry'.[72] He was a romantic and idealist, much like Sassoon.

Blunden had first written to Sassoon at the *Daily Herald* on 3 May 1919, calling his attention to two 'chap-books' of poems, written at school but not printed until 1916 when he was out in France as a young army officer. His second letter to Sassoon fills in the details of his war career: that he had joined the army in August 1915 straight from his school, Christ's Hospital, 'in a state of singular misery', then in May 1916 been posted to the Western Front with the 11th Battalion, the Royal Sussex Regiment. 'I was stigmatized with the usual ribbon [i.e. the Military Cross] in 1916,' he continued, 'and for a few weeks was on Brigade H.Q., but my free speech secured my return to the less disgusting front line, where I kept people's spirits up by letting loose any hope of returning world sanity I could collect. Your sonnets and excerpts in the CAMBRIDGE MAG[AZINE] were the principal joy-beams.'[73] By the time of this letter he had been demobilized and was living at Plymouth with the wife he had married in 1918.

Blunden's letter was a model of literary tact, down to the well-turned compliment with which it ends: 'With gratitude not only for your vivacious critica in THE HERALD but also for your great efforts throughout the war to bring the ferocity of the trenches home to a public more disturbed about rations than Passchendaele,/ I am, sir,/Yours truly,/ E.C. Blunden (Scholar-elect, Queen's College, Oxford).'

In submitting his work to Sassoon, Blunden could have expected a positive response to his anti-war views. It was not his war poetry he sent to Sassoon, however, but some earlier pastoral verse. Perhaps he had studied Sassoon's first successful collection, *The Old Huntsman* (1917), carefully and realized that Sassoon might be even more sympathetic to poems about nature, as indeed he turned out to be: 'Within five minutes,' Sassoon wrote in his autobiography, 'I knew that I had discovered a poet. Here was someone writing about a Kentish barn in a way I had always felt but had never been able to put into verse.' [74]

Their shared interest in nature poetry would become one of their greatest bonds. They would be united for life by their joint devotion to an older, less fashionable mode which would brand them both traditionalists. While other friends, such as Graves, Nichols and Turner, would lecture Sassoon in the twenties about being 'old-fashioned' and try desperately to be new-fashioned themselves, Blunden would seem to Sassoon the only one who 'talked sense'. [75] He actively urged Sassoon to write more 'rural' poetry like himself, the only problem he anticipated being arguments about who got certain parts of Kent, where they had both grown up.

Sassoon and Blunden had, then, at least two interests in common when they first met, at Nellie's rooms in Half Moon Street, and others would quickly emerge. Cricket, for example, a passion which arose partly out of their shared feeling for English landscape and country life, would become a frequent topic of conversation and playing cricket with Blunden, Sassoon felt, was the nearest he could get 'to sharing with beloved E.B. the essential fabric of my existence'. [76]

Book-collecting, too, kept them swapping stories and 'finds' from 1919 onwards. [77] It is revealing of both men that, according to Blunden, neither of them was primarily interested in costly first editions, but in the neglected by-ways, a taste which reflected their literary interests as a whole. Though both had a proper respect for the major writers of the past, it was the minor figures who intrigued them. As an ex-scholar of Christ's Hospital, Blunden was especially fond of a fellow-Bluecoat, Charles Lamb, who duly became Sassoon's staple reading. And Blunden's devotion to the eighteenth century generally and to John Clare in particular also infected Sassoon, whose poem 'To an Eighteenth Century Poet' is written in praise of another minor figure from the period, William Cowper. [78] And both were drawn to Henry Vaughan, who became the subject of a Sassoon poem greatly admired by Blunden, 'At the Grave of Henry Vaughan'. [79]

To begin with Blunden looked to Sassoon for direction. He was ten years younger than Sassoon, as well as virtually unknown, and Sassoon felt sufficiently confident of his own position and reassured by the modesty of his letter to want to help. To this end he mentioned Blunden's work in his next set of 'Literary Notes' for the *Herald* and arranged for three influential figures from the literary world to be present at their first meeting, Squire, Turner and Edward Shanks.[80] Blunden, who felt 'at once bewildered and happy' by the swift turn of events, was accordingly launched on the literary scene by Sassoon in much the same way Sassoon himself had been through Gosse's kindness. Blunden always maintained that, if Sassoon had not encouraged him in 1919, he would probably not have continued to write poetry.

Sassoon made it his business from then on to introduce him to all the friends he thought might be helpful: Marsh, Gosse, Cockerell, Tomlinson, Ottoline and Graves. All were of practical help. Sassoon also introduced Blunden to Hardy, but for different reasons. In doing so he felt that he was bringing two soul-mates together. Apart from superficial likenesses, such as their 'clear and graceful handwriting',[81] they shared what Sassoon most admired, 'a sort of old-fashioned seriousness about everything connected with authorship'.[82] Both seemed to him 'fundamentally countrified and homely' and loved talking about simple things.[83] (As he had anticipated, they took to each other at once.) In addition he found 'a similarly bird-like quality' in Blunden and Hardy, a reference to their quickness of perception and lightness of movement as well as their physical appearance. Blunden must surely have tired of having his 'beaky' face and diminutive stature compared to a bird, from a 'London house sparrow, that pecks and cheeps' (Virginia Woolf), to a nightjar (Barry Webb) or, less flatteringly, a crow (Virginia Woolf again). Whether he would have preferred Gosse's rather condescending though affectionate description of him as 'a dear little chinchilla', however, is doubtful.[84] The comparison had been inspired, Gosse told Sassoon, by Blunden's 'wonderful eyes', which he likened, inevitably, to Keats's.[85]

Sassoon almost always referred to his friend as '*little* Blunden' (my italics) and continued to feel protective towards him, in the way large, strong men often feel towards small women. He worried about Blunden's health (he was asthmatic), his finances and his complicated love life. But he insisted, as with Turner, that there was nothing sexual in the relationship: 'With Blunden I am my better self; I feel an intense sympathy and affection for him; the gross elements of sex are miraculously remote.'[86] Blunden's own powerful attraction to women probably helped.[87] It was an important factor in their relationship. With other male friendships, such as Graves and Osbert Sitwell, Sassoon's feelings were complicated by a lurking sexual element and both relationships would finally founder, whereas his friendship with Blunden would remain, in his own words, among 'the best and most fruitful' of his life.[88]

The flavour of that relationship comes through strongly in Sassoon's description of an early meeting between them which could stand for most of the many others that followed: 'for three days B and I talked about county cricket and the war and English poetry and our own poetry and East Anglia and our contemporaries .... He is, in fact, almost the ideal friend and fellow-craftsman.'[89] Sassoon was proud of his discovery and promotion of Blunden: 'I don't suppose anyone has done more for him than I have,' he wrote to Graves with some justification in 1920.[90] It was one of the few things that gave him any satisfaction in the immediate post-war years.

*

Sassoon's meeting with Blunden in late May or early June 1919 was the high point of his nine months with the *Daily Herald*. Until the end of June he was 'actively occupied, confident through success, and insolently healthy with youth and summer weather'.[91] His affair with Gabriel was going reasonably well, he was writing a fair amount of poetry and the literary editorship still interested him. But in early July sciatica struck, symbolizing in his own eyes 'the undoing of [his] blind belief in the beneficence of 1919'.[92] Perhaps, as he claimed, too much was expected of this first year after the War, which was for many a time of 'rootless re-beginnings and steadily developing disillusionments'.[93]

His own disillusionments started in July, as his diary records: 'July 1919-January 1920/ Very little poetry. Climax of bad health and discontent with G[abriel]./ Dissatisfaction with *Herald* work,/ and life in town.'[94] Yet to the outside world he appeared to be going from strength to strength, Heinemann and his friends making sure that he remained firmly in the public eye, Graves, for example, including his poems in both the first and second numbers of his new magazine, *The Owl,* in May and October. Harold Monro also kept his name before the reading public by arranging a Poetry Bookshop appearance for him on 9 October. The audience of 145, more than five times its usual size, suggests that Sassoon's work was still very popular with lovers of poetry. They probably heard very little of what Sassoon read that evening, since according to Monro he was as usual 'extremely inaudible'.[95]

To his friends' efforts, Sassoon added his own, bringing out a new volume of privately printed poems, *Picture Show*, in July 1919. Sassoon told Theo, who was helping to design *Picture Show* with Bruce Rogers, that it was a money-making venture, urging him to 'make it *look* as expensive' as possible, but it was more than money which concerned him. His endless revisions suggest that he was determined to include all his best work since January 1918, the point at which *Counter-Attack* broke off. Several pieces were written specially for the collection, notably 'Aftermath', 'Everyone Sang' and 'To a Very Wise Man', his homage to Rivers.

Less than half the poems in *Picture Show* deal directly with war, but as the title poem suggests the whole collection was written very much in its shadow, Sassoon not having yet settled on a new direction. Heinemann's next publication of Sassoon's work in October 1919, *War Poems*, reinforces the impression that he has still not found a satisfactory alternative to the subject matter and technique which had made him famous. Like *The Old Huntsman* and *Counter-Attack*, it is, in Sassoon's own words, another 'tract against war'.[96] Exploiting his continuing popularity in the genre, Heinemann has simply gathered together his war poems, with nearly a third of the weaker ones excluded. It was a shrewd choice on Heinemann's part, and when the first edition of 2,000 copies ran out in less than two months, *War Poems* was promptly reprinted. The most significant aspect of the collection, however, is that it contains no newly written work,[97] a factor which increased Sassoon's sense of unproductiveness in the second half of 1919 and added to his depression.

His most immediate cause for unhappiness, however, was his health. He had been suffering slightly from sciatica since the beginning of April but an attack in July immobilized him completely. He believed that his sciatica had been brought on by its commonest cause, a slipped disc. But conditions in the trenches had not helped either his back or his general health. He was still suffering occasional bouts of trench fever in 1918 and his teeth were already giving him trouble.

Sassoon would apologize to readers of his autobiography for the space devoted to the 'treacherous demon',[98] but it became so much the 'autocrat' of his existence in mid-1919 that it formed almost a 'constructive element' in his life. It led him, for example, to spend ten days with Osbert and Sachie Sitwell and, therefore, to a much closer relationship with them. This unplanned stay in their London house also turned into a whirlwind introduction to the latest trends in art and literature, a 'wholesome antidote', he believed, to his 'intolerance of the unusual' and 'instinctive preference for the traditional'.[99]

From the outside the Sitwells' house looked just like its neighbours in pretty Swan Walk. Inside, however, it was full of challenge, especially to someone like Sassoon, brought up on the paintings of G.F. Watts – startling and experimental pictures juxtaposed with early Victorian knick-knacks, all exemplifying for Sassoon 'a new aesthetic tendency to find beauty in the barbaric'.[100]

Sassoon had staggered to 5 Swan Walk in a state of near collapse one fine July day and been ushered solicitously to a small bedroom at the top of the narrow house by the Sitwells' housekeeper. And when Osbert and Sachie returned home, they too behaved like 'angelic and agitated turtle-doves'.[101] Sachie had quickly abandoned Oxford and both brothers now led a hectic social life, yet they found time to see Sassoon frequently during his ten-day stay and think up distractions for him, as well as arrange for a daily visit from a doctor and 'electricity' treatment.[102] And as long as Sassoon lay perfectly still, he was happy: 'being in bed in someone else's house gives one a great pull over the problems of life,' he believed, 'and permits the mind to move with unimpeded smoothness .... Quietude is essential to human happiness.'[103]

If Sassoon needed a reminder that, even in knowing the Sitwells, he had travelled a long way from his pre-war self, it arrived in the form of Norman Loder, who represented all that was decent, kind but essentially philistine. Sassoon had been due to stay with Loder at Peterborough to hunt with the Fitzwilliam, but was forced to cancel when sciatica struck.[104] Loder's appearance at the Sitwells' presented Sassoon with a problem, but not Loder: 'Norman never actively disapproved of anyone. He was too good-natured for that.'[105] Though he had not been happy about Sassoon's public protest against the War which he regarded as 'pro-Germanism', nor his 'Daily Herald Socialism', he had said very little. The Sitwells' pictures were also too much for his 'elementary taste in art',[106] but he merely made Sassoon promise to come and stay with him as soon as possible. His visit left Sassoon with a renewed sense of his sharply-divided personality, a dilemma he would fail to resolve for many years.

It was not a simple dichotomy between sport and art Sassoon faced in 1919. His affair with Gabriel and intense relationship with Rivers at Craiglockhart had made him aware of a number of other needs. Though he had made Forster laugh earlier in the year with his insistence that 'You *must* realize that I am *not* an intellectual,'[107] he did have intellectual needs, which were not met at the Loders'. This may have been the reason he took a week off during his stay with them in late July to visit Rivers and other friends in Cambridge.[108] And it is a sign of Rivers's stimulating effect on him that, while with him, he wrote one of his few poems of the period, 'Early Chronology', in which he describes an eminent colleague of Rivers's, Professor Elliot Smith, discussing 5,000 years of 'excavated History' to a chosen few in Rivers's rooms.[109]

Similarly, it was intellectual stimulation he hoped for when he left the agreeable but undemanding Loders to visit Robert Graves at the end of August. Graves, his wife Nancy and their new daughter Jenny, had gone to stay in Nancy's father's house at Harlech in March and were still there when Sassoon joined them. His initial resistance to Nancy seems to have weakened after their brief meeting the previous November, but he was evidently still jealous of her. The fact that she was pregnant again could not have helped, underlining as it did the sexual element in her relations with Graves. Nevertheless, Sassoon was probably being honest when he thanked the Graveses for an enjoyable three weeks. He was still 'passionately attached' to Graves, whom he numbered among his pantheon of heroes and, despite a growing difference in their approaches to literature, still needed to discuss it with him, especially poetry.[110]

By mid-1919 Graves believed that war poetry was 'played out' and that 'the most acceptable dope now' was 'Country Sentiment'.[111] Sassoon, whose *War Poems* were about to be published, was, as usual, not nearly so certain as Graves about his future direction. He was not even sure, at this point, that he would be able to continue writing poetry at all.

*

So the summer passed, divided between various friends and creating its own conflicts. One struggle it did not actively involve, however, was any attempt to resolve problems with Gabriel, since Sassoon deliberately kept away from him all summer. Drawn to him mainly by his youth and good looks, Sassoon was finding it increasingly difficult to accept his dissolute lifestyle. He had encouraged Gabriel to enrol at the Slade after their return from Oxford and had been pleased by his 'excellent drawing in the life school' during May.[112] But Gabriel could rarely sustain anything and by July Sassoon had reached his 'climax ... of discontent' with him.[113] His odd, rather unattractive behaviour may have stemmed not just from a determination to control his feckless young friend, but also from jealousy of the growing intimacy between Gabriel and Osbert. He may even have been already half aware of a sexual attraction towards Osbert himself, an element which would complicate their relationship greatly in future years.[114]

At all events, the situation added greatly to his post-war moodiness. Referring to later bouts of 'self-lacerating irritability against everything', which were liable to make him do something 'stupid and regrettable', he noted that it was 'nothing new, and I suspect ... not unconnected with my animal passions'.[115] Since those 'animal passions' could never, by their socially and legally forbidden nature, be easily satisfied, he would be subject to similar 'tigerish ill-temper' and 'capricious cruelty' until the passions themselves had weakened.[116] And his relationship with Gabriel would continue to resemble a ride on a rollercoaster for the next six years.

At the same time as Sassoon's trouble with Gabriel, he began to feel dissatisfied with his job at the *Daily Herald*. The literary columns were suspended for several months in August due to industrial action, and in any case he found that the literary editorship had 'simplified itself into an easy routine' and took less of his time than he would have liked.[117] By November Gould was suggesting to him a more businesslike approach, which worried him.[118] In any case, as Bennett shrewdly wrote to Nichols when he was thinking of editing a new periodical: 'I don't think this is quite your job – anymore than it is Siegfried's. You are too creative, temperamental, and wilful to be an editor.'[119]

One of Sassoon's main problems with the *Herald* remained his lack of real commitment to politics. An invitation to become British Secretary of *Clarté*, a movement started by Henri Barbusse to help unite French and English intellectuals, ended when the extent of Sassoon's political ignorance became clear at *Clarté*'s first British meeting.[120] At this point, with the War behind him, he had virtually abandoned politics.[121]

Sassoon had also finally left Weirleigh. It is ironic that, by the time he did so in October 1919, the main ground of dissent with his mother – his politics – was of little importance to him. But the cause of their other dissension – Gabriel and, behind Gabriel, Sassoon's unacknowledged homosexuality – was more important than ever and he needed freedom to explore it. A summer almost completely away from home, staying with sympathetic friends, may have prompted him to act, together with the knowledge that his brother Michael's return to Weirleigh with his family was imminent. In addition, his growing warmth towards Turner and his wife Delphine, who lived in London, made it seem an attractive alternative to Kent.

A few weeks back at Weirleigh in October seem to have decided him and by the middle of the month he had arranged to move into 54 Tufton Street, Westminster, with the Turners. Since Walter was always short of money, Sassoon had also agreed to lend him £1,300 to buy the house, a large sum which he probably borrowed against money he was expecting to inherit from his father's sister, Rachel Beer.[122] While the purchase of Tufton Street was being completed, he took temporary lodgings nearby, at 30 Hugh Street, which he quickly found 'sunless, stuffy-smelling, dingy and dispiriting'.[123]

*

Sassoon's unsettled state in the second half of 1919 was not due entirely to dissatisfaction with his lodgings, job, poetry or sex life. On 1 July he had received an invitation to lecture in America and, after further wooing from the lecture agent in person, had accepted. He was due to sail in January 1920, a prospect he found both exciting and disturbing.[124]

Mr Pond of Pond Lyceum Bureau, New York, had reassured Sassoon that he would not be expected to deliver 'professorial discourses';[125] he need only read his war poems and make a few informal remarks. But Sassoon doubted his ability to do even that audibly. After his reading at the Poetry Bookshop had underlined how bad a speaker he was, he enrolled at the Central School of Speech and Drama in a panic.

His misgivings about the enterprise were equalled only by his astonishment. While he knew that Masefield's generous praise of his work during his own lecture tour a few years earlier and Nichols's effusive introduction to the American edition of *Counter-Attack* and public readings from it, as well as a temporary interest in war poets, had made him known in the States, the last thing he had expected was a eulogistic letter from a well-known lecture agency.[126] The letter may have been prompted by the first reprint of *Counter-Attack* in April 1919, in which Nichols's romantic description of 'Sassoon the Man' with his 'air of a sullen falcon' again appears.

Sassoon was grateful for the praise, however high-flown, but his reasons for going to America were not to gratify his ego. He had pledged himself 'to oppose war' and a lecture tour on the subject seemed an effective way of doing so.[127] He also had a 'sudden impulse and longing to escape from the postwar complexities' of his life which had involved him with a bewildering number of new people.[128] The fact that Rivers advised him to accept and would himself be lecturing in America at the same time was another deciding factor. These were the reasons Sassoon gave for accepting Pond's invitation. The most convincing explanation for his uncharacteristic readiness to expose himself to the American public, however, was dissatisfaction with his life in post-war England and a general lack of direction.

21

Broadway and Beyond

January–August 1920

Under the fuscous canopy of heaven
Gold winking signs, façades of flickering fires,
Relentlessly proclaim the cheap-jack fame
Of Movie Stars and Chewing Gum and Tyres. ...
('Midnight on Broadway', *Recreations*)[1]

If Sassoon hoped to escape his problems by leaving England for America in January 1920, it was not for long. During the voyage itself, a leisurely crossing on the Dutch liner *Rotterdam* in a first-class cabin, he had a sense of putting the complexities of the past year into some 'sort of perspective'.[2] But when he landed in New York on 28 January, he was immediately faced with a new set of complications.

His arrival was not auspicious. Met at the boat by a Pond representative, he was driven in an ancient taxi through slush and snow to the Hotel Seville, which he found 'rather depressing'.[3] A 'nasty' dinner and two uninspired newspaper interviews were followed by a sleepless night with raging toothache in an overheated room. He started the next day with an emergency visit to the dentist, the first of nineteen hour-long appointments to deal with several decayed teeth and acute pyorrhoea. But this painful and expensive experience was not the worst of his problems. When he, next, presented himself at the Pond Lyceum Bureau at 50 East 42nd Street, he found a distinctly uneasy Mr Pond. By the terms of their contract Pond had undertaken to cover the cost of the transatlantic crossing and all rail and sleeping-car fares in America. More crucially, he had also guaranteed to pay $100 each for a minimum of twenty-five lectures. Yet by the time Sassoon was due to leave for America, he had managed to book only two paid engagements.

Pond had immediately cabled the bad news to Sassoon in England, urging him to cancel his trip. By catching an earlier boat, however, Sassoon had missed the cable, a fact he later appreciated. Pond claimed that the market had been glutted by British writers and also blamed a general reaction by the American public against 'war stuff', but did not admit something Sassoon subsequently discovered, that his agency had lost a great deal of money on a recent tour by the Belgian playwright Maeterlinck. The Pond Lyceum Bureau was, in fact, on the verge of bankruptcy.

Pond had, however, managed to arrange some publicity for Sassoon, who spent the afternoon being interviewed and photographed, the early evening at a reception in the National Arts Club and the evening itself at the annual dinner of the Poetry Society of America, where he had to give his first speech. Though this was unpaid, it gave him a valuable opportunity to advertise his skills and immediately brought in invitations to speak at two 'premier' ladies' clubs in the city.

The Poetry Society talk was a baptism by fire. Too busy to prepare himself mentally for the occasion and intimidated by the presence of Yeats as a fellow-speaker, Sassoon faced his first performance with dread. An absence of alcohol at the prohibition dinner itself added to his gloom. Thankful, however, for his smart new dress-suit and conscious of the fact that he was the most youthful, probably the youngest, man in the room, he decided on the 'natural' approach. The newspaper report of the event catches the tone well:

> Mr Sassoon, who arrived in New York from Europe recently, said he came with a toothache and would leave with a heartache. Asked by interviewers for his first impression of New York, he had replied, 'As I rode through the streets in a taxicab I kept saying to myself, Oh hell! Where's the nearest dentist?' Mr Sassoon said that if he should be asked to vote for the Prime Minister of living English poets he would cast his vote for a man whom most Americans probably knew only as a prose writer, Thomas Hardy. He read three of his own poems and gave a fourth – 'Everyone Sang' – in response to applause.[4]

The suggestion of spontaneity here is perhaps misleading. Judging from the detailed notes Sassoon made, he carefully prepared each of his presentations. Between his first official 'Commemorative Reading' at Bryn Mawr Women's College on 6 February and his last performance at the People's House Auditorium on 26 May, he revised his presentation at least eight times.

His increasing confidence is shown in a talk he gave to the women of Smith College a month after his first engagement. Judging his prepared line (about the effects of war on the individual soldier) unsuitable for a 'Talk About Poetry', he used his more recent experience in New York to bring his presentation to life. Sydney Cockerell, whose many contacts spanned the Atlantic, had given him an introduction to Miss Belle Greene, curator of the Pierpont Morgan Library, and Sassoon had used it gratefully as a retreat from an increasingly hectic social life. And he began his talk at Smith with a description of reading a Keats manuscript in the Morgan's 'sound-proof sanctuary',[5] which enabled him to lead on quite naturally to a consideration of Keats's views on poetry.

Smith was only one of the disproportionately large number of women's institutions he visited at the start and, just as he had not hesitated to exploit his youthfulness at the Poetry Society dinner, so he used his masculine charms to appeal to his female audiences. Though he claimed that addressing large audiences made him feel as if his soul had been 'undressed in public', he also admitted to the 'somewhat insidious allurement of doing it'.[6] He was certainly very conscious of the charm he exercised over American women, as his parody of his own war poem 'The General' shows:

'Good evening; good evening!' the lecturer bowed,
When we heard him last Monday in Carnegie Hall.
Now the charm of his smile has caught on with the crowd,
And he's promised to come here again in the fall.
'I'm afraid he's a Red!' whispered Dora to Daisy,
As he cursed the old men who in wartime were lazy.

. . . .

But the lilt of his eyebrow has sent them both crazy![7]

Ironically, in view of the fact that Sassoon laid the blame for the War largely on women in his preliminary address, five of Sassoon's first six engagements were at female institutions: Bryn Mawr, near Philadelphia, on 6 February was followed by Stamford's Women's Club in upstate New York on 18 February, the Cosmopolitan Club in New York City on 24 February, Smith College at Northampton, Massachusetts on 3 March (he also visited the nearby men's college, Amherst, on the 4th) and the Women's International League of Philadelphia on 10 March.[8] It was a relatively gentle introduction to the lecture circuit. And since all the engagements were either in New York or a few hours' train-ride from it, he was able to save himself the cost of hotel bills, which were not included in Pond's contract.

Most of February and early March, however, was spent in New York. Once free from toothache he started to find it more interesting. Though the population of Greater New York was less than that of Greater London in 1920, its centre was far more crowded and the pace of life already much faster. A recent large increase in Italian, Irish, German and Russian immigrants, many of whom were Jewish, gave New York an exotic, cosmopolitan flavour and Sassoon found the 'strange mixture of faces' exciting.[9]

Present-day landmarks, such as the Empire State Building and Rockefeller Center, were not then part of the scenery, but there were already a number of buildings over twenty storeys, impressively high to English eyes. To Sassoon New York seemed all skyscape: the night skies, in particular, he found 'strangely attractive', 'its lights and Whistler effects, and the ceaseless drone of activity and the towering buildings'.[10]

When he moved after his first few days to Westover Court at 210 West 44th Street, it was the night sky that dominated his impressions. Situated just off Broadway at Times Square in the heart of theatre-land, his small flat looked out on the Putnam Building and a huge neon sign advertising Wrigley's chewing gum. It was a district which never slept and Sassoon was often kept awake until 3 a.m. by the sound of heavy lorries collecting the first edition of the *New York Times*, printed next door to his own building. No wonder that he described New York as 'a sort of insomnia'.[11] As he observed with some restraint, living in Westover Court was 'an acclimatizing experience'.[12]

If Westover Court could not 'acclimatize' him, however, it was undeniably convenient, since he quickly found himself being invited to plays, concerts and operas in the surrounding neighbourhood. Within easy walking distance of the Pond Lyceum Bureau, Grand Central Station and most of the city's well-known clubs, such as the Century at 43rd Street, which had a reciprocal membership agreement with the Reform, it could hardly have been better placed. Part of the Vincent Astor Estate, Westover Court looked out on the Astor Hotel, where he sometimes ate.

Westover Court had another feature which suited Sassoon: it was a bachelor establishment, occupied largely by actors, artists and singers. He had soon tired of the constant attentions of the smart society hostesses and other well-meaning women who had welcomed him to New York. English friends, such as Masefield, Nichols and Cockerell, had supplied him, in all good faith, with numerous contacts, most of them female.[13] To begin with he had followed these up conscientiously, believing that the success of his lecture tour depended on it. Once the social machine had been set in motion, however, he began to panic and felt 'driven half off [his] head' by it. So much so that when one of his favourite hunting characters from the war years, 'The Mister', turned up from Limerick 'to see to his affairs', Sassoon was unable to appreciate him.[14] Looking just the same in a 'grand' overcoat with a bunch of violets in his buttonhole, he struck the distracted poet as an 'almost apparitional personality' and too forceful an addition to his already demanding schedule.[15] By 1 March he had started to rebel, refusing further invitations from unknown hostesses and gravitating instead towards a small circle of liberal-minded and intelligent people, preferably male. He was fortunate enough to meet three such men in New York, all of whom would remain friends long after he returned to England.

The first of these, Louis Untermeyer, had been an admirer of his poetry since at least August 1918, when he picked Sassoon out for special praise in his review of *Georgian Poetry: 1916-1917*.[16] He had sent Sassoon a collection of his own poems shortly afterwards, followed by a glowing review of *The Old Huntsman* and *Counter-Attack* of March 1919 and a copy of his anthology *Modern American Poetry* two months later.[17] Besides arranging for some of Sassoon's more recent work to be published in America, he also planned to include him in his projected anthology, *Modern British Poetry*.

Untermeyer was the sole person Sassoon knew on his arrival and he was grateful for his ebullient welcome. Invited immediately to Untermeyer's apartment on the Upper West Side, an area inhabited largely by artists and intellectuals, he was to spend many enjoyable evenings there with the dynamic little German Jew and his wife, Jean. They had married young and, although Louis was only a year older than Sassoon, he already had a teenage son who added to the domesticity.[18] Sassoon felt more at home there than anywhere else in New York and considered the Untermeyers two of the 'dearest friends' he made in America.[19] As with Turner, he found Untermeyer's exuberant, extrovert personality a useful balance to his own shyness and awkwardness. Though still working for the family jewellery business at the age of thirty-five, Untermeyer had created a rich cultural life for himself in the city and he admitted Sassoon to it with great generosity and enthusiasm. Louis's main interest was poetry and he and his wife, both practising poets, were proud to introduce Sassoon to some of America's most famous poets of the time at their apartment – Robert Frost, Vachel Lindsay and, later, Amy Lowell.[20]

Untermeyer's connections in the literary world were not limited to poets. His own prodigious output had also brought him into contact with publishers, editors, playwrights and university lecturers and he made it his business to help Sassoon remedy Pond's failure. As early as 5 February he was writing to Professor Gauss at Princeton to offer Sassoon's services and Sassoon was duly booked to speak to Princeton's Freneau Club on 11 March at the 'special' fee of $50. Untermeyer was equally successful with Yale, where Sassoon spoke to the Elizabethan Club for the same 'special' rate five days later. It is not difficult to see why Untermeyer's family were reluctant to lose his services as a jewellery salesman.

A highly practical man, Untermeyer also introduced Sassoon to several magazine and newspaper editors. One of the first of these worked for the *New York Tribune*, where Sassoon was subsequently given a blaze of publicity in an article written by – who else? – Untermeyer: 'Lilting Poet. Back from War. Speaks in Trumpet Tones'.[21] Untermeyer was also responsible for Sassoon's lucrative connection with Frank Crowninshield of *Vanity Fair*, who commissioned several articles from him and published at least eleven of his poems.[22]

Appreciative as Sassoon was of such efforts, he felt grateful above all for Untermeyer's introduction to New York's 'magnificent music'.[23] Before leaving school at fifteen, Untermeyer had wanted to be a composer, and his wife shared his strong musical interests.[24] One of their earliest invitations to Sassoon was to a recital by the world-class pianist Richard Buhlig, another of Louis's protégés. Sassoon had admired Buhlig greatly in pre-war England, and forty-five years after hearing him play Schumann's 'Fantastic' in C major in the Untermeyers' flat he would still be able to recall the thrill.[25]

Others in the musical world whom he met through the Untermeyers included Helen Tas, a talented violinist married to a Dutch diamond merchant, whom Sassoon would later visit in Holland in the 1920s. Such contacts, together with all the concerts and operas Louis and Jean took him to, gave him less reason than usual to miss his piano, as he often did on holiday.

Louis also took him to plays and one of these, a lavish production of *Richard III*, was responsible for a rare poem written in America, 'First Night: Richard III'.[26] Though not of great interest in itself, as Sassoon noted, it has technical significance as one of his first experiments in a genre he would explore for the next five years, social satire.[27]

A more successful attempt in the same genre, 'Storm on Fifth Avenue', written about the same time and almost certainly also inspired by an evening with Untermeyer, suggests that Sassoon was better at self-satire than satire of others:

A sallow waiter brings me beans and pork ...
Outside there's fury in the firmament.
Ice-cream, of course, will follow; and I'm content.
O Babylon! O Carthage! O New York!   (*CP*, p. 143)

There is no doubt that Sassoon appreciated Untermeyer, and not just his shrewd, practical help in the New York jungle. He particularly enjoyed his sense of humour, which was fairly similar to his own. A jokey verse-letter from him, for example, would elicit an equally witty rhymed response from his American friend.[28] Above all he loved Louis's enormous gusto for life. One of his fondest memories of New York would be 'a sudden glimpse of Louis's face behind a mound of vanilla ice-cream'.[29] Untermeyer undoubtedly valued Sassoon's friendship and continued to be an ardent admirer of his poetry.

It was, however, an admiration Sassoon could not wholeheartedly return. For theirs was largely an attraction of opposites. A certain brashness about Untermeyer – tactfully referred to as 'smart-minded immaturity' by Sassoon[30] – would prevent a deeper understanding developing. Even during his stay in New York there were things Sassoon felt unable to share with Untermeyer. He needed someone more mature, more sensitive or less worldly on occasions and was lucky enough to find it in two people who happened to be friends of Untermeyer, both, like him, of German-Jewish origin, both part of his literary and musical spheres.

He met the first of these, Ben Huebsch, directly through Untermeyer. Like Untermeyer and many other first-generation immigrants, Huebsch had had to start work young, first as an apprentice lithographer, then running a printing works with his brother, but had made up for his lack of university education by taking night classes. He had studied art at the Cooper Union and violin under Sam Franko, eventually becoming music critic for the *New York Sun*. His greatest commitment, however, was to literature. By the time Sassoon arrived in New York, Huebsch had launched his own small publishing house, which had already brought out Joyce's *Dubliners*, and had also started a weekly magazine of some repute, *The Freeman*. And when Huebsch went on to merge his own small firm with Viking in 1925, he would become, with one exception, the sole publisher of Sassoon's poetry in America.[31]

Sassoon himself described Huebsch as 'one of the most likeable men' in America and found his 'calmly judicious and benevolent personality' a welcome antidote to his own still occasionally juvenile behaviour.[32] Ten years older than Sassoon and about to marry, he gave him a much-needed feeling of 'serenity'.[33] 'Good and dear Ben' was how Sassoon would think of him throughout their long friendship.

Another side to Huebsch that Sassoon particularly appreciated in 1920, when he was still planning to be a good socialist, was his commitment to left-wing causes. An activist in the American Civil Liberties Union, he introduced Sassoon to labour circles, which led to invitations to address the Inter-Collegiate

Socialist Society, the Cooper Union and the Rand School.[34] At one point in his visit Sassoon was intending to stay on for the presidential elections. And it was probably Huebsch who introduced him to his fellow-countryman Harold Laski, then lecturing at Harvard, where Sassoon was subsequently invited to talk.[35]

Huebsch was also responsible for arranging a very different kind of engagement for Sassoon at the Free Synagogue in Carnegie Hall. 'As regards the Rabbi – I leave it to you,' Sassoon wrote to him in March 1920. The event itself, on 25 April, made him more conscious than he had previously been of his own Jewish blood. (He had made no close Jewish friends until his arrival in New York.) Faced with a 'prosperous and complacent' audience of over 2,000 at the Free Synagogue, he found himself behaving as though some 'angry prophet in [his] Jewish ancestry' had taken over.[36] Instead of simply reading his poems, as arranged, he delivered a blistering attack on his listeners for their ignorance of war's realities, surprising himself as well as his audience by his 'stern and dispassionate ferocity'.[37] This direct identification with Jewishness may be the most significant effect of his American visit.

It was an awareness which had been growing since his arrival in New York, one which had been stimulated unintentionally by his greatest friend of all in America, Sam Behrman.[38] Sam, the son of a rabbi from Worcester, Massachusetts, had mainly Jewish friends. Knowing Sassoon's love of music, he had taken him to visit the sister of one of them, the violinist Emily Gresser. Emily's father, a nineteenth-century Russian liberal, seemed awed at meeting a Sassoon and immediately asked him about his ancestry. When Sassoon showed little interest in it, Mr Gresser ran to the bookshelves and brought over the 'S' volume of the *Jewish Encyclopaedia*. 'He confronted Siegfried with pages about his ancestors,' Behrman recalled, 'enlivened by engravings of turbaned ancestors. One dignitary, with an immense white beard and magisterial expression, seemed to interest him particularly.'[39] This was almost certainly Sassoon's great-grandfather, the patriarch David Sassoon, an impressive reminder of all that was noblest in his father's family.

Sassoon had first met Behrman when he arrived at Westover Court to find himself living next door to 'a crashing old-young spectacled admirer who rushed in, and bored [him] at intervals'.[40] Behrman, who worked for the *New York Times*, also interviewed him for his paper.[41] Like Huebsch and Untermeyer he had strong musical interests, and would marry the sister of the Russian musician Jaffa Heifetz. One of his great friends was the Russian pianist Chotzinoff, who became another brother-in-law, and the Gershwin brothers were also close.

A graduate of Harvard and Columbia, Behrman was working as a freelance journalist while he struggled to establish himself as a playwright. Neither he nor Sassoon could foresee just how successful he would become and in 1920 he was the one person in New York with whom Sassoon could be what he called his 'ordinary' self.[42] Though Behrman found him far from 'ordinary', he had the good playwright's firm grasp of character and understood Sassoon's needs.

When the flood of social invitations was at its height, he was able to reassure Sassoon and guide him through what he delighted to call his 'praeternatural popularity',[43] becoming in effect his unpaid social secretary.

Though Behrman could be ruthless in dealing with Sassoon's social engagements, he was personally the 'nicest' of people according to Sassoon, who often used the word 'angelic' to describe him.[44] While maintaining that Sam was 'really too nice for words', he found plenty of other words for him too.[45] One of his favourites was 'little', a term used not just to emphasize his own superior height, but, as with Blunden, to indicate a strongly protective feeling. Sam was not quite as young as Blunden, but still seven years younger than Sassoon and not nearly so successful at that point. He also lacked the good looks of Sassoon, who appeared in Sam's eyes as 'tall, lithe and extraordinarily handsome'.[46] Ted Morgan, who knew Sam well, said that Sam believed he was physically ugly and Morgan's description certainly makes him seem so: 'On a squat body perched a large head with a high forehead and nearsighted eyes that blinked through thick-lensed glasses .... He never looked freshly shaven because his beard successfully resisted all razors. His walk was like the waddle of a penguin.' Yet, as a friend, Ted Morgan, testifies there was something very attractive about Behrman, 'an extraordinary warmth and charm'.[47]

Part of Behrman's charm for Sassoon lay in his humour, which insisted on assigning his friend the role of a gangling English eccentric. Sam chose to regard him as a 'quaintly trustful person on whom life was playing a series of practical jokes', a part Sassoon found himself involuntarily adopting in his company.[48] He tripped over things, forgot what he was doing and continually fulfilled Sam's idea of him. On one occasion, absent-mindedly stretching out his long legs in a very small, very ramshackle taxi, he broke the glass in the driver's partition. To Sam's glee the driver instantly leapt out, demanded 'Twenty dollars!' and advised his passenger to 'leave his legs at home next time'.[49] When particularly delighted by Sassoon's unworldliness, Sam would speak of him in the third person: 'He hasn't yet called on his publisher,' he crowed, after they had known each other about a month: 'Another example of his deeply organized business instinct!'[50]

Sassoon enjoyed Behrman's humour for the same reason Behrman appreciated his, that it was so different. He loved Sam's 'wisecracking' remarks and 'smart slang phrases', which seemed so much more expressive than the conversation of the highly cultivated New York society he was trying to avoid. Only someone as unashamedly American as Sam, for example, after racking his brains for something to send Sassoon's larger-than-life friend Nellie Burton, could say, 'I'd like to send her Niagara Falls.'[51]

Sassoon's best moments were spent with Sam in modest restaurants or cafés near Times Square, eating, say, a club sandwich, while Sam lectured him on playwriting or journalism. At such times he felt he was in touch with the 'reality' of New York.[52] His own attempts to satisfy Sam's interest in the British literary scene are revealing. 'His love for some of them – Edmund Blunden and

Wilfred Owen for example – was passionate,' Behrman remembered: 'He read their works aloud to me; he talked for hours about their distilled virtues.'[53]

*

Behrman would ultimately become for Sassoon the 'main human fact' of his visit to America, 'superseding' all the other friends he made there.[54] And it was Behrman he turned to when trouble arose. Writing to Turner on 21 February, Sassoon had reported that he was emerging from his initial crises and beginning to find New York 'great fun'.[55] A week later he was sending Meiklejohn a hundred pounds for Gabriel to join him at the end of April and all seemed well. Only two weeks after that, however, he was telling Ottoline that there were 'complications' and that he had cancelled Gabriel's visit, which would have been 'a great mistake'.[56] Clearly something dramatic had happened to account for his odd behaviour. The explanation was that he had become completely infatuated with someone else. But almost as soon as he cancelled Gabriel's visit the affair had (in his own words) 'ended disastrously'.[57]

It is possible that he had already met the young man concerned by 21 February, when he had ended a letter to Turner: 'All will be well if I can avoid falling in love!'[58] But it is more likely that he merely feared his own propensity for sudden and violent infatuations. Whatever lay behind his statement to Turner, it was a prophetic one, for by 10 March he had become deeply involved in the affair and by 16 March it was over.

Glenn Hunter was an American actor eleven years younger than Sassoon.[59] Sassoon may first have seen him on one of his many visits to the theatre with Untermeyer and Behrman. Hunter's theatre, the Hudson, was only a few blocks from Westover Court, which explains Sassoon's reference to being 'led such a devilish dance up and down West 44th Street' in March 1920.[60] Hunter was appearing in a highly successful play, *Clarence*. He had been cast as the ne'er-do-well son and his boyish good looks may have drawn Sassoon to the stage door after the performance.[61]

Judging from several later affairs, Sassoon felt a particular attraction to young male actors. It was not simply that they tended to be handsome and at least sympathetic towards homosexuals, if not homosexual themselves; they were also, he believed, involved in an important artistic profession. Behrman, who knew Hunter, called him 'talented, good-looking and absolutely empty ... a thoroughly commonplace young man'.[62] He had been taken into Sassoon's confidence only after the affair had run its violent course, leaving its victim humiliated and in deep despair. Though Sassoon was reluctant to give details, even in his diary, he did say that Hunter treated him 'like dirt' and that it would be years before he felt able to trust anyone again.[63]

But in 1920 there was one man he *could* trust, Behrman. (Rivers, whom he might have turned to, had just left for Baltimore after a few days in New York.) Young, inexperienced and heterosexual, Sam was at first 'bewildered, horrified and shocked' by a 'variety of love' about which he knew little.[64] But in the face of 'such suffering, such unmitigated agony' as Sassoon's, he quickly surmounted his prejudice and became, as far as Sassoon was concerned, 'an absolute darling, full of sympathy and understanding'.[65] Though neither of them describes the affair in their autobiographies, Behrman refers obliquely to his friend's 'private agony'.[66] Sassoon told no one else to begin with, though Ottoline, one of his closest confidantes in England, probably guessed what he meant when he alluded to an 'amazing experience' which had brought him close to breakdown.[67]

He was saved from complete collapse by Sam's sympathy; also by his lecture itinerary, which became more demanding in mid-March, providing a much-needed distraction. By then Pond's troubles had reached crisis point and he was obliged to tell Sassoon that he was on his own. Before doing so, however, he had booked him an engagement near Chicago through his branch office there, and two days after Hunter's final, brutal rejection, Sassoon set out for the Midwest. Stopping overnight at Rochester in upstate New York to lecture to the Associate Alumnae of Vassar, he continued on to Chicago and arrived in the city on 20 March.[68]

*

When Sassoon arrived in Chicago in 1920 it was still the most important railhead, grain market, livestock and meat-packing centre and lumber exchange in the world. Though he showed no awareness of these facts, he did know that it had a population of over two million and was second only to New York in importance. There is also a strong possibility that he had read Upton Sinclair's grim picture of the Chicago stockyards, *The Jungle* (1906). So that it would almost certainly have come as a surprise to see the beauty of the city: not just the strange beauty of a towering skyline, already encountered in New York – though Chicago was known as 'Skyscraper City' – but its dramatic architecture and the attractiveness of its waterfront setting. ('The lake is very fine,' he told his mother.[69]) Situated on the south-west corner of Lake Michigan with views protected by extensive parkland, it was also called the Garden City. And since Sassoon's first night was spent at the Auditorium Hotel, a magnificent building overlooking the lake, he might well have wondered why Chicago was mainly associated with its slaughterhouses.

Before visiting those stockyards, however, or discovering more about the city, he was obliged to leave it. His first, and only pre-booked, engagement was about thirty miles north of Chicago at Lake Forest, where he had agreed to talk to the girls of Ferry Hall School. After a successful performance in the school chapel ('Poems went well. Voice improving', he noted), he spent the night and the following week with a retired lawyer and his wife. The Horace Martins, whose low, rambling house in wooded grounds was only a few minutes' walk from the school, were ideal company for the exhausted Sassoon.[70] Long walks by Lake Michigan and desultory reading of outdated London journals restored his energy and after a few days he was ready to follow up the contacts they kindly offered.

The first of these, an introduction to the composer John Alden Carpenter, was also Sassoon's first taste of Chicago's rich cultural life.[71] Carpenter, who was later to set several of Sassoon's poems to music, invited him to a recital by the cellist Pablo Casals, who happened to be playing some of Sassoon's favourite music by Bach the day they met. Sassoon was deeply moved by Casals' performance and would attend other concerts during his stay, but it was the literary rather than musical life of the city which interested him most. Chicago in 1920 was associated with some of the best-known American writers of the time, such as the novelists Upton Sinclair, Theodore Dreiser, Sinclair Lewis and John Dos Passos, and the poets Carl Sandburg and Edgar Lee Masters. It was also home to Harriet Monroe's groundbreaking *Poetry* magazine, which played a prominent part in the movement known as the Chicago Renaissance.[72]

Sassoon would not have had much sympathy with *Poetry*'s Modernist aims, but he was delighted to meet one of its main contributors, Carl Sandburg[73] Sandburg's *Chicago Poems* (1916) had already established him as a major poet, but he continued to work as labour editor for the *Chicago Daily News*. It seemed to Sassoon an appropriate setting for the man he called 'the Whitmanesque poet of the Middle West':[74] 'forty years old, grey and tired-looking, with a deep voice and something wonderful about him – really big'.[75]

Sandburg appeared to Sassoon built on a larger scale than either Lindsay or Frost, though he shared the latter's 'deeply serious' humour.[76] Whereas Frost observed the 'minutiae of nature', Sandburg dealt in harsher realities. No one, Sassoon felt, had described Chicago better than Sandburg, its 'polyglot raw material', its 'teeming rudimentariness', which Sandburg had insisted on showing him and which he might otherwise not have seen. As he stood with Sandburg on the roof of a huge building, staring across Chicago's canyon-like streets and façades, a stormy sunset transformed the city and he noticed how it coloured not just the elegant boulevards but also the drifting clouds of factory smoke. It was indeed a place of extreme contrasts, as Sandburg had shown in his poem addressed to the city he called the 'Hog Butcher' of the world.[77]

Sassoon did not agree with Sandburg's definition of poetry as 'a series of explanations of life, fading off into horizons too swift for explanations', but he did respect his opinion in other areas.[78] It was Sandburg who made him realize that bullets, bombs, bayonets and gas were 'nothing more than words' to the majority of Americans and in doing so he provided the 'central point' of Sassoon's trip.[79] His mainly female audiences had been either too charmed or too inexperienced to question his message that 'war doesn't pay', his only challenge coming from a man whose son had been killed in the conflict.[80] But with more than half his lectures left to give, Sandburg's suggestion was an unsettling thought.

*

Sassoon's main motive in visiting Chicago had been to escape his unhappy affair in New York, the reason he accepted a another more impractical invitation to lecture at the University of Toronto: it would take him almost two days to get there and two days to get back by train for less than two days' stay. Not only was it a further distraction, however, but it also meant that he could see Frank Prewett, who still seemed to him as 'sweet' and 'loveable' as ever.[81] 'Toronto' had returned home from studying English at Oxford to take an organ course at the university, but he was missing England badly. One result of Sassoon's visit would be his promise to take Prewett back on the boat with him, an offer which would delay his own return by several months. With Prewett's help both the talk and the poetry-reading went well, one of the local newspapers comparing Sassoon to 'an avenging angel through whom the voice of slaughtered youth was speaking'.[82] His facility for playing on the emotions of his hearers was, he felt, becoming dangerously enjoyable.

Back in Chicago for his final fortnight he was exposed once more to the hectic social life he dreaded. His hostess on this occasion was a well-known local novelist, Janet Ayer, also, through her marriage to the owner of a large meat-packing firm, Kellogg Fairbank, one of the wealthiest and most influential people in Chicago society. So that Sassoon found himself staying in an elegant town house in an expensive area of the city[83] and, besides the concerts he craved, being taken to dine with a wealthy railway director, lunch with a millionaire meat-packer and politician, attend several evening parties and take a 'regular watering-place tittup' with Mrs Fairbank along Lake Drive.[84] Mrs Fairbank was also a woman of strong political concerns and he was obliged in addition to inspect two large maternity hospitals, as well as the stockyards, and to meet the famous social reformer Jane Addams.[85]

His hostess's energy and connections seemed limitless and she was no doubt responsible for some of the lectures he was asked to give in his final week. He was also helped by another socialite, Mrs Vaughan Moody, wife of an English professor at Chicago University, where he was asked to lecture to both the Friday Club and the Poetry Club.[86] His flattering letter to her from Rochester suggests that, however scornful he might be about such women, he was prepared to use them without hesitation when necessary.[87] Lectures to the Winnetka Women's Club, the Council of Jewish Women and the Arts Club completed his hectic schedule.[88]

*

Sassoon's greatest problem on arrival in New York had been a lack of engagements. Now, on his return to the city, he encountered the opposite. His own and his friends' efforts to fill the gaps had been almost too successful. But they had taken time to bear fruit, so that more than half his lectures had to be crammed into April or May. His five engagements in one week at Chicago had been followed by a rushed overnight stop at Cornell University on 15 April, with the result that he was already tired to start with.

Even before he had time to recover from his fourth long journey in four weeks, he was on the stage of the Greenwich Village Theater, which Pond had hired on 18 April. Columbia University on the 20th, Vassar College on the 23rd and appearances at both the Free Synagogue and the MacDowell Club on the 25 April concluded another exhausting week.

His final engagement for the month, the Harvard Poetry Club, was the one he most and least looked forward to. He was delighted to be staying with Harold Laski, who had already done a great deal to help and encourage him in America, and he was anxious to meet Amy Lowell, whom he believed responsible for his invitation.[89] But he had come straight to Boston from a talk to the women of Wellesley College and was so 'thoroughly overtired' that he had to 'screw [himself] up' to appear on the platform at all.[90] He had also been told to expect some strong militarist opposition. In the event, after a day in bed and some skilful chairing by Amy Lowell, the meeting passed off peacefully. Though he had been too exhausted to meet any of the interesting people Laski had lined up for him, he was able to enjoy an evening after his lecture with the two who most fascinated him, Lowell and Laski themselves.

There was one curious footnote to Sassoon's stay in Boston which probably brought the War nearer for him than any of his talks or war poems. This was a meeting with one of his best friends from the 1st Royal Welch Fusiliers, 'Birdie' Stansfield. As fat and cheerful as ever, he was doing well as a wool-broker in North America, the trenches firmly behind him.

Fearing himself close to breakdown at the end of April, Sassoon cancelled all further engagements with the exception of a few minor ones in New York. Thus ended what he called his 'diminutive attempt to make known to Americans an interpretation of the war as seen by the fighting man'.[91] Judging from the grateful letters he received from ex-soldiers, it seemed to him that his campaign had been moderately successful, though it is difficult to believe that it made much difference overall. Its main significance appears to have been in helping to purge his own system of the War.

He had intended to cover the presidential election in San Francisco in June for one of the big papers, but stayed in New York instead, hoping to relax and enjoy his remaining time in America. By waiting for Prewett to make up his mind whether to return with him or not, he had forfeited the possibility of sailing home before August, leaving him three whole months to fill. With Behrman's encouragement and help he moved into a larger flat at Westover Court, hired a grand piano, bought himself a straw hat and started to write again. Apart from a few poems, he had attempted nothing serious since his arrival. But Behrman, who thought it would be therapeutic, urged him to write a story about his unhappy affair with Hunter. Though he knew that this particular story was 'quite unpublishable', owing to its homosexual theme, it helped him through a bad phase: 'Work is the only anodyne.'[92] He eventually abandoned the story as 'too personal', but it is an intriguing forerunner of his prose trilogies.

Even before he stopped writing his story in early July, Sassoon had found something other than 'drifting round Broadway' to fill his time.[93] Rivers had introduced him to his neurologist friend John MacCurdy, who had a country house about thirty miles north of the city.[94] As the fierce New York summer got under way Sassoon began to spend several days a week there, playing golf at the Westchester County Club and enjoying the peace of the country. He was also invited to spend time on Staten Island with Russell Loines and his family. Loines, who was a marine-insurance lawyer, was also a devotee of poets and welcomed many of them to America.

By July such escapes from New York became increasingly attractive as the city grew ever more stifling. So that, when an invitation arrived to stay in Maine with a man he had met briefly at Wellesley College, Edward Percy Warren, it seemed an attractive idea. Sassoon claimed that what finally convinced him to take a 300-mile train journey to stay with an almost total stranger was that Warren had known Ross. He fails to mention that the 'freemasonry' he says this created was specifically that of fellow-homosexuals.[95] Warren, who wrote homoerotic verse about adolescents under the pseudonym Arthur Lyon Raile, was already ten years into his life's work, *The Defence of Uranian Love*, when they met.[96] At the age of sixty he was still unmarried. A wealthy art collector, respected connoisseur and classical scholar, with degrees from both Harvard and Oxford, Warren had been made a fellow of Corpus Christi College in 1915.

Warren's American estate, Fewacres, was organized along English country house lines, complete with a butler who served afternoon tea. Though modest in scale, Fewacres was an aesthete's delight of 'Doric porches, golden torsos, etc.'.[97] Only a few miles out of the town of Westbrook, where Warren's father had founded a highly profitable paper mill, the house was surrounded by half-wild countryside, which gave Sassoon the impression that 'the landscape was its garden and the darkness of the distant wood its boundary'.[98] From the plain but perfect country food to his host's daily study of the classics, he is at pains to suggest an atmosphere of high-minded but luxurious simplicity. He does not mention something he almost certainly knew, which is that Warren's 'serenely civilized existence' centred round his still unfinished *magnum opus*, his attempt to justify what he euphemistically termed 'lad's love'.[99]

Read in this light, Sassoon's description of his visit abounds in ambiguities. When, for example, he wrote that Warren had a temperament 'which excels in intimacy with the young', it is difficult not to read that as an oblique reference to his pederasty.[100] Or when Sassoon claims that Warren found his stay 'memorably delightful', the reader starts to wonder exactly what kind of relationship the older man had with his attractive, still very youthful-looking guest.[101] Did he discuss his theories during the long, 'sort of one-sided platonic dialogue' he carried on with Sassoon over his four-week stay? And did Sassoon, whose only confidant in America had been the puzzled, heterosexual Behrman, find relief in telling Warren about Glenn Hunter? Such questions can only be speculative. What is more certain is the physical benefit Sassoon derived from his stay. Warren had been a keen rider in his youth and, though he no longer kept a stable of Arab horses, he did have an old grey mare which he encouraged his guest to ride.

It seemed to Sassoon the best antidote to the past few months of hectic city life he could imagine. The old mare soothed him greatly, offering both mental as well as physical benefit and reminding him how much he missed the activity. One of the first things he did on returning to England a month later would be to buy himself a horse, a minor but positive result of his American trip. His mental peace was added to by Warren's resolute refusal to discuss either his lecture tour or war poetry. A man of great physical energy and needs, Sassoon was glad of other outlets at Fewacres, from swimming and canoeing to chopping down trees.

Evenings were equally relaxing. After a plain but excellent dinner he would sit and watch the sun go down with Warren before an early bedtime. For the first time since the War, when the contrast with the trenches had made him fully appreciate the countryside behind the lines, he felt he was in 'Arcadia' and Warren had no difficulty in persuading him to remain far longer than he had intended. It was the land of the Lotus Eaters. Sassoon felt that at Fewacres he had completed an exploration which had begun when he left England. And in a sense he had. For less than a fortnight after returning to New York, on 12 August, he was boarding the *Imperator*, an ex-German liner bound for Southampton.

*

Sassoon's journey home was very different from his voyage out. Not only was he sailing on a much larger ship, but it was one which carried a party of Hollywood stars. When he arrived at the dock, such celebrities of the silent screen as Olive Thomas, Jack Pickford and Alma Rubens were being given a high-profile send-off by their vociferous fans and an eager press. Pickford was so drunk he could hardly stand and Sassoon was amused to think how puzzled he would be when he woke the next morning to find himself at sea.

Though not the centre of this exuberant farewell, Sassoon was far from solitary, as he had been on the way out. Behrman, convinced that they would never meet again, had come to see him off and his other great friend, Huebsch, was actually travelling with him. (Prewett, when it came to it, was not.) Whereas Sassoon had spent the ten days' journey from Portsmouth contemplating his post-war problems, the eight days' journey home was passed more convivially in Huebsch's company.

He was also feeling much fitter. Expert dental treatment and a long stay in the country had left him full of physical energy, so that when the other passengers went below for their meals he often raced round the deck, jumping the railings like a hurdler. One of Huebsch's abiding memories of the trip was the sight of his unpredictable friend climbing dangerously high up a ship's mast.[102]

The greatest difference in Sassoon's return journey, however, was not in external circumstances but in himself. For America had affected him far more than he or any of his English friends could have predicted. His seven months there, he told Behrman shortly after his arrival home, had been 'in a way the most extraordinary I shall ever experience'.[103] They had undoubtedly broadened his horizons. It was not until he reached America that he had been fully exposed to another culture, and this contact with a completely new, often alien, environment, which at least one of his friends could not imagine him surviving for two days, had brought him out of himself to a surprising degree. And his growing enjoyment of his 'performances' during his tour suggests a significant increase in confidence. Behrman, Huebsch and Untermeyer in particular, had strengthened that confidence with their firm belief in his literary powers. They had also added to his circle of close friends. Behrman, moreover, was responsible for another important development in New York, Sassoon's first serious attempt at prose-writing, which would lead to his greatest prose success, *Memoirs of a Fox-Hunting Man*.[104]

More immediately, his American stay had helped Sassoon to 'get right away from all the Georgians and their conventional poetic vocabularies', as he put it to Ottoline.[105] Distancing himself from Marsh and his friends geographically had helped him separate himself from them mentally. Though far from agreeing fully with the technical experiments of Lindsay, Sandburg and Amy Lowell, meeting them and other Modernist poets had made him realize the limitations of an increasingly effete Georgian tradition. He had written little poetry of his own during his stay and felt 'rather hopeless' about the future direction of his work,[106] but he returned to England at least knowing what he wanted to avoid. In fact his few American poems, all experiments in 'occasional' or satirical verse, suggest that his American experience would shape the course of his poetry over the next five years. It had also convinced him that what he really wanted was 'to go on being a poet'.[107] It was partly for this reason, partly because America created a distance between himself and English politics, that he had decided by the end of his stay to give up his *Daily Herald* post.

On a more practical level his trip had provided him with a direction and the money to pursue it at a time of great personal bewilderment. Quite apart from money from magazine publications, he had earned a great deal from his tour – $2,562, at a time when the rent of a pleasant flat in central New York cost $35 per month. Despite Pond's failure, he had earned about $90 a lecture, almost twice as much as de la Mare had on a similar tour in 1917. Though it is doubtful that he arrived in England with much in his pocket, he had lived well, travelled widely and felt more sense of purpose and success than he had in post-war England.

Yet Sassoon would claim in 1924 that he was 'completely disintegrated' when he returned from America.[108] His 'ghastly cardiac enterprise', as he described his affair to Forster, his physical and mental exhaustion during a hectic lecture tour, his failure to write more than a few minor poems and his acute loneliness at times would support this interpretation of his trip. On the other hand, he told Ottoline that he felt 'stronger' for his stay.[109] By the time he arrived in England on 20 August 1920 he felt that he had 'come to the end of the journey on which [he] had set out when [he] enlisted in the army six years before'.[110] Both statements have some truth in them. Only by facing extreme change and trying to purge himself completely of his war poetry could he gain the strength to continue with what still seemed to him a fairly meaningless existence.

22

Tufton Street Blues

August 1920–November 1925

Sassoon brings his published autobiography to a neat conclusion in August 1920 with the assertion that his American trip had freed him from the War. But the most cursory look at his life in the early 1920s suggests that this was not so. While his frequent references to his 'fiendish' or 'vile' temper in his diary might be explained as simply a character trait, other allusions to a 'poisoned mind; an unwholesome unhappiness' pervading his 'healthy body' show that he regarded his state as an unnatural one.[1]

His main problem was his failure to find a 'moral equivalent' for war.[2] Though he had stopped thinking about the War consciously, there were still times when it seemed more real than events around him. Men like Lance-Corporal Gibson, whose death at Mametz Wood in July 1916 had provoked one of his most daring raids,[3] returned to haunt him, asking in effect the question Sassoon himself had posed in 'Sick Leave': 'Why are you here with all your watches ended?'[4] On such occasions Sassoon felt that he was only 'half-alive', that a part of him had 'died with all the Gibsons I used to know'.[5]

His 'sheet-anchor' in this slow recuperation from the War was Turner.[6] Together with his wife, Delphine, he formed the 'rock' on which Sassoon hoped to build his 'lighthouse'.[7] Before leaving for America Sassoon had already moved into the house they had agreed to share in Westminster, so that it was with a sense of belonging, however frail, that he returned to London. Turner, more than anyone he knew except Rivers, imposed 'sanity and half-humorous scrutiny' on him.[8]

Both Turner and Sassoon have left accounts of their relationship which suggest that it was one of more than ordinary warmth and closeness in the early 1920s. Sassoon's description of their many late-night talks in Tufton Street gives the flavour: 'We discuss the arts of Music and Poetry; we arrive at the most downright and irrefutable conclusions, half-pitiful and half-contemptuous of the human race, we are infinitely thankful that we, at any rate, are not as other mortals. We do not so much *debate* as discover our own dazzling notions. Quite as often we argue about Love (or Sex).'[9]

Turner's account, in the third volume of his autobiographical novel, *The Duchess of Popocatapetl*, while equally positive, is much fuller. Perhaps because he half-conceals Sassoon's identity by introducing him under two names (as himself and as the protagonist, Airbubble's great friend, Blow), it is also franker and more revealing. Portraying Blow as a strikingly handsome young man very like Sassoon, he relates how Blow had become a hero in the War but had quickly grown critical of it. Almost too daring in the Front Line, he was nevertheless terrified of women, with the exception of the protagonist's wife (the real-life Delphine Turner, whom Sassoon indeed trusted). Details of Sassoon's actual army career are slightly altered and something of Rupert Brooke's character added, possibly to forestall charges of libel, but he is unmistakably the model for Blow. So that it is revealing to read that he is very irritated by 'the normal attitude in English middle-class society towards homosexuality' and greatly relieved to be able to confide in Airbubble (alias Turner) with his 'completely free and unprejudiced mind'.[10] He admits to spending 'hours hanging around the stage-door of a theatre madly in love with a young actor', a reference to either Glenn Hunter or one or two other young actors with whom Sassoon became infatuated in the early 1920s.[11]

In at least one respect, then, Tufton Street was of some significance to Sassoon. It was also important as his first serious London base and the one he would live in longest. Quite different from the large and rambling country house he had inhabited most of his life, it stood on the site of a former slum and the area still retained some of the small artisan dwellings and businesses which had sprung up there in the late eighteenth and nineteenth centuries. But as the working-class houses were first abandoned, then demolished at the beginning of the twentieth century, the developers had moved in and so had the middle classes. No. 54 Tufton Street, crammed on a small plot in what had been formerly a builder's yard (Bennett's Yard), was a typical developer's attempt to pack as much as possible onto a tiny site. It had no garden and was overshadowed on three sides by larger buildings, an effect which was exacerbated by the fact that it was set several feet down from the street. But in the first flush of enthusiasm Sassoon could see none of the disadvantages of these conditions, referring affectionately to his new dwelling as looking 'not unlike a very large doll's house'.[12]

Fortunately his own flat was on the second floor, so was not quite as dark as the rooms below it. He had the whole floor to himself, though this consisted of only two small rooms, each measuring about twelve feet by ten feet. His one regret was the lack of space for his baby grand piano, which had to go into the Turners' much larger living room on the first floor. Above him on the top floor were Walter's and Delphine's bedrooms, separate because, as Walter explained with characteristic frankness, their sexual relationship had been a failure due to his wife's frigidity. On the ground floor was a small kitchen, a dining room and a minute room which Turner rented to another Georgian poet, Edward Shanks, for his use on his once- or twice-weekly visits to London.

To live in someone else's house, however small, seemed to Sassoon 'an obvious way of simplifying the domiciliary problem'.[13] He did not want to live alone and was equally anxious not to take on the responsibility of organizing his own domestic arrangements. He also preferred to live as austerely as possible, his survival of the War having left him with a general sense of guilt which he tried to assuage by this means. (He was encouraged in this by Dr Rivers.) By twenty-first-century standards, however, his life was far from spartan. The Turners' daily help would clean his rooms and make his breakfast, always a cooked one. He would take his lunch and dinner at the Reform, which became, in effect, an extension of his living quarters, serving as both dining and drawing room for him and his friends. His daily walk there would be part of his routine for many years.

Another advantage at the start was his nearness to Chelsea, where Gabriel lived at 120 Cheyne Walk, a pleasant stroll along the Embankment. And if the evening there went well, the Thames seemed a suitable companion to Sassoon's mood as he walked back in the early hours – 'sombre and lit by silver ripples of a new understanding'.[14] He sometimes joked about the convenience of Westminster generally – if he lived there long enough, he claimed, his corpse would be within easy reach of Poets' Corner – but it was a decisive factor in the success of Tufton Street at the start. One of the most important benefits of his move had been his final escape from Weirleigh. Yet it had left him feeling intensely guilty about his mother. 'She belongs now to a different life from mine,' he wrote in his diary in June 1921, 'a remote worn-out life from which I've escaped into the adventurous uncertainties and perplexities of active experience.'[15] He still felt obliged to visit his mother, or entertain her on her fairly frequent trips to London, and it was useful to live so centrally. The greatest advantage of all, however, was the chance to make a new start after the War:

> *I am clear about one thing* [he wrote in September 1922]: my present life (since I met Turner) has been a struggle to shake off the past (sexual fetishism, vague piano-playing, athleticism of golf, cricket and hunting, etc.). I have been trying to catch up with the intellectualism of Turner, the Sitwells, and all the rest of my post-war friends ... I have consciously repressed the past; trying to *discard* it (avoiding Weirleigh).[16]

In Turner, Sassoon had found the ideal landlord for such an experiment, since Turner had already created a cultural centre of sorts at Tufton Street by the time Sassoon returned from America. Sassoon often joined the Turners and their guests in the evening and even when his post-war moodiness made him slip past their door to his own room on returning from the Reform, the constant hum of discussion and debate below made him feel 'vicariously involved in the activities of the intellectual and artistic world'.[17]

One of the Turners' most regular guests and the one Sassoon identified most closely with at Tufton Street, was the poet Ralph Hodgson, whom he had tried but failed to meet in 1914. Sassoon calculated that, from the time Hodgson started visiting in early 1920, to July 1924, when he left to take up a professorship at Sendai University in Japan, he must at a reasonable estimate have been '150 times and have smoked at least 1,000 pipes on our premises'.[18]

Hodgson's appearance, like everything else about him, was singular. Of only medium height and build and already forty-nine by the time Sassoon met him, he was nevertheless a physically impressive figure, with broad shoulders tapering down to narrow waist and hips. His strong, muscular features and dark, expressive eyes were set in what his friend Enid Bagnold described as a 'long-lipped lantern face'.[19] His slightly saturnine air, a reflection of what Sassoon called his 'dark side', made Blunden see him at times as 'a very dyspeptic Eagle'.[20] This may help to explain his attractiveness to women, who apparently sensed something 'passionate and sensuous' in him.[21] His own strong attraction towards them, however, was kept rigidly under control by a pronounced puritanism, which occasionally made him seem fanatical. As Sassoon noted, he was 'a passionate denouncer who would have sent you to the stake' for a cause he believed in.[22]

Hodgson was, above all, himself. From the old bowler hat he always wore, to the cheap, strong-smelling tobacco he constantly smoked in a long churchwarden pipe, or the faithful bull terrier which accompanied him and which was sorrowfully replaced when it died of old age, or his refusal to drink anything but ginger beer, or even his habit of lying down to talk in an effort to relieve the pain of chronic piles from which he suffered, he was instantly recognizable.

Hodgson is now remembered, if at all, for a striking poem or two (such as 'Time You Old Gipsy Man', 'The Bells of Heaven', or 'Eve'), in anthologies read in childhood. But to Sassoon and many others he seemed at the time 'a prodigious genius' and 'much the strongest of the Georgian poets', with whom he became connected.[23] A brilliant talker, he cast a spell over his listeners and left them with a sense of loss afterwards. Much of Hodgson's energy seems to have been dissipated in talk. After *The Song of Honour* in 1913 he did not produce another work of any substance until *The Muse and the Mastiff* in 1942 and even that was a disappointment to some of his greatest admirers, though not to the loyal Sassoon. Sassoon brings 'Hoddy' vividly to life, lying on the sofa at Tufton Street, stabbing his pipe in the air for emphasis, bull terrier at his feet, while he rides one of his many hobby-horses into the early hours of the morning.

It is not surprising that Sassoon found Hodgson fascinating. What is less predictable is that he should have become one of his closest and lifelong friends. They were so different in many ways. Hodgson, born to a lower-middle-class family in the North, had had little formal education. He was a great believer in science and very positive about most modern developments, infuriating the drama critic Turner by arguing that 'cinema should supersede the theatre'[24] and disturbing Sassoon with his receptiveness towards Modernist poetry. (He became a friend of T.S. Eliot.) Three times married, he was flamboyantly heterosexual: for proof that the world was improving, he argued, you had only 'to look at the legs of the girls ... in the street and think what they were twenty-five years ago', not a convincing argument as far as Sassoon was concerned.[25] He was opposed to one of Sassoon's favourite sports, hunting, and worst of all did not admire Hardy, whose pessimism was a direct contradiction of his own fervent belief in progress.

Yet it was Hodgson's similarity to Hardy in some respects which attracted Sassoon to him, his 'unique quality of flavour and intensity', for example, his unworldliness and the 'startling freshness' of his poetic voice.[26] Like Hardy – and Sassoon himself – he had a great reverence for originality, which they all found in unexpected places. Blunden, Hodgson and Sassoon agreed, had more of this 'flavour' than anyone they had met. A minor writer, discovered in the old, out-of-the-way books they both loved to collect, might also have 'flavour'.[27]

What all these writers and Hodgson himself shared was an intense belief in literature, in his case poetry. More than 'any man alive' Hodgson made Sassoon want to 'serve the art of poetry faithfully'.[28] For both of them poetry was a sacred calling. There were other things they shared – an interest in graphic art, a love of animals, an appreciation of the absurd – but it was their strong sense of vocation as poets which kept the friendship alive. They would be still writing to each other until a few years before Hodgson's death in 1962 at the age of ninety, long, enthusiastic letters about their respective lives, especially their work. Distance seems to have made no difference to their relationship, if anything increasing their closeness, affection and respect.

*

Sassoon met other people beside Hodgson at Tufton Street, the painter Mark Gertler, the poet Edgell Rickword, the novelist Romer Wilson among them, but none of them interested him as much.[29] His friends remained largely those he had made either during or just after the war. Lacking a house of his own, it seemed to him that '[his] friends [were his] house'.[30]

Living in London made it easier to cultivate his relationships, though there were exceptions. Graves, for instance, was still in Oxford and would usually turn up unannounced at Tufton Street, which meant that they sometimes missed each other. Sassoon continued to enjoy his company, in spite of their increasingly divergent views on life and art, and to rely on him for advice about his work, as Graves did on him. Sassoon claimed that Graves was one of the few people who stimulated him intellectually and he was sad that his marriage prevented them seeing more of each other. It was not so much the geographical distance between them which mattered, for Graves frequently invited Sassoon to stay with him and his family at Islip, as Sassoon's jealousy of Nancy and hers of him.

Sassoon suffered from the marriage of a number of other friends besides Graves during this period, a situation which added to his sense of isolation. Blunden was already married when they met in 1919 and Robert Nichols became engaged before he left to work in Japan in 1921. In Blunden's case, his wife Mary appears to have handled Sassoon more tactfully than Nancy Graves and he paid several successful visits to the Blundens at their cottage near Clare in Suffolk, where Edmund was working on his edition of John Clare's poems. His appointment as Professor of English at Tokyo University in 1924 would bring an end to the visits but not the friendship which was, if anything, strengthened by the numerous letters they exchanged. (Over 500 would pass between them during their lifetimes.)

Blunden was one of a number of people Sassoon introduced to Turner. Another was Ottoline, who took Walter and Delphine under her wing, inviting them to spend several Christmases at Garsington. Not everyone liked Turner, however, as Sassoon discovered when he tried to introduce other friends to him. Gosse, for instance, 'cut' him at the Savile Club to which both men belonged; Wells 'disliked' him and the Sitwells 'loathed' him.[31]

In spite of such incompatibilities, Sassoon was nearer to the centre of the literary world at Tufton Street than he had ever been, or would be again. Though not fully aware of it at the time, he was present at the making of several important moments in literary history. This was nowhere more clearly demonstrated than in his friendships with E.M. Forster and T.E. Lawrence, both of which were cemented at the small house in Westminster.

Sassoon had met Lawrence only once before moving into Tufton Street, which was a few minutes' walk from Lawrence's London lodgings in Barton Street.[32] Over the next four years he would see him on a number of occasions. By July 1923 Lawrence was offering to let him read *Seven Pillars of Wisdom*, still at an embryonic stage. This was a rare privilege granted only to his most trusted friends and Sassoon was greatly excited when one of the eight privately printed copies arrived in November. By the time Lawrence wrote to ask on 23 November, with a diffidence Sassoon found hard to credit, 'Is any of it worthwhile?'[33] he was able to reply to the anxious author, with a sly reference to his job as a mechanic in the Royal Tank Corps: 'Damn you, how long do you expect me to go on reassuring you about your bloody masterpiece. It is a GREAT BOOK, blast you. Are you satisfied? You tank-investigating eremite.'[34]

In thanking him for his 'wonderful letter', Lawrence confessed that he still felt doubts about the book. 'Only judgements like yours and [George Bernard] Shaw's can give me any rest upon the point,' he told Sassoon, then added, alarmingly, 'It means a lot, because I'd like to act a "Nunc dimittis" ... if I were convinced.'[35] His suicide was certainly not what Sassoon intended.

Lawrence had become a 'queer figure' in the landscape of Sassoon's thoughts by 1923.[36] Reading *Seven Pillars*, even in execrably small print, had converted his feelings to hero-worship. So that when Lawrence arrived in person at Tufton Street a week after his 'Nunc dimittis' letter, it seemed like a miracle. Sassoon had been relighting the fire in the Turners' drawing room one evening, when the doorbell rang. There, standing under the porch in a new soft grey hat and light-coloured overcoat with a large brown paper parcel under his arm, was Lawrence, the last person he expected, but the one man he had been 'craving to talk to for weeks'.[37]

In town on leave from the army, to see General Trenchard about transferring back to the RAF, Lawrence had called to discuss *Seven Pillars* further. Overwhelmed by the honour and feeling 'enormous' beside his small, self-contained visitor, Sassoon remembered reacting in his usual excitable fashion.[38] While reading Lawrence's masterpiece, Sassoon had seen its author as an 'infallible superman', but watching him drink tea and nibble shortbread and sponge cakes, he felt protective towards him, in much the same way as towards Owen and Blunden. As with them, he wanted to be of practical help. No expert on prose himself at the time, he felt that the best reassurance he could offer was the opinion of an experienced prose-writer and brilliant critic, E.M. Forster. Forster could also be counted on to sympathize with Lawrence's mysticism, his homosexuality and his passion for the East.

By the time Sassoon asked Lawrence's permission to show Forster *Seven Pillars* in December 1923, he had come to think of Forster as one of the 'nicest' men he knew, as well as a 'real friend'.[39] Their relationship had started in earnest early in 1922 on Forster's return from a year in India. After giving him dinner at the Reform one evening, Sassoon had tried to analyse Forster's appeal for him. It was not a sexual one, though their homosexuality united them to some extent. Nor was it a complete sharing of ideas, since Forster made Sassoon feel 'youthful and impetuous and intellectually clumsy', a 'bit of a blunderbuss', as he told Graves. It was partly the relation of master and pupil, Sassoon finding Forster so 'stimulating' that he felt he might 'explode' in his company.[40] He always ended by telling the older man all his secrets, even inviting him to read his most intimate diaries, a confidence Forster returned by giving him his unpublished homosexual novel, *Maurice*, to read. He admired Forster's prose as much as Forster appreciated his poetry, concluding at their reunion in March 1922 that Forster was 'one of the very few who signify anything in our wilderness of best-sellers'.

On that same occasion he had also wished that he could help Forster to conquer the writer's block from which he was suffering, and by reintroducing him to Lawrence in a sense he did.[41] For Forster's reading of *Seven Pillars*, Lawrence's mystical response to Arabia, at a time when he was struggling to finish his own exploration of the East, had a significant effect on the last two chapters of *A Passage to India*, as well as influencing the final version of *Seven Pillars*. No wonder Lawrence found Forster's novel's ending 'breathlessly exciting'; he might almost be said to have written it himself.[42]

Like most people, Forster was as intrigued by Lawrence the man as by his work. While reading *Seven Pillars* he had felt neither emotion nor affection for its author, who seemed to him well able to look after himself. But when he met

Lawrence to discuss the 'immense' letter he had written him about the book in March 1924, he had to 'stop [himself] going to pieces before him'.[43] 'I have no right to go to pieces,' he told Sassoon, 'not enough beauty.'[44] By the end of his Dorset visit to Lawrence, when they talked 'for hours', Forster was able to be more objective about him.[45] In particular he noticed his 'flabby handshake' and his tendency to lapse into the 'close-lipped Oxford M.A.', or even 'the dashing free-booter'.[46] It seemed to him that Lawrence's chosen career as a private in the army was 'preposterous'. 'He is inside a membrane of absurdity which has worn so thin that it is amazing he cannot see the light,' he wrote to Sassoon. 'Those damned Arabs are all right and he knows it.'[47]

After another stay with Lawrence in June 1924, helping him to revise *Seven Pillars*, Forster summarized his conclusions for Sassoon:

> He is a rare, remote creature, uncanny, yet attractive. I suspect him of 'practices' – i.e. of some equivalent of yoga, otherwise I cannot understand his attitude towards the body – his own and other people's. He thinks the body dirty, and so disapproves of all voluntary physical contact with the bodies of others. Hence that flabby handshake, no doubt. I should like to know whether he held that view *before* he was tortured at Deraa.

Since Forster's sexual requirements included physical contact as well as 'beauty', he finally managed to maintain his equilibrium with Lawrence, as did Sassoon.

Sassoon's case, however, was slightly different. Like Forster, he was bowled over by Lawrence in some ways, but it is quite clear from one of his earliest descriptions that he felt scant physical attraction: 'a little man in a long, ready-made-looking, rough brown "ulster"'.[48] His description of him less than a year later, when he met Lawrence in his army mechanic's uniform, makes him seem even less physically attractive: 'a queer little figure in dark motor-overalls, his brown and grimy face framed in a fur-lined cap'.[49] There is more than a hint of snobbishness in both reactions. It is no coincidence that Sassoon's lovers, actors apart, tended to be of aristocratic or upper-middle-class origin. They were also inclined to be conspicuously 'pretty' and a great deal younger than himself, which Lawrence was not. Nevertheless, like Forster, he was intrigued by Lawrence's sexuality. When finally invited to tea with him at his cottage in Dorset, his main interest was in Lawrence's relationship to another guest, a fellow-private in the army, 'little Russell'.[50] Although he concluded that Russell was the 'Patroclus', or male lover, of the piece, both men were so discreet that he found it impossible to tell.

It would be many years before Lawrence's predilection for being flogged, sparked off by his rape at Deraa, became public knowledge. Lawrence might privately and quite rightly suspect that Sassoon had a 'savage' side to him, but it did not extend to physical violence of the kind Lawrence appeared to need.[51]

The effect, then, of the triangular relationship which developed in Tufton Street between Sassoon, Forster and Lawrence was mainly literary. And at the time it was confined largely to Forster and Lawrence, though it would eventually have a powerful influence on Sassoon.

*

Despite such distractions, Sassoon found himself with a great deal of time on his hands at Tufton Street. Part of his answer to the problem lay in an elaborate daily routine which rarely varied. While making life seem 'a very limited affair', it gave him what he needed in his fight to recover from the War, 'a grip on the details of everyday existence'.[52] His day started late, though not through any choice of his own to begin with. Since the one servant at Tufton Street did not arrive till 8.30 a.m., the Turners' breakfast was not ready until 9.30 and Sassoon had to wait until 10.30 for his. He had never been able to write poetry in the afternoon, so felt obliged to work late into the night. Eventually his first meal, taken at any time between noon and 6 p.m., became 'brunch', a rather odd affair of grilled fish and a milk or steam pudding reminiscent of the nursery or the gentlemen's clubs he frequented.

Graves, who discovered Sassoon still in bed on several afternoon calls, thought Sassoon 'lazy'[53] and Sassoon himself confessed to a tendency to 'indolence', which he blamed on his partly Oriental blood. His inertia did not extend to letter-writing and, if there was any of the morning left, he spent it writing to friends. After his first meal of the day, he might stroll through Mayfair to his barber's in Curzon Street, or visit the National Gallery, the Tate or one of the museums. Many afternoons were spent at concerts. And when the weather was particularly good, he walked in Hyde Park, or just sat and viewed the scene there.

All these activities are reflected in his poetry of the period, which suggests that he was not entirely satisfied as a gentleman of leisure. Just as he had satirized the Establishment in his war poems, so he now cast a satiric eye on the fashionable world as seen at musical performances ('Concert-Interpretation', 'Sheldonian Soliloquy', 'Hommage à Mendelssohn'), plays ('A Post-Elizabethan Tragedy'), art galleries ('In the Turner Rooms', 'In the National Gallery', 'On Some Portraits by Sargent') and museums ('The London Museum') or while promenading round London ('Observations in Hyde Park', 'Evensong in Westminster Abbey').

Unlike his war poetry, however, it is the criticism of the insider, of someone who had himself succumbed to the lure of the leisured life. While those with jobs looked forward at 4.30 p.m. to the end of the working day, for example, he would be sitting down to afternoon tea. It was often an excuse to visit Nellie Burton, after picking up strawberries and cream or a pound of fresh raspberries from nearby Fortnum and Mason. On one occasion he took 'Dame' Nellie to Hampton Court for tea and was amply rewarded by her reactions. She was, according to Sassoon, 'in her very best form, mispronouncing the names of the flowers, dipping wildly into English History ... and remembering how she saw a white blackbird in the wistaria last time she was here. "I do love the tapestries of the Seven Deadly Sins, don't you?" she ejaculated, her voluminous face brimming over with good-humour. (She meant the Mantegna frescoes.)'[54] Yet another trip with her to Wembley in April 1924 was the inspiration for a satirical poem on the more absurd aspects of public ceremonies (which Nellie loved), 'Afterthoughts on the Opening of the British Empire Exhibition'.[55]

Sassoon also used tea to fulfil his obligations as a nephew, sometimes visiting his Thornycroft relatives at Melbury Road, or inviting his great-aunt Mozelle to Tufton Street, duty teas which seemed to go on for ever. Nevertheless it was one of the advantages of his Westminster flat that he could entertain there, however modestly; Forster came for tea on several occasions, only afterwards complaining that the rock cakes were stale.

It was fortunate that Sassoon liked exercise since dinner, usually at the Reform, followed tea fairly quickly. He was sometimes invited to dine with friends, like the Gosses, but if dining alone he would often follow dinner with a play or a concert, sometimes the second of the day. Occasionally he succumbed to invitations from society hostesses, such as Lady Sybil Colefax or Lady 'Ettie' Desborough, which he invariably regretted. After one particularly vacuous dinner with 'nobby-snobby canary-haired' Lady Emerald Cunard, accepted (he said) with the intention of 'acquiring satirical material', he admitted his failure to achieve the 'detachment' he desired. The scorn expressed in his poem on the event, 'Breach of Decorum', is perhaps partly directed at himself for keeping such company:[56]

> I have seen a man at Lady Lucre's table
> Who stuck to serious subjects; spoke of Art
> As if he were in earnest and unable
> To ascertain its functions in the smart
> World where it shares a recreational part
> With Bridge, best-selling Fiction, and the Stable.
>   . . . . .
> I have seen her fail, with petulant replies,
> To localize him in his social senses:
> I have observed her evening-party eyes
> Evicted from their savoir-faire defences.
> And while his intellectual gloom encroached
> Upon the scintillance of champagne chatter,
> In impotent embarrassment she broached
> Golf, Goodwood Races, and the Cowes Regatta ...   (*CP*, pp. 135-6)

However Sassoon's evening had been spent, it usually ended at his writing desk. If poetry would not come, he filled his diary with detailed accounts of his day's activities. He had always 'seen and felt the present as material for memories' and would rely on his diary heavily when he came to write prose.[57] And because his homosexuality inhibited him from talking frankly to all but a few friends, he found it a relief to express his true feelings in its pages. Though realizing that he would probably never be able to publish such views, he was nevertheless consciously 'accumulating material' for an autobiography.[58] He would later, for various reasons, censor the material, but in the early 1920s it seemed vital to record it fully. 'I have formed an inflexible resolve to reveal my real self; my inner self; my secret self; the self that never sees the light of day,' he wrote in February 1922.[59]

This need to stand back from experience as it was taking place helps to explain why, even in the midst of his highly sociable life, he felt solitary. He frequently compared himself to Enoch Arden, Tennyson's tragic sailor-figure, who returns from a shipwreck in which he is thought to have died, and deliberately remains an onlooker when he finds his wife happily married to his best friend.[60] But as Sassoon admitted, except at Weirleigh where he had some grounds for feeling like a ghost from the past, his decision to stand apart stemmed from less noble motives than Enoch's. It had something to do with his belief that he needed to be alone to produce any poetry, though that was not the full explanation.

Forster, who understood Sassoon well, thought that his 'anti-social and self-centred life' had a 'good deal to say for it' if he would 'face its consequences and not hanker after the best of two worlds'.[61] But it would be some time, if ever, before Sassoon managed to resolve his highly ambivalent attitude towards society.

*

Sassoon's ambivalence and turmoil in the first half of the 1920s emerges clearly from his poetry of the period. In the 'new life' he was attempting to build for himself on the 'confusion and exhaustion of 1914-19', he told Professor Lewis Chase in 1922, he needed a 'new form' and a 'new vocabulary'. Though his whole life revolved around the determination to be a poet, he spent most of the Tufton Street years lamenting his sterility as a writer. '*Why* can't I create something?' he wailed in September 1921: 'I am as dry as a biscuit.'[62]

Since his lyric vein had temporarily dried up and would not come to order, he turned to his other talent, satire. Even that proved difficult. Following a trip to Rome in autumn 1921, he wrote despairingly to Graves: 'I have tried writing in clubs, churches, hotels, taxis, trains de luxe, Colosseums, Vaticans, Baths of Caracalla, channel steamers, latrines, chestnut mares, Tufton Street, etc., etc. Am definitely settled down as an ex-author now.'[63] He ended his letter: 'Damn poetry, say I,' but he was unable to do so and his painful efforts to write it late into the night, combined with his inability to sleep afterwards, contributed to his 'self-lacerating irritability' at this time.[64] Wilfred Owen's younger brother, Harold, who was grateful for Sassoon's kindness and generous help as he struggled to establish himself as an artist in the early 1920s, nevertheless found him moody and difficult. 'Morose', 'sardonic', 'distant', 'abstracted', 'sombre' and 'self-absorbed' are only some of the words he used to describe his contradictory benefactor.[65]

Sassoon's dissatisfaction and difficulty with his work was such that it took him nearly three years to gather sufficient material for the first of two volumes produced at Tufton Street, *Recreations*. Yet it was a collection of only twenty-four shortish poems, three of which had already appeared in *Picture Show*.[66] His lack of confidence in the work is reflected in his decision to have only seventy-five copies privately printed for friends, though he had initially intended to publish it with Heinemann.[67] The response to his gift was mainly polite praise. Gosse, Marsh, Wells, Blunden, Graves, Hodgson, Masefield, T.E. Lawrence, Lytton Strachey and others all wrote to say that they had enjoyed the book, though Strachey voiced a general concern when he tactfully wished that Sassoon could produce 'something with still more of yourself in it'.[68]

Bennett, rather more frankly, asked Sassoon when he intended to emerge from 'the carping school', for something 'more benevolent, more sublime, and more ideally beautiful?'[69] And Sassoon was even more annoyed when Vivian de Sola Pinto, *not* a poet he admired, added some equally perceptive criticism: 'As poetry, although some of it is exquisite art, it lacks something. A faith, a passion – that was what made the Shakespeares and the Donnes .... You had it for a moment during the war, but now there is only a fine technique and the languid interest of a half-amused spectator.'[70] Sassoon himself might dismiss *Recreations* as 'an unusually tidy little collection of verses',[71] 'not intended to be very exciting as poetry',[72] and admit that they were 'only a form of recreation' as the title implied; that they were 'futile – a series of disgusts'.[73] He might also tell Theo that the poems could have been written 'almost as effectively in prose'.[74] But he particularly resented criticism from Pinto, who had become a professor of English, considering it 'pedantic'.[75]

He found it no easier to accumulate sufficient poems for a second volume at Tufton Street and, when he did, there was an element of self-mockery in the elaborate title he gave it: *Lingual Exercises for Advanced Vocabularians* (1925). Again he had the book privately printed in a small edition 'for friends only'.[76] And again they responded politely but warily. Finally, however, a trade edition did appear: Heinemann, who published his *Selected Poems* in 1925, were anxious to bring out another collection of original verse and, with some cuts and a few additions, *Recreations* and *Lingual Exercises* were reprinted as *Satirical Poems* in 1926.[77]

In calling his collection *Satirical Poems*, Blunden argued, Sassoon was suggesting a shade of meaning other than straight satire: 'A satirical person is not a satirist.'[78] It was an ingenious defence from a loyal friend, but most readers of *Satirical Poems* will regret the absence of the angry Sassoon of the war poems. There are exceptions. A poem like 'Concert-Interpretations', for example, shows that when fully engaged (and music was something he cared about passionately) Sassoon could convey his message with some of his old verve. Contrasting the initially hostile reaction to Stravinsky's work with the later rapturous reception given to his *Rite of Spring* by polite English society, Sassoon notes another even more startling contrast between the 'vibroatmospheric copulations' of the music celebrating fertility rites and the bland, uncomprehending audience, and the effect this has on the narrator:

> ... This matter is most indelicate indeed!
> Yet one perceives no symptom of stampede.
> The Stalls remain unruffled: craniums gleam:
> Swept by a storm of pizzicato chords,
> Elaborate ladies re-assure their lords
> With lifting brows that signify 'Supreme!'
> While orchestrated gallantry of goats
> Impugns the astigmatic programme-notes ...   (*CP*, p. 159)

The narrator's 'savagery' here makes for biting and effective satire, the ending reminiscent of war poems such as 'Blighters' or 'Fight to a Finish'. The tone varies from that of the urbane, detached onlooker, with what Sassoon described as his 'laconic, legato' voice, in the stanza quoted, to the violently committed enthusiast of the second, the message reinforced by frequent alliteration, exclamation and a deliberately absurd mixture of Latinate polysyllables with Anglo-Saxon monosyllables ('Lynch the conductor! Jugulate the drums!/ Butcher the brass! Ensanguinate the strings!'). In this particular case, Sassoon's 'excessive verbal dexterity' (to quote Blunden) achieves its aim, which is (in Blunden's words) 'to illustrate brilliantly the genuine culture and the imitative clap-trap of our times'.[79]

A comparable contrast is achieved at the end of one of Forster's favourites, 'Sheldonian Soliloquy', where the narrator is listening to Bach's B minor Mass in the packed Sheldonian Theatre at Oxford on a fine summer's day.[80] Best of all, according to Edith Sitwell, is 'On Reading the War Diary of a Defunct Ambassador', which lulls the reader into a face-value acceptance of the 'fine old gentleman' through its cosy colloquialisms ('So that's your Diary – that's your private mind'), only to incite him savagely at the close with its deliberately pompous vocabulary and absurd rhymes:

> ... The world will find no pity in your pages;
> No exercise of spirit worthy of mention;
> Only a public-funeral grief-convention;
> And all the circumspection of the ages.
> But I, for one, am grateful, overjoyed,
> And unindignant that your punctual pen
> Should have been so constructively employed
> In manifesting to unprivileged men
> The visionless officialized fatuity
> That once kept Europe safe for perpetuity.   (*CP*, p. 130)[81]

All too often, however, *Satirical Poems* reads like a series of exercises. As Desmond

MacCarthy, a critic as well as a friend, observed in the *New Statesman*, the reader sometimes gets the impression that Sassoon had been 'looking round him for an occasion for satire because he [had] a satiric gift' and needed 'to vent his scorn, instead of having been provoked to utterance by the subject itself'.[82] Like Pinto, MacCarthy contrasted *Satirical Poems* with the 'memorable satiric poems' of the War: 'then there was no need to hunt for a subject ... because his subject was forced upon him, and he responded with all the rage and grief he was capable of feeling'.[83]

Sassoon himself believed that his collection was a failure owing to his 'undiscardable habit of strict versification and condensed form', which prevented him from acquiring the necessary flexibility and freedom of expression. But his dislike of free verse was 'unconquerable' and from this time onwards he was to remain, in his own words, 'traditional'.[84]

*

Satirical Poems, Sassoon realized, was a turning-point in his career, representing his failure to escape traditional verse for something more modern. Yet there were at least two groups of people in the early 1920s who might have helped him if he had wanted, the Sitwells and Bloomsbury.

He had become friendly with several members of the Bloomsbury Group after the War. Apart from Ottoline Morrell and Forster, who hovered on its fringes, he was on good terms with at least two of its inner circle, Lytton Strachey and Desmond MacCarthy.[85] MacCarthy, who wrote as 'Affable Hawk' in the *New Statesman*, he thought 'one of the best modern critics'[86] and Strachey seemed to him a 'lovely' writer.[87] But Strachey also made him feel like 'a beefy young rowing blue with the intellectual equipment of a New York policeman'.[88] And, however much he enjoyed reading Strachey's historical essays, he thought that his 'pry[ing]' into his subjects' private lives was a 'bad influence' on biography.[89]

Maynard Keynes, whom he knew reasonably well by the early 1920s, made him feel similarly inadequate, an effect Bloomsbury had on him generally.[90] Responding to an invitation from Virginia Woolf to dine with her and Leonard in May 1923, for example, he considered it necessary to explain, as he had to Forster: 'I am not at all intellectual – in fact I have a very cumbersome mind.'[91]

Virginia thought he exaggerated the 'horrors of our intellectuality ... it does not go deep, I hope'.[92] She remembered how pleased she had been when he wrote to thank her, through Ottoline, for her review of *The Old Huntsman* in 1917 and was gratified by his praise of her recent novel, *Jacob's Room*. And when Sassoon did eventually have dinner with the Woolfs in January 1924, it looked for a time as though he and Virginia might become close. Instead of the 'rarefied intellectual atmosphere' he had feared, he found the evening 'a gossipy affair, very pleasant and unconstrained'.[93] Though Leonard struck him as 'reticent and rather weary', Virginia was 'charming', drawing him out adroitly to gossip about mutual friends and acquaintances – Hardy, Gosse, Wells, Bennett, Lady Colefax, Middleton Murry, Graves, Huxley and T.S.

Eliot.[94] He was especially pleased by her attitude towards Eliot, whom she described as 'rather an old prig, really', who needed to be 'chaffed out of it'.[95] Such irreverence from another important Modernist delighted Sassoon. He was also flattered to be urged to write something for the Hogarth Press. For her part, Virginia found him 'a nice dear kind sensitive warm-hearted fellow'.[96] Coming from a group which prided itself on its frankness and sexual tolerance, she was unperturbed by his homosexuality. She also admired his work.

After a second meeting, however, the differences began to emerge, with Virginia wishing (in a misquotation of a Meredith sonnet) for 'more brain, O God, more brain!' from Sassoon.[97] And though Sassoon had agreed to write something on satire for the Woolfs' Hogarth Essays series by mid-1924, he quickly abandoned the idea and returned to less intellectual pursuits.[98] His whole philosophy of life and art was diametrically opposed to Virginia's cry for 'more brain'. He eventually came to believe that 'Bloomsbury lack[ed] generosity' and would refuse to be 'patronized and palavered over' by a group which seemed to think itself so superior.[99] 'They live in such a tiny world,' he wrote to Ottoline in 1928, 'and I sometimes think that they know next to nothing about life, in spite of having read all the great authors.'[100]

Osbert Sitwell believed that Sassoon's dislike of Modernism, which lay behind his antagonism to Bloomsbury, stunted his growth as a poet. He himself, together with Edith and Sachie, had enthusiastically embraced it and were another potentially modernizing influence for Sassoon in the 1920s.

Partly because he had first met Osbert through Ross and associated him with his last meeting with Owen, Sassoon felt almost wholly positive about him at the start. In spite of their different attitudes towards poetry, he had been impressed by Osbert's work and published it in his *Daily Herald* columns. Osbert returned the compliment by including Sassoon's poems in the first two issues of the magazine he edited, *Art and Letters*, where he found himself in the company of Eliot and another Modernist, Wyndham Lewis. Though Osbert saw no sign of his own rebellious attitude to traditional verse technique in Sassoon, he could (and did) admire his defiance of the Establishment in making his public protest against the War.[101] This was combined with a strong personal liking for Sassoon. In a verse-letter to Sassoon (a response to one from him) he highlights their differences, suggesting at the same time that Sassoon is afraid of anything but 'Georgian plaid'.[102] Osbert's scorn for the Georgian poets became the main cause of the rift which developed between him and Sassoon in the early 1920s and which lasted for a good part of Sassoon's time at Tufton Street.[103] For, in attacking the Georgians, even though he carefully excluded Sassoon and Nichols, Osbert was criticizing some of Sassoon's nearest friends, particularly Turner. Though Osbert later exempted Turner from his criticism in a conscious effort to placate Sassoon, the damage had been done and the battle-lines were drawn.

Osbert's first instinct under pressure was to strengthen the attack and his anti-Georgian pamphlet, *Who Killed Cock-Robin?*, followed in December

1921. Turner would eventually retaliate with a satirical play about the Sitwells, *Smaragdas Lover*, in 1924, though by that time the situation would have changed.

There were other factors at work. Sassoon himself was beginning to dissociate himself from *Georgian Poetry*, refusing (politely) to appear in Marsh's fifth volume of 1922, and his reaction to Osbert was much more personal than he admitted at the time. In the same diary entry which records his intense annoyance at Osbert's 'doggerel satire' against Turner, Graves and Blunden, he suggests that Osbert was motivated by jealousy of their friendship with him.[104] Osbert did later admit that his 'exaggerated ideas of friendship' had made him 'jealous', but it is also likely that Sassoon was projecting his own feelings onto Osbert.[105] Only three months after the break in November 1921, Sassoon deliberately followed him out of a concert at the Wigmore Hall for the pleasure of 'cutting' him outside. Thinking about it afterwards, he suddenly realized that his attitude towards Osbert was 'strongly sadistic': 'I saw, quite calmly, that my (supposed) stab at his feelings ... aroused in me acute sexual feelings ... (I'd never before been conscious of any sexual feelings toward him except a slight repugnance.)'[106] Osbert's comment to Sassoon on this aspect of his nature shows how shrewd an opponent he faced: 'You have a streak in your character that makes you derive a little pleasure, as well as much pain from humiliating your friends.'[107]

Sassoon's emotional instability at this time was certainly a factor in the prolonged row between himself and Osbert. 'You are a difficult friend,' Osbert wrote to him at the end of it, '– if one goes to see you, you become tired, and feel that your blood is being sucked, I believe – and if one doesn't go to see you, where are you to be found?'[108] Forster was to make a similar observation.

Differences of temperament and background also played a part. While still finding Osbert 'a tonic' in mid-1921, Sassoon had begun to think him 'frivolous, always'.[109] As early as December 1920 he had complained to Marsh: 'All this Sitwell spite and trivial charade-satire makes me tired.' 'What a brilliant, disintegrating family they are!' he wrote in his diary at the height of his dissatisfaction with Osbert: 'And why can't they be just a little different, just a little more tolerant and human and free from their perennial spirit of mockery?'[110] Staying at the family home, Renishaw, with the trio and their extraordinary father, Sir George ('Ginger'), and mother, Ida, in August 1921 underlined these differences, making him feel hostile, malicious and oppressed.[111] The Sitwells, he concluded, were 'an absolute climax! Regency relics', their trouble being 'too much taste'.[112]

Osbert himself, who practised what Sassoon called 'passive resistance' throughout their feud, sending 'amiable' notes via mutual friends, claimed: 'Much mischief was made for us both before you quarrelled with me, and more, I imagine, since.'[113] His chief suspect was Gosse, who was still highly critical of the Sitwells' literary experiments in 1923, though Sassoon would later partly win him over.

What emerges most clearly from Sassoon's comments during the eighteen months' quarrel is how obsessed he was by Osbert. Pride prevents him making any move towards reconciliation. Another seven months pass and he is still 'grim' and 'unkind' to Osbert when they meet at Nellie Burton's house in June 1923. But by the end of June 1923 he realizes that he is paying heavily for his feud, which by now seems to him 'futile'.[114] The end is in sight. When he meets Osbert unexpectedly the next day at the Reform, he forgets to scowl, though abstains from smiling. There is a slight hitch in the reconciliation process when he discovers that Osbert has left him a 'funny' post-card with the hall-porter and, 'infuriated', he sends a 'silly' one back.[115] But he immediately regrets it and, when Osbert then sends him a jokey Valentine in response, he finally capitulates: 'He always gets the last word and scores off me.'[116]

Defeated, he writes Osbert a 'very decent letter', explaining his position and is greatly relieved to receive a serious eight-page reply by return of post. 'Don't think for a moment,' Osbert writes, 'that you are the only person who has felt pain over our differences. In spite of all the silly little things I have done since, there have been moments when I felt so miserable at it, that I hardly knew what to do.'[117] Referring to their 'different ideas of literature and art', he says that they should 'never argue about that', a tacit acceptance of the fact that he has failed to win Sassoon over to his Modernist ideas.[118]

It would take nearly another year for the relationship to settle down to its former easy amiability, but by 17 June 1924, Sassoon could write with great relief in his diary: 'Peace is signed.'[119] It was a peace which would last until 1949, when Osbert's description of him and mutual friends in *Laughter in the Next Room* would bring about a second, less dramatic withdrawal on Sassoon's part. For, as he observed to a close friend in 1927: 'What should we do without the Sitwells to amuse us, and where shall we find a more intelligent and attractive trio?'[120]

One benefit of his reconciliation with Osbert in 1924 was a renewal of friendship with Edith. She was as fiercely loyal to her brothers as they were to her and had naturally taken Osbert's side in the feud with Sassoon. Even Sassoon's generous review of her highly experimental work, *Façade*, in May 1922 had failed to win her over.[121] Sassoon had first met Edith in October 1918, also through Ross, but it was not until late the following year that he really got to know her. Edith had published seven of Wilfred Owen's poems in her 1919 cycle of *Wheels* and hoped to bring out a wider selection of them in a separate edition. She worked hard on the difficult task of producing final texts from the several draughts in varying states of revision and was extremely disappointed when, on consulting Sassoon about the last two, he told her self-importantly that it would have been Owen's 'wish that he (Captain Sassoon) should see to the publication of the poems'.[122] It may be that Sassoon, who knew of her intentions, felt that Owen's reputation might suffer from the association with *Wheels* and the *avant-garde*, or it may simply be, as Dennis Welland suggested after talking to Sassoon, that he became jealous.[123] Whatever his motives, Edith felt obliged to accept his claim and did so with a surprisingly good grace.

Sassoon's next move was even more difficult to take. 'Captain Sassoon has suddenly gone off to America,' she wrote to Owen's mother in late January 1920, 'leaving all your son's manuscripts with me to get ready for the printers by February 1st.'[124] As she pointed out, Sassoon had done 'nothing' at that point except arrange for Chatto & Windus to publish them. Though credited with editing the poems, which were finally published in December 1920, his sole contribution to the first edition was a short introduction.[125]

Yet the 'stormy spinster petrel' meekly accepted Sassoon's lordly behaviour, possibly because she admired his work greatly and was strongly attracted to him as a man. Though she never admitted it outright, it is more than likely that she was in love with him. Sassoon himself thought so, as did her brother Sachie.[126] The very condition which prevented such a situation developing – Sassoon's homosexuality – also, ironically, made it 'safe' for Edith.

Sassoon, who had been pursued by Ottoline with much greater determination and far fewer inhibitions, would in any case have found Edith's unconventional appearance as challenging as he had Ottoline's.[127] Unfashionably tall and thin by contemporary standards, with a pronounced nose and wispy hair of indeterminate colour, Edith chose to make a feature of what she grandly called her 'Plantagenet' looks. Concealing her hair beneath highly coloured turbans but emphasizing her long, bony figure with exotic medieval robes and enormous pieces of dramatic jewellery, she deliberately attracted attention wherever she went.

Edith's admiration for his poetry, on the other hand, he both approved and reciprocated. Her recognition of his war poems was probably more to do with their anti-Establishment content than their largely traditional technique but her praise of *Satirical Poems* stemmed from a true appreciation of his poetic method: 'it cuts right down to the bone – and moves one most profoundly.'[128] When he, in turn, praised one of her poems from *Rustic Elegies* (1927), she replied: 'I don't really care a toss for the insults one has to put up with, if a poet who has written some of the most magnificent poetry of the time – I mean yourself – cares for my work –.'[129]

After seeing the completed manuscript of *The Heart's Journey* (1928), she praised it in terms which indicate the point at which these two very different poets met: 'Poetry doesn't come by bellowing to attract the attention of the crowd. It is much more like taming a wild bird in a wood – one has to do it in silence. You have tamed the wild bird and no mistake.'[130] For both of them, poetry was more to do with instinct than with intellect, a patient waiting on the Muse combined with a sensitivity to words and sounds, and in this respect Edith differed as much from Eliot and other Modernists as Sassoon did. Their techniques might differ widely but their aims at this time were very similar.

Sassoon was as admiring of Edith's poetry as she was of his. As early as July 1919 he had suggested to Marsh that Edith be included in the next *Georgian Poetry* anthology instead of Fredegond Shove.[131] By June 1924, he is linking her 'genuine poetry' with that of his favourite poet of the period, Charlotte Mew.[132] His admiration for Edith's poetry would continue until at least 1933, when he

52. SS with Stephen Tennant and Poll the parrot.

53. SS preparing to chop wood at Breitenau, 1929.

54. SS with Edith Oliver at the Daye House, Wilton.

55. William Walton in the early 1930s.

56. Max and Florence Beerbohm with SS, in characteristic pose, on the Beerbohms' roof terrace at Rapallo, *c.* 1930.

57. Max's caricature of SS.

58. Rex Whistler at 20 Fitzroy Street, London, c. 1927.

60. SS as an Elizabethan bard at the Wilton Pageant, June 1933.

59. Doris Westwood in the early 1930s.

61. Mr and Mrs Siegfried Sassoon, 18 December 1933.

62. The return of the fox-hunting man, Wiltshire, 1934/5.

63. Like father, like son.

64. SS seeing Dennis Silk off on his travels, Summer 1955.

65. SS alone at Heytesbury House.

66. SS, Angela Baddeley and Glen Byam Shaw at Heytesbury House, August 1952.

67. Downside Abbey.

68. Mother Margaret Mary Ross McFarlin.

SIEGFRIED

69. Dom Hubert van Zeller's impression of SS 'sitting cross-legged on the floor with his thermos and paper bag of cake and biscuit crumbs'.

70. 'He drove a car in the way that he rode a horse – at an uneven trot until lost in composition and then at a spanking gallop.' (Dom Hubert van Zeller)

71. Edmund Blunden and Rupert Hart-Davis opening the batting for Jonathan Cape *versus* the Alden Press, Oxford.

72. Blunden, SS and Silk listening to the Test Match results at Heytesbury in the early 1960s.

73. SS in what his friends referred to as his 'awful old hat'.

74. SS in meditative mood.

GOLDEN WEEKEND continued

Off again on another
of the dazzling runs
that have made him
the most exciting
player in the Ameri-
can Football League.

75. Haro Hodson's caricature of SS 'whizzing about in the library' with the coal scuttle in 1964. The caption reads 'GOLDEN WEEKEND. Off again on another of the dazzling runs that have made him the most exciting player in the American Football League'.

was instrumental in persuading the Royal Society of Literature to award her the A.C. Benson Silver Medal for Poetry.

The two of them did not always agree about poets – Eliot was a particular stumbling block – but they were generally united, and amusingly so, on those they thought frauds. When John Drinkwater, a popular contemporary poet and playwright whom Sassoon had already dismissed as 'a pompous literary humbug', dared to praise Squire's verse above Sassoon's, Edith flew to his defence with a deliberately absurd suggestion: '... would it matter if I killed Drinkwater? I'll promise not to if you say I'd better not.'[133]

Humbert Wolfe, another popular contemporary poet, was also a favourite target, Edith egging Sassoon on to write his parodies of Wolfe, *Poems by Pinchbeck Lyre* (1931).[134] (One of her favourite opening lines from the selection was 'Swing tripe, swing tosh!'.) The book itself was published by Edith's own publishers, Duckworth, and Wolfe stopped speaking to her.

Altogether it was an extraordinary relationship which grew up between Sassoon and Sitwell in the 1920s. Though it never developed into the romantic love Edith had hoped for, it was a loving relationship. When Edith's troubles, which were often numerous, became too much for her, Sassoon was ready to help with advice and (though he did this indirectly through Sachie) with money.[135] He was, as she noted in an unpublished memoir written in 1930 and 1931, 'fantastically loyal' whilst his friendships lasted and 'the most generous minded man' she knew.[136] Most importantly of all, he was 'one of the very first poets', indeed 'one of the very first people', to 'uphold' her.[137]

For her part, Edith showed a side to Sassoon which is in direct contradiction to the picture often painted of her as an acerbic personality, merciless towards all but her closest family. The tone of her letters is generally kind, concerned, almost motherly. When a mutual friend tells her he is worried that Sassoon is forgetting to eat or take care of himself, she writes to him anxiously and even offers to teach him to cook chops for himself.[138] Her invitations to tea were endless and when, in 1928, three of his closest friends died within the year, she did her best to console him. She presented him with proofs of one of her favourite collections, *Gold Coast Customs*, and dedicated another work, *Jane Barston*, to him.

With Sassoon's switch to prose in *Memoirs of a Fox-Hunting Man* (1928), *Memoirs of an Infantry Officer* (1930) and *Sherston's Progress* (1936) and Edith's own attempts to earn money with a number of prose books during the 1930s, however, their relationship began to change. Edith was noticeably less extravagant in her praise of Sassoon's prose and he himself found it impossible to praise hers. His copy of her *Aspects of Modern Poetry* (1933), lavishly annotated and 'decorated', is a collage of press cuttings, cartoons and sub-headings such as 'Literary Ass' under Edith's name on the title page. He also started a series of caricatures on the Sitwell siblings which depicts Edith in a number of absurd roles.[139] Without poetry to unite them their differences became more obvious.

Distinct cracks started to appear in the relationship by the early 1930s, as

Sassoon retreated further into conservatism and Edith's experiments grew more pronounced. By 1942 he could no longer believe in the poet he had admired so much in the 1920s, responding ungratefully to the presentation copy she had sent of her *Street Songs*:

> Whereas Miss Sitwell's use doth stray
> 'Twixt Cassiopeia and Cathay,
> One wonders – in one's humdrum way –
> Where *is* the ruddy border-line
> Between the foolish and the fine?
> And does Miss Sitwell while she spins
> Ask where Art ends and Bosh begins?[140]

On reading an article in 1954 about Edith's career as 'a publicity personality', and her insistence on the 'rôle of a Literary Queen', he noted in his diary the differences which had finally divided them, particularly her assumption of 'the robes of a prophetess ... much influenced by Yeats and Eliot'.[141] Edith had 'cooled off' him, he concluded, because he had resisted her influence and had remained 'old-fashioned'.[142]

*

Sassoon's original feud with the Sitwells marred his Tufton Street years in a number of ways. One effect, for example, was to prevent him from continuing his visits to their family estate in Derbyshire, a decided disadvantage for someone who longed to escape from London whenever possible. The arrival of his brother and family at Weirleigh in 1920, though it helped him feel less anxious about his mother, also made him unwilling to return home, however briefly. The death of his dog Topper there in September 1920 seemed to him to symbolize the end of an era.

Even on his most enjoyable days in London, he missed the country. Though nothing would induce him to return to an existence like the one he had led in Kent until 1914, memories of it persisted. Town life and social amenities, he claimed, were not 'natural' to him.[143] And though he did not share his mother's belief that Tufton Street was unhealthy because built on a former marsh, he did agree that it would be bad for him to spend all his time there. Both she and Loder urged him to hunt again, Loder offering to keep a horse for him. After only a brief struggle with the remnants of his Socialist conscience, Sassoon succumbed. When Geoffrey Harbord invited him to Weedon Equitation School for a few days' cubbing with the Grafton in October 1920, he bought himself a horse, Lady Jill, one of the best hunters he would ever ride. 'Inconsistency – double life – as usual,' he noted in his diary in December 1920, '– trying to be serious about life and work – buying a horse and dreaming of winning V[ale of] W[hite] H[orse] point-to-point!'[144]

There is a myth that Sassoon abandoned hunting after the War because he was so sickened by the killing he had witnessed there. Far from rejecting the sport for its violence, however, he had actually retreated from the violence of the War *into* hunting, which for him represented a peaceful and innocent world, the continuation of a long country tradition.

Significantly, in his many personal descriptions of hunting, Sassoon rarely refers to killing foxes. If he thought about it at all, he almost certainly shared the view of another friend and fellow-writer, T.H. White, that it was far better to give foxes a sporting chance than to trap, shoot or poison them. He thought of hunting in very different terms from its present-day opponents. His most precious memories were of 'the smell of a soft southerly wind on a dark December morning' as he opened his bedroom window onto a clouded sky.[145] His imagination would 'fondly re-create the whole day', from the time he was pulling on his boots by the light of a few candles to 'that last bit of hunting at the end of the afternoon when half the field had gone home' and his zest for jumping was only dampened by his horse being much tireder than he was.[146] At that point, he would get off and walk, anxious to spare his mount. For he loved horses, another important factor in his feeling for the hunt. By the 1940s he believed that the world had become 'too large and unlocalised' and that 'the parish and county boundaries of personal existence [were] being obliterated'.[147] Horses, he argued, being essentially unmodernisable and 'absolutely refusing to move with the times', could redeem the situation.[148]

If hunting was a way of discovering 'the secrets and manners of rural life' for Sassoon, it was also a link with a long literary tradition.[149] He loved writers like Beckford, Whyte-Melville, Trollope and Somerville and Ross. But his favourite was Surtees, whose characters reminded him of the many wonderful eccentrics, as well as good friends, he had met out hunting. Then there was the sheer physical thrill of hunting.

Sassoon was not unaware of the class connotations attached to the sport. For him it was inevitably associated with the pleasant country-house life of the past, which he knew gave it an undemocratic flavour. (There is a reference in his poem 'Reynardism Revisited' to 'Foxes Torn to Bits in Smart Society'.)[150] But was this élitism any worse, he wondered, than the attempts of urban-minded politicians to reduce everyone to equality and mediocrity of mind?

Sassoon continued to hunt into the mid-1930s and his decision to stop was a practical not a moral one. According to a close friend in later life, he would have been 'absolutely appalled' at the present attempt to ban the sport.[151] He believed that it was up to the individual to make up his or her own mind.

*

Sassoon's decision to start hunting again in 1920, though frustrated by his horse's lameness the first winter, provided him with a great deal of pleasure in the early 1920s. During the season, from mid-October to April, he would leave town regularly on a Thursday afternoon for the Loders.

It was a relief to escape London for the weekend and a very real pleasure riding across country on a good hunter. He derived even greater enjoyment from competing in point-to-point races, buying a second horse, Higham Destiny, for this purpose in 1922. But, increasingly, he connected sport with 'mindlessness'.[152] In addition he began to feel uncomfortable about the 'secret life' he was forced to conceal from his 'unintellectual Loders'.[153] It was not simply his homosexuality he could not discuss with them, but a wide variety of cultural subjects. They seemed to him 'conventional grown-up children'.[154] He could see that they had their own 'solid' values and he enjoyed some aspects of his visits to them: 'But not more than once a week, please!' he begged in his diary.[155]

He often took refuge with Ottoline at Garsington after visiting the Loders, as an antidote to their philistinism. He was able to value Ottoline more in the 1920s, and not simply as a confidante. His visits to her manor house offered not just another escape from London but a cultural world as rich, if not richer than Turner's. After the 'genial avidity and *Tatlerism* of Loder-land and sport', Garsington and its 'ever-dear Ottoline' seemed above all 'enriching'.[156]

Another retreat both from philistinism and London was Cambridge, where he continued to visit Rivers. Of all his friends, he believed Rivers was the person who had done most to help him resolve his divided self. It was Rivers who had encouraged him to study politics at Oxford in 1919, yet had understood when he gave it up. A committed socialist himself – he agreed to stand as Labour Party candidate for the University of London in 1922 – he appeared to accept Sassoon's decreasing commitment to politics without criticism. But he made him want to be a better, more serious person. It was with his guidance that Sassoon made several efforts to help those less privileged than himself in the early 1920s. Besides giving money to his ex-army servant, Law, he visited Wales to report on the miners' strike for the *Nation* in 1921, wrote a poem about it in 'A Case for the Miners' and started prison-visiting shortly afterwards.[157]

His 'dutiful pilgrimages' to Pentonville Gaol were harrowing but colourful, his assigned prisoners including a bigamist Yorkshire farmer and a scout-master who became '"over-enthusiastic" about some of his troops'.[158] By 1925 he was being allotted newly arrived prisoners, but most of them seemed already hardened cases. There were exceptions but, as his poem 'To One in Prison' shows, he despaired of being any real help even to those who did care. It is also clear from the same piece that he became emotionally involved with the young men he visited, an echo of his relationship with the young army private Jim Linthwaite in 1918:[159]

> And now – what use the pity that I am heaping
> Upon your head? Who knows? ... My heart, not yours, can tell.
>   (*CP*, p. 186)[160]

In this and his other attempts to be a 'serious' person, Sassoon was grateful for Rivers's support. He was, therefore, devastated when Rivers died suddenly on 4 June 1922 at the age of only fifty-eight.[161] But even by his death, Sassoon believed, Rivers had helped him: 'He has awakened in me a passionate consciousness of the significance of life,' he wrote in his diary the day after hearing the news. 'In a few hours I have recognized as never before the intensity of life which Rivers communicated to his friends.'[162] Attending the funeral at Cambridge with one of Rivers's closest friends and colleagues, Sir Henry Head, who would to some extent replace Rivers as one of several father-figures, he felt 'profound gratitude to the dead man for all that he wrote and lived'.[163]

Sassoon's descriptions of Rivers, even before his death, make him sound almost oppressively selfless, as though he gave everything and received nothing. But the Rev. Cyril Tompkinson, a friend of both men, was probably right to claim that Sassoon also 'did a great deal for [Rivers], bringing colour, delight and a deep affection into his life, just when it was needed'.[164]

Sassoon continued to visit Cambridge after Rivers's death, but less frequently and with less pleasure. He began to spend noticeably more time at Frankie Schuster's house on the Thames at Bray, which started to represent for him a compromise between the 'mindlessness' but physical well-being of the Loders' world and the high-mindedness of Garsington. By the time Rivers died, Sassoon had already paid several visits to the Hut, or the Long White Cloud, as Schuster's house became known after extensive enlargement. And in 1924 and 1925 he spent virtually the whole summer in what he rechristened 'Schuster's Retreat from Reality on the river'.[165] When planning a fourth volume of autobiography which would cover some of his time at Bray, Sassoon believed that 'the Schuster material alone should make it pretty good'.[166] Though he never completed the book, he clearly enjoyed writing about his 'lotus-eating by the Thames'.[167] His descriptions are full of verbs like 'idle' and 'saunter' and leisurely accounts of days spent weeding the lawn, pulling dead wood out of poplar trees or 'lumbering up and down' on one of Schuster's several grand pianos.[168] He told Graves, who had followed his slow recovery from the War with fellow-feeling, that Bray helped greatly in the healing process.[169]

The Long White Cloud was an idyllic place to be in summer. Though less than thirty miles from London, it was surrounded by fields on three sides, with the fourth facing the Thames. Its large grounds included a tennis court bordered with lilacs and poplars, croquet grounds, a terrace for moonlit dinners, a separate garden music room and well-kept lawns running down to the river. The house itself, long, low and rambling, was architecturally undistinguished but beautifully furnished, exuding an air of tranquillity, order and civilized living.[170] There was a staff of six, who provided Schuster and his numerous guests with the service and fine food and wine he expected.

Music was another source of pleasure for Sassoon at Bray. When they were not travelling up to London in Frankie's Rolls-Royce to hear an opera or concert, Schuster would often invite well-known musicians to his house for private recitals. The most famous of these and the one Sassoon came to know best was Elgar.[171] Sassoon had admired Elgar long before he met him at Schuster's, comparing him to Handel in his ability to design on a big scale, yet remaining 'so beautifully English' in feeling.[172] Elgar's appearance, that of a 'smartly dressed "military"-looking grey-haired man, with [a] carefully-trimmed moustache and curved nose', was so different from the 'magnificence' of his music that Sassoon had difficulty reconciling the two.[173] Elgar returned his admiration, asking him on one occasion to write him five or six poems to set to music, for instance.[174] Though Sassoon failed to produce the poems, he enjoyed being treated as a fellow-craftsman by the great man.

His fondest memory of the composer was an hour spent in Schuster's music room in 1924, with Elgar playing snatches from Sassoon's piano music (Mozart's A major Concerto and Bach's Fugues and Chaconne), some of his own choral works ('Death on the Hills', 'Te Deum' and 'Light of Life') and parts of Schubert's Rondo Brillante, which he loved. Watching him 'glowing with delight' in the music, Sassoon felt he was seeing the 'real' Elgar.[175] It helped him to forget the other side of Elgar, the one who told long-winded anecdotes about himself at lunch and who seemed to him 'just a type of club bore'.[176] Unfortunately, this side was never absent for long and Sassoon's overall impression was of someone 'a bit petty and disappointing'.[177] He was particularly critical of Elgar's treatment of Schuster, which was sometimes very unkind. Yet Schuster had done more than anyone, Sassoon believed, to establish Elgar's success.

Schuster's devotion to music helped Sassoon accept other aspects of him he found less attractive. His carefulness with money, for example, was completely alien to Sassoon, who found it especially irritating in someone so rich. He was even more critical of Schuster's social life, disliking the 'socially insincere smartly-dressed people with uninspected and protected lives' who descended on Bray at weekends.[178]

After Schuster's death Sassoon would come to feel that he had been unfair to him. It was true that Schuster loved a title, and if its recipient were wealthy so much the better. But he loved music more and his guests were expected either to provide it or to appreciate it. There is one group photograph taken at Bray which epitomizes the special kind of mix he created; it is of the powerful socialite Lady Randolph Churchill, Lady Maud Warrender, herself a good amateur singer, and the legendary Australian soprano Dame 'Nellie' Melba.

Sassoon would sometimes escape such gatherings. Though he was not nearly as immune to their social appeal as he suggests, he valued friendship more and preferred to visit de la Mare, for example, once he had moved to Taplow, only three miles from Bray. And there is no doubt that Sassoon felt happier in de la Mare's relatively modest house than at nearby Taplow Court, where he was sometimes invited by de la Mare's landlords, Lord and Lady Desborough.[179]

It was partly as a protest against the 'shams and insincerities of social intercourse' that Sassoon took his mother to visit Bray in 1924. Her shabby clothes, unsophisticated manner and artless appreciation of her surroundings filled him with both pride and pain. Only Schuster's much younger companion, 'Anzie' Wylde, seemed to appreciate his mother at a human level.[180]

Anzie's presence at Bray was often the only thing which stopped Sassoon leaving in disgust. A New Zealander by birth, he had acquired his nickname as a captain in the Canterbury Regiment with the ANZAC forces during the War. Wounded at Gallipoli, he was invalided back to England with severe chest wounds and a leg amputated up to the thigh. Schuster had met him while visiting the troops at Lady Astor's hospital and by the time Sassoon met Anzie he had been informally adopted by Schuster, whom he called 'Uncle', or 'Unkie'.

What struck Sassoon most about Anzie was his 'unfailing good nature and cheerfulness', his acceptance of everything that came to him, 'whether it was a leg lost at Gallipoli or the Rolls-Royce, which he'd been driving Frankie about in' since 1919.[181] He particularly admired Anzie's 'simple wisdom', a quality he detected in all his favourite people, from the greatest, like Hardy, to the most ordinary, like Nellie.[182] Anzie never elaborated or over-intellectualized problems, as 'clever' people like Forster did. At Bray especially he helped Sassoon take a down-to-earth view of things.

Besides himself, Anzie introduced another redeeming feature to Bray in the woman he married in 1924, Wendela Boreel.[183] The daughter of a Dutch diplomat father and wealthy American mother, 'Wendy' as she was known, had been a neighbour of Schuster and Anzie in Tite Street before they moved to Old Queen Street. Studying art under Tonks and Sickert, she had become romantically involved with Anzie while painting his portrait in 1923. Schuster, who must have realized early on that the handsome New Zealander did not share his own preference for young men, accepted their marriage in 1924 with a good grace. Sassoon himself found Wendela 'delightful' and was happy to sit for her.[184] She and her painting sometimes seemed to him 'the only "serious" element' in life at Bray.[185]

By 1925 Sassoon had decided that the advantages of the Schusterian existence were outweighed by its 'lack of serious foundations'.[186] 'Its froth-de-luxe,' he wrote, rather self-righteously considering the time he had voluntarily spent there, 'conceals nothing but materialism and refusal to face life seriously.'[187] After even a few days at Bray he felt bursting with good health but 'mentally slack and sluggish'[188] and his attempts to write poetry there almost always failed.

He might long for 'austerity and solitude; to be back with Rivers at Cambridge',[189] but he would go on visiting Bray for several years after leaving Tufton Street, a sign of his continuing lack of direction in the mid-1920s.

23

'*Love* is the Test'

1921-1925

Staying with Frankie Schuster was only one of the reasons Sassoon gave for his difficulty in writing poetry during the Tufton Street years. Another related to the 'cursed complication of sex', which dominated this period.[1] While his sexual frustration before and during the War and his initial euphoria over Gabriel had fuelled his creative urge, the restless experiments which followed had the opposite effect. Starting with his unhappy affair with Glenn Hunter in New York, these never fully satisfied him, though it is clear from a poem written at this time that he still believed that physical passion could inspire the artist:

> While we are sober, sage, and sane,
> We plough and plant a sterile plain.
> But passion's climax storming by
> With phallic imageries of art
> Creates in pomp along the sky
> Dazzling cloud-rhapsodies of heart. ...[2]

Another poem written at the same time, 'A Last Judgement', orders the protagonist to 'look for love' but, if it cannot be found, to 'look for lust', the piece containing the despairing admission: '... mocked and maimed, he knew,/ For scrawls on dungeon walls his priapismic devils.'[3] In the light of Sassoon's own development in the early 1920s, it is impossible not to read both poems autobiographically. He himself claimed that his best poetry was the result of 'repressed sex' and the lacklustre nature of the verse written during this, his period of greatest sexual activity, appears to support the theory.[4] From October 1921, when he started an affair with a young German prince, to early 1925, when his disastrous relationship with a well-known actor came to a painful end, he wrote little that either he or posterity would wish to keep.

Side by side with the sexual adventures – one sometimes leading to the other – were his actual travels, which formed an important part of his routine at Tufton Street. Partly because Turner needed to let the house for extra income at times, partly because it was possible to live more cheaply abroad, but mainly because his experiences during the War and in America had given him a taste for it, Sassoon spent long periods travelling between 1920 and 1925. He also quite self-consciously set out to broaden his cultural horizons.

In many ways these trips were simply an extension of the life he lived in England, with a great deal of his time devoted to concerts, art galleries and museums. 'My travels are food for the mind,' he wrote in 1922, 'and a liberal education in arts and manners.'[5] For this reason, no doubt, his favourite countries were Italy and Germany, though he visited the South of France with Schuster on at least two occasions.[6] He particularly enjoyed Munich, where he stayed more than once during the opera season.

One reason for his restlessness was an increasing dissatisfaction with Gabriel. His first trip abroad after America, planned for April 1921, was to be with Gabriel, but only because, as he told Ottoline, there was 'no one else to go with'.[7] He was already beginning to find Gabriel 'silly and second-rate'.[8] Everything they did together now seemed to him 'flabby and sterile' and he could only 'flog' himself into emotions by having rows with him about his 'rather squalid habits and associates'.[9]

His periodic agonies about Gabriel's lifestyle were partly caused by the realization that the 'poor little soul' tried very hard to follow his sensible advice: 'but I am a hard master,' Sassoon admitted, 'and my prejudice against alcohol is more than he can swallow.'[10] Turner had told him that he had 'never known anyone who had such a strong desire to dominate people's lives', a 'sort of half-paternal instinct', he called it, adding that Sassoon put 'an almost impossible strain' on the people he loved by 'demanding an intensity equal to [his] own'.[11]

Sassoon was still too attached to Gabriel to leave him completely but he was already looking for someone to replace him as a lover by 1921. And it was on his first trip abroad in September that year that he found a substitute. He had cancelled his trip to Venice in April because of a coal strike, spending a month in Somerset instead.[12] But he still wanted to see Italy. So that when Prewett, who had returned from Canada to study at Christ Church, enthused about his own recent trip to Rome, Sassoon suggested another visit with him.[13] Though Sassoon was helping Prewett financially at Oxford and paying all the expenses for the Rome trip, Prewett made it quite clear that there would be no sex between them. Yet his very presence aroused Sassoon sexually, as did the young Italian men he saw in the streets: 'Is it my own fault,' he asked after twenty-four hours in Rome, 'that I am under this cursed obsession of sex-cravings. If Gabriel were here it would be no better. Worse, probably. The fact is that I am not interested in the Roman Empire, or the Renaissance, or Baroque effects. My tastes are neither historical nor antiquarian, nor artistic. I am interested in the physical aspect of Italy.'[14]

It was not with an Italian but with a German, however, that Sassoon was to experience the physical side of Italy. Conveniently, as it turned out, Prewett became ill on reaching Rome and had to go into a nursing home with a gastric ulcer. This left Sassoon very much to his own devices and free for what was to follow.

The one person he knew in Rome apart from Prewett was Lord Berners, who had an apartment at 6 Via Varese. Berners, born Gerald Tyrwhitt in 1883, had inherited his title in 1918 and with it the Faringdon estate, which Sassoon had already visited and would return to several times in the early 1920s.[15] Monocled, bowler-hatted and urbane, the Old Etonian was a friend of the Sitwells and Morrells and rented rooms from Nellie at Half Moon Street before buying his own house in Chesham Place. A colourful eccentric and aesthete, he famously had the doves on his estate dyed magenta, green and sky-blue.

There was, however, a more serious side to Berners, who was also a composer, novelist and painter.[16] Wherever he went he took with him his clavichord, strapped to the back seat of his chauffeur-driven Rolls-Royce, and Sassoon derived great pleasure from his impromptu recitals, writing at least one poem on the subject.[17] He also enjoyed Berners' wit and practical jokes, particularly the idea of a hoax telegram Berners planned to send his fellow-homosexual

Osbert Sitwell in 1924, from a lady Osbert had fled to Dieppe to escape; it announced her imminent arrival there. From thinking Berners 'consistently inhuman' and 'exclusively intellectual' at the start, Sassoon would come to find him quite human and easy to get on with.[18] Whatever his criticism of Schuster and his friends, he enjoyed being with rich, titled people, especially when, unlike Schuster, they were generous with their money.

It was at Berners' house at the beginning of October 1921 that he first met the young German who was to dominate his life for the next two years, Prince Philipp of Hesse. A few days later he was invited to lunch with Berners and Philipp again, this time just outside Rome at the Castel Gandolfo above Lake Albano. As the diplomat Harold Nicolson, who was also there with his wife, Vita Sackville-West, and their friends Gerald and Dorothy Wellesley, recorded in his diary, it was a romantic affair. After lunching exquisitely beneath the leaves of a vine, they all launched paper boats down a nearby waterfall and Sassoon became so excited that he threw his hat in too. He was in love again.

His attraction towards Prince Philipp was not primarily a physical one, though it would be a sexually active relationship, Philipp moving into his hotel only three days after their first meeting. 'Physically I have never been really infatuated by him,' Sassoon would note a year later.[19] Heavier than Gabriel and already balding, Philipp had none of his physical charm for Sassoon. But Philipp interested him more. Sassoon wanted a connection founded on 'a firmer basis than mere sensualism'.[20] He also hoped that Philipp would be his 'link with Europe' and a 'social experience'.[21]

Philipp's standing in society was one of his main attractions for Sassoon. His mother, Princess Margarethe of Prussia, was the daughter of Kaiser Frederick, Emperor of Germany, and granddaughter of Queen Victoria. She was also the sister of Kaiser Wilhelm II, then in exile in Holland, and of Princess Sophie who, through her marriage to the Duke of Sparta, had become Queen of Greece.[22] Philipp's father, Friedrich Karl, was next in line to become Landgrave of Hesse, when his brother died, and Philipp after him.[23] Philipp himself would marry the daughter of the King of Italy.

Though the family prestige and fortunes had suffered greatly from Germany's defeat in the War, a fact which made him not unnaturally bitter, he still carried with him the consciousness and confidence of his heritage, a large part of his appeal for Sassoon. To be intimate with the great-grandson of Queen Victoria and nephew of the King of Greece was irresistible, even if Philipp's link with his disgraced uncle, the Kaiser, was less appealing to one who had seen the carnage of the First World War.

A more positive side to Philipp's inheritance was that it had turned him into a highly cultivated person with 'beautiful' manners.[24] And since their relationship coincided with Sassoon's 'grand tour in quest of culture', he fully appreciated Philipp's ability to distinguish between baroque and rococo art, for example, or his detailed knowledge of music.[25] (He was later to regret the conventionality and limitations of Philipp's taste – he thought Sassoon 'wrong' to 'tolerate' Gauguin, Van Gogh and Stravinsky, for example.)

Sassoon also admired Philipp's 'essential amiability' and imperturbable manner, which made it impossible for him to inflict his 'tigerish ill-temper' or 'tantrums' on Philipp as he did on Gabriel: 'he has a way of disarming me by a sort of placidity, quite different to the long-suffering flimsiness of poor G, who only takes refuge in tears and silence.'[26] Philipp's charm was his greatest asset. He had only to appear with the little dog and Greek servant who always accompanied him, and any reservations Sassoon felt would vanish.

For he had begun to have reservations about Philipp within a comparatively short time, soon after their passionate ten-day idyll in Rome had ended. Philipp had returned to Germany via Venice and his first few letters were gratifyingly romantic. But in his third letter, three days later, he mentions a possible visit from another English male lover. And although his next letter is full of enthusiasm for Sassoon's poems, which he has sent for Philipp's birthday, there is another reference to the English lover. A six-week silence then follows during which, it emerges, Philipp has resumed his affair with a married woman in Berlin. While describing the whole thing as a 'torture and agony', he nevertheless gives vivid details of their love-making, which has only ended because she has to leave Berlin.

It was probably at this point that Sassoon realized something he had only suspected in Rome, that Philipp was 'wholly unimaginative and rather coarsely sensual'.[27] No one of any sensitivity could have failed to understand the effect his letter would have on another lover. And after spending a much longer period with Philipp, from August to October 1922, Sassoon felt even more convinced that he lacked imagination.[28] This made Philipp far more matter-of-fact than Sassoon, who tried to keep love romantic and who wished his noble lover were not quite so 'sophisticated' about his numerous affairs.[29]

It is hardly surprising, therefore, that he failed to inspire Sassoon to write much in the way of love poetry. Apart from an indirect reference to Philipp in the 'Villa d'Este Gardens', which he had visited with the prince in October 1921, there is only one poem directly devoted to him, 'Vigil'. Written while Sassoon waited to see Philipp again in 1922, it is as conventional and formal as the man himself.[30]

Heavily derivative in general terms, the piece ends 'The Paradise of your imperfect lover', an actual phrase taken from Sassoon's far livelier poem to Gabriel, 'The Imperfect Lover'.

Philipp's lack of imagination accounted, Sassoon felt, for most of his other faults, particularly his conventional response to the arts. This irritated Sassoon most when it concerned his own poems, which Philipp professed to admire greatly. Gabriel, for all his limitations, was preferable in this respect.

There were, however, a number of similarities between Philipp and Gabriel: both ten years younger than Sassoon, they shared an enthusiasm he did not understand for 'silly chattering smart women', cocktail bars and old brandy late at night.[31] They were both promiscuous and far less puritanical than Sassoon,

Philipp, for instance, being fond of 'filthy' stories and 'obscene' statues.[32] But Sassoon was conscious mainly of Philipp's difference from Gabriel when he met him for the second time at Munich in August 1922.

To begin with the contrast was all in Philipp's favour, Sassoon finding his imperturbability a relief after Gabriel's weak and emotional nature. But by the time he moved to Venice with Philipp in October 1922, he had started to appreciate Gabriel's more creative approach to life: 'G at any rate aspires to become an artist. P is merely a cultured person.'[33]

Nevertheless, by the end of this second holiday with Philipp, he realized that his relationship with him had become very similar to that with Gabriel. He attributed this to the fact that, as with Gabriel, he had 'all the money' and 'dole[d] it out' to his young lovers, a situation which he confessed added to his 'feeling of increased domination'.[34] He had noted early on in their relationship that Philipp's sexual attitude to him was 'identical' to Gabriel's – 'passive surrender, with hero-worship; passionate desire to be adored'.[35] But he had not yet accepted that the need to dominate people (noted by Turner), together with the sadistic streak (suspected by Osbert), made it most unlikely that he would ever achieve a successful sexual liaison. Only in relationships where, to repeat his own words, 'the gross elements of sex' were 'miraculously remote', as with Blunden, would he find genuine fulfilment.[36]

He himself explained his increasing dissatisfaction with Philipp in different terms. The young prince, he noted, had 'not got a first-class mind'.[37] Worse still, he could imagine him getting 'heavier and heavier from year to year'.[38] He had taught Sassoon a great deal that he 'needed to know – worldliness', but he seemed to him 'fundamentally *stupid*' and as 'heavy as a German oratorio'.[39]

Philipp made several attempts to see Sassoon again between their parting at Naples in October 1922 and his marriage to Princess Mafalda of Italy in 1925. But Sassoon, disappointed and disillusioned by Philipp and possibly repelled by his growing interest in the Nazis (which would end with collaboration with Hitler and the death of his wife in a concentration camp), had already started on a series of new relationships by early 1923.[40]

*

Sassoon had become increasingly obsessed by Walter de la Mare's son, Colin, since he had met him as a thirteen-year-old in 1918. By 1922 he confessed that the fifteen-month break in his visits to the de la Mare family had 'probably' something to do with his attraction to Colin. 'He is an uncomfortably attractive creature – one of the most attractive I've met,' he wrote after a visit to the de la Mares in July 1922: 'Instinct warns me once again to avoid seeing him often.'[41] By the following Easter, however, he was asking Ottoline if he could bring Colin with him to Garsington: 'I have seen a great deal of him lately, and I want you to share my very deep affection for him, and to help me keep it worthy of the trust which his father puts in me, (little guessing I am afraid, the perilous complications involved!)'[42]

There was a 'deep wound', he told Ottoline two months later, but it was not Colin's fault. Judging from the pages torn from his diary for mid- to late August 1924, when he spent a week with the de la Mares at Manorbier in Wales, his fascination continued to be a sexual one, fed mainly by Colin's youth and his 'queer eyes'.[43]

It was the same two qualities which attracted him to Lord David Cecil, whom he met in March 1922, just a month before Cecil's twentieth birthday. He had already heard of the precocious young man, who visited Garsington at weekends with his Oxford undergraduate friends, Eddy Sackville-West, L.P. Hartley and Robert Gathorne-Hardy, and had looked forward 'with secret curiosity and eagerness' to meeting him, his title an added incentive.[44] When they eventually did so, he found Cecil 'fragile, intellectual, and charming, with a very delicate profile' and disturbing pale-grey eyes,[45] which he 'avoided'.[46] He felt deeply self-conscious with the youth, too aware of Cecil's attractiveness to behave naturally, and it is clear from his letters to Ottoline that he tried to become more intimate with him, assuming that someone who moved in homosexual circles was himself homosexual.

But by July 1923, when Cecil failed to keep an appointment for dinner with him at the Reform, Sassoon seems to have given up. 'The way he "put me through it" is not easy to forget,' he wrote subsequently to a sympathetic friend, Henry Festing-Jones, 'though excusable in one so young and wildflower eyed.'[47] His later references to Cecil suggest that he never really forgave him, though the two remained on civil terms for the rest of Sassoon's life, meeting very occasionally once Sassoon had moved to the West Country.[48] For his part, after his first awe of the well-known poet had passed, Cecil found Sassoon 'strangely uncouth', remembering him most vividly after his death for his 'sudden laughter'.[49]

At the height of Sassoon's attempts to engage the young aristocrat more deeply, however, he was already involved with another undergraduate of a very different kind, Richardson ('Dick') Wood. Even younger than Cecil, he was an American who had come to England to study at King's College, Cambridge.[50] He had been there a year when Sassoon first met him in August 1923 through Bartholomew. Sassoon was deeply smitten by Dick and spent many weekends with him, either in Cambridge or London. This may explain why he did not travel to the Continent at all in 1923, instead renting the whole of Tufton Street from the Turners in late September while they went to Italy.

By the following March, however, Sassoon was happy to leave England for a month in the South of France with Schuster, which suggests that his affair with Dick was over, or at least cooling. Certainly by 13 June 1924 he was 'worrying about Dick' and by the end felt in 'need of a new sexual adventure'.[51] This seems to have arrived, very conveniently, in the form of another young American, John Philbin, a friend of Schuster's. Philbin, who claimed to be a qualified mining engineer with a PhD from the University of California, arrived back in England in mid-June after a five-year absence in a poor financial state and came to stay at Bray, where he met Sassoon. In the same diary entry that refers to his need of a new sexual adventure, Sassoon also mentions Philbin. 'Sunburnt and wild-westerly', Philbin was physically very attractive, and his straitened circumstances added to his charms, since Sassoon 'like[d] to feel that [he could] help him'. That same summer he took Philbin to lunch at the Reform, tea with Nellie and dinner at Tufton Street with the Turners and Hodgsons, as well as a visit to Henry Head and his wife, and to his mother at Weirleigh, all rituals usually gone through with lovers. He also invited Philbin on a tour of the West Country and, his greatest sign of approval, took him to meet Hardy and T.E. Lawrence. The most convincing indication of a physical involvement, however, is the fact that they shared a hotel room at Bournemouth, after which Sassoon tore a page out of his diary.

It was during his tour of the West Country with Philbin that Sassoon was inspired to write one of the few poems of this period he believed showed his true poetic voice, 'Stonehenge'. But Philbin turned out to be 'rather a fraud', according to a disillusioned Sassoon, and the relationship was short-lived. By late summer 1924 he is describing himself as a man suffering from 'sexual starvation' and by mid-September his frustration has reached the point where he finds himself attracted to almost every passably handsome youth he sees.[52] Another torn-out page in his September diary and a poem written a day later suggest that he is prepared to settle for at least one casual sexual encounter on a trip round the Midlands that month.[53] Other passing attractions appear to have included the poet Edward O'Brien, judging from his reaction to O'Brien's subsequent marriage to the novelist Romer Wilson.[54]

Despite Sassoon's wish to write a *Madame Bovary* of 'sexual inversion', he was not bold enough to leave an explicit account of his sexual adventures,[55] and it is significant that his diary for 1924, when his sexual frustration was at its height, has a disproportionately large number of pages torn out of it. The most intriguing of these is his destruction of entries from early October 1924 to the middle of February 1925, the period covering one of his most painful affairs of all, with Ivor Novello.

Novello had first achieved fame with his wartime song 'Keep the Home-fires Burning' and Sassoon's initial response to him was one of intense dislike: 'Someday I will kill the man who wrote keep the home fires burning,' he had told Dent in 1916.[56] When he actually met Novello at Eddie Marsh's in January 1919, he was again critical, though at the same time acknowledging the young Welshman's talents. Partly because Sassoon identified him with Marsh, for whom Novello had become a substitute Rupert Brooke, he already regarded him as highly superficial. And when he encountered the young actor filming in Venice in October 1922, he was positively rude to him.[57]

This made his infatuation with Novello, when they met for the third time in September 1924, all the more unexpected. He had been invited to tea on the 28th by the actress Constance Collier, a friend of both Marsh and Schuster. She was also close to Novello, having only recently helped him adapt his current hit,

The Rat, from a film script to a stage play. (He, of course, played the male lead.) It was, therefore, quite natural that she should invite him to meet Sassoon, whom she had got to know that summer at Schuster's. She also invited another equally attractive and even younger actor, Glen Byam Shaw.

In the event Sassoon, unwisely, chose Novello, who promptly pitched him into an 'unblinking little hell', an 'inferno' far worse than that created by Hunter in New York.[58] Spoilt by his doting mother and early success and inordinately proud of his Italianate good looks, Novello deliberately cultivated a charm which concealed his essential egotism. Adored by men and women alike, he seems to have satisfied his sexual appetite with very little concern for the person involved. Though Sassoon destroyed the details of their affair, he did tell a close friend later that Novello had 'outraged and betrayed [his] decent feelings to an incredible degree'.[59]

After the first raptures of the meetings in Novello's dressing room and supper at one of his favourite restaurants, the Savoy Grill, had subsided, Sassoon began to think of him as 'something very inhuman'.[60] Sitting in the 'blinding glare of unshaded bulbs and mirrors, applying Californian sun-burn to his successful countenance', he struck Sassoon as nothing but a 'stage-self', a 'victim of his own vanity and weakness', yet he was unable to extricate himself from the affair, appearing to derive a masochistic pleasure from it. He was still suffering intensely when he went to see Novello in his dressing room for the last time alone at the beginning of May 1925. There is little doubt that it was Novello who ended the relationship and, though Sassoon denied feeling bitter about him, his subsequent references are very resentful indeed.

Sassoon found his relationship with Novello humiliating perhaps because, for once, he was not the one in control. His usual advantages of age, fame and money did not apply.[61] Instead of 'doling out' allowances to a much younger man who worshipped him, he found himself expected to do the worshipping. By late February 1925 the affair was over. Sassoon was ready to accompany Schuster to the South of France for a month again and to spend most of the summer at Bray recuperating. He even arranged to meet Gabriel during his stay in France and to take him on a tour of the West Country in mid-July.[62]

One reason for Sassoon's apparent change of heart towards Gabriel, apart from needing balm for his bruised ego, was the acquisition of a car in June 1924, a new Gwynne Eight, given by Ross's friend Richmond Temple. Once Anzie had taught Sassoon to drive, he left his cramped flat in Tufton Street as often as possible. And when he stayed at Bray, he was no longer dependent on Anzie to ferry him around but could come and go as he pleased. He relished his new-found freedom and spent the summer of 1924 exploring various parts of the country with Philbin. Once he had gained confidence, he started driving alone. Turning up for weekends with H.G. Wells in Essex, Ottoline at Garsington or even the Hardys in Dorset, for instance, he would proudly offer rides in his little two-seater. Sometimes an unsuspecting friend would accept, though rarely a second time.

The problem was that Sassoon, however physically co-ordinated on the hunting field or cricket pitch, was hopeless with anything mechanical, a curious anomaly in someone related to the well-known engineering Thornycrofts. Even the telephone 'annihilated' him, according to one friend.[63] It had something to do with a general resistance to change, stemming partly from a deep reverence for the past, which also informed his attitude toward poetic techniques. Cars were a particular challenge and several witnesses have suggested that he drove them as though riding a horse.[64] Stories about his bad driving abound. His cousin Lettice, for example, said that it was a 'traumatic' experience to be driven by him.[65] She remembered replying meaningfully, when he asked her during one drive whether she liked cars, that she 'wasn't frightened that they wouldn't start, but that they wouldn't stop'.[66] Even T.E. Lawrence, who hardly knew the meaning of fear, was, by Sassoon's own account, terrified after only five minutes of his driving; 'my methods of turning from side roads into main roads were abrupt in those days', Sassoon added by way of explanation.[67]

Sassoon was prosecuted on at least one occasion and only with great difficulty managed to have the charge changed from 'dangerous driving' to a lesser charge and to retain his licence.[68] On his very first drive alone he had run into a dog-cart, then the next day knocked down a cyclist, but he seemed unaware of how dangerous he was and loved driving. On one occasion he killed a sheep, narrowly missing its accompanying shepherd. Yet less than a month after being given the Gwynne he noted that his 'increasing confidence' made him 'genuinely enjoy the car. It makes me feel more human and less pathological. It is a substitute for my hunter, I suppose.'[69] Not only that but a car was also, he told Graves, 'much less trouble than a horse and much more mobile'.[70]

His preference for horses would return in due course; the Gwynne would be replaced first by a Morris Oxford, which he promptly crashed, then by a Chrysler, a Packard and, finally, by a Humber Snipe 80 Drophead Coupé; but the driving would remain completely erratic. Only in the era before the compulsory driving test would he have been allowed a licence at all.

The one thing which worried Sassoon about owning a car was the fear of becoming dependent on material things, in his efforts of 'continually trying to escape from acquisitiveness' during this period.[71] He hoped to achieve this by sharing the Gwynne with the Turners, but suspected that, once he started to enjoy driving, his resolution might crumble. And, in any case, the situation at Tufton Street had begun to deteriorate badly by mid-1924.

*

Sassoon's first serious dissatisfaction with Tufton Street had started in late 1923, when he had rented the whole house from the Turners for several months during their visit to Italy. Much as he enjoyed this period of 'unmolested piano-playing, and using the only nice (though dark) room' in the 'poky' house, he was conscious that it must soon end and that he would be forced to revert to a routine of 'club-lunches and sitting upstairs listening to the Turners playing my piano'.[72] To his dismay he began to 'feel like a cuckoo in a linnet's nest, anxious to elbow them out of it'.[73] Back in his own rooms in December they seemed to him even more cramped by comparison. And he could scarcely fail to remember that it was his own money, still not repaid, which had bought the house originally.

Another cause for irritation was the arrival of a permanent fair on a piece of nearby waste ground in January 1924. The blaring of the hurdy-gurdy organ went on till midnight, adding considerably to the noise of tipsy singing and loud music from down the street, the booming of Big Ben and even the Turners' conversation below or above him in the poorly insulated house. Concentration became almost impossible.

During the Turners' absence he had been able to eat at home, waited on happily by the one servant, Mrs Binks. Since he worked late, slept late and combined breakfast with lunch, she had a much lighter workload than usual, coming in only half a day, and was not unnaturally sorry to see the Turners arrive back. By trying to make him comfortable, he believed, she brought about her own dismissal in February 1924 as well as creating a 'rift' in his relations with the Turners, who resented the extra time she devoted to him. Waited on all his life, even in the army, Sassoon could not understand the fuss: 'I never have more than one meal a day cooked here, and that's only a bit of fish and some coffee.'[74] But it was one meal more than the original agreement and with Mrs Binks's departure it stopped. By spending most of spring and summer at Bray, Sassoon survived 1924 at Tufton Street, but by 1925 he knew he must leave what had become for him 'a poisoned house'.[75]

Turner himself, the main inducement for Sassoon to live there in the first place, had become the one problem he could not ignore. Since their successful holiday together in 1922, when Sassoon had paid for Turner to accompany him to Munich, their relationship had slowly deteriorated. By April 1925 everything Turner 'says, does, and is' irritated him.[76] He also grew resentful at having given money to Turner, which he suspected made Turner resentful too.

Sassoon's hostility to Turner did not extend to his wife, whom he continued to admire. It was for Delphine's sake, he told Ottoline, that he tried to forget his resentment against her husband. He and Ottoline had been outraged when Walter, having visited Garsington regularly with his wife since 1920, turned up suddenly in 1925 with his current mistress, Cynthia Noble, especially since they believed he was only interested in her money. Though they successfully thwarted Turner's plans, Sassoon could not forgive him for his 'unpardonable cruelty' towards the long-suffering Delphine. He was also antagonized by Turner's lack of gratitude towards Ottoline, who had treated him with great generosity. Turner's 'insulting caricature' of her in his skit *The Aesthetes* had not been published by 1925 and Ottoline herself had not yet seen it but he had already shown it to Sassoon, who was deeply shocked.[77]

Even at this point – early August 1925 – Sassoon was prepared to try again. When Ottoline told him that the Turners would be quite happy if only they had a car, he gave them the money to buy one, though he made it clear that it was for Delphine's sake. And he still felt obliged to remain at Tufton Street. When friends urged him to go and live comfortably by himself, he pointed out that if he did so the Turners would also have to leave their house, which they might then be unable to sell or let.

So things might have continued for some time longer, had it not been for Graves's intervention in mid-August. Graves had been staying at Sutton Veny in Somerset with his father-in-law, William Nicholson, who told him that the impecunious Turners were 'coming down in a car'.[78] Greatly surprised, Graves suggested that Sassoon must have bought it for them, but Nicholson rejected the idea, since Turner had told him that 'S.S. was very mean, and never helped anyone unless it helped him to dominate them'.[79] He had talked of Sassoon 'with great dislike' and had expressed a 'strong desire' that Sassoon should 'cease to live in *his* house' (my italics).[80] Most provokingly of all, Turner had complained that Sassoon annoyed him by playing *his* piano.

Delphine, who wrote a long letter of explanation to Sassoon as soon as she heard of Graves's action, believed that he was either very 'clumsy and literal-minded' or that he was deliberately trying to destroy the relationship between Sassoon and Turner.[81] Richard Perceval Graves, argues that his uncle was particularly 'anxious' about his own affairs at the time and simply being 'tactless'.[82]

Jealousy and a lack of tact were almost certainly behind Nellie's actions too when, a few days later, she related her own bit of gossip to Sassoon: that Turner had told Romer Wilson that Sassoon had prevented him and Delphine from 'ever going away when they wanted to'.[83]

The result was immediate. Sassoon decided finally to leave Tufton Street, though felt unable to tell Turner so directly. Instead he asked Ottoline to explain to Delphine that he 'wanted to live more comfortably' and that he was 'deeply hurt' by Turner's reported remarks.[84] In spite of Delphine's eloquent defence – that there was something 'fine and worthwhile' in her husband under his surface roughness – Sassoon stuck to his decision and by late August was looking for other rooms.

His anxieties about house-hunting were made worse by a growing sense of hopelessness over his love life. His long series of unsatisfactory relationships had finally made him realize that he would find 'no happiness or serenity through "falling in love" with people because they look nice'.[85] Reading J.R. Ackerley's play *The Prisoners of War* in April 1925, when he was still suffering intensely from his humiliating affair with Ivor Novello, he identified closely with Ackerley's tormented homosexual officer:

And all today [he wrote in his diary for 22 April 1925] I have carried about with me an inward sense of homesickness for that land where I would be – that Elysium, forever deluding me with its mirage in the desert of my frustrated and distorted desires. I know that real happiness cannot be created by any sensual Elysium. But even a ramshackle Elysium is alluring, when the discredited oasis beckons me toward its disenchanted groves, though I know that the reality would leave me desolate and dissatisfied.[86]

Only six months after writing these words he was to embark on an affair which would bring him nearer to that Elysium than any he had yet experienced. It would also, in more prosaic terms, provide him with a new flat.

*

By December 1925, Sassoon was experiencing a 'new sense of proportion as regards the trivial details of life', he told his diary. The main reason for his optimism, Glen Byam Shaw, was only twenty when Sassoon started an affair with him in October that year. Yet Glen was in many ways the wisest and most grounded of all Sassoon's lovers and their two years together were to be among the happiest, calmest and most productive of Sassoon's life. As creative as Gabriel, if not more so, Glen suffered from neither his dissoluteness nor his lack of discipline. And though less well-educated than Philipp, he had a natural intelligence and a more genuine thirst for culture that delighted Sassoon. He was also tall, slim and good-looking.

Had Sassoon not chosen Ivor Novello at his first meeting with Glen at Constance Collier's in September 1924, he might have escaped a year of misery and frustration. For he had found Glen attractive from the start. Unfortunately, Glen had been about to leave on tour when Sassoon's first postcard arrived the month they met and failed to respond to it. Nor did he answer a second, sent after Sassoon's affair with Novello had reached its sorry end. But when a third arrived, posted by Sassoon on his thirty-ninth birthday from the Gloucester Music Festival, Glen was sufficiently intrigued to ask Constance for Sassoon's address. And when Sassoon arrived back in Tufton Street on 10 October 1925, he found a card from Glen waiting.

Glen now seemed equally anxious to meet him and, even more gratifyingly, to read his poems. But Sassoon, diffident at the best of times and especially so when dealing with someone young enough to be his son, was so vague in his invitation to dinner the following week, that Glen failed to turn up. It would be 20 October before they finally met again, more than a year after their initial encounter.

Once Glen realized his mistake over the first invitation, he had written to apologize, wanting to be reassured that Sassoon did not think he had acquired Novello's heartless 'method of treating his friends'.[87] Novello was a subject close to both their hearts, Glen having also suffered an emotional bruising at his hands, and he formed one of the main topics of conversation at their first dinner.

Even more importantly from Sassoon's viewpoint, Glen asked for his help. Though he loved acting, which he had taken up professionally on leaving Westminster School at eighteen, he was finding actors extremely philistine and did not want to 'get like them'.[88] He knew something of art, since his father, Byam Shaw, had been a painter and run an art school until his death in 1919. But he felt almost entirely ignorant about literature and music.

Sassoon was delighted to oblige. It was reassuring to be regarded as a 'great poet', especially at a time when he felt poetry had deserted him, and a genuine pleasure to share his enthusiasms with an intelligent and imaginative young disciple. He responded at once with a book of his own poems, together with a photograph. Best of all, it was clear from Glen's thank-you letter that he had enjoyed Sassoon's company as much as Sassoon had his. It was more than just a strong sense of humour they shared: 'I felt so awfully peaceful and happy when I came home yesterday,' Glen wrote, unknowingly echoing Sassoon's own diary response to the event.[89]

The evening also had a practical outcome. It had seemed quite natural when they arrived back at Tufton Street from the Reform for Sassoon to refer to his increasingly pressing need to find alternative accommodation, Glen knew of possible rooms near his home at 18 Campden Hill Gardens; a family friend, the painter Harold Speed,[90] had converted the top floor of his house at 23 Campden Hill Square into a flat, which was still empty. Less than a week later Sassoon was viewing Speed's flat. Having meantime spent another 'happy' evening with Glen, he was already predisposed towards it, since it was only three minutes' walk away from Glen, his 'bosom's best friend'.[91] (Whether he was deterred by the fact that his 'ex-bosom friend', Gabriel, lived only a few hundred yards in the other direction across Holland Park Avenue he does not say, though he does note the fact.)[92]

Campden Hill Square rises steeply and No. 23, an elegant and spacious house, lies on the south side at its highest point. It struck Sassoon at once as the very opposite of cramped, dank Tufton Street, jammed in below street level. Instead of neighbouring tenements, the top floor of 23 looked out over the treetops of the gated central garden below, towards distant church spires. He wrote at least two poems based specifically on the view which suggest that his move to Campden Hill Square inspired a return to nature in his work. Looking down from his 'silent-soliloquied windows of thought' on the 'sun-slanted green of the Square' returned him to an awareness of the natural world that he had loved as a child and young man. It was an influence which would make itself strongly felt in his next collection of poems.[93]

Even on the top attic floor, the rooms at 23 Campden Hill Square were far larger than at Tufton Street, especially after Speed had agreed to remove the partition wall between the two front ones. Having just bought a new Bechstein, space for a grand piano was extremely important to Sassoon. So too was the fact that the flat was self-contained, with a bedroom, bathroom and small kitchen at the back. Instead of having to take all his meals out, he could look forward to eating at least one of them at home. A Mrs Dingle was to replace Mrs Binks (could two domestics really have had such Dickensian names?) and supply a brunch of sole and coffee at 11 o'clock, an hour after Sassoon woke up.[94] It was a routine which would allow him time to play the piano and write some of his many letters before setting out on his daily walk. More like a marathon by modern standards, this would often last from two o'clock till five and usually take him across Kensington Gardens and Hyde Park to Mayfair, where he continued to buy his special Dunhill tobacco and Earl Grey tea.[95] If he was dining at the Reform, he would stay on in the area for tea, either at Nellie Burton's or the club itself. But more often than not he would walk all the way back to Campden Hill for dinner at one of the nearby hotels. The move would shake him out of some of his most hallowed rituals but, a creature of habit, he quickly formed new ones.

On his first visit to 23 Campden Hill Square Sassoon had been gratified to learn that the previous owner, J.M. Barrie, had written *Peter Pan* there, the idea of 'the lost boy' in that play having been inspired by Barrie's predecessors in the house, the Llewellyn-Davieses, whose son had died tragically young.[96] Barrie's success with *Peter Pan* seemed a reassuring literary precedent.

His first visit also alerted him to one possible deterrent, the character of his landlord. Speed, who struck Sassoon as a *Punch* caricature of an artist with his beard, pipe and blue smock, greeted him with ominous effusiveness, insisting that Sassoon first inspect his paintings before allowing him to see the flat. He could only hope that Speed was 'sufficiently commonplace and complacent' to be no trouble to him.[97] For at a rent of £150 a year he was ready to overlook most drawbacks, rejoicing in the thought of being 'safely detached from Turner and his gloomy house and heroic wife'.[98] Moving into Campden Hill Square, an event intimately linked in his mind with his closer acquaintance with Glen, was, he believed, a 'turning-point' in his life.[99] And the 'emotional tranquillity' he would feel for at least the first two of his six years' tenancy there, was a reflection of his 'happy experience' with Glen.[100]

Sassoon had had to stay on at Tufton Street until 29 November, while alterations were completed, and when it came to it, leaving Turner's gloomy house was not quite so joyful as he had anticipated. Once he had found alternative accommodation, Turner did not seem nearly so impossible, in fact Sassoon would voluntarily spend Christmas with him and Delphine at Garsington a month later. Furthermore, he had loved and grown part of his room, as his nostalgic 'Farewell to a Room', written a week before his departure, shows. It is a poem which anticipates the change of style his change of situation would help develop, a move away from the detached, ironic tone he had cultivated in *Satirical Poems* to a more meditative, inward-looking verse:

> Room, while I stand outside you in the gloom,
> Your tranquil-toned interior, void of me,
> Seems part of my own self which I can see ....   (*CP*, p. 179)[101]

In spite of such evident nostalgia, it was finally with a sense of relief and some excitement that Sassoon left Tufton Street. After a few days with his Treasury friend, Meiklejohn, at 22 Connaught Square and a weekend at Oxford with Glen, he installed himself in his new flat on 7 December 1925. The motherly Nellie, he told Ottoline, 'flying to and fro with sticks and straws and scraps of moss in her beak', had saved one of her favourite chicks all the usual 'bother' of moving, 'bless her'.[102]

Nellie was also his first guest, having tea with him the same day; and Glen, just back from Oxford, the second. He and Sassoon celebrated both the move and his return with dinner at the Reform that same evening, retiring to his new flat afterwards. After two more evenings with Glen, both of which ended at Campden Hill Square, Sassoon could write gratefully in his diary: 'I am being compensated for much unhappiness in the past.'[103]

There is no doubt that Glen made Sassoon very happy. Yet it was a happiness which depended on his frequent absences, either at the Oxford Playhouse or on tour. Sassoon needed complete solitude to work, as well as time to savour his emotions. And the pattern he established for himself in Glen's absence, of a day virtually free of human contact, goes some way to explaining his extraordinary creative productivity at Campden Hill Square. His need to be alone, yet his craving for a lasting relationship, was a problem which dominated his life after the War. One of the finest poems he wrote during this time centres on this crucial subject:

> '*When I'm alone*' – the words tripped off his tongue
> As though to be alone were nothing strange.
> '*When I was young*,' he said; '*when I was young ...*'
>
> I thought of age, and loneliness, and change.
> I thought how strange we grow when we're alone,
> And how unlike the selves that meet, and talk,
> And blow the candles out, and say good-night.
>
> *Alone* ... The word is life endured and known.
> It is the stillness where our spirits walk
> And all but inmost faith is overthrown.   (*CP*, p. 180)[104]

Sassoon valued this poem greatly, he told Dame Hildelith Cumming in 1964, 'because it was the first of my post-war poems in which I discovered my mature mode of utterance (what I call "my cello voice")'.[105] It seemed to him in retrospect that he had never written a truer line than the eighth: '*Alone* ... The word is life endured and known.' It was one of a number of poems he wrote on the theme in the 1920s.

Glen was not just a negative blessing, however, merely someone who allowed Sassoon freedom to work. He also brought a number of positive things to the relationship. While there was undeniably an element of the master-disciple syndrome between them – Glen almost certainly found in Sassoon the father-figure Sassoon himself had looked for – Glen gave as much as he received. And though Sassoon generally preferred the position of control that 'giving' allowed, the younger man's tact and sympathy were such that Sassoon, for once, was able to accept what he offered.

Glen's most immediate gift was to renew Sassoon's idealistic view of love, which had been badly damaged since his first idyllic venture into the world of sex with Gabriel in 1918. Glen, he believed, had made this happiness possible by his simplicity and sincerity, as well as an instinctive capacity for avoiding misunderstandings. And he would continue to maintain, long after their affair was over, that Glen was the only friend who really understood him.[106]

Glen also made Sassoon more relaxed and far more tolerant for a time, and not just with himself. When Sassoon visited the Graveses, just before they left for Cairo in November 1925, for instance, instead of finding it the usual strain, he felt 'very peaceful and happy'.[107] More remarkably he even wrote to Nancy Graves asking her to forgive him for all his 'cussedness' in the past and to allow him 'to try and be a good friend again'.[108] Glen's own equable nature enabled him to dispel the 'demons' which accumulated round Sassoon in his long periods of solitude and self-analysis.[109]

Having always looked more youthful than his years, Sassoon had found his recent thirty-ninth birthday, with its threat of a fortieth, a depressing experience and the eighteen years' age gap between himself and Glen might have made this worse. But Glen's boyish enthusiasm sent Sassoon back in time, making him feel young again. On giving him a driving lesson in the Gwynne, for instance, he had felt rejuvenated by Glen's childlike delight. Their shared jokes were often reminiscent of the game Sassoon had played with Gordon in his early twenties. Only instead of Surtees, it was *The Diary of a Nobody* or O'Casey's controversial play *Juno and the Paycock* that supplied the humour.

Sassoon had first seen *Juno and the Paycock* with Meiklejohn a few days before Glen's return from Oxford.[110] It was his seventh visit to the theatre in six weeks, clearly an attempt to draw nearer to the young actor. Only two days after their first dinner, instead of his more usual concert or opera, he had gone to *The Seagull* and Chekhov had quickly become a favourite playwright for both of them. Sassoon would always be grateful to Glen for his reintroduction to an area of culture that had not interested him greatly. He was thrilled when Glen introduced him to one of theatre's legendary figures, Ellen Terry, with whom they spent a whole weekend in 1927.[111] And some of their happiest times together later on would be at Stratford-upon-Avon during Glen's directorship of the Royal Shakespeare Company.[112]

Glen also restored Sassoon's faith in himself as a poet. For the first time in years he found himself wanting to write, rather than forcing himself to do so. Appropriately, one of the first poems to emerge was inspired by Glen, an attempt to explain the difference he had made to Sassoon's solitary existence that ends: '... But you are with me in this voiceless air;/ My hands are empty, but my heart is filled.'[113]

Another more successful poem almost certainly inspired by Glen, 'The Power and the Glory', was also the first to be written in his new room. Though it would be an oversimplification to equate Glen entirely with the 'glorious angel' of the piece and the direct cause of the poet's 'rapture', there is little doubt that the renewed energy, intensity and sense of direction in it sprang mainly from their relationship:

> *Let there be life*, said God. And what He wrought
> Went past in myriad marching lives, and brought
> This hour, this quiet room, and my small thought
> Holding invisible vastness in its hands.
>
> ...
> *Let life be God* ... What wail of fiend or wraith
> Dare mock my glorious angel where he stands
> To fill my dark with fire, my heart with faith?   (*CP*, pp. 193-4)[114]

With the move to more peaceful surroundings, the 'quiet room' becomes a central motif of his later poetry, generally used to suggest the private self looking out on the world.[115]

Sassoon had already started 'escaping' into a more lyrical mode in several poems,[116] some of which had appeared in the privately printed *Picture Show* and *Lingual Exercises*.[117] Intending to exclude these from *Satirical Poems*, he was saving them for a separate volume of 'Love and lyrical poems' which he had been planning as early as October 1923, *The Heart's Journey*.[118] As the title implies, this would be in the nature of an exploration into his own being.

To begin with, all the pieces meant for this collection were, according to him, 'idyllic poems' deriving from the 'old days in the garden at Weirleigh', which continued to be the 'background' of his every dream.[119] And though this would not remain true for the completed book, it is remarkable how many of the poems in *The Heart's Journey* hark back to his moments of revelation at dawn in his childhood garden.[120] One of the earliest to be written, 'Song, be my Soul', which opens the sequence, shows what a powerful epiphany that had been, symbolizing a purity which the 'way-worn traveller' has lost, together with the loves that he has 'wronged and slain'. Its simplicity both of form and language reinforces the sense of the poet trying to get back to his childhood innocence through the recreation of it in his verse, or 'song'. The soul, clothed appropriately in pure white, leads the narrator through a garden full of his past ghosts at the moment when dawn is about to break. The theme and the tone set the mood for the whole collection:

> ... Soul, be my song; return arrayed in white;
> Lead home the loves that I have wronged and slain:
> Bring back the summer dawns that banished night

With distant-warbling bird-notes after rain. ...
Time's way-worn traveller I. And you, O song,
O soul, my Paradise laid waste so long.   (*CP*, p. 175)

This quiet, meditative sonnet of surface simplicity but some technical
complexity – the insistent repetition of soft consonants (s's, l's and w's), for
example, underlines the ethereal quality of the scene – heralds a poetic voice
quite different from the angry tones of the war satires. The subject matter might
vary, from a consideration of physical passion,[121] great men of the past,[122] the
death of someone known[123] or social problems,[124] to the power of music[125] or
the state of solitude,[126] and there are even two further poems on the War,[127] but
the reflective voice of the poet remains constant, giving unity to the volume.

Edith Sitwell, who found the 'quiet unfaltering beginning' of 'Song, be my
Soul' very 'beautiful', believed that Sassoon had finally found his true voice.[128]
Even Graves 'like[d it] extremely' at first, much to the surprise of Sassoon, who
had expected him to condemn it as '1902 poetry' or 'only anthology stuff'.
(Graves was later to dismiss the whole volume as 'lace-Valentine vulgarity', a
'monument to [Sassoon's] emotional shortcoming'.)[129] Blunden believed that
it belonged to a 'Sassoonian tradition older than his vision of war's realities
and his subordinate satires', arguing that he 'took the mystery of things upon
him in the beautiful though tentative poems of his boyhood' and that he had
'always responded in verse of great grace and significance to "invisible vastness"
immanent in quiet and solitude'.[130]

The poems in *The Heart's Journey*, however, are not simply echoes of the
pantheistic poems of his youth. As Thorpe argues, there is a 'lucid sense' of
being on 'the threshold of a new and more vital life', which 'cannot be entered
on with the old innocence: that, once lost cannot be regained by shrugging
off the knowledge and experience of harsh life already undergone'.[131] It is
this conflict which lies at the centre of the collection. Shelley's *Ozymandias* is
only one of a number of literary influences in this sequence. Cowper's homely
imagery and his tranquil, fire-lit interiors appear side by side with verbal
echoes from Shakespeare's sonnets, and Graves found at least two phrases from
Housman's *Shropshire Lad* in 'Conclusion'. But the greatest single debt is to the
seventeenth-century devotional poets, Vaughan in particular. One of Sassoon's
own favourites in *The Heart's Journey* is a Vaughan-like meditation on his visit
to the poet's grave.[132]

Like Vaughan, to whom Blunden and others have compared him, in this
and later collections Sassoon is trying to 'see into the heart of things'.[133] And in
setting out and reflecting on a possible correspondence between this world and
another, he frequently resorts to images of flowers and light, as Vaughan and
his fellow-mystics had done:

A flower has opened in my heart ...
What flower is this, what flower of spring,

What simple, secret thing?
It is the peace that shines apart,
The peace of daybreak skies that bring
Clear song and wild swift wing. ...   (*CP*, p. 195)[134]

Sassoon's own comment on Vaughan – that he 'seldom wrote a perfected poem' – applies equally to his own poetry of this second period.[135] As with Vaughan, the intensity comes and goes, but at its best it is so full of what Sassoon found in Vaughan – 'radiant naturalness' – that it fully justifies his belief that *The Heart's Journey* was the 'strongest work' he produced in the 1920s.[136] Most of his friends agreed with him. Apart from Blunden and Edith Sitwell's endorsements, he received lavish praise from Gosse, Nichols and, even more importantly to him, Hardy, Forster and T.E. Lawrence.

Reviews were slower in coming, since Crosby Gaige, the wealthy American connoisseur who first produced *The Heart's Journey* as a limited edition in 1927, did not send out review copies.[137] It was not until Heinemann published a trade edition in 1928 that they started to appear.[138] One of the first was by a poet Sassoon despised, Humbert Wolfe, and was so lavish in its praise that, to Sassoon's embarrassment, it boosted his sales dramatically.[139]

*

Though Glen inspired some of the finest poems in *The Heart's Journey*, whenever he reappeared in London from his current acting engagement, Sassoon would stop writing to be with him. On his first return from Oxford in December 1925, for instance, in addition to a round of dinners and plays, Sassoon treated him to a five-day tour of the West Country for what had become a statutory visit to Hardy, his equivalent of taking a partner home for parental approval.[140]

Sassoon found the visit 'perfect',[141] which even the death of his uncle Hamo, announced in the *Evening Standard* on the second day of their journey, could not spoil. But it formed a sad end to the trip as he set off from Max Gate in wet, windy weather on 22 December with Hardy's laurel wreath to his old friend Hamo in the back of the Gwynne. Parting from Glen in Oxford the next day, he hurried out to Garsington to borrow a black suit from Philip Morrell, then made his way sombrely to his uncle's funeral at Christ Church Cathedral.

Relieved that his mother had not come to Oxford for the 'desolate business', which signified for her even more than himself the end of an era, he drove to Garsington, where he spent Christmas.[142] After the excitement of his trip with Glen it seemed a tedious period, filled with too many people, too many card games and largely trivial talk, though it was cheered up by visits to Bridges, Masefield and the painter Gilbert Spencer, a recent acquaintance.[143]

Glen spent Christmas with his family, then left shortly afterwards to join Fagan's company for a tour of the provinces. So that, apart from occasional snatched meetings with him, Sassoon was left alone once more to write, happy in the knowledge of Glen's existence and anxious to see him again but undistracted by his actual presence. At the end of April he could happily anticipate Glen being back in London.

He was also looking forward to the appearance of *Satirical Poems*. Publication date was set for 29 April 1926 and Heinemann had arranged maximum publicity for it. In the event both Glen's return and the launch of the book were overtaken by the General Strike, which started on 3 May.[144]

Sassoon's sympathies, which had been with the miners in their strike of 1921, were now more divided. It was not simply that the strike had killed his book 'stone-dead', but that, though he still felt for the workers, he could not fully endorse the methods they had chosen. Nor did he think much would change, a prognosis that turned out to be largely correct. He believed that Asquith, Grey and Balfour were failing to address the situation and described Winston Churchill, with his 'Napoleon complex', as 'the main obstruction to the reasonable settlement which can and ought to be made at once'.

The strike itself, one of the most controversial and significant events of the inter-war years, was (like the previous one) brought about by the miners, who faced severe cuts in their wages. The Government, in anticipation, had set up an 'Organization for the Maintenance of Supplies', so that when the three big unions struck – the miners first, followed by the railwaymen and transport workers – it was ready for the situation. Soldiers and a large body of volunteers were brought in to staff essential services and, though life did not proceed quite as usual, it carried on.

Sassoon's own part in the strike, though hardly dramatic, was more active than his waning socialist beliefs would lead one to expect. Osbert Sitwell, now on the best of terms with Sassoon, had been drawn into a behind-the-scenes attempt to settle the dispute through his connection with the Liberal peer Lord Wimborne and his wife.[145] Following the Labour M.P. and railwaymen's leader J.H. Thomas's admission that the miners were ready for a compromise, he contacted Sassoon, whose experience on the *Daily Herald* he believed might help.

Together they 'exerted and exhausted' every possible legitimate connection they had between them, including an unsympathetic Arnold Bennett and the editor of the *Daily Express*, Beverley Baxter, who was readier to listen.[146] Considering that he had been virtually ambushed by Sassoon and Sitwell, who lay in wait for him as he returned to his Chelsea flat at two in the morning, and that (according to his own account) the 'gallant eccentric' Sassoon had been highly excitable, pacing his sitting room and 'brandishing his fists at the ceiling' while Osbert remained 'unnaturally calm', Baxter showed exemplary fairmindedness.[147] Having accepted that Sitwell's formula for peace was 'clear, sane and wise', he agreed to approach his paper's owner, Lord Beaverbrook, in the hope of being allowed to modify the *Express*'s 'bellicose' views of the strike.[148]

While Baxter shrewdly suspected that Sassoon was 'riding some tempest of the soul that would not give him peace' – his own guilt, perhaps, at having more or less abandoned his socialist principles – Sassoon admitted no such thing to himself in his diary, merely dismissing Baxter as an enemy of the unions. He was very surprised indeed when, contrary to his gloomy predictions, the strike came to an end on 12 May. And, unlike either Baxter or Sitwell, he did not believe that it had anything to do with 'the work of two poets'.[149]

The end of the strike brought the stranded Glen home from the North. But it was only a brief interval between tours and he was soon off again. For Sassoon, meantime, the summer stretched emptily ahead. He had resisted going to Bray again, partly because Campden Hill Square seemed even lovelier in late spring, unlike Tufton Street, but he spent several weekends at Garsington and Whitsun at 'Painshanger' with Lord and Lady Desborough. By the end of June, however, he was becoming bored.

It was in this mood that Ottoline persuaded him to join her husband Philip, their daughter Julian and herself for a tour of Europe. To begin with, knowing how badly Julian was getting on with her mother, Sassoon sensibly limited his commitment to three weeks. But when another friend of the Morrells, the 26-year-old Robert ('Bob') Gathorne-Hardy, was added to the party, he suddenly found that he could manage the full six weeks.[150]

The only drawback from Sassoon's viewpoint was that Bob's partner, Kyrle Leng, was also invited. The two younger men were already living together and when, on arrival at Versailles, it became clear to Kyrle that Bob was as 'mad about' Sassoon as Sassoon was about him, he decided to return home.[151] Bob evidently wanted an affair and, deeply smitten himself, Sassoon had found it very difficult to resist. 'I wanted you to stay with me,' he wrote to Bob; 'the thought was Paradise.' Only the sight of Kyrle's unhappy face, 'like the troubled face of my own good angel', he told Bob, had prevented him from succumbing.[152] Instead, and at the risk of sounding 'frightfully priggish', he talked of his own 'strict moral code'.[153] As his fortieth birthday approached he was more aware than ever of the importance of forming a permanent bond: 'I have lived long enough to know that such a relationship [as yours and Kyrle's] does not happen twice in life.' Eight restless years of flitting from one relationship to another had finally convinced him that 'the paradise of the spirit is the only one worth entering'.[154] He could no longer enjoy the paradise of the flesh 'with a light heart and blinded eyes'.[155]

It seemed a sign that he was finally growing up. It was also a decision which enabled him to remain friends with Bob for the rest of his life. But his infatuation with Bob in the first place suggests that he was not fully satisfied by Glen, whom he deliberately misled about Bob's reasons for returning to England.[156] Perhaps the long periods apart, forced on them by Glen's profession, had weakened his initial intensity of feeling. Whatever the explanation, when the next serious temptation came along, Sassoon would not resist a second time.

Meanwhile, feeling like the 'Sorrows of Werther', he continued 'drearily' on with the Morrells across France and Italy to Venice, as Ottoline had wished.[157] He arrived back six weeks later, exhausted, ill, underweight, but surprisingly positive about the Morrells considering the strain of trying to 'lubricate the friction between mother and daughter'.[158] Apart from a promise to read his poems to the Literary Society of University College, London, there seemed no compelling reason to go back to England at all – 'except to see my mother'.[159]

Fortunately, filial love triumphed and Sassoon returned with the Morrells on 11 September. For it was during a short visit to his mother only a week later that the idea of his prose classic, *Memoirs of a Fox-Hunting Man*, was conceived.

24

Memoirs of a Fox-Hunting Man: 'The Testament of my Youth'

1925-1927

No one was more surprised than Sassoon himself when *Memoirs of a Fox-Hunting Man*, his nostalgic *roman à clef* so different from the grandiose prose work he had envisaged, became an instant success. So uncertain was he of its reception that he published it anonymously to begin with,[1] but it sold 15,000 copies in three months and continued to sell year after year.[2] It also won him the prestigious James Tait Black Memorial Prize in 1928 and the Hawthornden Prize in 1929.[3] Just as importantly the book would extend his appeal to include people who might find poetry intimidating but could enjoy a simple tale of a young boy, mad about horses and cricket, growing up in rural Kent, before being catapulted into the very different landscape of the First World War. It seems extraordinary that someone who had written nothing more ambitious in prose than a handful of indifferent short stories came to equal his heroes, Hardy and Meredith, in their successful transition from one genre to another. Relatively few writers in any language have managed to excel in two different mediums. What was it that led a well-known poet with no proven record in prose to turn to novel-writing at the age of forty?

The first, and very pressing, 'condition' which led him to write *Fox-Hunting Man* was his age.[4] He had an almost 'superstitious' feeling about being forty, since he had often excused any unproductiveness in the past by quoting Robert Louis Stevenson: 'Everything in a writer's life is preparation for what he does when over forty.' Rivalry also entered into it. He felt particularly threatened by Osbert Sitwell, who had also started his career as a poet yet produced his first novel, *Before the Bombardment*, in 1926 to great acclaim.

The most surprising of all Sassoon's 'conditions' for writing *Fox-Hunting Man*, at first glance, is 'the fact that [he'd] given up hunting in 1923 and hadn't been on a horse since'. But he was convinced that he could not have achieved the 'detachment' necessary to describe his hunting days if he had still been mixing with horsey people. In effect, hunting, at this stage in his life, had for a time become part of his past and, therefore, fit material for reminiscence.

For nostalgia lies at the heart of *Fox-Hunting Man*. The book, he claimed, was a direct result of a weekend spent with his mother at Weirleigh from 18 to 20 September 1925 and having tea with two childhood friends there, when he made 'the discovery of the pre-1914 past as being rich literary material'. Talking to the deceased Squire Marchant's daughters he had suddenly felt himself 'invaded by all the strangeness of the past'.[5] Sparked off by two living reminders of that past, the 'little world' of his hero George Sherston's boyhood began to 'shape itself with spectroscopic distinctness'. His own childhood began to take on a peculiar intensity, 'simply because it was no longer possible for people to live in that candle and oil lamp lit, telephoneless, unmotorised Arcadia'. It is nostalgia for this world which lights up *Fox-Hunting Man* from its first to its last page.

He started the same day on his attempt to recapture that past. But his first effort, two foolscap pages of reminiscence, was far too much of a 'conscious literary performance' to satisfy him: the voice he wanted had to be a natural speaking one, innocent, even naïve, to reflect the reality of a small boy and unsophisticated young man. So the work was abandoned as quickly as it had been begun.[6]

And there his efforts might have ended, had it not been for his old rival-friend, Osbert, his new love, Glen, and two good bottles of wine. Happening to complain to Osbert about his 'urgent need for mental employment' a few weeks later over one of his host's bottles of 'lovely old Moselle', Osbert had advised him to write an essay on hunting. Though Sassoon rejected the idea initially, the seed had been planted and a few days later, under the 'genial influence of Reform Club burgundy', he found himself telling Glen stories of his hunting days. Glen, like Osbert, cared little for horses,[7] but he listened with genuine enjoyment to the colourful characters and situations Sassoon described and begged him to write it all down. This, according to Sassoon, was the birth of *Fox-Hunting Man*.

Successful books are rarely the result of a single influence, however, and there were other factors at work. Sassoon had already begun to revisit his past more than a year before his weekend at Weirleigh in mid-September, his recently-acquired car giving him the freedom to explore his childhood haunts. A nostalgic visit to the New Beacon School at Sevenoaks with Philbin on 27 July 1924 had been followed by a solitary trip to a childhood holiday house at Edingthorpe in Norfolk less than two months later.[8] Noting in his diary various details of Edingthorpe Rectory, which his mother had rented for eight weeks in 1897, he was already subconsciously recreating the past as literature: 'Mistily I memorized an elongated old shandrydan of a vehicle with an elderly horse, in which we used to drive to North Walsham. Also I remembered the donkeys we used to ride; I rode mine in a donkey-race at a local flower-show and came in last in a "field" mainly composed of fat farmers. (That was my first race!)'[9] Though this particular episode of childhood would not be included in *Fox-Hunting Man*, it would provide one of the most successful chapters in his autobiography ten years later.

Another reminder of his past followed in February 1926, when a letter arrived from the 2nd RWF's Dr Dunn, asking him to write an account of his bombing raid in the Hindenburg Trench nine years earlier.[10] Sassoon's initial response was in verse, not prose as requested, and it was to decline to contribute to Dunn's history of the 2nd RWF, *The War the Infantry Knew*.[11] Almost immediately he relented, however, and produced a twelve-page account of his experiences with the 2nd Battalion, which he sent to Dunn a month later.[12]

In the meantime, as a result of Dunn's request, no doubt, he had arranged to spend an evening with one of his closest friends from the 2nd Battalion, Ralph Greaves, resulting in a second poem about the past, 'To One Who was With Me in the War'.[13] Addressed directly to Greaves, it traces Sassoon's reluctant involvement in painful memories.[14]

Shortly after seeing Ralph, Sassoon spent another evening reminiscing about the War with his brother, Edward Greaves.[15] He also wrote to his old quartermaster friend from the 1st RWF, Joe Cottrill, but was sad to learn that he had died the previous January. And though neither effort resulted in further poems, they did complete his engagement with that particular time in his past and bring into being the last section of *Fox-Hunting Man*. Just as he had needed to be detached enough from hunting to write about it, so he had required an even longer period to feel sufficiently recovered from the War to describe his part in it. As for many other writers on the First World War, it took approximately a decade for this to happen.

Once made, the decision to include his war experience in *Fox-Hunting Man* seemed to Sassoon the only way to end the book. Since it was to be the story of a young man 'being brought gradually to the reality of human experience', Sherston's confrontation of the deaths, first of his boyhood friend Stephen Colwood, then of his ex-groom, Dixon, and finally of his closest army companion, Dick Tiltwood, were essential. By 20 November 1926, less than six weeks after the start of the writing, the decision to include war material had been made and the germ of a sequel, *Memoirs of an Infantry Officer*, been planted.

Though this material is naturally quite different in tone from the childhood and hunting scenes, *Fox-Hunting Man* is unified by an equal intensity of feeling throughout, partly because of the book's autobiographical nature, partly because Sassoon is a poet even in prose. The earlier scenes, though lying so far back in time, are as sharply realized as the later ones.

Gosse had anticipated the benefits for Sassoon in returning to his roots when he had advised him in 1918 to draw on his 'sporting experiences for typical country figures'.[16] Seven years after Gosse had voiced what turned out to be a sound literary intuition, Nichols had written to Sassoon from his scriptwriting job in Hollywood with a similar suggestion. He was presumably thinking of a screenplay, but Sassoon had been determined to write a novel since at least 1921 and he continued to think of his *magnum opus* as prose. He had also contemplated writing an autobiography, but in purely practical terms novels appeared to pay much better and to reach a wider audience. He had the evidence of Wells's and Bennett's affluence and fame almost daily before his eyes at the Reform. In addition, both novelists had on separate occasions 'urged' him to switch to their own medium.[17]

So when Forster showed enthusiasm for his diary entries, in particular their 'range of incidents and characters' and humour, he took notice.[18] It was these aspects, together with the first-person speaking voice, which Sassoon carried over from his diary to *Fox-Hunting Man*. His 'descriptive diary' at the Front was an important contributory factor in his prose-writing career.[19]

Sassoon believed that the 'naturalness' of *Fox-Hunting Man* was 'entirely the result of assiduous diarising', just as the quest for self-knowledge in it derived from Rivers.[20] And his favourite novelists, Surtees and Somerville and Ross[21] with their casts of eccentric hunting 'types', lie behind the creation of such 'characters' as 'Gentleman George' and Bill Jaggett in *Fox-Hunting Man*, though both are also based on real-life people.

Sassoon argued that Dickens had modelled his style partly on Surtees, which may be one reason he had started to re-read Dickens in 1922, finding him 'a *beautiful* writer'.[22] Dickens's careful choice of adjectives, the 'gusto and picturesqueness' of his kaleidoscopic scenes, together with his 'humanity' and 'fine ... descriptive writing' would all contribute to Sassoon's own creation of a teeming microcosm in *Fox-Hunting Man*.[23] Well aware that Dickens might be thought 'too sentimental' by some, Sassoon was nevertheless deeply affected by *Bleak House*, especially Esther's first-person narration. Dickens's use of this device, particularly in *Great Expectations*, which was also to influence Graham Greene more than twenty years later in *The End of the Affair*, would leave its mark on George Sherston's deliberately unpolished account of his early experiences.

Another very different writer, whom Sassoon had also been reading before starting his novel, was Proust. The first part of *À la recherche du temps perdu* had been published in 1918 but, with his fairly basic French, Sassoon had not felt able to tackle it until Scott Moncrieff's translation appeared in November 1922. He was reading 'a lot of Proust' the autumn he started his own excursion into the past. In addition to certain similarities of character and background to Proust – his homosexuality, his half-Jewishness, his love of music,[24] his sensitivity – Sassoon's work shows sufficient specific likenesses to suggest that he was directly influenced by the French writer. Proust's title alone, which Moncrieff translated as *Remembrance of Things Past*, would seem equally appropriate to Sassoon's own attempt to recreate the past. Told in the first person, both semi-autobiographical novels open with the narrator remembering himself as a young, somewhat isolated child. Both describe in highly evocative poetic prose an older social order which is brought largely to an end by the First

World War. 'A few pages of Proust,' Sassoon wrote in his diary before starting *Fox-Hunting Man*, 'have made me wonder whether insignificant episodes aren't the most significant',[25] a sentiment which lies behind such revealing scenes as George Sherston losing his pony on his first ride alone and having to walk ignominiously home. It may not have been madeleines Sassoon ate at Weirleigh in September 1926, but whatever his mother provided for tea that day had a similar effect.

Less than a year before starting *Fox-Hunting Man*, Sassoon read another novelist who reminded him strongly of Proust, his fellow-Frenchman Romain Rolland.[26] Reading Rolland's *Jean Christophe*, a monumental work in ten volumes, four of which appeared in English, Sassoon found his saga of a sensitive musician 'by far the most stimulating' book he had read since discovering Proust: 'It gives me courage and reminds me that I must learn to go my way alone as far as possible, if I am ever to be any good to the world.'[27] These are words that the 'shy and solitary' George Sherston himself might have spoken as the shrouded body of his beloved Dick Tiltwood was lowered into the ground towards the end of *Fox-Hunting Man*.

*

These were just some of the influences and events which went into the making of *Fox-Hunting Man*, the most important of them all, Sassoon insisted, being Glen's encouragement. It was with Glen's request for hunting stories in mind that he sat down on 8 October 1926 and scribbled a few notes about a retired colonel living in Cheltenham. Though these were promptly torn up, the next day he began in earnest, producing the first four pages of his book. A month later his scheme had expanded to include Sherston's first year and a half in the army. By 2 December he had written '41,500 unprofessional words (including about 3,000 "wrong 'uns")' in fifty-four days and had 'worked himself to a standstill'.

Sassoon claimed that his main reason for stopping was the arrival of Sam Behrman, whom he had not seen for six years, but it is more likely that he was simply exhausted. His writing methods had always been demanding, requiring him to start work at a time when most people are going to bed. With a pot of strong tea at his elbow, a pipe in hand and a few rough notes made earlier in the day, he would stare at the blank page of notebook on his knee 'waiting for something to happen'. (Later he learnt that an hour on the sofa with the light out made all the difference.) When inspiration did come, he would scribble it down quickly in pencil, which he found less inhibiting than typewriter or pen. His method of revision was simply to ink over what he had written, making a few alterations as he went. These amateurish practices seemed to him a crucial part of the final product. 'Had I been a more practised performer,' he pointed out, 'The Fox-Hunting Man would have lacked its essential quality, which is youngness – recaptured youngness of feeling and expression. My inexpertness was appropriate to the subject matter. It was the testament of my youth.' It was also, like his relationships with much younger men, an attempt to recapture his own vanishing youth.

By the time Sam arrived in London on 18 December, Glen had been back from the Oxford Playhouse for nearly a fortnight and any plans Sassoon had for continuing his novel were abandoned. As usual in Sam's presence he became over-excited, unconsciously playing up to the caricature of the vague Englishman which so delighted his American friend. Sam, Glen and Christmas, which he spent with his Aunt Mozelle and Schuster at Brighton, kept him busy until early January. And a visit to Dorset in the middle of the month provided a further distraction while he visited both Hardy and the Heads who, having moved from London to Lyme Regis in the early 1920s, had moved again and were now living only a few miles from Max Gate.[28] They were, like the Hardys, playing an increasingly parental role in Sassoon's life – even as Sir Henry himself declined into the hell of Parkinson's Disease – and Sassoon shuttled between them and the Hardys like a loving and obedient son.

Sassoon finally got back to his writing on 27 January 1927, but it was verse not prose he produced, 'Everyman'. The first he had attempted for eight months, his poem conveys his own 'weariness' as he struggled to complete *Fox-Hunting Man*. It also reveals its ambiguous creative origins, since it can be read as either poetry or poetic prose: written originally in prose, according to Sassoon, it 'turned out, almost without alteration, to be a poem',[29] which attempts to recreate the effort needed to 'climb the steepening hill'.[30]

As 'Everyman' suggests, the beginning of 1927, except for his visits to Glen (again on tour), was a time of 'nerviness and dissatisfaction'. Without his car, which he had generously given to Glen, there was no excuse for impromptu excursions, but he was still not able to get back to work. So, on April Fool's Day, he bought himself a new Morris Oxford, 'a cosy, complacent boudoir of a car'.[31] The date of his purchase turned out to be highly appropriate, since a mere fortnight later, driving along a completely empty street in Bayswater at midnight, perfectly sober according to him, he crashed into a lamppost, damaging both the car and himself.

The only positive aspect of the affair was the devotion of Nellie, who made the most of this opportunity to mother her 'favourite boy'. Glen, out of town for a few days, was very alarmed when Nellie reported the incident to him, but reassured to hear that one of her most trusted tenants, and a great admirer of Sassoon, Mr Fleming, had sat up all night with him to make sure that it was only a broken rib Sassoon suffered. He was less thrilled to learn that Sassoon had, after three days, been whisked off to Bray by Schuster to convalesce.

By the time of Sassoon's accident there was already some antagonism between Glen and Schuster, stemming probably from possessiveness on both their parts. When Glen arrived to visit Sassoon at his retreat by the Thames on 24 April, Schuster made him less than welcome and Glen, normally the most easy-going of people, was deeply offended: Schuster, he declared, had 'the manners of a pig', an unfortunate choice of imagery for someone as Jewish as Frankie.[32] Caught in the middle, Sassoon tried to placate Glen, who nevertheless continued to think Schuster a 'jealous, mean vampire'.[33] It was an uneasy situation and one which was not improved by Sassoon's suggestion that the three of them should take a holiday together later in the year.

One reason for his idea was that, by the end of April, he found himself a wealthy man. His Aunt Rachel, whom he had not seen for twenty years, had died on 29 April, leaving him a quarter of her substantial fortune. After her husband Frederick Beer's death from syphilis in 1902, she had slowly declined into madness brought on by the same disease. By 1927 she had been ill for so long that Sassoon claimed to have almost completely forgotten his expectation of inheriting money from her until by 1926 the expectation had been 'almost dismissed' from his mind. Only a few weeks before her death, he had sent a self-righteous poem to the *Labour Weekly:*

> I accuse the Rich of what they've always done before –
> Of lifting worldly faces to a diamond star,
> I accuse the Rich of being what they always are –
> The enemies of Lazarus lying at their door.[34]

Sassoon made no attempt to attend Rachel's funeral, using his still slightly painful rib as an excuse, and felt virtually unmoved by the whole affair: 'The idea of being "much better off" has brought me no particular sense of pleasure,' he wrote in his diary. 'I can't see what good it will do me in my everyday life; and it certainly won't help me to write better poetry. I can be generous to my friends, and give lots of it to my mother. That seems to be about all there is in it.'[35] His claim to have trained himself to be 'non-acquisitive' seems a hollow boast for someone who had recently bought himself both a Bechstein grand piano and a new sports car. Edith Sitwell's comment on the subject also suggests that Sassoon was more interested in Rachel Beer's money than he admitted. Referring to Graves's well-documented liaison with Laura Riding, who had not only accompanied him and his wife to Cairo but also back again, she wrote to Sassoon: 'Osbert and I were so delighted to get your letter and hear the splendid news ... I only hope [it] ... won't lead Robert [Graves] to increase his harem.'[36]

Sassoon would have been less than human if he had not rejoiced in his newly acquired riches. Whether knowing, from the age of fifteen onwards, that he would one day inherit had helped or hindered him is debatable.

During his two months' convalescence at Bray, Sassoon had been persuaded by Anzie to spend some of his inheritance on an expensive touring car, a Chrysler.[37] After two years of marriage the Wyldes were expecting their first child, which meant that Anzie would be unable to chauffeur Schuster round Europe in his Rolls as usual that summer, and Sassoon, with some misgivings, agreed to drive him to Bayreuth for the annual music festival.[38] Crossing the Channel on 24 July with Schuster and Glen, he decided to travel by way of

Ypres where the New Menin Gate had been unveiled the previous day. As he studied the large white monument, covered with the thousands of names of those who died there, he felt a fresh surge of bitterness about the War and the way in which one of its worst battlefields had become 'a sight-seer's centre'.[39] Who, he asked, in a sonnet written the same day, would remember the 'unheroic Dead who fed the guns?' Who would 'absolve the foulness of their fate?':

> ... Here was the world's worst wound. And here with pride
> 'Their name liveth for ever,' the Gateway claims.
> Was ever an immolation so belied
> As these intolerably nameless names?
> Well might the Dead who struggled in the slime
> Rise and deride this sepulchre of crime.   (*CP*, p. 188)[40]

'On Passing the New Menin Gate' is among Sassoon's most vehement poems about the War. (Gordon Harbord had died at Ypres.) Sassoon would later describe this poem as his 'final word about the 1914 War'.[41] While it may have been his 'final word' in poetry, however, he had still a great deal to say on the subject in prose and his visit to Ypres almost certainly strengthened his decision to continue *Fox-Hunting Man* into the War itself.

The rest of the trip was relatively uneventful, though it is clear from his letters to Glen afterwards that they had both found Schuster redundant in what Sassoon described as their 'halo of hurried happiness', which seemed to him 'as near perfection as possible'.[42] Less than six months later, 'old Shuffling Shu', as Sassoon and Glen nicknamed him, was to die from a perforated ulcer and Sassoon would eventually come to feel that he had failed fully to appreciate Schuster's very real affection for him, as well as his love and knowledge of music. As it was, he said goodbye to Schuster at Munich in mid-August with some relief and, though he had had to part with Glen too, started on his long drive to Berlin in high spirits. Numerous breakdowns, flat tyres and a broken fan-belt failed to daunt him. His meetings with several attractive young hitchhikers on the way, one a sixteen-year-old sailor, more than compensated for the drawbacks of the journey and he arrived at the northern capital in good form.[43]

He knew that there would be friends waiting to meet him there, since he had invited the Sitwell brothers to join him as his guests, together with Nellie. Nellie, delighted to be sharing a holiday with three of her favourites, already knew Berlin from previous visits to another of her 'boys', Ross's friend, the writer Max Meyerfeld.[44] Meyerfeld, who introduced the 'stately' Nellie to his friends as an 'illegal' daughter of Queen Victoria ('Can't you see it?' he asked Sassoon), was himself one of Sassoon's greatest admirers and more than a little in love with him.[45] They all celebrated Sassoon's forty-first birthday on 8 September and, although his *magnum opus* was still not completed and could even be said to be suffering from this prolonged holiday, Sassoon was happy.

Berlin was followed by Dresden, Dresden by Vienna and Vienna by Budapest, where they listened to gypsy music and saw the El Grecos in the Herzog Collection. Then on 29 September, more than two months after leaving England, Sassoon was home again, to see Glen off on a seven-month season in New York, an absence he was dreading.[46] With Glen gone there were no more excuses for delay and on 6 October, two days before the anniversary of his start on *Fox-Hunting Man*, he was back at work on it.

Two things conspired to bring him to a halt again only a week after he had restarted. The first was when Edmund Blunden returned after three years in Japan and took him away from his work for almost a day.[47] But the second event, a weekend with a young man who was rapidly replacing the absent Glen in his affections, was more serious and on 14 October *Fox-Hunting Man* was again abandoned. It would take nearly three and a half months and the absence of the young man concerned for him to return to his writing. When he did so in January 1928, it was with a grim determination to finish it before his new lover returned in April.

By dint of avoiding almost all his friends, especially Graves, he completed the rest of the book (more than half) in less than three months. Conducting Sherston from his steeplechasing victories and further hunting experiences in the Midlands to his enlistment at the outbreak of war, he leaves him at the end on the Western Front, facing the loss of two of his closest friends, Dixon and Dick Tiltwood. Emotionally gruelling as well as hugely satisfying, the writing of *Fox-Hunting Man* was a result of both desperation and inspiration and his greatest sustained effort to date.

*

T.E. Lawrence told Marsh that if he were 'trying to export the ideal Englishman to an international exhibition' he would choose Sassoon as his 'chief exhibit'[48] (an irony considering that Sassoon was only half English). It seems therefore appropriate that a main theme of *Fox-Hunting Man* should be Englishness. From its title-page onwards, with its reference to that most English of sports, fox-hunting, and its epigraph, taken from England's best-known writer Shakespeare's own praise of his fellow-countrymen in *Richard II* – 'This happy breed of men, this little world' – the novel is a celebration of the microcosm in which Sassoon himself grew up.

Set mainly in one of England's most beautiful landscapes, the Weald of Kent, *Fox-Hunting Man* celebrates the English countryside at the end of the nineteenth and beginning of the twentieth century in nostalgic detail. The young Sherston also yearningly describes such English pursuits as summer cricket matches on village greens, exhilarating hunts on crisp autumn and winter days and that dying institution, the local flower show. His description of Butley and Rotherden's cricket teams covers a wide range of English social types, from William Dodd, the saddler, with his 'Did-I-Say-Myself', to Parson Yalden, with his most 'unevangelical expression' when he is bowled out.[49]

But the more socially exclusive Packlestone Hunt is no less representative of Englishness in its own way, from the 'massive and white-moustached' Captain Harry Hinnycraft riding one of his 'magnificent weight-carriers ... with the air of a monarch' and that 'paragon of natural proficiency', Mrs Oakfield, who 'sailed over the fences in her tall hat and perfectly fitting black habit with a bunch of violets in her buttonhole', down to the pompous Sir Jocelyn Porteus-Porteous ('note the majestic variation in spelling') and the intrepid 'brothers Peppermore'.[50]

The protagonist himself, as Sassoon points out, is a 'very typical English character'. His first name, George, conjures up England's patron saint, while his surname, Sherston, refers to two typically English villages, one in the Cotswolds in an area Sassoon had hunted over with Loder, and the second in Wiltshire, named Sherston Magna, which Sassoon believed to be the original home of the Byam Shaws.[51] For *Fox-Hunting Man* is also a homage to Glen, especially its first half, and it is no coincidence that its hero's initials are the same as its most important, if not 'onlie begetter'.

Even the last fifth of the book, when Sherston leaves his idyllic rural surroundings for the army and the harsh conditions of wartime France, is dominated by notions of Englishness. For it is in order to defend England and Englishness that he leaves it all behind. Though he will later, in two sequels to *Fox-Hunting Man*, become disillusioned with the cause, it is in the spirit of another Shakespeare play, *Henry V*, that he sets out to defend his country.

All these aspects of Englishness are combined to produce a skilfully shaped account of Sherston's development from childhood to manhood, within a loose structure of apparently random recollections. Introducing the subject of cricket indirectly on the first page, by way of a contrast between George's elderly tutor, Mr Star and his aunt's robust young groom, Tom Dixon, he follows this up quite naturally with a reference to Dixon teaching the boy to ride. From then on he alternates between the narrator's progress in the two sports, culminating in his triumph at cricket in 'The Flower Show Match' and his winning of 'the Colonel's Cup' at a point-to-point. Starting with a vivid recreation of George's childhood, with all its joys and woes, he ends with his realization of love and death at the Front, a conclusion which has been anticipated in Book Eight by Sherston's goodbye to his childhood drawing room at the outbreak of war, when he notes a 'fiery patch of light' resting on his aunt's reproduction of Watts's picture 'Love and Death'.[52] The book opens as it closes with a sense of Sherston's isolation.

'It is a lovely book,' Forster wrote to Sassoon, 'so beautifully shaped, and full of something I often think about at present, and have to call "tenderness", something that isn't affection though it often accompanies it, and isn't sentimentality.'[53] Other friends and critics would be for the most part as positive as Forster, with few of the reservations that had marked their response to his poetry of the early 1920s. A notable exception was Graves. Unlike Forster he believed that Sassoon had 'missed out' a great deal that mattered. By writing in the guise of George Sherston, he argued, Sassoon avoided facing the moral problems inherent in the autobiographical presentation of one's experience and left the reader 'to decide for him whether the book is sincere or ironical'.[54]

By the time Graves's review appeared the two of them were on uneasy terms and Sassoon did not respond directly to his charge. But it clearly rankled, for when he finally wrote to Graves after a gap of several years, he was still anxious to explain why he could never entirely 'be himself' as Graves had advised:

> Everyone wants to be himself, if he is any good, I imagine. Is it so easy when one is in my quandary – for the duration of my life – as regards 'temperament'. But if you had read my diaries for the past nine years I think you would retract your remark. No one is more aware than I am that the 'Fox-Hunting Man' is mere make-believe compared with the reality of my experience. But it isn't (as your review implied) a piece of facile autobiographic writing. Sherston is only a fifth of myself, but his narrative is carefully thought out and constructed. I don't see how it could have been done differently.[55]

As long as society continued to place homosexuality outside the law, which it did, ironically, until the year of Sassoon's death, he would continue to suffer both as an artist and a man. In *Fox-Hunting Man* it prevented him, for example, describing his true feelings for the Dick Tiltwood character and thus diminishing the full impact of Sherston's loss when Tiltwood is killed.

But it was not just his homosexuality which Sassoon excluded from his first novel, however autobiographical it might first appear. He also quite deliberately omitted any literary aspirations from his hero's character, as well as any hint of Jewishness. Unlike Proust, whose narrator charts his progress towards his artistic goal, Sassoon's narrator's ambitions are sporting. (So much so that when Sassoon allows himself to describe his love of poetry in the first draft of his manuscript, he feels obliged to cross all three pages out.) Sherston's symbolic role as a typical Englishman does not allow for strong literary interests. Sherston is a deliberately 'simplified version' of himself, Sassoon explained, because he is intended to represent and speak for the generation to which he belongs and that, in his creator's opinion, did not 'typically' include a love of poetry.

When Sassoon alters any of the autobiographical material on which *Fox-Hunting Man* is based, it is never arbitrary. When, for instance, George announces in the opening paragraph that he is an only child, orphaned young and brought up by an unmarried aunt, it is partly to get round the disagreeable fact that Sassoon's own father left home before he was five, partly a reflection of his feelings of isolation from his two brothers after the age of ten and partly because he needed to keep his mother 'separate' from his emotions.[56]

Other changes are made for the sake of dramatic tension. 'The Flower Show Match', for example, is based on an actual match in which Sassoon played as a schoolboy for Brenchley ('Butley' in *Fox-Hunting Man*) against the village of

Rolvenden ('Rotherden'). Whereas in the novel George scores the winning run for his team in a nail-biting finish, in real life Brenchley lost the match, with Sassoon making only a minor contribution.[57]

A more significant alteration of autobiographical material occurs towards the end of the book, when Sherston meets Dick Tiltwood, assumed by most Sassoon critics to be based exclusively on David Thomas, since Tiltwood dies in almost identical circumstances. It is only when one studies the original manuscript and sees a photograph of another young Welch Fusilier, Robert Hanmer, pasted in opposite the description of Tiltwood, that it becomes clear that Tiltwood is a composite character. He represents Hanmer as well as Thomas, a fact which makes sense when one knows that Sassoon became infatuated with both of them in quick succession.

The most interesting departure from autobiography in *Fox-Hunting Man* concerns another crucial structural device, the death of Dixon. As Sassoon indicated, the book 'culminates' in the deaths of Dixon and Tiltwood in order to bring its hero face to face with reality. In fact, Tom Richardson, the model for Dixon, did not die until 1928.

Though Sassoon's primary reason for renaming his characters is to disguise their identity, like Dickens he enjoys finding names to suit his characters and often makes more than one attempt to get it right, while at the same time avoiding offence. After calling one particularly aggressive 'would-be thruster' of the Atherstone 'Bill Hoggerell', to convey his brutishness as well as echo his real name, Lindsay-Hogg, he changed it in manuscript to the even more negative but less give-away 'Bill Jaggett'. The timidity of another rider is suggested through his surname, 'Croplady'. His success at capturing the nature of his real-life models would in a few cases ('Jaggett' was one) provoke angry letters. At least with horses he did not have to worry about offending them and many of their names are taken from life. 'Cockbird', for example, remains himself.

Sassoon's choice of names is never random and a biographical link can usually be traced. The link to real life was clearly important to him, as the manuscript of *Fox-Hunting Man* also shows. Lovingly bound by its author in three hessian-covered notebooks, it is crammed with photographs, press cuttings and other ephemera from his own life. There are, for instance, two photographs of Richardson, looking just as Sassoon describes Dixon, one of Cockbird, another of his mother (to whom he felt obliged to explain that 'in Aunt Evelyn' he had 'only ... drawn a very faint portrait of a very small part of your character – (certainly no one could have described you as a "timid and incompetent horsewoman"!!)'), an article on and an obituary of his 'Denis Milden' figure, Loder, a map of the Southdown Hunt country and an obituary of Captain Ruxton. Many of these items were added long after the book was published and all suggest how 'real' his fictional world was for him.[58]

Much of the humour of *Fox-Hunting Man* – and it is very funny indeed in parts – lies in its characterization. Like Pip in *Great Expectations*, Sherston is able to laugh at himself as he looks back on his youthful absurdities and it is a laughter the reader is invited to share. But George's superstitious methods of working out his chances of cricketing success from cricketers' names in his local paper, for example, or his attempts to become a 'hard-bitten hunting-man' in spite of several humiliations on the field, are not just amusing: they are also insights into his character and the self-deceptions of youth in general.

Aunt Evelyn, too, provides moments of rich comedy while she adds to the reader's knowledge of both Sherston and herself. Her flustered attempts to make tea on a spirit lamp in a railway carriage under the 'scandalized glances' of her fellow first-class passengers, including her craven and snobbish nephew, is one of the high points of the book.[59]

As in Dickens, minor characters are generally more comical than the main ones. Virtually every member of the Butley and Rotherden cricket teams in 'The Flower Show Match' could stand as an example. This much anthologized section manages to convey the singularity of each player while, at the same time, glorying in the rich flavour of village cricket at the end of the nineteenth century.[60] Tom Seamark, the Rotherden umpire, a red-faced sporting publican who bulks 'as large as a lighthouse' and Bill Sutler, Butley's one-legged, 'grossly partisan' umpire, are particularly good examples of this.[61]

Comedy plays such a large part in *Fox-Hunting Man* that its near absence at the end in France points up the stark difference between the grim realities Sherston has finally to face and his earlier carefree life. It is interesting to note that when Sassoon looked back on the book forty years later, he saw it not as the comic masterpiece it undoubtedly is, but as 'a work of innocently insidious anti-war propaganda'.[62] He might complain about being branded as a war poet but he could never, even in his most light-hearted moments, escape his experiences of 1914 to 1918.

25

'The Old Earl and Little Lord Fauntleroy'

1927-1931

Sassoon always insisted that Glen was his main inspiration for *Fox-Hunting Man*.[1] Yet more than half of it was written under the influence of the person who had supplanted Glen long before its completion, Stephen Tennant. This helps to explain why the last part of the book, with its themes of love and death, is so different from the rest. For Tennant was to be the most consuming love of Sassoon's life, taking him back to his first great passion for David Thomas, which comes through thinly disguised in his book. The TB from which Stephen suffered, then a life-threatening illness, was to make death a present reality for Sassoon as he struggled to finish *Fox-Hunting Man*.[2]

Sassoon had already met the young aristocrat and aesthete the Honourable

Stephen Tennant before Glen left for America at the beginning of October 1927. The fourth son of Lord Glenconner, Stephen was a prominent member of the Bright Young Things so gleefully satirized by Evelyn Waugh. Said to be the model for Miles Malpractice in *Decline and Fall* and Sebastian Flyte in *Brideshead Revisited*, Tennant was wealthy, privileged and beautiful, his effeminate manner and provocative behaviour attracting attention wherever he went.[3] A great favourite of his fellow-exhibitionists the Sitwells, they appeared particularly keen to interest Sassoon in him. They were responsible for Stephen and Sassoon's first meeting, for example, which was at a dinner party given by Sachie and Georgia Sitwell to celebrate the christening of their son Reresby. (Sassoon had also attended the ceremony itself, which was performed by the Archbishop of Canterbury in the private chapel of Lambeth Palace, accompanied by Nellie in a splendid hat.) The Sitwells had been careful to tell him in advance that Stephen was 'avid' to meet him and after the dinner, at which Sassoon found himself talking very excitably 'for the benefit of S. Tennant ... a very good audience', he was equally 'avid' to see Stephen again.[4] 'He is 21, very affected (in a nice way), very witty and intelligent and divinely beautiful,' Sassoon told the writer Henry Festing-Jones; 'But, alas, very fragile.'[5] Perhaps it was fear of being thought snobbish that prevented him adding the other details he noted in his diary, Stephen's 'ultra-refined voice' and 'well-bred' manner.

Despite his fascination with Stephen, however, Sassoon continued to protest his complete devotion to Glen. And while Stephen and his fashionable friends spent the summer of 1927 at increasingly wild parties, stretching aristocratic privilege and social tolerance to their limits, Sassoon passed his three weeks with Glen in Germany dreading Glen's departure for America. When he sailed for New York on 1 October Sassoon felt desolate. Yet only a fortnight later he was suffering from a bad case of what he called 'Stephenitis'.[6]

Stephen's invitation to spend the weekend at his family house in Wiltshire had arrived on 10 October, when Sassoon had just started work again on *Fox-Hunting Man*. Knowing that it would be a distraction, Sassoon was nevertheless unable to resist. Squaring his conscience with the promise of an 'hour-by-hour' account of his visit to Glen, he set off in the Chrysler on Saturday, 15 October, for Wilsford, the large Elizabethan-style manor house designed by Detmar Blow for Stephen's mother, Pamela, shortly after her marriage to Edward Tennant.[7] Beautifully situated in a hollow of the Wiltshire Downs near Amesbury, on the banks of the Avon, it represented all that Sassoon himself had wanted from a country house in his youth and everything that Weirleigh, for all its dearness to him, did not possess – elegance, charm and distinction. But its perfection, as Stephen's niece Emma Tennant would observe, also made it seem to the critical eye rather unreal, like a stage set. 'Anyone who had spent their life in these surroundings,' she argued, '– and especially Stephen, with his adoring mother Pamela – would continue to expect a pageant, a pantomime, every time he went out of the house.'[8]

The curtain went up the very night of Sassoon's arrival. Coming in to dinner tired and late after losing his way in the tortuous Wiltshire lanes, he was at once transported into Stephen's fantasy world. Osbert, who had known the Tennants for years through his friendship with the eldest son, Edward ('Bim', killed in the First World War), was curious to know its effect on the puritanical Sassoon: 'Will you hate Wilsford?' he asked Sassoon just before the visit.[9]

Apart from Osbert and other people Sassoon already knew – Sachie and his wife Georgia, the Sitwells' musical protégé, William Walton, and Osbert's 'crony' Christabel McLaren[10] – Stephen had gathered together some of his most extrovert friends. If this had been done to impress Sassoon it was not entirely successful, since the first of these, the budding society photographer Cecil Beaton, had already been dismissed by Sassoon as 'clever, very affected, effeminate, *arriviste*' on the one occasion they had met.[11] And though he would agree to be photographed for *Vogue* by Beaton only a few weeks later and accept invitations to his weekend retreat at nearby Ashcombe, he was never to change his initial opinion. He was almost equally dismissive of the Jungmann sisters, Zita and 'Baby', whose mother's second marriage to Richard Guinness had thrown them into London's fashionable set. And though he would become intimately involved with the last of Stephen's younger friends, the painter Rex Whistler (just starting out on his successful career with a commission for murals at the Tate Gallery restaurant), he scarcely registered his existence at this their first meeting.

Altogether, Sassoon felt very much out of things when he arrived at Wilsford. Exhausted from his writing efforts of the week, as well as the journey, and conscious that he was nearly twice the age of Stephen and most of his friends, he felt every inch the 'tired and middle-aged author'.[12] But as dinner progressed he found himself talking volubly to impress his host and noted with gratification that Stephen seemed to hang on his words. When it came to dressing up after dinner, however, he felt isolated again. Refusing to participate himself, he watched the young people, of both sexes, dressing up first as nuns, then in pyjamas, shocking choices in the context of the times. Even allowing for a reaction against the austerities of the War, it was the kind of deliberately provocative behaviour that was beginning to scandalize London society. Sassoon himself did 'not quite like it', though he could see that it was 'very amusing',[13] an ambivalence that would characterize his whole relationship with Stephen.

The 'high jinks' continued relentlessly the next day.[14] Stephen had ordered elaborate eighteenth-century shepherd's costumes. (With his love of cross-dressing, on this occasion the women had to wear male clothes.) Beaton was to film the various tableaux into which the actors were organized by Stephen. Whereas Sassoon had been thrilled as a child by his mother's innocent *tableaux vivants*, he was clearly uneasy at Stephen's subtle subversion of the form and again refused to join in. As a result he does not appear in Beaton's photographs, which have been described as 'the most evocative images of wealthy young England in the 1920s'.[15]

It may have been in an effort to escape from this unreal world and assert his own literary authority that Sassoon suggested driving Stephen, Osbert and Christabel to see Lytton Strachey the same afternoon. Strachey lived not too far away at Ham Spray in the north-west of the county, but Sassoon got lost on the way, driving eventually into a haystack, and they arrived very late for tea. Though fascinated by this 'strange eruption of unexpected visitors from the expensive classes', Strachey resisted their pleas to accompany them back to Wilsford for more dressing up and 'shudder[ed] to think of the horrors of their return journey'.[16] 'Strange creatures,' he told his friend Roger Senhouse, 'with just a few feathers where brains should be.'[17]

Strachey added as an afterthought, 'though Siegfried is rather different', and that was Sassoon's main problem. Whilst magnetized by Stephen even at his most *outré*, he could never enter unselfconsciously into his world. And it was not simply a matter of age and upbringing. For Edith Olivier, who joined them for dinner on their return from Ham Spray, was thirty-four years older than Stephen and the spinster daughter of a vicar, yet she loved being garbed and made up extravagantly for the fancy-dress dinner and charades which followed.

Edith's only complaint that Sunday evening at Wilsford was the lateness of the meal, delayed by Stephen's agonizings over his own costume – 'a white Russian suit with silver train and a bandeau round his head', she remembered.[18] But when he finally made his appearance, he seemed to her to move 'like Mercurius with winged feet'.[19] Sassoon was equally dazzled, realizing for the first time how dangerous the situation had become. Stephen, as Sassoon later recorded, was actively encouraging him 'with eyes that could persuade'.[20] Instead of withdrawing, however, as he had with Gathorne-Hardy, he made a deliberate advance, suggesting a late-night drive to Stephen, who readily agreed. It was 6.30 a.m. before they arrived back, their relationship clearly on a very different footing from when they set out.

By the time Sassoon had driven Stephen back to London and deposited him at his mother's house in Smith Square, only a few hundred yards from his old lodgings in Tufton Street, he was completely infatuated. He instantly abandoned all attempts to finish *Fox-Hunting Man*, though alternately guilty and resentful about it, and tried to put Glen out of his mind. His promised account of the Wilsford weekend for Glen was put off a whole week and, when finally dispatched, was singularly misleading, referring to Stephen only once and then simply with his name.

It was Stephen he needed, however, and Stephen needed him. Writing to Sassoon on 5 November after three tempestuous weeks together, he assured him that he was thinking 'of one vast beautiful thing that warms my heart and mind and body and soul'.[21] And though usually an assiduous diarist, he noted in his almost empty journal, with a deliberate sexual pun: 'I've been too gay to write in my diary.'[22]

Sassoon, on the other hand, scribbled copiously in his, though he knew it was *Fox-Hunting Man* he should be writing. Instead of grim midnight sessions with Sherston, however, he found himself entertaining Stephen or posing unwillingly for Stephen's commissioned photographs of him in Beaton's studio. Stephen on the other hand loved posing, the more artificially the better: Stephen in a leopard skin perching on rocks, Stephen as Romeo lying on his tomb in velvet doublet and pearls, Stephen in a black, shiny mackintosh with carefully made-up face, all show the same love of the camera. Whereas he relished attracting attention to himself, Sassoon loathed it. He was already worried that their relationship would be talked about and begged Stephen to be discreet. It was a proof of Stephen's deep commitment that he agreed to such an uncharacteristic thing.

Too many people had already witnessed and talked about their evident infatuation with each other, however, and soon the only real interest of the affair for onlookers was not *whether* they were involved but *how* they could possibly have become so. It was, as Beaton observed, 'such a paradoxical combination of characters, the one so flamboyant and the other so retiring'.[23] Peter Quennell, a young Oxford graduate and aspiring poet, who knew both Stephen and Sassoon by 1927, was equally intrigued by the contrast between them: 'Sassoon was like the worthy vicar of a parish coming to town and meeting this great society beauty.'[24] And it was not simply jealousy which caused Edith Sitwell to christen the lovers 'The Old Earl and Little Lord Fauntleroy': they were conspicuously different.

To some extent this was part of their mutual attraction. Sassoon struck many people, including Anthony Powell, as 'melancholy' and 'saturnine'.[25] Ottoline had detected something '*sauvage*' in him at their first meeting, comparing him to a stag or faun, and part of his attraction for Stephen was that 'like some charming wild animal – one never felt that he was really tame (or tameable)'.[26] Though he sometimes called Sassoon by his army nickname, 'Kangar', he thought it not quite fierce enough; a moose or grizzly bear seemed to him more appropriate.

As such similes imply, Sassoon did not always find it easy to fit into society, especially after the War. Whereas for Stephen, with what he himself called his 'light, gay nature', life was all fun.[27] He was Sassoon's obverse, his unrealized flip side. He enabled the man he once described as a 'tortured, scarred hermit' to 'remember the joy of life, to share his amazing ecstasies'. Even as Stephen grew older he retained his childlike appreciation of things, but when Sassoon first met him at twenty-one, it was at its peak. It was the age which most appealed to Sassoon, the age Gabriel and Glen had been when he first met them, the age when a youth is just turning into a man. And Sassoon found it 'impossible, or intolerable' to imagine Stephen as 'anything but young', an ominous admission for any long-term future together.[28]

Stephen's effeminate manners and appearance, his willowy slenderness and delicate features, provided another strong contrast to Sassoon, of whom the words 'rugged', 'masculine' and 'military' were frequently used. Just as he had been drawn to Glenn Hunter, Ivor Novello and Glen Byam Shaw, for whom make-up and stage-costume were second nature, so he found Stephen's magenta lips, necklaces and exotic scents a powerful attraction, where some might have found them repulsive.

Sassoon's mother, remembering Gabriel's golden curls and girlish features among others, would refer later to Stephen, as she had to Gabriel, as 'just another of Sieg's pretty boys'.[29] But it was more than prettiness that attracted Sassoon to Stephen. He also needed to feel protective towards his lovers and Stephen's fragile, almost ethereal beauty seems to have enhanced his own sense of dominance and control. The more vulnerable Stephen became, the deeper Sassoon's commitment.

They were opposites in so many ways. While Stephen admired Sassoon's ideals and loved his earnestness, his unworldliness, his austerity, even his tidiness, his own lifestyle was frivolous, sophisticated and luxurious, his surroundings lavishly cluttered, and his morals far more relaxed. But what the two did undoubtedly share from the start was a powerful sexual attraction.[30] Stephen had only to be absent from his 'Tristan and Galahad and Launcelot' to be 'hungry for the sense of [his] arms around [him] and [his] mouth'.[31]

Had sex been the only dimension to their relationship, however, it would neither have lasted as long as it did, nor survived such problems. On first meeting Stephen, Sassoon had not just found him 'divinely beautiful' but also 'very witty and intelligent'. Edith Olivier thought him 'the most sparkling talker' she had ever met 'and perhaps the most amusing'.[32]

Stephen's intelligence was largely untutored, but he delighted Sassoon with his love of literature, especially poetry. By the time he met Sassoon, his favourites included Shelley, Tennyson, Keats, Housman, Charlotte Mew and de la Mare, all poets Sassoon admired. Stephen wrote poetry himself, but it was perhaps fortunate that it was not very good, since the main thing Sassoon brought to their relationship was his poetic authority. Secure in his role of mentor he introduced Stephen to some of his own more recent discoveries, such as Vaughan and Landor, and revelled in his disciple's lavish praise of his own work.

Their shared interest in the other arts also drew them together, music being the one partial exception. (Sassoon never learnt to like jazz, which Stephen adored.) They both enjoyed art galleries, museums, ballet and theatre. Stephen himself was constantly drawing and painting and in this area Sassoon was happy to concede his 'delightful talent'.[33] He particularly admired Stephen's delicate and intricate designs of orchids and shells, making no public comment on his numerous sketches of sailors and missionaries, many of them indecent.[34] He arranged for Stephen to decorate three of his own works in Faber's 'Ariel' series.[35]

Stephen was a combination of all that had attracted Sassoon to his previous lovers. Even Prince Philipp, though apparently so different from Stephen, shared one important characteristic, his social standing, which had given both of them impeccable manners and the charm and confidence of the privileged.

Not quite so dazzling as Philipp's, Stephen's connections nevertheless impressed Sassoon greatly. In addition to his father, the 1st Baron Glenconner, there was his aunt Margot Tennant, who had married the Liberal Prime Minister Herbert Asquith, later the 1st Earl of Oxford and Asquith. And Margot's stepdaughter Violet had created yet another well-known clan, the Bonham Carters, when she married her father's private secretary. Stephen's mother's family, the Wyndhams, though not belonging to the aristocracy, moved in elevated artistic circles, and when Lord Glenconner died Pamela had married Asquith's Foreign Secretary, Lord Grey of Fallodon, a figure who inspired both awe and deep affection in Sassoon.

Stephen's was also a moneyed world and it is unlikely that Sassoon would have felt able to venture into it without his recent legacy; he began responding to Stephen's interest in him only two months after Rachel Beer's death. On the other hand one of the few things he regretted about Stephen at the start *was* his money. Money had often been a means of controlling relationships for Sassoon, but there was to be none of that with Stephen.

*

'You are the person I've most loved in my life,' Sassoon told Stephen.[36] He may not have been able to 'treat' him in the way he had indulged Gabriel, Philipp and Glen, but there were still the other rituals of courtship to enjoy. Confident that his friends would find Stephen's beauty, charm and background as irresistible as he did, he entered with even greater relish than usual on a round of introductions – the Hardys, the Heads, his mother, Forster, Blunden, Nellie.

The majority of these introductions took place during the first few crowded months of the relationship, which also included further visits to Wilsford to meet Stephen's own mother and stepfather. While Pamela and Sassoon, who may both have sensed competition for Stephen's affection, failed to bond, Sassoon got on well with Lord Grey, who seemed like a breath of reality in Wilsford's unreal world. What he admired most about the elderly politician was not his statesmanlike qualities but his 'perfect simplicity and kindness' or, as he would put it in a poem written nearly twenty years later, his 'native humour, human – simple yet profound'.[37] The 'strength of spirit' which was helping Grey deal with his own failing eyesight in late 1927 would convince Sassoon that he was the one member of what Ruth Head called 'that curiously hard family' whom Sassoon could trust when Stephen became seriously ill.[38]

Stephen was still free from a recurrence of his TB in January 1928 but Pamela, whose 'fussing' Edith Olivier believed was turning her son into a chronic invalid, decided that he needed to go abroad for his health. Her decision may have resulted in part from a wish to separate him from Sassoon. It is ironic if it did, since it had the opposite effect by giving Sassoon a much-needed respite.[39] At the beginning of 1928, just before Pamela announced her plan, he had reached a crisis which would have seemed unimaginable to him three months previously: 'My feelings about Stephen have changed lately,' he wrote in his diary, 'owing to the conflict between my desire to get on with my book and his inability to keep away from me. This has caused me to wake out of my entrancement and to see him with the more critical eyes of commonsense. He symbolizes all that I should ordinarily regard as idle and pleasure-loving and self-indulgent.'[40] Though still charmed by the 'grace' with which Stephen performed, he was beginning to realize that he was 'essentially childish' beneath his 'veneer of sophistication'.[41] This was brought home to him sharply by Stephen's reaction, or rather lack of reaction, to Hardy's death.

Hardy, who had taken to his bed only five days after their visit the previous December, died on 11 January 1928 at the age of eighty-seven. Sassoon, who had scarcely registered Schuster's death a few weeks previously, was devastated.[42] He valued his visits to Max Gate more than anything else in his adult life and, however much he had prepared himself for the inevitable, it was a heavy blow when it came. So that Stephen's breezy announcement to him on 12 January – 'I came to tell you about darling Mr Hardy – he's dead' – underlined his shallowness for Sassoon.[43] (To be fair to Stephen, he had only met Hardy once.) 'I sometimes doubt whether he is capable of feeling deeply,' Sassoon confessed on 18 January.[44] He had spent the intervening week trying to help Florence Hardy through her ordeal, shuttling between Wilsford and Max Gate on the 14th and 15th and facing his own severe trial at Hardy's funeral in Westminster Abbey on 16 January. Florence had given him a front-row seat in the Abbey but, unable to face the very public and, to him, unfeeling ceremony, he 'slunk in' and stood at a side door until he saw Hardy's ashes lowered into the ground, then rushed out overwhelmed by grief.[45]

Sassoon wrote more than one poem on Hardy's death.[46] Hardy's funeral, surrounded by publicity, controversy and outright wrangling, seemed to him the last straw. Like Hardy and Florence themselves, he believed Hardy's body should be in the family churchyard at Stinsford, near to their Dorset home, and was enraged by Cockerell's insistence, as co-executor, that it should be buried in Poets' Corner. The gruesome compromise eventually reached, that Hardy's heart should go to Stinsford, his ashes to the Abbey, seemed to him lacking in any kind of dignity or appropriateness and depressed him even further. He was equally disgusted by Graves's 'presumptuous' article on Hardy in the *Sphere*, 'a vulgar and hasty exploitation', he felt, of the fact that Graves had stayed one night at Max Gate in 1920.[47]

In this context and with the added worry of his unfinished novel hanging over him, Stephen's departure for Germany a few days after the funeral was almost a relief. He would be in safe hands, since his aunt, 'Nan' Tennant,[48] had agreed to go with him to the Bavarian *pension* she had recommended for its mountain air and nursing facilities, Haus Hirth. And Sassoon would be able to devote himself to *Fox-Hunting Man*.

By 31 January he was hard at work. Avoiding most of his friends in February and March and missing Stephen during his long absence, he aimed to complete the book by his return in April. Appropriately, since *Fox-Hunting Man* ends on Easter Sunday 1916 with Sherston staring across no man's land, he finished at 5 a.m. on 8 April, another Easter Sunday. He arranged with his new publishers, Faber and Gwyer, to have the book published anonymously later in the year and put it out of his mind.[49]

In spite of his great relief at finishing *Fox-Hunting Man* and Stephen's imminent return, the grim start to the year continued. Scarcely had he recovered from Hardy's death when another poet he greatly admired, Charlotte Mew, died in tragic circumstances, committing suicide on 24 March at the age of fifty-nine, a death Sassoon could just about rationalize: 'She must have wanted to be in peace very much to have done that,' he wrote to Edith Sitwell. 'And we have her magnificent poetry.'[50]

He could even accept Ottoline's cancer of the jaw, diagnosed in mid-April, since there was a reasonable chance that she would survive it. But he found it very difficult indeed to come to terms with Edmund Gosse's death on 16 May. Like Hardy's, it was not entirely unexpected: Gosse had become increasingly frail and his operation for prostate (itself a dangerous undertaking in the 1920s) at the age of nearly eighty was considered a serious risk. Nevertheless Sassoon felt almost as shocked as he had when Hardy died. He had remained grateful to Gosse over the years for his early encouragement. Even in Gosse's old age, when his resolute conservatism in literature and increasing prickliness had made him seem slightly absurd to some, Sassoon went on admiring his complete devotion to letters.

Sassoon had already made a link between the deaths of Hardy and Gosse, though not conscious of it at the time. After visiting Gosse's sickbed on 28 October 1927, he had written a sonnet, 'One Who Watches', which he subsequently revised for Hardy's death less than three months later. Without telling Gosse that it was *his* possible death which had inspired the poem, Sassoon then sent it to him 'as a consoling comment' on Hardy's death.[51] Gosse found it 'very beautiful', little realizing that it had been written in anticipation of his own end four months on.[52]

Before Gosse died he had agreed to edit Hardy's letters as Florence had requested. She had also asked that Sassoon be approached to write the *English Men of Letters* volume on Hardy, an honour he declined. Not only did the thought of another prose book horrify him, but it seemed almost disloyal to write about him publicly. 'I never Boswellized T.H. when staying at Max Gate,' he told Tomlinson. 'When I went upstairs [to bed] I felt that it would be a sort of betrayal of the hospitality.'[53] He would later write an article in *John O'London's Weekly* for Hardy's centenary in 1940 and draw up a list of his favourite Hardy poems, first for Cockerell, then for a BBC programme in 1956.[54] He would even contemplate a book on Hardy after finishing *Meredith* in 1948, but his only sustained account of the writer he admired most in the whole of English literature would be in *Siegfried's Journey*.

*

Both Hardy's and Gosse's death had made Sassoon more conscious of his own age, an effect heightened by the return of Stephen. Whether in an attempt to make up for his own absence or, as Philip Hoare suggests, as a 'minder',[55] Sassoon had paid for William Walton to join Stephen in Bavaria and their accounts of the light-hearted holiday together on Stephen's return in mid-April underlined his own sense of mortality.[56] 'I think I am happiest, really, with elderly people,' he wrote shortly afterwards, 'because they can talk about the past.' He was still deeply in love with Stephen and extremely jealous when he heard how much Stephen had enjoyed meeting Edith Sitwell's protégé, the Russian painter Tchelitchew, in Paris on his way home. But Sassoon was increasingly antagonized by Stephen's lifestyle, especially society friends like Beaton, who seemed to be 'silly people whose behaviour really cannot be exaggerated in its folly and extravagance'.[57] By the time Stephen left London again in late April for Preston Deanery, a health farm near Northampton, Sassoon had begun to wonder if he understood young people and their world at all.

Temperamentally averse to dressing up, or performance of any kind, he avoided the numerous parties thrown by the Bright Young Things in that last hectic season, before the Depression put an end to their cavortings. Pyjama parties, bottle parties, even swimming-bath parties, all designed to shock, filled Stephen's diary that summer and Sassoon grew worried that people were talking about the outrageous doings of him and his friends. Like Edith Olivier, he believed Stephen's behaviour stemmed mainly from exuberance, with a little light-hearted ribaldry added. 'All that is only a mask,' he tried to reassure himself. 'All the rest of his character is lovable and witty and intelligent.'[58]

The outside world was not as tolerant, however, and eventually Stephen's own class turned against him. It was not so much the incident itself – Stephen and David Plunket-Greene bringing two uninvited guests to Lady Ellesmere's Ball on 10 July – as a refusal on the part of the soberer members of the upper classes to accept any more. As a matter of principle Lady Ellesmere complained to the press of Stephen's flouting of social etiquette, and his name was splashed across the nation's newspapers.

Pamela Grey panicked and Sassoon's chance to win her over arrived. She and Lord Grey had been warned that it was 'the beginning of a "Round-up" of Stephen and his foppish friends', Edith Olivier wrote in her diary.[59] 'She fears he may be suspected of real immorality if he continues to be written of in the papers in this company.' Pamela, 'quite broken' by events, begged Edith to help prevent further trouble and Edith suggested writing to Sassoon.[60]

Sassoon, who had spent his summer enjoying Russian opera and ballet in Stephen's private box, was fully committed to Stephen by this time. His references to Glen suggest that he appreciated him more than ever, perhaps by comparison with Stephen's silliness. But he was still infatuated with Stephen and in any case Glen's return in late May had put their relationship on an entirely different footing.

Glen had been back from America a week before he contacted Sassoon at the Reform on 4 June. 'When are you coming home, my darling?' Sassoon had asked him in February, but he could not have looked forward to his return. Believing that the moment of truth had now arrived and feeling very guilty indeed, he agreed to meet Glen later that evening at Glen's house in Campden Hill Gardens. But his return from the cinema with Stephen was delayed, perhaps deliberately, by Stephen, who also insisted on coming to see Glen with him. It was the last thing Sassoon wanted. Using their lateness as an excuse for not visiting Glen, he took Stephen back to his own flat in Campden Hill Square and was in the kitchen making tea when Glen announced his arrival by hooting the car horn. To his horror Sassoon heard Stephen shout airily from the window: 'Siegfried is on his way down.'[61] It was a scene either from nightmare or a Whitehall farce. 'You'll find Stephen Tennant in there,' Sassoon announced at the top of the stairs and the next hour of strained conversation and suppressed emotions may be imagined.[62]

It was only after Stephen had been driven home by a self-righteously injured Glen and they were back at Glen's house, that Sassoon attempted to explain. The irony was that, after making a 'slight scene' about Sassoon's infidelity, Glen then confessed to his own; he, too, had fallen in love with someone else.[63] The irony was strengthened by the fact that the person in question was a woman, the actress Angela Baddeley, and the sister of Stephen's brother David's new wife, Hermione.[64]

The denouement with Glen behind him, Pamela's plea for help in late July encouraged Sassoon to hope for an even closer involvement with Stephen. And when he arrived at Lord Grey's Northumberland estate, Fallodon, in mid-August to spend a few days with the exiled and decidedly bored Stephen, he presented Pamela and her husband with a plan. Both he and Stephen had been invited to hear Edith Sitwell and William Walton's collaboration, *Façade*, performed at Siena on 14 September and to spend a week at Sir George Sitwell's Italian estate, Montegufoni, afterwards: Sassoon proposed to take Stephen there, then on to Venice, at his own expense. Stephen could travel by the Orient Express with his childhood nanny, Rebecca Trusler, to Munich, where Sassoon would drive to meet them and they could spend a few days at the Bavarian *pension*, Haus Hirth, for Stephen to recover from the journey.

The whole plan, like everything else in Stephen's adult life, was based on the assumption that he was still a child and still suffering from TB, neither of which was at this point true. Sassoon may have been trying to reassure Pamela, who was nevertheless only satisfied when they added another of their servants, William, to the party as Stephen's valet.

Buying a luxurious new red Packard especially for the trip, Sassoon set off in it a few days before Stephen, Nannie and William, arriving in Munich on 29 August. To begin with things went very well. Meeting the Wilsford trio off the train at Munich the day after his own arrival, Sassoon spent the next four days there sharing Stephen's most attractive quality, his love of art. He responded joyfully to the operas, concerts and art galleries to which Sassoon took him, reverting to a routine he had first established during his stay in Munich with Philipp in 1922.[65] And they both read avidly, Stephen grateful for the eclectic but serious mixture of books he had asked Sassoon to bring in his car, among them Shelley's poems, Maugham's *Of Human Bondage*, Forster's *Aspects of the Novel* and Sassoon's own work.

Against this reassuring background Sassoon seems to have been happy to join in Stephen's lighter entertainments, buying 'lovely bounderish caps with long peaks and saucy patterns', tinsel paper and postcards, or simply eating pink ices in a teashop.[66]

Their visit to Haus Hirth on 4 September also went well. Situated in the village of Untergrainau near Garmisch, a two hours' drive south-west of Munich, it was on the border of Austria and surrounded by snow-covered mountains. Set in a sheltered valley, where tinkling cow bells and fir-covered slopes created a fairy-tale atmosphere, there was something magical about it for most of its visitors. Like Stephen, Sassoon fell 'in love with everything at once ... the miraculous cleanliness of the house, the atmosphere of gaiety and happiness'.[67]

The owners of this 'holiday or rest home', as it was advertised, were Walther and Johanna Hirth. They had lost all of Walther's considerable fortune in Germany's post-war inflation, but seemed quite contented with their simple, hard-working life. Taking in guests at a very reasonable rate, they provided them with 'plain but perfect' food (according to Sassoon) and, if necessary, nursing care, as Stephen had discovered eight months earlier.

The Hirths welcomed Stephen back and made an equally great fuss of Sassoon, insisting on a special breakfast with a scarlet-candled cake and chair festooned with flowers for his forty-second birthday on 8 September. When he and Stephen set out for Italy in the Packard after four days' rest, it was with their laps full of dahlias from the Hirths' garden and a 'divine' picnic from Tante Johanna, which they ate on a mountainside as they crossed Austria to Italy.[68] Stephen found the drive over the Brenner to Bolzano 'breathtaking' and he was not being ironic about Sassoon's handling of the car, which fortunately struck him as bold rather than erratic. 'Siegfried drove masterfully and tirelessly,' he wrote in his diary that evening, 'whisking round bend after bend, dodging touring cars and lymphatic peasants – swooping from Bavaria to Austria and finally into Italy, mellow, much warmer, *too* lovely!!'

Their second day was even more successful. Following the longer, more scenic route to Bologna, Sassoon drove over the Mendola Pass to Lake Garda, where they stayed the night at Riva, 'the most romantic place' Stephen had ever seen: 'hot, raucous, southern, slouching Italian sailors roll along the wharves and groups of giggling peasant girls cluster outside the "Ristorantes"'.[69]

Sassoon, however, became increasingly tired, in spite of a much shorter drive than was planned the next day, to Gardone further down the lake. For he also found himself having to act as Stephen's valet in William's absence. So that, while Stephen strolled about the town, Sassoon did the packing of Stephen's many suitcases. And when Stephen brought back peaches, it was Sassoon who washed them for him to eat. Again it was Sassoon who had to prepare the car for their journey via Brescia to Cremona on their fourth day, and he who, in an attempt to make up for lost time, had the long drive from Cremona to Bologna on their fifth, followed by a last fruitless dash to reach Siena in time for *Façade* on their sixth.

But it was Stephen who complained. Having done nothing more arduous than go to the cinema, visit a few sights or eat a peach, and waited on hand and foot the whole way, he was nevertheless (in his own words) 'sulky and temperfull' by the time they reached Siena: 'We had arrived too late for *Façade* to my great grief. I thought I should die of temper. I felt eaten up with rage and hate. RAGE & HATE.'[70]

He was, however, mollified by a week at Montegufoni, an imposing eleventh-century castle with superb views of the surrounding Tuscan hills.[71] It was now Sassoon's turn to react. He was in trouble with Edith for missing *Façade*, he disliked most house parties and would have much preferred to be in Florence visiting picture galleries, and he was finally beginning to 'resent the fact that Stephen never stir[red] a finger to help facilitate [their] arrangements'.[72] For the first time on their journey he longed to be alone.

'For really happy companionship I rely on Glen more than Stephen, who has yet to prove that his feelings for me are more than physical,' he wrote in his diary shortly after their arrival in Venice on 29 September.[73] It was the mid-point in their journey and Stephen seemed to him more physically desirable than ever. But his self-centredness and callousness could no longer be ignored and Sassoon was now determined to try to 'influence him towards behaving sensibly'.[74] It was a re-run of his relationship with Gabriel and doomed to failure, but a resolution that would rule his life for the next three and a half years.

*

Venice marked a turning point not only in Sassoon's relations with Stephen and the journey, but also in his career as a writer. *Fox-Hunting Man* had been published on 28 September, the day before his arrival there, and was reviewed glowingly the day after. Sitting in the sunshine with Stephen in St Mark's Square drinking hot chocolate, Sassoon was delighted to find a long and enthusiastic review by J.C. Squire in the *Observer*.[75] To have his first serious attempt at prose praised so warmly and discriminatingly by someone as authoritative as Squire gave him hope for his writing future just as he had begun to despair of it.[76]

It was also a pleasure to return to a city that he had first visited with Philipp in 1922. His second stay, with the Morrells in 1926, had given him an even greater appreciation of its art and he enjoyed acting as Stephen's guide, Baedeker in hand. Stephen improved somewhat during their three-day stay, genuinely excited by the wealth of art and truly appreciative of the 'exquisite' Guardi reproductions Sassoon bought him at the Accademia.[77]

Once they had put Nannie and William, who had joined them, back on the train for Munich and started on their own return by car to Haus Hirth, however, Stephen's childishness reasserted itself. Instead of sympathizing with Sassoon's frustration when he discovered at Vicenza that he had left his case of vital travel documents in Venice, he simply escaped to the nearest cinema to see a film called *The Gorilla*. By this point in the journey Sassoon was exhausted as well as bad-tempered. The weather had also deteriorated and when they finally arrived at Haus Hirth on 4 October he was suffering from bronchitis. In a reversal of what was to come, a Dr Kaltenbach was called in to examine his lungs, always his weak point. A 'few spots' were found and the return to Paris delayed while Sassoon was nursed back to health by a willing Tante Johanna. Like Florence Hardy she was more than a little in love with Sassoon.[78]

He enjoyed his convalescence. The countryside, as Stephen rather fancifully put it, was 'molten in the autumn blur', with 'dazzling days, mountains glittering like bride-cakes, gentians and the last late golden-rod'.[79] And there were 'sheaves of press-cuttings' waiting of *Fox-Hunting Man*, *The Heart's Journey* and even, to Stephen's particular delight, of the Ariel poem he had illustrated for Sassoon, 'To My Mother'.[80] There was fresh company too, in the person of his aunt, Nan Tennant, whom Sassoon instantly liked. Nearer her age than Stephen's, he found her 'a cultivated, grey-haired, alert, well-connected woman – a cut above E.M. F[orster]'s fictional spinsters'.[81]

After a fortnight's peace on Tante Johanna's sunny balcony, Sassoon made the long drive back to Paris to join Stephen, Nannie and William, who had preceded him by train.[82] He arrived on 23 October with another cold, which again turned to bronchitis. Having driven approximately 2,000 miles in just under two months he longed for rest, yet was once more frustrated by Stephen, who wanted to socialize, but was looking unwell. Stepping into the role which was shortly to antagonize almost all Stephen's friends, Sassoon took control, and when Brian Howard, Cynthia Mosley, Meraud Guinness and Mrs Barrymore telephoned to invite themselves to lunch, pretended to be what he had in fact become on their travels, Stephen's valet, and put them off. Eventually, at the end of October, he persuaded Stephen to move out of central Paris to Versailles. It would be even more expensive at the Hotel Trianon Palace than at the Hotel Foyot, where Stephen had run up enormous bills, but at least they would get what they both needed, 'a dose of quietude'.[83]

It should have been a successful end to a trip designed largely with Stephen's health in mind. For the rest of their stay they planned to visit only two friends, Miss Fleming-Jones and Madame Duclaux. Both of them elderly females, neither seemed likely to over-excite Stephen. But they were not calculated to cheer him either, the main topic of conversation with each being death, in particular those of Hardy and Henry Festing-Jones.

Sad as the deaths of his old friends were for Sassoon, none of them was entirely unexpected. A far more sudden and catastrophic loss awaited Stephen, one which would also affect Sassoon in its own way. While they had been paying a second visit to Madame Duclaux on 17 November, the day before Stephen planned to return to England with Nannie, Stephen's mother Pamela had suffered a severe stroke in the garden at Wilsford and had died four hours later. She was only fifty-seven and, though known to have a heart condition, had certainly not been expected to die.

Stephen, who had remained completely dependent on his mother and would normally have turned to her in such a situation, had no resources to deal with her death. Sassoon felt he had no choice but to take over Pamela's role. He had had almost three months' practice at the job by this point. Their holiday had made him more aware of Stephen's faults, but Pamela's death showed him, unexpectedly, a more positive side to her son: 'Stephen is ... very courageous in this desolation,' Sassoon wrote to the Heads on 1 December 1928.[84] His New Year resolution for 1928 had been to see less of Stephen, but fate had intervened and by the end of the year he found himself more deeply committed than ever.

*

Only two things were needed to make Stephen's dependence on Sassoon almost complete, Stephen's ill health and that of Nannie Trusler. When both followed quickly on Pamela's death in November 1928, Sassoon took charge, though with some apprehension. His greatest fear was that Stephen would demand even more attention and prevent him writing again. Ironically, it was this threat that made him write far more and more successfully during the first three years of their relationship than either before or after. One of his greatest problems, except in the war years, had been motivation. Now, threatened by too little rather than too much time for writing, he was fully motivated.

Apart from Stephen's few days at Wilsford for Pamela's funeral and his brief visit to one of her friends at Oxford, Sassoon had to be with him 'constantly' after their arrival back from France.[85] It was only when Stephen left for Fallodon with Lord Grey on 10 December that he was able to concentrate for the first time on his new book. Willingly contemplating Christmas on his own, he worked hard and by the end of December had written well over 6,500 words of 'Memoirs Continued' (later retitled *Memoirs of an Infantry Officer*). But his progress was brought to an abrupt halt in the new year, first by a summons to join Stephen at Wilsford, then, more dramatically, by the news that Stephen's tuberculosis had recurred.[86] The doctors predicted that he would 'probably be dead ... within a year'.[87]

Whether Stephen's TB had been brought on by stress at losing his mother, as the doctors believed, or whether the long car journeys through Europe had affected *his* lungs as well as Sassoon's, or whether the disease had simply been missed by previous tests, the result was the same, to stop Sassoon working until Stephen was packed off to Haus Hirth again at the end of January. In an almost exact repetition of the previous year Sassoon instantly returned to his book, determined to finish at least half of it before he joined Stephen for Easter. Nan Tennant would see her nephew safely to Bavaria and Nannie (Sassoon still believed) would look after him there till his arrival.

Then the second blow fell. Tante Johanna wrote in February 1929 to say that she was 'terribly anxious not about Stephen but about *Nannie*'.[88] Like Pamela, Nannie had a heart condition, which had started to get worse. She was also, at seventy, growing increasingly confused. For Stephen, who had depended on her since childhood and loved her as much, 'possibly more so', as his mother, the situation was grave.[89] But for Sassoon, who saw Stephen's last prop beside himself vanishing, it was extremely threatening and he redoubled what had come to seem to him his 'awful drudgery'.[90]

As in the previous year he cut himself off from almost everyone, and by 23 February had squeezed out nearly 30,000 words, a third of the projected book. He had conducted Sherston from the point at which his adventures had ended in *Fox-Hunting Man* – on the Front opposite Mametz at Easter 1916 – through an army training course at Flixécourt and his daring rescue of Corporal O'Brien during a failed raid in May, to the Battle of the Somme and its unheroic aftermath for Sherston, trench fever, which took him back to England in July. Celebrating his achievement with a rare break, Sassoon spent the weekend with the two friends of Stephen he liked most, Edith Olivier and Rex Whistler.

Edith was not a typical parson's daughter, though she had retained her father's strong religious principles. Until the death of her sister, with whom she lived on the Wilton estate, she had enjoyed a genteel, relatively quiet life on the fringes of the aristocracy. Then in 1925, at the age of fifty-three, everything had changed. Meeting Rex during a holiday with Stephen designed to console her for her sister's death, she had fallen deeply in love with the young art student. Rex liked her greatly but, as his friend Beaton put it, 'Rex, so romantic with his luminous face, Roman nose, and large crown to his head, exud[ing] warm-heartedness and sympathy,' was nevertheless a 'strangely remote person'.[91] Quite apart from an age gap of over thirty years, he was also predominantly homosexual and Edith had to be content with the role of confidante.

It was a part she also played with Sassoon, who was already consulting her frequently about Stephen by February 1929. Her own late entry into writing, with the moderately successful romantic novels she began to produce at the age of fifty-five, gave them another interest in common. But like most of her homosexual friends he found the small, dynamic woman 'too vivacious and feminine to be a comfortable crony'.[92] She was to remain, nonetheless, a lifelong friend, to whom he would make a generous allowance when her own meagre income eventually failed.[93]

Edith had become very fond of Sassoon by February 1929 – he seemed to her the 'most natural, independent man' she had ever met – and probably invited him down to Wiltshire with Rex to make sure the two men did not fall out over Stephen. She may have imagined a jealousy which, according to Rex's brother, Laurence Whistler, did not exist.[94]

What did exist, however, entirely unsuspected by Edith, was a strong sexual attraction between Rex and Sassoon, which her innocent manoeuvre unwittingly encouraged. Their long crawl down to Wiltshire in Sassoon's car through thick fog gave them hours of intimacy together. And Rex's ardour, which Sassoon noted in his diary with some concern, was unextinguished by the icy pond Sassoon drove him into towards the end of their journey, though it caused the waiting Edith great anxiety. (The pond's owner, far from responding to their request for help, merely erected a notice which read THIS POND IS PRIVATE.)

By the time the two men arrived back in London after their weekend together, Sassoon was actively 'worried' about Rex's evident attraction for him,[95] fearing that Rex was 'on the verge of the precipice'.[96] He liked Rex, was grateful for his company during Stephen's absence and flattered by his delicate drawings of him. He even found him 'desirable' and thought it 'easy enough to succumb' but he knew that it would be 'no joke once it started'. It was an awkward situation and one he had faced a number of times in the 1920s from both sexes. Forced to choose between two attractive young men, he picked Stephen, a decision which would cause him years of unhappiness.

The most revealing feature of the affair is the strength of Sassoon's commitment to Stephen at the very point when he might be expected to fear the effects of too great an involvement. It is characteristic of him that he found the two happiest years of their relationship those covering Stephen's deepest dependence on him.

*

Sassoon was in high spirits when he arrived at Haus Hirth on 5 April. He had written nearly 50,000 words of *Infantry Officer*, over half of its eventual 82,000.[97] Parts 5, 6 and 7, describing Sherston's progress from his regimental depot at 'Clitherland' to the infantry base depot at Rouen, then on to the Battle of Arras, were virtually finished and the end almost in sight. Even better, he was rejoining Stephen.

Happiness made him even more generous than usual, especially if he thought it would help Stephen. William Walton and Edith, who were there entertaining the invalid when he arrived, had both had their expenses paid by him, and when Rex turned up on 20 April it was thanks to Sassoon's money. Hearing of the Hirths' financial difficulties over a badly needed new roof, Sassoon insisted on giving them £500, a large amount matched by Stephen the next day. He also 'lent' the Hirths an even bigger sum two months later that he clearly did not expect them to repay.[98] A 'marvellous generous creature', as Edith noted,[99] it was his proud boast that he had spent none of the considerable royalties already earned from *Fox-Hunting Man* on himself, his first act being to buy Glen (now engaged to Angela Baddeley) a new car.[100] His wedding present to them when they married in September would be even more lavish, half payment for their first house.[101] He would also buy a house for Nellie when her lease at Half Moon Street expired.

As Edith also noted, Sassoon was 'happy as a boy' in his generosity that spring in Bavaria.[102] His evident love for Stephen made him in turn very 'lovable'.[103] Nobody could resist him; host, hostess, servants, guests and Stephen most of all, succumbed to the extraordinary charm which normally lay concealed beneath a stiff, somewhat awkward, exterior. Stephen's health especially pleased him, having improved rapidly in the hands of the specialist from Heidelberg, Dr Kaltenbach. (Sassoon would probably have approved of Kaltenbach's view of Stephen as a mixture of a Fra Angelico and Botticelli angel, but less so of Stephen's description of the doctor as 'blond, young and fascinating', a deliberate attempt to make Sassoon jealous.[104])

Kaltenbach's decision to rest Stephen's affected lung in March by collapsing it with a process known as pneumothorax, had produced hopeful results by the time Sassoon arrived in April and full recovery seemed possible. Stephen, who had been confined to his bed upstairs with visitors strictly limited, was allowed to come down on 21 April for his twenty-third birthday.

The peak of their joy lay just ahead. Stephen's improvement continued and by mid-May Sassoon decided that he was well enough to move to a small house in the nearby village of Schmölz. He had reluctantly started thinking of his work again and needed more solitude than the gregarious Haus Hirth allowed. He also wanted to be alone with Stephen, or as alone as Stephen ever was. Nannie and William were still with them and an English nurse had to be added to the party to look after Stephen and the increasingly frail Nannie, but at least it meant that Sassoon was able to concentrate on revising *Infantry Officer*.

'You would love this house,' Sassoon wrote to Glen from 'Breitenau' on 22 May. 'It is approached from the main road by a plank footbridge over the river; then a path through [Himalayan cedars] and silver pines to the actual shack which is, in places, 250 years old, full of creaks and rattles and charm.'[105] For Sassoon it was the Bavarian equivalent of an enchanted house from a de la Mare poem or story and Stephen found the grounds equally fairy-tale. Five acres of lawns thickly covered with gentians and lily of the valley, they backed on to virgin pine forest, 'hot and scented in the sunshine, full of giant butterflies, snakes and lizards'.[106] 'It's paradise!' he wrote to a friend, echoing Sassoon's own word for it.

Sassoon, who had written at least two poems during his stay at Haus Hirth, now resolved to concentrate on his prose.[107] But the combination of Breitenau's exotic beauty and his passion for Stephen made verse irresistible: 'Every day we pack more wealth away –/ Every night we welcome new delight', he wrote in 'Song Without Words' a week after arrival in their own house, lines he eventually rejected as perhaps too explicit.[108] On the same day, however, he wrote a poem which would be included in his *Collected Poems* and remain one of the most haunting of his non-war pieces, 'The Heart's Paradise'. In it he tried to convey the magical nature of his experience at Breitenau that summer:

At the end of all wrong roads I came
To the gates of the garden without a name.
There, till the spell should fail, I found
Sudden Elysium, strange with sound
Of unknown birds and waters wild
With voices unresolved for rest.
There every flower was fancy's child,
And every tree was glory's guest,
And Love, by darkness undefiled,
Went like the sun from east to west.   (*CP*, p. 216)[109]

After the many false turnings taken since leaving his childhood garden at Weirleigh, Sassoon believed that he had finally found its equivalent, the Garden of Eden. For the first time he dared to hope that he had arrived at his goal, true love.

Yet the poem also suggests that he was aware at some level that it *was* an enchantment and unlikely to last, that the 'spell' (as he anticipates in the third line) would eventually 'fail'. Looking back on the scene three years later he remembered moments of unease, staring at the old house with its two sick inhabitants as though, in the words of another unpublished poem written there, 'halfway through some long, unhappy story'.[110]

Nevertheless, the ten weeks at Breitenau were to remain among his happiest memories. Two days after writing 'The Heart's Paradise' he was back at work on his prose, adding just one new passage to his original 50,000 words, thus bringing Sherston from his nostalgic chat with Wilmot about the Kentish Weald to his rash foray in the Hindenburg Trench, where he receives his first wound. It took the author himself to within a few hundred words of the end of Part 8.[111] The rest of his time was spent on revision.

No greater proof of Sassoon's devotion to Stephen exists than his decision to change his working hours from night to morning to suit the invalid. So that while Stephen visited a nearby hospital for daily treatment, he sat down to work, and by the middle of June had rewritten and fair-copied almost half his manuscript in the old library on the ground floor. He had taken this for his room and, apart from hundreds of battered German books, it contained a bed, a writing table, where he also ate, and a grand piano imported from Munich especially for him. After finishing work for the day, he would relax with Bach's organ fugues adapted for piano, 'with a lot of exuberant octaves added' to reflect his mood.[112] Two floors above, Stephen would be reading or playing with several small aquaria he had set up on his balcony.

Nannie, who was confined to her room on the first floor, struggled on till mid-June, when she had to return to England for greater medical care. Stephen now became Sassoon's full responsibility and when Eddie Marsh wrote to tell him of the Hawthornden Prize-giving on 12 July, he replied, 'I must remain here with Stephen,' nominating Blunden to receive the award on his behalf as he had once done for Blunden.[113]

It was no real hardship. The skies were cloudless, the sun grew hotter and their isolated retreat even lovelier. There are photographs of Sassoon stripped to the waist, muscular, axe in hand, looking rested if a little self-conscious as he prepares to chop wood for the evening fire. Others show him with Stephen at his side, slim and girlish in a variety of fanciful outfits. They could be shots from a successful honeymoon. And the first half of *Infantry Officer*, in spite of its sombre material, reflects some of this happiness, the sections on Sherston's training at Flixécourt and convalescence at Oxford in particular.

The idyll came to an end in late July with news of Nannie's sudden deterioration and admission to hospital. Sassoon, dreading a repetition of the circumstances of Pamela's death, decided that he must take Stephen back immediately. He had difficulty in getting him through the journey. Nannie lingered on, however, rallying slightly at the beginning of August. But by 14 August she was dead and Stephen distraught again. From this point on it would be Sassoon who must try to find the answers. He had become, as Strachey noted, Stephen's *'garde-malade'*.[114]

To this end Sassoon spent most of the next two months at Wilsford looking after Stephen. He had in any case begun to tire of 23 Campden Hill Square, a rather modest place after the grand hotels and romantic settings of his travels with Stephen. It was effectively the end of his time at the flat, though he would stay there occasionally on visits to London during the next few years and would not officially move out until 1932. One obvious effect of his relationship with Stephen had been to make him abandon his resolve not to let money change his way of life. Keeping up with Stephen's extravagant habits had quickly seen to that.

So on his arrival back in England he had installed himself with Stephen in the Hyde Park Hotel, an expensive establishment he was to return to several times during the coming years. With Pamela's death Stephen's luxurious, silver-lined apartment in Smith Square had gone: Pamela had left her town house to his older brother, David, together with Wilsford. Stephen himself had been given Pamela's parents' home at Lake with its extensive grounds. But it was Wilsford he wanted and he eventually succeeded in persuading his brother to rent it to him. What Stephen wanted he usually got.

It was, therefore, to Wilsford Stephen returned when Nannie's funeral was over. And it was at Wilsford that Sassoon would spend the better part of a year, on and off, becoming in the process dependent on both Wiltshire and large houses, not to mention their grounds. For Wilsford's grounds were enchanting and Sassoon's stay there represented a journey from one idyllic garden to another. 'This is a sort of earthly paradise,' Blunden noted on 28 September 1929 during one of several visits arranged by Sassoon, '– trees, birds, dogs, reptiles, fishes and all!'[115] 'If this is autumn,' he concluded, 'what splendid flowers and bird-music must be here in spring?'

Sassoon was not to experience spring at Wilsford, however. Dr Kaltenbach, who had been flown over especially from Germany to inspect Stephen's lungs in late October, decreed that, though 'cured', he needed a milder climate for the next six months. Sicily was chosen.

Sassoon, possibly in anticipation, had packed all the visits he considered important into the three months since his return. His mother's health was worrying him almost as much as Stephen's and he had made the tortuous journey from Wiltshire to Kent several times to see her. He had also stayed with the Heads and the Wyldes regularly on his way to and from London, where he paid numerous visits to the dentist. He had even managed a visit, with Blunden, to the ageing poet laureate. Bridges had become very fond of Sassoon, who had organized a present of a harpsichord for him on his eightieth birthday, and Sassoon was anxious to introduce Blunden to him before it was too late.

Sassoon's only real worry about the trip to Sicily, as always with Stephen, was his writing. He had got back to *Infantry Officer* on 21 September and carried on with it at intervals throughout October, sitting at his table on the second floor of Wilsford's thatched wing close to Stephen's open-air loggia. He was determined to keep it up and it was on the understanding that he would be allowed to complete the final half of the book in Sicily that he set off on their second long tour of the year. So that while the Great Depression of 1929 deepened into the hardships of the early 1930s the two men started for the south with Stephen's extravagant entourage, which included not only his valet and innumerable suitcases but also his pet parrot.

Their journey began in mid-November with a week in Paris to please Stephen, who was much fonder of the city than Sassoon. He also hoped to see one of his literary heroes, André Gide, there and was thrilled when Sassoon managed to arrange a meeting. Sassoon liked Gide greatly, though he realized that the Frenchman was more interested in his pretty young friend than in himself.[116]

Sassoon's turn came next with a visit to one of *his* literary heroes, Max Beerbohm, at his home on the Italian Riviera. He had been sending Beerbohm copies of his privately printed books since their first meeting in 1916, But 'my Max', as he put it 'began in November 1929', that is on this visit to Rapallo, where Max had settled with his wife Florence in 1910. The invitation had come about through a chance meeting with Max on New Year's Eve 1928 at the house of William Nicholson. Sassoon's admiration for him amounted to hero-worship by this time; he had read *Zuleika Dobson* and most of Beerbohm's essays and had bought eight of his caricatures in recent exhibitions.

Max was almost all Sassoon looked for in a man and an artist. The wit which characterized his delicate drawings and mannered prose style made conversation with him a delight. Like his friend Ross, he rarely allowed his own wit to dominate and Sassoon always left him feeling nourished. From the start Max symbolized for him everything that was 'delightful and diverting and stimulating'.[117] Fourteen years older than Sassoon, he was in his late fifties when their 'real' friendship began, but he seemed to his disciple 'neither young nor old. Just wise, witty and sweetly civilized.'[118] As with that other dapper

Edwardian dandy, Ross, he was more like a jolly bachelor uncle than a father-figure for Sassoon.

Unlike Ross, however, Max was sexually ambiguous. 'The usual judgement,' Anthony Powell wrote, tactfully, 'was that Beerbohm was not very active in the field of sex.'[119] Max himself told Sassoon that 'the best thing in life is to be in bed', not with a person but 'with a book'.[120]

Sassoon identified strongly with Max, who confirmed many of his own prejudices. Despite his wit, Max was not 'clever' in the way Sassoon disliked so much in Modernists such as Eliot or Graves. A fellow-reactionary, Max preferred the past to the present. 'Modern writers pride themselves on being tough experts,' Sassoon wrote in notes for his description of Max in *The Weald of Youth*: 'Show that Max is faultlessly efficient in his use of words ... Let them be as *expert* as Max!'[121] Paradoxically, however, the quality which most impressed him in Max's prose and one he deliberately cultivated in his own, was its apparent amateurishness: it had, he claimed, 'the spontaneous charm of good amateur work'.[122] Max had become what he himself aimed to be, 'a completely expert amateur'.[123]

It is a highly subjective view of a writer whose style Wilde compared to a silver dagger, but there is no doubting the admiration which lies behind it. Together with Hardy and de la Mare, Max would remain one of the three writers Sassoon had known who meant more to him than any others: 'Max so different from the other two ... *gave* me something quite different.'[124] By 1952 he was to describe his visits to Max as 'the nearest thing to Paradise' or 'Elysium' he had ever experienced.[125]

The spell was cast immediately on the first visit in November 1929. Sassoon and Stephen had caught the train from Paris on 22 November, booking into the Excelsior Hotel on the 23rd. They had presented themselves for lunch the next day at the Villino Chiaro, Max's modest but dramatically situated house in the via Aurelia, just outside Rapallo on the main Genoa road. Steep stairs led up to the living quarters, then on up to a large roof terrace and Max's study. Lunch was eaten in one of the four small rooms overlooking the Bay of Genoa, and the conversation so lively that it was 6.30 p.m. before the guests left.

They stayed a week in all, visiting the hospitable Beerbohms on alternate days for a vastly extended lunch – 'absolute bliss' to Sassoon, who spent most of his time talking to Max while Stephen engaged in stage gossip with Florence, an ex-actress.

Despairing of the Boswellian task of summarizing three or four six-hour sessions of sparkling conversation, Sassoon left much of it unrecorded. But he could not resist reporting his own remark about Yeats (whom he and Stephen had also visited at Rapallo), that 'he *was* a bit of a *poseur*', and Max's shrewd reply, 'that the brilliant Irishmen in London had often been "poseurs", but had helped to keep London alive and amused – from Goldsmith, Sheridan, Burke, Tom Moore, on to Wilde, George Moore, and Bernard Shaw'.[126] He also thought Max's sharper comments worth preserving: 'Of Norman Douglas:

"There is a touch of the 'codger' about him." Of Galsworthy: "He does the old uncles beautifully, but goes to pieces when describing 'the way of a man with a maid' ..." Of H.G. Wells: "His novels are like collapsed blancmanges, but always contain enjoyable passages.'"[127]

Reluctant as he was to leave such 'exquisitely civilized conversation',[128] Sassoon knew that they must continue their journey south. Rapallo at the beginning of December was too cold and wet for Stephen's lungs and he himself needed to start work, as he planned to do in Sicily. They landed at the island's capital, Palermo, on 20 December after a twelve-hour crossing from Naples, where they had lingered for two weeks.

Even in Palermo, where they stayed just over a fortnight, Sassoon was unable to get on with his prose. His main problem remained Stephen. With only William and Poll, the parrot, to distract him he was even more demanding of Sassoon's time than in Bavaria. Sassoon, who 'dread[ed] any relationship' which would 'make demands on' him, saw a conflict looming, but was still too infatuated to do anything about it. So for the next month he devoted himself to Stephen's entertainment, exploring the island with him, first from Palermo, then from Girgenti, where they moved on 6 January 1930.

It was a strange time for Sassoon, a mixture of intense happiness as they discovered Sicily's ancient beauties and strong foreboding as he contemplated his unfinished work. Whereas his Breitenau poem 'At the End of All Wrong Roads' had used the metaphor of the journey to lead to 'sudden Elysium', his poem 'In Sicily' uses it negatively: 'Life's one forward track' can 'never again come back.' It is also much darker in tone: 'the unreturning day must die', the word 'grave' ends the piece and the echoes from Arnold's 'Dover Beach' in line eight and Owen's 'The Unreturning' in line ten reinforce the sense of melancholy. (The poem's original title was 'Elegy in Sicily'.) Consciously or unconsciously, Sassoon is already anticipating the end of the relationship:

> Because we two can never again come back
> On life's one forward track, –
> Never again first-happily explore
> This valley of rocks and vines and orange-trees,
> Half Biblical and half Hesperides,
> With dark blue seas calling from a shell-strewn shore:
> By the strange power of Spring's resistless green,
> Let us be true to what we have shared and seen,
> And as our amulet this idyll save.
> And since the unreturning day must die,
> Let it for ever be lit by an evening sky
> And the wild myrtle grow upon its grave.　　(*CP*, p. 214)[129]

By mid-January Sassoon knew he had to start writing again. So on 18 January, just three days before he and Stephen made their final move to Syracuse, he returned to his half-finished manuscript. The compromise he was forced to arrive at with Stephen was less than perfect from his point of view, but it had a positive effect on his writing habits. By sitting down to his work every morning in his room at the Hotel Villa Politi while Stephen sunbathed or sketched on the balcony next to his, and abandoning it every afternoon to collect the shells Stephen loved on the beach, he established a routine he could maintain.[130]

Two and a half months and just over 30,000 words later he had, to his enormous relief, completed *Infantry Officer*; Sherston had been taken back to England, had convalesced at Nutwood (i.e. Chapelwood) Manor and, partly as a result of it, made his public protest and faced the consequences. '82,000 words all written out twice, and much of it three times, and endless hours spent revising and correcting the typescripts' had exhausted Sassoon.[131]

The manuscript, densely written on both sides of the page, crossed out and rewritten, indicates that he had worked with a pronounced sense of urgency. And a letter to Blunden of 28 March suggests that the circumstances under which the book was written materially affected its finished form. In it he refers to his elimination of the episode with which he had originally intended to close Sherston's story, his stay at 'Slateford' (Craiglockhart). Three days after writing to Blunden, however, he had brought *Infantry Officer* to a slightly abrupt halt with Sherston's journey to the hospital: 'And with my arrival at Slateford War Hospital this volume can conveniently be concluded.'[132] Apart from other considerations he had been too exhausted to continue and acknowledged that if the last chapters had been written 'in strict solitude they might have been stronger'.[133]

Stephen's biographer has argued that Sicily, rather than Bavaria, was the couple's true honeymoon. If so, it was a far stricter and more prolonged test of their compatibility and Sassoon would have saved himself a great deal of suffering had he heeded the warning signs. It is clear that Stephen, beside making it difficult for him to work, could not satisfy one of his most important needs, intelligent discussion. By the end of February he was already yearning for a long talk with Blunden: 'life here – with all its compensations, – *is* a sort of exile,' he confessed.[134] He was also eagerly looking forward to Max's stimulating conversation, having grown 'rusty' with Stephen.[135]

When he and Stephen had left Rapallo they had arranged to return on their way home and once his book was finished he could hardly wait. Travelling via Taormina[136] he transported Stephen and his numerous belongings by boat from Messina to Genoa and by 8 April was back in Rapallo having tea with the Beerbohms.

During the next three weeks Sassoon revelled in Max's 'delectable gossip', recording far more of it than on his first visit.[137] Though he maintained that Max was 'never malicious', unlike Gosse, of whom he otherwise reminded him, some of Max's judgements were decidedly astringent. T.S. Eliot, for instance, seemed to him 'a case of the Emperor wearing no clothes', D.H. Lawrence was 'a clumsy writer' with 'a diseased mind', and he 'gladdened' Sassoon by 'demolishing' Wyndham Lewis as a writer altogether.[138] Browning, he argued, was 'a gigantic and fertile continent of creative resourcefulness compared with the melancholy backyard of Tom Eliot, who sits there ironically analyzing an empty sardine-tin'.[139] The relish with which Sassoon repeats such remarks is evident. But he also enjoyed the more positive side of Max's talk, his admiration for Henry James and Walter de la Mare, for example, or his detailed knowledge of more obscure literary figures of the 1890s. Strolling about his roof terrace, or darting into his little indigo-coloured study for a book, Max delighted his guest, who could only thank him 'a thousand times for restoring my faith in delicacy, and perfection of manners, mental and hospitable, in the graces of life and philosophy'.[140] Sassoon's own way of life from the mid-1930s onwards would owe much to the model he had studied so carefully at Rapallo, as his poem, 'Memento for Max', suggests.[141]

Max's effect on Sassoon's writing was even more apparent than on his lifestyle. Sassoon had submitted *Infantry Officer* to him on arrival and was quite intoxicated by his praise of it. From this time on he was to send all his prose books to Max for him to check their style and would dedicate *The Old Century* to him in 1938. More importantly, his enthusiasm had restored Sassoon's own faith in his work, and he left for Aix-les-Bains and Biarritz at the beginning of May 'feeling very happy about my book, and quite eager to revise the proofs ... Getting my manuscript back reminds me that I am in love with it (although it has seemed such weary work) and it makes me eager to begin another book.'[142]

He was less happy with Stephen and in Paris, where they arrived in May, they had their first serious argument. 'A sad ending,' Sassoon reflected, 'to our half year abroad.'[143] They were both tired and Sassoon was determined to prevent Stephen being further exhausted by friends in Paris, who only wanted to 'plunge' him into 'a vortex of silly and vicious circles of cosmopolitan cocktail consumers'.[144] Stephen, however, insisted on paying several visits to be painted by Tchelitchew, who had already made Sassoon so jealous the previous year. After six months together they were more aware of each other's faults, Sassoon oppressed by Stephen's 'possessiveness'.[145] Yet he was also conscious of his own tendency to be 'egotistical and domineering' and was still at a stage where he blamed himself for their differences.[146] He resolved to be less 'clumsy' with Stephen, to learn how to 'manage' him, terminology more appropriate in a parent or an animal-trainer than a lover.[147]

It was clearly time for a break and when they arrived back in England on 14 May, Sassoon stayed in London while Stephen went to Wilsford. But once again fate intervened and he was not free of his responsibilities for long. With the doctors' announcement on 14 June that Stephen's TB was still active, Sassoon felt obliged to take charge, installing himself at Wilsford for the rest of the summer.

With Stephen's complete dependence on him, all his past feelings revived: 'he needs me so much and is so touchingly grateful', he told the Heads.[148] His goal now was to make sure that Stephen had the best medical attention possible and to prevent him from exerting himself.

Both aims were very worthy, but in carrying them out he managed to antagonize Stephen's doctors, family and friends. Whereas someone more tactful and less impetuous might have found a smoother way of insisting on second and third opinions about Stephen's health, Sassoon bluntly declared his lack of faith in both the local doctor, Kempe, and the London consultant, Chandler, demanding that a specialist from nearer at hand should be brought in. Even he recognized that to fly Dr Kaltenbach over from Germany again would be going too far, though he did have another German doctor, Hausen, called in. He also succeeded in getting an English lung specialist, Dr Snowden, from a neighbouring sanatorium near Cadnam, to see Stephen, and in having another X-ray taken. While all this may have been medically desirable, it did not endear him to Stephen's doctors and placed Stephen's eldest brother, Lord Glenconner, in an awkward position.[149] Only Lord Grey, won over partly by Sir Henry Head's tactful letter of professional advice, seemed to be on Sassoon's side.[150]

A similar situation developed with Stephen's friends, whom Sassoon had vowed to prevent 'descending on him in selfish shoals'.[151] Edith Olivier was exempted from this charge, but Beaton was seen as a prime suspect and became deeply offended. Even the mild and well-inclined Rex felt put out. Noting that Sassoon's own friends, like Blunden, Forster and Byam Shaw, were allowed to visit, he and Beaton believed that Stephen was deliberately being taken away from them by a possessive Sassoon. The Sitwells, who according to Edith Olivier had become increasingly jealous of the intimacy between Sassoon and Stephen, were outraged.

Sassoon, who referred to himself jokingly as an 'old watch-dog', ignored them all.[152] From mid-June to mid-September he kept guard at Wilsford, taking time off only to visit his mother and the dentist. Stephen, terrified of a further relapse, behaved 'angelically' and Sassoon still found it a 'great consolation' that 'he needs me and that I can help him'.[153] He quickly settled into a new routine, which combined as many elements from his past life as possible and would provide a pattern for the future.

'My salvation as regards nerves,' he told Nan Tennant, 'is due to "Bruno"; the cob who ought to be pulling the Victoria, but is ridden by me about two hours every afternoon.'[154] It was seven years since he had last ridden, but it quickly became a daily necessity that he would continue until well into his seventies. He also managed an occasional game of cricket. His other remedy for 'nerves' was the new piano Stephen had ordered specially for him and several more hours were passed stumbling his way through Bach.

With *Infantry Officer* at the printers he had only the proofs to deal with and was able to revert to the pre-*Memoirs* habit of more or less vegetating through the summer, saving his serious writing for autumn and winter.[155] He had longed to get back to 'the Elysium of poetry' after such a 'plodding prose expedition', but when the opportunity came it was prose not poetry he planned.[156] The story, about a man waking up in Antediluvium and creating a retrospective existence of people and episodes for himself, was never written, but the notes for it are revealing, suggesting that by the end of August he was beginning to tire of Stephen's possessiveness again.[157] The idea behind the story, as Sassoon himself recognized, expressed his 'need for solitude and reflection'.

Stephen's need of autonomy was equally powerful, however, and by 22 September he expressed a wish to be alone for at least ten days and a game of cat-and-mouse began. Summoned back to Wilsford in early October, Sassoon was banished for a second time at the end of that month, after an ominous entry in Stephen's diary, 'I'm better alone.'[158] And though Sassoon was recalled at short notice at the beginning of November and again in mid-December, even spending Christmas with Stephen at his request, it was in effect the end of their relationship.

A poem written on Christmas Eve at Wilsford suggests that Sassoon himself suspected as much. Entitled 'December Stillness', it is a melancholy poem, set at 'nightfall, sad and spacious' among 'loom[ing]' trees. Following a flock of birds 'in lone remote migration beating by', the poet appears to identify with their state, begging the wintry stillness to 'teach me to travel far and bear my loads'.[159] Sassoon and sympathetic friends like Edith Olivier might blame Stephen's quixotic behaviour on his physical condition and his most recent help, Nurse May, who indulged his whims, but by January 1931 it was clear that he no longer wanted Sassoon with him.

26

The Turn of the Screw

1931-1933

Fortunately for Sassoon, Stephen's first banishment of him came a few days after the publication of *Memoirs of an Infantry Officer* on 18 September 1930; at the time it was more convenient to be in London than Wiltshire, and he had plenty to distract him.[1] Following its serialization in the *Daily Telegraph*, Blunden had reviewed it enthusiastically in the *News Chronicle* on publication day, setting the tone for the other reviews that quickly followed.[2] During the crisis over Stephen's health Sassoon had seen much less of Blunden than he wanted and his return to London now gave him a chance to catch up on their friendship.

Sassoon had been worried about Blunden since his return from Japan in August 1927. Blunden had left for Japan in 1924 without his wife Mary, who had refused to go with him, and he returned after his long absence expecting to separate from her. She had hardly bothered to conceal her relationships with other men and he, possibly in response, had brought his Japanese mistress, Aki Hayashi, back to England with him. He had no money and no job with which to support his extended *ménage* of mistress, wife and two children. An unexpected reconciliation with Mary on his arrival home had only complicated things further and in any case had not lasted. By spring 1929 he had filed for divorce.

Sassoon wanted to help, but was wary of interfering in his private life. So that when Ottoline wrote, urging him to advise Blunden to persuade Miss Hayashi to return to Japan, he felt his 'flawless friendship' with Blunden was being threatened and refused to do so.[3] He did, however, offer to be guardian to Blunden's son John, a suggestion made mainly in the hope that it would help Edmund to remain close to his child. Mary indignantly rejected Sassoon's offer[4] and he confined himself on the whole to more practical assistance. A generous present of money was followed by a great deal of string-pulling on Blunden's behalf with members of the Royal Literary Fund, which resulted in a grant of £500 for Blunden in February 1928. But Blunden, through a mixture of unworldliness, generosity and heavy financial commitments, was never solvent for long. By early 1928 he was in desperate need of more money and set about earning it in the only way he knew, his pen. An avalanche of reviews, articles and books poured from him, including the work he had been trying to write since the War itself and by which he would become best known, *Undertones of War*.

Both *Undertones* and *Infantry Officer* are, in one sense, a reaction to Eric Remarque's *All Quiet on the Western Front*, which had irritated Sassoon not just because of its sensationalism, but also because it gave 'no place names' and left 'everything vague'.[5] It seemed to him the 'exact opposite' of Blunden's approach. He had been reading Remarque's book while writing *Infantry Officer* in 1929 and it undoubtedly strengthened his determination to be factually precise. Like Tolstoy's *War and Peace*, which he was also rereading while he wrote his own book, it is the combination of factual detail and direct personal experience vividly rendered that makes *Infantry Officer* a convincing and compelling picture of war.

When Graves's autobiography, *Goodbye to All That*, was published in 1929, it represented all that Sassoon was anxious to avoid. (Ironically, it would become, together with *Undertones* and *Infantry Officer*, one of the three most popular war books of this period.) His criticisms of *Goodbye* are, in a sense, a reverse manifesto of what he was trying to achieve in *Infantry Officer*. He had read it in November 1929 while he was writing *Infantry Officer* and felt it could not have appeared at a worse moment: the book 'landed on my little edifice like a Zeppelin bomb', he told Graves.[6] It seemed to him that Graves had 'blurted out [his] hasty version' like a hack journalist with scant regard for accuracy, the 'antithesis' of his own method.

Sassoon ended by saying that he was 'extremely glad' that Graves was making a lot of money from the book and informing him that he had left him money in his new will, a provocation, intended or otherwise, that Graves dealt with in his usual robust and witty fashion: 'Signing fat cheques for your friends: the indelicate irony of it is that had you thought of signing one when you heard of "my troubles" – which left us all without money – I would not have been forced to write *Goodbye* to contribute to the work of restoration, and you would not have had the Zeppelin-bomb.'[7]

Sassoon believed that Graves was jealous of his 'affinity' with Blunden,[8] but it is possible that the reverse was true and that Blunden was not averse to widening the growing rift between Sassoon and Graves.

Even without Blunden's intervention, however, it is unlikely that Sassoon could have accepted Graves's book, which was the last of a series of irritants in their relationship.

As Sassoon admitted to several friends later, however, his 'quarrel' with Graves was caused almost entirely by the latter's 'subjection to Laura Riding'.[9] Graves himself had argued, in his pithy reply to Sassoon's long letter of complaint, that Sassoon's 'homosexual leanings' had already created 'several cross-currents' in their relationship before Laura's advent, notably his jealousy of Nancy and his fear of her when, according to Graves, she fell in love with him.[10] Ironically, it was just as Sassoon was finally becoming reconciled to Nancy that Laura had taken her place in Graves's life. In spite of repeated efforts to like the American poet, Sassoon was 'finally driven away by her intense egotism and eccentricity'.[11]

He was also unable to accept Laura's extreme Modernist views and their effect on Graves, which made Sassoon feel like a lumbering 'intellectual Pickford Van'.[12] Nor could his essentially conservative nature accept the extraordinary *ménage à quatre* Laura set up with Graves, Nancy and a married Irish poet, Geoffrey Phibbs. So that when Laura, suspecting that she was losing Phibbs to Nancy, attempted suicide by swallowing poison and jumping from a fourth-floor window, he was unable to sympathize. He did not go quite as far as Nellie who, on hearing incorrectly that Laura would certainly die, said 'good riddens [*sic*] to bad Rubbish'; *he* was simply 'appal[led]'.[13]

The most significant aspect of this interminable quarrel, which like most had two sides to it, was its effect on *Infantry Officer*. Apart from making Sassoon determined to get his own facts right, it also presented him with a problem. His mounting hostility towards Graves had already caused him to omit his meeting with him in November 1915 from *Fox-Hunting Man*, important though it was. And this was what he first resolved to do in *Infantry Officer*. He had though eventually to include him as a crucial element of the plot, but their relationship was essentially finished.

Sassoon's struggle with the Graves material is only one of a number of confrontations with his past he was forced to make in writing *Infantry Officer*. As he told Ottoline the day after completing it: 'Psychologically it has been an extraordinary tussle, but I hope it has relieved my mind.'[14] If it had relieved his mind, however, it had not done so sufficiently, since there were four more books of reminiscence to come.

Sequels rarely sell as well as the book that spawned them and *Memoirs of an Infantry Officer* was no exception. But its sales fell very little short of those of *Fox-Hunting Man* at the start.[15] This was due partly to lucky timing. Just as Sassoon's war poems had been published at a point when the public was ready to respond to their anti-war message, so his first two prose accounts of the War appeared at the height of the genre's popularity. A few years earlier and they might, like Ford Madox Ford's Tietjens tetralogy of 1924 to 1928, have attracted little attention. A few years later and they would possibly have suffered the fate of the last book in Sassoon's trilogy, *Sherston's Progress*, which was not published until 1936 and is the least well-known of the three.

Sassoon had intended to complete *Sherston's Progress* much earlier. Fired by the success of *Infantry Officer* in autumn 1930, he planned to start work at once on another volume of memoirs. Not only would this enable him to utilize the Craiglockhart material he had reluctantly abandoned at the end of *Infantry Officer* and write about Rivers, as he longed to do, but it might also distract him from the deteriorating situation at Wilsford. By late 1930 Nurse May was making life very 'uncomfortable' for him there because (he believed) the 'vixen' was 'jealous' of his relationship with Stephen. So he sat down resolutely to write a third volume of Sherston's 'Further Experiences',[16] but by the beginning of January 1931 he had abandoned the project.

He faced a number of problems; he was dealing with the least exciting period of his war-time experience and he would find it difficult to explain his stay at Craiglockhart without reference to his literary side. The main reason for his failure to continue with Sherston, however, was Stephen's behaviour. Sassoon's poetic sensibilities had exposed him to intense suffering in the past, but he had never felt so desperate as he did during this period. It was, he told Robert Nichols with only a little of the latter's tendency to exaggerate, 'death in life'.[17] (The echo of Coleridge's suffering Ancient Mariner was probably deliberate.) Sassoon was no stranger to uncertainties and he had actually enjoyed the dangers of hunting and even the perils of life at the Front, but this constant playing with his most powerful feelings was to lead him for the first time in his life to contemplate suicide:

> Just to go out and leave my life behind, –
> This writing left unsigned; click off the light,
> Close the door quietly on the house; and find
> An empty road and windless winter night.
>
> Not like a traveller starting before day,
> Who smells adventure on the early air;
> But asking only peace to be away
> From Time's mean street and those who wrangle there.

Just to forget and be myself no more.
Thus have I mused. Yet life still guards the door.[18]

It may have been a subconscious death wish which led to his unusually high number of accidents and illnesses during this period.[19]

He had found it difficult enough to write his two previous prose books, being naturally more drawn to poetry. Now, profoundly depressed by Stephen's behaviour, he could write only verse and filled his notebooks with attempts to express his desolation. Though the majority of them fall short of his best work, they are an invaluable record of his feelings. [20]

One effect of Stephen's rejection was to make him even more conscious of his age, and the passing of youth is a recurrent theme. He specifically called one poem 'Farewell to Youth' and another, untitled, unpublished piece opens with the stark words, 'Youth gone. Midnight and winter', and closes with a clear reference to Stephen: '... and the last syllable said/ Of the one love that gave him back his youth,/ And then betrayed him.'[21] His most successful exploration of the theme, published, like 'Farewell to Youth', in *Vigils*, is 'The Hour-Glass', which centres round the arresting image of himself, rather than Father Time, 'holding an hourglass in his hand':

> ... Deriving intimate omens from the trickling sand:
> Intent on Time's device which casually contains
> The world's enigma in its quietly falling grains.
> Myself I see; for whom the idle moments pass
> From *is* to *was* in that *memento mori* glass; ...   (*CP*, p. 224)[22]

Another effect of Stephen's withdrawal was to force Sassoon to look for other meanings in life, and the poems of the early 1930s reveal a search for spiritual values. In July 1932, at the height of his suffering, he told Edith Olivier that 'religion [was] the mainspring of his life and that he [thought] a Poet is a Prophet'.[23] This belief emerges in his poems not just in an increasingly religious vocabulary[24] but, more significantly, in their content. 'The mind of man environing its thought', for example, which Edith Sitwell considered among the best poems he had ever written, was originally called 'World Invisible' and ends with a plea for spiritual enlightenment:[25]

> World undiscovered within us, radiant-white,
> Through miracles of sight unmastered still,
> Grant us the power to follow and to fulfil.[26]

It would be many more years before Sassoon turned fully to religion, but the process was undoubtedly started here in the early 1930s.

For the time being, however, his verse was his religion. Edith Olivier believed that he found in poetry-writing 'a complete release from the cloud over him', as he had during the War, and his output increased dramatically. So that, although Stephen may be held largely responsible for the delay and possibly the comparative failure of *Sherston's Progress*, he can also be seen as the goad which led to the writing or revising of all seven poems in *The Road to Ruin* (1933), half of the thirty-five poems in the trade edition of *Vigils* (1935) and half a dozen of the forty-two poems in *Rhymed Ruminations* (1939, 1940). Sassoon himself was convinced that the deprivations imposed on him by Stephen resulted in some very good work between 1930 and 1933, resulting partly from 'sublimated sexual energy'.[27]

However consoling he found poetry, Sassoon still needed his friends, particularly those who were close but not too close to Stephen. Edith Olivier, for example, grasped the situation better than most and proved a great comfort. Her understanding of Stephen's temperament prevented her from antagonizing Sassoon, who was still not ready to hear any real criticisms of his beloved. 'The problem,' she wrote in her diary on 26 February 1931, 'is really insoluble. Sieg. adores Stephen so much that he can't endure separation and is convinced that he alone can make him better ... Stephen believes only Nurse May can cure him so that he *must* stick to *her* now and [that he and Sassoon] are not compatible.'[28] On the other hand, she knew how 'wounded' Sassoon must be by Stephen's 'unkind' behaviour: 'But Stephen is quite irresponsible,' she noted a month later. 'He's like a half fairy creature – captivating and cruel.'[29] She did her best to soften each blow as it came. The most practical way in which she helped was to offer Sassoon somewhere to stay in the district now that Wilsford was closed to him, and they were to spend many evenings together in the next few years. Edith was at the centre of a large circle of people and kept Sassoon in touch with the outside world.

Another lifeline during this time was the company of two people who were even nearer to news of Stephen, being part of the Wilsford staff. They were the sisters Beryl and Eileen Hunter, who worked in the garden. Sassoon's friendship with 'Really and Truly', as he nicknamed them, had begun when he had taken up riding again in July 1930.[30] They were both horse lovers and had gladly helped him look after Bruno. The middle-aged daughters of a Captain Hunter, who lived in the nearby village of Lake, they were better read than most of the Wilsford staff. They had started buying Sassoon's books long before they met him and he rewarded their admiration with signed copies of his later works. Like many other local people, who nicknamed him 'Don Quixote', they saw him as a valiant knight coming to the rescue of their 'young lord', Stephen.

Sassoon delighted in the Hunters' devotion; his bruised ego needed all the comfort it could get after Stephen's battering. Nevertheless, it was an odd alliance that grew up between himself and the sisters during his exile from Wilsford. For a start they were unmarried and almost the same age as himself, whereas most of his female friends had previously been either safely married, like Delphine Turner, or significantly older, like Ottoline and Edith Olivier. But it is clear that for all their adoration, Beryl and Eileen were no threat to him sexually. Rather masculine in their ways, they were manual workers at a time when that was much less usual for women, they rode a motorbike together, knew all about cars and seemed more interested in animals than people on the whole. Their greatest devotion was to each other.

The other initially odd aspect of this relationship was Sassoon's readiness to become friendly with Stephen's gardeners. The Hunters, however, were less working-class than their occupation suggested at the time and less of a challenge to Sassoon's class consciousness than might at first appear. Impoverished circumstances had forced both their father and themselves to find work at Wilsford after the War, which had brought about great social changes. But they remained essentially middle class.

One useful aspect of Beryl and Eileen's former social standing was that it enabled them to provide Sassoon with an introduction to the local hunt. So on 17 January 1931, after almost eight years' abstinence, he had a day out with the Wylye Valley Hounds.[31] Edith, who had driven over to the meet at Berwick St James with Walton's mistress, Princess Imma von Doernberg, delighted in the irony of the situation: 'The rest of the field little knew that they had the "Fox-Hunting Man" with them, but thought he and his horse were both beginners!'[32]

The experience, for all its shortcomings, left Sassoon determined to buy himself a real hunter and less than a fortnight later he was in possession of a twelve-year-old mare, Silvermane. Unfortunately, he had bought the horse while still under the impression that Stephen would 'want him to be with him a good deal'.[33] When the opposite proved true, the Hunter sisters came to his help, putting Silvermane up in their own stables and doing their best to exercise the high-spirited horse.

Sassoon came to rely on them heavily, especially for news of Stephen. Shrewd, outspoken and down-to-earth, with a healthy sense of humour, they were ideal informants. Anyone less sympathetic to Stephen would have angered him, anyone more so could not have identified with Sassoon as completely as they did. They quietened any guilt they felt about their role as spies by telling themselves that it was for Stephen's own good and that a reconciliation with Sassoon was his only hope.

Sassoon was particularly dependent on the Hunters during the first year of his exile while he was still trying to establish his own base in the district. He had moved temporarily to a nearby hotel after the sisters' attempts to find him suitable rented accommodation had failed.[34] And in March he decided to accept Walton's suggestion that he should join him and Imma in Switzerland for a break. For the moment his patience had run out. Still unable to live without news of Stephen, however, he was grateful for Beryl's and Eileen's promise to keep him informed.

Walton had written to Sassoon on 8 March from Ascona, almost certainly at Imma's suggestion. She had met Edith's handsome friend only very briefly before they went to see him hunt in January, but had followed Edith's report of the unfolding 'catastrophe' with Nurse May indignantly.[35] Walton had to

be in England on 23 March to hear his Viola Concerto played by the great
Lionel Tertis and to discuss the performance of *Belshazzar's Feast* at the coming
Leeds Music Festival[36] and Sassoon could return with him to Switzerland on 29
March for an 'entire change'.[37] As an added incentive he argued that Sassoon
would be able to settle down and do some work.

Hoping Walton was right, Sassoon agreed to his plan and duly travelled
back with him to Switzerland. But in spite of Walton's industrious example,
he wrote very little successful verse during his two months there. Apart from
tinkering with old poems, he produced four new poems at Ascona, but only one
('To a Red Rose') was published.[38] He was beginning to despair of producing
anything significant in poetry. His parodies of Humbert Wolfe, *Pinchbeck Lyre*,
were published by Duckworth on 15 May, but it was two years since he had
produced a serious book of poems.[39]

In spite of his inability to work well at Ascona, however, he did feel 'much
more at liberty in [his] mind' and stayed six weeks longer than his intended
fortnight, suggesting that he enjoyed himself there.[40] Situated in southern
Switzerland on Lake Maggiore, it had all the advantages of magnificent views,
constant sun and mountain air. Being only two miles from the Italian border,
it offered the amenities of ordered Swiss life without any of its drawbacks, an
attractive mix of two very different cultures.

Walton was by no means the first to discover this Utopia. It had been colonized
by artists and freethinkers since the end of the nineteenth century, including a
wealthy Belgian, Henri Oedenkoven, who had bought a hilltop overlooking the
little fishing village and named it Monte Verità, the Mountain of Truth.[41] It was
here, in a hotel founded by Oedenkoven, that Sassoon stayed. Thinking his own
pension too modest for his wealthy friend, Walton had recommended the Monte
Verità as much for its extraordinary art collection of Picassos, Matisses, Braques
and Chinese painters as for its dramatic views. Its only fault in Sassoon's eyes
was its inability to serve a 'decent' cup of tea, a situation he quickly remedied:
'You would laugh if you could see me with my electric kettle, making myself
secret cups of tea in my room,' he wrote to Ottoline towards the end of April. 'I
am like an old Almsman – content with "a pinch of tea and a twist of bacca".'[42]
Already settled into lifelong routines, he was beginning to lose what youthful
flexibility he had once possessed. His tea-making activities would become a
familiar ritual to his friends in his old age. Walton and Imma walked over from
the nearby Casa Angelo most evenings for coffee and a chat.

Until this point Sassoon's relationship with Walton had consisted mainly of
favours granted on his side and requests for further help on Walton's. Both of
them lived mainly for themselves and their art. But with the introduction of
Imma into the equation this changed and they grew closer for a time. Imma
herself became especially fond of Sassoon and was clearly attracted to him
physically.[43] There is evidence to suggest that Sassoon also felt some sexual
attraction towards her.

Sassoon was still obsessed with Stephen, however, and waited anxiously for news of him from the Hunters at Ascona. In April Beryl reported the negative effect his leaving had had on Stephen and Nurse May's increasing domination over her patient, though she was finding it difficult to ward off Stephen's undesirable friends without Sassoon's help. Beryl also promised they would let him know the results of Dr Snowden's imminent visit and on 23 April Eileen told Sassoon the good news that Stephen had been pronounced free of TB. He now seemed much happier, promising to show Beryl Sassoon's 'lovely' postcards from Ascona and 'murmuring about the prospect of a future that includes you'.[44]

Sassoon was not deceived. Doubly exiled as he was in Switzerland and able to rely only on Stephen's unreliability by this time, he wrote in resignation and despair:

> To all my happiness I say
> Farewell. I tell my listening heart
> 'Put all your deep desires away
> Henceforth we two must live apart.'[45]

Even when Beryl wrote to tell Sassoon on 16 May that Stephen had sent Nurse May packing – 'Oh marvellous jubilant day!' – and that her replacement, Miss Turnbull, seemed 'an awfully good sort', he was unable to rejoice.[46] He could only hope that Stephen would be led by wiser counsels, such as his aunt, Margot Asquith, and Edith Olivier, to a full reconciliation with himself.

Encouraged by some more positive reports, Sassoon decided to return to England at the end of May[47] and was rewarded by a few days with Stephen in late June. Though the patient was 'full of affection' and invited him to return to Wilsford the following weekend, however, Sassoon's trust had been destroyed. He was by now convinced of what Stephen's new nurse had warned him, that Stephen played on his feelings about his health to an 'unfair degree', and he resolved to 'try to be more firm' and 'assert [his] independence'.[48]

Stephen's invitation was, predictably, cancelled and Sassoon set about asserting his independence. He decided to stop hanging about Wilsford and embarked on a 'five-weeks "season" of Operas and Sitwells and asking old friends to lunch at the Hyde Park Hotel'.[49] The Sitwells' friendliness seems to have increased as his closeness to Stephen declined and June and early July passed pleasantly enough.[50]

Sassoon's next assertion of independence was to accept Anzie and Wendela Boreel's generous invitation to stay at Bray in their absence, 'the Ideal Invitation' he wrote to Max, who knew and sympathized with the Stephen situation,[51] pinpointing unintentionally what was, in fact, his own most serious bar to a close relationship: 'No one is so sociable as I am, when I am alone.' It is significant that the majority of his strongest friendships were kept up mainly by letter. But he did accept the Wyldes' invitation to join them at Cannes, where they had a yacht, and spent part of August with them.

By 25 August he was alone again and more depressed than ever about Stephen. His mood was not helped by the political situation, which was at crisis point. While he had been toying with the idea of taking a luxurious holiday at Ascona in March, Britain had been facing an economic slump. Sharp rises in unemployment in July and dire warnings by the Bank of England shook national confidence further, prompting Sassoon to return briefly to his all but abandoned satiric vein 'Mammoniac Ode'.[52] By 23 August 1931 the entire Labour Cabinet of Ramsay MacDonald had resigned. The following day MacDonald had been invited to form a national government with the Conservatives and the Liberals to deal with the emergency.

The situation was equally precarious abroad. As Sassoon's stay with Walton and his German princess had made him aware, the Nazis were increasing their hold in Germany. Worse even than the private implications for people like Imma was the threat to international peace. As Maynard Keynes had warned at the Treaty of Versailles, the punitive treatment of Germany and her war reparations had inevitably led to great hardship and Hitler was now exploiting his countrymen's discontent. By the summer of 1931, less than thirteen years after the Armistice, Sassoon to his dismay saw war looming again.

His depression about this and his own personal situation persisted throughout September, which he spent at Ipsden near Oxford, in an attractive Queen Anne house he had rented from the writer Rosamond Lehmann. Lehmann, who had established her reputation with her first novel, *Dusty Answer*, in 1927, had been a friend of Stephen's since before her marriage to Wogan Philipps (later Baron Milford) in 1928 and Sassoon had first met her at Wilsford. One of a series of women friends he appealed to in this crisis, she had tried her best to help, having reason to be grateful to him for his advice over her brother John Lehmann's first book of poems.[53] But like all his other allies, she was unable to make any headway with Stephen, who by early September had refused to see Sassoon 'ever again'. Sassoon's alleged crime had been to turn up at Wilsford unannounced and catch Stephen without his make-up. 'I have given up expecting to see him,' Sassoon told Ottoline at the end of the month.[54]

Unfortunately Sassoon could still not resign himself to the inevitable and was looking for rented accommodation near Stephen. Yet his decision to live near Wilsford at such a time was not as perverse as it seems. He had missed Wiltshire, which gave him 'a sense of freedom and untouched country life', had lived for the whole summer in large, well-appointed houses in the midst of beautiful surroundings, and returning to a small flat in London appealed to him less and less.[55] 'I get so nervy and distracted in London,' he told Hodgson.[56] He had also grown to love riding again and his horse added to the equation.

By the end of September he had made his choice from the 'wad' of house descriptions sent by Beryl at his request, Fitz House in the village of Teffont Magna, ten miles from Salisbury. 'It looks simply topping,' Eileen Hunter reported; 'the flagstones, lavender and mullion windows are certainly all there, to say nothing of a burbling, crystal-clear stream, and a steep little orchard at the back.'[57] The trout-filled stream ran past the front gate and the house could only be reached by a small bridge. Described (rather misleadingly to modern eyes) as a 'Gentleman's Country Cottage Residence', it was an impressive, stone-built, thatched edifice dating from about the fifteenth century, standing in three acres of ground. A converted barn served as a garage.[58] Edith Olivier, who had rented it with her sister from the owner, Lord Bledisloe, just after the War, was equally enthusiastic about the interior.[59] A stone-flagged hall led to drawing room, dining room and library, all of them oak-beamed, with servants' quarters behind. Upstairs there were three good-sized bedrooms and a fourth single one, ideal for a small sitting room.

The village and its surroundings were equally attractive. It was also a good centre for hunting and, at fourteen miles from Wilsford, Teffont Magna was sufficiently far for Sassoon to keep away if he wished, but near enough to reach it when necessary. If Sassoon needed company Edith was only a few miles away at Wilton. A 'sort of rural Heaven', according to one of Sassoon's first guests there, Ralph Hodgson, Fitz House represented the pre-industrial England to which Sassoon was emotionally drawn, 'that "pre-lapsarian" world he so much preferred to the real one', as Hodgson's biographer puts it.[60]

After some perfunctory bargaining Sassoon agreed to the landlord's terms, which included taking on Fitz House's existing staff, a married couple named Lapworth, and a full-time gardener. Though when Sassoon signed the lease in November 1931 he intended Fitz House only as a weekend retreat, he quickly settled down to live there.

The effect on his work is noticeable. Living permanently in the country hastened his return to what Blunden believed to be his true path, pastoral poetry. 'November Dusk', for example, clearly emerges from his rural situation, as well as giving some of the flavour of his life at Fitz House.[61] A related effect of living in the country again was to remind him sharply of his childhood love of nature, and several of the poems written at Fitz House are a celebration of that time, like '6' in *Vigils*, originally entitled 'First and Last Love':

> It was the love of life, when I was young,
> Which led me out in summer to explore
> The daybreak world. A bird's first notes were sung
> For childhood standing at the garden door ...   (*CP*, p. 211)[62]

One poem, first called 'Childhood Recovered', opens: 'Down the glimmering staircase, past the pensive clock,/ Childhood creeps on tiptoe, fumbles at the lock'. Another piece, originally entitled 'Past and Present', explicitly refers to his early years at Weirleigh and mourns 'Simplicities unlearned long since and left behind'.[63]

Without Stephen to entertain, Sassoon reverted to former habits and wrote what poems he could after dinner, leaving the mornings free for riding. The Hunters were delighted at 'Captain' Sassoon's almost daily visits to their stables and continued to report on Stephen's doings. Having become almost as critical of his new nurse as his old, they were convinced that Miss Turnbull's well-meaning intercession on Sassoon's behalf had actually made matters worse. Stephen simply felt 'coerced'.[64] After another of his aunts, Mrs Adeane, had failed to bring him to his senses, Nan Tennant had attempted, no more successfully, to plead Sassoon's cause. The only good news was that Stephen's general health had improved and that the latest X-rays still showed no recurrence of TB.

Sassoon had, with some misgivings, decided to tell Stephen of his move to Fitz House, secretly hoping that he would relent and agree to see him. When he refused, Sassoon was forced to find other distractions, book-buying chief among them. His youthful taste for book-collecting had been sharpened over the years by Blunden and Hodgson, and it was Hodgson who now stimulated his revival of interest. Since leaving for Japan in 1923, Hodgson had kept in close touch with Sassoon, responding enthusiastically to each of his poetry books as they were sent to him. He had been equally positive about Sassoon's prose, describing *Fox-Hunting Man* as 'nature (human) with a pen! A thing of glory!'[65] and urging him to continue the series.

Sassoon had been too busy with *Fox-Hunting Man* when Hodgson took his first sabbatical from the University of Sendai in 1927 for them to see as much of each other as they would have liked. But in October 1931, when he returned for his second furlough, Sassoon had almost unlimited time for him and on 10 November they set out in Sassoon's Packard on a book-buying tour of the north-east. Having decided to start at Hull, little as it appealed to Sassoon's romantic soul, they worked their way down through Yorkshire, Lincolnshire, Norfolk and Suffolk, visiting at least seventeen bookshops on the way.[66]

'Those five days were a joy for ever,' Sassoon told Hodgson, echoing a mutual favourite of theirs, Keats. He had loved the way Hodgson sang on the journey, 'usually without words', though on one occasion he included the lines of an old song taught to him by the poet Edward Thomas.[67] They also planned an anthology together of the 'small, neglected authors' they loved so much, like Thomas Ashe, Primovard Dugard or Charles Dalmon. This was never completed but their detailed notes for it reveal the extraordinary breadth of their reading in out-of-the-way places. One extract they intended to include from William Camden's *Remains*, 'Epitaph for a Man Killed by Falling from His Horse', is particularly interesting since it led directly to the writing of one of Sassoon's favourite poems. The words 'Betwixt the stirrup and the ground/ Mercy I asked, mercy I found' haunted Sassoon from the moment Hodgson quoted them to him on their trip and lay behind the writing of 'The Merciful Knight' eight months later.[68] Though Graves could not see 'any use in appealing for "mercy from long ago"',[69] Sassoon seldom derived such pleasure from one of his own poems: 'I keep repeating it to myself in a quiet ecstasy,' he told Hodgson, 'and loving its music and the Pre-Raphaelite pictures it evokes.'[70] The concept of 'mercy' had become even more attractive to him since Stephen's apparent lack of it had caused him so much suffering.

Hodgson was one of Sassoon's few visitors at Fitz House when he came to stay with his latest bull terrier, 'Pickwick', in June 1932. Sam Behrman, unable to entice Sassoon up to London, had visited briefly in April on his way back to America via Southampton, but other close friends were too busy. Blunden had been elected a Fellow of Merton College, Oxford, in March 1931 and was in any case preoccupied with a new collection of Owen's poems he was editing at Sassoon's suggestion. Sassoon still felt too emotionally involved with Owen to undertake it himself, as he explained to Blunden: 'I have always suffered from an obscure difficulty in clarifying my friendship with him – perhaps because the loss of him was a shock which I never faced squarely – coming as it did at the most difficult time, when I was emotionally and physically without any foundations.'[71] Blunden's own emotional involvement with the young journalist, Sylva Norman, which began in early 1932, was another reason he saw so little of Sassoon this year.

Glen also was too busy to visit Fitz House much in 1932. His first child had been born in September 1930 and christened George, partly in Sherston's honour.[72] (Sassoon had naturally been asked to be godfather.) Trying to combine his family and career left Glen little free time, but he wrote to Sassoon regularly, as he would continue to do until the latter's death.

For a social life Sassoon had to rely on Edith Olivier and other sympathetic neighbours. By mid-1932 he was already on close terms with the Bonham Carters at nearby Stockton House. As he told Hodgson, he became 'very attached to Cressida and Laura and their little brother Mark'.[73] The omission of the young Bonham Carters' mother, Lady Violet, from the list is noticeable.[74] Sassoon had reason to be grateful to her, since she persuaded Stephen to see him twice that August. She also introduced him to a distinguished circle of people, which clearly impressed him however blasé he appeared to be. Viscount Esher and his wife, for instance, were regular visitors and became keen collectors of his books. And Lord and Lady Desborough, whom he had not visited for seven years, managed to persuade him back to Taplow Court when they invited themselves to Stockton House with the express purpose of seeing him. Sassoon was not quite so pleased to meet Winston Churchill again at Violet's, this time dismissing Churchill as a 'fiend', presumably for his lone rearmament campaign from the back benches.

Sassoon openly admired Violet's political acumen and was very appreciative of her hospitality, but he also had serious reservations about her. For one thing he suspected that she was in love with him, a suspicion her letters to him appear to support.[75] He also felt that, in spite of her avowed devotion to poetry, his in particular, Violet held very different values from his own and was probably no less worldly than her stepmother, Margot Asquith. (His nickname for Violet was 'Flamingo'.[76]) Literature, like politics, was an elaborate game to Violet and her kind, he believed.

When she left on holiday with her family for North Berwick in September 1932, however, he missed her greatly and felt lonelier than ever. It had been a bad year overall, though he had been comforted by the award of an Honorary D.Litt. from the University of Liverpool in December 1931.[77] He had been saddened by the death of Helen Wirgmann in March. And his mother had developed an abscess on her appendix at Christmas, which became so serious that she was encouraged to make her will early the following January.[78] Then on 21 January, the day of her operation, Stephen suffered another severe haemorrhage, suggesting a return of TB. Nellie had also been very ill during the winter and was not expected to live.

As 1932 passed it became clear that Stephen's physical health was not the only problem. His family grew increasingly anxious about his behaviour, which was becoming more outrageous than ever. Not only had there been an 'incident' with a soldier on Salisbury Station during one of his rare outings in 1931, but he was in trouble with the police again in summer 1932. They had managed to hush things up when he had got into difficulties over soliciting soldiers as a teenager, but he was now a grown man and responsible for his actions. When Sassoon took Sam to Wilsford in April 1932, in the faint hope of being allowed to see Stephen, the visit left the American with 'an impression of evil, intensified, somehow by the surrounding beauty'.[79] Sassoon had bitterly compared this 'poisoned beauty' to Henry James's sinister setting in *The Turn of the Screw*, and as Sam watched an unsavoury 'flamboyantly dressed and arrogant young man' admitted to Stephen's quarters directly after Sassoon had been refused access, he could only agree.

Sassoon explanation to himself was that Stephen was 'a "dual personality". One part, vain and chic and sophisticated – behaving in terms of his abnormal temperament; the other ... as he won my devotion.'[80] Sir Henry Head was inclined to agree with him and recommended a nerve specialist, Dr George Riddoch, with whom he and Rivers had worked in 1920. Riddoch, in turn, advised treatment at the Cassel Hospital for Functional Nervous Disorders, known as 'Swaylands'. Founded in 1919 by Sir Edward Cassel, it based its treatment on experience gained from shell-shock cases during the War and was not unlike Craiglockhart. Situated at Penshurst in Kent, it was only ten miles east of Weirleigh, a factor which influenced Sassoon in its favour.

After a great deal of cajoling by Violet Bonham Carter and some straight talking from Nan Tennant, Stephen was persuaded to accept Riddoch's advice and left for Swaylands in the autumn of 1932. He had already started his game of cat-and-mouse again, encouraging Sassoon to pay fortnightly visits to him at the hospital, then telling him 'not this week'.[81] But Sassoon allowed himself to hope again. Stephen's new specialist, Dr Ross, had told him that Sassoon was 'good' for him, and Stephen was very much under the influence of his new doctor. Ross had persuaded him to talk about his 'tragic disability', Sassoon told the Heads – a coy reference to impotence, which Sassoon believed to be the source of all Stephen's difficulties. And Stephen loved talking to Ross, 'who banish[ed] bogies very cleverly', he told Sassoon. Stephen seemed positive about his relationship with Sassoon for the first time in two years.

Sassoon had suffered too deeply from Stephen's capriciousness, however, ever to trust him fully again. He was also conscious of the truth of Forster's shrewd analysis that Stephen might 'get much better, but ... will be worried by his own behaviour to you, and will incline to see people who know nothing about it'.[82] So that when Stephen once more refused to see him, at the end of February 1933, only a week after sending him a Valentine message, 'O Siegfried, how faithful is this heart', he was not wholly unprepared.[83] Though still 'loitering about in his vicinity', he had already started to think of Stephen as 'a sort of idea of happiness which will not return'.[84] In fact, he seems to have hastened the end, consciously or not, by issuing an ultimatum to Stephen. 'Can't you hear the best thing in your life being strangled, while you lie there locked in with your obsession?'[85] he asked him, finally prepared to 'say goodbye' if the response was negative.[86]

Nevertheless, when the end came he was devastated. Stephen's cruel response was severe. Conveyed through an embarrassed Dr Ross, it left no room for doubt:

> 22 May [1933]
> Dear Captain Sassoon,
> Thank you for your letter. Mr Tennant told me that he had received a letter from you, but he has not read it and I do not think he intends to.
> What I am now going to say is something I have nothing whatever to do with, except that I have been asked to pass it on to you as a message from him. I do not know why, but since your last visit his feelings towards you have not been what they were. He says that you upset him and make him feel ill, and that he cannot see you again. I know that he has done this before, and that you will probably feel he is a very impossible person. He is of course not well, and that is about all there is to be said for it. I know also that I encouraged you to come in the Autumn, because I thought that your visit did him good: but as he says he does not wish to see you now, I can obviously do nothing further in the matter.
> Yours sincerely,
> J.A. Ross[87]

It was the last turn of the screw, one of the most important turning points in Sassoon's life, and one that would lead him in directions he could never have predicted.

27

'O, Hester, You Must Redeem My Life'[1]

1933-1938

Stephen had overplayed his hand and would come to regret it bitterly. In rejecting Sassoon so callously through his doctor he had underestimated Sassoon's pride and overestimated his patience.[2] He had also made no allowance for chance – or Edith Olivier.

Edith was still sympathetic towards Stephen in 1933. Like most of his friends she believed that his mental breakdown was largely a delayed reaction to the deaths of the two people he had needed most, his mother and Nannie. But she was also shocked by the effect his behaviour had on Sassoon, who was unable to hide his suffering from her. In a deliberate attempt to distract him she insisted that he accompany her to the George Herbert Pageant at Wilton on 7 and 8 June 1933. And for it she provided him, rather optimistically, with a female partner, Hester Gatty.

Edith had known the 27-year-old all her life. Hester's mother's family, the Morrisons of nearby Fonthill Abbey, had been famous collectors and patrons of the arts and Edith had been close to two of their four children.[3] She had campaigned for their son, Hugh Morrison, when he became Conservative M.P. for Salisbury in 1918 and would later help their daughter (Hester's mother) Katherine, Lady Gatty, with her own mother's unfinished account of her life at Fonthill and Carlton House Terrace. Hester, like Sassoon, was suffering from the after-effects of a failed love affair and Edith undoubtedly hoped that they might help each other to recover. One of Hester's two younger brothers, Richard Gatty, was also invited to join the Wilton party, together with Glen Byam Shaw and his wife Angela.[4]

Sassoon was clearly more interested in the company of Glen and Angela, who were staying with him, than that of a young lady, however well connected. He was no more enthusiastic at the pageant itself, feeling both embarrassed and hot in his elaborate costume of an Elizabethan bard. Caught on camera, he stares uncomfortably into its lens, awkward in his velvet doublet, ruff and knickerbockers, frozen in time at the very moment his life is about to take one of its most unexpected turns. He is not yet aware that Hester Gatty, looking 'a dream in an oyster silk Caroline dress' according to Edith, will shortly replace Stephen in his affections and, in less than six months, become his wife.[5]

Though Sassoon afterwards claimed to have felt a 'strong affinity' with Hester, at the time she merely struck him as a charming young woman and he made no effort to see her again.[6] Hester herself seems to have had other ideas and at the beginning of September booked herself into the Black Horse Inn at Teffont Magna, only a few hundred yards from Sassoon's house. Her ostensible reason was artistic, to paint the village and its surroundings, but it is more likely that she was hoping to meet Sassoon again. Unfortunately, Sassoon failed even to recognize her when he passed her painting in the village street on 3 September. It was hardly an auspicious start, but Hester was determined, and, when they exchanged pleasantries two days later, identified herself as his fellow-guest at Wilton. An invitation to Fitz House for dinner that evening duly followed. Good manners dictated that he should be hospitable to a friend of Edith's and in any case he was very lonely.

Sensitive, well-read and artistic (she wrote poetry, composed music and played the piano as well as painted), Hester evidently shared enough with Sassoon to make her interesting company.[7] She also had a 'good brain' and 'lovely nature', according to Edith, who also enthused about her 'quiet serene beauty' and 'voice like an echo'.[8] Sassoon's first impression had been of her 'clear and gentle voice' and 'wide bluish-grey eyes'.[9] Just as importantly, like Stephen, she was twenty years younger than Sassoon, a great admirer of his work and ready to play the devoted acolyte.[10]

Love quickly followed that first evening, especially once Sassoon was convinced that, like all his previous lovers except Novello, 'she needed protecting'.[11] She herself had invited his pity when she told him of her recent recovery from a nervous breakdown after her failed love affair. Slim, dark and not unduly feminine in figure, she had a boyish look and reminded Edith, for one, of Stephen. It was not a huge transition from the young male figure to hers and Sassoon quickly found himself attracted to her. He began to entertain her daily, driving her about the Wiltshire countryside, taking her to visit the Hunter sisters (perhaps for their approval) and giving her dinner each evening at Fitz House. By the time she left she had spent more time painting in his garden than the village and they had made arrangements to meet again soon. 'Strong affection' was turning into romantic love.[12]

There was one major stumbling block in the way. Though Sassoon had mentioned his 'friendship' with Stephen, he had been unable to match her frankness about her past love life. 'What can I do?' he asked himself at the beginning of October. 'I can't say to her, "Look here, I am forty-seven, and have never had a love affair with a woman. The best thing you can do is never see me again."' After being taken home to meet her widowed mother at Ossemsley Manor near Bournemouth, however, he realized that Hester was 'gently leading' him away from Stephen.[13] For his strongest impulse had been to rescue Hester from the rather stifling atmosphere of Lady Gatty's ornate, over-furnished house.

The crisis came when they met again only five days later on 7 October in London. Sassoon now felt that he was in love with her 'physically as well as mentally' and the last obstacle crumbled.[14] That afternoon he talked to her explicitly about the past six years of his life and her sympathetic response convinced him that a future together was possible. When they travelled back to Salisbury together the next day he told her of his feelings. The following day, Sunday, 9 October, he formally proposed and was accepted. The white swan flying across the sky at the pageant rehearsal, he told the 'ecstatically happy' Edith, had clearly been 'Stephen passing out of his life'.[15]

It was a huge relief to Sassoon, Edith's account of him at this time suggests: 'He looks well and unnervy – laughing and chuckling and kicking up his heels. Like a young *hunter*, as well as a fox-hunting man!'[16] 'I can only sum all up,' he wrote to the Heads, who had shared most of his suffering over Stephen, 'by saying it is as though my good angel had arrived in human form. My previous life seems to have been a sort of purgatory in which I was being taught to use the real happiness which has come at last with a sense of peace and security I can't describe.'[17] Henry Head, he knew, would understand how extraordinary the psychological impact had been for him. For a younger man to turn from homosexuality to heterosexuality, as Robert Graves and Glen Byam Shaw had done, is not so unusual, but for someone of forty-seven it was a complete overturn.

The most obvious explanation is that he was on the rebound from Stephen and punishing him, though Stephen himself put a more flattering interpretation on it: 'Don't you think, Siegfried, [he asked] that it was because you and I had set such a high standard of happiness together – that when it all smashed, you had to marry in the endeavour to create a state of happiness as much like it as possible.'[18] Another strong motive was undoubtedly social. The difficulties of homosexual relationships in the days before it was legalized may have attracted men like Auden, who appears to have felt it added spice to them, but Sassoon needed social respectability. Hester may have represented the solution.

Hester's family background was an equally important factor. Solidly upper-middle-class, they had some distinguished connections. Not only was her mother a Morrison of Fonthill, her mother's brother married to a lady and her mother's sister married to a viscount, but Hester's father had been knighted for his services as Chief Justice of Gibraltar.[19] Sassoon was even more impressed by the fact that Sir Stephen was the younger brother of the popular nineteenth-century children's writer Juliana Horatia Ewing, whose books he had already started collecting. Sir Stephen Gatty's mother, Margaret Gatty, also a successful children's writer, was herself the daughter of Nelson's private secretary and chaplain on the *Victory*, Alexander Scott.[20] It was a reassuring mix of the Establishment and the artistic. In addition, Hester's family had money.[21]

Hester was not the first well-connected, wealthy young woman to pursue him, however, and there were other equally important considerations. Apart from the sexual frustration of a highly sexed man, he had strong needs in a different direction. 'I, too, have longed for children,' he had written at Weirleigh as long ago as January 1919, when his passion for Gabriel was at its height, and time had increased that longing. The birth of Glen's son in 1930 and his affection for the Bonham Carter children had brought it to the forefront of his mind, as had his growing reputation: sales from his work were so high that he had to pay £739 super-tax in 1933, a large amount of money for the time. But there was no one to whom he could pass on his name. A friend who knew him and Hester well later on had no hesitation in saying that 'he married to have a son' and that he viewed her mainly as 'the mother of his child'.[22] And with all those 'gifted Gattys' and 'financially famous Morrisons' behind her, she promised to be good breeding stock.[23]

Sassoon was almost certainly influenced too by Glen's successful switch from a homosexual to heterosexual lifestyle. (Graves's marriage had not been so successful, but his taunt about Sassoon's 'emotional shortcomings' in October 1933 may have helped propel him towards matrimony.)[24] Glen's wife, Angela Baddeley, may also have contributed to his change of heart. For she was one of an increasing number of women he had grown fond of in the late 1920s and early 1930s. Beryl and Eileen Hunter, Imma von Doernberg, Edith Olivier and Rosamond Lehmann had all made him feel that he could trust women, and, where none of his male friends had volunteered, had tried to help him over Stephen.

There was no real question of a romantic interest with these women. But there was one curious relationship between 1930 and 1933 which he concealed from all his friends and which may have paved the way for Hester.[25] The person concerned was Doris Gertrude Westwood, an unmarried woman in her thirties of middle-class background and independent means, who wrote to him mainly from Digby House, Sutton Coldfield, where she lived with her mother when not staying at the Ladies International Club in Bayswater, London. A writer herself, who had studied playwriting at RADA and had had one novel published by the time she contacted Sassoon, she was intelligent, educated and cultured.[26] She was also sensitive, romantic and vaguely religious, a follower of Mahatma Gandhi and half-believer in Christian Science.

An ardent supporter of animal rights, Doris first wrote to Sassoon on 25 February 1930 after reading *Fox-Hunting Man*. She admired him as a poet, particularly one who had protested publicly against the War, in which she appears to have lost her fiancé. But she was shocked to think of him hunting, a sport of which she strongly disapproved, and had refused to read the book on publication. When she eventually did so, however, she felt that 'no book could have told the story of fox-hunting with less cruelty or, perhaps, less enthusiasm for the "kill" itself', and praised its 'gentleness and humanity'. Her ostensible reason for writing was to 'apologize' for misjudging him, but it is clear that she was hoping to strike up a correspondence.

Though Doris's letters started as fan mail, they quickly developed into something more personal. At first this centred round her sympathy for Sassoon as his relationship with Stephen deteriorated, the tone very rapidly becomes even more intimate: she has already requested a photograph of him and sent one of her own; now she addresses him (where he is staying in Switzerland) as 'O Kangar-among-the-mountains' and tells him that spring has refused to arrive in England in his absence.[27] By the beginning of 1932 she is assuring him of her 'love' and offering to come to Teffont Magna 'if [she] thought it would be any help to [him]'.[28] Her suggestion that she should book herself into the village inn contrasts revealingly with Hester's much bolder decision to stay at Teffont Magna *without* asking Sassoon and indicates less insight into his character.

It is at this point that Sassoon appears to panic, since shortly after his reply there is a long silence from Doris. Her next letter, on 5 November 1933, is one of shock at having read of his engagement in the newspapers: 'It is the last thing I ever expected to happen and I feel like you did when S[tephen] shut you out. Only this is worse because I have always been outside waiting for the day when you would let me in and you have never done it.' Two more letters follow and, in July 1934, he finally has to ask her to stop writing to him now that he is married. Her final letter is one of embarrassed apology and a horrified refusal of his invitation to meet him and his wife when they are next in London.

Though Doris's letters end, however, she continues to explore her powerful feelings for Sassoon in fictional terms. In *An April Day* (1934), her third novel, almost certainly written during the most intense period of their relationship in 1933 and early 1934, the heroine falls in love with 'the lonely hermit' Kester Carmichael, who eventually rejects her advances in spite of an evident attraction to her. Not only is the allusion to 'Hester' obvious in Doris's choice of her hero's unusual first name, but Kester himself strongly resembles Sassoon. Even his house closely resembles Fitz House, which Doris knew from a secret pilgrimage she made to the West Country to visit all the places Sassoon had mentioned in his letters.

Doris's fourth and final novel, *Humble Servant* (1936), suggests that she is still struggling with her unrequited love for Sassoon and attempting to exorcise her feelings in a more radical way. With a similar mingling of real-life details, or subversions of them, and a plot of her own invention, she makes her hero a young German prince reminiscent of Sassoon's young lover Prince Philipp of Hesse, who bears a strong physical resemblance to Sassoon as well as his unusual middle name (for a man), Loraine, with its distinctive single 'r' spelling. In this version of events, there are two main bars to a successful relationship with the novel's heroine, the prince's royal responsibilities, which he is reluctant to shoulder, and the heroine's age: at forty-two she is approximately the same age as her creator, Doris, and more than twenty years older than the hero. His attraction for her is never in question and they fall deeply in love, the problems of a future together conveniently resolved by the prince's assassination on the last page of the novel. Having killed Sassoon off in fictional terms, Doris writes no more novels.

Edith Olivier, who knew nothing of Doris Westwood, believed that Sassoon was eventually 'inspired ... to leave Stephen for Hester' by a quite different woman, whom he scarcely knew, Rachel MacCarthy.[29] She was convinced that it was seeing the newly-married David Cecil, who had come to live nearby, 'watch his dear little elfin wife [Rachel] with satisfied eyes of love' that had finally persuaded him.[30] Another marriage which certainly did influence him was that of Edmund Blunden and Sylva Norman in July 1933, which appeared to make Blunden very happy.

An even more decisive factor in Sassoon's conversion, however, was his meeting in 1933 with Geoffrey Keynes, later an eminent surgeon and bibliophile. A friend of Bartholomew and younger brother of the economist and prominent member of the Bloomsbury Group, Maynard Keynes, Geoffrey appeared to have no problems with his bisexuality. Influenced perhaps by Bloomsbury's frankness on sexual matters, he made no secret of his attraction to men. Sassoon would later warn a young friend about to set out on a camping trip with Keynes: 'You'd better be careful; he likes young men.'[31] The poet Andrew Motion, who was introduced to Keynes because of his schoolboy pilgrimage to Rupert Brooke's grave on Skyros and stayed with him fairly often after that, remembers that his host's goodnights were 'fairly intimate'.[32] It was 'quite clear', Motion said, that 'I was more interested in boys than girls' at eighteen (his age at the time) and Keynes would come into his room last thing at night and sit on his bed, though not go 'beyond a certain point'.[33]

Yet Keynes was happily married and the father of four sons. Sassoon had assumed from an early age that his own sexuality was fixed for life and confined to one sex, but Keynes's attitude challenged both those assumptions when they met in June 1933, just a few months before Sassoon's second meeting with Hester. Geoffrey made marriage seem attractive as well as possible. Though one of Sassoon's most recent friends when he married, Keynes would be among the few he invited to his wedding.

Keynes had first written to Sassoon on 10 April 1933 as Bartholomew's literary executor, to tell him of the librarian's early death at the age of fifty and to offer Sassoon his choice of book from his valuable collection. In his reply Sassoon had told Keynes to 'look [him] up' sometime, a suggestion which quickly became an invitation to spend a weekend at Fitz House as soon as possible.[34] Flattered by Keynes's praise of both his poetry and prose, *Fox-Hunting Man* in particular, he also saw him as a potentially useful and interesting contact. Keynes had been the literary executor of Festing-Jones as well as Festing-Jones's great friend Samuel Butler. In addition he had an expert knowledge of typography and shared Sassoon's love of old books. Not only could he be relied on to prevent the sale of Sassoon's letters to Bartholomew and the privately printed books they had produced together, but he would make an ideal replacement for him as a designer of future productions by Sassoon.

Keynes's own collection of books was, to use Sassoon's word, 'scrumptious', including such priceless items as original loose plates from Blake's *Songs of Experience* printed by the poet himself, together with several of his paintings.[35] A man of enormous energy as well as enthusiasm, Keynes was an insatiable and also highly competitive collector, unable to let a bargain slip through his hands. And once he had bought one book by an author who really interested him, he might begin to collect the rest of their works, often going on to compile their bibliography, usually the first in the field.[36]

A further point of contact between him and Sassoon was the fact that Keynes had served as a major in the Royal Army Medical Corps during the War. Sassoon had always respected the regimental doctors and was still in touch with Dr Dunn. Keynes's pioneering work in blood transfusion methods with badly wounded soldiers was particularly impressive, one more manifestation of his extraordinary range of abilities.

Like most of his friends, Sassoon found Keynes's energy both admirable and daunting. The young Dennis Silk, with the advantage of forty-four years over Keynes, felt 'stupefied' with tiredness by the end of a stay with him: 'he had the energy of ten men'.[37] The wide spread of his interests, which included entomology, woodcarving, bricklaying, croquet and mountaineering, added to his knowledge of both the arts and the sciences, made him seem out of place in the twentieth century. 'I always think of him as a seventeenth-century man,' Sassoon told de la Mare after knowing Keynes almost twenty years, but Keynes might have seemed even more at home in the Renaissance or the Victorian age. (Either would have been appropriate, Andrew Motion believed, 'so long as it emphasized his pioneering spirit'.)[38]

One of Keynes's favourite roles was that of host, either in his London house or current weekend retreat. The poet Jon Stallworthy remembers hearing Keynes talk to the English Club at Rugby about his contemporary there, Rupert Brooke, and being invited shortly afterwards to stay with him in the country. 'Hospitality at Lammas House', Stallworthy writes, 'was absolute.'[39] So that, while Keynes enjoyed his weekend at Fitz House on 24 June 1933, he was insistent that for their second meeting he must be host. Only a fortnight after the Wiltshire visit, therefore, Sassoon found himself staying at the Keynes's family home in Arkwright Road, Hampstead.

One of Keynes's motives in persuading Sassoon to visit him in London was to show off his library, also another of his enthusiasms, the ballet. His brother Maynard, whose homosexual liaisons had been a feature of the early Bloomsbury Group, had surprised many people by marrying the Russian ballerina Lydia Lopokova in middle age and Geoffrey himself was enchanted by the Russian Ballet. He took Sassoon to see them twice during his first London visit from the 10-12 July and sympathized when Sassoon expressed interest in a male dancer called Shabelevsky . Encouraged by Keynes's openness about his attraction to men, and having told him about his affair with Stephen at their first meeting, Sassoon arrived in London carrying his diaries for the period, which Keynes pronounced 'the story of two splendid lovers'.[40] Sassoon also gave him photographs of himself and Stephen, whimsically captioned 'the oak and the butterfly'.[41]

Another important feature of Sassoon's first visit was his introduction to Keynes's wife, Margaret, one of the four Darwin sisters and granddaughter of Charles Darwin. She made him an ideal wife, running his busy household, bringing up their children yet accepting his interest in young men.[42] Supportive but not interfering, she conformed closely to the role Sassoon believed wives should play. Many of the marriages Sassoon had witnessed previously had seemed a constraining rather than enlarging influence and he had been critical of a number of his friends' wives. The Keyneses' suggested that other models existed and he found Margaret 'the kindest and best of souls'.[43]

Sassoon's second stay with the Keyneses, at a house they had rented for a family holiday in August, certainly seems to have increased his receptiveness to marriage, and Keynes was one of the first people he told of his engagement in October. Two days after that he took Hester to meet Geoffrey and Margaret.

Keynes believed that marriage would help Sassoon recover from Stephen, a relationship which could never have succeeded in his opinion. His concern was all for Sassoon, whom he was anxious to help in any way possible. As Stallworthy notes: 'He had his vanity – he knew he was a good craftsman (in some crafts "the best") – but his formidable energies were directed by a deeper modesty in the service of other people: patients, friends and artists.'[44] For Keynes, Sassoon was 'Merlin', a creature of magical powers, who had every right to stay in his cave if he so wished and to demand service of himself, 'Pellinore'.[45] When Sassoon asked his advice on a limited edition of his poems in June 1933, for example, he organized the whole production of what would become *Vigils* with both taste and efficiency. In spite of a rather brusque manner, which went with his clipped moustache and tall, spare figure, Keynes was exceptionally kind and helpful towards Sassoon. Not only would he take charge of his privately printed books for the next twenty-five years, with one exception, but he would also deal with any medical problems that arose. And though only six months younger than Sassoon, he would frequently chauffeur him round the country in later years. He was, in Sassoon's own words, an 'unfailing friend'.[46]

Sadly, Sassoon would quickly begin to take Keynes's many good qualities for granted and fasten on his weaker points. His favourite jibe, initiated unwittingly by Keynes himself in relation to his book-collecting, was 'Jackdaw Keynes'. Sassoon interpreted it more negatively; he seriously believed that Keynes lacked 'the finer shades' and had 'no aesthetic absorption of beauty'.[47] The difference between Keynes and himself, he asserted with an evident sense of superiority, was 'the difference between a typewriter and sensitive handwriting'.[48]

It was an extraordinary and unfair claim for Sassoon to make, considering how much he would profit from Keynes's counsel. That he should frequently ask Keynes's advice about which poems to include in his collections over the years is hardly the act of a man who believed that Keynes lacked literary judgement.[49] Dennis Silk, Jon Stallworthy and Andrew Motion all testify to Keynes's love of literature. Keynes had encouraged the young Stallworthy to read the poems of John Cornford (his godson), for example, and had insisted on giving an edition of them to him, together with many other books. And he loved his wife to read Jane Austen to him as they drove up to London from their weekend house.

It may be that Sassoon and Keynes were just too unlike to be really close friends. Apart from superficial differences in taste – Keynes was not remotely interested in cricket or riding, nor Sassoon in mountaineering or croquet – they were completely opposite personalities, Keynes a practical, energetic extrovert in direct contrast to the (as he saw it) 'illogical', introverted Sassoon.[50] Sassoon once described Keynes as his 'antithesis'.[51] Nevertheless they *were* friends and remained so, with only a few minor differences, until the end of Sassoon's life. And in his fairer moments Sassoon acknowledged that Keynes was 'a man of very fine quality'.[52]

*

On 9 November 1933, a month after his engagement to Hester, *The Road to Ruin* was published and Sassoon was able to show her proof of his credentials as a writer.[53] The collection, unfortunately, contains neither the best nor the most characteristic of his poetry, but it does highlight his growing concern with the international situation. Five of its original seven poems appeared in the *Spectator* and the *New Statesman* in March 1933, the month Sassoon had written to Ottoline: 'The state of the world, as seen in *The Times*, alarms me. The bullying of intelligent people in Germany must be perfectly horrible.'[54] His despair is even more evident and the causes of it much clearer in a second letter to her a week later: 'To me it is as though the powers of darkness were winning. Poor old Ramsay [MacDonald] letting off his perorations about peace, with all that cynicism and armament manufacturing in the background, and the French really believing that the Germans will bomb Paris .... And P[hilip]Sassoon playing Winston's game at the Air Ministry.'[55] He found it difficult to believe that there were individuals all over England who still 'derided "pacifism"' and that the Church appeared to be supporting the idea of war. He was particularly shocked by a letter from Archbishop Temple in *The Times* and wrote to Temple himself on 19 April 1933 to argue the pacifist cause.[56]

Sassoon's own position was virtually unchanged from 1918 and the media had used him throughout the 1920s and early 1930s to represent the pacifist cause. His *War Poems* had been published to mark the anniversary of Armistice in 1920, for example, and the *Daily Mail* had reprinted 'Aftermath', with its persistent question: 'Have you forgotten yet?' in November 1927 for the same purpose. As late as 1934 the *Spectator* would offer its readers 'Ex-Service', two mordant stanzas by Sassoon to mark the sixteenth anniversary of the Armistice.[57] And he would still be appearing on the Reverend 'Dick' Sheppard's Peace Pledge Union platform to read his anti-war poems as late as 1937.

While working on *The Road to Ruin* Sassoon had been reading *Why War? Open Letters between Albert Einstein and Sigmund Freud*, and his slim volume is prefaced with a quotation from Einstein which represents his own position in 1933 and highlights his scorn of the profiteers that had marked his position in the First World War.[58]

Sassoon himself must have suspected that *The Road to Ruin*, like *Satirical Poems,* was a wrong turning since, apart from the two poems added when it was reprinted in *Collected Poems* and a few more included in *Vigils* and *Rhymed Ruminations*, it was his last concerted attempt at war poetry. The gap between the idealistic young army officer and the older, more disillusioned civilian was simply too wide to bridge.

The failure of *The Road to Ruin*, which Sassoon himself later described as 'just a nightmare',[59] affected him less severely than usual, however, since the week it was published he and Hester suddenly decided to bring forward the date of their wedding and there was a great deal to do. Any poetry he had written before he met her now felt like something he had 'discarded'.[60]

The ceremony had originally been planned for April 1934, but by 9 November, Sassoon was anxious on several fronts. As Nellie had triumphantly reminded him the previous week, his engagement had been in 'a good many papers' and he feared further media intrusion.[61] He also wanted to get the wedding over as soon as possible: 'I begin to feel that by getting engaged and then hiding I am affronting all my (few) real friends,' he explained to Keynes in late November.[62] Part of the strain he felt was in dealing with his friends' evident surprise at the event and answering their many letters. He was also very much in love with Hester – 'Rapture reigns over us,' he wrote a month after their engagement[63] – and may have been impatient for the consummation of their marriage. On the other hand he may have feared such a radical change and be anxious to have it behind him.

Whatever the explanation, he and Hester were married 'very quietly' by private licence at Christchurch Priory, near Bournemouth, on 18 December 1933, a Canon Gay (by chance) officiating.[64] The choice of church had been fairly straightforward. Christchurch was approximately five miles from Hester's family home and a relatively easy drive from Fitz House; it was also convenient for the most illustrious of the wedding guests, T.E. Lawrence, who was serving as 'Aircraftsman Shaw' at Southampton, no distance at all for the powerful motorbike he liked to ride.

Lawrence was one of only five friends Sassoon invited to the wedding, the others being Glen, Geoffrey Keynes, Rex Whistler and Edith Olivier. His mother was not well enough to attend, though she had expressed complete approval of Hester when Sassoon took her to visit in late October, and the matchmaker, Edith, appropriately stood in for her. Hester, attended by her mother, two brothers and a Morrison cousin, had also invited very few friends and the wedding, as planned, was a quiet and solemn affair.

While T.E. Lawrence had his doubts about the wisdom of the marriage, Keynes rejoiced in it, though his greatest excitement was the 'heaven-sent opportunity' to meet at last with Lawrence of Arabia, who had long been one of his 'top heroes'.[65] Placed opposite him in the church, he could 'gaze [his] fill at the small but strongly built man, with a pink face and a shock of yellow hair'.[66] He was even more delighted when, at the end of the ceremony, he had a long conversation with Lawrence, the two of them leaning on opposite sides of his motorbike, 'Boanerges'.

Edith was equally thrilled by the marriage, for which she felt largely responsible. But she was also worried by Stephen's reaction to the news, which was to retire back to the bed he had so recently left. He was to remain in bed until the following April, his mental state still very precarious, as Edith realized when he appeared late and unannounced at her house one night, clothes thrown on carelessly over his pyjamas. She was shocked by the bloated appearance of the once willowy Stephen, but relieved to note that he remained 'so utterly his wayward self in spite of the disguise of the fat'.[67]

Sassoon had written Stephen a 'kindly-worded letter' about his engagement at Keynes's charitable suggestion,[68] but he found it hard to sympathize with him after his recent behaviour and had ignored his plaintive question, 'Would you like me still to be your friend?' For the rest of his life Stephen would swing between self-condemnation – 'This evening I am unhappy thinking how selfish

I was to you' – and self-pity – 'All my friends chucked me away – as you did when you married.'[69] Rex he considered one of the worst traitors and even Edith came in for some criticism. But since no one really held him responsible for his actions, most of his friends went on humouring him and the only thing he really lost by Sassoon's marriage was Sassoon himself.

Stephen's immediate reaction on first hearing of Hester had been to hope that she was not too attractive, but when he eventually met her in the early 1940s he quite liked her. So did Sassoon's other homosexual friends. Though they were probably all as amazed as Stephen at Sassoon's sudden change of allegiance, only Bob Gathorne-Hardy and Forster were frank enough to question it, though Forster was quick to reassure Sassoon as well:

> I didn't suppose you had acted other than rightly, [he wrote on 8 November 1933] and I shan't seek T.E. [Lawrence]'s or anyone else's opinion on her and shall like to meet her. But Siegfried, you mustn't expect me at my age to take on new intimacies. I am wonderfully pliable but I am nearly 55. You are entwined with my past and with my future so far as I can come at it with that past. To ask what doctors might call a 'certain question' and which I shouldn't ask unless I was very fond of you: – Have you had an emotional and physical overturn? Your news, though I accepted it as good news, startled me.

Even T.E. Lawrence, who feared among other things that 'marriage would conventionalize' Sassoon, quickly succumbed to Hester's charms, though he had serious doubts about the marriage's chance of survival.[70] 'Fancy taking on SS,' he wrote to another friend, Nancy Astor, describing Hester as a 'foolhardy creature'.[71]

Sassoon's married friends were equally enthusiastic about Hester. Blunden and his new wife Sylva showed their approval with their own 'Amalgamation' of 'Prose and Verse in Honour of Siegfried and Hester', including an original poem by Blunden and some prose by Sylva, the whole written out beautifully by hand.[72] Glen and Angela rejoiced for Sassoon, and the Heads were relieved and delighted. Even Graves, whose cool request for 'about £1,000' Sassoon had indignantly refused that year, sent his 'good wishes'. [73]

Sassoon's women friends, some of whom were also close to Stephen, were equally pleased for him, with one or two significant exceptions. Nan Tennant, Beryl and Eileen Hunter and even more emotionally involved friends like Ottoline and Florence Hardy, rejoiced at his escape from Stephen. Nellie's loyalty to Sassoon overcame her deep-rooted suspicion of young women: 'and, above all, what a score off on [sic] Stephen', she wrote gleefully on receipt of the news: 'He will ... now find out who is [sic] true friend was.'[74] And Rosamond Lehmann was so happy at the news that she presented the Sassoons with her dog 'Sheltie', to whom Sassoon had become greatly attached while renting her house.[75]

Violet Bonham Carter and Edith Sitwell were manifestly less happy. 'V.B.C. has been a bit odd about it,' Sassoon told Nan Tennant: 'Her only reference to Hester so far was in a long and hysterical letter asking me to go and see her – "Bring Miss Gatty". "Bring your umbrella", would have been much the same!'[76] Edith made her jealousy less obvious, telling Sassoon she was 'thrilled and delighted' at his engagement, but remarking caustically in private to her sister-in-law: 'I suppose the bridal pair will want to adopt S[tephen] T[ennant].'[77]

Hester and Siegfried's honeymoon in Spain completed what was, according to someone who knew them both well, 'a dream thing' – the meeting at a pageant in exotic clothes, the whirlwind courtship, the romantic marriage in a beautiful old priory, the ancient manor house they were negotiating to buy.[78]

Algeciras had been chosen not just for its warmth, but because it was Hester's favourite place.[79] (Her father had retired as Chief Justice of Gibraltar the year before her birth, but she knew and loved southern Spain.) By a fortunate coincidence it was also *not* Germany or Italy, the two countries in which Sassoon had spent his previous 'honeymoons' with Philipp, Glen and Stephen. This did not prevent him suggesting a visit to Sicily, however, and after a few days at Malaga he and Hester passed three weeks at Syracuse, the scene of so many memories of Stephen.[80]

Then, in an almost exact repetition of that previous visit, on their way back to England, he took Hester to Rapallo to meet the Beerbohms. Staying at the same hotel (the Bristol) and following a similar routine of long lunches with Max and Florence and return dinners at their hotel, it might almost have been winter 1929 or spring 1930 again. Since, for once, Sassoon kept no record of the visit it is impossible to know how he felt about this. Nor do we know for sure how the Beerbohms regarded his change of partner. Like the rest of his married friends, they probably rejoiced for him. 'He only cares for himself,' would be Max's caustic, final word on Stephen.[81]

*

In May 1934, only a year and a few months younger than he had planned, Sassoon took possession of the house he had imagined in his diary on 27 March 1923 and looked forward to the lifestyle he had then envisaged. After their marriage, he and Hester had stayed for a short time at Tunbridge Wells to be near Sassoon's mother for Christmas, then spent a week in a suite at the Hyde Park Hotel, London, before returning to live in Fitz House until they left for their honeymoon at the end of January 1934. When they came back from Spain and Italy in May, however, it was to the place they had discovered together during their engagement, Heytesbury House.

Hester had liked Fitz House, but the lease was short and indefinite and in any case Sassoon had grander ideas. He wanted somewhere even more suited to the fairy-tale nature of their romance. He also still missed the luxuriousness of Wilsford Manor and may even have needed to compete with it. When it came to buying his own house, he was determined to erase his childhood shame at

Weirleigh's lack of elegance, which Hester's substantial income added to his own now enabled him to do.

Neither of them wished to leave the district, so counted themselves lucky when they discovered that Heytesbury House, two miles from Warminster and only fifteen miles from Teffont Magna, was for sale. A great yellow-grey stone mansion standing in 220 acres of park and woodland in the heart of the Wylye Valley on the edge of Salisbury Plain, it was the kind of house Sassoon had dreamed of. All his life he had been drawn, perhaps partly because of his foreign blood, to characteristically English things – hunting, cricket, English landscapes – and Heytesbury House seemed to him 'the epitome of timeless and unchangeable England'.[82] Set well back from the village of Heytesbury and the main road, it was visible only in glimpses through the magnificent trees that surrounded it.

Heytesbury had a long and romantic history, another of its attractions for Sassoon. Occupying the site of what was thought to have been a manor house belonging to the twelfth-century Queen Matilda, it still retained a medieval dovecote and barn.[83] The house itself had been rebuilt several times, most recently about 1700 as a red-brick house with a clock tower and garrets. In 1780 this was re-faced in Bath stone and later given other classical touches, including an imposing Grecian portico on the entrance front.[84] The last Lord Heytesbury to live there had died in Sassoon's own lifetime, another inspiration for a poem.[85]

With its seventeen bedrooms, six large reception rooms, separate service wing and numerous additions, Heytesbury House was already an anachronism in an age when servants were rapidly becoming a thing of the past. Its high ceilings, numerous large windows and long stone passages also threatened exorbitant heating bills in winter. The sale price was high, more money would have to be spent restoring the estate to its former glory and a small army of servants hired to maintain it.[86] But none of this deterred Sassoon, who clearly relished the thought of becoming lord of the manor and squire of Heytesbury. 'Captain' Sassoon, ambling along on horseback, was to become a proud feature of village life, a fact Sassoon very much enjoyed.

He was not unaware of the inconsistencies of his position as a one-time socialist and his attempts to rationalize his situation are diverting. 'I must break it to you that Heytesbury is a *large* house,' he wrote to the most egalitarian of his friends, Hodgson, about the fifty-two-room mansion he was about to buy, 'but you will not mind its size when you see it. We shall live very simply and quietly there, and at last I shall have a home which will be an earthly paradise for my few real friends to see me in. So don't be alarmed. Everything will be just the same, only nicer.'[87]

Sassoon did succeed in making Heytesbury what a later friend, Joe Ackerley, agreed was 'an earthly paradise' and Keynes thought a perfect setting for a writer who 'valued solitude but could no longer complain that he was lonely'.[88] He failed conspicuously, however, in his resolve to live 'very simply and quietly'.

He and Hester returned to a lifestyle of some grandeur, though they both denied their need for it. One of Sassoon's biggest outlays over the next few years would be the replanting of Heytesbury's sadly depleted wood. He wanted an avenue of acacia and lime and forty new bay trees, each representing one of his favourite poets, a scheme which gave rise to 'An Emblem', the opening of his next volume, *Vigils*.[89] In another poem Sassoon envisaged old Lord Heytesbury returning from the dead to take his favourite woodland walk and seeing:

> ... plumed acacia and the nobly tranquil bay;
> Laburnums too, now small as in the prosperous prime
> Of your well-ordered distant mid-Victorian time ...
>
> ('In Heytesbury Wood', *CP*, p. 234)

Heytesbury appears regularly in Sassoon's poetry from 1934 onwards, often as setting, sometimes as the subject itself.[90] But it is doubtful whether the move benefited his work as a whole. Representing as it did a further retreat from the modern world, it seems to have strengthened his already reactionary views on literature. For as Ackerley noted when he visited Heytesbury in the 1940s:

> One could fade away here, of course, like a plant, flower and fade and never be seen. It is the enclosed eighteenth- and nineteenth-century world. In all the houses I was brought up in, when one walked out of the front door one walked smack into the life of the world, passers-by, tradesmen, cars, one jostled against life; here no, one walks into such a vast Garden of Eden of one's own, pre- or post-Eve, that one is entranced and has not the desire to go beyond, to go out of the great gates, for all one wants lies inside. No adventures, therefore, except the adventures of nature, the turn and fall of the leaves, song of birds, encounters with rabbits, squirrels and foxes – no adventures here.[91]

Sassoon's most successful poetry had arisen out of conflict; glimpses of paradise tended to slacken his verse, though he refused to accept this himself. He was convinced that Heytesbury was an ideal setting for the kind of poetry he believed he wrote best, the meditative, pastoral verse which its privileged rural calm invited.

Yet another effect of Heytesbury on his poetry, at least to begin with, was to dry it up. Captivated by the enchantment that the estate laid on its inhabitants, he had little time for verse in 1934 and his output dropped dramatically. He and Hester remained under its spell for the rest of the year 'like children alone in the world', as T.E. Lawrence observed.[92] One of the Sassoons' first guests in July, he felt as if he were making an invasive 'raid': 'All visitors there intrude, as yet, I think,' he told Keynes: 'The huge house ... the gardens, so lavishly kept up, the quiet sun-impregnated park: the two laughing strangers running about it, making pretence to own it. Yes, Heytesbury was rather like one of the great villas of Roman Britain, after the Legions had gone.'[93] A shrewd observer of mankind, Lawrence could not help thinking that Sassoon seemed 'abnormally' happy, though he rejoiced to see the change in his friend.

This feeling of almost unreal happiness continued throughout the summer. The first edition of *Vigils* had been printed in May 1934 and finished copies were ready by August, all twenty-two poems of this limited edition having been engraved on copper by Charles Sigrist. Keynes had taken immense care and Sassoon and Hester were 'enraptured' by the 'beauty' of the production.[94] It was partly to 'gloat' over *Vigils'* attractions that the equally enthusiastic bibliophile, Lawrence, had visited in July.[95] 'What an iconic stillness there is about his images now! He has progressed from flesh-and-blood (in *Counter-Attack*) to bronze ...One of the good things about S.S. is that he changes freely and completely.'[96] Lawrence's lavish praise would not be echoed by the majority of the critics when *Vigils* appeared in a trade edition the following year, but for the moment Sassoon could enjoy a feeling of success. He was to include all twenty-two of the pieces, plus the thirteen added to the trade edition, in his *Collected Poems*.

*

A more immediate pleasure than work was entertaining friends, who came for long weekends during the summer in a pattern that would continue throughout the 1930s, old friends like Marsh, de la Mare, Cockerell, Tomlinson, Lord Berners and H.G. Wells. (Bennett had died in 1931.) In their first summer at Heytesbury in 1934, besides Lawrence and Edith Olivier, he invited Ottoline, who had met and liked Edith but had still to inspect Hester. Geoffrey and Margaret Keynes also came and Sassoon's favourite nephew, Hamo, his brother's youngest child, who stayed for a few days on his way back to Sherborne School. Blunden also brought Sylva, a visit Siegfried and Hester had rather feared since she was reputed to be a determined, intense, somewhat neurotic woman, obsessed by physical fitness. In the event they both liked her and she became a regular visitor with Blunden for the next few years.

One reason the Blundens began to visit so often had to do with Blunden's own particular obsession, cricket. Unlike Sassoon, who had played only occasionally since his pre-war games, Blunden had remained loyal to the sport and was delighted when Sassoon took it up again in earnest. One of Sassoon's first tasks on returning from honeymoon had been to organize the renovation of the village cricket pitch, which lay within his own grounds a few hundred yards from the house.

Naturally he became captain of the local team, though he was by no means its best player. He could not sack any of his outdoor staff, he told Swinnerton, because 'three-quarters of the gardeners represent our two best bowlers and the wicket-keeper'.[97] One of his greatest pleasures in the game was arranging annual matches between the Heytesbury XI and Blunden's Mertonians (the Barnacles), an enjoyment unspoilt by Blunden's superiority as a cricketer. Another pleasure was the blow-by-blow analysis which followed each match, either at tea in Heytesbury's old kitchen wing, or over supper in one of Merton's lecture rooms.

As autumn approached cricket was replaced by hunting. And just as he had tried to involve Hester in his cricketing activities (she was allowed to keep the score), so he now made sure that she was included in the hunt, finding a suitable horse for her as a matter of priority. The day the opening meet of the local hunt set out from Heytesbury House marked his real 'comeback', he told the Heads, from his miseries over Stephen, 'a sort of apotheosis of my apotheosis!'[98]

As T.E. Lawrence had predicted, however, 'the barometer [could] not always stand so high' and 1935 opened badly, with Hester suffering from 'internal troubles' following an attack of chicken pox the previous October.[99] Almost certainly a reference to gynaecological problems, this probably explains the fact that she was not yet pregnant. From Sassoon's pride in announcing her pregnancy later in the year (September), it is clear that they were both hoping for a child. The reference to her 'internal troubles' may even be a euphemism for a miscarriage, which is how her September pregnancy would end.

But it was not just Sassoon's disappointment over the 'little Sass' he had so gleefully announced to all his friends that marred 1935. Hester's problems in September also put an end for a while to visitors while she rested upstairs in a vain attempt to save the pregnancy. Hamo Sassoon, for instance, was not invited to stay as usual on his way to Sherborne School in the autumn, but had to wait until Hester was thought strong enough for visitors. At the age of fifteen Hamo already had many interests in common with his uncle – cricket, music, art, literature, the countryside. He also formed a link for Sassoon with life at Matfield, on which he reported regularly, including the sad fact that one of Sassoon's childhood friends there, the carrier Tom Homewood, was dying of cancer and a shadow of his former self.

During his early visits to Heytesbury, Hamo noted a curious feature of the Sassoons' marriage, which would become more significant later on: as he and his aunt prepared to retire for the night, Sassoon would sit down at his large writing table with the words 'I stay', resisting all Hester's pleas to accompany her to bed. After almost a year's rest from writing, by late 1935 he felt an urgent need to get back to it. This was partly for financial reasons, since the upkeep of Heytesbury was even higher than expected, but also because writing was his *raison d'être* in a way that Hester, however miraculous she still seemed, could never be. The problem was that marriage made it even more difficult to write than living with Stephen had, mainly because of his irregular working habits. All his 'best writing', he explained to Hamo, was achieved when he stayed in bed most of the day and worked till 5 a.m.[100] It did not bode well for the future of his marriage.

Sassoon had already sounded an ominous note in his diary in late 1934, less than a year after the wedding: 'Protective and possessive love can never realise that it can be a bit boring at times – lovely sweet Hester, why can't you realise this?' Hester, he was complaining to Keynes by August 1935, allowed him no time to 'relax and ruminate' and he was beginning to find her constant attention suffocating.[101] It made it virtually impossible for him to carry on with *Sherston's Progress*, which he had taken up but quickly abandoned in the spring of 1933. Now, in November 1935, he was determined to complete it. Considering that Hester had just suffered a miscarriage, however, his attitude towards her was remarkably self-centred. He actually 'banished' her from Heytesbury for five weeks that same month at a time when she must have been feeling very low indeed.[102]

The trade edition of *Vigils* was published by Faber on 4 November 1935, with thirteen poems added to Keynes's limited edition of 1934. The fact that none of these additional poems were inspired by Hester is significant. Though the book was dedicated to her, it was largely inspired by Stephen. The absence of love poetry from his work, noted by a curious fellow-soldier in 1916, had been rectified after the War by a succession of male lovers, but would not return with Hester. Sassoon may even have blamed her, subconsciously, for *Vigils*' poor reception, another cause for unhappiness in 1935. Certainly the largely negative reviews of *Vigils* help to explain his determination to finish another prose book. His poetry was increasingly becoming the target of Modernist critics.

Friends rallied round in private. It was reassuring to read that Edith Sitwell, herself a pioneer of Modernism, believed that *Vigils* included 'some of the finest poems' he had ever written: 'They are so truthful, bare, controlled, and fiery, and deeply moving.'[103] She picked out for particular praise 'Presences Perfected', 'Elected Silence', 'The mind of man environing its thought', 'At the end of all wrong roads I came' and 'Ex-Service', which she declared 'magnificent'.

'All that a poet can do is warn,' Wilfred Owen had written and Sassoon did so clearly in *The Road to Ruin*, *Vigils* and, later, *Rhymed Ruminations* (1939, 1940). He also took political action. Hitler's Night of the Long Knives in July 1934 and his growing closeness to Mussolini in 1935 added to Sassoon's unease and convinced him of the need for greater commitment to the pacifist cause. By mid-1935, like 80,000 other British subjects, he had joined Canon 'Dick' Sheppard's Peace Pledge Union and appeared on the PPU platform in July that year.[104] Sheppard, a radio preacher of great popular appeal as well as former vicar of St Martin-in-the-Fields, had founded the PPU in October 1934 with the express purpose of averting another war and had attracted many well-known figures to his cause, Bertrand Russell, Vera Brittain and Aldous Huxley among them.

Sassoon's contribution to the PPU's inaugural rally on 14 July 1935 at the Albert Hall was a reading of his poems which included 'Everyone Sang' and 'Credo', though he declined to make a speech. It was the first of a number of appearances, his readings apparently moving Vera Brittain to tears.[105] He was to compose a poem specially for his appearance at a PPU rally on 27 November 1936, which followed the Italians' brutal invasion of Abyssinia, Hitler and Mussolini's support of Franco in the Spanish Civil War, which broke out that year, and their Rome-Berlin Axis agreement in the autumn. Not one of Sassoon's most effective anti-war poems, it nevertheless shows the strength of his pacifist commitment as late as November 1936.[106] The poem opens 'We are souls in hell' and by the time it was written on 20 October 1936, Sassoon could well have meant it literally. For in 1935 an event had occurred which not only added to his depression that year, but also affected his whole system of beliefs. For the death of T.E. Lawrence in May 1935 dramatically convinced him of the existence of an after-life.

Lawrence was not the only close friend who died that year – Sassoon was 'much saddened' by the loss of 'Anzie' Wylde and the death of Nellie left an even bigger gap. Their deaths, however, were not a complete surprise, whereas Lawrence's was totally unexpected. And, while Sassoon's friendships with Anzie and Nellie had been diluted by his retirement to Wiltshire, the same move had brought him closer to Lawrence. So that, when news of Lawrence's serious motorbike accident and subsequent coma reached him on 13 May 1935, he was devastated. Even before Lawrence's actual death five days later Sassoon had received a ghoulish request from the *Observer* for a 'personal appreciation ... in the unfortunate event of the accident proving fatal'.[107] Though he indignantly refused to oblige, he did write a poem about Lawrence a week after his death, which he sent to Marsh for *The Times*. Marsh rejected it, ostensibly as a 'technical indiscretion', but more probably because of its rather startling contents. Addressed directly to Lawrence, it was, in effect, a claim that Lawrence had appeared to him after his death.[108]

Lawrence had already impressed Sassoon directly with his 'extraordinary powers' in the autumn of 1933, when he had performed an 'act of healing' on Sassoon, who had been in danger of losing the sight in one eye after a bout of shingles.[109] His 'visitation' after death completed the process and was a significant factor in the poet's developing spirituality, the 'closest [he] had ever come to religion', he told Tomlinson.[110]

The importance of Lawrence to Sassoon emerged in the violence of his reaction at Lawrence's funeral. Sickened by its carnival-like atmosphere, he had knocked a camera from the hand of a man who was trying to photograph the coffin at the open grave. And his disgust at what he called Robert Graves's 'performance' after the burial resulted in a further distancing of himself from Graves. When Hester, who had quite legitimately considered herself a friend of Lawrence, tried to share his grief, he felt even more threatened by her: 'Let me have my feelings to myself,' he begged in his diary.

While Lawrence was still alive, Sassoon had declined Cape's invitation to write about him, passing the offer on to Graves,[111] but after his death he agreed to help with a script for a film planned by the Korda brothers. Though the Kordas were known to pay generously and the renovation of Heytesbury yawned like a bottomless pit, Sassoon's main motive was not mercenary: what money he did eventually earn he gave to the local almshouses on whose committee he proudly served. He simply feared that the film would be a 'travesty' and hoped to be able to 'purify' it.[112] He also liked Lawrence's brother, Arnold, who visited Heytesbury in June 1935 to discuss the project.[113]

By this point Sassoon had re-read 170 pages of *Seven Pillars of Wisdom* in preparation, but if he hoped to make the film a literary one he was sadly mistaken. While his fellow-writer on the project, Colonel W.F. ('Michael') Stirling, seemed sympathetic to his aims, it is clear from the polite but firm rejection of their initial efforts that the Kordas had quite different ideas. By August a professional scriptwriter had been added to the team. Though Sassoon's involvement nominally continued into September, his part in it had virtually ceased by the 22nd of that month.

A second poem about Lawrence, written by Sassoon the day the Kordas' new scriptwriter was due to visit Heytesbury, suggests why he had failed to satisfy the film-makers. His efforts to convey the real-life Lawrence he had known were not what they wanted; *they* were looking, as he points out in this second poem, for the 'unanswering myth' and 'legend mask of stone', which was precisely what Sassoon was determined to avoid.[114] The whole episode epitomises Sassoon's frustration and sense of failure in 1935.

*

By early 1936, however, the prospect looked distinctly more cheerful at Heytesbury. After fourteen weeks of solitary grind Sassoon had managed by 9 January to finish a first draft of *Sherston's Progress*, his shortest book at approximately 52,000 words. He had already written the first chapter of 6,000 words by the time he took it up again in October 1935 and the third of the four sections was lifted with very few changes from his diary for the period. Nevertheless it was a huge relief to reach the end of his trilogy, a relief which turned to joy in February when Hester announced that she was pregnant again. With his book largely behind him he was a great deal more supportive than in the previous autumn and she safely negotiated the first three critical months. Even at this happy moment, however, the warning note is still sounding in Sassoon's diary: 'I love her deeply and gratefully, but it is a love that has learnt, by previous experience, to safeguard itself – or try to.'

Having completed *Sherston's Progress,* by the end of January 1936 Sassoon started on a series of articles for the *Spectator* which managed to strike a more reasonable note than his attempt to reply to the critics of *Vigils* in 'A Poet on Poetry', which had been commissioned but never published by Ackerley for the *Listener.* This was mainly through the witty use of an imaginary 'Aunt Eudora'. By placing all his more anti-Modernist views in the mouth of a charming old lady (who strongly resembles his mother) he manages to avoid the hectoring tone of 'A Poet on Poetry'. This time all three articles were published; the first and second, 'Aunt Eudora and the Poets' and 'Educating Aunt Eudora' (ostensibly reviews of the Bodley Head's *The Year's Poetry 1935* and Walter de la Mare's *Collected Poems*, respectively), provoked a lively correspondence in the magazine between Sassoon and his critics, and the third, 'Querkes, Farmonger and Dusp', appears to be a response to this interest.[115] He followed it up in August with 'A Personal View on How to Write' for the *Manchester Evening News.*[116]

Then, on 3 September 1936, just two months before his first child was due, his third prose offspring, *Sherston's Progress*, was published.[117] In direct contrast to *Vigils* the previous year, the reviews were almost universally good, in some cases ecstatic, underlining the fact that his prose fared much better than his poetry in the Modernist era.

Sassoon himself thought the most important quality in *Sherston's Progress* was the 'naturalness' of its 'speaking voice'.[118] For today's readers the portrait of Dr Rivers, which provided Pat Barker with important material for her novel *Regeneration*, is likely to be of greatest interest. Even taking this into account, however, it is impossible to agree with Sassoon's claim that *Sherston's Progress* is 'prime vintage' and the best of his three fictional works. It seems, rather, a falling-off, proof perhaps that he was right to worry about the effect of marriage on his writing. Forster, the most perceptive of his prose critics, was uncharacteristically non-committal in his response to it. The book nevertheless sold very well, helping considerably towards the renovation and upkeep of Heytesbury. Together with a legacy from Hester's aunt, Lady St Cyres, it provided the Sassoons with a very healthy income in 1936.

*

If the reception of *Sherston's Progress* raised Sassoon's spirits at the beginning of September 1936, the birth of a son less than two months later carried them to unimagined heights.

'Son both well,' he telegrammed to Blunden on 30 October, the day of the birth. He and Hester had rented 18 Hanover Terrace in Regent's Park, next to Gosse's old house, for October and November, to be near specialist help in London. As it turned out no complications occurred and Hester was allowed a home delivery. The baby was christened George Thornycroft Sassoon at St Martin-in-the-Fields on 28 November by its former vicar Dick Sheppard, by now a good friend. Blunden, Glen, Edith Olivier and both the Beerbohms were godparents, all but the last two being present, together with Rex Whistler, Osbert Sitwell and, in spite of increasing ill-health, Ottoline. Theresa Sassoon, suffering from severe arthritis and angina, did not attend, though she was delighted by the arrival of another grandson and would visit Heytesbury shortly afterwards to inspect him.

Most people are thrilled by the birth of their first child, awed by the realization that they have helped create another, independent life. For Sassoon, who had resigned himself to childlessness, the experience was overwhelming: it was, Glen would claim after his friend's death, 'one of the two supreme happinesses in his life'.[119] His son would quickly replace Hester in his already fluctuating feelings for her. From the moment of his birth it was George, not Hester, who represented Sassoon's 'whole future'.[120]

Even before the birth it had become clear that Sassoon's suspicion of women as domineering, over-possessive creatures had not been entirely overcome. His son offered no such threat. He was able to identify almost completely with a son, especially with one who resembled him closely; as he looked down at the child in his arms he saw, in the words of one of his many poems on the subject, his 'self reborn':

> Meeting and Parting
> My self reborn, I look into your eyes;
> While you, unknowing, look your first time on me.
> Thus will *you* stand when life within me dies.
> And you, full knowing, my parting presence see.   (*CP*, p. 251)[121]

Through George, Sassoon was transported mentally to the period when he had experienced life most intensely. In addition George also represented not just the continuity Sassoon had longed for when he married, but the perpetuation of his name. Before the child was a year old he had written at least one poem about future great-grandchildren.[122] Equally importantly George seemed to him a refuge from the 'cleverness and intellectual elaboration of the modern world'.[123] From now on he would invest virtually his whole reason for living in his son. George was to be, as Hester had been, his redemption.

It was too heavy a responsibility for one child to bear. Had there been other children things might have been different, but Hester had been so traumatized by the birth, possibly also by her miscarriage, that she would refuse to have a second child until it was too late. So that George alone had to bear the weight of his father's almost idolatrous affection. And, as Ackerley would observe during his visit to Heytesbury, it was not only George who suffered. By doing what he, Ackerley, had done with his dog Queenie and becoming 'fixated' on his child, Sassoon had unwisely put 'all [his] eggs in [one] basket'.[124]

None of this was apparent at the start, however. The birth initially made Sassoon more, not less, appreciative of Hester and Christmas with her and George in 1936 seemed to him 'the happiest ... ever'.[125] But when he tried to get back to work in January 1937, the difficulties quickly resurfaced. Spurred on by the success of *Sherston's Progress*, reminded by George of his own childhood and confident that he was now sufficiently well known to justify it, he planned to start on his real autobiography, the first volume to take him to the age of thirteen in 1900 and be called *The Old Century*.

Once again he insisted that the only way he could write was to stay up half the night and sleep half the day. Whether he was using work partly as an excuse to be alone, or whether he was simply incapable of real adjustment, the results were the same, an increasing irritation on his part with Hester's attempts to establish a more regular married life and bewilderment and hurt on hers. While formally acknowledging that few women of her age would be content with the large chunks of time alone he expected for his work, he resented her 'inability to control her intense devotion' to him, an extraordinary complaint considering how much he had needed it at the start.[126] It seems as if, once certain of her love, he no longer fully appreciated it and that once she had 'given' him George, his emotional fulfilment lay elsewhere. Rather than George being a 'safeguard' for their marriage, as Sassoon claimed, he was one of a number of reasons for Sassoon's increasing dissatisfaction with Hester in 1937.[127]

His greatest fear remained her possessiveness. There was also her occasional 'nerviness', Sassoon's euphemism for what he was secretly beginning to believe were pronounced neurotic tendencies. Their celebration of the coronation of King George VI in May that year was more successful, meliorated by the company of H.G. Wells, who stayed eight days at Heytesbury, and Hamo, who caught flu and stayed eighteen. Theresa Sassoon's visit in July also passed without a hitch.

So long as he and Hester did things together the calm continued. But when he tried to see Glen and Angela on his own in August, Hester felt excluded; some 'ghastly scenes' ensued and he was forced to cancel his visit.[128] And any attempt to be alone with George failed miserably. By November 1937 he reported gloomily to Glen that Hester had become 'impossibly possessive ... refusing to take her eye off [him]'.[129] In December there was a confrontation and the marriage reached crisis point.

Still struggling to finish *The Old Century*, Sassoon put his foot down at the beginning of 1938 and insisted that Hester leave him alone, even though this meant being without George, whom she took to her mother's. Another month together with the Beerbohms in the spring of 1938[130] failed to work its usual magic for Sassoon and by the beginning of July he once more banished Hester from Heytesbury. This time she was instructed to take George to the seaside for a fortnight and the situation was not improved when she returned two days later complaining of the state of the hotel. Since at that point Sassoon had not only completed *The Old Century* but also corrected the proofs, it is obvious that he simply wanted to get rid of her. While Ralph Hodgson's visit in August on his final return from Japan cheered Sassoon up, it almost certainly made Hester feel more excluded as the two old friends talked endlessly about the past and about Hodgson's future in America. A final showdown between husband and wife seems to have been averted, however, by two events of considerable importance to Sassoon in September, the publication of *The Old Century* on the 15th and Chamberlain's return from Munich on the 29th after what many would later come to regard as his appeasement of Hitler.

28

War Within and Without

1939-1945

In one sense *The Old Century and Seven More Years* was a direct result of the threat of war.[1] Writing to an admirer only three days after Chamberlain's return from Munich in September 1938, Sassoon told him that he created his book quite deliberately 'as an antidote to the times we live in' and that he wanted it to be 'completely harmonious and secure'.[2] Knowing that he would be accused of 'escapism' by 'sophisticated clever people' and of lack of 'realism' by the Modernists, he nevertheless believed that *The Old Century* was far more than an escape: 'It is a reassurance for decent people, that decency still exists.'[3]

It was as much to reassure himself as others, however, that Sassoon wrote it: he, too, needed 'mental release from Hitler and Mussolini' and the war that seemed to him a certainty, despite Chamberlain's soundbite, 'Peace in our time'. While admiring the Prime Minister's efforts, which he believed to be in the spirit of Dick Sheppard, by mid-1937 he no longer felt that such action was enough. Influenced by Max Beerbohm's change of heart in Fascist Italy and seeing for himself the growing power of Mussolini, who had passed through Rapallo during Sassoon's stay there in spring 1937, he had finally given up the pacifist cause.[4] His visit to Max the following year had increased his awareness of the preparations for war in Europe, especially in Paris, where he and Hester had stayed with her cousin at the Embassy on their way home. He was still ready to protest against the situation, gladly allowing his name to be read out at a meeting, 'Writers Declare Against Fascism', organized by the Association of Writers for Intellectual Liberty on 8 June 1938, but his attitude had changed.[5] And as the hopes of averting a major conflict receded, it seemed to him more important than ever to provide 'some peaceful pages' within the enclosed, distant world of his book, that 'drowsy, homespun age' of long ago.

It was a passive rather than an active response to the situation and in direct contrast to his strident verse-warnings of the First World War. Similarly his reluctant acceptance of the need to fight the Second World War was very different from his outspoken opposition to the continuation of the First. Like Bertrand Russell and many other eminent opponents of the earlier conflict, he felt forced to acknowledge that the only effective way of stopping Hitler was to fight him.

It was not simply as an antidote to war, however, that Sassoon wrote *The Old Century*. There were more practical motives. He needed the money to maintain Heytesbury and the success of *Sherston's Progress* encouraged him to concentrate on prose. He had ruled out a fourth fictionalized volume covering his life in the 1920s as being too sensitive, but he saw nothing to prevent him returning to his early life. Ever since completing his account of the sporting aspect of his childhood in *Fox-Hunting Man*, he had wanted to make good his omissions by describing his other 'strange dream side'.[6] Gathorne-Hardy had once suggested, no doubt with Wordsworth's *Prelude* in mind, that this might take the form of a long poem, to be called *The Growth of a Poet's Mind*, but only three weeks after the publication of *Sherston's Progress* Sassoon was asking him: 'Could it be done, in prose, as a sort of parcelled portrait of Sherston (the "country cousin"), do you think?'[7] From there it was only a short step to actual autobiography. With his son George as a stimulus and a daily reminder of his own childhood, it should not be difficult to recreate it.

Sassoon had intended to finish his book at the end of the nineteenth century, with perhaps a coda on his belated departure for prep school and the death of his Uncle Beer in 1902. Its title was to be *Memoirs of Myself,* a clear allusion to the first two, and most popular, volumes of the Sherston trilogy. He had worked to this plan from late December 1936 and had completed eight of his proposed eleven chapters by the time he and Hester set out for Rapallo in early April 1937, the speed of execution suggesting how much he enjoyed writing them. Hester, delighted by the success of *Sherston's Progress* and during a temporary lull in hostilities, had typed them up for Sassoon to show to Max. Max praised them lavishly, and not just because he was the book's dedicatee; for the pleasure with which Sassoon had written comes through clearly in the writing and conveys itself to most sensitive readers.

When Sassoon returned to work on what he thought would be the final three chapters, however, he found the going harder, not completing his plan until late November 1937. By this time the omnibus *Complete Memoirs of George Sherston* had been published and, possibly fearing repetition, he changed his title, *Memoirs of Myself,* to *The Old Century.*[8] It was an excellent choice. The only problem was that it had taken him less than 40,000 words to cover the nineteenth-century period of his life, barely half the 75,000 words he had agreed to deliver for his £900 advance. His publishers, Faber, were convinced that to be 'easily marketable' something more substantial was needed.[9] Rejecting Sassoon's own suggestion of an appendix of his early privately printed poems, Faber insisted that he add at least 'seven more years' to his life story.[10]

The task reduced Sassoon to near despair. Whereas he had found his early childhood a joy to recreate, he groaned his way through the next seven years, the period covering his formal education away from Weirleigh. Only the determination to take a completed manuscript to Max when he visited him again in late April 1938 enabled him to complete the final chapter and to bring his word-count up to 63,000. All in all *The Old Century* cost him '1500 hours of dumb donkey-work', he told de la Mare, many of them concentrated into this last third of the book.[11]

Few readers would deny the entertainment value of *The Old Century,* but some have questioned whether it fulfils the purpose its author sets out in his 'Prelude': 'to tell whither the water journeyed from its source, and how the seed came up'.[12] Apart from the young Sassoon's convalescence on the lawn and his teenage awakening to the power of poetry through reading Thomas Hood at Marlborough College, there are no direct attempts to explain how he became a poet. Yet in its very reluctance to describe and its determination instead to 'show' the working of the young Sassoon's consciousness, *The Old Century* succeeds in conveying the slow, often jerky development of his imagination. A key scene in the book, for instance, and one chosen by him to illustrate the title-page wood-engraving by Geoffrey Keynes's sister-in-law, Gwen Raverat, is the one showing him fishing as a ten-year-old in the orchard pond. There is no direct discussion of poetry-writing here, but rather a demonstration of the future poet's imagination at work, transforming the outer world until the fairly ordinary pond becomes the banks of the Zambesi River.

The Old Century was treated well by reviewers, with only 'three gadflies' settling on it, according to its author.[13] Of these three Malcolm Muggeridge alone irritated Sassoon sufficiently for him to repeat Muggeridge's criticism to Keynes, that '*The Old Century* [is] like an anaemic fairy story – something belonging to a remote past and with no bearing on the so ominous present.'[14] As far as Sassoon was concerned its remoteness from the present was precisely the point, but he doubted whether younger critics like Muggeridge could understand that and was grateful to be spared the critical onslaught of *Vigils*. Blunden, as usual, was euphoric, Tomlinson too.

Friends from the period covered by the book also wrote to congratulate Sassoon. (One reason why so many of the characters in *The Old Century* emerge as 'extremely nice people' may be that its author knew that the majority of them were still alive and was afraid of offending them. Having to use real names made him feel far more vulnerable.)

Max Beerbohm was proud to have such a 'perfectly lovely thing' dedicated to him, though, like Forster, his enthusiasm was reserved mainly for Book I. 'It is like going out into a garden at 6 o'clock on a summer morning!' he told Sassoon. 'You have put the dewy cobwebs and dewdrops on to the paper without breaking a single dewdrop. You have shown childhood as it seemed to a child.'[15] Enchanted by its delicacy, he predicted that it would be an '*enormous success*'.[16] To which Sassoon, in gratitude for Max's unstinting help with proof-correcting, especially his punctuation, replied:

> Ah, what avails enormous sales!
> Ah, what unstinted praise!
> This book, with proud remembrance, hails
> Page-proof Rapallo days.
> Max, punctuation's pioneer
> The unbound *Old Century* through,
> Its every thought and cadence here
> I dedicate to you.[17]

Sassoon was not quite so lofty about sales as he affected to be, however, and by January 1939 was writing sadly to Keynes that, 'owing to the crisis' of approaching war, *The Old Century* had sold half what he and his publishers had expected.[18] It was not so much the money he minded, though the disappointing sales made domestic economy a 'drastic necessity' at Heytesbury in 1939; he was 'irked' that *The Old Century* was so little known by comparison with *Fox-Hunting Man*.[19] '*The Old Century* is a daisy of a book,' he wrote to a close friend towards the end of his life: 'I can't think how I did it.'[20] Of all his prose works, it would remain his favourite.

*

By the time Britain declared war on Germany on 3 September 1939, Sassoon was already fully engaged in his own personal battle with Hester. The two conflicts would run side by side for the next five years, each affecting his attitude towards the other and both exerting a significant influence on his work.

To begin with the national emergency brought about a stand-off in his private warfare, as he and Hester faced the consequences of a second world war. Hester, who had been warned in August to expect at least twenty evacuees at Heytesbury House, was caught up in preparations for their arrival, while Sassoon braced himself to deal with the influx of army officers threatened by a visiting military man earlier in the year.

The evacuees quickly materialized and Hester, whose untidiness and lack of organization increasingly irritated her obsessively neat husband, was fully occupied trying to house and feed them. She was far more concerned about their fate than Sassoon, whose attitude was both detached and lofty, the socialism of his *Daily Herald* period now completely dead. She was also busy helping a maid sew black-out curtains, an occupation Sassoon thought entirely appropriate to her sex: 'Nothing can alter the fact,' he wrote in his diary with the full force of his male chauvinism, 'that women are only effective when they stick to their appropriate concerns.'[21] Since he regarded domestic duties as the chief of those concerns and since no army officers had presented themselves for his own attention, he himself contributed almost nothing of a practical nature during the first seven months of the War, a period which came to be known as the 'phoney' war because so little appeared to be happening. There were a few skirmishes in the Maginot Line, the series of fortifications built by the French against Germany after the First World War, and some activity at sea, but no bombing, and the War itself, which had seemed a very real threat during the year leading up to it, became rather unreal to the majority of civilian English.

Sassoon's own battle with Hester also became less prominent as she concentrated her energies elsewhere, allowing him more of the solitude he craved. Left largely to his own devices and 'sick to death' of the War after less than two months of it, he finally overcame eighteen months of writer's block to begin a second volume of autobiography, *The Weald of Youth*, on 25 October 1939.[22]

'It was the War that did it, I think,' he wrote to Max, who had left Fascist Italy with Florence in February 1939 and settled at Abinger, Surrey, in a cottage lent to them by Sydney and Violet Schiff.[23] 'The newspapers just drove me away from *1939*; and how happy I've been during my six days' revisitation of *1909!*' By avoiding Hester, even at meal times, by sacrificing even his son's company except for his third birthday tea and, most importantly, by ignoring news of the War, he managed to write 3,200 words by 1 November 1939. It was a great deal by his standards and a sign of his complete involvement not in the present but in the past. For *The Weald of Youth*, like *The Old Century* and his fictional trilogy, would result largely from his need to 'give the present the slip' and 'escape' to what seemed in retrospect a much happier time, in this case the years covering his 'country squire' period at Weirleigh followed by an attempt to make a life for himself in London in the summer of 1914. Though the shadow of the First World War would fall across the last few pages, it was essentially a pre-war world to which he retreated. His intense nostalgia for it comes through clearly in a poem written a year previously, 'Heart and Soul', which gave *The Weald of Youth* its title and central metaphor:

> Growing older, the heart's not colder:
> Losing youngness, the eye sees clearer.
> (Inward eye, while our sight grows blurred.)
> Living longer, the soul grows stronger.
> Looked on, the darkening weald grows dearer.
> (Weald of youth, a remembered word.) ...   (*CP*, p. 247)[24]

Sassoon's poem was also a response to his own accelerated sense of ageing at this time. The outbreak of another world war reminded him that a quarter of a century had passed since his headlong entry into the previous one,[25] adding to his consciousness of the half century which lay between himself and his son.[26] And *The Weald*, like his poem, was an attempt to recapture that earlier life. He might claim that it was written with 'the deliberate purpose of providing mental relief' for his 'kind readers',[27] but it was (as with *The Old Century*) as much for his own sake as theirs that he wrote it.

His problem was that, faced with a second world war, he could not deal with it directly, either in verse or prose. In 1919 he had asked, rhetorically, 'Is it all going to happen again?' and now that the answer was yes, he felt unable to comment further. During the three years he spent 'toiling, off and on' at *The Weald*, he told de la Mare, 'the muse deserted [him], except for a few snatches of contrived writing'.[28]

The verse to which he refers is very 'contrived' indeed and, fortunately for his reputation, largely unpublished.[29] The few war poems which did appear in print are mediocre efforts at best. Dismissed by Stephen Spender as 'lamentable', they are the kind of jingoistic outpourings Sassoon had challenged in the First World War. That they were published at all was due mainly to the fact that he was still thought of primarily as a war poet. The *Observer*, for instance, published two of what he called his 'duty' poems, 'The English Spirit' and 'Silent Service', in May and June 1940, when the War was entering its second, more aggressive phase.

Sassoon's few successful poems about the Second World War are those in a lower key that touch on the subject only incidentally, pieces such as 'A 1940 Memory' or 'On Scratchbury Camp', where this particular conflict is placed in the context of nature and history:

Shadows outspread in spacious movement, always you
Have dappled the downs and valleys at this time of year,
While larks, ascending shrill, praised freedom as they flew.
Now, through that song, a fighter-squadron's drone I hear
From Scratchbury Camp, whose turfed and cowslip'd rampart seems
More hill than history, ageless and oblivion-blurred.   (*CP*, p. 279)[30]

It is a detached vision of events, as far from his passionate engagement of the First World War as he felt in years, but it is truer to himself as a poet in the early 1940s than the militant call to arms of 'The English Spirit'. He was not indifferent to the War; it was rather that the aspects which moved him most were mainly personal. Whereas from 1916 to 1918 he had been taken out of himself into a larger world of love and pity for his fellow-soldiers, so that he had daily and willingly sacrificed self-interest to a greater cause, this later war drove him deeper into himself and his own concerns, as he freely admitted in an unpublished poem of the period:

... I sometimes felt before this war broke out,
That when it came I'd leave all else behind,
Setting myself alight to move about
In ardent acts, with reawakened mind.
Yet here I ride, a landscape figure still,
No hint of new emergence in my eyes:
Throughout this war I've done what looks like nil;
And no one, to my knowledge, has expressed surprise ...[31]

Where he had once rushed to enlist in the army even before war was declared, he now contemplated the situation from the sidelines. There was nothing to prevent him volunteering for meaningful war-work, such as the Home Guard. His contemporary Geoffrey Keynes, who had also served with honour in the First World War, instantly volunteered for the Second and became a consultant surgeon to the RAF. And younger friends, such as Glen Byam Shaw, Rex Whistler and his brother Laurence, all enlisted at the first opportunity. Even his nephew Hamo, whom he could still remember playing on the lawn at Weirleigh as a small child, deferred his place at Merton College, Oxford, to serve his country.

Sassoon was immensely proud of their willingness and highly critical of those he suspected of evading their responsibilities, unaware, it seems, of any irony in his own uncommitted position. 'I feel like a semi-submerged barge on a derelict canal,' he told Keynes, after congratulating him on his RAF appointment.[32] There were many days when he wished 'that the July 1918 bullet had finished me'.[33]

Nevertheless, apart from a half-hearted offer (through Marsh) of his services as a writer and the donation of two manuscripts illustrated by him to Red Cross sales in July 1940 and October 1942, he made no effort to become involved.[34] He found Hester's avid following of the news just one more cause of irritation with her. Only when personal concerns were at stake did he take any interest in events. When Hamo, for example, who had joined his older brother Leo in the North African Campaign, narrowly escaped with his life from a burning tank, Sassoon was moved to write to Angela Baddeley: 'I sometimes feel that if it wasn't for George I should have my face lifted and enlist as a private.' And when Angela's husband Glen was posted to India, he felt equally strongly.

He was also concerned about Hitler's treatment of the Jews, again partly for personal reasons. The fact that he himself was on the Nazis' list of banned books made him more conscious of his own Jewishness and readier to identify and sympathize. And a visit from one of T.E. Lawrence's friends, L.B. Namier, a naturalized Russian Jew who was second-in-command of the Zionist Federation, confirmed his belief that the Nazis' ethnic cleansing programme was 'unspeakable cold devil's work' and Hitler a 'blind fanatic and egomaniac'.[35] One of the few aspects of the War which he felt compelled to write about in verse was Belsen: 'Something has happened to the human soul/ Which needs long decontamination by time', he would warn in his angriest poem of the period.[36] He did not feel 'genuinely humane' about the German people, he admitted, though he had made good friends of the Hirths in Bavaria and still cared about them. For the first time since his anti-war protest of 1917, Sassoon and his mother were united in their hatred of the Germans.

His overwhelming feeling, however, was one of remoteness from the War, like 'a spider in his web among the weeds – at the foot of the Tower of Babel', or 'a leaning eighteenth-century gravestone in a village churchyard'.[37] Whole army camps would be built in his grounds and his house would be filled with army officers and their staff several times during the course of the War, but Heytesbury was physically distant from the main centres of action. The only real reminders of it would be the sound of planes overhead on their way to Bristol and a single, stray bomb exploding in his garden.

'All I want to do is to forget,' he wrote in his diary as 1939 turned into 1940, '– and have no arc-lights of practical-mindedness turned on to my loathing of this Second Great War, by which I am being reduced to an impotent absurdity.' His position was evidently deliberately taken and stemmed mainly from what he saw as 'a more and more intimate and personal' outlook on the world, but what looks very like self-absorption to an outsider.[38]

Looking back to the First World War, what surprised him was that he had 'had the temerity to express any opinions at all about a phenomenon which is, apparently, as uncontrollable as an earthquake'.[39] He now viewed his past self as a 'booby-trapped idealist', his present attitude to war being quite different: 'The only effective answer that a poet can make to barbarism is poetry, for the only answer to death is the life of the spirit.'[40]

Yet his difficulty in writing poetry continued. His struggle with Hester, though temporarily in abeyance, had left him too emotionally drained for verse. 'My mental life is in ruins,' he wrote in his diary. 'I feel self-destructive and defeated.' Equally significant was his fear of the critics. Their reaction to *Vigils* in 1934 continued to discourage him. Unable to alter a technique the majority of them considered out of date, he anticipated further savaging at their hands for any subsequent volumes. It was one thing to let Keynes produce a private collection of thirty-three poems, *Rhymed Ruminations*, in 1939, just two months before the War, since private editions were rarely reviewed.[41] But it was with great reluctance that he allowed Faber to publish a trade edition in October 1940, with nine poems added to make it 'a little less pamphlet-like'.[42] His motive was almost certainly money, about which he was worrying again.

Of the poems added to the trade edition, only two ('The English Spirit' and 'Silent Service') directly concern war, though the majority were written after its outbreak. The remaining seven are a similar mix to the main body of the collection, meditations on elemental human experience such as a young child at his window watching his father return home.

It would be another eleven years before any new volume of poems appeared, and then only in a private edition. Instead Sassoon concentrated on prose. By February 1940, he had written 30,000 words of *The Weald* and was frankly delighted when Hester felt obliged to take George to her mother's that same month because of German measles among the evacuees. One of his main problems with his marriage remained his inability to work with his wife in the house. By the time she returned in mid-March, far from having missed her, he could only rejoice in the 'quiet time' without her. His temporary sense of freedom had made him more determined than ever to be independent of her and in early April, with the news of Glen's posting to Yorkshire with the Royal Scots Regiment, he insisted on going to London alone to wish him goodbye. A small rebellion, it nevertheless marked the beginning of the end of their marriage.

By this point the War was entering a more threatening phase. In May 1940, when Chamberlain resigned and the more belligerent Churchill took charge of a coalition government, British troops landed in Norway but were forced to withdraw. By the end of May they had to begin their humiliating retreat from Dunkirk. The Germans had overrun the Low Countries and by mid-June had also invaded France. That same month Italy joined Germany in the fight. Only the Battle of Britain, a fierce struggle for air superiority over the Channel in July, August and September, saved Britain itself from invasion. In Churchill's famous words: 'Never in the field of human conflict was so much owed by so many to so few.'

The situation seemed to Sassoon 'too abysmal' for words, an effect reinforced by the loss of several friends in 1940.[43] The death of Norman Loder coincided somewhat eerily with his attempt to recreate the period of their greatest intimacy, his six-month stay with him in Warwickshire during the winter of 1913-14. Though he would in any case have wanted to describe his time there, Loder's premature death seems to have added both pathos and affection to his account of him in *The Weald*.[44]

Sassoon had not seen Loder for almost twenty years, however, and he felt sadder about the death of Ottoline, for instance, who had died in 1938.[45] But the death of a more recent friend, Sir Henry Head, seemed the greatest loss of the period. Head and his devoted wife, Ruth, who had died in 1939, had been like parents to him during his many crises with Stephen, and among the chief rejoicers when he married Hester. Theoretically Head's death was a merciful release both from the Parkinson's Disease that had rendered him completely helpless by 1940, and the misery of a life without Ruth. But his death for Sassoon meant one more blow at a deeply unhappy time. His general feeling of waste and destruction was increased by another death in the summer of 1940, that of Hester's younger brother Oliver, a brilliant physicist who had died while carrying out dangerous experiments for the Government.

During the heroisms of the Dunkirk evacuations in May and June, Sassoon had believed that 'the spirit of man is *not* going to be conquered by the abominable' and that the Nazis had 'underestimated the forces that had been built up against them', sentiments he could easily have repeated during the Battle of Britain.[46] But by the end of 1940 he had begun to despair of the situation.

Dr Dunn, his former guide in military matters, was no support this time round. Dunn had visited Heytesbury that very summer, but when Sassoon wrote to him for 'elucidations' about the War later in the year, there was no response.[47] This was hardly surprising since Dunn, like Blunden, had changed roles with Sassoon and was now a pacifist, an irony completely lost on Sassoon, who merely felt abandoned. He could not agree with them that England was the real villain of the piece. He was in any case finding Dunn, now nearing his seventies, increasingly 'crotchety', and his attempts to make England responsible for the Second World War seemed to Sassoon 'a distortion of reasonableness'.[48] Though he had himself been extremely critical of Churchill's 'war-mongering' during the mid-1930s, he now entirely disagreed with Dunn's and Blunden's charge that the Prime Minister was playing into Hitler's hands on almost every occasion. In Dunn's case, at least, the profound difference of opinion between them seems gradually to have eroded their friendship.

Blunden he found harder to dismiss. Sensitive, passionate and persuasive, he was a far subtler opponent than the blunt Scotsman. When Sassoon thought of the 'essential wickedness of the Nazi Party machine' and their determination to 'impose their will on the rest of Europe by brute force', he simply could not agree with Blunden's pacifist views. On the other hand he did not want to lose an old and trusted friend, and one of his last explicit letters on the subject shows how anxious he was to preserve peace between them, by moving the debate to common ground: 'If only the Germans would cultivate Cricket instead of frontier expansion! We might then establish a workable human relationship.'[49] He and Blunden had already agreed that cricket and poetry were the two best things in life. The threat to both in late 1940 was one more factor in his growing unhappiness.

Not all the news was gloomy. The Italians had failed in their attempt to invade Greece, the Royal Air Force had knocked out three Italian battleships at Taranto in November and General Wavell had chased them out of Egypt, driving them 500 miles back to Benghazi in December. But 1941 brought more reverses as British troops were expelled from Greece and Crete and the Axis powers took over the whole of the Balkan peninsula, extracting a promise of neutrality from Turkey in consequence. The Royal Navy, meanwhile, was being severely challenged both in the Mediterranean and the Atlantic.

Sassoon in his Heytesbury retreat ignored the news as best he could, preferring to tell Blunden and other friends in lengthy letters of his progress (or lack of) on *The Weald*. He was trying to write chapters 6 to 9, covering his first formal visit to Gosse, his musical education with Helen Wirgman and the writing of his first successful work, *The Daffodil Murderer*, which led to his introduction into the London literary scene through Gosse and Marsh. He was also rewriting chapter 2, an attempt to make his development as a poet in his early twenties sound interesting. As summer approached he abandoned his writing, as usual, and started to organize local cricket matches, another attempt to defy the realities of war. When he did think about the War he now felt vaguely optimistic, though there was little outward justification for it in the first five months of 1941.

The first real sign of hope came in June, when Germany attacked Russia and the Russians entered the fighting on Britain's side; the second in December, when Japan blew up American warships at Pearl Harbor and the Americans likewise joined the Allies. This entry of two of the world's greatest powers into the War was an important turning point. It also transformed what had been an essentially European war into a global conflict.

As public morale in Britain rose, however, Sassoon sank deeper into despair over his private troubles. With Hester he could find no peace: 'Behind that "gentleness" there is cast-iron selfishness and lack of consideration for others.'[50] It was almost certainly how Hester saw his own behaviour by mid-1941. The War, which had initially delayed open conflict between them, now exerted extra pressures on their crumbling relationship. By this stage every able-bodied man and woman was needed to help with the War effort and life at Heytesbury was correspondingly affected. As first the younger male staff, then the female and finally all the servants left, with only an occasional cook or charlady to help out, the situation between Sassoon and Hester deteriorated badly. The smooth running of the house by numerous servants, their very presence even, had to some extent cushioned the friction: without them things rapidly fell apart. Hester found herself, for the first time in her privileged life, having to do the housework, as well as look after George when his nanny left. Already bored by a severe reduction in her social life as a result of the War, she took her frustrations out on Sassoon – or so it seemed to him.

To begin with he simply stayed in bed, the quietest place he could find, spending six or seven hours a day there at his writing. Blunden's new love,

Claire Poynting, who visited Heytesbury for the first time in the summer of 1941, remembered that Sassoon did not appear till lunchtime, spent the afternoon out riding alone, and retired to his room at night, still refusing (as Claire put it) to 'go to bed with Hester'.[51]

Blunden's decision to abandon his increasingly unhappy relationship with his wife Sylva in favour of Claire in itself encouraged Sassoon to take a stand against Hester, but his greatest incentive was his work. Once he had decided that Hester prevented him from writing, their marriage was effectively over. His dread of confrontation led him first to try evasive tactics, and he began sending her away to stay with her family and friends as much as possible. He still could not concentrate, however, and spent most of 1941 struggling in vain to complete *The Weald*. He also tried going away himself, paying a visit in June to Merton College, where Blunden had arranged for him to talk on Beerbohm's prose. Then, in October, with the news of a fresh posting for Glen and, therefore, a short leave, he hurried to London to see him again, taking the opportunity to refresh his memory with a visit to his old flat in Raymond Buildings. On the point of describing the circumstances of his stay there in summer 1914, he was disturbed to find that it alone, of the many apartments at Gray's Inn, had been completely destroyed, like the leisured life it represented.

He also tried to distract himself with visitors to Heytesbury. Apart from Blunden and Claire, Hamo came from nearby Warminster Camp, and two friends from the 1920s, Will Rothenstein, who wanted to draw him again, and Lord Berners,[52] who helped satisfy his craving for music. And with a house full of fine pictures, his own collection now supplemented by his solicitor Lousada's valuable paintings, which he had placed at Heytesbury for safe-keeping, he drew daily comfort from art. A chance meeting with the painter Edward Seago, a camouflage officer with the Southern Command, would lead to the purchase of several more pictures by Seago's teacher (and Hamo Thornycroft's old friend) Sir Arnesby Brown, as well as one by Seago himself.[53]

None of these diversions was fully effective and the strain started to show itself physically. He suffered increasingly bad indigestion, not the result of Hester's inexperienced cooking, as he liked to claim, but almost certainly a reaction to the strains in their relationship. It was the beginning of the duodenal ulcer which would take him into hospital in 1948. He also had several bad bouts of lumbago and flu and began to feel old. He had always looked – and acted – far younger than his years; now, suddenly, he felt much older. Walking past fit young soldiers camped in Heytesbury's grounds and talking to a 40-year-old colonel about the First World War made him particularly conscious of his years, though he was still only fifty-five. It was not so much his physical infirmities as his loss of hope which made him feel that 'the fire [was] burning low'.[54]

While George was too young to be sent to boarding school, and in the absence of anyone else to look after him, Sassoon still needed Hester, but he found the situation extremely unpleasant, as his description of Heytesbury's daily routine in 1942 shows. Writing to Keynes in September that year he complained bitterly about Hester, though he continued to do little to help himself. Her inability to control George in the mornings, he told Keynes indignantly, interrupted his peaceful reading in bed: 'Then a pandemonium lunch with Hester and George. Then shave and pull my boots on and hack ride till 5.30. Then make myself some tea; and by 6.15 G[eorge] is having his bath just outside my door, with frequent altercations, and comes in to consume the cup of cocoa which I prepare for him. I then sift wheat till dinner, and continue the process till 1 a.m., when I sometimes write a letter, as now.'[55]

The gulf between husband and wife emerges starkly from this description and though the situation improved slightly when George started attending the local school at the end of September, by that time the marriage was past saving. It lurched on, as far as Sassoon was concerned, for the sake of convenience only.

The War, too, dragged on, but with more to hope for. There were some reverses for the Allies in 1942, such as the Japanese conquest of the Philippines and the new German Commander Rommel's capture of Tobruk in North Africa, but as the British and Americans joined forces to save Europe, the victories began to outweigh the defeats. And when General Montgomery routed Rommel's Afrika Korps at Alamein in late October and early November, Churchill declared in another of his memorable speeches that the real turning point of the War had been reached: 'Up to Alamein we survived. After Alamein we conquered.'

Since two of Sassoon's nephews, Hamo and Leo, were in North Africa and Glen was on his way to Burma by 1942, Sassoon was more involved with the War this year than at any other stage, though only the parts that concerned his nearest and dearest. Whereas he found it hard to imagine conditions in Russia, dramatic as the Germans' attempts to defeat the Red Army were, he could only too vividly envisage the dangers faced by Glen and Hamo. As in the First World War he needed to be imaginatively engaged for war to become real to him. 'I have been much relieved to hear ... that my beloved nephew Hamo is in hospital with [only] slight burns,' he wrote to Cockerell in June 1942. 'His Tank battalion had been in the thick of the Libyan battle, and I have had three weeks of acute anxiety.'[56] A temporary lull in the Far East gave him a short respite as far as Glen was concerned.

Apart from his personal involvement in these two theatres of war, however, his greatest concern in 1942 was the completion of *The Weald*, which would be dedicated to Glen as a 'final remembrance' of their friendship.[57]

*

Promised to Faber for mid-1941, *The Weald of Youth* was not completed until April 1942. From conception to birth it had taken three years to write. Faber, desperate to publish, got page proofs to Sassoon in less than a month. Further delays followed, however, when Sassoon forwarded them to his 'prince of proof-readers', Beerbohm, so 'charmingly forgetful of time'.[58] It was October before *The Weald* was finally published.[59]

Sassoon predictably blamed Hester for the delay and the domestic responsibilities she had at last insisted he share. He found himself for the first time in his life having to lay the table, wash dishes, fetch food from the kitchen, make fires, scrub baths and even clean out lavatories. It was only by sending Hester and George away again in March 1942 and living on snacks that he had managed to meet his second deadline of April. His dreary living conditions at Heytesbury as he finished *The Weald* help to account for the heavily nostalgic tone of the final section, which includes the young Sassoon's excited, sole possession of his freshly decorated London flat and the solicitous care of his housekeeper, Mrs Fretter, who seems, in this context, to be everything Hester is not, 'young and pleasant-faced' and doing 'things in a shy unobtrusive way'.[60] 'I liked the aroma of frying bacon and well-made coffee; I liked the company of my own mind and the certainty I couldn't be interfered with,' the older man causes the younger man to write, with evident yearning.

Such passages, harking lovingly back to a leisured, pre-war England, held an obvious appeal for many readers in wartime conditions and won praise from public and critics alike. Howard Spring in the *Daily Mail* was followed by other influential reviewers, such as Blunden in the *Spectator*, Desmond MacCarthy in the *New Statesman* and an anonymous writer in the *Times Literary Supplement*.[61] Most of the reviews were 'first-rate', according to Sassoon, only a few critics, like Peter Quennell in the *Observer*, demurring.[62] It was clearly a case of the right book at the right time: the first edition of *The Weald* sold out within a few months and a reprint was talked of before the end of the year.[63]

Delighted as he was by its reception, Sassoon had reservations about *The Weald*. He agreed with Tomlinson's tactful but honest opinion that it was 'a perilous sort of performance', in danger of being thought sentimental.[64] He could have written a 'bad-tempered' book about the years 1908 to 1914, Sassoon replied, but deliberately chose not to.[65] The result is undeniably anodyne, or as he himself put it, 'a syllabub of amiabilities from start to finish'.[66]

Opening with his first public recognition as a poet in Crosland's *Academy* magazine, *The Weald* closes with the decision which will define him in that role, his enlistment in the army. Looked at from this angle it is easy to understand why he argued that *The Old Century* and *The Weald* were 'really *one* book', with the latter serving as a 'kind of bridge' to another instalment.[67]

He was so exhausted when he finished *The Weald* in April 1942, however, that he was unable to face starting the projected third volume for another year. Instead of feeling relieved, he became very depressed, especially about relations with Hester, as a poem written the same month shows:

> How could he think to find
> That life beloved had lied –
> Its promise undesigned
> Discordant to his dream?   (*CP*, p. 265)[68]

Sassoon could not yet free himself from Hester in October 1942, the month *The Weald of Youth* was published, but he could and did try to shut out the realities of war. His favourite authors at this time are Jane Austen, Dickens, Trollope, Scott and Stevenson: 'I can only keep going ... by reading civilised literature,' he had written to Cockerell in 1940.[69] Having also read many of Henry James's novels, with their 'vanished world of parties in large country houses and elaborate conversations in London drawing-rooms',[70] by 1943 he was begging Keynes to send him James's *Letters*. For poetry he returned to an old favourite, Fitzgerald, whose world of the 1870s seemed to him 'perpetual Sunday afternoon' by comparison with wartime England.[71]

It was impossible to escape the War for long, however. Rationing of food and petrol made entertaining difficult so there were far fewer visitors to distract him by 1942, and what few there were were not entirely comforting; even Forster failed to cheer him. A more unexpected visit from Bobby Hanmer's sister Dorothy, to whom he had been 'rather flimsily engaged' in 1916, was another unavoidable reminder of war, since she had come to Wiltshire to visit her only son in nearby barracks.[72] Now a 'placid, plump and cosy lady with grey hair, very lame' and 'hobbling slowly on two sticks', she nevertheless took Sassoon back to the first time they had met through Loder in Warwickshire, the very period he had just finished describing in *The Weald*.[73] His next visitor, Marsh, who had been forced to leave Gray's Inn through heavy bombing, brought further reminders of war; he had just lunched with Churchill, who told him that British reinforcements had reached Alexandria. And Cockerell, paying his first visit for three years in August, was hardly more comforting, addicted as he was to daily radio bulletins and newspapers.

The only visitor in 1942 who did not remind Sassoon of the War, though he brought many memories with him, not all of them pleasant, was Stephen Tennant. Stephen had arrived unexpectedly at Heytesbury one evening three years earlier, ostensibly in response to the copy of *Rhymed Ruminations* Sassoon had sent him. The visit had been constrained but not impossible, Hester behaving better than Sassoon had expected and Stephen ecstatic: 'You look so young ... Oh Sieg, – wasn't it nice meeting? ... I thought you might be rather shirty and ritzy – but all our dignity collapsed and we just giggled ....'[74] Since then, as Sassoon's relationship with Hester deteriorated, he had actually invited Stephen to 'call' on him.[75] When Stephen did eventually materialize, again unannounced, in September 1942, Sassoon was out walking with George, and Hester felt obliged to entertain him for two and a half hours. His charm undiminished, in spite of now looking like an overweight chorus boy,[76] he managed to make her feel quite sympathetic towards him. Full of 'complaints and self-pityings' about Sassoon's 'treatment' of him, according to Sassoon, he threatened to 'destroy everything [he] had built up' at Heytesbury.[77] Sassoon's reaction to Stephen sounds very similar to the accusations he was levelling at Hester by the end of 1942: 'I think his egotism and inconsiderateness have made him slightly crazy,' he wrote to Keynes shortly after this visit. 'His point of view of things doesn't fit in with normality – and other people. He complains about my heartless treatment of him. (A heart was the only thing I couldn't give him.)'[78] Hester herself seems to have identified with Stephen, urging her husband to 'be kind to him', a volte-face Sassoon found extraordinary: 'All *I* want,' he told Keynes revealingly, 'is a quiet life.'[79]

Only George and his dog, Sheltie, could be guaranteed to comfort Sassoon. His old Dandie Dinmont seemed to him one of the few 'decent things' left to him by the middle of the War. So that he was very sad indeed when Sheltie had to be put to sleep at the beginning of June 1942. A wedding present from Rosamond Lehmann, his end was symbolic. 'I still miss [Sheltie], and can't bear to look at his photograph,' Sassoon wrote to Hamo at the end of 1942.[80] He knew that he should have been feeling more cheerful: Montgomery's historic victory at Alamein had given heart to many. But Sassoon was still worried about Glen: by October 1942 he was undergoing jungle training in India to prepare him for Burma, which had been invaded by the Japanese in 1941. Sassoon was also anxious about the planned 'Second Front' in Europe; though he could see the need for it, he dreaded the 'loss of good men' it would cause, friends like Rex Whistler, who had been visiting Heytesbury since the end of 1941 from the nearby Welsh Guards camp.[81]

By April 1943 Glen was en route for Burma and Sassoon was devastated to hear the news he had been dreading, that Glen had been seriously wounded.[82] (Robert Graves's son, David, was killed in the same campaign.) Only when it became certain that Glen would recover could Sassoon join in the general feeling of hope in mid-1943, that it would be only a matter of time before the Axis powers were defeated.

The complete rout of German and Italian troops in North Africa by May that year opened up Italy and the Balkans to the Allies. Italy was invaded in July, Mussolini deposed and the Italians forced to help fight the Germans by September. (Rome would fall to the Allies in June 1944, Florence two months later.) The situation in the Balkans was equally cheering and by August 1943 even Sassoon felt more 'hopeful' as the occupied countries there began to revolt against their oppressors. Meanwhile the British and Americans had started their round-the-clock 'thousand-bomber' raids on German cities, a relentless attack on industrial centres and communications. As Sassoon rightly suspected, the Nazi leaders were by this point 'in extremis', though not quite ready to 'remove' Hitler as he predicted they would.[83]

It was a buoyant and confident Sassoon, therefore, who met Field-Marshal Sir Archibald Wavell on 30 June 1943 at the house of one of the few rich Sassoon relatives he would know personally, Sir Philip Sassoon's sister, Lady Sybil Cholmondeley. In 1913, Sybil Sassoon had married the 5th Marquess of Cholmondeley, to whom she brought a large dowry. It was she who had suggested this first meeting to Sassoon, regretting as she did so that Philip was no longer alive to join them.

Wavell's war, as the leader of the early North African Campaign, then Commander-in-Chief of India, concerned the two areas of any real interest to Sassoon and he was delighted to be introduced to the great general. But their talk was more of poetry than fighting. Wavell had specifically asked to meet Sassoon, whose work he admired, and was anxious to discuss his anthology of war poetry due out in the autumn, *Other Men's Flowers*. Sassoon was more than ready to listen and advise, despite his objections to being known as a war poet: he was too flattered to do otherwise.

Somewhat overawed by his 'charming and swell cousin' and her illustrious guests, who included the diplomat Sir Ronald Storrs as well as Wavell, and exhausted by his first visit to London in eighteen months, Sassoon nevertheless thoroughly enjoyed his evening at Kensington Palace Gardens,[84] which made him feel twenty years younger. Not only was Wavell himself 'a very likeable modest man', but Sassoon was pleased to find that one of the other guests was the well-inclined editor of the *Observer*, Ivor Brown, another his old friend Desmond MacCarthy.[85]

There was to be no second talk with Wavell, Sassoon being sad to have to turn down an invitation to meet him again in 1945, but this sole meeting left a deep impression. It was almost certainly with Wavell in mind that Sassoon agreed to write an introduction to another anthology of Second World War verse, *Poems from Italy*.[86] Ten years after the meeting, and three years after Wavell himself was dead, Cockerell would introduce Sassoon to Wavell's son, Major Earl Wavell. When, just a few months later, he was killed in action in Kenya, it left Sassoon with 'permanent heart-ache'.[87] They met only five times, but 'Archie John', as he was called, was to make Sassoon feel that he had 'gained a wonderful new friend' whose admiration for, and understanding of his work encouraged him at a time of great despair.[88] Young Wavell's sincere religious-mindedness would also influence Sassoon's own movement towards the Church a few years later.

*

Sassoon's failure to take Hester with him to meet Wavell senior was one more sign of how bad things were between them by mid-1943. After accepting his cousin Sybil's invitation for himself only in June, he had been kept up till three in the morning by Hester's 'scenes', he told Keynes, clearly wondering what all the fuss was about.[89] By this point he had dropped all pretence with his close friends and was openly accusing his wife of mental instability. From another account to Keynes of one of their many rows it is obvious not only that he was entirely unaware of her point of view, but also that she was beginning to fight back.

Her first serious act of defiance, calculated to hurt Sassoon where he was most vulnerable, was to pursue an affair with one of his close friends and former aspiring lover, Rex Whistler. Her visits to stay with him in London in the autumn of 1943 were quite blatant. She was clearly being provocative, but then she had herself been severely provoked. Though June 1943 had been the worst month ever at Heytesbury, with no servants at all, not even a charlady, Sassoon had left most of the housework to her. By the end of the year he went on strike altogether, retiring to his music room and taking the handle off the outside of the door. His one concession was to help look after George: his 'sanity', he told Keynes, now depended on his son.[90] 'The worst thing of all' in the whole sorry business, he told his mother, was Hester's jealousy of his love for George: 'She made scenes whenever I tried to be alone with him.'[91]

The breaking point had been reached. Knowing that *The Weald* had been a financial success and confident that *Siegfried's Journey*, a third volume of autobiography started in October 1943, would do equally well, he believed he was now in a position to run Heytesbury independently of Hester.[92] His first Christmas alone since his marriage reminded him of the joys of solitude. So that as soon as George started boarding at Greenways, a nearby prep school, in January 1944, he decided to act.[93] Using his need to work as his pretext, Sassoon insisted that Hester should go to stay with her mother and leave him entirely alone. Though not fully complying with the second edict, by the end of April 1944 she had effectively left Heytesbury. Neither the pleas of her mother, Lady Gatty, whom Sassoon liked but thought 'weak and silly' with her daughter, nor Hester's own desperate offer to have the second child she had hitherto denied him, could change his mind.[94] Had her offer come earlier, it might well have kept the marriage going, since it is clear from a poem written in 1947 that Sassoon had once longed for a second child.[95] Sassoon was profoundly relieved when Hester finally left, after giving him 'fifteen successive days of domestic hell'.[96]

One of the many irritants for Sassoon in the months leading up to the separation had been Hester's incessant 'grieving' about the long-awaited 'Second Front'. Since Rex Whistler was involved in the elaborate staff-work surrounding the Normandy landings, Sassoon strongly suspected that it was Rex, not the War, which concerned her. He was even more incensed when, after the news of Rex's death arrived in late July 1944, Hester started behaving as though she were his widow. His own grief was great, 'the worst ... I've felt since the War began. I somehow felt [Rex] would be killed,' he wrote in his diary after reading the announcement in the *Daily Telegraph*.[97] But his main concern was for Edith Olivier, who had adored Rex since the early 1920s. She, if anyone, was entitled to behave like a widow, though she did no such thing.

'Operation Overlord', popularly known as 'D-Day', had started on 6 June 1944 with the convergence of 4,000 ships on the coast of Normandy. A combined effort of British, American and Canadian troops, by the end of August the Allies had a million men in France and the Germans had been driven back to the old Siegfried Line, known so well to Sassoon and his fellow-soldiers in 1917 as the Hindenburg.

Like Hester, who had herself been driven back to Siegfried's limits, the Germans continued to harass the enemy as often as they could, their dropping of 'buzz-bombs' on London being one particularly unpleasant case in point. Hester's harassment consisted of about four visits a week and three telephone calls a day in November 1944. But in both cases the battle was essentially over. By March 1945 the Germans were forced to sign a peace treaty. The War in Europe, like Sassoon's marriage, was at an end.

It is hard to imagine Sassoon not getting caught up to some extent in the mounting euphoria of the final struggles, but his main feeling in the case of the War was one of detachment. In his old hat and worn-out clothes, he told Blunden, he was no nearer the current conflict than the blackbirds and lilac bushes in his garden, merely a ghostly survivor from the First World War. And when Victory in Europe (VE Day) was celebrated on 8 May 1945, rather than jubilation he felt weighed down by 'mental flatness'.[98]

Instead of celebrating he spent the day quietly with his eight-year-old son, after putting his wife firmly back on a bus to Salisbury. Oppressed by thoughts of concentration camps and millions of lost lives, he was unable to satisfy the *Observer*'s request for a celebratory poem. Instead the piece which emerges is one of mourning. Could human nature ever 'escape responsibility for such horrors?' he asked Tomlinson. Added to his guilt and sorrow, there was also anger, as in the First World War, at those he believed had profited by the War, as his poem, 'To Some Who Say Production Won the War' shows:

> What now of those, on land, in air, at sea,
> Who – ardent or unafraid – went forth to be
> Defenders of the soul of man assailed
> By foul aggression and its creed of crime?
> How *their* productive fortitude prevailed,
> Ask, and be answered till the end of Time.[99]

Published in the *Observer* on 6 May 1945, this poem is the nearest Sassoon came to his bitter satires of the First World War, though it lacks their force. The two atomic bombs dropped on Hiroshima and Nagasaki later that year in a horrifying but successful effort to end the War in the Far East would pass virtually without comment from him. Perhaps beyond a certain point, as in his battle with Hester, he felt too numbed to care. From now on, he told Keynes in August 1945, 'my human existence is centred in George. I literally live for nothing else. As his concerns broaden out, mine will follow him. I have no literary ambition at all now.'[100]

It was a highly vulnerable position to be in, as the next ten years would show.

29

The Wilderness Years

1945-1950

How lonely – how lonely – how lifeless – how forsaken.

(Diary entry for 1947)

Once Hester had been ejected from Heytesbury, Sassoon's life quickly reverted to its pre-marital routine. Apart from school holidays devoted to George, a sacrifice he welcomed, by 1945 he was back in the round of daily rituals that had been his lifeline up to 1933. Its two main props were friends and work.

He had always valued friends highly and they now became more important than ever to him. But the break-up of a marriage can be a great divider, friends often polarizing into allies and enemies, few managing to remain convincingly neutral. Even if they try, as Keynes and his wife did, their efforts are not always appreciated. Sassoon, who had regarded Keynes as *his* property, was resentful when he and Margaret continued to visit Hester as well as himself. Edith Olivier, who had known Hester from a child yet had remained open-minded about the separation, was also judged 'a disappointment over the Hester business'.[1] Sassoon demanded complete support, not fair-mindedness. He failed to appreciate the fact that no one, not even Hester's mother, condemned him outright. Anyone who could see Hester's viewpoint, like Forster, for instance, was phased out as a close friend. Averse to confrontation, Sassoon went on seeing Edith and continued to write to both Forster and Keynes, but he secretly regarded them as traitors. In 1946, before the strength of Keynes's commitment to Hester as well as himself became clear, he had appointed him as his joint literary executor together with Blunden. Afterwards he regretted his choice of Keynes, eventually replacing him with another friend, largely because of Keynes's loyalty to Hester.

He cared even more about Blunden's 'defection' (though kept him as his literary executor), since he had regarded Blunden as his best friend. And in this particular case there is probably some truth in his charge that Hester had deliberately tried to 'nobble' those closest to him.[2] She not only appealed directly to Blunden for help, but also invited him, his new wife Claire and their baby daughter to stay with her several times once she bought her own house in mid-1945.[3] Blunden's sympathetic nature disposed him to understand Hester's point of view, which was partly his own, that Sassoon's 'egotism was defeating his invention and imagination'.[4] By July 1947 Blunden was writing to regret Sassoon's apparent 'disinclin[ation] to see' him and a break of almost three years followed.[5] Whereas their letters had multiplied during Blunden's first professorship in Japan in the 1920s, by the time his second post started there in 1947 their correspondence had ceased. Blunden would later come to feel that he had been 'trapped' by Hester and relations would be resumed,[6] but the situation had hurt both men deeply and damaged what Sassoon had previously considered their 'flawless friendship'.[7] He seems conveniently to have forgotten his earlier refusal to take sides in Blunden's own marital problems.

One of the people who helped to salvage their friendship was Laurence Whistler, who visited Heytesbury more regularly after the death of his brother Rex in 1944. Both Sassoon and Hester had attended his wedding to the actress Jill Furse in 1939 and when she died tragically young, leaving Laurence with two small children, they were mutually sympathetic. 'Laurie' was one of their few friends who managed to remain neutral without endangering his relationship with Sassoon, and would continue to visit Heytesbury with his second wife, Theresa, well into the 1950s, while also staying with Hester. Sydney Cockerell was another. But then neither Whistler nor Cockerell had ever been as close to Sassoon as Blunden.

Fortunately, all the people he really cared about, apart from Blunden, seem to have taken his side. Friends of long standing, like Tomlinson, Hodgson, Swinnerton and de la Mare made no effort to defend her and their letters continued to comfort him in the late 1940s and early 50s, together with those of more recent friends like Gathorne-Hardy and Nan Tennant. His family, too, were a great support, his nephew Hamo making no attempt to keep in touch with Hester after the separation and his mother telling him that she had 'sized Hester's character up' adversely years earlier.[8] Though disappointed in the failure of her son's marriage and concerned, like Lady Gatty, about its effect on George, she believed that 'a true artist should never marry'.[9]

When Sassoon first heard of Blunden's sympathy for Hester, he had written sadly in his diary: 'I must cling to Glen.' Glen had been his earliest and main confidant until the War claimed him, when his wife Angela replaced him as a sympathetic listener; Sassoon's long, unhappy letters to them both make painful reading. One of Glen's first acts on his return to England in 1945 was to invite Sassoon and George to join him and his family for a seaside holiday at Minehead.[10] The holiday ended with the Byam Shaws visiting Heytesbury on their way home, as Sassoon had longed, so that they could 'see me at my best'.[11] The only flaw in his happiness was Glen's lameness as a result of his wound, but even that was dealt with by the ever-willing Keynes, who arranged for expert medical help.

Shortly before dividing his friends up into allies and enemies, Sassoon had told Blunden that he had only six 'real' friends left beside Blunden – Glen, Keynes, Cockerell, Edith Olivier, Sam Behrman, and his son George. (Beerbohm was excluded on the grounds that he rarely answered his letters.) By his grudge against anyone who remained in contact with Hester he eliminated at least three people from this list, leaving only Glen, Sam and George as 'real' friends. But Glen, who had been 'nothing but a blessing' since 1925,[12] returned to a busy post-war career as Director of the Old Vic Theatre Centre, which made meeting difficult; Sam was even more elusive, visiting Heytesbury only infrequently on his rare visits to England, and George was at boarding school.

That left Sassoon very much on his own. 'Without Hester this place is heaven,' he told Keynes shortly after she left. Heytesbury in the mid-1940s was a very different scene from the 1930s, however, when he and Hester had entertained almost continuously.[13] Not only had the War and loss of servants severely curtailed its social life, but Hester's departure in 1944, together with the removal of all her valuable furniture in 1945, had continued the process. By the time the full effect of Sassoon's resentment of her supporters became apparent in 1947, Heytesbury was no longer quite as inviting as it had been. And Sassoon himself was in danger of becoming almost totally isolated.

One of the few regular visitors to the 'hermit of Heytesbury', as he became known in the second half of the 1940s, was the owner of George's school, Vivien Hancock. Sassoon had got to know her well on his almost daily rides to Codford St Peter to see George. Mrs Hancock had disliked Hester from the start and she and Sassoon grew particularly close after Hester left.[14]

Hester was jealous of their intimacy, though she had no cause to suspect any sexual interest on either side. By 1945, when she accused them of being 'too close', Mrs Hancock was already involved with the man who would become her second husband within the year and Sassoon was still appreciating his independence.[15] His main interest was to keep the school going, since he did not want George sent to a more distant establishment. Hester, who wished him to go to Winchester, had announced her intention of taking him away from Greenways and sending him to a feeder-school for Winchester sixty-three miles away. Sassoon, who favoured Oundle over Winchester as being more suited to George's scientific bent, was determined to thwart her at any cost. (Keynes, whose sons had attended Oundle, had strongly influenced Sassoon in this respect.) Where his son was concerned, his usual mildness deserted him: 'In me the tiger sniffs the rose,' he wrote to Keynes, quoting his own words, when he heard of Hester's scheme.[16] Vivien Hancock was an important player in his strategy to outwit her.

She was also useful in other ways. When, by coincidence, he received a letter from a master at Oundle, Rolf Barber, shortly after deciding on it for George, he passed Barber on to Mrs Hancock,[17] who took him as a paying guest with riding included at a very reasonable rate. In this way Sassoon hoped to establish a useful connection at the school in advance of George's arrival there. Everything he did now was with George's advancement in mind.

Despite his fairly cynical motives for cultivating the friendship initially, Sassoon learnt to enjoy Barber's company, his love of books and horses in particular. Sensitive, unmarried and prone to depression, Barber had sufficient qualities in common with him to make occasional visits and more regular letters from him pleasant. (Barber's own description of Sassoon included words like 'sensitive', 'generous' and 'spontaneous'.) The relationship would become closer once George started at Oundle, when Sassoon would, in the words of one close friend, find Barber a 'lifeline'.[18]

Another link through Mrs Hancock, and who cheered up Sassoon's life during this period, was Haro Hodson, a 24-year-old undergraduate at Oxford, previously a wartime major in the British Army. Mrs Hancock had allowed Haro, whose parents she knew well, to use her name (Mrs Gibbons by now) to introduce himself to Sassoon in 1948. An aspiring poet and artist with a particular gift for caricature – he was already 'drawing wittily for *Punch*' – Haro greatly admired Max Beerbohm and saw Sassoon initially as a possible way of getting to know his hero on a forthcoming trip to Rapallo.[19] Having read nothing of Sassoon's own work by the time he was invited to tea at Heytesbury, he admits to bluffing his way through their first meeting, though he subsequently came to read and admire almost everything Sassoon wrote. There was only one exception and that, ironically, was the main cause of the friendship which grew up between them. Haro never learnt to like *Meredith*, the biography Sassoon had just completed when they met. Yet it was proofs of this book which Sassoon asked Haro to deliver personally to Beerbohm on his visit to Rapallo in June 1948. (Haro was so terrified of losing the proofs that he sat on them all the way to Italy in his third-class railway carriage.) Following this introduction to Max and in the years leading up to his marriage to the writer Elizabeth Mavor in 1953, Haro would stay with Sassoon seven or eight times and get to know him well. Sassoon continued his efforts to help him, introducing him to Keynes when he learnt of his passion for Blake[20] and putting him in touch with his godson, George Byam Shaw, at Oxford.

Sassoon's evident affection for an attractive, artistic young man in the late 1940s inevitably raises questions. He had enough in common with Haro to explain his interest in terms of straightforward friendship – poetry, art, worship of Beerbohm, a whimsical humour and strong sense of the absurd, as well as shared army experience.[21] But Haro himself believes that 'the dear old boy "fell in love" with [him]'.[22] He had wondered why Hester, who had appeared during some of his early visits looking 'rather beautiful, like a ravaged medallion', had so evidently disliked him, but later concluded that she was suspicious and jealous of any young man who visited her husband.[23]

Haro's first impression of Sassoon had been of 'a nervous being, extremely shy and kindly', who would 'talk non-stop' for several hours when his guest first appeared, never looking at him at all: 'then at one juncture the eye would quickly glance at you and, that having happened, he would calm down and conversation of a kind could occur'.[24] It was, he recalled, like catching a horse; you had to take the indirect approach.

Sassoon's response to Haro and his attitude towards Hester and women in general suggest that his deepest instincts had not changed by 1947. But the existence of George made any further relationships with men unthinkable to him. One of his greatest fears was that George would be 'contaminated' by his past: the 'very thought of [Stephen Tennant] being anywhere near George', for instance, horrified him.[25] His frustrated sexual needs in the late 1940s go some way to explain his growing sense of desolation at the time, despite being 'enormously happy' with George.[26]

Hester did not hesitate to use his past, so trustingly confided to her in 1933, against him. When he tried to have George made a ward of court in the custody battle which developed after she left, she told him that he would stand no chance at all because of his 'association' with Stephen, of which her lawyers would make full use.[27] The threat worked and Sassoon instantly abandoned the idea. Instead he made Glen his executor, assigning him the role of George's 'personal trustee' if he died.

*

In this deeply unhappy situation Sassoon was no nearer to the peace and quiet he needed to write poetry. By the end of 1945 he had produced little of the verse he had expected to flow from him once Hester had left. He had not even been able to work on the edition of his collected poems Faber planned to publish.

He did, however, manage to complete the third volume of his autobiography, *Siegfried's Journey*, which he had been struggling with since April 1943. His double anxiety, about Hester and the War, had almost caused him to give up, but her timely decision to take George to her mother's again in January 1944 and leave him to work in peace had saved the book. In the weeks following her departure he wrote one of his most successful sections, his first visit to Hardy in chapter 9. By April 1944 he had completed 15 (of 23) chapters, 56,000 of his projected 90,000 words, and had reached another of what he thought the 'best things' in *Siegfried's Journey*, his meeting with the poets Wilfrid Scawen Blunt and Hilaire Belloc. Once Cockerell had 'vetted' it, Sassoon felt free to go ahead with the final eight chapters, which largely cover his lecture tour in America. By 7 April 1945 only the revising of the book remained.

One reason it had taken almost two years to complete was that he had never written a book he 'liked so little',[28] finding it 'weary-minded drudgery'.[29] After the first 40,000 words, which took him up to his meeting with Walter de la Mare, he began to feel that he was 'reporting' rather than 'recreating' the past,[30] a process which is reflected in the less spontaneous writing of the second half.

Siegfried's Journey was the least satisfactory of Sassoon's memoirs artistically and his friends' response to it was largely muted. It also did less well in America, where Edmund Wilson dismissed the book in the *New Yorker* as 'narcissistic fatuity'.[31] A highly influential reviewer, Wilson's piece may help to explain the book's disappointing sales in America, despite the fact that part of it was set there. Only four months after publication, Sassoon was forced to accept the fact that the 'Yanks' did not appear to understand him; most of them were too 'crude and provincial' to do so, he told Hodgson.[32] With Blunden he was even more critical, telling him that Americans were entirely lacking in the 'intellectual finesse' of the French: 'French letters are as far as they get.'[33]

Even before *Siegfried's Journey* was published in December 1945 Sassoon had been searching for something to succeed it. But the very reason he wanted to distract himself with work – the struggle over custody of George – was the same reason he found it difficult to begin another book.

He had started on nothing new by January 1946 and was beginning to panic at the thought of empty days ahead. Then into this void the same month dropped an invitation from Otto Kyllman of Constable to write a life of George Meredith, an offer he accepted with relief. 'It will provide literary occupation,' he told de la Mare, 'while I am "filling up the cistern" for another tap-turning of "Memoirs".'[34] It was not simply a matter of plugging a gap; he was actively 'excited', he told Blunden, at the prospect.[35]

Meredith had remained one of his favourite authors since Helen Wirgman had first introduced him to his poetry. Prompted almost certainly by his description of that conversion in *The Weald of Youth*, he had been re-reading Meredith since 1942 and by January 1946 was discussing the idea of a Meredith biography with another editor from Constable, Helen Waddell.[36] It was probably two more references to Meredith in *Siegfried's Journey* which triggered Constable's formal approach.

Though the biography itself was to lead nowhere in professional terms, the friendship it brought about with Helen Waddell would prove important to him, a very special relationship in a time of great need. Helen Waddell, a distinguished medieval scholar, translator and novelist, whose *Wandering Scholars* had swept her to fame in 1927, would form a bridge between the long line of female confidantes of his past and those of his future. From Wirgie onwards, he had always needed a sympathetic, intelligent, preferably well-read woman friend who could be close but not too close, a role which Ottoline, Nellie, Delphine, Ruth Head, the Hunter sisters, Edith Olivier, Vivien Hancock and others had fulfilled with varying degrees of success. By the time his friendship with Helen Waddell started in earnest in 1946, Ottoline, Nellie, Ruth Head and the Hunter sisters were dead, Mrs Hancock had remarried and Edith Olivier had been demoted for her loyalty to Hester. He was, therefore, in need of fresh comfort, which Helen, with her ready Irish wit and abundant kindness, was able to give.

Sassoon came to believe that Helen had 'one of the finest minds of any woman writer alive – possibly the finest', a reference to her scholarship in books such as *Medieval Latin Lyrics* (1929).[37] He also told a mutual friend, T.H. White, that she was the 'greatest' woman he had ever known.[38] But it was her imagination and insight rather than her intellect which enabled her to get through to him in his growing isolation, qualities which he admired in her brilliant recreation of the legendary lovers Heloise and Abelard in *Peter Abelard* (1933).[39] Her letter to him about Meredith in 1947, for example, written as he approached the end of his biographical labours, shows her insight into both biographer and subject, whom she sees as kindred spirits: 'for he had your exceedingly rare power of being completely aware of yourself and, at the same moment, of other people. For *The Egoist* is only half of Meredith. And I think you both know something of what Emily Brontë meant when she said anguish.'[40]

The daughter of a Presbyterian missionary, Helen, like Edith Olivier, had grown up with a deep respect for spiritual values and was able to give Sassoon more than understanding alone. She also reminded him of another possible element in life, one which he had begun to explore for himself in *Vigils*, anticipating by a decade the women who would become his spiritual guides and support in the last years of his life.

When agreeing to write a biography of Meredith, Sassoon had made it quite clear that he was not aiming at a work of great scholarship, though he hoped it would establish him as 'quite a serious writer' with university dons.[41] All he could try to do, he felt, 'was to show what sort of a man he was, the nature of his writings, and how far they remain readable and rewarding'.[42] Based almost solely on Meredith's published *Letters* and Buxton Forman's collection of Meredithiana which Constable had acquired, Sassoon's biography makes no attempt to be comprehensive, including few references to anything outside these two.

Even as the 'commonsense' account of Meredith's life it set out to be, *Meredith* is not altogether satisfactory.[43] At the very beginning of the book its author indicates that he will not be going into 'the details of [Meredith's] intellectual and emotional development'.[44] He also makes it clear that he does not consider himself a professional critic. Written in the first person, his is a frankly subjective approach, full of his own likes and dislikes – his interest in rare books and 'black and white' artists of the nineteenth century, his love of Fitzgerald and Hardy, or his suspicion of the highly analytical mind, for instance. He himself found the critical analysis of Meredith's numerous novels 'a weary game', he confessed to Blunden, and frequently wanted to tell his readers to 'Read the b—y book and decide for yourself.'[45]

Constable had faith in Sassoon's work and published 10,000 copies of *Meredith* in September 1948. But in spite of mainly favourable reviews, it sold slowly and there was no reprint.[46] Sassoon believed that its disappointing sales were due to the unfashionableness of Meredith's novels. Another explanation is that his biography falls between two stools, being neither a work of serious scholarship nor a 'popular' biography. It remains the least read of all his prose works.

It was also his last book of prose. Once his lack of scholarship had been criticized he decided against a biography of Hardy and finally abandoned the fourth volume of autobiography he had started. His unpublished manuscript of about a hundred pages is full of lively scenes from his life in the 1920s – a meeting with W.B. Yeats over 'large pink ice[s]' in Gunther's tea-shop, a weekend at H.G. Wells's with the Sitwells, a hilarious tea at Gosse's with Sam Behrman and Edith Sitwell, another visit to Thomas and Florence Hardy. But the long, false start, partly quoted by Rupert Hart-Davis in his Prelude to *Diaries 1920-1922*, shows the difficulties he was still experiencing. 'The vital problem is *what to try and express* by the book,' he wrote in his diary. '*The Old Century* expressed childhood and adolescence. *The Weald* – unsophisticated youth, *Siegfried's Journey* – youth finding its feet, but still undeveloped and bewildered. This one must be an adventure in the gaining of self-understanding.' Encouraged by friends like Cockerell and Keynes, who feared for the emptiness of his life, he persevered. But when it became clear that the only 'adventure' he felt free to describe in the 1920s was how he came to write *Fox-Hunting Man*, he finally gave up. He had arrived at that extraordinary moment when his writing had turned in on itself; in describing the past he had reached the point where to write about it was to write about himself writing about it. As he put it to Tomlinson, he was no longer 'writing' but merely 'editing that other self'.[47] It is hardly necessary to point out the irony of the working title of the abandoned volume, *Know Thyself*.

Otto Kyllman's explanation for Sassoon's problems with prose work in the late 1940s was rather different from Sassoon's. Sassoon had submitted a selection of Meredith's poems with an introduction to Constable shortly after the publication of *Meredith*, and in rejecting it in February 1949 Kyllman explained that it 'show[ed] signs that you were tired and ... under the weather'.[48] Kyllman's rejection, however sympathetically expressed, seemed to Sassoon his death-knell as a writer. Yet the analysis was perceptive; Sassoon had been both tired and physically down as he prepared his proposed selection and someone of less 'anemone-shrinking sensitiveness' (Helen Waddell's words) might have accepted Kyllman's advice rather than giving up at that point.

*

Sassoon's illness had started years before with digestive problems, brought on, he believed by Hester. Though the symptoms had improved temporarily after her departure in 1944, her repeated visits to Heytesbury, together with the strain of being responsible for George for long periods during his school holidays and the effort of completing *Meredith*, had caused them to return in a more acute form. A four-week holiday with George on Mull in September 1948 had brought things to a head. Hester was in the process of settling down on the island, which she had known and loved since childhood, and had suggested they visit her there.[49] The combination of an unsuitable diet, the 'restless routine' of minding George and above all the daily contact with Hester had brought Sassoon to a point where he felt ready to accept medical help. Keynes and his local doctor Falk both diagnosed a duodenal ulcer.

Keynes, whose admiration and sympathy for Sassoon had remained unaffected by Sassoon's own cooling off, at once arranged for him to have treatment in the Central Middlesex County Hospital at Park Royal, West London. Sassoon made only one condition, that Hester should not be allowed to visit him, though he hoped to see his friends there.

Keynes was less sure about the desirability of any visitors at all for someone as excitable as Sassoon, but they came nevertheless. During Sassoon's six weeks at what he variously called, with recovered light-heartedness, 'Ovaltine Mansions' or 'Duodenal Mansion', he was entertained daily. There were not just friends of long standing, but more recent ones like Haro Hodson, Helen Waddell and Joe Ackerley. Apart from a natural desire to cheer him up, it was so much easier to get to West London than Wiltshire. 'Since 1939 I have seen so few of my friends and got stuck in my silly shell, hermit crab-like,' Sassoon wrote to de la Mare, revelling in his renewed social life.[50]

De la Mare himself was too frail to travel, but Sassoon ventured out of the hospital twice towards the end of his stay to have tea with him, occasions which brought back all the old magic. Writing to thank Angela Baddeley for driving him to de la Mare's house in Twickenham, Sassoon notes that it was like seeing 'Coleridge and Lewis Carroll rolled into one'.[51] As with Hardy and Beerbohm, he tried not to think of age creeping up on de la Mare.

All in all he thoroughly enjoyed his six weeks away from Heytesbury. His treatment had been gentle – luminol tablets to quieten him down, milk every two hours, bland food and a great deal of rest. Immunity from Hester had also helped him, mentally as well as physically. He needed little encouragement to lie in bed reading and got through the complete works of Shakespeare, Lamb's *Letters*, James's *Notebooks*, *Middlemarch*, as well as some Cowper, Browning and Jane Austen. But it was the company he enjoyed most, writing to Haro only three days after his arrival at Park Royal on 19 October: 'I am becoming so popular here that I begin to feel like inviting the whole staff of the "Sick Bay" to stay at Heytesbury next summer!'[52]

It was a strong contrast to his life at Heytesbury, which seemed all the more solitary when he returned there at the end of November 1948. Still a 'paradise' to him in summer, it was at its bleakest and coldest in mid-winter. To make matters worse his cook, Mrs Bailey, and head gardener, Gearing, had taken advantage of his absence to get rid of two members of staff they disliked, the woodman, Johnson, and his wife, who helped in the house. Sassoon arrived back to be given notice by his 'staff and prop', Johnson, and was then so furious with Gearing that his notice quickly followed.

Though the domestic situation gradually improved in 1949, his loneliness grew worse. Keynes visited as frequently as possible, but that was not often; Laurence Whistler came to lunch occasionally on his way to Dorset, and George spent part of his school holidays at Heytesbury. Otherwise Sassoon was on his own for long periods. Without friends or work to distract him he became deeply depressed, the only bar to suicide being George's need of him. He could see no other meaning in life. 'Comforting and sustaining' though he found Helen Waddell's belief in the power of 'the continuity of learning and spiritual decency', by 1949 it was not enough to save him from despair.[53]

His depression had been growing on him since his sixtieth birthday in 1946.[54]

H.G. Wells's death in August 1946 had increased his gloom. Critical as he had been of certain aspects of Wells's work and character, he readily acknowledged that Wells was 'a world-scale dreamer of things that might be, a breeder of big loose ideas and ideals. Vastly stimulating as he went along.'[55]

The death of his mother the year after Wells, in July 1947, affected him even more deeply, though not immediately.[56] He had 'long prepared' himself for her death, which was hardly unexpected at the age of ninety-three, so that he 'felt very little emotion' when his brother Michael rang to tell him of it.[57] Nevertheless he 'couldn't face the funeral', or a return to Weirleigh; as he explained in his diary, it would only cause him 'the needless pain of emotion. I just resolved not to indulge in feelings (Hester has cured me of that!).'[58] And he strictly forbade Hester, who felt she ought to go in his place, to attend, possibly fearing further manipulation. As the days passed, however, his mind turned more and more to the time before his mother had become old and sick. 'I can now think of her in the reality of her prime,' he told Glen, 'and bring her to life in my mind with the full realisation of her qualities which were wonderful.'[59] Their earlier misunderstandings were long forgotten and her recent sympathy with him against Hester had brought them very close. Her death also eased his financial situation, releasing him from the £400 annuity he paid her and bringing the promise of money from his half-share in the sale of Weirleigh. In addition, the Weirleigh furniture would help to fill the empty spaces left by the removal of Hester's belongings from Heytesbury.

His mother's death was another reminder of how alone he was by 1947. Edith Olivier's death the following year and Lady Gatty's in 1949 increased this sense of being gradually abandoned. The award of an Order of Merit to T.S. Eliot in 1948, a coveted honour limited to twenty-four holders only, had made him feel even more of a back number. He had secretly hoped for it himself. The offer of a Companion of the British Empire award in 1951 would do little to reassure him and was accepted somewhat grudgingly. 'Geoffrey is driving me to Buckingham Palace on February 28 – to be "invested",' he was to write to Haro on the occasion. 'He thinks it fun, but I am dreading it, and feel affronted by the whole affair.'[60] In the event he rather enjoyed it, writing with some complacency in his diary that evening: 'I think the King was pleased to see me, as my writings are liked by the Queen and I was undoubtedly the most famous person there. He spoke nicely with a charming, genial smile.'

But a sense of slight remained. And however much he expressed horror at the idea of being nominated for the laureateship when Masefield died, he was clearly disappointed not to be asked. Though he should have been forewarned by the lukewarm to downright dismissive reception of his *Collected Poems* in 1947, he found it hard to take.

When Ackerley visited him in the summer of 1949, it was his grievances, his melancholy and, above all, his isolation which struck him most forcibly. Ackerley had been publishing poems, reviews and articles by him since 1935, and would continue to do so till 1954, but they had never been close friends

and Sassoon's invitation to Ackerley to stay at Heytesbury for as long as he liked
in itself smacks of loneliness:

> Siegfried sweet, kind, loquacious, absent-minded, lonely, dreadfully self-
> centred and self-absorbed [Ackerley noted in his diary]. I like him very
> much, there is something very touching about his aged, beautiful, worn
> face, the light in the eyes dimmed from constant looking inwards. He
> scarcely ever meets one's eye – he never has, I think – but talks, talks away
> from one, from side to side, or into his lap or over one's head, always about
> himself, his life, his past fame, his present neglect, his unhappy marriage,
> his passionate love for his son. It is all intensely subjective (he scarcely
> ever asks one about oneself – a flash or two of effortful interest, but always
> reminding him about himself) and threnodic, it is a man who has spent
> years and years of loneliness, talking his thoughts at last aloud to an ear. It
> is all delivered in a low, mumbling, self-absorbed, almost inaudible voice,
> a whisper sometimes, very refined, accompanied by gestures of pain or
> feeling – hand on heart, clasping his face.[61]

'But why is he like this?' Ackerley asked himself.[62] His name and fame were
assured, as far as this literary editor was concerned; though his poems, memoirs
and heroic exploits in the First World War might be 'temporarily out of mind'
and a new kind of experimental poetry in fashion, he believed that Sassoon's
work had 'a permanent place in our literature'.[63] 'Dear Siegfried, he has taken
a wrong turning somewhere. There is no happiness in self, self as a permanent
diet is melancholic and poisonous, it kills, one dies, as he is dying, talking,
talking away about his lost fame, his loneliness, his domestic affairs – his aged,
worn, fine face turned sideways, sightless, towards the window.'[64] Ackerley
thought by contrast of their mutual friend, Forster, with his perennial interest
in people and things, his ability to get outside himself. Ten years Sassoon's
senior, he seemed to Ackerley 'eternally young, eternally gay, cushioned in fat –
the fat of secure love and personal esteem'.[65]

Ackerley's attempts to help Sassoon make diverting reading, particularly in
view of the fact that Sassoon believed that *he* was helping Ackerley. 'He was
desperately in need of a holiday and peace,' Sassoon wrote in his own diary,
'owing to a bad time he's had with his sister ... I have asked J.A. to stay as long
as he likes, as it is doing him so much good.'[66] While Ackerley looked pityingly
on Sassoon in his threadbare clothes, his lean shank peeping through a hole in
his trousers, Sassoon was feeling sorry for Ackerley, who was, he noted, going
deaf. 'Ten years younger than me,' he added, 'he is old and disillusioned .... Sad
and used up.'[67]

By the end of a fortnight Ackerley was relieved to be going. He had started to
feel resentful at what seemed to him the meanness, or at the very least carefulness,
of the rich: Sassoon's evident reluctance to keep on opening his good wine for
him, his unnecessary reminder to Ackerley to 'reward' the housekeeper, Miss

Benn, for looking after his dog so well, his unwillingness to ask the young poet James Kirkup (whom he wanted Ackerley to meet) to stay in advance, or to invite him to do so more than one night at a time when he arrived.[68] Then there was his unawareness; when Kirkup was leaving it was Ackerley not Sassoon who realized that he needed some tea before he caught his bus to the station for the long journey home. And though Ackerley understood Sassoon's treatment of Hester, who visited daily with her 'pale, lined, ravaged face', he found the situation uncomfortable.[69] Finally, and most exhaustingly, there was Sassoon's craving for continual praise and recognition and his all-absorbing egotism.

In spite of which, Ackerley left Heytesbury with the impression that Sassoon was 'very kind and nice, and ... charming'.[70] His behaviour to both Ackerley and Kirkup overall had shown how generous he could be. Yet the overriding impression remained of a man locked up in himself, unable to find the key.

30

An Asking

1950-1956

Solitude, Sassoon realized by 1949, 'compels one to discover what one's mental resources amount to', and his own, he concluded, were 'very limited'.[1] Having made all the discoveries he was likely to make in poetry and come to an end of his prose-writing, he could no longer rely on work to give his life meaning. Nor, by 1950, could he expect George to do so; his departure for Oundle on a scholarship that year was the first step towards increasing independence. Sassoon had dreaded the moment when George would leave his nearby prep school for a public school nearly 200 miles away on the other side of England, and it had now arrived.

Post-war Britain also filled him with gloom and foreboding. He was openly resentful of Clement Attlee's Labour Government and the heavy taxes it imposed on wealthy people like himself, regardless of the benefits these might bring to those less fortunate. Worse still was the development of the atomic bomb, which he believed would lead to a 'suicidal conflict', a threat he thought all the more likely because of the growing tension between Russia and America.[2]

Hardy's *The Dynasts*, which Sassoon re-read in 1949, had first made him ask the question that had been forming in his mind for several years: 'What *do* I really believe in?'[3] And it was this question which lay behind a series of poems written between 1946 and 1954 and privately printed in three slim volumes, *Common Chords* (1950), *Emblems of Experience* (1951) and *The Tasking* (1954).[4] Written under the same kind of intense emotions which had given rise to his First World War satires, these poems of his spiritual odyssey resemble them also in what Sassoon called 'direct utterance of dramatized emotion'.[5] As in the 1914-18 period he had again discovered a theme which inspired him. The difference is that by 1950 the drama is largely internal rather than external and that, while the earlier poems chart his gradual loss of faith when confronted with the horrors of the First World War, the later pieces show his developing need to rediscover it as he faces threats of a different sort.

Reading these later poems as they were arranged by Sassoon in his private volumes and in Faber's trade edition of the three, *Sequences* (1956), it is possible to identify the various states of mind he experienced. They provide a revealing account of his stumbling progress towards faith, particularly of its beginnings.

The first three in the series to be written, for example, 'Solitudes at Sixty', 'A Prayer to Time' and 'In Time of Decivilisation', suggest that the initial stimulus had been the pronounced sense of lost youth which followed his sixtieth birthday and an accelerated awareness of the passing of time (a theme to which later poems in the series, such as 'A Proprietor' and 'Associates', would return).

The religious terminology with which 'A Prayer to Time' opens and closes indicates that, though its theme may be Shakespearian, its author, unlike Shakespeare, is looking beyond his own creative powers for answers. This terminology is taken up again in 'Praise Persistent', 'An Asking' and 'An Absentee', all three written a few months later in early 1948. And it is at this point that the concept of a living, listening God as a possibility is introduced, the first convincing sign of the birth of religious awareness. Sassoon's posing of the question in 'An Asking' – 'Primordial Cause, your creature questions why/ Law has empowered him with this central I;/ Asks how to carnal consciousness you brought/ Spirit, the unexplained of sovereign thought' (*CP*, p. 270) – shows him starting out on a spiritual quest. The reference in 'Praise Persistent' to mankind pursuing 'their one hope on earth .../ In perishable pilgrimage' suggests that he suspects that the journey will not be easy and that, in the words of 'An Absentee', he will need 'God's Mercy ... a word/ Seldom in these times heard'.[6] Nevertheless, the question has been asked and the journey begun. Like St Augustine, whom he resembles in his searching and openness, Sassoon will continue to ask many questions on the way, but it is clear that he has had his first glimpse of 'the soul – a star – a gift he yet might save'.[7]

As with Christian's progress towards the Celestial City, Sassoon was to experience distractions and take false turnings on his pilgrimage. In 'Ultimate Values', for instance, written at the end of 1948, he appears to be still clinging to the memory of 'out-live[d]' friends for meaning in life, and depending for 'consolement .../ On hoarded time, enriched and redesigned'.[8]

Less than three months later he is back on track with what he describes as 'the first "spiritual" poem of the collection, which "cried out for the living God" *in me*' – 'Resurrection'.[9] It is here that he introduces another possibility, that of forgiveness for what increasingly seems to him a life misspent:

> Suppose, some quiet afternoon in spring,
> The hour of judgement came

For me and my mistakes when journeying
Along with that defence for nullity, my name.
Suppose, while sauntering in the primrosed wood,
To body and soul's dispute a voice cried *halt*,
And I that instant stood
Absolved of unfulfilment and essential fault ...   (*CP*, p. 270)

Sassoon referred in the last line of this poem to 'marred and mystic me' and
Blunden would make a similar point in his review of *Sequences* in the *Times
Literary Supplement*. In reading the collection, Blunden wrote, he had been
reminded of Sassoon's 1920s sonnet 'At the Grave of Henry Vaughan', because
of a 'spiritual affinity' between the twentieth-century poet and seventeenth-
century mystic: 'The impression given [in *Sequences*] is of a recluse seeking
some spiritual light, often under the stars, and of a solitary wayfarer pausing
beneath a tree, noting the primrose, riding along the farm track.' Sassoon
himself had referred in 'A Fallodon Memory' (written in March 1948) to Lord
Grey's 'Wordsworthian slow self-communing',[10] a phrase that describes his own
method in the poem which immediately precedes 'Resurrection', 'The Message'.
'Riding slowly homeward' on a still November day, the narrator sees 'the sky/
Transfigured as by beneficence fulfilled':

Cloud streaks and shoals, like silver wings outspread,
Spanned innocent serenities of blue,
As though, enharmonised with life below,
Some heavenly minded message had been said.
Thus, childlike, I imagined. Yet it might be true.   (*CP*, p. 264)[11]

In 'Euphrasy', the poem which follows 'Resurrection', there is a similar sense
of Nature suggesting to the poet a meaning beyond its outward appearance of
'large untidy February skies', 'low-shot sunlight' and 'cheerful starlings screeling
on a tree'.[12] Though viewed at times as 'beguilements', the charms of Nature,
particularly those of spring, are presented in these and other poems, such as
'An Example', 'Wren and Man' and 'Release', as a potential gateway to God.[13]

Where once Sassoon would have extended these descriptive passages, he
now, in poems like 'Early March', lets them stand as significant in themselves.
Sassoon the nature poet has not disappeared; he has simply moved on a stage.
And in concluding the first of his private volumes with 'Redemption', he makes
the clearest statement to date of his transcendental yearnings by the end of
1949.[14] Its final stanza, centring round the idea of the body as a vehicle through
which God's glory might shine, is Vaughan-like in its mystical acceptance of
different possible ways of knowing and serving:

... I think; if through some chink in me could shine
But once – O but one ray

From that all-hallowing and eternal day,
Asking no more of Heaven I would go hence.   (*CP*, p. 271)

Seizing on this, one of the few but highly effective metaphors in *Common Chords*, Helen Waddell wrote to Sassoon in terms which gave him more hope than he had experienced for years: 'You do not know what you have done,' she wrote, 'and I have not the words to tell you. The soul's dark cottage in these poems has not only let in the light through chinks that time has made: it has itself become a light shining in the darkness.'[15]

Gathorne-Hardy, too, recognized the mysticism behind such poems, his chosen comparison being with Wordsworth rather than Vaughan. It was Gathorne-Hardy, not Keynes, who issued the first collection of spiritual outpourings, *Common Chords*, from his private Mill House Press in 1950.[16]

The most likely explanation for Sassoon's departure from his usual practice of printing his private volumes with Keynes was that he suspected that the rationalist Keynes would not appreciate the new direction he was taking. By the time he was ready with a second collection along similar lines, he was confident enough to return to Keynes for the production of it. Gathorne-Hardy's response to *Emblems of Experience* (1951) was more generous than Keynes's had been to his efforts. 'I was entranced,' he told Sassoon, 'by that quiet, wise, ruminative music.'[17] It seemed to him that the voice was now more like another seventeenth-century mystic, George Herbert. Sassoon was gratified by the comparison, though he had been aiming at something nearer to Emily Brontë's 'Last Lines'.

It had taken him just over a year to accumulate the twenty poems for *Emblems of Experience*, a year in which nothing had occurred to lessen his despair. The verses in it, even more so than those of *Common Chords*, are a cry for salvation. '"Take not Thy holy Spirit from us" is all they amount to,' Sassoon concluded.[18]

One of them, 'A Dream', suggests that he had been thinking a great deal about his past.[19] An account of the narrator's meeting with 'a stranger', who turns out to be himself, the poem ends: '"Stranger," I said, "since you and I are one,/ Let us go back. Let us undo what's done."' (*CP*, p. 284). The echoes of Owen's 'Strange Meeting' are more than coincidental. Owen had been much in his mind and the previous month he had written a sonnet about the two of them (never published) which underlines just how depressed he had become by January 1950, the month of its composition:

> *An Incident in Literary History*
> Sassoon and Owen – names that found their niche
> In literary history. Owen's dead.
> The other one survived the bullet which
> Toward that War's end just grazed him on the head.
> Yes; *his* career continued. But of late,
> His state of mind has made him wonder whether

Sassoon's continuance was appropriate ...
Should not these soldier poets have died together?

For thirty years a person of that name
Has done his level best to supplement
The scraps that opportunely earned him fame.
Yet literature's cold chronicles resent
The existence of this ghost. He should have kept
Silence, and out in France forever slept.[20]

One of the most successful poems in the collection is 'Befriending Star'. Like Cardinal Newman's 'Lead Kindly Light', of which there are echoes, this is a plea for simple faith expressed in language which becomes progressively more direct throughout its two quatrains until the narrator's final appeal to the star.

... Heart-simplified, appear
Not in ferocity of elemental fire,
But, for my lowly faith, a sign by which to steer.   (*CP*, p. 285)

'Such little things go to make up one's meditative existence,'[21] Sassoon noted at this time. He had been reading Helen Waddell's *Medieval Latin Lyrics* as he worked on his own poems and her translations of five poems by Alcuin had made him conscious of the similarities between men of faith in all ages. Sitting in his 'tall-windowed Wiltshire room,/ (Birds overheard from chill March twilight's close)', he imagined the medieval poet undergoing a similar experience to his own, especially the comfort he derives from the night sky:

Alcuin, from temporalities at rest,
Sought grace within him, given from afar;
Noting how sunsets worked around to west;
Watching, at spring's approach, that beckoning star;
And hearing, while one thrush sang through the rain,
Youth, which his soul in Paradise might regain.   (*CP*, p. 283)

Together with his unpublished poem 'Brevis Quod Gratia Florum Est', 'Awareness of Alcuin' is Sassoon's formal tribute to Helen Waddell at the moment when, though he did not know it, she was beginning her long, slow descent into complete mental extinction.[22]

By the time he came to write the bulk of the poems in *Emblem*, Sassoon, like Bunyan's Christian, had already passed through the Slough of Despond but not yet reached the Cross where Christian's burden rolls away. Nevertheless there is acceptance in these poems and an urgent desire for God to 'speak' to him.

Emblems closes with two poems almost certainly written last, 'The Present Writer', where the poet describes a further step in his spiritual progress, an

awareness of 'how little' the 'gnomic mind' can understand without the 'soul',
and 'The Messenger':

> Mind, busy in the body's life-lit room;
> Seldom in strength, unpiloted at best;
> How ignorant you admit from outer gloom
> The soul, in all God's world, most welcome guest.
> ...
> Poor mortal mind, when you, in me, decay –
> When once delighting faculties grow dim –
> Cry on the parting soul for power to say,
> With passion, 'I befriended was by Him.'   (*CP*, pp. 286-7)

With his ingrained suspicion of the intellect, Sassoon welcomed a revelation,
which he now implies – in 'World Without End' – he had been working
his way back to all his life. Ultimately it came down to a blind and trusting
'Acceptance', as his poem of that name argues. But the next step was one he
was not yet able to take. For by the time *Emblems of Experience* came out in
November 1951, his life had undergone a dramatic change which threatened
to distract him from spiritual matters altogether.

*

It is an intriguing story. Sassoon had been corresponding since 1945 with a
young Australian woman, Dorothy Wallis, who had written from Melbourne
initially to say how much she admired his work. Her letters showed her to be,
in his own words, 'a very nice person', of good education, who shared his love
of music and ballet.[23] She also started sending fruit cake, chocolate and other
luxuries, for which Sassoon was grateful, since rationing continued in England
for some time after the War. When Dorothy arrived in England with her
mother early in 1951, Sassoon invited her to visit him at Heytesbury. The fact
that he waited until December to do so and was 'somewhat hesitant' (according
to Dorothy who was longing to meet him) suggests that he feared as well as
wanted a further involvement, and his return to work on a fourth volume of
autobiography in September that year may indicate a sense of renewed energy
and hope.

   When Dorothy eventually visited Heytesbury in December 1951, Sassoon
insisted that she stay a whole week, 'long enough', she told Glen, 'to decide that
he wanted [her] to remain in his life'.[24] Weekends followed (Dorothy worked in
London during the week) until her mother, disapproving of what she suspected
was more than simply friendship, made her daughter's life so 'miserable' that
Dorothy temporarily stopped seeing Sassoon.[25] Once her mother returned to
Australia in August 1952, however, the relationship was resumed with renewed
intensity. Dorothy claimed that Sassoon made it quite clear that he wanted
her to come to live with him, though not until 1954, when George would

be eighteen. He was anxious that neither George nor Hester should know of Dorothy, nor did he talk to any of his friends. He had at first wanted to tell Glen 'everything about us', Dorothy wrote, but later changed his mind.[26]

Edmund and Claire Blunden were the only ones to know of the relationship, since it was Dorothy who had brought about a reconciliation with Sassoon. Hearing him speak of Blunden and their estrangement, without telling Sassoon she had visited Blunden at the office of the *Times Literary Supplement* where he was working by early 1952 and told him how much Sassoon missed him. By August the Blundens had spent several weekends again at Heytesbury. Claire, who believed that Sassoon approved of her for Blunden in spite of a significant age difference, thought that Sassoon was subconsciously influenced by their relationship in his own with Dorothy, who was thirty-six years his junior. She also suggested that Sassoon might still secretly be hoping for more children. Dorothy, she remembered, was an attractive though not conventionally pretty woman, tallish, slim and vivacious, a 'very lively' person. Her great admiration for Sassoon's work at a time when he felt neglected and undervalued as a poet, Claire maintained, was an important factor in the equation.[27]

By September 1952 when Dorothy resumed her visits to Heytesbury, it seemed to her that 'everything ... promise[d] well' for the future: 'I had seen Siegfried change from the man who believed there was only loneliness ahead of him to one who could say I had been "sent to deliver him" and that he could have "complete trust in my love".'[28] The fact that Blunden claimed to have witnessed the same change in his friend convinced her that she was not deluding herself.

Sassoon's poetry of that period offers strong proof of a renewed hope in life. After a significant gap in his religious questionings in the second half of 1951, when he wrote little or no poetry, the poems of 1952 (following his first meeting with Dorothy) reveal a zest for life long absent from his work. 'The Best of It', written on 27 February 1952, for instance, opens:

> Spring, surgent in the sense-delighted blood;
> In daybreak being all the burst of bud.
> This, beyond argument, was well begun.   (*CP*, p. 298)

'Another Spring', which appeared in the *Times Literary Supplement* on 20 March 1952, shortly after it was written, conveys an even greater sense of renewal of life and hope: 'Eyes, ears are old,' he concedes, 'But not the sense of spring' (*CP*, pp. 296-7).[29]

Such poems alone suggest that Sassoon's relationship with Dorothy was an invigorating one, as she claimed, revealing as they do a fresh exuberance and joy in earthly things. Claire Blunden believed that the relationship had a physical side to it, though other friends questioned this.[30] After nearly a decade without a sexual relationship it is not impossible that Sassoon responded to an attractive and willing young woman, as she claims he did. A letter to Tomlinson telling him that 1952 was his 'most unworried yet' strengthens the likelihood that his life had changed significantly that year.[31] He also told Tomlinson in October 1952 that his 'inner consciousness' was prompting him with speculations about the problem of body and spirit and that his next volume of verse would be 'a series of variations on that theme'.[32] Having so recently set off on a spiritual quest, a physical relationship with Dorothy would explain his claim in 'The Alliance' that:

> 'Of body and soul there can be no division;
> 'Soul should embrace it, cherish and control.
> 'Our two great halves must share a single vision.
> 'Let mutual services unite them whole.' ...   (*CP*, p. 299)

When things began to go wrong with Dorothy it was not because of the sexual side, she believed, but a result of her unintentional confrontation with Sassoon's housekeeper, Miss Benn. After a series of disastrous cooks, the last of whom had removed all the silver as she left, at the end of 1949 he had finally discovered Miss Kathleen Benn. An ex-kennel-maid, she brought with her her large poodle, Caesar, whom Sassoon adored. Short, squat and mannish, with cropped hair, she reminded Haro Hodson of a 'shaving brush in specs'.[33] But like all Sassoon's friends he was impressed by her excellent cooking and general efficiency. When the old housekeeper, Mrs Angus, left, Miss Benn took over the whole upkeep of Heytesbury and ran it as if it were a military operation. It was a rule of iron, as Dorothy discovered. Even Sassoon, who was abjectly grateful for a well-run house and first-class cuisine, grew tired at times of Miss Benn's bleak manner, which he complained of to Dorothy.

Ostensibly a row about Dorothy daring to clean the candelabrum in the music room, when Miss Benn considered it her province, Dorothy's difference with Miss Benn was really a battle for control. Miss Benn felt her supremacy threatened and presented Sassoon with a choice between herself and Dorothy. He had become so dependent on her for the smooth running of Heytesbury by that point that he chose Miss Benn. She had not only made herself particularly obliging to him during this period, but had also managed to portray Dorothy as domineering and managerial, playing to all his deepest fears about women. (Ironically Miss Benn was much nearer to this stereotype herself and her tyranny over him would increase until he became desperate enough to dismiss her in the late 1950s.) What *he* wanted, he told Dorothy in a letter terminating their relationship, was 'another Florence Hardy; ... She would have abased herself to Miss Benn and all would have been well.'[34]

Claire Blunden ultimately held Sassoon responsible for events. Though he had 'obviously enjoyed it all', she said, when the first 'glorious romance' became more ordinary, he shied away from commitment.[35] 'Such a charmer,' she remembered, 'but always dodging away from people.'[36]

Another factor which neither Claire nor Dorothy took into account was guilt, since neither was fully aware of Sassoon's spiritual searchings by 1951. While 'The Alliance' expresses the positive aspect of Sassoon's thoughts on the relationship between body and spirit, 'Human Bondage', written in October 1952 at the height of his affair, indicates that there were times when the physical seemed to him a threat to the spiritual enlightenment he had earlier glimpsed, ending: 'I, this blithe structure of sensation,/ Prisoned and impassioned by my clay' (*CP*, p. 300).

Sassoon's longing for Dr Rivers to return from the dead to clear up his 'confusion' in January 1953 suggests that he was suffering a conflict as powerful as the one Rivers had tried to resolve for him between his pacifism and his devotion to his soldiers. It was shortly after that, according to Dorothy, that he decided she was not the answer to his problems. By the end of January he was focused once more on the 'faithful pilgrimage' on which he had embarked, 'zealous to walk the way of Henry Vaughan', though more aware than ever of the difficulties, as poems like 'The Trial' show.[37]

Dorothy did not let go without a struggle. After receiving Sassoon's letter, she wrote at length to Glen, whom Sassoon had described as the only person who understood him.[38] But Glen, knowing how fiercely Sassoon reacted to disloyalty in his friends, refused to become involved. 'You must remember that he is one of my dearest friends,' he replied to her desperate plea, 'and that I should naturally tend to see things from his point of view.'[39] Even more cogently he argued, in terms which show how well he understood Sassoon's character by 1953: 'I know he is a man who hates upsets and quarrelling. Also when he makes a decision about anything he usually sticks to it.'[40] So Dorothy was forced to accept defeat and Sassoon was faced again with a lonely life at Heytesbury.

He did not return immediately to his spiritual quest, however. His relationship with Dorothy, whatever its outcome, had given him a taste for more human pleasures, for company in particular. Yet every year fewer friends made their way to Wiltshire. Either they were too busy, like Glen and Keynes, or too infirm, like Tomlinson or de la Mare, or simply no longer alive, like Marsh who had died in January that year. Though too deeply rooted in Heytesbury to live elsewhere, Sassoon felt he must 'compel' himself to leave it more often.[41] Apart from other considerations Miss Benn, whose triumph over Dorothy had strengthened her hold over Sassoon, quite reasonably insisted on a holiday periodically. So, less than a fortnight after his final letter to Dorothy of 6 May 1953, he set out for a ten-day visit to Cambridge, the first of many such trips in the 1950s.

His choice of Cambridge was relatively easy. Just as he had cultivated Rolf Barber's company initially for the sake of his son's future at Oundle, so he now planned to make Cambridge a 'centre' in advance of George's arrival there.[42] In addition most of what he dolefully called his 'few remaining connexions' were there.[43] E.M. Forster had been made a Fellow at King's College in 1946 and had rooms there and Keynes, whose company Sassoon still sought whatever his reservations, not only lived nearby but had also introduced him to a number of his friends and relatives in or on the outskirts of the town. In addition Sassoon's work on *Meredith* had brought him into contact with G.M. Trevelyan and his circle, one of whom was S.C. Roberts, the Master of Pembroke. He had also by 1953 resumed relations with Edmund Gosse's son, Philip, who had retired to Cambridge, with the poet, Frances Cornford, and the artist, Gwen Raverat. The deaths, first of Philip's wife, the poet, Anna Keown, and Gwen Raverat in 1957, then of Frances Cornford in 1960, would be factors in his decision not to make Cambridge his second home.

Sassoon admired Raverat's paintings and bought a number of them over the years.[44] His favourite, which hung in his bedroom, was a view of the River Cam looking towards Queen's and the boathouse of his usual stopping place in Cambridge, the Garden House Hotel. It was at this hotel on the evening of his arrival in town from the Keyneses on 19 May 1953 that he entertained the young man who was to 'nourish and enliven' him for the next fourteen years, Dennis Silk.[45] The meeting came about through Blunden who, like all Sassoon's friends, worried about his isolation. Blunden and Silk were both old boys of Christ's Hospital and had met at a school reunion. On hearing of Sassoon's trip to Cambridge, Blunden suggested Sassoon look the young man up at the university cricket grounds. The combination of Blunden's recommendation and cricket had been irresistible and Sassoon was at Fenners within hours of his arrival. Dennis Silk, a 21-year-old history student in his second year at Sidney Sussex College, retains a vivid memory of 'the gaunt, handsome stranger in moth-eaten blue blazer and faded trilby hat who marched up to the pavilion with a long forked hazel staff in his hand'.[46] Looking up at the rows of seated spectators, he said 'in a tone of enquiry and a little awkwardly: "Dennis Silk"?', identifying himself simply as 'Siegfried Sassoon'.[47] It was a name which, even by 1953, needed no explanation.

Sassoon's enthusiasm was immediate. Within a short time Dennis would get to know all Sassoon's closest friends. Some he would meet at Heytesbury, where he would stay many times in the following years.

In asking to bring Dennis with him to the Gosses, Sassoon described him as 'quite exceptionally nice and intelligent' and one of 'the most successful of this year's University cricketers'.[48] And it was this mix of physical and mental prowess, together with his 'modesty' and 'gentleness', which particularly appealed to him.[49] Dennis would go on to achieve great things in sport, playing cricket for the MCC several years running, as well as rugby to county standard.

Equally important to him, however, was Dennis's great love of literature. He found 'instructing young Silk about literature' just as enjoyable as discussing cricket with him, according to his diary, and talked to him at length about his own work. Dennis's public readings of Sassoon's poetry suggest that he had found a perceptive and appreciative audience in the young man. And it was not just for his work. Silk loved hearing Sassoon expound 'endlessly and unforgettably' about the First World War: '"my old war" as he called it, exorcising the ghosts of 1914-1918'.[50]

Sometimes they would sit down in the library after dinner and, before either of them realized it, dawn had risen. Sassoon felt he was again reliving the past, particularly the time when he made his 'agonizing protest'.[51] Dennis brought back his youth to him at a time when he was feeling his age badly. 'He blossomed in the company of young people,' Dennis remembered, 'and gave richly of his energy and vitality.'[52]

In a short time Dennis became indispensable to Sassoon, who was delighted when he accepted a teaching post at Marlborough College, only thirty miles from Heytesbury. He bought Dennis a half-share in an old car so that he could come to see him more easily[53] and, as he grew less willing to drive himself, Dennis would also chauffeur him in his ancient Humber. They both looked forward to the annual visits they made to Glen and Angela at Stratford, for instance, where Glen was first co-director, then director of the Shakespeare Memorial Theatre from 1952 to 1959. Seeing stars like Laurence Olivier and Peggy Ashcroft nightly was an unforgettable experience. They also met there the Shakespearian scholar Dover Wilson, whom Dennis charmed into addressing the Marlborough Literary Society. Sassoon was invited to the talk and would start to correspond with Wilson, whose work he greatly admired.

Being approved by Glen was one of the tests Sassoon set for new friends and he had no hesitation in introducing Dennis, who passed at once. Dennis came to occupy a similar place to Glen and Blunden in Sassoon's affections. Dennis's heterosexuality freed Sassoon, as it had with Blunden, from the 'cursed complication of sex' and when Dennis married in 1963 Sassoon's feelings for him would remain unchanged, except that they would expand to include his wife, Diana, whom he would pronounce 'quite perfect'.[54] According to Dennis, his relationship with Sassoon was entirely 'uncomplicated'.[55] He 'never sniffed any hint of homosexuality' about him and was very surprised indeed when he detected it in Sassoon's published diaries after his death.[56] The relationship seemed to them both like that of father and son. When in 1955, at the age of eighteen, Sassoon's own son married very suddenly and without telling his parents, Sassoon, 'bewildered, puzzled and hurt', would turn gratefully to Dennis for consolation.[57] Dennis was an ideal friend for Sassoon, bringing youth, vitality, idealism and hope to him at a crucial point in his life. After Blunden left England again for the University of Hong Kong in September 1953, Sassoon would rely increasingly on Silk for sympathy and stimulation, and his presence at Cambridge in 1953 and 1954 added greatly to its attraction during those years.

So, too, did the award of an honorary fellowship at his old college, Clare, at the end of 1953.[58] Though he claimed not to be interested in worldly honours, Sassoon was intensely gratified by the suggestion that his name should be put forward for a fellowship in October 1953. It took him completely by surprise, he told the Master of Clare, Sir Henry Thirkhill, but he had no hesitation in accepting the idea. Thirkhill's confirmation of his unanimous election on 3 November helped to make up for the long years of neglect he felt he had suffered. He agreed with S.C. Roberts, who wrote in his letter of congratulation that 'Honorary Fellowships constitute one of the few honours that remain very strictly and exclusively honourable' and that he would enjoy 'the highest possible status' at Clare.[59] For someone who had come down from Cambridge without a degree and suffered from a sense of intellectual inferiority all his life, it was a heady moment. From this point on he would include a few days' residence at Clare in spring and autumn as part of his Cambridge season.

On one such visit in late 1954 he agreed to give an informal talk to students in the rooms of Professor John Northam, head of English. 'There was no society behind the occasion to guarantee a reasonable attendance,' Professor Northam remembers; 'I had simply let it be known that Sassoon was to speak.'[60] He therefore 'ate an anxious dinner' in Sassoon's company, 'mentally coining phrases of regret suitable to an audience of six, four, even of two'.[61] After all, as he pointed out, the Great War, to which Sassoon's name was 'riveted', had long passed:

> In the event my rooms were packed; the atmosphere was intense and it remained so throughout the evening. Not because of anything in Sassoon's performance. He did not perform. His only response to the occasion was to read from his own works in a quiet near-mumble. My recollection is that he pipe-smoked as he talked. He made few comments, none of them memorable. And yet not only did he keep the attention of his audience for the duration of the talk proper, but he mesmerized them into staying long after the talk had ended. In the end he had to be rescued.
>
> I have often wondered why he worked so powerfully upon those much younger men. Only a few, I fancy, knew his writings with any intimacy. Some, I suppose, had come out of curiosity to see a hero from a great and terrible enterprise that had become a legend. But for most, I believe, Sassoon was more than a writer or a relic. What excited their interest and admiration was his other kind of courage, the courage that made him reject war and the prestige that he had won through war. It was not the V.C. quality they had come to pay respect to, but the man who had thrown his decorations away in protest. What gripped them that evening was his integrity.[62]

One student present, Tim Rix, agrees that 'integrity' is 'exactly the right word' for Sassoon's appeal that evening.[63] Like the rest of the young men he found Sassoon 'mesmerizing'. It was partly because of the habit Northam noted of pipe-smoking throughout his performance – 'He lit and relit his pipe about eighty times in all and spoke in bursts in between puffs,' Rix remembers, leaving a large pyramid of used matches on the arm of his chair. But he was also riveted by Sassoon's appearance as he sat alone in the centre of the room with his 'great hawk-like head', a 'tremendous presence' in the midst of them.

*

However pleasing such public recognition of his work and however many new friends Sassoon made in the early 1950s, they could not satisfy his deepest needs. By the end of 1953, without even wanting or willing it, he believed that 'creative existence as a whole is what matters to the future' and that 'the spirit of God (or good) should pervade and prevail'.[64] He felt he was being gradually compelled to believe, recording each stage of his journey in poems marking moments of illumination, many of them seeming to arrive from nowhere. It was, as he describes in 'The Visitant' (a poem Masefield considered one of his best), almost like being possessed:

Someone else I know of – neither young nor old –
Seated late at night in my accustomed chair,
Willed to an intended thing which must be told,
Catches intimations brought from otherwhere.

Someone else invades me for an hour or two.
Clocked occluded self wrote never lines like his.
Me he has no need of. And I know not who
Or from what irrational inwardness he is.   (*CP*, p. 292)

The poems written between 1952 and 1954, published as *The Tasking*, show a greater spiritual awareness and sense of inwardness than any previous volume. 'Renewals', for instance, records an experience very close to T.S. Eliot's 'Teach us to sit still' in 'Ash Wednesday' in its final line: 'Be silent and grow still'.[65]

Sassoon's earlier reading of the seventeenth-century mystic John Norris of Bemerton, a small parish not far from Heytesbury, suggests that he was already searching for inner stillness when he quoted Norris in *Siegfried's Journey* in 1946: 'Quietude is essential to human happiness ... The solitary and contemplative man sits as safe in his retirement as of Homer's heroes in a cloud, and has this only trouble from the follies and extravagances of men, that he pities them.'[66] His own favourite poem from *The Tasking*, 'A Chord', centres on a similar theme, conveying an experience of God anticipated by his habit of sitting down to the piano for inspiration long before he started on his spiritual quest:

On stillness came a chord,
While I, the instrument,
Knew long-withheld reward:
Gradual the glory went;
Vibrating, on and on,
Toward harmony unheard,
Till dark where sanctus shone;
Lost, once a living word.

> But in me yet abode
> The given grace though gone;
> The love, the lifted load,
> The answered orison.   (*CP*, p. 303)

But there are also signs of doubt and despair in *The Tasking*. These feelings may have resulted partly from outward events, such as the death of Wavell's son, Archie, at the end of 1953, or George's increasing independence which kept him away from Heytesbury for months at a time. They sprang, however, from what Sassoon subsequently recognized as also an essential stage in the spiritual process. The paradox of his position emerges most clearly in the last poem to be written in *The Tasking*, 'Faith Unfaithful':

> Mute, with signs I speak:
> Blind, by groping seek:
> Heed; yet nothing hear:
> Feel; find no one near.
>
> Deaf, eclipsed, and dumb,
> Through this gloom I come
> On the time-path trod
> Toward ungranted God ...   (*CP*, p. 294)

The Tasking was privately printed by Keynes in November.[67] The 'complete absence of emotional excitement or preliminary mental chemistry' Sassoon experienced as he struggled to express each new insight may help to explain their spareness and condensed force.[68] Not a word or image is wasted. Sassoon's own description of his work in *The Tasking* is 'plainsong and essential expression'.[69] Though very different in both content and technique from his war satires, the poetry of this last period shares its muscularity and rawness.

Sassoon was enormously relieved at his friends' responses to *The Tasking*. 'The poems evidently do well,' he wrote to the man he claimed as the book's 'godfather', Tomlinson.[70] He was 'especially pleased' by Swinnerton saying that he found them '*refreshing* – and not depressing', since he had thought of them as 'a rather gloomy offering'.[71] And George Trevelyan, who could be 'a bit forbidding', had said he 'love[d] them and was deeply moved'.[72] John Betjeman boldly declared that the poems '*must* be immortal' and Keynes forwarded 'kind comments' from Rupert Hart-Davis, remarks that helped offset Sassoon's fears of dismissal by Modernist critics like Graves, Edith Sitwell and Geoffrey Grigson.[73]

*

The last stage of Sassoon's spiritual odyssey was the hardest. Following the composition of the final poem of *The Tasking* in March 1954, he suffered nearly three years of 'dark night'.[74] Helen Waddell's mental decline and the death of Archie Wavell in Kenya had deprived him of the two people he believed could have helped him find his way through it. 1953 and 1954 were 'special years of frustration and discouragement and solitude' and 1955 and 1956 'little better'.[75] The deaths of two old friends who had been of particular importance to him, Max Beerbohm and Walter de la Mare, made 1956 even more of a trial.[76]

Outwardly his life followed a familiar pattern of spring and autumn breaks at Cambridge, with summer trips to Glen at Stratford beginning in 1955. There were a few new developments. In 1953, for instance, he got to know the Warden of All Soul's, Oxford, John Sparrow, and a young man Sparrow brought with him on a visit to Heytesbury that year, Colin Fenton.[77] (It would be Fenton, rather than any of Sassoon's closer friends, who would write his obituary in *The Times*.)[78]

There were other distractions to break up the monotony of Sassoon's existence. He enjoyed a visit to the Whistlers at Lyme Regis in June 1954, for example, and a reunion of the Royal Welch Fusiliers at Swindon in July, when he met a number of officers he had known in the First World War and was presented to the Queen. And he was pleased to encounter Robert Graves again in October 1954 after a gap of twenty-seven years. Graves, who was delivering the Clark lectures at Cambridge, seemed to him as 'provocative' as ever, but 'personally likeable' in a way he had forgotten over the years.[79] He would remain for Sassoon an intriguing opposite, a 'queer fish'.[80] While he appreciated Graves's renewed admiration for his work, for instance, he felt it could only be perverseness which made Graves irreverent about Tennyson and Wordsworth and dismissive of Pope's technique in his Clark lectures. (Sassoon himself turned down an invitation to deliver the lectures the following year because he felt he had nothing to say.)

Sassoon was delighted, too, when George won a science scholarship to King's College, Cambridge, in 1955, though his son's sudden marriage a few months later devastated him. A disagreement with Keynes over his plans to publish an edition of Rupert Brooke's letters left him more marooned than ever at Heytesbury. By November 1956 the Suez crisis and the 'ghastly state of the world' generally added to his gloom and he began to complain once more of solitude.[81]

The publication of *Sequences*, Faber's collected trade edition of *Common Chords*, *Emblems of Experience* and *The Tasking*, on 9 November 1956 brought matters to a head. After sixteen years of 'patience and silence' on his part, he had hoped that the reviewers would at least appreciate his painful efforts to bare his soul.[82] Instead he was largely dismissed or ignored, a situation he found 'heartbreaking'.[83] Blunden alone appeared to recognize his aims and achievement, arguing, as he had from the start, that Sassoon was 'essentially a religious poet'.[84]

Yet it was this least publicly acclaimed of all his works which was to have a more powerful effect on Sassoon's fate than anything since his First World War poetry. Not only would it win him the prestigious Queen's Gold Medal for Poetry in June 1957, but it would also lead to the complete transformation of the last ten years of his life. For it was one of *Sequences*' first readers, Mother Margaret Mary McFarlin, who recognized the spiritual darkness with which Sassoon had struggled for almost three years and who was eventually able to lead him out of it.

31
'It Has Been a Long Journey'
1957-1967

Mother Margaret Mary McFarlin, according to Sassoon, was 'the greatest benefactor' of his life.[1] Mother Superior of the Convent of the Assumption in Kensington Square, London, she first wrote to him about *Sequences* at the beginning of January 1957. Reading his poems while convalescing from flu, she had felt an overwhelming urge to tell him that she was praying he might (in his own words) 'through the Darkness divine God's Presence'.[2] 'I was in a complete black-out,' Sassoon remembered, '... and somehow was helped to realize that deliverance had arrived.'[3] His reply by return on 10 January was the first step in his entry into the Roman Catholic Church eight months later.

Sensitive, intelligent and devout without being in the least stuffy, Mother Margaret, as Sassoon recognized, 'never made a glimmer of mistake in her guidance and influence'.[4] Sensing that his faith sprang from emotions rather than intellect, she avoided overwhelming him with ponderous theology, appealing first to his love of literature. Her early letters deal mainly with their shared love of the Jesuit poet Gerard Manley Hopkins, Thomas Hardy and Robert Browning and the metaphysicals Henry Vaughan and George Herbert. She also suggested that he read the mystical writings of St John of the Cross and directed him towards the sermons of one of the Catholic Church's greatest converts, John Henry Newman. 'Reading Newman,' Sassoon would write in 1960, 'I wonder what effect it would have made if someone had given it to me ten years ago. Everything I needed is there, waiting for me! All clear as daylight. And as simple as falling off a log – just unconditional surrender!'[5]

The 'unconditional surrender' was not long in coming, thanks largely to the stream of letters between the 54-year-old nun from Liverpool, who began each of hers with the confident words 'Beloved Son in Christ' and the 70-year-old poet, who addressed her as his 'Dear Mother', sometimes 'Cornucopia Mother'.[6] His lengthy weekly reports, describing his spiritual progress and much else, quickly replaced his lonely diary musings and, unlike his diary, always produced a reply, except in Lent, when Mother Margaret was not allowed to write.

By Lent, however – more specifically by Ash Wednesday, 5 March 1957 – less than two months after his first letter to Mother Margaret, Sassoon had begun to face up to 'the proposition of becoming a Catholic'.[7] And by Easter he had regained his belief in God, an intense experience he described in a poem written the day following Good Friday:

Deliverance
No comfort came until I looked for light
Beyond the darkened thickets of my brain.
With nothingness I strove. And inward sight
No omen but oblivion could obtain.

He spoke. He held my spirit in His hand.
Through prayer my password from the gloom was given.
This Eastertide, absolved, in strength I stand.
Feet firm upon the ground. My heart in heaven.[8]

Overwhelmed with relief and happiness, Sassoon rushed up to London and presented himself, unannounced, at Mother Margaret's convent in Kensington Square. She would later recall the 'tall, wiry, nervy man' who talked to her in 'bursts of speech' that often seemed 'barely intelligible', and her surprise at his shabby clothing, though she recognized an 'innate elegance'.[9] Tiny, bubbly, outgoing and highly articulate herself, she was in many ways his opposite and an unlikely candidate for the sainthood he bestowed on her.[10] An inspiring teacher, she was quite ready to liven up events by unconventional means, dancing the Charleston on feast days, for example, or singing Fred Astaire and Ginger Rogers hits to hold her students' attention, behaviour which would have horrified Sassoon in earlier years.

She was also very practical, however, and it was at her suggestion that he started instruction in the Catholic faith with Dom Sebastian Moore at Downside Abbey, only fifteen miles from Heytesbury. Beginning on 30 May and continuing throughout June and July, he drove there once a week to 'converse' with the Benedictine monk. Dom Sebastian still remembered in his eighties Sassoon's arrival every Wednesday afternoon in his dark-green Humber, its antiquated hood secured not altogether effectively by yellow adhesive plaster, which 'glistened bravely in the sun' and matched Sassoon's equally ancient hat.[11]

One of the younger monks, 'dear old Sebby' (as he quickly became to Sassoon) had not been Mother Margaret's first choice. He seemed an ideal person to instruct Sassoon, however, being himself a poet as well as an authority on another First World War writer, David Jones.[12] Like Mother Margaret, he immediately sensed Sassoon's needs and kept things informal, holding their weekly sessions in the abbey's rock garden. He 'asked no questions', according to Sassoon, 'just let it happen through self-expression on both sides'.[13] By

August Sassoon felt ready to commit himself completely to what he called the 'Old Faith'.

Part of the explanation for the speed of Sassoon's conversion was that he was already well prepared when he started his instruction, having read widely on the subject under Mother Margaret's skilful direction. Dom Sebastian had also noted at their first meeting, both in Sassoon's vocabulary and his stillness, the qualities of the mystic for whom no detailed intellectual argument was needed. Sassoon had been particularly struck by Hilaire Belloc's letter to another devout Catholic, Lady Katharine Asquith, which opens: 'The Faith, the Catholic Church, is discovered, is recognized, triumphantly enters reality like a landfall at sea ....'[14]

Sassoon had also been helped by another close friend of Katharine Asquith, Monsignor Ronald Knox.[15] It was Knox's more serious works, especially his sermons, that he read and re-read in the lead-up to his conversion and he found it impossible to 'measure [his] debt' to Knox's instructive writings.[16] He had got to know Knox reasonably well in 1954 when he was reintroduced to Katherine Asquith by Violet Bonham Carter's daughter, Cressida. Knox, who was two years younger than Sassoon, had gone to live in the Asquith household after the Second World War, having by then retired as Catholic chaplain to the University of Oxford. Officially there to complete his new translation of the Bible based on the Vulgate text, he unofficially acted as private chaplain to the Asquith family and his presence reinforced Mells as a Catholic centre, its nearness to Downside (only eight miles away) adding to its attractions. Like Newman, Knox had himself been a convert, which may help to explain the appeal of both writers for Sassoon.

Though Sassoon never referred directly to his spiritual needs to Knox on his frequent visits to Mells Manor between 1954 and 1957, Knox reached him, he claimed, 'with a living voice through his writings, as no one else'.[17] He certainly gave intellectual respectability to Rome in Sassoon's eyes. In addition to that, behind the 'incredibly brilliant and accomplished' front of the Old Etonian and Balliol scholar, Sassoon detected a 'creative sanctity' and 'near-saint[liness]', an 'incomparable expositor of alive religion'. Above all he found that Knox *'gave* with both hands – spiritual help, scholarship, entertainment'.[18] On his last visit to the priest, shortly before Knox's death from cancer at the age of sixty-nine, he had taken Blunden to meet him and Knox had talked to them for three and a half hours 'with full enjoyment of seeing us', almost making Sassoon forget 'how heartbreaking it was, that farewell'.[19]

Knox's illness was the reason he gave Mother Margaret for not taking on Sassoon's instruction as she had suggested in 1957. Mother Margaret had got to know him well during his period as chaplain to her convent at Aldenham during the Second World War. It is quite likely that they had subsequently discussed Sassoon once he started visiting Mells in 1954 and that Mother Margaret's first letter to Sassoon had been prompted by something more than a voice from above. Knox himself was far too subtle to have broached the subject of Sassoon's evident needs directly with him when it was clear that Sassoon himself was not ready to ask for help. Yet in all essential respects it was Knox who seems to have guided him towards the Catholic Church, suggesting that what might otherwise appear as a hasty conversion had been really a more gradual process over a number of years.

When Sassoon was received into the Church at Downside on 14 August 1957, the Eve of the Feast of the Assumption, it was, therefore, the culmination of years of thought and reading. Yet his inward experience during the next few days seemed to him 'something unfathomable by the mind'.[20] He 'just allowed it to happen, knowing and yet unknowing', finally feeling at peace with himself and the world.[21]

However private the experience, Sassoon was fully aware of his news value as a high-profile convert and was greatly relieved that the Catholic papers had been persuaded to say nothing. But the 'gutter press', to his disgust, 'found out somehow and were all after [him]'.[22] The news of his conversion, leaked publicly by the *News of the World*, surprised almost everyone, including those closest to him, since he had told no one of his intentions, not even Glen, Blunden or Dennis. But he had no real cause for worry; his friends appeared to be delighted for him, with two exceptions: Laurence Whistler, whose violent reaction startled him, and Swinnerton, a 'rational sceptic' who had 'no sympathy', he wrote, with Sassoon's 'final acceptance of clerical supervision'.[23]

Even Keynes, a confirmed agnostic married to a Darwin, responded positively to the news. Sassoon had feared that he would be 'unsympathetic and insensitive',[24] but like all his true friends Keynes welcomed anything that might help offset the desolation of his life in the late 1940s and early 50s. Whatever his own position, he had 'always recognized Sassoon's spiritual leanings'.[25] However critical he might be of Keynes, Sassoon acknowledged that he was 'good' for him and a 'truly reliable friend'.[26] By 1958, their differences over the Rupert Brooke *Letters* had been buried and Keynes was hard at work on another project to boost Sassoon's morale, a bibliography of all his verse and prose works. Though he had told Keynes that he was not particularly keen on a bibliography, even taking a perverse pleasure in concealing information from him at times, he was secretly reassured by this sign of his importance as a writer.

Keynes would also be responsible for managing an even more gratifying recognition of his achievements, when he arranged to receive his own honorary doctorate from Oxford at the same time as the one offered to Sassoon, 'knowing how difficult it might be to prise Sassoon out of his shell' otherwise.[27] Together with the Russian poetess Anna Akhmatova and Professor Gianfranco Contini, the two of them would be invested with their honours at a special ceremony the day before Encaenia to protect Sassoon as much as possible from the exhaustions of the more public occasion, Keynes making sure that all went smoothly.

Hester was not quite so understanding as Keynes; for her the Mass was 'only a ceremony' and 'God was mostly "out of doors"'.[28] She could not begin to understand her husband's need for dogma and an organized religion.

Nevertheless, she too came round when she saw how happy Sassoon's conversion had made him and was duly taken to visit Mother Margaret, to whom she presented a huge box of Heytesbury snowdrops.

There was no such ambivalence on the part of Sassoon's three closest friends, though Blunden discovered the change only by chance, an indication that the distance between them had not been fully bridged. Sassoon had inadvertently pulled out a rosary with his handkerchief as they lunched together during Blunden's leave from Hong Kong shortly after Sassoon's reception at Downside. Claire remembered Sassoon picking it up but not saying a word. When he did finally tell Blunden, Blunden rejoiced for him and yet another visit to Mother Margaret took place.

Sassoon had told Glen and Dennis almost immediately of the change during his annual trip to Stratford with Dennis, the month after his Downside reception. On arrival at their hotel, the Welcombe, Dennis had been summoned to Sassoon's room to find him sitting nervously on the edge of his bed, rosary in hand. He feared that, as the son of an Anglican clergyman, Dennis might disapprove and was anxious to 'explain'.[29] The explanation, when it eventually emerged, was revealing: 'I'm very highly sexed, you know,' he told Dennis in his abrupt way, '– had a lot of trouble down there,' pointing awkwardly at his genitals. Dennis, who knew nothing of his homosexual past, nor of his more recent affair with Dorothy Wallis, was understandably puzzled. But he was also delighted, since it was clear that Sassoon's conversion had made him 'transparently happy'.[30] One of the most powerful attractions of the Catholic Church for Sassoon appears to have been the notion of confession and absolution. There is no doubting the sense of guilt he carried with him up to his entry into the Church.

Glen, though suffering none of Sassoon's guilt over sex and his youthful homosexuality, nevertheless responded as positively as Dennis to what he recognized as Sassoon's 'infinite happiness and heart's ease'.[31] He felt privileged to be told about such a private matter: 'it showed me that you still love and trust me'.[32] Tactfully avoiding any reference to the failed relationship with Dorothy, or her letter to him, he nevertheless concluded with a shrewd analysis of Sassoon's frustrated needs throughout his life, sexual and otherwise:

> Above all else I have longed for you to be happy and at peace. I hoped that Hester would be able to give you that, and when she wasn't, I thought George would do so. Of course it wasn't their fault that they couldn't. You needed so much, because you are capable of so much, and I see now that you could only find supreme comfort in the way you have.[33]

Vivian de Sola Pinto believed that Sassoon had always been 'in a very real sense, a religious man'.[34] His condemnation of war, Pinto argued, was 'essentially religious, a protest against the maiming of the divine image in man'.[35] Another close friend would trace Sassoon's spiritual leanings even further back, arguing that it was 'not a sudden conversion: it was the movement of a straight line from the age of eight to seventy, it was the small boy arms outstretched calling to God across the Weald, it was George Sherston, the infantry officer, adding to his memoirs the curious epigraph: "I told him that I was a Pilgrim going to the Celestial City"'.[36]

A more complex question is why Sassoon chose to become a Catholic rather than simply returning to the Anglican faith of his upbringing. In responding to Tomlinson, who sympathized with his spiritual needs but found his choice of Church puzzling, he told him that the Catholic Church gave him a 'sustenance' the Church of England could not; it seemed 'so real' and its followers so different from the 'inhibiting reticence' which characterized the average Anglican.[37] He had been particularly impressed by the warmth and uninhibitedness of Mother Margaret and the fact that the Downside Benedictines were 'not a bit monastic'.[38]

Dennis Silk believes that a decisive factor in Sassoon's turning to Rome was his despair at world events, Korea and Suez in particular. He also maintained that Sassoon 'wanted to be told what to do' in his old age, and that the Catholic Church, with its claim to be the 'One True Church' and belief in the infallibility of its leader, the Pope, provided that authority. Sassoon himself, in his attempt to explain his decision, had written: 'My faith needs Authority to sustain it, I suppose. And this great traditional edifice of Catholicism makes Anglicanism seem unreal and ineffective. The faith I am now blessed with came to me through Catholic influence ....'[39] In becoming a Catholic he had found similar relief to the kind he had experienced in joining the army: he was once more 'under orders'. And as Maurice Wiggin, who met him towards the end of his life, suggested, his 'instinct for order' was very important to him.[40]

Robert Graves, who wrote to Sassoon less unsympathetically than might have been expected about his conversion, told a friend privately that it suited Sassoon 'as it suits a lot of frustrated homosexuals; but I am not one and so remain an ex-Protestant'.[41] He was almost certainly referring to the aesthetic appeal of the Catholic Church's elaborate rituals. There is no doubt that Sassoon had been influenced by these, as his long poem tracing his spiritual needs, 'Lenten Illuminations', shows:

> The aids were manifest; but only for your eyes and ears,
> In anthems, organ music, shaft-aspiring stone,
> And jewelled windows into which your mind might melt.[42]

The appeal to Sassoon's Romantic instincts was powerful, as also to what he called his 'self-sacrificing complex'.[43] Adrian Caesar sums it up well when he describes the Catholic Church as 'an entirely appropriate mental destination for a soldier poet who had sought and seen "sacrifice" in war, who had imagined himself and others as Christ-like in their suffering and who subscribed to the Romantic view that art was also dependent upon suffering and sacrifice'.[44]

Sassoon once described Catholicism to Dennis Silk as 'so civilized' and there is little doubt that Lady Katharine Asquith and her circle at Mells gave Catholicism a social as well as aesthetic appeal for Sassoon. But it would also be true to say that Katharine meant a great deal to him personally and influenced his final decision, quite apart from her impressive connections. His visits to her became an important part of his life even before his conversion and were undiminished by Knox's death in 1957. The numerous letters between them show how precious her friendship was to him in the last ten years of his life. She is always 'dearest' or 'darling' Katharine and he her 'loving Siegfried'.[45]

Through Katharine Sassoon also became friends with other Catholics in the district, like the Hollises whom he first met at Mells. Christopher Hollis, an 'extraordinarily gruff' but kind man, according to Dennis, had more than his Catholic publishing and writing in common with Sassoon, being, as Dennis put it, 'mad about cricket'.[46] Hollis's obituary of Sassoon in the *Spectator* would show how well he understood his complex personality.[47]

It was cricket, too, which added to the attraction of Katharine's other good friends, the monks of Downside Abbey. Sassoon had got to know a number of the Benedictine brothers at Mells several years before his instruction at Downside in 1957; his reception into their Church only increased an existing admiration and affection for them, Dom Sebastian Moore, Dom Martin Salmon, Dom Hubert Van Zeller and Dom Philip Jebb, in particular.

With all these men Sassoon appeared to feel, more strongly than at any time since early childhood, even more than in the army, a sense of belonging. The thought of Downside was 'a sanctuary' for his mind, its 'providential nearness' having 'dissolved all the formidableness of "becoming a Catholic"'.[48] For most of his life he had felt isolated in various ways, first by his homosexuality and poetry-writing, then by his public protest and later, physically, by his retreat to Heytesbury and the breakdown of his marriage. Now, finally, he saw himself as part of a community, with no need for apology or explanation. It seemed to him one of Catholicism's most precious gifts.

He experienced a similar sense of belonging at Stanbrook Abbey, which he first visited in June 1960. Curiously, it was not the Downside monks who introduced him to their Benedictine sisters, but his old agnostic friend Sydney Cockerell. Cockerell's interest in medieval manuscripts and fine printing had led him, in spite of his rationalism, to Stanbrook, which had a much respected press run by the sisters under Dame Hildelith Cumming. His long correspondence with the former Abbess of Stanbrook, Dame Laurentia McLachlan, between 1907 and 1953 had been published by 1959 and was known to Sassoon, as was George Bernard Shaw's equally interesting correspondence with Dame Laurentia. Sassoon also owned and admired editions of *The Stanbrook Carols* and *The Little Breviary*.

So that when Cockerell wrote to Sassoon in October 1959 enclosing a letter from one of the Stanbrook nuns, Dame Felicitas Corrigan, he was already familiar with that remarkable collection of ladies. The letter itself pleased him greatly, being a perceptive and positive critique of *Siegfried's Journey*, which Cockerell had sent Dame Felicitas to read.[49] Sassoon's instant response to her, with the photograph she had requested, was followed equally quickly by her reply and marked the start of a series of letters which chart his life in some detail over his last eight years. Not only does he speak to her frankly about his spiritual life and the joy he has experienced in entering the Catholic Church, he also talks to her fully about his past work and gives a running commentary on each new poem as he writes it.

They discuss music too. Dame Felicitas, a contemporary of Mother Margaret at Liverpool University, was the organist at Stanbrook Abbey and a fine musician, much to Sassoon's delight. She remembers how, on one of his visits to Stanbrook – a twice-yearly ritual from 1960 onwards – he begged her to play to him, requesting Bach's Prelude and Fugue in F. Her admiration for 'A Chord', a poem that depends on an understanding of musical technique for full effect, almost certainly explains his decision to make it the concluding poem of his revised *Collected Poems* in 1961.[50] Dame Felicitas, who had written two books herself by the time she met Sassoon, would go on to write her own formal evaluation of Sassoon based on his co-operation with her.[51] Sassoon evidently basked in her admiration and that of the other nuns at Stanbrook Abbey. He was persuaded to read and give a talk to them and though both performances were complete failures in terms of audibility – his speech being more indistinct and slurred than ever – yet 'one and all were enthusiastic' according to Dame Felicitas.[52]

Sassoon closed his reading to the nuns on his first visit to them in June 1960 with three poems written since his conversion. The earliest of these, 'Lenten Illuminations', an 81-line account, he explained, of 'my present self telling my pre-1957 self' what had led him to the Catholic Church (written 'quite easily' in three days after only two short pieces in the previous four years), had already been published in the *Downside Review* in June 1958.[53] The opening lines of this ('Not properly Catholic, some might say ...') promise well. Their easy, conversational tone suits the self-examination of the subject, as do the long, irregular lines of the verse, and convinces the reader that the poem came, as Sassoon claimed, 'unbidden and spontaneous'.[54] That it is 'the real thing', as he also argued, is sadly not the case, and Faber's refusal to distribute it is understandable.[55] Sassoon's Catholic friends, however, encouraged him to write verses they believed helped him clarify both his thoughts and emotions about his faith, and Dame Felicitas published a selection of his spiritual poems, *The Path to Peace* with the Stanbrook Abbey Press in 1960.

Overjoyed by the renewal of his poetic urge, long after he had assumed it dead, Sassoon seems to have been untroubled by doubts as to the relative worth of his religious verse. His relief, together with his connoisseur's appreciation of the beautifully produced *Path to Peace*, which he had helped design, emerges clearly in the jokey punning of his letter to Dom Martin Salmon on the subject: 'Just fancy – *Stanbrook* is printing a super de-luxe limited selection of my verse

... in Romulus Cancelleresca Bastarda fount – so I'm not such a cancelled old bastard as some of the modern critics think!'[56]

Stanbrook Abbey Press went on to print two smaller but equally beautiful productions, a short story from Sassoon's childhood to celebrate his eightieth birthday, *Something About Myself*, and a collection of his last four poems, *Ave Atque Vale*, in 1967, but *The Path to Peace* was his last significant production. As Michael Thorpe observes, it must be left for a Catholic writer to say 'Here is the story of a soul as shapely as any poet could want his verse to be.'[57] For those more interested in his poetry than his Catholicism, the most shapely ending would have been, as Thorpe notes, *The Tasking*.

*

Catholicism ensured that the last six years of Sassoon's life were his happiest. Rather than isolating him from people even more, as Keynes claimed, his religious belief (in the words of another close friend) 'gave him back to the world of men'.[58] Dame Felicitas, who readily acknowledged Keynes's affectionate charge of 'patent egocentricity' against Sassoon, believed that 'he tried to face up to it and at least combat it in the last years of his life' and that he '*was* endowed with a power of imaginative sympathy and compassion that rang absolutely true'.[59] She saw Sassoon's life as 'the breaking down of an immense egocentricity by the continuous hammer blows of human affliction and failure into something very like Christian holiness and humility'.[60] Whatever the truth of her theory, there is no doubt that Sassoon was more open to people after his conversion than at almost any other period in his adult life. They were not all Catholics, though these predominated.

Ian Balding, an outstanding amateur steeplechaser, was only one of a number of non-Catholics to whom Sassoon responded enthusiastically in his seventies. While Balding was a pupil at Marlborough, Dennis had given him *The Complete Memoirs of George Sherston*, which he subsequently asked Sassoon to sign for the horse-mad boy. When Balding eventually met Sassoon in the spring of 1963 he had already won an important National Hunt Chase race at Cheltenham (on a horse called 'Time') and Sassoon was keen to hear all about it. Balding, who had arrived late for tea at Heytesbury and mistaken 'an old boy mooching about in an overcoat and muffler' for the gardener, when it was in fact his host, nevertheless felt immediately at ease with Sassoon, who could not resist punning about him 'not being on "Time"'.[61] Their talk was largely of horses and cricket, at which Balding also excelled. Sassoon invited him back regularly after that and Balding still recalls his visits 'very fondly'.[62] The young sportsman was, according to Dennis, 'everything Sassoon would love to have been' and it would no doubt have gratified him greatly to hear Balding's retrospective praise of his 'nice seat' on a horse.[63]

Another friendship formed after his conversion underlines how open Sassoon's faith had made him. He had been corresponding with Rupert Hart-Davis since 1931, when Hart-Davis was a 24-year-old assistant at his first publisher's, Heinemann. The correspondence became more frequent in 1946 after Hart-Davis had returned from fighting in the Second World War and started his own small publishing house. But it was not until 1958, the year after Sassoon's conversion, that Hart-Davis felt confident enough of a warm reception to suggest lunch with Sassoon. The poet's welcoming response was the start of one of the most important friendships of his last years.

Sassoon was 'naturally nervous' to begin with and unable to look at his visitor for almost an hour, a phenomenon the actor Alec Guinness would observe when he visited the poet the following year to discuss T.E. Lawrence with him.[64] But he plied Hart-Davis with sherry and some 'terrifically good' Beycheville 1933, 'with which I washed down some fine roast duck'.[65] Sassoon himself was not drinking, but he gradually relaxed and they were soon talking 'nineteen to the dozen'.[66]

Less than a month after Hart-Davis's first visit to Heytesbury Sassoon appointed him his third literary executor, 'to defend Blunden' against Keynes, in his words.[67] And in 1961 came the dismissal of Keynes as literary executor altogether. It followed complaints from Hart-Davis of the many errors he had had to correct in Keynes's bibliography of Sassoon, which Hart-Davis was about to publish.

An even greater proof of Sassoon's openness at this time was his friendship with Sir Alan ('Tommy') Lascelles. Sassoon's letter to Dame Felicitas after their first meeting at Heytesbury on 2 May 1960 sets out Lascelles' appeal for him: 'Yesterday I was visited by Sir Alan Lascelles, brought here by a young friend [Colin Fenton], and new to me, though he was at Marlborough with me.'[68] After pointing out that Lascelles had been Private Secretary to the last three kings, 'so an outstanding contrast to *this* avoider of what is known as "the great world" ', Sassoon continued: 'A charming and cultivated man – drew me out about Hardy and Max Beerbohm – and was at Oxford with Ronald [Knox], and knew Katharine [Asquith]'s brother Edward Horner and her husband well – so all went easily.'[69] Other topics of conversation are likely to have been music and horses, which Lascelles also loved, and the Great War, in which he, like Sassoon, had won an M.C.

Sassoon would be persuaded to stay with Tommy and his wife Joan at their splendid apartment in the Old Stables at Kensington Palace at least eleven times between 1960 and 1965. Equally impressive was Lascelles' success in persuading Sassoon to become a member of the Literary Society, a dining club of which he was president and Hart-Davis secretary. Its meetings at the Garrick Club were always an excuse for Lascelles to insist that Sassoon pay another visit to the Old Stables, where he made sure the company was of the best.

For all their thrill, Sassoon found Lascelle's dinners in brilliant intellectual company wearying and much preferred being taken to watch cricket at Lords. Sassoon thought of him as 'a second Geoffrey [Keynes]', though 'much more sensitive'.[70] He was quickly exhausted by the constant social events the hospitable Lascelles laid on for him, particularly when on one occasion he was taken to meet royalty.[71]

There were some introductions he did appreciate, especially to literary figures, the most interesting of these being with another First World War writer who had also served in the Royal Welch Fusiliers, David Jones. Jones, whom Sassoon thought 'undoubtedly a man of genius', was invited to the Old Stables to meet Sassoon in July 1964. He enjoyed his talk with Sassoon – 'about Blunden and Graves and the Welch Fusiliers – Mametz, Limerick, etc. (he said that however much he tried he could never get that First War business out of his system)' – but found that he 'couldn't make much contact, if any' with Sassoon 'about poetry'.[72] Highly experimental himself, as *In Parenthesis* and his later, even more abstruse *Anathemata* show, he stood for all that Sassoon most feared in Modernism. Curiously, though Jones, who had converted to Catholicism in 1921, longed to discuss their common faith, Sassoon gently and politely evaded the topic and Jones's sad conclusion was 'that we seem *all* to live in separated worlds, and as far as I could make out, his particular literary outlook offered few openings that I could infiltrate'.[73] Jones's partial deafness combined with Sassoon's mumbling made communication even more difficult. Nevertheless Jones found Sassoon 'extremely nice, gentle and pleasant', if older than he expected.[74] Sassoon's own account of the working-class Jones was less charitable and rather patronizing: a 'pathetic, helpless seeming little man, ultra-sensitive', was how he described him to Dame Felicitas.[75]

Sassoon's visits to the Lascelles started at a time when his attempts to make Cambridge a second 'centre' in his life had failed, mainly because so many of his friends there had died. Now London, together with Downside, Stanbrook and Mells, would form an alternative 'centre', providing him with a more active social life than at any time since the 1930s.

*

A typical year between 1959 and 1965 might start with a week's stay at Cambridge to see Mother Margaret at Hengrave Hall, followed by a few days at Stanbrook Abbey Guest House in June and (until his marriage to Diana Milton in April 1963) an extended visit from Dennis Silk in August.[76] Even without Dennis, Sassoon would go regularly to Downside to play cricket throughout the summer and entertain the monks in turn at Heytesbury during the cricketless winter months. In September came the second of his biannual visits to Stanbrook to celebrate his birthday, which he was proud to remind people fell on the Feast Day of the Virgin Mary. By 1960, in an attempt at reconciliation with Hester, he had started inviting her to spend Christmas at Heytesbury, so that December and early January became a family affair once more. And though he found these visits exhausting he felt amply rewarded by a clearer conscience and a renewed sense of closeness to George, whose marriage had broken down in 1959 and who once again became a 'great comfort' to him.[77]

If any gaps remained in this fairly full timetable, they were filled by newer friends he had made since becoming a Catholic. One of these was Muriel

Galsworthy, a niece of John Galsworthy (who had died in 1933). Miss Galsworthy had been at Downside cheering her nephew on at cricket when they first saw each other, one of the meetings Sassoon felt had been 'arranged by our Lady of Consolation'.[78] She was quickly invited to Heytesbury and became a regular visitor in his last years.

The parish priest also visited, at first Father Joseph Renehan, later Father Nicholas McCarthy, arriving weekly to celebrate Mass with him. Sassoon looked forward to these occasions and the 'lovely talks' which followed.[79] He was greatly amused, even a little flattered, by Father McCarthy's adaptation of his nickname 'the hermit of Heytesbury' to 'the *Abbot* of Heytesbury'.[80]

By 1964, the year Blunden finally left Hong Kong, he too resumed visiting. He had, as usual, been in some financial difficulty trying to find the money to buy a house for his family. Just as predictably it was Sassoon who provided the bulk of it.[81] He was delighted to have Blunden back in the country again, even if he did choose to settle on the other side of England at Long Melford in Suffolk. He would also rejoice for Blunden's sake when he succeeded Robert Graves as Professor of Poetry at Oxford in 1966.

Another visitor to Heytesbury about this time has left an equally revealing account of Sassoon during his last years.[82] Anthony Powell, who met Sassoon at the Literary Society with Tommy Lascelles, was struck forcibly by the apparent contradictions in him: though he talked 'very much in the army idiom' of Powell's father, he did so 'with a gentle, remote, almost embarrassed air'.[83] He reminded the younger man, who like most people, and despite Dame Felicitas's efforts, associated him with his war poetry, of 'a ghost haunting the fields of Passchendaele or Bapaume', his 'unusually tall, gauntly thin' appearance making him seem 'almost transparent'.[84] On learning that they were neighbours in the West Country, Sassoon had invited Powell and his wife Violet to tea, but when Powell rang up (as suggested) a week later, he sounded as though he was already regretting it.

A date was nevertheless agreed and the Powells arrived for tea at Heytesbury on a 'crisp luminous autumn afternoon'.[85] The house's grey façade, 'dignified and massive like its owner', and the stillness of the surrounding gardens, woods and rolling downs, made them feel that they had arrived at an enchanted castle, an effect heightened by their difficulty in gaining access.[86] When, finally, they simply stepped into the drawing room through a long, open sash window, it was as though life had 'stopped perhaps half a century before'.[87] Sassoon, who suddenly materialized from nowhere, appeared not in the least disconcerted. He seemed 'to walk in a dream through a dream world', repeating several times in response to their murmurs of Heytesbury's beauty, 'Tennysonian. Absolutely Tennysonian.'

This visit from Powell, himself a successful novelist by 1963, indicates Sassoon's own growing status as a writer. Though this second flowering of his reputation had begun as far back as 1957, when he had been awarded the Queen's Gold Medal for Poetry, his lionization proper had started with his visits to Lascelles and re-introduction to the wider world in 1960. Though

Lascelles failed to get him the O.M. Sassoon still secretly coveted, he did believe he could get Sassoon the Laureateship and might have done so, if Sassoon had not been within months of his own death when Masefield died.

It may not have been a coincidence that shortly after meeting Lascelles Sassoon was honoured by a request to unveil a plaque in St Paul's Cathedral crypt to one of his dearest friends, Walter de la Mare, on 18 December 1961.[88] It is also likely that Lascelles had used his considerable influence at his old university, Oxford, in 1965, when Sassoon was offered an honorary doctorate there, though a number of other friends are also reputed to have applied pressure.[89]

By his eightieth birthday on 8 September 1966, therefore, Sassoon's stock had risen considerably and his long-time admirer Charles Causley had no difficulty in persuading the Literature Panel of the Arts Council on which he served to celebrate the event appropriately. After a long discussion at Heytesbury House, in which Causley and the Literature Director of the Arts Council, Eric Walter White, had urged Sassoon to allow them to print subscription copies of some of his poems along similarly lavish lines to the volume marking David Jones's seventieth birthday, he agreed to let them have his last eight poems. The first six pieces from *An Octave*, as it was called, had already been printed in *The Path to Peace*.[90] Only 'Proven Purpose' and 'A Prayer in Old Age' were new and they too would appear in the final Stanbrook Abbey Press production, *Ave Atque Vale*, the following year.

The subscription list, which ran to over 200 names, suggests that by 1966 Sassoon was respected by young and old alike and that this was by no means confined to his friends. The latter were there, with the notable exception of Forster and Swinnerton, who may have objected to the wholly religious nature of the poetry, but some of the Modernists, such as Auden and Day-Lewis, and many of the younger poets of the 1950s and 60s, like Roy Fuller, Ted Hughes and Philip Larkin, also subscribed, a sign of ultimate acceptance. And in his graceful introduction Causley stressed that this represented only a small section of Sassoon's 'many friends and admirers'.

Causley, who had been drawn to the 'suggestion beyond the words' in Sassoon's poetry since childhood, was also behind a BBC Bristol programme celebrating his birthday. He had already recorded two radio programmes with him at Heytesbury in 1955.[91] Though Sassoon complained of being ignored by the BBC Third Programme and 'all those clever people up in London', he was heard a number of times on radio in the last twenty years of his life and would even make a brief appearance on television, all part of his growing public recognition.[92] The first full-length book of critical appraisal of Sassoon was also published that year, *Siegfried Sassoon* by Michael Thorpe.

'Lionized by Lords in excelsis', was how Sassoon described this late flowering of his reputation.[93] His reaction to it was as ambivalent as the phrase suggests. In the 1930s, 40s and 50s he had passionately wanted recognition as a poet, greatly resenting the obscurity to which he felt he had been relegated. Yet he did not wholly enjoy the limelight, continuing to find public occasions torture. Perhaps, as he argued, it had returned to him too late.

Sassoon's eightieth birthday was his last. He had enjoyed reasonable good health throughout his adult life, apart from his duodenal ulcer in 1948, and when he suffered a blackout and stomach haemorrhage in late December 1964 he assumed that his old 'digestive' problems had returned. 'Exploiting the event for all [he was] worth', he indulged in 'a glorious rest cure', spending the next month in bed, with Hester allowed to fuss over him all she liked.[94] For the first time in years he genuinely welcomed her presence at Heytesbury, rather than taking it on sufferance. She had been seeing to the upkeep of the house for years but he had not really appreciated her efforts. Now, with his need of her and the softening of her attitude towards his religious beliefs, something like harmony prevailed.

Though she, too, claimed to think that it was his ancient ulcer resurfacing, the episode – an alarming one in which he had lain for some time in a freezing passage unable to move – worried Hester sufficiently for her to insist on a valuation of Heytesbury. As she pointed out, they did not want George to have to sell the estate to pay off death duties.

Sassoon still believed he was suffering from an ulcer, even after a second 'episode' in September 1965 had prevented his usual Stanbrook visit, and it was not until the beginning of 1966, when he confessed to a noticeable loss of vitality and weight, that he began to suspect something more serious. His condition was aggravated by prostate problems, which eventually took him into the Lansdown Hospital, Bath, for an operation. It seems ironic that while the robust Keynes had suffered complications and nearly died from the same operation a month earlier, the much frailer Sassoon sailed through it, feeling much 'relieved', as he punned, after it. But his eightieth birthday and the attendant fuss three months later exhausted him again and by January 1967 he was completely housebound.

Though Sassoon realized that his end was approaching, he was not afraid of death. He had found the idea of Purgatory difficult to accept and utterly rejected the notion of Hell for his non-Catholic friends, but firmly believed in Heaven. And as his physical state weakened further, he began to long for it.

It had, in his own phrase, 'been a long journey', but by July 1967 it was almost over. Incredible as it seems by today's standards, he did not learn of his inoperable stomach cancer until the month before he died from its secondaries of the liver and peritoneum. 'He knows the full facts,' his GP, Dr Falk, wrote to Mother Margaret in August at Sassoon's request, 'and accepts wonderfully the truth that there is nothing we can do that can alter the outcome.'[95]

Hospital was clearly not the answer. Though he had been sent to one in Warminster as soon as the full truth was suspected, he had asked to be sent home to die 'back in his own bed and by his familiar things'.[96] Once back at Heytesbury Sassoon settled down to die. On 15 August, the tenth anniversary to the day of his First Communion in the Catholic Church, he was anointed and given holy communion by Father McCarthy.

It was the signal for a round of last visits from close friends, with the exception of Dennis Silk and Edmund Blunden who were out of the country. It is not certain, in any case, that Blunden could have faced saying goodbye. He had found his visits to Heytesbury increasingly painful, describing Sassoon as irritable, moody and difficult to bear, a rather different picture from that painted by his other friends. Blunden had dreaded the death, which he realized was imminent. Claire Blunden believed that once he heard of Sassoon's death 'he turned his face to the wall'.[97] (Though not yet seventy, he would suffer a serious collapse shortly afterwards and retreat inexorably into senile dementia, dying himself at the age of seventy-eight.)[98]

Mother Margaret Mary, on the other hand, made every effort to be at Sassoon's bedside. She had been in retreat in Suffolk when she heard of the diagnosis, but arrived towards the end of August with the fruits of his – and her – proselytizing, his niece Jessica Gatty. She was grateful to have been warned of his skeletal appearance and relieved to find him still lucid. He seemed to her fully prepared for death.

Hart-Davis, alerted by Mother Margaret Mary, also spent several days with him in late August, and was reminded by the gaunt figure stretched out on his large bed of a saint in a medieval painting. But Sassoon's thoughts were not all of the afterlife:

'My poems; they were all right, weren't they?' he asked his literary executor.
'Yes, Sieg, *more* than all right,' Hart-Davis assured him.
'Every one a bull's-eye?'
'No, Sieg,' Hart-Davis felt compelled to reply, 'not *every* one.'[99]

Fortunately, Sassoon's humour had not deserted him and he found his friend's painful attempt at honesty immensely funny. Hart-Davis in turn was amused by Sassoon's response to his own anxious question: 'Would you like me to get Hester down from Scotland?' 'Good Heavens no,' the dying man replied, 'we're in enough trouble as it is!'[100] Hester, in fact, was herself ill, having suffered a stroke which paralyzed her down one side. But George came as planned when Dr Falk believed the end was near. He was struck by his father's anxiety not to be 'a bore or a nuisance'.[101] Stoical to the last and buoyed up by his faith, he told his son, 'This is the final test of my endurance and I intend to put up a good show.'[102] Less than twenty-four hours later, at 8 o'clock on the evening of 1 September 1967, just a week short of his eighty-first birthday, he died.[103]

'It may not be significant, but it is perhaps worth mentioning,' George wrote to Charles Causley shortly afterwards, 'that Heytesbury cricket team played their match here as usual on Saturday after a two-minute silence on the field, and soundly defeated a team from whom they usually got a hammering.'[104] Nothing, Causley felt, 'could have been more appropriate for Old Sig'.[105]

THORNICROFT or THORNYCROFT

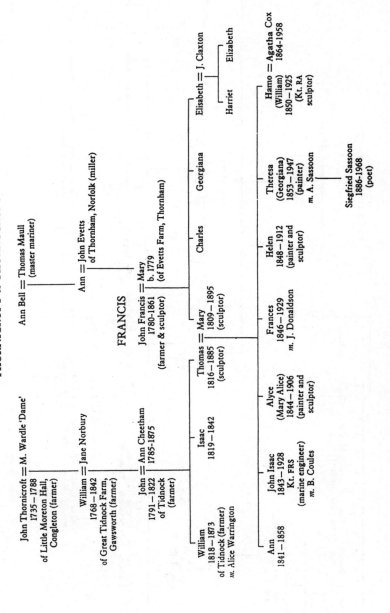

John Thornicroft = M. Wardle 'Dame'
1735—1788
of Little Moreton Hall,
Congleton (farmer)

Ann Bell = Thomas Maull
(master mariner)

William = Jane Norbury
1768—1842
of Great Tidnock Farm,
Gawsworth (farmer)

Ann = John Evetts
of Thornham, Norfolk (miller)

John = Ann Cheetham
1791—1822   1785—1875
of Tidnock
(farmer)

FRANCIS

John Francis = Mary
1780—1861   b. 1779
(farmer & sculptor)   (of Evetts Farm, Thornham)

William
1818—1873
of Tidnock (farmer)
m. Alice Warrington

Isaac
1819—1842

Thomas = Mary
1816—1885   1809—1895
(sculptor)   (sculptor)

Charles

Georgiana

Elisabeth = J. Claxton

Harriet   Elizabeth

Ann
1841—1858

John Isaac
1843—1928
Kt. FRS
(marine engineer)
m. B. Coules

Alyce
(Mary Alice)
1844—1906
(painter and
sculptor)

Frances
1846—1929
m. J. Donaldson

Helen
1848—1912
(painter and
sculptor)

Theresa
(Georgiana)
1853—1947
(painter)
m. A. Sassoon

Hamo = Agatha Cox
(William)   1864—1958
1850—1925
(Kt. RA
sculptor)

Siegfried Sassoon
1886-1968
(poet)

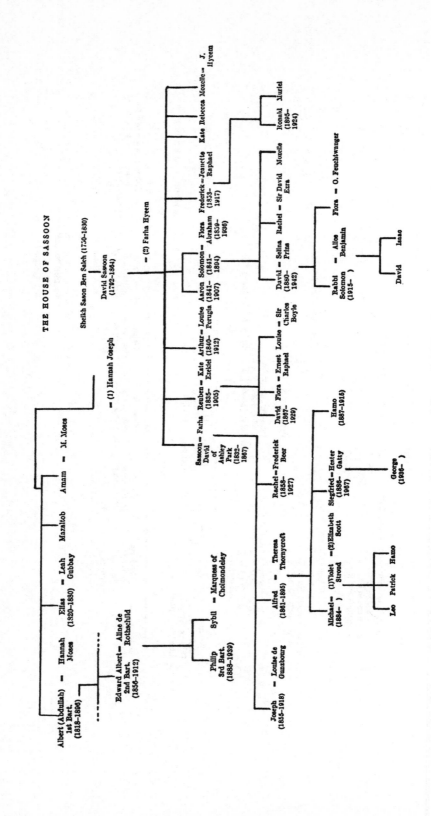

THE HOUSE OF SASSOON

Acknowledgements

My first acknowledgement must go to the late George Sassoon, who encouraged me to write this life of his father and allowed me to quote extensively from his work. Other members of the family have also been helpful, in particular Hamo Sassoon, Lady Lettice Strickland-Constable, Mrs Leo Sassoon, Timothy Thornycroft, Jacques Sassoon and Sister Jessica Gatty. Sassoon's godson, George Byam Shaw, and his wife Maggie have likewise contributed a great deal.

I have been fortunate in having the advice of experts at every stage, especially Philip Guest, Dominic Hibberd, Tony Laughton, Patrick Quinn, David West, Charles Wheeler and Patrick Campbell.

I have also been lucky in being able to talk to an appreciable number of Sassoon's friends, or to those who knew his friends well, and should like to express my gratitude here to Lord Oxford and Asquith, Lady Helen Asquith, Ian Balding, Rolf Barber, Claire Blunden, James Byam Shaw, Vivien Clarke, Nicholas Herbert, Haro Hodson, Dom Philip Jebb, Milo Keynes, Mother Margaret Mary Ross McFarlin, Dom Sebastian Moore, Andrew Motion, Dennis Silk, Jon Stallworthy and Theresa Whistler.

In addition I am grateful to those who gave me access to their collections and the fruits of their research, in particular Timothy Atkinson and his wife, Angela, Timothy d'Arch-Smith, Nicholas Barrington, Bryan Connon, Dame Felicitas Corrigan, Stewart Craggs, Lionel Dakers, Roy Davids, Sister Clemente Davlin, Terry Halladay, John Harding, Anne Hill, Philip Hoare, William Reese, Keith Simpson, Harry and Cookie Spiro, Michael Thorpe, Len Weaver and Burton Weiss.

I should also like to thank librarians and archivists throughout Britain and America, especially of Cambridge University Library, the Berg Collection, New York Public Library, the Butler Library, Columbia University, the Beinecke Rare Book Library, University of Yale, the Regenstein Library, University of Chicago, the Lilly Library, University of Indiana, Special Collections, Southern Illinois University at Carbondale, the Harry Ransom Humanities Research Center, University of Texas at Austin, the University of Washington at Pullman, the Brotherton Library, University of Leeds, the Laing Art Gallery, Newcastle, the Houghton Library, University of Harvard, the Imperial War Museum Library, the Royal Welch Fusiliers Archives, the Fitzwilliam Museum, Cambridge, the Bodleian Library, University of Oxford, Clare College Library, University of Cambridge, Sutton Coldfield Reference Library, the British Library, Rutgers University Library, the State University of New York at Buffalo Library, McMaster University Library, University of Marquette Library, the Library of Congress, University of Delaware Library, University of Arkansas Library,

Vassar College, King's College Library, University of Cambridge, Wichita State University Library, the Public Record Office and the National Army Museum, both of London.

My warmest thanks are due also to the following individuals, who have helped me in different areas; Tony Badger, Jenny Barty-King, Gavin Beattie, Eleanor Birne, Maureen Borland, Laurel Brake, Keith Budge, Russell Burlingham, Jonathan Cecil, Charles Cholmondeley, Roland Constantine, Anthony Curtis, Sarah Curtis, Jonathan Cutbill, Roger Daniell, Joan Draper, Geraldine Elwes, Shu-Yiu Fenton, James Fergusson, Robert Fessenden, Hilary and Byron Gangnes, Jonathan Gathorne-Hardy, Pom Gibbons, Martyn Goff, David Handforth, Annie Hasted, Charles Hastings, Anthony Head, Bill Hetherington, Pat and Stuart Laurence, Jim Lewton-Brain, Elizabeth Mavor, Michael MacGarvie, Noel Morgan, Maureen Murray, John Northam, Michael O'Regan, Giles Payne, Judiyh Perle, Michael Pierson, Wendy Pollard, Anthony Powell and Lady Violet Powell, Anne and Jeremy Powell, Susan Rand, Willie Reardon, John Richardson, Tim Rix, Karen Robertson, Pat Robertson, Peggy Rust, Rose Sanguinetti, Siobhan Santry, Daphne Sayed, Winifred Stevenson, June Stubbs, Sarah Such, Elizabeth Tagert, Gertrud Watson, Vivien Whelpton, Charles Wilson, Renée Wylde, Marjorie Wynne, and Gill Yudkin. Some are no longer alive to receive my thanks, but their relatives are.

I am grateful too for the help and forbearance of Ray Davies, Deborah Blake, Judith Perle and John Wells in the preparation of this book for the press.

Full acknowledgement has been made, either in the text or in endnotes, of all sources quoted in this book.

Finally, I must thank my family, who deserve medals for their encouragement, forbearance and practical help throughout this whole project: my children, Kate, Philip, Emma, Alice and Trim, and, above all, my husband, Cecil Woolf.

J.M.W.

Notes

Abbreviations

Sources

Arkansas = University of Arkansas
Beinecke = Beinecke Rare Books Library, Yale University
Berg = Berg Collection, New York Public Library
BL = Department of Manuscripts, British Library, London
BLL = Brotherton Library, University of Leeds
Bodley = Bodleian Library, Oxford
Buffalo = University of New York at Buffalo
Columbia = Columbia University Library, New York
Congress = Library of Congress, Washington DC
CUL = Cambridge University Library, Cambridge
Delaware = Delaware University Library
Harvard = Harvard University Library
HMC = Henry Moore Centre for Study of Sculpture, Leeds
HRHRC = Harry Ransom Humanities Research Center, University of Texas at Austin
IWM = Imperial War Museum, London
Lilly = Lilly Library, Indiana University
NAM = National Army Museum, London
Pullman = Pullman Library, University of Washington
Rutgers = Rutgers University Library
USI = Special Collections, University of Southern Illinois at Carbondale
Syracuse = University of New York at Syracuse
Wichita = Wichita State University Library, Kansas

Published works

CA = Siegfried Sassoon, *Counter-Attack* (Heinemann, 1918)
CC = Siegfried Sassoon, *Common Chords* (Mill House Press, 1950)
CP = Siegfried Sassoon, *Collected Poems* (Faber paperback, 1961)
D1 = *Siegfried Sassoon Diaries 1915-1918* (Faber, 1983)

D2 = *Siegfried Sassoon Diaries 1920-1922* (Faber, 1981)
D3 = *Siegfried Sassoon Diaries 1923-1925* (Faber, 1985)
EE = Siegfried Sassoon, *Emblems of Experience* (Rampant Lions Press, 1951)
GTAT = Robert Graves, *Goodbye to All That* (Penguin Books, 1960)
Hassall = Christopher Hassall, *Edward Marsh* (Longmans, 1959)
HJ = Siegfried Sassoon, *The Heart's Journey* (Heinemann, 1928)
Keynes = Geoffrey Keynes, *Bibliography of Siegfried Sassoon* (Hart-Davis, 1962)
MFM = Siegfried Sassoon, *Memoirs of a Fox-Hunting Man* (Faber, 1928; Faber Library edition, 1943, used)
MIO = Siegfried Sassoon, *Memoirs of an Infantry Officer* (Faber, 1930; Faber paperback, 1973, used)
OAG = *Ottoline at Garsington: Memoirs of Lady Ottoline Morrell, 1915-1918*, ed. Robert Gathorne-Hardy (Faber, 1974)
OC = Siegfried Sassoon, *The Old Century and Seven Years More* (Faber, 1938; Faber paperback, 1968, used)
OH = Siegfried Sassoon, *The Old Huntsman* (Heinemann, 1917)
O'Prey = P. O'Prey (ed.), *In Broken Images: Selected Letters of Robert Graves, 1914-1946* (Hutchinson, 1982).
RR = Siegfried Sassoon, *The Road to Ruin* (Faber, 1933)
RRu = Siegfried Sassoon, *Rhymed Ruminations* (Faber, 1940)
RR:RWF = *Regimental Records of the Royal Welch Fusiliers*, compiled by C.H. Dudley Ward (London, Forster Groom, 1928), vol. 3.
SJ = Siegfried Sassoon, *Siegfried's Journey* (London, Faber, 1945)
SP = Siegfried Sassoon, *Sherston's Progress* (Faber, 1936; Penguin Books edn, 1948, used)
SS:MWP = Jean Moorcroft Wilson, *Siegfried Sassoon: The Making of a War Poet* (Duckworth, 1998)

SS:PP = Dame Felicitas Corrigan, *Siegfried Sassoon: Poet's Pilgrimage* (Victor Gollancz, 1973)

Thorpe = M. Thorpe, *Siegfried Sassoon: A Critical Study* (OUP & Leiden University Press, 1966)

UV4 = Siegfried Sassoon, unpublished and unfinished 4th vol. of autobiography

WIK = J.C. Dunn (ed.), *The War the Infantry Knew 1914-1919: A Chronicle of Service in France and Belgium with the Second Battalion, His Majesty's Twenty-Third Foot, the Royal Welch Fusiliers* (P.S. King, 1938)

WP = Siegfried Sassoon, *The War Poems* (Faber, 1983)

WY = Siegfried Sassoon, *The Weald of Youth* (London, Faber, 1942)

Correspondents

AB = Arnold Bennett
AL = Sir Alan Lascelles
AT= Anne Tennant
ATB = A.T. Bartholomew ('Theo')
BH = Ben Huebsch
DFC = Dame Felicitas Corrigan
DS = Dennis Silk
EB = Edmund Blunden
EG = Edmund Gosse
EH = Eileen Hunter
EJD = Edward Dent
EM = Edward Marsh
EMF = E.M. Forster
EO = Edith Oliver
ES = Edith Sitwell
FS = Frank Schuster
FSw = Frank Swinnerton
GA = William Atkin ('Gabriel')
GBS = Glen Byam Shaw
GK = Geoffrey Keynes
GS = George Sassoon
HFJ = Henry Festing-Jones ('Enrico')
HGW = H.G. Wells
HH = Haro Hodson
HMT = H.M. Tomlindon ('Tommy')
HS = Hamo Sassoon
HT = Hamo Thornycroft
JC = Joe Cottrell
JD = Julian Dadd
JG = Sister Jessica Gatty
KA = Lady Katharine Asquith
LG = Lady Gatty
LOM = Lady Ottoline Morrell
LU = Louis Untermeyer
LW = Laurence Whistler
MB = Max Beerbohm

MMM = Mother Margaret Mary McFarlin
NB = Nellie Burton
OS = Osbert Sitwell
PG = Philp Gosse
RG = Robert Graves
RGH = Robert Gathorne-Hardy ('Bob')
RH = Ralph Hodgson
RHD = Rupert Hart-Davis
RM = Roderick Meiklejohn
RN = Robert Nichols ('Crikey')
RR = Robert Ross
SB = S.N. Behrman ('Sam')
SCC = Sydney Carlyle Cockerell
SS = Siegfried Sassoon
SSi = Sacheverell Sitwell
ST = Stephen Tennant ('Steenie')
TEL = T.E. Lawrence
TH = Thomas Hardy
TS = Theresa Sassoon ('Ash')
WdlM = Walter de la Mare
WJT = Walter James Redfern Turner
WO = Wilfred Owen
WW = Sir William Walton

Introduction

1. Bonham's cat., London, 8 May 2013, p.151.
2. DFC to SS, 30 Oct. 1966.
3. 'Siegfried Sassoon', *The Author*, Winter 1989, p.125.
4. SS:PP, p.23.
5. T.H. White to SCC [c.1958], Cockerell, *The Best of Friends,* p.166.
6. D2, p.53.
7. SJ, p.105.
8. ibid.
9. SS:PP, p.16. She may have had in mind John Henry Newman's 'Definition of a Gentleman' in his *Idea of a University.*
10. OAG, p.152.
11. Letter from Geoffrey Keynes to DFC on the publication of SS:PP in 1973 (quoted in 'Siegfried Loraine Sassoon: a Centenary Essay' by DFC).
12. SS's 4th unpub., unfinished vol. of autobiography (private collector).
13. Stephen Tennant to G.A. David (of the Sorbonne),12 Nov. 1971, collection of Hugo Vickers.
14. SS:PP, p.15.
15. *Meredith* (London, Constable, 1948), pp.98-9.
16. Jackson Page to RHD, 31 Aug. 1967, CUL.

Chapter 1

1. MIO, pp.230-1.
2. For information about the Sassoon family my main sources have been Cecil Roth, *The Sassoon Dynasty* (Robert Hale, 1941), Stanley Jackson, *The Sassoons* (Heinemann, 1968) and Jacques Sassoon, whose father shared a grand-father with SS.
3. SS:PP, p.47.
4. When I talked to Siegfried Sassoon's neph-ew, Hamo Sassoon, in Apr. 1991, in answer to my question about the two sides of the family, he said, 'I'm a Thornycroft,' adding that Sieg-fried had made the same remark to him when they got to know each other in the 1930s. Cf. SS to Mr Carter, 27 Sept. 1948, HRHRC.
5. OC, p.45.
6. ibid., p.67.
7. SS to RG, undated, USI.
8. SJ, p.32 and a letter from SS's wife, Hes-ter Gatty, to her sister-in-law, Pamela Gatty, *c.*1960 in the Gatty Papers at CUL.
9. SS:PP, p.36.
10. Letter from Stephen Tennant to G.A. Da-vid, 12 Nov. 1971, collection of Hugo Vickers.
11. SS to DFC, 25 Jun. 1965; SS:PP, p.47 and SJ, p.202.
12. WY, p.251.
13. SS to DFC, 25 Jun. 1965; SS:PP, p.47.
14. SS to HH, 4 Nov. 1948, in the possession of the recipient.
15. SS to SCC, 31 Oct. 1942, HRHRC.
16. SS to DFC, 25 Jun. 1965; SS:PP, p.47.
17. OC, p.39.
18. ibid., p.41.
19. ibid., p.298.
20. 'Pop' concerts in the 19th century appear to have been the equivalent of our modern-day 'Proms'.
21. The following account of Alfred and The-resa's engagement and marriage is based mainly on Hamo Thornycroft's letters to his fiancée, Agatha Cox, from Nov. 1883 to Feb. 1884 at HMC.
22. HT to Agatha Cox, 1 Feb. 1884, HMC.

Chapter 2

1. St Stephen's, where SS was christened on 10 Oct. 1886, was in Stanley Road, Tunbridge Wells.
2. OC, p.107.
3. The 'tower' or spire was demolished as un-safe in the 1950s. Sassoon owned a book illus-trated by Harrison Weir (*The Poultry Book* by W.B. Teget-Meier), which he inscribed 'bought at Newbury – these drawings were made at Weirleigh 20 years before I was born there' (Phillips' Bath Sale Catalogue, 31 Oct. 1994). Weir also invented cat shows in 1871.
4. SS to SCC, 20 Jul. 1947, HRHRC.
5. Advertisement in *The Times*, 23 Apr. 1884.
6. MFM, p.23.
7. *London Mercury*, Jun. 1929.
8. MFM, pp.78-9.
9. ibid., p.73.
10. See 'Memoirs of a Poetry-Writing Boy' by Jean Moorcroft Wilson, *The Times*, 11 Nov. 2008.
11. A dog-cart is a two-wheeled driving-cart with cross seats back to back.
12. OC, p.35.
13. ibid., p.29.
14. Interview with Mary's daughter, Lady Strickland-Constable. See also OC, p.294.
15. OC, pp.24-5.
16. ibid.
17. It is likely that Alfred's artist friend was not 'Randall' but Henry Ryland, who moved into the newly-built Pembroke Studios from Bolton Studios in 1891 and was living at no. 2 while Alfred was at no. 8.
18. HMC.
19. OC, p.77.
20. SS to DFC, 25 Jun. 1965; SS:PP, p.48.
21. SS to Lady Lettice Strickland-Constable, 6 Nov. 1947 (Lady Lettice Strickland-Consta-ble).
22. OC, pp.13-14.
23. 'Celebrated Storeys', Brenchley [*c.*1894-5], a ms collection of stories in SS's hand, Columbia.
24. OC, p.149.
25. ibid., p.55.
26. ibid., pp.26 & 162.
27. Called 'Some of my favourites' and writ-ten about 1894, this 20-page manuscript note-book is now at Columbia. It contains a series of little essays on various butterflies.
28. OC, p.60.
29. ibid., pp.31-2.
30. Maskelyne was a famous conjurer of the period.
31. Sassoon claims, in OC (p.39), that the HMS *Speedy* was launched by Princess May, but I have found nothing to support this.
32. Information on Alfred Sassoon's illness has been taken from his will and Siegfried's

account in OC, pp.30-1.

33. See ibid., pp.12-13.
34. ibid., pp.45-6.
35. ibid., p.50.
36. ibid., p.56.
37. ibid., p.65.

Chapter 3

1. OC, p.55.
2. ibid., p.59.
3. ibid., p.???.
4. MFM, p.10.
5. OC, p.150.
6. ibid., p.153.
7. 'The Painting of Cockbird', unpub. article by the late John Richardson, written Nov. 1986, p.5.
8. OC, p.85.
9. *The Best of Friends: Further Letters to Sir Sydney Carlyle Cockerell*, ed. Viola Meynell (London, Hart-Davis, 1956), p.67; SS to SCC, 18 Jun. 1939.
10. SS:PP, p.31.
11. WY, p.60.
12. This and the three previous quotations are taken from OC, pp.104-5.
13. See 'A Short History of the Sassoon Family' by Sue Edwards, *Siegfried Sassoon Centenary* brochure, 1986, p.3.
14. Michael married Violet Mildred Stroud, one of twins like himself, in 1907. They had three sons: Alfred Lionel Thornycroft (b.1909), Norman Basil Arundel (b.1910) and Hamo (b.1920).
15. See SS to Edward Carpenter of 27 Jul. 1911 & 2 Aug. 1911 (Sheffield City Libraries), and OAG, p.230.
16. See D1, p.46.
17. ibid., pp.41-2.
18. CP, p.212
19. (i) 'The poems, Brenchley, 1896-97' ('For Mamsy'); (ii) Volume of poems for Theresa Sassoon's birthday, Mar. 1897; (iii) More Poems by S.L. Sassoon, Oct 20-Dec 25, 1897; (iv) The Poems by Siegfried Sassoon, 1898; (v) The Blue Poetry Book, 1898 ('For Wirgie'); (vi) The Poems, 1898 ('For Aunty Lula'); (vii) The Red Poetry Book, Christmas 1898 ('For Uncle Hamo'); (viii) A Book of Verses, Jan 1899; (ix) The Poems. 1899.
20. A number of poems in this 4th vol. are repeated in the following 3 vols, also produced in 1898: *Poems*, *The Blue Poetry Book*, and *The Red Poetry Book*.

21. D3, p.174.
22. OC, p.86.
23. Quoted from *More Poems 1897* by DFC in SS:PP, p.54.
24. OC, pp.75-6.
25. MFM, p.10.
26. Major Edgeworth Horrocks, J.P., lived at Mascalls House and died in 1908.
27. WY, p.90.
28. D2, p.237. Letters from Helen Wirgman to SS at CUL. Quotes attributed to her are from this coll.
29. OC, p.119.
30. ibid., p.123.
31. SS to DFC, 14 Feb. 1961; SS:PP, pp.69-70.

Chapter 4

1. OC, p.199.
2. Rupert Croft-Cooke, *The Glittering Pastures* (Putnam, 1962), p.102.
3. SS inscribed one copy of *Sonnets* (1909) to 'My Dear Mr Norman'.
4. Jean Moorcroft Wilson, *Charles Hamilton Sorley* (Cecil Woolf, 1985), p.51.
5. See Walter Pater's *Marius the Epicurean* (1885), in which Marius seeks spiritual truths rather than worldly satisfaction.
6. OC, p.209.
7. John & Michael O'Regan, *John O'Regan and his Family Background*, p.196.
8. OAG, p.230.
9. OC, p.228.
10. ibid., p.230.
11. i.e. SS's attempt to win the Chancellor's Medal at Cambridge in 1905-6.
12. Sold at Sotheby's saleroom, Bond Street, Jul. 1992.
13. OC, p.227.
14. The Corps, part of the Cadet Movement, was started at MC in 1860 and attached to the 2nd Volunteer Battalion of the 2nd Wilts. in 1870. See also WY, p.275.
15. OC, p.241.
16. ibid., p.239.
17. ibid., pp.240-1. 'The Extra Inch' appeared in *Cricket* xxii, no. 623, 9 Apr. 1903, signed 'Siegfried Loraine Sassoon'.
18. 1903: 'Spring (With all due deference to Lord Tennyson's opinions)', *Cricket* xxii, no. 625, 23 Apr., p.91, signed 'S.L.S.'; 'To Wilfred – Bowling (A reminiscence of the Second Test Match) (When Wilfred Rhodes a'bowling goes)', *Cricket* xxiii, no. 650, 28 Jan. [probably

1904], p.13, signed 'S.L.S.' 1904: 'Yuletide Thoughts (At Yuletide all my thoughts are far remote)', *Cricket* xxiii, no. 679, 2 Dec., p.476, signed 'S.L.S.' 1905: 'Dies Irae (What of the days to be?)', *Cricket* xxiv, no. 700, 10 Aug., p.332, signed 'S.L.S.'

19. D2, p.267.
20. OC, p.243.

Chapter 5

1. OC, p.244.
2. William Paley's *Evidences of Christianity* (1794), a work became a textbook for Oxford and Cambridge entrance.
3. WY, p.159.
4. SS to Arthur E. Risdale, 4 Aug. 1940, CUL.
5. OC, p.249.
6. ibid., p.262.
7. It was Michael's last term there; he left without taking a degree.
8. Alastair Donaldson entered Jesus College and in 1907 his brother, Eric, would follow Malcolm to Trinity.
9. Sassoon rented 4 Market Hill from Oct. 1905 to Apr. 1907, sharing his flat with Hamo for the first year. See his jokey cartoon in the First World War, showing an equestrian memorial to him on Market Hill.
10. OC, p.266.
11. S. Jackson, *The Sassoons* (London, Heinemann, 1968), p.134.
12. OC, p.268.
13. SS:PP, p.55.
14. ibid.
15. SS bought the *Poems* by William Watson (London, John Lane, 2 vols, 1905) in 1906.
16. 1906: 'To a Blood', *Cambridge Review* xxviii, no.678, p.317; 'Prospice', *Granta* xix, no.424, 19 May, pp.335-6; 'Darak and Daimla – an Inanity', *Granta* xix, no.425, May, pp.340, 342; 'Par-les-Eaux-du-Perrier' , *Granta* xix, no.426, 2 Jun., p.369; 'The Bomb', *Granta* xix, May Week no., 9 Jun., pp.24-5.
17. SS had added a poem called 'Aspiration' meantime.
18. SS:PP, pp.55-6.
19. SS to LU, 11 Oct. [1920], Lilly.
20. SS:PP, p.56.
21. OC, p.282.
22. D2, pp.130-1 for more details of Hamo.
23. OC, pp.273-4.
24. *Marble and Bronze*, p.159.
25. HT to SS, 20 Mar. 1907, CUL.

26. See SS's brief *CV* for Ernest Benn's sixpenny 'Augustan Books of English Poetry' series, edited by Edward Thompson, Bodley.

Chapter 6

1. OC, p.289.
2. WY, p.214.
3. ibid., p.50.
4. The Blue Mantles (sometimes styled Bluemantles) was founded in either 1862 or 1864 by the Bluemantle Pursuivant at Arms. By 1896 it was playing about 36 matches a year and had over 140 members.
5. WY, p.63.
6. Dennis Silk, *Siegfried Sassoon*.
7. David Foot, *Beyond Bat and Ball*, p.51. See also SS:MWP for details of SS's cricket books.
8. Letters from HT to TS, 2 Oct. 1908 & 10 May 1909, CUL.
9. SS:PP, p.31.
10. 'Rambling Thoughts on Horses and Hunting', MS at HRHRC.
11. WY, p.70.
12. Cockbird won 4 out of the 11 races he ran between 1911 and 1914, came 2nd once, and 3rd 3 times.
13. Gordon Harbord to SS, 2 Feb. 1917, IWM.
14. Robert Smith Surtees (1805-64); principal works *Jorrocks's Jaunts and Jollities* (1838); *Handley Cross* (1843), *Hillingdon Hall* (1845) and *Mr Sponge's Sporting Tour* (1853).
15. D2, p.141.
16. D2, p.63, WY, pp.41-7.
17. WY, p.135.
18. ibid., pp.29-33.
19. D2, p.192.
20. ibid., pp.280-1.
21. WY, p.111.
22. Bars of music are given as a guide to metre in 'Rough Drafts' (1906) at Columbia.
23. WY, p.107.
24. See 'Rough Drafts' (1906), Columbia.
25. WY, p.15.
26. Helen Wirgman to SS, 26 Aug. 1908, CUL.
27. EG to SS, 28 Mar. 1908, Rutgers.
28. OC, p.300.
29. WY, p.9.
30. SS to RH, 14 Jun. 1932, Beinecke.
31. SS to SCC, 26 Feb. 1942, HRHRC.
32. WY, p.18.
33. ibid., p.28.
34. EG to SS, 6 Dec. 1911, Rutgers.

35. SS wrote in a proof copy of *Amyntas*, 'This proof copy is the only one in existence, as no copies were printed. SS'. *Amyntas* did appear in the *Antidote*, 8 Mar. 1913; parts of it later included in *Discoveries* (1915), as 'Romance'.

36. SS to EM, 6 Jul. 1914, Berg. SS asks Marsh his opinion of the abandoned play.

37. SS also owned *Ioläus: an Anthology of Friendship* (1906) and Carpenter's *Sonnets* (1912).

38. *Coming Out* (London, Quartet, 1977), p.80.

39. SS to EC, 2 Aug. 1911, Sheffield City Libraries.

40. This handwritten sonnet was included in the copy of *Twelve Sonnets* sent to Edward Carpenter.

41. D1, p.166.

42. Carpenter to SS of 17 Aug. 1918.

43. WY, p.121.

44. ibid., p.122.

45. ibid., p.127.

46. ibid., p.124.

47. ibid., pp.25-6.

48. ibid., p.129.

49. SS to DFC, 14 Feb. 1961; SS:PP, p.68.

50. EG to SS, 13 Feb. 1913, Rutgers.

51. EG to HT, 2 Jul. 1883, HMC.

52. See *The Lyttleton Hart-Davis Letters*, vol.3, 1981, p.141.

53. SS dates this visit as 1911 in WY, but the 'Book of Gosse' (CUL) gives it as 6 May 1909.

54. Aldous Huxley to Julian Huxley, 13 Dec. 1917, *Letters*, ed. Grover Smith (London, 1969).

55. WY, p.145.

Chapter 7

1. Hassall, p.501.

2. Early Imagists members included Ezra Pound, Amy Lowell, Richard Aldington, Hilda Doolittle, John Gould Fletcher and F.S. Flint.

3. WY, p.139.

4. i.e. Robert Ross.

5. WY, p.142.

6. Berg.

7. WY, p.195.

8. ibid., p.196.

9. Berg.

10. WY, p.188.

11. ibid., p.175.

12. ibid., p.206.

13. See CP, p.60.

14. TLS, 31 May 1917.

15. WY, p.216.

16. ibid., p.203.

17. RR to SS, 13 Jun. 1914, Lilly.

18. WY, p.221.

19. Note SS's echo of Brooke in 'A Footnote on the War' (WP, p.149).

20. SS to EM, 6 Jul. 1914, Berg.

21. SS to DFC, 28 Jul. 1965; SS:PP, p.66.

22. WY, p.254.

23. ibid., p.255.

24. ibid., p.265.

25. ibid., p.264.

26. ibid., p.217.

27. ibid., p.218.

Chapter 8

1. WY, p.274.

2. ibid., p.272.

3. See Wilson, *Charles Hamilton Sorley, a Biography*, pp.157-60.

4. MIO, p.128.

5. MFM, p.225.

6. ibid., p.219.

7. ibid.

8. ibid.

9. SS to EM, 17 Aug. 1914, Berg.

10. 'Romance' is a song taken from *Amyntas*.

11. CP, p.58.

12. *Cambridge Magazine*, 2 Jun. 1917.

13. SS states in MFM that Capt. Ruxton had served in the RWF, but there is no record of a Capt. Ruxton in the Regiment at the time SS suggests. He may deliberately have concealed the true identity of the man who used his influence to smooth SS's way to a commission.

14. MFM, p.233.

15. D1, p.130. See articles in the *Crosby Herald* of 28 Mar., 4 & 11 Apr. 1996.

16. MIO, pp.224 & 236.

17. SJ, p.17.

18. *Taking It Like a Man* (Manchester University Press, 1993), pp.67-8.

19. *The Collected Letters of Charles Hamilton Sorley*, ed. J.M. Wilson (Cecil Woolf, 1990), pp.218-19.

20. RWF Archives, Caernarvon.

21. MFM, pp.240-3 and D1, pp.44-5.

22. DT to SS, 26.8.15., CUL.

23. D1, p.45.

24. SJ, p.148.

25. ibid.

26. Edward Joseph Dent (1876-1957).

27. SS to EJD, Aug. 1915, CUL.

28. D1, p.106.
29. RG to RR, 24 Nov. 1916, Lilly.
30. SS to RG, 9 Apr. 1917, USI.
31. D1, p.94.
32. Robert Baldwin Ross, 1869-1918.
33. Letter from Maureen Borland, Ross's biographer, 26 Oct. 1993.
34. SJ, p.6.
35. D1, p.131.
36. SJ, p.31.
37. SS to John Bain, 12 May [1917], IWM.
38. *The Marlburian*, 21 Jun. 1917, pp.89-90.
39. GH was to die in Aug. 1917, not Nov. 1915; but since SS had made his self-portrait, George Sherston, an only child in MFM he could not describe the death of a brother, substituting that of the character based on Gordon in the story.
40. MFM, p.242.
41. SS to EJD, n.d., Nov. 1915, CUL.
42. D1, p.126.
43. ibid., pp.26-7.
44. Related to me by Peter Haworth, whose family knew Michael Sassoon in Canada and who visited TS at Weirleigh.
45. MFM, p.244.

Chapter 9

1. See W. Allison & J. Fairley, *The Monocled Mutineer* (London, Quartet Books, 1979), p.53.
2. D1, p.20.
3. JD's sister, Elfreda, wrote to SS on 15 Jan. 1937 after her brother's death: 'I've always felt since I read "A Whispered Tale" that you understood him well and greatly cared for him.' CUL.
4. SS wrote about Edmund Dadd as 'Edmunds' in his fiction, concealing the brotherhood of Julian and Edmund, just as he concealed that of Edward and Ralph Greaves, perhaps because he felt it would give too strong a clue as to their real identity.
5. JD to SS, 20 Jan. 1929, IWM.
6. MFM, p.253.
7. *The Collected Letters of Charles Hamilton Sorley*, p.243.
8. MIO, pp.76-80, 94, GTAT, p.146.
9. D1, p.21.
10. SS to RG, 2 Mar. 1930, Buffalo.
11. D2, p.162.
12. Hassell, p.79.
13. SS to EM, 14 Jul. 1916, Berg.
14. Brig.-Gen. C.I. Stockwell to SS, included in a letter to JD, 3 Mar. 1931, IWM.

15. MIO, p.108.
16. ibid.
17. ibid.
18. D1, p.21.
19. *In Broken Image*, ed. Paul O'Prey (Hutchinson, 1982), p.37.
20. See Robert Graves, *Fairies and Fusiliers* (Heinemann, 1917).
21. MFM, p.247.
22. D1, p.20.
23. ibid., p.21.
24. SS changed the last two lines of this stanza, which read originally 'And dimly in his pain he hopes to die/ That Brummagen be safe beyond the seas'.
25. Fragment dated 7 Aug. 1916, HRHRC.
26. *The Great War and Modern Memory* (OUP, 1975), p.282.
27. Undated letter from V. King to SS, CUL.
28. D1, p.22.
29. ibid., pp.22-3.
30. GTAT, p.149.
31. MFM, p.257.
32. D1, p.31.
33. ibid., p.28.
34. BL.
35. WP, p.20.
36. D1, p.32.
37. SJ, p.8.
38. e.g. between 10 Jan. & 14 Feb. 1916 SS drafted 'January', 'Druids', Glory: 1916', 'The Silver Stems', Love', 'The Rainbow', 'Pastoral'.
39. D1, pp.36-7.
40. MFM, p.257.
41. NAM, SS coll., Army Book 152.
42. D1, pp.43-4.
43. SS to EJD, 17 Feb. 1916, CUL.
44. WP, p.22. SS also included a poem in a letter to EM on 10 Feb. 1916, 'Winter in Picardy'.
45. SJ, p.29.
46. ibid., p.28.
47. SS to EJD, 11 Mar. 1916, CUL.
48. Anthony Powell, *To Keep the Ball Rolling* (Penguin, 1983), p.348.
49. ibid.
50. M. Borland, *Wilde's Devoted Friend*, p.272.
51. ibid., p.42.
52. ibid., p.16.
53. Prob. Moffat-Smith, see D1, p.80.
54. D1, p.40.
55. Clifford Inglis Stockwell D.S.O. is described in Frank Richards's *Old Soldiers Never Die* (p.35).
56. D1, p.39.

57. Trench diary 1916, CUL.
58. WP, p.25.
59. D1, p.44.
60. MFM, p.274.
61. D1, p.45.
62. ibid.
63. ibid.
64. In a letter from SS to EJD, 5 Apr. 1916, CUL.
65. See ts. of the poem made from SS's ms. original by EJD in his collection of SS letters, CUL.
66. By 18 May 1918 SS thought all his poems 'tosh', he told EJD 'except the "Last Meeting" and "The Working Party".' CUL.

Chapter 10

1. RG is the main source for the 'Mad Jack' legend.
2. D1, p.52.
3. ibid., p.53.
4. *The Diary of Virginia Woolf*, vol.IV, 28 Apr. 1935, p.307.
5. SS to EJD, 5 Apr. 1916, CUL.
6. Cpl. 'Mick' R. O'Brien joined the RWF in Nov. 1914, fought at Neuve Chapelle, Festubert and Loos, killed in action 26 May 1916.
7. D1, pp.47-8.
8. ibid., p.48.
9. ibid.
10. 'stuffy' in the original.
11. See typed copy in EJD's coll. CUL.
12. Berg.
13. Letter from GH to 'Ken/Sig/Geoff', 8 Apr. 1916, IWM.
14. For one rejected poem, 'The Giant-Killer', see D1, p.56.
15. SJ, p.17.
16. Thorpe, p.24.
17. Perhaps because SS had had a horse of this name and was slightly jerky in his movements on occasions.
18. D1, pp.57-8.
19. ibid., p.60.
20. See GTAT, p.226.
21. SS to EJD, 17 Apr. 1916 & 30 Apr. 1916.
22. 'The Last Meeting', CP, p.35.
23. Goodall had joined Jan. 1909, the term after Sorley, whom he knew.
24. MIO, p.116.
25. SS to EJD, 5 Jun. 1915, CUL.
26. D1, p.66.
27. ibid.

28. RR:RWF, p.186.
29. See JD's notes to RG's GTAT, IWM.
30. Beinecke.
31. D1, p.67.
32. ibid., pp.74-5. RG's reference to 'Limbo' comes from *Over the Brazier* (1916).
33. D1, p.75.
34. SS to EJD, 5 Jun. 1916, CUL.
35. This, and next quote are from D1, pp. 78-9.
36. D1, p.79.
37. MIO, p.47.
38. D1, p.83.
39. MIO, p.56.
40. ibid., p.58, 'The Road' (CP, p.32).
41. D1, p.88.
42. Hassall, p.398.
43. MIO, p.67.
44. RR:RWF, p.202.
45. WP, pp.42-3.
46. ibid. The ms.
47. MIO, p.69.
48. ibid., p.70.
49. ibid., p.77.
50. D1, p.92.
51. ibid., p.93.
52. ibid., p.94.
53. ibid.
54. The ms. of this poem (HRHRC) dated 18 Jul.
55. 'Letter to SS from Mametz Wood' is from *Poems 1914-1926*.
56. D1, p.98. 'Oh my songs never sung' is from RG's 'The Shadow of Death', *Over the Brazier*.
57. ibid., p.97.
58. CUL.
59. See D1, p.99, WP, p.44. All the mss referred to are at HRHRC.
60. MIO, p.88.
61. *Westminster Gazette*, 28 Sept. 1916.
62. TLS, 31 May 1917.

Chapter 11

1. SJ, p.41.
2. CUL.
3. WP, p.46.
4. SS:PP, pp.80-2.
5. This and next quote: SJ, p.19.
6. SJ, p.19.
7. The Hon. Dorothy Brett (1883-1977) daughter of the 2nd Viscount Esher, friend of Dora Carrington, Mark Gertler, D.H. Lawrence.

8. OAG, 1974, p.121.
9. ibid., p.122.
10. Emslie John Horniman (1863-1932), connoisseur of art and travel.
11. D1, p.101.
12. ibid., p.102.
13. ibid.
14. SS to EJD, 23 Feb. 1916, CUL.
15. R.P. Graves, *Robert Graves: the Assault Heroic (1895-1926)* (London, 1986), p.160.
16. ibid.
17. GTAT, p.191.
18. See SS:MWP, p.294 for the problems of dating here.
19. SJ, pp.20-4.
20. ibid., p.21.
21. ibid., p.23.
22. ibid.
23. In SS's annotated copy there are approx. 5,631 words of annotation on 250 of its 448 pages.
24. GTAT, p.191.
25. D1, p.125.
26. GTAT, p.192.
27. RG to RR, 16 Sept. 1916, Lilly.
28. B.H. Liddell Hart, *History of the First World War* (London, Papermac edition, 1992), p.249.
29. Jacques Sassoon's father, David, was SS's cousin.
30. See SS:MWP, p.301 for this poem.
31. D1, p.71.
32. CUL.
33. SS was especially proud of 'The General'.
34. WP, p.57.
35. D1, p.95.
36. ibid., p.106.
37. ibid., p.107.
38. D3, p.140.
39. MIO, pp.101-2.
40. SS to EJD, 3 Dec. 1916, CUL.
41. Caesar, *Taking It Like a Man*, pp.82-3.
42. D1, p.121.
43. WP, p.61.
44. See EG to SS, 17 Feb. 1917, Rutgers.
45. SS to EG, 27 Feb. 1917, BLL.
46. RG to SS, 30 Nov. 1916, Berg.
47. ibid.
48. D1, pp.118-19.
49. ibid., p.124.
50. ibid., p.124, SJ, p.44.
51. WP, p.64.
52. D1, pp.107-8.
53. ibid., p.107.
54. EB's note on the MS of 'Enemies' at HRHRC.
55. D1, p.120.
56. ibid., p.126.
57. SJ, p.40.
58. ibid., p.43.
59. ibid., p.40.
60. *Mr Britling Sees It Through* (1916), bk II, ch. 4.
61. D1, p.127.

Chapter 12

1. D1, p.132.
2. See ibid., pp.133 & 134.
3. MIO, p.119.
4. SS to RR, 22 Feb. 1917, Lilly.
5. D1, p.133.
6. SS to EJD, 23 Feb. 1917, CUL.
7. SS to RR, 8 Mar. 1917, Lilly.
8. D1, pp.139-40.
9. WP, p.73.
10. SS to RR, 1 Apr. 1917, Lilly.
11. WIK, p.308.
12. ibid.
13. GTAT, p.196.
14. JC to SS, 29 Mar. 1917, IWM, Capt. John Dunn to SS, 31 Jan. 1927, CUL.
15. WIK, p.308.
16. MIO, p.137.
17. WIK, p.308.
18. MIO, p.163.
19. SS names Orme as his companion on a trip into Amiens on 21 Mar. 1917 (D1, p.144), but not for his trip to Heilly sur l'Ancre.
20. Yates had been Q.M. with the 2nd RWF since 1912.
21. MIO, p.136.
22. GTAT, p.173.
23. SS to RG, 14 Mar. 1917, USI.
24. MIO, p.135.
25. WIK, p.468.
26. ibid., p.468.
27. ibid., p.401.
28. WP, pp.147-8.
29. MIO, p.141.
30. WIK, p.298.
31. ibid., p.310.
32. ibid., p.369.
33. SS to RR, 1 Apr. 1917, Lilly.
34. WIK, p.326.
35. ibid., p.306.
36. CP, p.67.
37. D1, p.149.
38. WIK, p.309.

39. MIO, p.142.
40. D1, p.151.
41. WIK, p.311.
42. SJ, pp.46-7.
43. WIK, p.311.
44. MIO, p.145.
45. WIK, p.311.
46. *First World War* (London, 1994), p.322.
47. See WIK, p.317.
48. ibid., pp.315-16.
49. WP, p.77.
50. WIK, p.318.
51. Heinemann to RR, 21 Jan. 1918, Lilly.
52. WIK, p.320.
53. ibid., pp.320-1.
54. D1, p.156; the last words of RG's poem 'Escape'.

Chapter 13

1. *New Witness*, 18 Oct. 1918.
2. D1, pp.161-2.
3. SS to LOM, 26 Apr. 1917, HRHRC.
4. MIO, p.176.
5. ibid.
6. Reprints of 350 in Aug. 1917 and 500 in Jan. 1918 wd. follow.
7. *Beginning Again* (Hogarth Press, 1964), p.123.
8. SJ, p.50.
9. Ts, private collector.
10. D1, p.245.
11. SS gives the date as 10 May.
12. *Marble and Bronze*, p.173.
13. SS to RG, 23 May 1917, USI.
14. D1, p.168.
15. WO to his father, 26 Aug. 1917, *Collected Letters* (OUP, 1967), p.488.
16. SS to LOM, 4 Feb. 1917, HRHRC.
17. TLS, 31 May 1917.
18. *Nation*, 16 Jun. 1917.
19. 'The Bayreuth-Baghdad Line', *New Witness*, 28 Jun. 1917.
20. Letter from Charles Scott Moncrieff to SS, 8 Jul. [1917], from SS's press-cutting book (William Reese).
21. RR to SS, 2 Jun. 1917, Lilly.
22. EG to SS, 29 May 1917, Rutgers.
23. RR to SS, 18 May 1917, Lilly.
24. See *Robert Ross: Friend of Friends* (Cape, 1952), p.313.
25. SS to RG, 23 May 1917, USI.
26. SS to EJD, 14 May 1917, CUL.
27. D1, p.165.
28. ibid., pp.165-6.

29. ibid., p.166.
30. ibid., p.167.
31. ibid.
32. ibid., pp.173.
33. ibid., p.172.
34. SJ, p.48.
35. JC to JD, 17 May 1917; JC to SS, 30 May 1917, IWM.
36. 'The Supreme Sacrifice', WP, p.81, 1st pub. in *Cambridge Magazine*, 9 Jun. 1917.
37. SS to RG, 23 May 1917, USI.
38. D1, p.157.
39. SS to EJD, 2 Jun. 1917, CUL.
40. WP, p.80.
41. Both pub. in *Cambridge Magazine*.
42. D1, p.167.
43. See SS to EJD, [6 & 8 Jun. 1917], CUL.
44. SJ, pp.49 & 50.
45. D2, p.158.
46. *Tatler*, 27 Feb. 1918.
47. SJ, p.51.
48. SJ, p.50.
49. ibid., p.49.
50. Bertrand Russell (1872-1970) had lost his teaching job at Cambridge in July 1916 as a result of his pacifism.
51. See Christie, Manson & Wood's sale catalogue, 4 Jun. 1975, p.93, SJ, pp.48 & 52.
52. Lees-Smith later became Postmaster-General in a Labour Government.
53. SS acknowledged this later, in talking to Dr W.H.R. Rivers at Craiglockhart. He may have wished to spare his superiors further embarrassment.
54. The original statement at IWM differs very slightly from the version SS included in MIO and other places.
55. D1, p.176.
56. MIO, p.203.
57. SS to LOM, 3 Jul. 1917, HRHRC.
58. SS to ATB, 4 Jul. 1917, quoted in Keynes, p.37.
59. SS owned both the French and English editions of *Le Feu* (*Under Fire*).
60. D1, p.176.
61. ibid., p.175.
62. SJ, p.56.
63. ibid., p.54.
64. SS to DFC, 17 May 1965, SS:PP, p.65.
65. MIO, pp.210-14.
66. See MIO, pp.207-10.
67. RG to SS, 30 Jun. 1917, Berg.
68. D1, p.177.
69. ibid., p.178.
70. ibid., p.180.

71. SJ, p.56.
72. See RG to RR, 9 Jul. 1917 (Lilly), D1, p.178.
73. D1, p.179.
74. ibid., pp.180-1.
75. *Marble and Bronze*, p.174.
76. See *Wilde's Devoted Friend*, p.259.
77. D1, p.179.
78. *Wilde's Devoted Friend*, p.271.
79. SS to RR, [n.d.] Jul. 1917, Lilly.
80. ibid.
81. JC to SS, 11 Jul. 1917, IWM.
82. Lilly.
83. GTAT, p.214.
84. D1, p.192.
85. Hassall, p.416.
86. i.e. 'Lamentations' and 'The Effect'.
87. MIO, p.235.
88. GTAT, p.216.
89. PRO/WO/ 339/SI 440/49289.
90. HGW to SS, Jul. [1917], McMasters.
91. JD to SS, 1 Jan. 1929, IWM.
92. *The Times*, 31 Jul. 1917.
93. The *Bradford Pioneer* had pub. the statement in full on 27 Jul.; *The Times, Manchester Guardian, Morning Post, Daily Telegraph, Daily Chronicle, Burton Evening Gazette, Southampton Echo* and others followed.
94. SJ, p.57.

Chapter 14

1. Liddell Hart, *History of the First World War*, p.327.
2. SP, p.30.
3. ibid., p.31.
4. ibid., p.7.
5. Harper is 'Hooper' in SP.
6. Now Napier College.
7. SS to LOM, 19 Aug. 1917. D1, p.184.
8. SS to EJD, 25 Jul. 1917, CUL; SP, p.7.
9. SP, p.53.
10. SS to RG, 4 Oct. 1917, USI.
11. William Halse Rivers Rivers (1864-1922).
12. SP, p.7.
13. ibid., p.27.
14. *Conflict and Dream* (Kegan Paul, 1923), p.167.
15. ibid., p.171.
16. ibid.
17. P. Fussell, *The Great War and Modern Memory*, p.101.
18. SP, p.7.
19. SS to EM, Aug. 1918, Berg.

20. See 'Revisitation', CP, p.221.
21. See *CP*, p.106.
22. SP, p.8.
23. Fussell, *Sassoon's Long Journey*, p.135.
24. *Behind the Lines* (Yale, 1987), pp.65ff.
25. *Taking It Like a Man*, p.88.
26. *Behind the Lines,* p.65.
27. SS to LOM, 30 Jul. 1917; D1, pp.183-4.
28. Gordon and Geoffrey Harbord's letters to SS are at IWM.
29. Geoffrey Harbord to SS, 5 Aug.1917, IWM.
30. SS to Carpenter, 29 Aug. 1918, Sheffield City Libraries.
31. D1, pp.185-6.
32. SJ, p.58.
33. WO to Susan Owen, 11 Sept. 1917 & WO to Leslie Gunston, 22 Aug. 1917, *Collected Letters,* pp.494 & 485.
34. SJ, p.58.
35. Related by Peter Parker, *The Old Lie, the Great War and the Public School Ethos* (Constable, 1987), p.193.
36. WO to Susan Owen, 8 Aug. 1917, *Collected Letters*, p.482.
37. *Collected Letters*, pp.484-5.
38. WO to Susan Owen, [12] Sept. 1917, *Collected Letters*, p.494.
39. WO To Mary Owen, 29 Aug. 1917, *Collected Letters*, p.489.
40. *War Poems and Others*, ed. D. Hibberd (Chatto & Windus, 1975), p.73.
41. WO to Leslie Gunston, 22 Aug. 1917, *Collected Letters*, p.486.
42. SJ, p.59.
43. See WO's *War Poems*.
44. SJ, p.60.
45. ibid., p.59.
46. D.J. Enright brought this to my attention.
47. SJ, p.71.
48. 'Wirers', WP, p.90.
49. WP, p.92.
50. ibid., p.93.
51. SS to RR, 3 Oct. 1917; D1, p.187.
52. D1, p.194.
53. CP, p.77.
54. SS to LOM, 28 Oct. 1917, HRHRC.
55. SS to RR, 3 Oct. 1917; D1, p.188.
56. WO to SS, 5 Nov. 1917, *Collected Letters*, p.505.
57. WO to Susan Owen, [12] Sept. 1917, *Collected Letters*, p.494.
58. ibid., 7 Sept. 1917, *Collected Letters*, p.492.

59. WO to SS, *Collected Letters*, p.512.
60. WO to Susan Owen, Sat. [29 Oct. 1917], *Collected Letters*, p.503.
61. Related to me by Gabrielle Cross, a close friend of Harold Owen.
62. WO to Susan Owen, [12] Sept. 1917, *Collected Letters*, p.494.
63. SJ, p.63.
64. ibid.
65. SS's diary, 7 Feb. 1954; SS:PP, p.87.
66. D1, p.157.
67. R.A. Sampson was still writing to SS in 1933, CUL.
68. Margaret Sackville (d. 1963) pub. her own war poems, *Pageant of War* (London, 1914).
69. SS to RR, 3 Oct. 1917; D1, p.188.
70. WO to Susan Owen, 14 Oct. 1917, *Collected Letters*, p.499.
71. See *CP*, pp.82-3.
72. *London Mercury*, Jun. 1929.
73. See SS's diary entries for 2 Jul. 1916 (D1, p.85) & 6 Jul. 1916 (D1, pp.88-9).
74. SS to LOM, 11 Oct. 1917, HRHRC.
75. SP, p.36.
76. ibid.
77. SS to LOM, [17 Oct. 1917]; D1, pp.190-1.
78. SP, pp.34-5.
79. OAG, p.230.
80. *The Old Huntsman* had sold 700 copies by 17 Aug., which SS considered 'quite good'.
81. RG to SS, 25 Jan. 1917, Berg.
82. ibid., 21 Apr. 1917, Berg.
83. ibid., 3 Jul. 1917, Berg.
84. ibid., [1 Dec. 1917/e. Jan. 1918?], Berg.
85. By 15 May 1918 SS was writing to RG that 'Bob Nichols' was 'the best poet of the three', USI.
86. 'The Day's March', *Men Who March Away*, ed. I.M. Parsons (Chatto & Windus, 1966), pp.42-3.
87. SJ, p.68.
88. ibid.
89. Hassall, p.437.
90. SS to RR, 17 Aug. 1917, Lilly.
91. SS to RG, 21 Nov. 1917, Berg.
92. O'Prey, p.89.
93. SS to ATB, 15 Dec. [1917], CUL.
94. RG to SS [Dec?] 1917, Berg.

Chapter 15

1. SP, p.55.
2. SS to LOM, 22 Dec. 1917, HRHRC.
3. SP, p.57.
4. ibid.
5. SS to LOM, 4 Dec. 1917, HRHRC.
6. D1, pp.196-7.
7. See 'Current Literature' by J.C. Squire, *New Statesman*, 24 Nov. 1917; *TLS*, 27 Dec. 1917; *The Nation*, 19 Jan. 1918; *The Welsh Outlook*, Jul. 1918; *The Dial*, 15 Aug. 1918.
8. SP, p.60.
9. D1(19 Dec. 1917) pp.197-8.
10. SS to RN, 22 Dec. [1917], Bodley.
11. See Fussell, *The Great War and Modern Memory*.
12. SS to Goldsworthy Lowes Dickinson, 19 Dec. [post 1906], King's College, Cambridge.
13. SS to LOM, 21 Nov. 1917, HRHRC.
14. RG to SS, [1 Dec. 1917/ e. Jan. 1918], Berg.
15. SS to RM, 29 Dec. 1917, HRHRC.
16. D1, pp.201-2.
17. SS to RG, 14 Jan. 1918, USI.
18. D1, p.203.
19. ibid.
20. ibid.
21. SP, p.66.
22. ibid., p.81.
23. SS to LOM, 4 Feb. 1918, HRHRC.
24. SP, p.77.
25. SS to LOM, 26 Dec. [1917], HRHRC.
26. See CP, p.88.
27. TH to SS, 8 Jan. 1918, Eton College.
28. 'Idyll' was 1st pub. in the *New Statesman*, 29 Jun. 1918, then *Picture-Show* (1919).
29. 'Memory' 1st pub. *To-Day*, Mar. 1918, then *Picture-Show*.
30. SS to EM, 16 Jul. 1919, Berg.
31. e.g. RR, EM, RM & WHRR, William Heinemann & J.G. Lousada.
32. D1, p.212.
33. *Studies in the History of the Renaissance* (1873).
34. D1, p.218.
35. ibid.
36. ibid., p.212.
37. ibid., p.214.
38. ibid.
39. CUL.
40. SP, p.90.
41. D1, p.242.
42. ibid.
43. ibid., p.243.
44. ibid., p.235.
45. ibid., p.216.
46. SS to EJD, 19 Feb. 1918, CUL.
47. D1, p.227.

48. ibid., p.219.
49. ibid.
50. ibid.
51. ibid., p.222.
52. ibid., p.223.
53. SS to LOM, 20 Mar. [1918], HRHRC.
54. SP, p.130.
55. D1, p.236.
56. ibid., p.262.
57. D2, p.67.
58. D1, p.229.
59. ibid., p.240.
60. ibid.
61. ibid.
62. D1, p.224.
63. ibid., pp.226-7.
64. SS to EG, 25 Mar. [1918], Rutgers.
65. D1, p.229.
66. ibid.
67. ibid.
68. ibid., p.232.
69. ibid., p.234.
70. See ibid., pp.232-3.
71. ibid., p.237.
72. Lena Ashwell (1872-1957).
73. D1, p.236.
74. ibid., p.235.
75. ibid., p.238.
76. ibid., pp.239-40.
77. The *Leasowe Castle* sank on 27 May 1918 with the loss of most of her passengers.

Chapter 16

1. *Wilde's Devoted Friend*, p.277.
2. Hassall, p.348.
3. D1, pp.246-7.
4. 'Testament' was included in SS's letter of 9 May 1918 to LOM (HRHRC).
5. D1, p.247.
6. ibid., pp.252 & 269.
7. ibid., p.248.
8. ibid.
9. ibid.
10. This notebook, now at NAM, is signed 'T.B.B.' but is clearly written by SS.
11. SP, p.118.
12. D1, p.250.
13. ibid.
14. ibid., p.255.
15. *The New Book of English Martyrs* (Heinemann,1918), p.53.
16. D1, p.258.
17. ibid., p.263.
18. ibid., p.258.

19. ibid., p.259.
20. SS to EM, 30 May 1918, Berg.
21. D1, p.259.
22. ibid., p.261.
23. ibid., p.264.
24. ibid., p.266.
25. SP, p.132.
26. D1, p.269.
27. ibid., p.267.
28. SS to RN, 19 Jun. 1918, Bodley.
29. *Y Ddraig Goch*, Mar. 1968, vol.17, no. 1, p.13.
30. SP, p.140.
31. op.cit., p.13.
32. SS to RM, 7 Jul. 1918, HRHRC.
33. SP, p.141.
34. SS to EJD, 26 Jun. 1918, CUL.
35. SS to EM, 27 Jun. 1918, Berg.
36. SS to EG, 29 Jun. 1918, Rutgers.
37. 'Atrocities' was later pub. in *War Poems* (1919) in a modified form.
38. SS to OS, 3 Jul. 1918, HRHRC.
39. op.cit., p.14.
40. ibid.
41. D1, pp.272-3.
42. See WP, p.141.
43. SP, p.147.
44. ibid., pp.151-2.
45. D1, p.252.
46. See SJ, p.71.
47. SP, p.154.
48. ibid., p.157.
49. ibid., p.158.
50. ibid., p.161.
51. Bodley.
52. Letter by Sir Wintringham Stable in the *Daily Telegraph* (13.9.67).
53. D1, p.275.
54. SS to RN, 2 Jun. [1918], Bodley.
55. D1, p.275.

Chapter 17

1. 'Moon Street' was a reference to Ross; 'Ardoursandendurans' referred to RN's *Ardours and Endurances* in 1917.
2. Included RG's to SS, 16 Jul. [1918].
3. See WP, pp.130ff.
4. 'I stood with the Dead' printed in *Nation*, 13 Jul. 1918, the day Sassoon was wounded.
5. SP, p.170.
6. ibid.
7. SS to SCC, 4 Aug. 1918, Berg.
8. SS to RN, 15 Aug. [1918], Bodley.

9. 'Via Crucis' was a revision of a poem of 12 Aug. 1916; 'The Dug-Out', annotated 'St Venant, July 1918', was probably started there.

10. SS to EM, [Aug. 1918], Berg.

11. ibid., [Jul. 1918], Berg.

12. From 'Recessional'.

13. From 'For the Fallen'.

14. D1, p.278.

15. SS to C.K. Ogden, 10 Aug. 1918, McMasters & WP, p.134.

16. SS to EM, [Aug. 1918], Berg.

17. *The Morning Post*, 2 Aug. 1918.

18. OS to SS, 26 Jun. 1918, Pullman.

19. SS to OS, 3 Jul. 1918, HRHRC.

20. SS to EJD, 26 Jun. 1918, CUL.

21. *Noble Essences*, p.109.

22. See SS to EM, [1918], Berg; *Wilfred Owen: Collected Letters*, p.571.

23. SJ, p.72.

24. WO to SS, 31 Aug. 1918, *Collected Letters*, p.571.

25. SS to EM, [1918], Berg.

26. SS to EC, 15 Aug. 1918, Sheffield City Libraries.

27. ibid., 3 Sept. [1918].

28. SJ, p.73.

29. ibid., p.75.

30. SS to EM, 26 [Aug. 1918], Berg.

31. SS to RM, 18 Sept. 1918, HRHRC.

32. SJ, p.75.

33. Guilhermina Suggia (1888-1950).

34. SJ, p.76.

35. D2, p.162.

36. RG had written on 11 Sept. 1918: '"Ancient History" is wonderful ...'. SS sent it to the *Nation*; pub. there 28 Sept. 1918.

37. SS to EG, 20 Sept. 1918, Rutgers.

38. SJ, p.84.

39. SS to RR, 6 Oct. 1918, Lilly.

40. SJ, p.84.

41. RG to SS, 12 Oct. 1918, Berg.

42. WO to Susan Owen, 15 Oct. 1918, *Collected Letters*, p.585.

43. SJ, p.87.

44. D1, p.280.

45. ibid.

46. ibid.

47. Since 1912 EM had asked poets to copy their verses into his rather coyly named Little Book.

48. SJ, p.89.

49. ibid.p.92.

50. ibid., p.91.

51. LOM to SS, 10 Jan. 1923, Columbia.

52. SJ, p.91.

53. Letter from Virginia Woolf to Vanessa Bell [19 Nov. 1918], *Letters*, vol. II, p.297.

54. SS to Lewis Chase, 25 Jan. 1922, Congress.

55. See SJ, p.50 & SS to RG, 24 Jun. 1917, USI.

56. SJ, p.95.

57. ibid.

58. WO to Susan Owen, 29 Oct. 1918, *Collected Letters*, p.590.

59. D1, p.282.

Chapter 18

1. SJ, p.26; title quotation SJ, p.109.

2. 'Lovers' 1st pub. May 1919 in *Oxford Outlook*.

3. SJ, p.106.

4. See SS:MWP, pp.391-5.

5. SJ, p.106.

6. SJ, p.97.

7. SS to RHD, 12 Dec. 1963, CUL.

8. D1, p.282.

9. Unpub. section of SS's diary, CUL.

10. SJ, p.98.

11. SS to DFC, 28 Jul. 1965, SS:PP, p.66.

12. John Drinkwater (1882-1937).

13. Walter James Redfern Turner (?1889-1946).

14. Wilfrid Wilson Gibson (1878-1962).

15. John Freeman (1880-1929).

16. D2, p.189.

17. John Galsworthy (1867-1933).

18. SS to FSw, 17 Sept. 1940, Arkansas.

19. 'Night on the Convoy' published in vol. III of *Reveille*, Feb. 1919.

20. H.W. Massingham (1860-1924).

21. Hamo Sassoon was wounded at Gallipoli in Nov. 1915.

22. SJ, p.105.

23. ibid.

24. ibid.

25. ATB's diary, 25 Aug. 1915, CUL.

26. GA's unpub. memoirs, Wichita.

27. Famous American book designer.

28. GA (1897-1937) was with 222nd Mixed Brigade at Margate.

29. SS to EJD, [*c.*Nov. 1917], CUL.

30. GA to EJD, 30 Oct. 1918, Dent Collection, CUL.

31. ibid.

32. ibid., [*c.*11 Nov. 1918].

33. William ('Gabriel') Park Atkin painted mainly watercolours but also did drawings for book illustrations and was a gifted cartoonist.

34. GA to EJD, 30 Oct. 1918, CUL.
35. SS would give his Broadwood piano to GA.
36. EJD to SS, 20 Feb. 1918, CUL.
37. Diary of ATB for 29 Jun. 1919, CUL.
38. GA to EJD, 30 Oct. 1918, CUL.
39. ibid., 15 Aug. 1918.
40. SS to ATB, 26 Nov. 1918, CUL.
41. ibid.
42. GA to EJD, 28 Dec. 1918, CUL.
43. ATB's diary, 16 Dec. 1918, CUL.
44. GA to EJD, 24 Nov. 1918, CUL.
45. This and next quotation, SS to GA, 23 Nov. 1918, Berg.
46. D2, p.71.
47. ibid., p.72.
48. Interview with Lady Lettice Strickland-Constable.
49. SS's notes on OC, CUL.
50. ibid.
51. SS told LU he had written 'fake' love sonnets in his twenties.
52. E.B.C. Jones's review of *Picture Show*, *Cambridge Magazine*, 8 Nov. 1919.
53. 'Parted' is dated 'Gray's Inn, 25 Nov.' in HRHRC ms. of *Picture Show*.

Chapter 19

1. SJ, p.127.
2. 'Picture-Show' written at Weirleigh in Jan. 1919.
3. CP, p.116.
4. SS to GA, [6 Dec. 1918], Berg.
5. 'The Imperfect Lover', CP, p.116.
6. D2, p.86.
7. CP, p.116.
8. SS to RG, 9 Feb. [1924], USI.
9. 'Memory', CP, p.105.
10. i.e. Corrigan, *Siegfried Sassoon*.
11. *Centenary Essay* on SS by DFC (1986).
12. SJ, pp.119-20.
13. ibid., p.119.
14. SS to GA, 27 Dec. 1918, Berg.
15. CP, p.106.
16. SS to GA, 27 Dec. 1918, Berg.
17. ibid., 31 Dec. 1918, Berg.
18. SS was at Blackburn 10 to 15 Dec. 1918.
19. SJ, p.111.
20. Unpub. diary entry, 10 Dec. 1918, CUL.
21. ibid., 13 Dec. 1918, CUL.
22. ibid.
23. L. Woolf, *Downhill All the Way*, p.84.
24. Snowden (1864-1937) son of a weaver in Yorkshire, was injured aged 22.

25. Unpub. diary, entry for 14 Dec. 1918, CUL.
26. SJ, p.115.
27. SS to LOM, [n.d.] Dec. 1918, HRHRC.
28. Unpub. diary, entry for 13 Dec. 1918, CUL.
29. D2, p.294.
30. ibid.
31. SS to RN, 5 Nov. [1923], Berg.
32. SJ, p.126.
33. ibid., p.118.
34. SS to LOM, 4 Jan. 1919, HRHRC.
35. SS to EM, Dec. 1919; SJ, p.128.
36. SS to GA, 20 [Jan. 1919], Berg.
37. SJ, p.128.
38. Cyril Bradley Rootham (1875-1938).
39. DS says SS seemed unconcerned or unaware of the interruptions created.
40. SS to ATB, [16] Dec. 1918, CUL.
41. SS ms. poems are at the Berg.
42. See D2, pp.78, 255 & 274.
43. SJ, p.127.
44. SS proposed by AB and seconded by His Honour Judge Hugh Murray Sturgis in Nov. 1918.
45. SJ, p.127.
46. D2, p.32.
47. ibid.
48. SJ, p.132.
49. Letter from John Langdon Davies to *New Statesman* letters column, 22 Sept. 1967.
50. ibid.
51. ibid.; SJ, p.133.
52. SJ, p.134.
53. SS to RG, 9 Jan. 1919, USI.
54. R.P. Graves describes Boar's Hill at this period as a 'miniature Parnassus' in *Robert Graves: The Assault Heroic*.
55. SS to RG, 2 Mar. 1919, USI.
56. WW to his mother: 'I met John Masefield and Siegfried Sassoon, the poets.' Kennedy, p.14.
57. See Osbert Sitwell's *Laughter in the Next Room* (Macmillan, 1950), p.171.
58. SJ, p.135.
59. ibid.
60. ibid., p.137.
61. D2, p.73.
62. SJ, p.137.
63. See Bryan Connon's *Beverley Nichols: A Life* (Constable, 1991).
64. Nichols printed Sassoon's 'Lovers' in full in the first issue of the *Oxford Outlook*, May 1919.
65. Once SS had made the decision to leave

Oxford, he wrote another poem on his last day there, 'Cinema Hero'.

66. SJ, p.141.

67. On 11 Mar. 1919 the *London Gazette* announced SS's retirement from the Army.

68. SJ, p.137.

69. SS to ATB, 19 Mar. 1919, CUL.

70. SS to LOM, 4 Jan.1919, HRHRC.

71. SS to RG, 13 Mar. 1919, USI.

72. ibid.

Chapter 20

1. SJ, p.138.

2.See *Gravesiana*, vol.1, no.1, p.42.

3. SS to Mr Hillyer, 2 Oct. 1960 (Syracuse): 'Everyone Sang' has brought him 'several hundred pounds in anthology fees!'

4. SJ, p.141.

5. ibid.

6. The *Daily Citizen*, the official organ of the Labour Party, had folded by 1919, leaving only the *Daily Herald*.

7. L. Woolf, *Downhill All the Way*, p.244.

8. The *Daily Herald* suffered from the post-war slump and would need help from the trade unions in the early twenties.

9. Gerald Gould (1885-1936) presented Sassoon with a copy of his *The Happy Tree and Other Poems* (1919), which contained a section of war verse.

10. See SS:MWP, p.522.

11. SS to Harold Laski, 13 Feb. 1920, William Reese Collection.

12. L. Woolf, *Beginning Again*, p.223.

13. Turner publications including *The Dark Fire* (1918), *Pursuit of Psyche* (1931), *Songs and Incantations* (1936), *The Man Who Ate Popomack* (1922), and books on music.

14. SS to RG, 23 May 1917, USI.

15. Lytton Strachey to Virginia Woolf, 19 Sept. 1922.

16. D3, p.81.

17. D2, pp.109 & 16.

18. ibid., p.236.

19. ibid., p.162.

20. ibid., p.103.

21. ibid., p.271.

22. ibid., pp.271-2.

23. Sassoon sent Irene Clephane *Recreations* (1923) and *Lingual Exercises* (1925).

24. See SJ, p.143.

25. ibid., p.143.

26. ibid., p.142.

27. R.P. Graves, *Robert Graves: The Assault*

Heroic, p.215.

28. Graves, op.cit.

29. GTAT, p.236.

30. ibid.

31. See SS to RG, 9 Apr. 1919, USI.

32. SJ, p.145.

33. ibid., p.138.

34. 'Base Details', 'The Hawthorn Tree', 'The Investiture' and 'Together'.

35. After the first 3 literary pages there is virtually no book advertising.

36. SS to RG, 30 Mar. 1919 (USI): 'I only get six half-columns a week.'

37. SS to RG, 13 Mar. 1919, USI.

38. Robert Nichols (1893-1944). See SS:MWP, pp.420-3, for more details.

39. ES submitted a review of George Willis's *Any Soldier to his Son* on 4 Jun. 1919.

40. This was published by Mr Henderson at the Bomb Shop, 66 Charing Cross Road, in 1919.

41. SS to GA, [Apr.] 1919, Berg.

42. See Waugh, *Resentment* (1918); D2, p.160; D3, p.156.

43. Review of 21 May 1919.

44. e.g. SS asked Lascelles Abercrombie for an article on TH and WdlM for one on *Robinson Crusoe*.

45. i.e. 6 Hogarth Studios, 64 Charlotte Street, London W1.

46. TEL to SCC, 19 Mar. 1924 ('I'm frigid towards women, so I can withstand her: so that I want to withstand her') and SS to WdlM, 30 Mar. 1932, Beinecke.

47. See D3, p.186.

48. See ibid., p.46.

49. SJ, p.151.

50. ibid.

51. ibid., p.154.

52. ibid., p.153.

53. ibid., p.154.

54. ibid., p.149. The tribute was delayed and delivered to TH in Nov.

55. SJ, p.150.

56. ibid.

57. Henry Major Tomlinson (1873-1958).

58. C. Causley, 'Writers Remembered: Siegfried Sassoon', *The Author*, Winter 1989.

59. D3, p.185.

60. Diary entry for 12 Mar. 1924.

61. L. Woolf, *Downhill All the Way*, p.92.

62. D3, p.189.

63. SS to HH, 4 Nov. 1948, in possession of HH.

64. SS to HMT, 25 Dec. 1942, HRHRC.

65. SS's notes to OC (CUL) and D3, p.189.

66. See HMT to SS, 2 Dec. 1927, Columbia, where HMT questions SS's charge.

67. SS to WdlM, 14 Nov. 1948, Beinecke.

68. Frank Arthur Swinnerton (1884-1982) contributed at least four reviews to the *Daily Herald* between Apr. & Jun. 1919.

69. SS to FSw, 26 Jun. 1931, Arkansas.

70. There would be one significant break in SS's correspondence with FSw following SS's conversion to Roman Catholicism in 1957.

71. D2, pp.162-3.

72. ibid., p.174.

73. EB to SS, 7 May 1919, HRHRC.

74. SJ, p.146.

75. SS to WdlM, 10 Feb. 1952, Beinecke.

76. SS to Dame Hildelith Cumming, 3 Jul. 1962; SS:PP, p.229.

77. See SS:MWP, pp.103-4.

78. CP, p.183.

79. ibid., p.189.

80. Edward Shanks (1892-1953) was a poet, novelist and critic.

81. SJ, p.146.

82. D2, p.177.

83. ibid.

84. EG to SS, 14 Jan. 1923, BLL.

85. ibid.

86. D2, p.171.

87. EB was married three times, divorced twice and supported an early mistress all his life.

88. SJ, p.146.

89. D2, p.174.

90. SS to RG, 3 Sept. 1920, USI.

91. SJ, p.160.

92. ibid.

93. ibid.

94. D2, p.33.

95. SJ, p.172.

96. Keynes, *The Gates of Memory*, p.53.

97. The three poems which had not already appeared in print – 'In an Underground Dressing-Station', 'Atrocities' and 'Return' – had been written much earlier. All three had been considered too outrageous for publication. See Bonham's London Sale cat., 8 May 2013

98. SJ, p.160.

99. ibid., p.163.

100. ibid.

101. ibid., p.161.

102. SS stayed with the Sitwells 7-17 Jul. 1919.

103. SJ, pp.161-2.

104. Loder had transferred from the Atherstone to the Fitzwilliam in 1914 with his new wife Phyllis.

105. SJ, p.165

106. ibid., p.164.

107. ibid., p.170.

108. SS was staying at St John's, Cambridge, 11-18 Aug. 1919.

109. CP, p.162.

110. SS to WdlM, 10 Sept.1919, Beinecke.

111. RG to EB, 12 Jul. 1919, USI.

112. SS to ATB, 24 May 1919, CUL.

113. D2, p.33.

114. SS to ATB, 12 Nov. 1919, CUL.

115. D2, pp.88-9.

116. ibid., p.240.

117. SJ, p.168.

118. See Gerald Gould to SS, 2 Nov. 1919, William Reese.

119. AB to RN, 14 Aug. 1923, Bennett, *Letters*, p.195.

120. ibid., p.169.

121. See SS to RH, 27 Jun. 1937, Beinecke: '... my politics ended in 1919, I think'.

122. See SS:MWP, pp.76-9 for details on Rachel Beer.

123. SJ, p.167.

124. SS told GA that he had been invited to lecture in America as early as Jan. 1919.

125. SJ, p.171.

126. CA was pub. by Dutton in America in Dec. 1918.

127. SJ, p.172.

128. ibid.

Chapter 21

1. 'Midnight on Broadway' 1st pub. in the *London Mercury* in Apr. 1921.

2. SJ, p.174.

3. ibid.

4. ibid. SS to GA, 5 Feb. 1920, Berg.

5. ibid., p.184.

6. SJ, p.178.

7. Included in a letter from SS to WJT, 9 Jul. [1920], Berg.

8. Dates taken from diary SS kept of his trip, CUL.

9. SS to LOM, 17 Jun. [1920], HRHRC.

10. SS to LU, 25 May [1921], Delaware, and SS to LOM, 15 Jul. [1920], HRHRC.

11. SS to SCC, 24 Oct. 1920, Berg.

12. SJ, p.181.

13. e.g. Masefield wrote SS a letter of introd. to Mrs Thomas Lamont.

14. SS to AL, 12 May 1960, CUL.

15. ibid. 'The Mister' fell on hard times; in the 1930s, his old house crumbling around him, he wandered the lanes fuddled and poor.

16. See *The Dial*, 15 Mar. 1918. Louis Untermeyer (1885-1980).

17. LU's review of OH and CA appeared in the *Evening Post*, 15 Mar. 1919.

18. The Untermeyers were to divorce. LU married 3 more times and had 3 more sons.

19. SS to LU, 27 Mar. [1920], Delaware.

20. Jean Untermeyer (as Jean Starr) produced at least 5 bks of poetry between 1918 and 1940.

21. SJ, p.182.

22. SS wrote an article on war poetry, one on TH, a 'spoof' interview with himself and a 'Set of Parodies of the Work of Some Famous Modern Poets' in *Vanity Fair* between Feb. & Jul. 1920.

23. SS to LU, 7 Mar. [1921], Delaware.

24. Jean trained as a singer.

25. SS to Jean Untermeyer, 23 Mar. 1965, Buffalo.

26. SS saw *Richard III* on 6 Mar. 1919.

27. See CP, p.155.

28. SS to LU, 2 May [1922] & LU to SS, 28 May 1922, Lilly.

29. SS to BH, 28 Dec. 1920, Congress.

30. SJ, p.182.

31. *Satirical Poems* (1926), *Vigils* (1936), RRu (1941), CP (1949), *Sequences* (1947), but not HJ (1928), published by Harper & Brothers.

32. SJ, pp.218 & 219.

33. SS to BH, 18 Jun. 1929, Congress.

34. i.e. Inter-Collegiate Socialist Society, 7 May 1919, Rand School, 16 May & Cooper Union on 10 Aug.

35. SS spoke to the Harvard Poetry Club on 29 Apr. 1919. Harold Laski (1893-1950).

36. SJ, p.202.

37. ibid.

38. Samuel Nathaniel Behrman (1893-1973).

39. *Tribulations and Laughter*, p.14.

40. SS to GA, 5 Feb. 1920, Berg.

41. SB interviewed SS for *New York Times*.

42. SJ, p.204.

43. ibid., p.205.

44. e.g., SS to GBS, 25 Nov.1927, CUL.

45. SS to GBS, 23 Apr. 1932, CUL.

46. *Tribulations and Laughter*, p.11.

47. T. Morgan, *Somerset Maugham* (Jonathan Cape, 1980), pp.447-8.

48. SJ, p.206.

49. ibid., p.207.

50. ibid., p.206.

51. ibid.

52. ibid., p.207.

53. *Tribulations and Laughter*, p.13.

54. SJ, p.207.

55. SS to WJT, 21 Feb. 1920, Berg.

56. SS to LOM, 6 Apr. [1920], HRHRC.

57. ibid.

58. SS to WJT, 21 Feb. 1920, Berg.

59. Glenn Hunter (1897-1945).

60. D2, p.276.

61. *Clarence* played 20 Sept. 1919 for 300 performances.

62. SB to RHD, 14 Mar. 1969, CUL.

63. D2, p.208.

64. SB to RHD, op.cit.

65. ibid. and D2, p.209.

66. *Tribulations and Laughter*, p.9.

67. SS to LOM, 16 Mar. [1920], HRHRC.

68. SS stayed at Powers Hotel, Rochester, NY.

69. SS to TS, 14 Apr. 1920, Berg. The letter quoted in the epigraph to this chapter is also from the Berg collection.

70. The Ferry Hall School was at 533 North Mayflower Road, now a block of flats.

71. John Alden Carpenter (1876-1951).

72. Harriet Monroe asked SS, 27 May 1922, if she could include 7 of his poems in her revised edition of *The New Poetry* (Regenstein Library, University of Chicago).

73. Carl Sandburg (1878-1967).

74. SJ, p.196.

75. SS to LOM, 6 Apr. 1920, HRHRC.

76. SJ, p.197.

77. 'Chicago', *Chicago Poems* (1918).

78. SJ, p.198.

79. ibid., p.197.

80. See SJ, pp.185-90, for John Jay Chapman's violent challenge to SS.

81. SS to LOM, 6 Apr. [1920], HRHRC.

82. SJ, p.200.

83. The Kellogg Fairbanks lived at 1244 North State Street.

84. SJ, p.200.

85. Mrs Kellogg Fairbank had attracted national attention during the suffrage movement by riding a white charger down Michigan Boulevard.

86. SS lectured to both clubs on 8 Apr. 1920.

87. See SS to Mrs Vaughan Moody, 18 Mar. 1920, Regenstein Library, Chicago.

88. On the 9, 12 & 13 Apr. respectively.

89. See SS to Mr Hillyer, 2 Oct. 1960, Syracuse. See also the minutes of the Harvard Poetry Society, 9 Feb.1920.

90. SJ, p.202.
91. Both this and the previous quotation are from SJ, p.203.
92. SS to LOM, 17 Jun. [1920], HRHRC.
93. SS to RG, 1 Jul. [1920], USI.
94. John Thompson MacCurdy (1886-1947).
95. SJ, p.213.
96. Edward Percy Warren (1860-1928).
97. SS to LU, 29 Jul. 1920, Delaware.
98. SJ, p.215.
99. ibid.
100. ibid.
101. ibid.
102. BH to SS, 13 Jul. 1945, Congress.
103. SS to SB, 3 Feb. 1921, CUL.
104. *Tribulations and Laughter*, p.9.
105. SS to LOM, 15 Jul. 1920, HRHRC.
106. SS to RG, 1 Jul. 1920, USI.
107. SJ, p.219.
108. SS to RG, 13 Feb. 1924, USI.
109. SS to LOM, 17 Jun. 1920, HRHRC.
110. SJ, p.224.

Chapter 22

1. See D2, pp.50, 52, 77-8.
2. ibid., p.73.
3. See SS:MWP, pp.269-70.
4. CP, p.85.
5. D2, p.73.
6. SS to RN, 5 Nov. 1923, Berg.
7. D2, p.162.
8. ibid.
9. ibid., p.119.
10. *The Duchess of Popocatapetl*, Dent, 1939, p.169.
11. ibid.
12. UV4.
13. ibid.
14. D2, p.31.
15. ibid., pp.71-2.
16. ibid., p.236.
17. UV4.
18. D3, p.163.
19. Bagnold's *Autobiography*, p.82.
20. Interview with Theresa Whistler, 29 Mar. 1999; EB to SS, 8 Aug. 1935, Columbia.
21. Interview with Theresa Whistler.
22. ibid.
23. ibid.
24. D3, p.77.
25. ibid., p.34.
26. SS to RN, 25 Dec. 1941, HRHRC; WY, p.216.
27. SS and RH started exchanging rare books early on.
28. SS to RH, 27 Jun. 1937, Beinecke.
29. But SS inscribed a copy of *Recreations* to Romer Wilson.
30. D3, p.253.
31. ibid., p.141.
32. See SS:MWP, pp.515-16.
33. TEL to SS, 23 Nov. 1923, collection of Harry and Cookie Spiro.
34. SS to TEL, 26 Nov. 1923, ibid.
35. TEL to SS, 2 Dec. 1923, ibid.
36. D3, p.66.
37. ibid., p.68.
38. ibid.
39. D2, p.148; EMF to SS, 12 Jun. 1922, private collection.
40. D3, p.135; D2, p.149.
41. EMF had met TEL only once before.
42. TEL to EMF, 24 Jul. 1924, Lawrence, *Selected Letters*.
43. EMF to SS, 25 Mar. 1924, private collection.
44. ibid.
45. ibid.
46. ibid.
47. ibid.
48. D2, p.151.
49. D3, p.53.
50. ibid., p.187.
51. D2, p.151.
52. ibid., p.29.
53. RG to EB, 10 Mar. 1921, O'Prey, p.123.
54. D3, p.248.
55. See CP, p.128.
56. D3, pp.101 & 102.
57. UV4.
58. D3, p.234.
59. 'Prelude to a Self-Revealing Journal', D2, p.104.
60. Cf. the 'Old Caspar' figure of 'The Utopian Times', CP, pp.164-6.
61. EMF to SS, 20.3.27, private collection.
62. SS to Lewis Chase, 25 Jan. 1922, Congress.
63. SS to RG, 21 Nov.1921, USI.
64. D2, p.88.
65. See Harold Owen's *Aftermath*.
66. 'Limitations', 'Early Chronology' and 'Falling Asleep'.
67. *Recreations* 1st printed at the Chiswick Press Jan. 1923.
68. D3, p.41.
69. ibid., p.39.
70. ibid., p.38.
71. ibid., p.40.

72. SS to TS, 25 Jun. 1923, Berg.

73. SS to RG, [Feb.] 1922 & 6 Jun. 1924, USI.

74. SS to ATB, 27 Apr. 1921, CUL.

75. D3, p.38.

76. 99 copies printed at CUP, Feb. 1925.

77. *Selected Poems*, 2,000 copies of which published by Heinemann on 23 Apr. 1925, contained 67 poems from OH (1917), CA (1918) & *Picture Show* (1919).

78. Blunden, *A Selection of His Poetry and Prose*, p.319.

79. ibid.

80. See CP, p.161.

81. SS told RG (letter of 5 Jan. 1925) that the ambassador was 'Lord Bertie of Thame'.

82. *New Statesman*, 23 May 1925.

83. ibid.

84. UV4.

85. LOM introduced SS to Desmond MacCarthy and Maynard Keynes; Keynes had introduced SS to Lytton Strachey.

86. SS to Lewis Chase, 25 Jan. 1922, Congress.

87. SS to HH, 19 Feb. 1949.

88. D2, p.155.

89. SS to HH, 19 Feb. 1949; SS to HMT, 4 May 1949, HRHRC.

90. See SS:MWP, pp.509-11.

91. SS to Virginia Woolf, 21 May 1923, Berg.

92. Virginia Woolf to SS, 22 May 1923, V. Woolf, *A Change of Perspective*, p.85.

93. D3, p.78.

94. ibid., p.79.

95. ibid.

96. V. Woolf, *Diary of Virginia Woolf*, vol.2, p.287.

97. V. Woolf, *A Change of Perspective*, p.85.

98. Notes for this essay are at the BL Manuscript Room.

99. SS to LOM, 28 Mar. 1928, HRHRC.

100. ibid., 2 Nov. 1928.

101. See O. Sitwell, *Laughter in the Next Room*, p.112.

102. 'A Letter to S.S.', undated ms. at HRHRC.

103. See also Philip Ziegler's *Osbert Sitwell* and 'The Letters of Edith Sitwell to Siegfried Sassoon', ed. Thomas W. Rand, dissertation, Pullman.

104. D2, p.90.

105. OS to SS, 4 Jul. 1923, Pullman.

106. D2, p.103.

107. OS to SS, op.cit.

108. ibid., [3/4 Jul. 1923].

109. D2, pp.69, 74. Following quote is from SS to EM, 18 Dec. 1920, Berg.

110. D2, p.255.

111. ibid., p.75.

112. ibid., p.77.

113. D3, pp.39-40; OS to SS, op.cit.

114. ibid., p.40.

115. ibid., p.44.

116. ibid.

117. OS to SS, op.cit.

118. ibid.

119. D3, p.141.

120. SS to GBS, 2 Dec. 1927, CUL.

121. 'Too Fantastic for Fat-Heads', *Daily Herald*, 24 May 1922.

122. ES to Susan Owen, Nov. 1919, E. Sitwell, *Selected Letters*, p.20.

123. 'Sassoon on Owen', *TLS*, 31 May 1974, pp.58-9.

124. E. Sitwell, p.23.

125. See D. Welland, *Wilfred Owen: A Critical Study* (1978), p.589.

126. SS told DS late in life that ES was in love with him.

127. See SS:MWP, pp.288-9. When ES read SS's description of LOM in SJ (1945) she wrote to John Lehmann: 'Have you seen Siegfried's deplorable book ... one mass of treachery, fawning and snobbishness. I didn't like the old Lady Ottoline Morrell, and she hated me – but she adored Siegfried and it is painful to see him "wishing she wouldn't look so extraordinary" ... and otherwise goring her' (Rand, p.49.) ES clearly identified with LOM in this respect.

128. ES to SS, 4 Jun. 1926, Pullman.

129. ibid., 9 Nov. 1926.

130. ibid., 14 Dec. 1926.

131. SS to EM, 16 Jul. 1919, Berg.

132. D3, p.134.

133. ES to SS, 2 Jan. 1927.

134. Humbert Wolfe (1885-1940).

135. See SS to SSi, 12 Jan. 1932, William Reese.

136. Elborn, p.98.

137. ES to SS, 3 May 1955, Pullman.

138. ibid., 25 Oct. 1928.

139. These caricatures were targeted mainly at Edith and Osbert (William Reese).

140. Written by SS into his copy of ES's *Street Songs* (Lionel Dakers Coll.).

141. Diary entry for 23 Jan. 1954 (SS:PP, p.157).

142. SS to Dame Hildelith Cumming, 17 Jun. 1961(SS:PP, p.209).

143. D2, p.232.
144. ibid., p.20
145. SJ, p.26.
146. ibid.
147. Sassoon, 'Thoughts on Horses and Hunting', *My First Horse* (P. Lunn, 1947), p.14.
148. ibid.
149. ibid., p.22.
150. D2, p.139.
151. Interview with DS.
152. D2, p.138.
153. ibid., p.109.
154. ibid., p.100.
155. ibid., p.110.
156. ibid., p.114.
157. See CP, p.137; D2, pp.57-61.
158. D3, p.221.
159. See SS:MWP, pp.220, 450 & 457.
160. SS helped a number of prisoners and their wives in 1920s.
161. *The Times* reported on 5 Jun. 1922 that the cause of death was 'strangulation of the intestines'.
162. D2, p.163.
163. ibid., p.166.
164. Cyril Tomkinson to SS, 5 Jun. 1922, CUL.
165. D3, p.265.
166. SS to GBS, *c.*1949, CUL.
167. D3, p.129.
168. SS to HFJ, 30 May 1927, CUL; SS to RG, 9 Jul. 1925, USI.
169. SS to RG, 9 Jul. 1925, USI.
170. The Long White Cloud still stands beside the Thames opposite Monkey Island.
171. Edward Elgar (1857-1934).
172. SS to TS, 21 Oct. 1941, Berg.
173. D2, p.80.
174. See D2, pp.124-5.
175. ibid., p.152.
176. ibid.
177. SS to WdlM, op.cit.
178. SS to RG, 9 Jul. 1925, USI.
179. WdlM had moved by 1925 to Hill House near Taplow Court.
180. 'Anzie's' real name was Leslie Wylde.
181. UV4.
182. See SS's notes on OC at CUL.
183. Born Edith Wandela Boreel in 1895.
184. SS to HFJ, 12 Jul. 1927, CUL.
185. SS owned four of Wendela's works.
186. D3, p.260.
187. ibid.
188. ibid., p.148.
189. ibid.

Chapter 23

1. D2, p.81.
2. 'The Power Ordained', dated '14.9.24', SS poetry notebook, CUL.
3. CP, p.196.
4. Notes by SS on OC, CUL.
5. D2, p.222.
6. SS travelled to France with FS and Anzie for a month in Mar. 1924 & Feb. 1925.
7. SS to LOM, 5 Apr. 1921, HRHRC.
8. ibid.
9. D2, p.201.
10. SS to LOM, op.cit.
11. D2, p.214.
12. SS stayed at Porlock Weir with GA from 5 May to 6 Jun. 1921.
13. SS stayed at the Hotel Angleterre in Rome from 28 Sept. to the end of Oct. 1921.
14. D2, p.86.
15. Sir Gerald Tyrwhitt-Wilson (1883-1950) was the 5th baronet and 14th Baron Berners.
16. Berners was a composer of light divertimenti-style music, several ballets and one opera.
17. 'Clavichord Recital' pub. in *Nation*, 30 Dec. 1922; D2, p.246.
18. D2, pp.119, 121.
19. ibid., p.280.
20. ibid., p.201.
21. ibid., pp.225 & 249.
22. Constantine I King of Greece 1913-17 & 1920-23.
23. Philipp's elder brother had died at the Battle of Dobrugia in 1916, leaving Philipp in line for the title, which he inherited in 1940 and held until his death in 1980.
24. D2, p.225.
25. ibid., p.272.
26. ibid., pp.244, 240, 208, 276.
27. ibid., p.225.
28. SS left Victoria Station on 20 Jul. 1922, arriving Munich on 1 Aug. 1922.
29. D2, p.216.
30. Pub. 1st in *Nation*, 30 Dec. 1922, with 'Clavichord Recital'.
31. D2, p.279.
32. ibid., p.232.
33. ibid., p.276.
34. ibid., p.284.
35. ibid., p.249.
36. ibid., p.161.
37. ibid., p.382.
38. ibid., p.279.

39. SS to the Heads, [Apr. 1933], HRHRC; D2, p.225.

40. Philipp was eventually sent to Buchenwald with his wife Mafalda, who died there in 1945.

41. D2, p.189.

42. SS to LOM, 15 Mar. 1923, HRHRC.

43. D2, p.189.

44. ibid., p.113. Lord Edward Christian David Gascoyne Cecil (1902-86).

45. D2, p.113.

46. ibid.

47. SS to HFJ, 27 Apr. 1927, CUL.

48. Ruth Head to SS, 3 Sept. 1936, CUL.

49. Telephone interview with Jonathan Cecil, 4 Mar. 2000.

50. Richardson King Wood (1903-76).

51. D3, pp.137 & 148. Following quotes from D3, pp.170 & 149.

52. e.g. D3, p.159.

53. See D3, p.197.

54. See O'Prey, *In Broken Images*, pp.150-5.

55. D2, p.53.

56. SS to EJD, 18 May 1916, CUL.

57. Novello was the male lead in the film *The Bohemian Girl*.

58. SS to GBS, [22/23 Oct. 1925], CUL.

59. ibid.

60. ibid.

61. Novello was 31, SS 38 in 1924.

62. SS travelled to the Riviera with FS and Anzie in late Feb. 1925, staying at Cannes and the Cap d'Ail, where GA visited him.

63. Interview with DS.

64. Both DS and HH suggested this.

65. Interview with Lady Lettice Strickland-Constable.

66. ibid.

67. SS to WdlM, 20 May 1949, Beinecke.

68. SS received a summons to appear at Wilton County Court Petty Sessions for 'driving without due care and attention' on 20 Mar. 1932.

69. D3, p.151.

70. SS to RG, 15 Aug. 1924, USI.

71. D3, p.133.

72. ibid., p.66.

73. ibid.

74. ibid., p.94.

75. ibid., p.276.

76. ibid., p.237.

77. ibid., p.268. *The Aesthetes*, pub. 1927.

78. ibid., p.270.

79. ibid.

80. ibid.

81. ibid., p.281.

82. R.P. Graves, *The Assault Heroic*, pp.315-16.

83. D3, p.272.

84. ibid., p.281.

85. SS to RG, 9 Feb. 1924, USI.

86. D3, p.235.

87. GBS to SS, 16 Oct. 1925, CUL.

88. ibid., 21 Oct. 1925.

89. D3, p.291.

90. Harold Speed (1872-1957) was known mainly as a portrait painter.

91. D3, pp.293 & 299.

92. ibid. GA lived at 9 Ladbroke Grove.

93. 'Summer Morning in London', dated 23 Jun. 1926, SS poetry notebook, CUL.

94. SS's domestic was called 'Dengel', not 'Dingle'.

95. SS shopped in Jermyn Street.

96. D3, p.299.

97. ibid.

98. ibid.

99. SS to GBS, 4 Nov. 1947, CUL.

100. D3, p.303.

101. 'Farewell to a Room' written at Tufton Street, 23 Nov. 1925.

102. SS to LOM, 25 Nov. 1925, HRHRC.

103. D3, p.299.

104. SS told LOM (6 Apr. 1925, HRHRC) that 'Alone' was written at Garsington at Christmas 1924 and suggested by a book by Gorky.

105. SS:PP, p.103.

106. Dorothy Wallis to GBS, 7 Apr. 1953 (George Byam Shaw).

107. SS to RG, 19 Nov. 1925, USI.

108. SS to Nancy Nicholson, 11 Nov. 1925, USI.

109. SS to RG, 'Mon. 11' [*c*.1927], USI.

110. SS saw *Juno and the Paycock* at the Vaudeville, 1 Dec. 1925.

111. Ellen Terry (1847-1928), leading lady to Henry Irving from 1878.

112. GBS co-director of the Shakespeare Memorial Theatre, Stratford 1952-1956 and Director 1956-1959.

113. SS to GBS, 24 Oct. 1925.

114. Written 12 Dec. 1925, 1st pub. *London Mercury*, Apr. 1926.

115. e.g. compare 'Vigils', 'Farewell to Youth', 'A Local Train of Thought', 'November Dusk', 'In Time of Decivilisation', 'Old Fashioned Weather', 'Awareness of Alcuin', 'The Messenger', 'The Present Writer', 'Retreat from Eternity' and 'The Visitant'.

116. SS to ATB, 19 Nov. 1924, CUL.

117. 'Lovers' and 'Elegy (to R.R.)' had appeared in *Picture Show*, and 'In me past, present, future meet', 'Stonehenge', 'Alone', 'Grandeur of Ghosts', 'To an Old Lady Dead', 'To One in Prison' and 'Conclusion' in *Lingual Exercises*.

118. D3, p.56.

119. ibid., p.60.

120. e.g. 'Song be my soul', 'Sing bravely in my heart', 'As I was walking in the gardens', 'Strangeness of Heart', 'Alone, I hear the wind about my walls', 'Conclusion' and 'A flower has opened in my heart'.

121. 'Lovers', 'Now when we two have been apart so long', 'While I seek you'.

122. 'Grandeur of Ghosts', 'To an 18th Century Poet'.

123. 'To an Old Lady Dead', 'To One Who Watches', 'Elegy (to R.R.)'.

124. 'To One in Prison'.

125. 'From a Fugue by Bach', 'When selfhood can discern'.

126. 'Alone'.

127. 'To One Who was With Me in the War', 'On Passing the New Menin Gate'.

128. Rand, 'The Letters of Edith Sitwell to Siegfried Sassoon', p.66.

129. SS to RG, 3 Oct. 1933, Buffalo.

130. 'The Watch-Tower', review of *Vigils* by EB.

131. Thorpe, p.210.

132. SS visited Vaughan's grave at Llansantffraed on 27 Aug. 1924.

133. Thorpe, DFC and Paul Moeyes all make the connection.

134. 'Nativity' pub. as No. 7 of Faber & Gwyer's 'Ariel Poems' series on 25 Aug. 1927.

135. SS:PP, p.104.

136. ibid.; SS to ATB, 6 Jan. [1927], CUL.

137. Crosby Gaige issued 599 copies of HJ in a ltd edn in Mar. 1928, though dated 1927.

138. Heinemann published 2,000 copies of a trade edn of HJ on 19 Jul. 1928 and reprinted it 7 times from Oct. 1928 to Jan. 1935.

139. See SS to HFJ, 12 Oct. 1928, CUL.

140. It seems significant that SS did *not* take GA to visit TH.

141. D3, p.304.

142. ibid., p.305.

143. SS described Gilbert Spencer (1893-1979) as 'good old Gil ... rubicund and charmingly simple as ever' (D3, p.246).

144. There is a telegram from Henley begging SS to collect GBS. SS did not do so.

145. Ivor Guest succeeded his father as the second Lord Wimborne in 1914.

146. O. Sitwell, *Laughter in the Next Room*, p.222.

147. B. Baxter, *Strange Street*, p.121.

148. ibid.

149. ibid.

150. Robert Gathorne-Hardy (1902-1973).

151. Eardley Knollys to Lady Anne Hill, 31 Jul. 1990, shown to me by Lady Anne Hill.

152. SS to RGH, 30 Jul. 1926, Lilly.

153. ibid.

154. SS to RGH, 19 Aug. 1926, Lilly.

155. ibid.

156. SS wrote to GBS on 29 Jul. 1926 (CUL): 'Bob Gathorne-Hardy and his friend ... returned to London yesterday, without saying exactly why.'

157. SS to RGH, 30 Jul. & 19 Aug. 1926, Lilly.

158. SS to RGH, 19 Aug. 1926, Lilly.

159. ibid.

Chapter 24

1. *Daily Mail* revealed SS's identity 2 Oct. 1928.

2. MFM became an optional text on the School Certificate English Paper in 1943 and in 1954 SS was amazed to learn that it was a set text for GCE English.

3. The James Tait Black Prize brought a cheque for £127 6s. 2d. as well as prestige.

4. UV4. All unattributed quotations from SS in this chapter are from this source, copy at CUL.

5. See SS:MWP, pp.70-74.

6. 'An Enquiry' is at BL.

7. GBS's only sporting activity was rowing.

8. See D3, pp.172-5, 201-3.

9. ibid., p.202.

10. J.C. Dunn to SS, 18 Feb. 1926, CUL. See SS:MWP, pp.347-50, for details.

11. *The War the Infantry Knew, 1914-1919* was published by P.S. King, anon., in 1938.

12. This material would be incorporated into MIO.

13. See SS:MWP, pp.331-2.

14. See CP, pp.186-7.

15. See SS:MWP, pp.211-12.

16. SJ, p.100.

17. D3, p.247 & pp.131-2.

18. EMF to SS, 23 Jun. 1923.

19. SS's notes on OC, CUL.

20. SS to Michael Thorpe, 12 Aug. 1966 (*Letters to a Critic*, p.13).

21. There are explicit references in MFM to Surtees, whom SS continued to read till the end of his life.

22. SS to the Turners, 13 Sept. 1922, Berg.

23. D2, pp.245, 256 & 286.

24. SS claimed reading Proust sent him 'back to Debussy' (D3, p.63).

25. D3, p.218.

26. Romain Rolland (1866-1944).

27. D3, p.301.

28. Sir Henry Head married Ruth Lawson, a headmistress, in 1904.

29. GK's notes on MFM, CUL.

31. SS to LOM, 31 Mar. 1927, HRHRC.

32. GBS to SS, 24 Apr. 1927, CUL.

33. ibid., 31 Jun. 1927.

34. SS records 'I Accuse the Rich' not included in CP.

35. SS's 1927 diary, UV4.

36. ES to SS, 11 May 1927, Pullman.

37. Anzie managed to sell the smashed Morris Oxford for £200.

38. James Wylde, born that summer, is no longer alive.

39. Diary entry for 25 Jul. 1927.

40. Started on 25 Jul. 1926, 'On Passing the New Menin Gate' was 1st pub. in *London Mercury* May1928.

41. SS to D.J. Enright, 23 Nov. 1960, shown to the author by the recipient.

42. SS to GBS, 23 Aug. 1927, CUL.

43. See SS letters to GBS, CUL.

44. Max Meyerfeld (1875-*c*.1952).

45. Max Meyerfeld to SS, 14 Oct. 1926, CUL.

46. GBS left England 1 Oct. 1927, arrived New York 9 Oct. 1927, remaining there until the end of Apr. 1928.

47. EB had both tea and dinner with SS on 12 Oct. 1927.

48. E. Marsh, *A Number of People*, p.236.

49. ibid., pp.52, 60.

50. ibid., pp.205, 206, 207, 210. Following quote from SS to RGH, 25 Sept. 1936 (Lilly).

51. GBS's son, George, says that the (Byam) Shaws came originally from Ayrshire.

52. MFM, p.228.

53. EMF to SS, 17 Dec. 1928.

54. 'An Author's Secret: Mr Sassoon's Anonymous Book of Memoirs', *Daily News and Westminster Gazette*, 9 Oct. 1928.

55. SS to RG, 2 Mar. 1930, Buffalo.

56. SS writes in 'An Enquiry' that Weirleigh

was 'all mixed up with mother, of course, but I must try to keep her separate from my emotions' (BL).

57. SS records details of this Brenchley vs Rolverden match on 27 Jul. 1904: 'They won the toss – made 157. Bishop 78 not out. Self bowled 5 overs, 2 maidens, 8 runs, 1 wicket. We made 132. Went in at 105 for 7 with W. Seymour took it to 120. Made 3. Caught at wkt.'

58. There are relatively few significant changes to this ms., now at BL.

59. MFM, p.75.

60. 'The Flower Show Match' provided the title, for example, of a collection of excerpts from SS's prose published by Faber & Faber on 24 Jul. 1941.

61. MFM, pp.55-6.

62. *Letters to a Critic*, p.14.

Chapter 25

1. SS gave GBS the desk on which MFM was written.

2. SS's father had died of TB.

3. e.g. P. Hoare, *Serious Pleasures*, p.32.

4. SS to HFJ, 21-24 Jun. 1927, CUL; SS's diary, 1 Jun. 1927.

5. SS to HFJ, ibid.

6. SS's diary, *c*.19 Oct. 1927.

7. SS to GBS, 10 Oct. 1927, CUL.

8. E. Tennant, *Strangers*, p.160.

9. OS to SS, 12 Oct. 1927, Pullman.

10. SS to GBS, 13 & 24 Oct. 1927, CUL.

11. Cecil Beaton (1904-1980). SS's diary, *c*.7 Jul. 1927.

12. SS's diary, *c*.15 Oct. 1927; S. Bradford, *Sacheverell Sitwell*, p.170.

13. ibid.

14. SS to GBS, 13 & 24 Oct. 1927, CUL.

15. *The Contents of Wilsford Manor* (Sotheby cat., London, Oct.1987), p.12.

16. M. Holroyd, *Lytton Strachey*, p.953.

17. ibid.

18. P. Middleboe, *Edith Olivier*, p.62.

19. ibid.

20. Untitled poem by SS, dated 26 Oct. 1927, poetry notebook, CUL.

21. ST to SS, 5 Nov. 1927, Berg.

22. Philip Hoare notes that ST uses the word 'gay' to imply homosexual.

23. C. Beaton, *Self-Portrait with Friends*, p.6.

24. P. Hoare, *Serious Pleasures*, p.132.

25. A. Powell, *To Keep the Ball Rolling*, p.135.

26. ST to Gilles David, 4 Dec. 1971, Philip

Hoare Coll.

27. ST to SS, [n.d.] Aug. 1938, Berg.

28. SS's diary, Oct. 1928.

29. Interview with Lady Lettice Strickland-Constable.

30. See sonnet dated 26 Oct. 1927, CUL.

31. ST to SS, 30 Dec. & 8 May 1928, Berg.

32. Middleboe, *Edith Olivier*, p.51.

33. ibid.

34. For ST's one commercially produced book, *Leaves from a Missionary's Notebook*, see *Serious Pleasures*, p.133.

35. *To My Mother*, pub. 24 Sept. 1928, *In Sicily*, pub. 25 Sept. 1930, *To the Red Rose*, pub. 8 Oct. 1931 in Faber's Ariel Poems series.

36. Hoare, *Serious Pleasures*, p.155.

37. SS to TS, 26 May 1929, Berg; 'A Fallodon Memory', CP, p.280.

38. Ruth Head to SS, 19 Sept. 1930, CUL.

39. Middleboe, *Edith Olivier*, p.50.

40. SS's diary, Jan. 1928.

41. ibid.

42. FS died of a perforated ulcer on 26 Dec. 1927.

43. SS's diary, 12 Jan. 1928.

44. ibid., 18 Jan. 1928.

45. SS to GBS, 17 Jan. 1928, CUL.

46. Another 1920s poetry notebook sold recently at Bonham's, London, contains 'Max Gate', written on 14 Jan. 1928 at Max Gate itself, and 'Thomas Hardy is Dead', both unpub.

47. SS's diary, 1 Jan. 1928.

48. Anne Tennant (*c.*1874-1961).

49. SS to EB, 14 Apr. 1928, HRHRC.

50. SS to ES, 28 Mar. 1928, Berg.

51. SS's note on letter from EG of 15 Jan. 1928 (BLL) praising 'One Who Watches'.

52. EG to SS, 15 Jan. 1928, BLL.

53. SS to HMT, 23 Mar. 1954, HRHRC.

54. See 'Writers Remembered: Siegfried Sassoon', *The Author*, Winter 1989.

55. *Serious Pleasures*, p.101.

56. SS gave WW £20 to visit and entertain ST at Haus Hirth.

57. SS's diary, Apr. 1928.

58. ibid.

59. Middleboe, *Edith Olivier*, p.77.

60. ibid.

61. SS's diary, 5 Jun. 1928.

62. ibid.

63. ibid.

64. David Tennant had married the actress Hermione Baddeley on 16 Apr. 1928.

65. SS and ST heard Elizabeth Schumann in *The Marriage of Figaro* at the Residenz Theater, the *Meistersingers* at the Prinzregenten Theater and a Mozart quintet in the courtyard of the Residenz.

66. ST's diary, 30 Aug. 1928, Berg.

67. ibid., 4 Sept. 1928, Berg.

68. The Hirths' route for their journey reads 'Garmisch, Innsbruck, Brenner, Bozen (i.e. Bolzano)'.

69. ST's diary, 10 Sept. 1928, Berg.

70. ibid., 15 Sept. 1928.

71. SS & ST stayed at Montegufoni from 17 to 24 Sept. 1928, then at the Hotel Helvetia, Florence for 2 days.

72. SS to GBS, 3 Oct. 1928, CUL.

73. SS & ST stayed at the Hotel d'Italie and Bauer Grunwald.

74. SS's diary, Sept./Oct. 1928.

75. SS had given J.C. Squire lunch at the Reform on 12 Jun. 1928.

76. MFM was 'noticed' favourably in *Shooting Times, Manchester Guardian, Sporting Life, TLS, Baptist Times, TP's Weekly & London Mercury*.

77. ST's diary, 1 Oct. 1928, Berg.

78. ES told EO that she 'had been very angry with Stephen ... says that SS has two patches on his lungs and blames ST for this' (Middleboe, *Edith Olivier*, p.85).

79. ST's diary, Oct. 1928, Berg.

80. ibid., 6 & 10 Oct. 1928.

81. SS to HFJ, 12 Oct. 1928, Berg.

82. They stayed at Hotel Foyot in Paris.

83. SS to LOM, 1 Nov. 1928, HRHRC.

84. SS to the Heads, 1 Dec. 1928, CUL.

85. SS to Ruth Head, 28 Feb. 1929, CUL.

86. ST's doctors diagnosed a recurrence of the disease on 8 Jan. 1929.

87. SS to RG, 2 Mar. 1930, Buffalo.

88. Johanna Hirth to SS, 24 Feb. 1929, CUL.

89. SS to the Heads, 4 Mar. 1929, HRHRC.

90. SS to Ruth Head, 4 Mar. 1929, CUL.

91. C. Beaton, *Self-Portrait with Friends*, p.6.

92. SS to RGH, 26 Sept. 1946, Lilly.

93. SS made EO an allowance of £200.

94. L. Whistler, *The Laughter and the Urn*, p.135.

95. ibid., p.131.

96. ibid.

97. The original ms of MIO is now at the IWM.

98. Frau Hirth sent SS interest on the loan of 10,000 marks, but SS tore up the cheque.

99. Middleboe, *Edith Olivier*, p.91.

100. MFM had already earned SS £1,500 by Apr. 1929.

101. GBS and Angela Baddeley married on 8 Sept. 1929.

102. Middleboe, op.cit.

103. ibid.

104. See ST to SS, *c.*Mar. 1929, Berg.

105. SS to GBS, 22 May 1929, CUL.

106. ST to Elizabeth Lowndes, 26 May 1929 (Hoare, p.138).

107. SS wrote 'War Experience' & 'Childhood Recovered' in Apr. 1929; ms. of both poems at Harvard.

108. Dated 25 May 1929 in SS's ms notebook of poetry and prose at the IWM.

109. This poem 1st pub. in *Nation*, 5 Apr. 1930.

110. 'At Breitenau, 23 May 1929' dated 22 Mar. 1932 in the Harvard ms.

111. SS would finish this section on 21 Sept. 1929.

112. SS to BH, 18 Jun. 1929, Congress.

113. EB awarded Hawthornden Prize for *The Shepherd* in 1922.

114. M. Holroyd, *Lytton Strachey*, p.1009.

115. EB to Aki Hayashi, 28 Sept. 1929 (Claire Blunden).

116. See message from Gide for SS at the Hotel Plaza Athenée, suggesting a meeting 18 Nov. 1929 (CUL).

117. SS to HH, 14 Feb. 1951.

118. ibid., 16 Nov. 1948.

119. A. Powell, *To Keep the Ball Rolling*, p.40.

120. SS to HH, 22 Oct. 1948.

121. SS wrote 2 pages of notes about MB for WY (Columbia).

122. ibid.

123. ibid.

124. SS:PP, p.137.

125. SS to SCC, 26 Aug. 1952, Cockerell, *The Best of Friends*, p.212. Copy of SS's BBC talk by SS of 28 Jun. 1956 (CUL).

126. Hart-Davis (ed.), *Letters to Max*, p.7.

127. ibid.

128. Home Service broadcast, 2 Jun. 1952.

129. 'In Sicily' was inspired by a valley on the way to Noto.

130. Cf. SS's shell simile in his lecture 'On Poetry' (University of Bristol Press, 16 Mar. 1939, p.18).

131. SS to LOM, 2 Apr. 1930, HRHRC.

132. MIO, p.236.

133. SS's diary, *c.*Apr. 1930.

134. SS to EB, 25 Feb. 1930, HRHRC.

135. SS's diary, 8 Apr. 1930.

136. SS & ST stayed at the Domenico Hotel at Taormina.

137. *Letters to Max*, p.11.

138. ibid., pp.9-11.

139. ibid., p.10.

140. ibid., p.11.

141. ibid., p.12.

142. SS's diary, 30 Apr. 1930 *Letters to Max*, p.13.

143. ibid., *c.*May 1930.

144. SS to LOM, 16 Apr. 1930, HRHRC.

145. SS's diary, *c.*May 1930.

146. ibid.

147. ibid.

148. SS to the Heads, undated letter of 1930, HRHRC.

149. Lord Glenconner later came to appreciate SS's help (EH to SS, 24 May 1931, CUL).

150. *Serious Pleasures*, p.162.

151. SS to Ruth Head, undated letter of 1930, CUL.

152. SS to LOM, 16 Apr. 1930, HRHRC.

153. ibid., 20 Jun. 1930.

154. SS to AT, 2 Aug. 1930, CUL.

155. SS had finished correcting proofs of MIO by mid-July.

156. SS to LOM, 2 Apr. 1930, HRHRC.

157. Copy of notes at CUL.

158. ST's diary for 25 Oct. 1930.

159. CP, p.211.

Chapter 26

1. Faber pub. 20,000 copies of MIO on 18 Sept. 1930 and 8 more editions in the following 4 years.

2. *Daily Telegraph* serialized portions 6-9, 11-16, 18-23 & 25 between 6 & 26 Aug. 1930 for the sum of £350. The *TLS* reviewed MIO on the day of publication.

3. SS to EB, 31 Oct. 1927.

4. SS made it clear to Mary Blunden in his letter of 15 Oct. 1929 that he was only 'offering to make [himself] responsible for all expenses concerned with John's education'.

5. SS to RH, 15 May 1929, HRHRC.

6. SS to RG, 7 Feb. 1930, Buffalo.

7. RG to SS, 20 Feb. 1930, Berg.

8. SS to EB, 20 Dec. 1928, Columbia.

9. SS, *Letters to a Critic*, p.21. EM (in C. Hassell, *Ambrosia and Small Beer*, p.29), says that he was the only pre-war friend RG had retained.

10. RG to SS, 20 Feb. 1930, Berg.

11. *Letters to a Critic*, p.21.

12. SS to RG, 11 Oct. 1926, USI.

13. NB to SS, n.d., Sotheby's cat., 14 Dec. 1992 & SS to GBS, 16 Jun. 1929, CUL. RG had jumped out of a lower floor window after Laura Riding but had escaped unhurt.

14. SS to LOM, 2 Apr. 1930, HRHRC.

15. By 1935 MIO had sold only 7,000 less than MFM, that is 48,000.

16. 'Further Experiences' is the working title of an ms. notebook containing Pt 1 and nearly all Pt 4 of *SP* (William Reese).

17. SS to RN, 20 Feb. 1932, Bodley.

18. 'Dateless oblivion and divine repose', Harvard poetry notebook, dated '18.2.32' & '28.1.33'.

19. In one year alone, from Feb. 1932 to Feb. 1933, Sassoon had three driving accidents, mumps and a broken collarbone.

20. See Harvard poetry notebook.

20. Harvard.

22. 'The Hour-Glass' is dated '20.9.32' and revised '9.11.32' in a 1930s poetry notebook at CUL.

23. Middleboe, *Edith Olivier*, p.136.

24. e.g., 'Vigils', 'Heaven' and 'Ode' from *Vigils*.

25. ES to SS, 22 Dec. 1934, Pullman.

26. CP, p.225. This was dated '11.9.32' a poetry notebook at CUL.

27. SS to the Heads, 17 Apr. 1933, HRHRC.

28. CP, p.123.

29. ibid., pp.123-4.

30. Beryl appears to have been 'Really' and Eileen 'Truly'.

31. SS often spells this 'Wylie'.

32. Middleboe, p.122.

33. SS to AT, 18 Mar. 1931, Berg.

34. Beryl Hunter told SS of the Mill Cottage on 16 Feb. 1931 after he had moved into the Avon Hotel.

35. WW to SS, 8 Mar. 1931, William Walton Collection, Ischia.

36. *Belshazzar's Feast* 1st performed by the Leeds Festival Chorus on 8 Oct. 1931, Malcolm Sargent conducting.

37. WW to SS, loc.cit.

38. 'To a Red Rose', musical in theme, illus. by ST, pub. in Ariel Series in Oct. 1931.

39. 'Did you like *Pinchbeck Lyre*?' SS asked MB on 8 Jul. 1931. 'Unkind; but the result of much piffle-provocation' (*Letters to Max*, p.167).

40. SS to LOM, 27 Apr. 1931, HRHRC.

41. For a more detailed picture of this colony see D. Hibberd, *Harold Monro Poet of the New Age*, Palgrave, 2001.

42. SS to LOM, 27 Apr. 1931, HRHRC.

43. ibid.

44. EH to SS, 23 Apr. 1931, CUL.

45. Harvard poetry notebook.

46. Beryl Hunter to SS, 16 May 1931, CUL.

47. SS stayed 3 days with Miss Fleming-Jones in Paris (SS to TS, 1 Jun. 1931, Berg).

48. SS to AT, 30 Jun. 1931, Berg.

49. SS to MB, 8 Jul. 1931, *Letters to Max*, p.17.

50. Later in 1931 ES, worried about SS's own health, would arrange for him to visit her friend Dr Lydiard Wilson in Bloomsbury.

51. SS to MB, 8 Jul. 1931, Hart-Davis, *Letters to Max*, p.16.

52. CP, p.166.

53. *A Garden Revisited and Other Poems*, 1931.

54. SS to LOM, 30 Sept. 1931, HRHRC.

55. SS to TS, 14 Aug. 1932, Berg.

56. SS to RH, 4 Dec. 1931, Beinecke.

57. EH to SS, 28 Sept. 1931, CUL.

58. Sales brochure of Fitz House at CUL.

59. SS rented Fitz House from Colonel Charles French, who had it on a long lease from Lord Bledisloe.

60. J. Harding, *Dreaming of Babylon*.

61. Dated 22/23 Nov. 1932, Harvard.

62. Dated 13 Jul. 1932 & 20 Jul. 1933, poetry notebook, CUL.

63. 'Childhood Recovered' was written 8 Apr. 1929 but revised at Fitz House.

64. Beryl Hunter to SS, 25 Jul. 1931, CUL.

65. *Dreaming of Babylon*.

66. See 'Our Tour Book-hunting, Nov. 10-14 (1931)' (Bodley) for booksellers visited.

67. SS's notes of this journey are included in the notebook headed 'Books bought while at Fitz House' at Columbia.

68. See CP, pp.221-2. Dated 16 Jul. 1932 & 14 Mar. 1933, Harvard.

69. RG to SS, undated letter of late 1933, O'Prey, p.232.

70. SS to RH, 5 Apr. 1933, Beinecke.

71. SS to EB, 12 Nov. 1931, HRHRC.

72. GBS's eldest brother was also called George.

73. SS to RH, 18 Sept. 1932, Beinecke.

74. Lady Violet Bonham Carter (née Asquith, 1887-1969).

75. Main collection at CUL.

76. *Letters to Max*, p.58.

77. SS was awarded his Hon.D.Litt. on 18

Dec. 1931.

78. TS signed her will on 6 Jan. 1932.

79. S. Behrman, *Tribulations and Laughter*, p.189.

80. SS to the Heads, 21 Jun. 1932, HRHRC.

81. ST to SS, 6 Mar. 1933, Berg.

82. EMF to SS, 11 Apr. 1932, private collection.

83. ST to SS, [Feb. 1933], Berg.

84. *Letters to Max*, p.18; SS to the Heads, 8 Apr. 1933, HRHRC.

85. SS to the Heads, 8 Apr. 1933.

86. ibid.

87. Dr Ross to SS, 22 May [1933], copied out in SS's hand and enclosed in a letter to the Heads.

Chapter 27

1. SS's diary for 8 Oct. 1933.

2. 'Thanksgiving', an unpub. poem dated 4 Oct. & 1 Nov. 1934, included in an illustrated collection of poems now at CUL.

3. Alfred Morrison (1821-97) and his wife Mabel (1847-1933) married in 1866; their first son, Hugh, was born in 1868 (d.1931) and their elder daughter, Katherine, in 1869 (d.1949).

4. Richard Gatty (1909-75).

5. EO's diary, quoted in J.S. Roberts, *Siegfried Sassoon*, p.249.

6. SS to RH, 16 Nov. 1933, Beinecke.

7. A large collection of HG's literary efforts, including a play, some stories and numerous poems are at the Berg.

8. EO to Ruth Head, 24 Oct. [1933], HRHRC.

9. SS to RH, 16 Nov. 1933, Beinecke.

10. Hester's mother approved of the age gap, approx. the same as that between her husband, Sir Stephen Gatty, and herself.

11. SS's diary, mid-Sept. 1933.

12. ibid.

13. ibid., c.Oct. 1933.

14. ibid., 7 Oct. 1933.

15. Middleboe, *Edith Olivier*, p.145.

16. EO to Ruth Head, 24 Oct. [1933], HRHRC.

17. SS to the Heads, 16 Nov. 1933, HRHRC.

18. ST to SS, 'January' 1942, Berg.

19. Sir Stephen Gatty, KC, had been Chief Justice of Gibraltar from 1895 until 1905, the year he married Katherine Gatty.

20. SS noted buying 'Three books by Mrs

Ewing' in his Fitz House notebook for 23 Nov. 1931 and 'Gatty, *Legendary Tales*, 1958 3/6' (Columbia).

21. HG had an income of £2,000 p.a. of her own and would be left a large amount of money by her aunt, Lady St Cyres, in Sept. 1936. Her mother would settle another £10,000 on her and give her £7,500 for a house of her own in the mid-1940s.

22. Interview with Mrs Hancock, 25 Apr. 1931.

23. SS to HMT, 15 Mar. 1956, Christie's catalogue, 3 Apr. 1992.

24. SS to RG, 3 Oct. 1933, quoted O'Prey, p.230.

25. 26 letters from Doris Westwood, 25 Feb. 1930 to Jul. 1934, are now in the Berg.

26. Doris Westwood's pub. 4 novels – *Starr Bladon* (1930), *The Hair Shirt* (1932), *An April Day* (1934), *Humble Servant* (1936) – a collection of poems and a theatrical diary.

27. Doris Westwood to SS, 25 Apr. 1931.

28. ibid., 20 Feb. 1932.

29. Middleboe, *Edith Olivier*, p.146.

30. ibid.

31. Interview with DS.

32. Interview with Andrew Motion, 4 Jul. 2001.

33. ibid.

34. SS's pc of Fitz House of 11 Apr. 1933, CUL.

35. SS to HH, 30 Oct. 1948.

36. GK compiled bibliographies of Jane Austen, Thomas Fuller, Sir Thomas Browne, Edward Gibbon, Donne, Blake, Hazlitt, and SS, among others.

37. Interview with DS.

38. Interview with Andrew Motion.

39. J. Stallworthy, *Singing School*, p.83.

40. GK to SS, 20 Jul. 1933, CUL.

41. Caption on one of the photographs of SS and ST, CUL.

42. GK had been first attracted to Margaret's sister, Gwen (later Raverat).

43. SS to HH, 30 Oct. 1948.

44. *Singing School*, p.90.

45. Nicknames GK used of SS and himself in his letters to SS's nephew, Hamo.

46. SS to HH, 30 Oct. 1948.

47. SS to HH, 30 May 1950, SS to PG, 6 Apr. 1955, HRHRC

48. SS to RHD, 24 Sept. 1964, CUL.

49. In Oct. 1938 SS felt very discouraged about producing another book of poems and told GK that if he would come to look at

his poetry notebooks he might help him put another collection together. The result was almost certainly *Rhymed Ruminations* (pp 1939, trade edn 1940).

50. GK to HS, 30 Jan. 1950.

51. SS to WdlM, 3 Feb. 1952, Beinecke.

52. SS to HH, 4 Nov. 1948.

53. Faber pub. the 7 poems of RR on 9 Nov. 1933.

54. SS to LOM, 10 Mar. 1933, HRHRC.

55. ibid., 18 Mar. 1933, HRHRC.

56. For Temple's reply to SS's letter on 25 Apr. 1933, see Sotheby's cat. 13 Dec. 1993.

57. 'Ex-Service', published in the *Spectator* on 9 Nov. 1934.

58. *Why War?* (pub. by the League of Nations and International Institute of Intellectual Co-operation 1933) was among SS's books when he died.

59. SS to RHD, 3 May 1967, CUL.

60. SS to GK, 30 Oct. 1933, CUL.

61. NB to SS, 2 Nov. 1933, CUL.

62. SS to GK, 29 Nov. 1933, CUL.

63. ibid.

64. SS to the Heads, 29 Dec. 1933, HRHRC.

65. Keynes, *The Gates of Memory*, p.234.

66. ibid., p.235.

67. Middleboe, *Edith Olivier*, p.153.

68. SS to GK, 8 Nov. 1933, CUL.

69. ST to SS, Jan. 1942 & 4 Nov. 1941 respectively, Berg.

70. SS to the Heads, 20 Oct. 1934, HRHRC.

71. TEL to Nancy Astor, 31 Dec. 1933.

72. The anthology, *The Coppice*, is at the University of Iowa.

73. SS to RG, 24 Nov. 1933, Buffalo: 'Many thanks for your good wishes'.

74. NB to SS, 25 Oct. 1933, CUL.

75. SS compared himself and Hester to the Brownings, who had a spaniel, 'Flush'.

76. SS to AT, [*c.*Nov. 1933], Berg.

77. ES to SS, [*c.*Nov. 1933], Pullman.

78. Interview with Claire Blunden.

79. SS to GK, 1 Feb. 1934, CUL.

80. The Sassoons stayed at the Grand Hotel Miramar, Malaga, before moving to Syracuse.

81. SS to HH, 22 Mar. 1950.

82. SS to LG, 1 Apr. 1941, Columbia.

83. SS would write a poem about that 'wild and warring Queen' (CP, p.238).

84. Work done in 1820 by Bath architect John Pinch.

85. Lord Heytesbury died in 1891. 'In

Heytesbury Wood', written in Mar. 1935.

86. SS sold £1,300 worth of shares in Feb. 1934 and put down a deposit of £1,290 on Heytesbury House, raising the balance of £11,746 by selling more stocks and shares.

87. SS to RH, 29 Dec. 1933, Beinecke.

88. Keynes, *The Gates of Memory*, p.235.

90. Half of the 13 poems added to GK's limited edition of *Vigils* in 1934 & 1935 make specific references to Heytesbury.

91. J.R. Ackerley, *My Sister and Myself*, p.173.

92. TEL to GK, 6 Aug. 1934, Lawrence, *Selected Letters*, p.357.

93. ibid.

94. SS to GK, 24 Aug. 1934, CUL.

95. TEL to GK, 6 Aug. 1934, Lawrence, *Selected Letters*, p.357.

96. ibid., p.358.

97. SS to FSw, 3 Oct. 1935, Arkansas.

98. SS to the Heads, 20 Oct. 1934, HRHRC.

99. TEL to GK, 6 Aug. 1934, in *Selected Letters*, p.357, and SS to LG, 9 Jan. 1935, Columbia.

100. SS to HS, 12 Dec. 1937, lent to me by HS.

101. SS to GK, 12 Aug. 1935, CUL.

103. ES to SS, 22 Dec. 1934, Pullman.

104. The Rev. H.R.L. Sheppard (1880-1937).

105. SS read his poems at a PPU rally at the Albert Hall on 27 Nov. 1936, at Bristol on 13 Jan. 1937, Salisbury on 31 Jan. 1937 & Southend-on-Sea on 6 Feb. 1937.

106. See 'A Prayer from 1936', CP, p.250, dated 20 Oct. 1936.

107. SS to MB, 17 May 1935, *Letters to Max*, p.27.

108. Dated 25 May 1935, a week after TEL's death on 19 May (1930s notebooks, CUL).

109. SS to PG, 18 Mar. 1955, BLL.

110. SS to HMT, 12 Nov. 1943, HRHRC.

111. RG pub. *Lawrence and the Arabs* with Cape in 1928.

112. SS to EB, 25 Jun. 1935, HRHRC.

113. Arnold Lawrence visited Heyesbury on 25 Jun. 1935.

114. Dated 9 Sept. 1935 and titled 'T.E.L.', unpub. poem in poetry notebooks, CUL.

115. 'Aunt Eudora and the Poets', *Spectator*, 31 Jan. 1936; 'Educating Aunt Eudora', *Spectator*, 28 Feb. 1936; 'Querkes, Farmonger and Dusp', *Spectator*, 19 Jun. 1936.

116. Pub. 7 Aug. 1936 in the *Manchester Evening News*.

117. The publication of 15,720 copies of

SP by Faber on 3 Sept. 1936, preceded by serialization from Jun. to Aug. in *Nash's Pall Mall Magazine*.

118. SS to RGH, 25 Sept. 1936, Lilly.

119. GBS to RHD, 28 Apr. 1974, CUL, re. an entry for SS in the *DNB*.

120. SS's diary (J.S. Roberts, *Siegfried Sassoon*, p.262).

121. SS told GK that this 'grand poem [he] wrote about seeing George for the first time', which he believed to be his 'very finest', was 'written in two minutes in a state of mental release induced by whiskey, orange juice, sugar, and hot water' (letter of 29 Aug. 1943, CUL).

122. 'Ancestral Admonition', 1930s poetry notebook, CUL.

123. SS to HMT, 20 Aug. 1937, HRHRC.

124. Ackerley, *My Sister and Myself*, p.168.

125. SS's diary, Christmas 1936.

126. SS to the Heads, *c.*summer 1937, HRHRC.

127. ibid.

128. SS to GBS, 11 Aug. 1937, CUL.

129. ibid., 28 Nov. 1937, CUL.

130. The Sassoons stayed at the Excelsior Hotel, Rapallo, from 21 Apr. to 18 May 1938.

Chapter 28

1. SS to Michael Thorpe, 14 Mar. 1967, *Letters to a Critic*, p.20.

2. SS to Mr Hardcastle, 2 Oct. 1938, HRHRC.

3. ibid., 29 Oct. 1938.

4. SS resigned in effect from the PPU in 1937.

5. SS wrote to Rosamond Lehmann (3 Jun. 1938, King's Coll., Cambridge).

6. ST's journal, 12 Oct. 1938, Berg.

7. SS to RGH, 25 Sept. 1936, Lilly.

8. 4,500 copies of *The Complete Memoirs of George Sherston* pub. 4 Oct. 1937 by Faber.

9. Hart-Davis, *Letters to Max*, p.67.

10. SS originally planned to call this last third of the book 'Educational Experiences'.

11. SS to WdlM, 15 Oct. 1938, Beinecke. Columbia has a fair copy of the ms of OC, which is written into 3 bound volumes by SS.

12. OC, p.25.

13. SS to RH, 15 Nov. 1938, Beinecke.

14. SS to GK, [Sept. 1938], CUL.

15. *Letters to Max*, p.40.

16. ibid.

17. Keynes, p.98.

18. SS to GK, 10 Jan.1939, CUL.

19. SS to AL, 21 Nov. 1961, CUL.

20. ibid.

21. SS's diary for 1939/1940.

22. SS to HS, 24 Sept. 1939.

23. SS to MB, 1 Nov. 1939, *Letters to Max*, p.80.

24. 'Heart and Soul' is dated 29 Oct. 1938 in SS's 1930 notebook at CUL.

25. An unpub. poem (1940s notebook of SS's, CUL) written the day after war was declared, opens: 'To-day I'm old by five and twenty years / Since "War Declared" tolled tocsins to my ears ....'

26. Unpub. poem in same CUL notebooks, dated 23 Sept. 1939, is titled '(Fifty Years Between Us) To a Child'.

27. SS to SCC, 24 Aug. 1942, HRHRC.

28. SS to WdlM, 28 Dec. 1942, Beinecke.

29. The bulk of these unpub. poems contained in SS's poetry notebooks, CUL.

30. 'On Scratchbury Camp', 1st pub. *Country Life*, 25 Jun. 1943.

31. SS's 1940s poetry notebooks, CUL.

32. SS to GK, 18 Sept. 1939, CUL.

33. SS's diary for 3 Sept. 1939.

34. SS wrote GK on 18 Sept. 1939 that the Ministry of Information had written to say that he was 'on their list of potentially useful authors', but that it signified nothing, since they just told him to go on doing what he usually did (CUL).

35. SS to HMT, 1 Mar. 1943 & 5 Feb. 1939.

36. Unpub. poem, f. 1940s notebooks, CUL.

37. SS to HMT, 1 May 1940 & 17 Nov. 1942.

38. SS to HMT, 21 Jul. 1941 (Christie's cat. 3 Apr. 1992, p.13).

39. SJ, p.193.

40. ibid.

41. 75 copies of RRu were printed for SS and GK at the Chiswick Press in Jul. 1939, with a title page designed by LW.

42. SS to BH, 30 Aug. 1940, Congress.

43. SS to HMT, 4 Dec. 1940, HRHRC.

44. WY, p.160.

45. 'I have felt sad about poor Lady Ottoline's sudden death,' SS wrote to TS on 26 Apr. 1938 (Berg).

46. SS to HMT, 28 May 1940, HRHRC.

47. ibid., 4 Dec. 1940.

48. ibid., 9 May 1941.

49. SS to EB, 18 Apr. 1943, CUL.

50. SS to GK, 18 Jul. 1945.

51. Interviews with Claire Blunden.

52. Will Rothenstein visited with a dozen

young architects serving with the Artillery Survey Companies in Jul. 1941.

53. Edward Seago, RWS, RBS (1910-55).

54. From an unpub. poem of 27 May 1942, CUL.

55. SS to GK, 25 Sept. 1942, CUL.

56. SS to SCC, 22 Jun. 1942, Cockerell, *The Best of Friends*, p.88.

57. SS to GBS, 18 Mar. 1941, CUL.

58. SS to SCC, 22 Jun. 1942 (*The Best of Friends*, p.88).

59. SS and GK had 50 copies of an extract from WY printed as a pamphlet, *Early Morning Long Ago*, in Mar. 1941.

60. WY, pp.206-7.

61. See *New Statesman* xxv, 6 Feb. 1943 and *TLS*, 31 Oct. 1942.

62. SS to HS, 1 Dec. 1942.

63. Keynes's *Bibliography* has no record of a reprint until 1948.

64. SS to HMT, 17 Nov. 1942, HRHRC.

65. ibid.

66. SS to EM, 27 Mar. 1941, Berg.

67. SS to GK, 19 Nov. 1942, CUL.

68. 'The Hardened Heart' dated Apr. 1942 in ms. at CUL.

69. SS to SCC, 5 Jun. 1940, *The Best of Friends*, pp.78-9.

70. SS to HMT, 27 Mar. 1943, HRHRC.

72. SS to Angela Baddeley, 12 Jun. 1942, letter in possession of George Byam Shaw.

74. ST to SS, 22 Aug. 1939, Berg.

75. See ST to SS, 4 Nov. 1941, Berg.

76. See SS to GBS: 'There he sat – an artificial person – outwardly very much like "one of the chorus"' (CUL).

77. SS to GBS, 23 Sept. 1942, CUL.

78. SS to GK, 25 Sept. 1942, CUL.

79. ibid.

80. SS to HS, 1 Dec. 1942.

81. See SS to SCC, 25 Dec. 1941 & 22 Jun. 1942, *The Best of Friends*, pp.86 & 88.

82. GBS had joined 1st Battalion, Royal Scots in 1940 with his brother James Byam and was sent with him to join 6th Brigade in Burma.

83. SS to GK, 29 Aug. 1943, CUL.

84. SS to WdlM, 1 Aug. 1943, Beinecke.

85. ibid.

86. Subtitled 'Verses Written by Members of the Eighth Army in Sicily and Italy, Jul. 1943-March 1944' (George G. Harrap, 1945).

87. SS to SCC, 30 Dec. 1953, *The Best of Friends*, p.228.

88. ibid.

89. SS to GK, 20 Jun. 1943, CUL.

90. ibid., 14 Dec. 1944.

91. SS to TS, 15 May 1944, Berg.

92. WY brought SS £1,374 in its first six months.

93. Greenways was owned and run by Vivien Hancock at Codford St Peter.

94. SS to TS, 1 May 1944, Berg.

95. Unpub. in SS's lifetime, this poem is in the CUL poetry notebooks, dated 25 Dec. 1947.

96. SS to GK, 4 May 1944, CUL.

97. SS's diary for 27 Jul. 1944.

98. SS to HMT, 16 May 1945, HRHRC.

99. Dated 3 May 1945 in the CUL poetry notebooks & pub. *Observer*, 6 May 1945.

100. SS to GK, 18 Jul. 1945, CUL.

Chapter 29

1. Roberts, *Siegfried Sassoon*, p.290.

2. SS to FSw, 9 Aug. 1945, Arkansas.

3. HG bought the Grange, Winterbourne Dauntsey, 22 miles from Heytesbury.

4. EB to RHD, Jul. 1948, CUL.

5. EB to SS, 29 Apr. 1947, HRHRC.

6. Interview with Claire Blunden.

7. SS to EB, 7 Aug. 1947, HRHRC.

8. Roberts, *Siegfried Sassoon*, p.285.

9. Lady Lettice Strickland-Constable.

10. SS and GS shared lodgings shared with the Byam Shaws in Minehead, 29 Aug. to 8 Sept. 1945.

11. SS to GK, 18 Jul. 1945, CUL.

12. SS's diary (Roberts, *Siegfried Sassoon*, p.43).

13. SS to GK, loc.cit.

14. Interview with Mrs Hancock.

15. ibid.

16. See SS to GK, 22 Nov.1944, CUL.

17. Interview with Rolf Barber, 20 Jun. 1991.

18. Interview with DS.

19. SS to MB, 28 Jun. 1948, *Letters to Max*, p.100.

20. GK owned several Blake paintings and some plates from his illuminated books.

21. HH had served with the Glosters in the WWII before becoming an official war artist.

22. HH to RHD, 29 Feb. 1968, CUL.

23. Interview with HH.

24. ibid.

25. SS's diary, Feb. 1948.

26. SS to SCC, 17 Dec. 1945, HRHRC.

27. SS to GBS, 30 Oct. 1945, CUL.

28. SS to GK, 14 Dec. 1944, CUL.

29. SS to HMT, 16 May 1945, HRHRC.
30. ibid., 23 Feb. 1944.
31. See SS to GK, 29 Apr. 1946, CUL.
32. SS to RH, 21 Jul. 1946, Beinecke.
33. SS to EB, 23 Jul. 1946, HRHRC.
34. SS to WdlM, 6 Feb. 1946, Beinecke.
35. SS to EB, 17 Jan. 1946, HRHRC.
36. SS first met Helen Waddell on 19 Jul. 1945.
37. SS to GBS, 19 May 1947, CUL.
38. SS to T.H. White, 21 Mar. 1951, HRHRC.
39. Helen Waddell presented SS with a signed copy of *Peter Abelard*.
40. Quoted by DFC in *Helen Waddell*, Gollancz, 1990, p.347.
41. SS to SCC, 11 Nov. 1947, HRHRC.
42. SS to L.P. Hartley, 25 Sept. 1948, CUL.
43. ibid.
44. SS, *Meredith*, p.4.
45. SS to EB, 15 Dec. 1946, HRHRC.
46. SS told Patrick Lawlor (18 Feb. 1950, Columbia) that *Meredith* had sold only about 4,500 copies.
47. SS to HMT, 16 Oct. 1951, HRHRC.
48. Otto Kyllman to SS, 18 Feb. 1949, HRHRC.
49. HG's family owned land in Mull.
50. SS to WdlM, 14 Nov. 1948, Beinecke.
51. SS to Angela Baddeley, 17 Jan. 1949 (George Byam Shaw).
52. SS to HH, 22 Oct. 1948.
53. SS to WdlM, 7 Dec. 1948, Beinecke.
54. See 'Solitudes at Sixty', CP, p.276.
55. SS's diary, 2 Jul. 1953, SS:PP, p.147.
56. TS died 11 Jul. 1947.
57. SS to GBS, 18 Jul. 1947, CUL.
58. SS's diary, Jul. 1947.
59. SS to GBS, 18 Jul. 1947, CUL.
60. SS to HH, 14 Feb. 1951.
61. Ackerley, *My Sister and Myself*, p.167.
62. ibid.
63. ibid.
64. ibid.
65. ibid.
66. P. Parker, *Ackerley*, p.302.
67. ibid., p.305.
68. James Kirkup referred to his visit to SS at Heytesbury in his autobiography, *I, of All People*, Weidenfeld & Nicolson, 1988, p.72.
69. Ackerley, *My Sister and Myself*, p.175.
70. ibid., p.179.

Chapter 30

1. SS:PP, pp.132.
2. 'Elsewhere', CP, p.267.
3. SS:PP, p.132.
4. CC dated 1950 but not issued until 1951.
5. SS's diary, 29 Mar. 1951.
6. CP, p.264.
7 'An Asking', CP, p.270.
8. CP, p.277.
9. SS:PP, p.130.
10. CP, p.280.
11. 'The Message' 1st pub. 3 Nov. 1949, *Everybody's Weekly*.
12. CP, p.262.
13. SS uses 'beguilements' in 'Early March', CP, pp.278-9.
14. See SS to HMT, 11 Oct. 1950, HRHRC.
15. Roberts, *Siegfried Sassoon*, p.306.
16. 107 copies of CC printed on handmade paper.
17. RGH to SS, 29 Sept. 1952, Lilly. 75 copies of EE were printed at Rampant Lions Press, Cambridge, Nov. 1951.
18. SS:PP, p.141.
19. 'The Dream' written Feb. 1950.
20. 1950s poetry notebooks, CUL.
21. SS to DFC, 17 Feb.1960, SS:PP, p.138.
22. 'Brevis Quod Gratia Florum Est', SS's 1950s poetry notebooks at CUL.
23. SS to GBS, 16 Dec. 1947, CUL.
24. Dorothy Wallis to GBS, 4 May 1953 (George Byam Shaw).
25. ibid.
26. ibid.
27. Interview with Claire Blunden.
28. Dorothy Wallis to GBS, 4 May 1953, loc. cit.
29. SS had this printed as an Easter card.
30. e.g. GBS's son, George, doubted any sexual dimension on SS's side.
31. SS to HMT, 1 Jan. 1953, Christie's cat., 3 Apr. 1992, p.14.
32. SS to HMT, 30 Oct. 1952, HRHRC.
33. Interview with HH.
34. Dorothy Wallis to GBS, 4 May 1953.
35. Interview with Claire Blunden.
36. ibid.
37. See CP, p.296.
38. Dorothy Wallis to GBS, 4 May 1953.
39. GBS to Dorothy Wallis, 11 May 1953.
40. ibid.
41. SS to PG, 30 Nov. 1953, BLL.

42. SS to DFC, 16 Feb. 1962, quoted in SS:PP, p.219.

43. SS to PG, 30 Nov. 1953, BLL.

44. SS presented a Raverat painting to Clare College, Cambridge.

45. SS to HMT, 15 Mar. 1956, Christie's cat., 3 Apr. 1992.

46. Dennis Silk, *Siegfried Sassoon*, p.27.

47. ibid.

48. ibid.

49. SS to HMT, 15 Aug. 1955, HRHRC.

50. Silk, *Siegfried Sassoon*, p.27.

51. ibid.

52. ibid., p.28.

53. SS to GK, 23 Mar. 1955, CUL.

54. SS to JG, 20 Jul. 1963, CUL.

55. Interview with DS.

56. ibid.

57. SS to PG, 6 Jun. 1955, BLL.

58. Oliver Thornycroft told SS that the idea of the fellowship 'was mainly instigated by an F.R. named H. Godwin'.

59. S.C. Roberts to SS, 4 Nov. 1953, CUL.

60. Obit. of SS in the Clare Association Annual, 1967, p.79.

61. ibid.

62. ibid.

63. ibid.

64. SS:PP, p.148.

65. CP, p.301.

66. SJ, p.162.

67. 100 copies of *The Tasking* printed for SS & GK at CUP.

68. SS:PP, p.149.

69. SS:PP, p.151.

70. SS to HMT, 22 Jan. 1955, HRHRC.

71. ibid.

72. ibid.

73. SS to GK, 18 Jan. 1955, CUL.

74. SS to DFC, 5 Aug. 1960 (SS:PP, p.167).

75. SS to DFC, 22 Feb. 1963 (SS:PP, p.169).

76. SS's 'A Tribute to Max' on BBC Home Service on 28 Jun. 1956, just after WdlM's death on 22 Jun.

77. Colin Fenton (1929-1982).

78. Eton College Lib. have SS's correspondence with Colin Fenton.

79. SS to HMT, 4 Dec. 1954, HRHRC.

80. ibid.

81. SS to PG, 5 Nov. 1956, BLL.

82. SS to Michael Thorpe, 12 Aug. 1966, *Letters to a Critic*, p.15.

83. ibid.

84. Quoted by SS from EB's review of *Sequences* in the *TLS*.

Chapter 31

1. SS to DFC, 30 Oct. 1959 (SS:PP, p.175).

2. Notebook of MMM, CUL.

3. SS to DFC, 30 Oct. 1959, in SS:PP, p.175.

4. ibid.

5. SS to DFC, 5 Aug. 1960 (SS:PP, p.167).

6. MMM to RHD, 16 Jun. 1969, CUL.

7. SS's notes, 1958-1964 notebook at CUL.

8. Dated '19.4.57'; quoted in SS:PP, p.173.

9. Notebook of MMM, CUL.

10. SS wrote a poem 'in anticipation of MMM' (' 22/23 Oct. 1952') entitled first 'Sainthood Sufficing', then 'Unknown Saint' (CUL).

11.SS:PP, p.198 and author's interviews with Dom Sebastian Moore, 1991 & 2002.

12. Dom Sebastian Moore was an authority on Jones's *The Anathemata*.

13. SS to DFC, 21 Jan. 1960 (SS:PP, p.177).

14. Read by SS in R. Speaight, *The Life of Hilaire Belloc*, p.377

15. The Rt. Rev. Monsignor Ronald Arbuthnott Knox (1888-1957).

16. SS to EB, 20 Feb. 1960, HRHRC.

17. SS quotes himself in a letter to DFC, 14 Apr. 1960 (SS:PP, p.185).

18. ibid.

19. ibid.

20. SS to DFC, 21 Jan. 1960, in SS:PP, p.177. SS was received into the Catholic Church by Fr Francis Little.

21. SS to DFC, 21 Jan. 1960.

22. SS to PG, 14 Oct. 1957, BLL.

23. F. Swinnerton, *Figures in the Foreground*, p.210.

24. SS to PG, 14 Oct. 1957, BLL.

25. GK to DFC, Aug. 1973, quoted by her in her *Centenary Essay* of 1986.

26. SS to PG, 24 Sept. 1958, BLL.

27. Keynes, *The Gates of Memory*, p.237.

28. SS to KA, 13 Nov. 1959 (Lord Oxford and Asquith).

29. Interview with DS.

30. ibid.

31. GBS to SS, 11 Sept. 1957, Columbia.

32. ibid.

33. ibid.

34. 'Memories of Siegfried Sassoon', *Journal of RWF*, Mar. 1968, p.15.

35. ibid.

36. DFC's *Centenary Essay* on SS.

37. SS to HMT, 10 Jan. 1958, HRHRC.

38. ibid.

39. Extract from the 3 sheets of journal entries by SS (Apr. to Oct. 1957).

40. *The Times*, 4 Sept. 1967.

41. RG to Timothy Budd, 4 Jun. 1971, private collection.

42. SS:PP, pp.178-9.

43. ibid., p.182.

44. A. Caesar, *Taking It Like a Man*, p.102.

45. SS's letters to KA are in the possession of Lord Oxford and Asquith.

46. Interview with author.

47. *Spectator*, 8 Sept. 1957.

48. SS's journal, 1957, CUL.

49. DFC refers to the 'lovely prose cadences' of SJ (*Centenary Essay*).

50. 3,000 copies of *Collected Poems 1908-1956* pub. by Faber, 3 May 1961.

51. See DFC's *Any Saint to Any Nun* (1947), *In a Great Tradition* (1956), *Siegfried Sassoon: Poet's Pilgrimage* (1973), *George Thomas of Soho* (1970) & *Helen Waddell* (1986).

52. SS:PP, p.192.

53. *Downside Review* lxxvi, no. 245, pp.129-32.

54. SS to Dom Martin Salmon, 16 May 1958, CUL.

55. ibid., 18 Mar. 1958.

56. *Something About Myself* was Stanbrook Abbey Press's first calligraphic book.

57. Thorpe, *Siegfried Sassoon*, p.250.

58. DFC to GK, 26 Aug. 1973, CUL.

59. ibid.

60. DFC's *Centenary Essay*.

61. Interview with Ian Balding on 21 Dec. 1998.

62. Interview with Ian Balding.

63. Interviews with DS and Ian Balding.

64. See R. Hart-Davis, *The Lyttleton-Hart-Davis Letters*, p.140.

65. ibid., p.141.

66. ibid.

67. SS to RHD, 6 Oct. 1958, CUL.

68. SS to DFC, 3 May 1960, in SS:PP, p.102.

69. ibid., pp.102-3.

70. SS to HH, 14 Jan. 1964.

71. SS introduced to Princess Marina on 9 Jun. 1965.

72. D. Jones, *Dai Greatcoat: Letters of David Jones*, p.210; SS to AL, 1 Jul. 1964, CUL.

73. ibid.

74. ibid.

75. SS to DFC, 5 Aug. 1964 (Roberts, *Siegfried Sassoon*, p.326).

76. SS did not attend DS's wedding but sent a generous present.

77. SS to DFC, 25 May 1966, in SS:PP, p.242.

78. Roberts, *Siegfried Sassoon*, p.320.

79. SS to DFC, 3 Jan. 1967 (SS:PP, p.248).

80. ibid., 25 Oct. 1965 (SS:PP, p.240).

81. SS left EB £4,000 in his will.

82. Anthony Powell and his wife visited SS at Heytesbury House in autumn 1963.

83. Powell, *To Keep the Ball Rolling*, pp.350-1.

84. ibid.

85. ibid.

86. ibid.

87. ibid., p.351.

88. SS told DFC that it was WdlM's son, Richard.

89. John Sparrow, Lord David Cecil and Rupert Hart-Davis almost certainly joined in the campaign to have SS awarded an Hon. D.Litt.

90. i.e. 'Rogation', 'Sight Sufficient', 'Arbor Vitae', 'Unfoldment', 'A Prayer at Pentecost' and 'Awaitment'.

91. Causley persuaded SS to read some of his best known poems on the BBC and recorded this at Heytesbury House on 16 Feb. 1955.

92. SS appeared briefly in 'T.E. Lawrence, 1888-1935', BBC, 27 Nov. 1962.

93. Interview with DS.

94. SS to Dame Hildelith Cumming, 1 Jan. 1965, in SS:PP, p.236.

95. Dr Falk to MMM, 13 Aug. 1967, CUL.

96. Dom Philip Jebb to his parents, 7 Sept. 1967.

97. Interview with the author.

98. EB did, however, write an obit. in the *Observer* on 3 Sept. 1967.

99. Related to DS by RHD in 1967.

100. Jonathan Gathorne-Hardy to author, letter of 17 Jul. 1990.

101. Charles Causley, 'Siegfried Sassoon', *The Author*, Winter 1989, p.127.

102. ibid.

103. See Judith Usher to RHD, 3 Sept. 1967, CUL.

104. GS to Charles Causley, loc.cit.

105. Causley, 'Siegfried Sassoon', op.cit.

Select Bibliography

Works by Siegfried Sassoon, in order of publication
(pp = privately printed)

The Daffodil Murderer (John Richmond, 1913)
The Old Huntsman and Other Poems (Heinemann, 1917)
Counter-Attack and Other Poems (Heinemann, 1918)
Picture Show (pp, 1919)
War Poems (Heinemann, 1919)
Recreations (pp, 1923)
Lingual Exercises (pp, 1925)
Selected Poems (Heinemann, 1925)
Satirical Poems (Heinemann, 1926)
The Heart's Journey (Heinemann, 1928)
Memoirs of a Fox-Hunting Man (Faber & Gwyer, 1928)
Memoirs of an Infantry Officer (Faber & Faber, 1930)
Poems by Pinchbeck Lyre (Duckworth, 1931)
The Road to Ruin (Faber & Faber, 1933)
Vigils (Heinemann, 1935)
Sherston's Progress (Faber & Faber, 1936)
Complete Memoirs of George Sherston (Faber & Faber, 1937)
The Old Century (Faber & Faber, 1938)
On Poetry (University of Bristol Press, 1939)
Rhymed Ruminations (Faber & Faber, 1940)
Poems Newly Selected (Faber & Faber, 1940)
The Weald of Youth (Faber & Faber, 1942)
Siegfried's Journey (Faber & Faber, 1945)
Collected Poems (Faber & Faber, 1947)
Meredith (Constable, 1948)
Common Chords (pp, 1950/51)
Emblems of Experience (pp, 1951)
The Tasking (pp, 1954)
Sequences (Faber & Faber, 1956)
Lenten Illuminations (pp, 1958)
The Path to Peace (Stanbrook Abbey Press, 1960)
Collected Poems 1908-1956 (Faber & Faber, 1961)
The War Poems (Faber & Faber, 1983)

Sassoon's early privately printed volumes are: *Poems* (1906), *Orpheus in Diloeryum* (1908), *Sonnets and Verses* (1909), *Sonnets* (1909), *Twelve Sonnets* (1911), *Poems* (1911), *Melodies* (1912), *Hyacinth* (1912), *Amyntas* (proof copy, abandoned 1912), *Ode for Music* (1912).

Secondary Sources

Ackerley, J.R., *My Father and Myself* (Penguin, 1971).
Ackerley, J.R., *My Sister and Myself: The Diaries of J.R. Ackerley*, ed. Francis King (Hutchinson, 1982).
Adams, B., *Nothing of Importance* (Methuen, 1917).

Amory, M., *Lord Berners: The Last Eccentric* (Chatto & Windus, 1998).

Bagnold, E., *Enid Bagnold's Autobiography* (Century, 1985).

Barbusse, H., *Under Fire (Le Feu)* tr. Fitzwater Wray (Dent, 1917).

Barker, P., *Regeneration* (Viking, 1991).

Baxter, B., *Strange Street* (Hutchinson, 1935).

Beaton, C., *Self-Portrait with Friends: The Selected Diaries of Cecil Beaton*, ed. R. Buckle (Penguin, 1982).

Behrman, S., *Portrait of Max: An Intimate Memoir of Sir Max Beerbohm* (Random House, 1960).

Behrman, S., *Tribulations and Laughter* (Hamish Hamilton, 1972).

Bennett, A., *The Journals of Arnold Bennett*, ed. F. Swinnerton (Penguin, 1954).

Bennett, A., *The Letters of Arnold Bennett*, ed. J. Hepburn (Oxford University Press, 1968).

Bergonzi, B., *Heroes' Twilight* (Carcanet, 1996).

Blunden, E., *Edmund Blunden: A Selection of his Poetry and Prose* (Rupert Hart-Davis, 1950).

Blunden, E., *Cricket Country* (Collins, 1944).

Blunden, E., *Undertones of War* (Penguin, 1982).

Blunden, E., *Overtones of War*, ed. M. Taylor (Duckworth, 1996).

Borland, M., *Wilde's Devoted Friend* (Lennard Publishing, 1990).

Bradford, S., *Sacheverell Sitwell: Splendours and Miseries* (Sinclair-Stevenson, 1993).

Butcher, D., *The Stanbrook Abbey Press Bibliography* (Whittington Press, 1992).

Caesar, A., *Taking It Like a Man: Suffering, Sexuality and the War Poets* (Manchester University Press, 1993).

Cecil, D., *Max: A Biography of Max Beerbohm* (Atheneum, 1985).

Cockerell, S.C., *The Best of Friends: Further Letters of Sir Sydney Carlyle Cockerell*, ed. Viola Meynell (Hart-Davis, 1956).

Connon, B., *Beverley Nichols: A Life* (Constable, 1991).

Corrigan, D.F., *Helen Waddell* (Gollancz, 1990).

Corrigan, F., *Siegfried Sassoon: Poet's Pilgrimage* (Gollancz, 1973).

Coward, N., *Diaries* (Little, Brown, 1982).

Cunningham, V., *British Writers of the Thirties* (Oxford University Press, 1988).

Darton, J.H., *From Surtees to Sassoon* (Morley & Mitchell, 1931).

Dickinson, G. Lowes, *The Autobiography of ...*, ed. D. Proctor (Duckworth, 1973).

Duhamel, G., *The New Book of Martyrs (Vie des Martyres)* tr. Florence Simmonds (Heinemann, 1918)

Dunn, J.C. (ed.), *The War the Infantry Knew 1914-1919: A Chronicle of Service in France and Belgium* (P.S. King, 1938).

Edwards, H.I. Powell, *The Sussex Yeomanry and 16th (Sussex Yeomanry) Battalion, Royal Sussex Regiment, 1914-1919)* (London, Andrew Melrose, 1921).

Egremont, Max, *Siegfried Sassoon: A Biography* (Picador, 2005).

Elborn, G., *Edith Sitwell* (Sheldon, 1981).

Fitzgerald, P., *Charlotte Mew and her Friends* (Collins, 1984).

Fitzgerald, P., *The Knox Brothers* (Macmillan, 1977).

Fletcher, F., *After Many Days* (Robert Hale, 1937).

Foot, D., *Beyond Bat and Ball* (Good Books, 1993).

Forster, E.M., *Selected Letters, 1921-1970*, ed. M. Lago and P.N. Furbank (Collins, 1985).

Furbank, P.N., *E.M. Forster: A Life* (Oxford University Press, 1979).

Fussell, P., *The Great War and Modern Memory* (Oxford University Press, 1975).

Fussell, P. (ed.), *Siegfried Sassoon's Long Journey* (Oxford University Press, 1983).

Gilbert, M., *First World War* (Weidenfeld & Nicolson, 1994).

Gilbert, M., *Second World War* (Phoenix, 1995).

Gittings, R., *The Older Hardy* (Heinemann, 1978).

Glendinning, V., *Edith Sitwell: A Unicorn Among Lions* (Oxford University Press, 1983).

Graves, R.P., *Robert Graves: The Assault Heroic 1895-1926* (Weidenfeld & Nicolson, 1986).

Graves, R.P., *Robert Graves: The Years with Laura 1926-1940* (Papermac, 1991).

Graves, R., *Goodbye to All That* (Penguin, 1976).

Harding, John, *Dreaming of Babylon: the Life and Times of Ralph Hodgson* (Greenwich Exchange, 2008).

Hardy, T., *Collected Letters*, vols 5 and 6, ed. R.L. Purdey and M. Millgate (Clarendon, 1978).

Hart-Davis, R., *Halfway to Heaven* (Sutton, 1998).

Hart-Davis, R., *The Lyttleton–Hart-Davis Letters*, vol. II (John Murray, 1986).

Hart-Davis, R., *Praise from the Past* (Stone Trough Books, 1996).

Hart-Davis, R., *Siegfried Sassoon: Letters to Max Beerbohm* (Faber & Faber, 1986).

Hassall, C., *Edward Marsh: Patron of the Arts* (Longman, 1959).

Hassall, C. (ed.), *Ambrosia and Small Beer: The Record of a Correspondence Between Edward Marsh and Christopher Hassall* (Longmans, 1964).

Hibberd, D., *Harold Monro* (Palgrave, 2001).

Hibberd, D., *Wilfred Owen* (Weidenfeld & Nicolson, 2002).

Hoare, P., *Serious Pleasures: The Life of Stephen Tennant* (Penguin, 1992).

Holroyd, M., *Lytton Strachey* (Penguin, 1971).

Hynes, S., *A War Imagined* (Bodley Head, 1990).

Jackson, S., *The Sassoons* (New York, Dutton, 1968).

James, L., *Lawrence of Arabia: The Golden Warrior* (Weidenfeld & Nicolson, 1991).

Johnston, J.H., *English Poetry of the First World War* (Princeton University Press).

Jones, D., *Dai Greatcoat: Letters of David Jones*, ed. René Hague (Faber & Faber, 1980).

Kennedy, M., *Portrait of Walton* (Oxford University Press, 1989).

Keynes, G., *A Bibliography of Siegfried Sassoon* (Hart-Davis, 1962).

Keynes, G., *The Gates of Memory* (Clarendon Press, 1981).

Lane, A., *An Adequate Response: the War Poetry of Wilfred Owen and Siegfried Sassoon* (Wayne State University Press, 1972).

Lawrence, T.E., *Selected Letters of T.E. Lawrence*, ed. D. Garnett (World Books, 1941).

Lawrence, T.E., *Seven Pillars of Wisdom* (Jonathan Cape, 1940).

Liddell Hart, B.N., *History of the First World War* (Macmillan, 1992).

Manning, E., *Bronze and Steel: Life of Thomas Thornycroft, Sculptor and Engineer* (Kingstone Press, 1932).

Manning, E., *Marble and Bronze: Life of Hamo Thornycroft* (Trefoil Books, 1982).

Marsh, E., *A Number of People* (Heinemann/Hamish Hamilton, 1939).

Middleboe, P., *Edith Olivier: From Her Journals 1924-1948* (Weidenfeld & Nicolson, 1989).

Moeyes, P., *Siegfried Sassoon: Scorched Glory, a Critical Study* (Macmillan, 1997).

Morrell, O., *Ottoline at Garsington, 1915-1928*, ed. R. Gathorne-Hardy (Faber & Faber, 1974).

O'Prey, P. (ed.), *In Broken Images: Selected Letters of Robert Graves, 1914-1946* (Hutchinson, 1982).

Owen, H., *Aftermath* (Oxford University Press, 1970).

Parfitt, G., *English Poetry of the First World War* (Harvester, 1990).

Parker, P., *Ackerley: A Life* (Constable, 1989).

Parker, P., *The Old Lie: the Great War and the Public School Ethos* (Constable, 1987).

Pearson, J., *Façades: Edith, Osbert and Sacheverell Sitwell* (Fontana, 1980).

Pinto, V. de S., *The City That Shone* (Hutchinson, 1969).

Pinto, V. de S., *Crises in English Poetry* (Hutchinson, 1939).

Porter, K. and Weekes, J. (eds), *Between the Acts: Lives of Homosexual Men 1885-1967* (Routledge, 1990).

Powell, A., *To Keep the Ball Rolling* (Penguin, 1983).

Quinn, P., *The Great War and the Missing Muse* (Susquehanna University Press, 1994).

Richards, F., *Old Soldiers Never Die* (Faber & Faber, 1933).

Richards, H., *The Bloody Circus: The Daily Herald and the Left* (Pluto Press, 1997).

Roberts, J.S., *Siegfried Sassoon* (Richard Cohen Books, 1999).

Ross, R., *Friend of Friends (1869-1918)*, ed. M. Ross (Jonathan Cape, 1952).

Roth, C., *The Sassoon Dynasty* (Robert Hale, 1941).

Rothkopf, Carol (ed.), *Letters of Siegfried Sassoon and Edmund Blunden, 1919-1967* (Pickering and Chatto, 2012).

Seymour, M., *Ottoline Morrell: Life on the Grand Scale* (Sceptre, 1992).

Seymour-Smith, M., *Robert Graves: His Life and Works* (Paladin, 1987).

Silk, D., *Siegfried Sassoon* (Tisbury, Wilts, Compton Russell, 1975).

Silkin, J., *Out of Battle: The Poetry of the Great War* (OUP, 1972).

Sitwell, E., *Selected Letters of Edith Sitwell*, ed. R. Greene (Virago, 1997).

Sitwell, O., *Laughter in the Next Room* (Macmillan, 1949).

Sitwell, O., *Noble Essences* (Macmillan,1950).

Skaife, Major E., *A Short History of the Royal Welch Fusiliers* (Gale & Polden, 1926).

Sox, D., *Bachelors of Art* (Fourth Estate, 1991).

Speaight, R., *The Life of Hilaire Belloc* (Hollis & Carter, 1957).

Stallworthy, J., *Singing School: The Making of a Poet* (John Murray, 1998).

Stallworthy, J., *Wilfred Owen* (Chatto & Windus and OUP, 1974).

Swinnerton, F., *A London Bookman* (Secker, 1928).

Swinnerton, F., *The Georgian Literary Scene* (Dent, 1946).

Swinnerton, F., *Figures in the Foreground* (Hutchinson, 1963).

Taylor, M., *Lads* (Constable, 1988).

Tennant, E., *Strangers: A Family Romance* (Jonathan Cape, 1998).

Thorpe, M. (ed.), *Letters to a Critic* (Kent editions, 1966).

Thorpe, M., *Siegfried Sassoon: A Critical Study* (Leiden University Press/Oxford University Press, 1966).

Thwaite, A., *Edmund Gosse: A Literary Landscape* (Secker & Warburg, 1984).

Turner, W.J., *Blow for Balloons* (Dent, 1935).

Turner, W.J., *The Duchess of Popocatapetl* (Dent, 1939).

Webb, B., *Edmund Blunden: A Biography* (Yale University Press, 1990).

Weeks, J., *Coming Out* (Quartet, 1977).

Whistler, L., *The Laughter and the Urn* (Weidenfeld & Nicolson, 1985).

Whistler, T., *Imagination of the Heart: The Life of Walter de la Mare* (Duckworth, 1993).

Woolf, L., *Beginning Again* (Chatto & Windus, 1964).

Woolf, L., *Downhill All the Way* (Chatto & Windus, 1967).

Woolf, V., *A Change of Perspective: The Letters, 1923-1928*, ed. N. Nicolson and J. Trautmann (Penguin, 1981).

Woolf, V., *The Diary of Virginia Woolf,* vol. 2: *1920-1924*, ed. A.O. Bell and A. McNeillie (Penguin, 1981).

Ziegler, P., *Osbert Sitwell* (Chatto & Windus, 1998).

Index